Articles Published in the *Journal of Abnormal and Social Psychology* and the *Journal of Personality and Social Psychology* on Selected Topics between 1944 and 1978

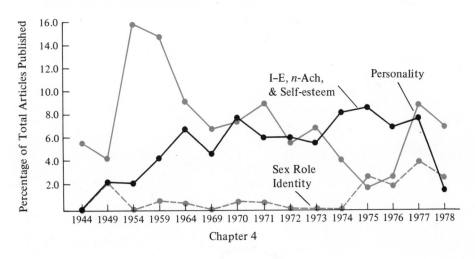

Chapter 4

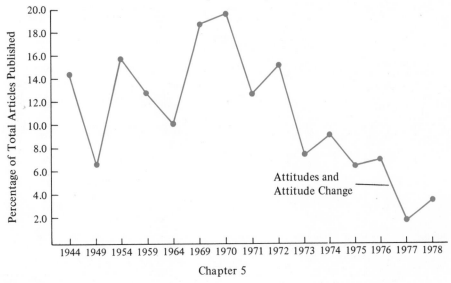

Chapter 5

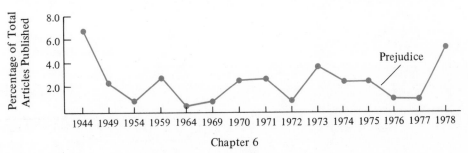

Chapter 6

Social Psychology

SOCIAL PSYCHOLOGY

JOHN LAMBERTH

TEMPLE UNIVERSITY

Macmillan Publishing Co., Inc.

NEW YORK

Collier Macmillan Publishers

LONDON

Macmillan Publishing Co., Inc.
866 Third Avenue, New York, New York 10022

Collier Macmillan Canada, Ltd.

Library of Congress Cataloging in Publication Data

Lamberth, John.
  Social psychology.

  Includes bibliographies and index.
  1. Social psychology. I. Title.
HM251.L233 1980   301.1   78-27747
ISBN 0-02-367310-9

    Printing: 1 2 3 4 5 6 7 8   Year: 0 1 2 3 4 5 6

To Shirley

Preface

My aim in writing this book has been to introduce students to the excitement of social psychology. In order to do so, I have found it advisable to keep three lesser goals in mind. First, it is vitally important to write in a way that reveals rather than obscures what my colleagues and I find so fascinating about social behavior. Those of us who deal with psychology daily have, of necessity, developed modes of thought and a language that are more abstract than is the behavior we study. I have attempted to emphasize first and foremost the concreteness of behavior, and only when this has been done to develop the abstractions that are necessary for scientific theorizing. If I have succeeded, students will find the book exciting, interesting, and informative.

My second goal has been to write a book that covers, in a complete and scholarly way, the most important topics of historical and contemporary social psychology. Deciding which of the many interesting topics to cover was the work of two surveys.

First, Macmillan constructed a survey that asked a large number of social psychologists what they thought was most needed in a social psychology text. Then I surveyed the contents of the *Journal of Abnormal and Social Psychology* (*JASP*) at five-year intervals until it became the *Journal of Personality and Social Psychology* in 1965. Starting with 1969, I surveyed the contents of *JPSP* yearly through 1978. Each article was categorized by title into subject areas, and the percentage of articles in a given area for each year surveyed was computed. The results of this work are presented by chapter in the form of graphs, printed on the endpapers of this book. These investigations revealed a high correlation between what social psychologists said they wanted covered in a text and the recent research in *JPSP*. This, of course, made my task somewhat easier, and the subject matter in this book reflects this correlation. As an added benefit of this study, the endpapers show at a glance a concise history of the main avenues of research in social psychology over the past four decades.

My third goal was to reflect my own views about the present state of social psychology and, more importantly, to anticipate its future. The rapid changes within this discipline in the last decade made this task more difficult than it would otherwise have been. I have made my own views known to students in sections labeled *Comments*. Boxed material is included to cover the latest research in each area. The boxes were written after the body of the text and were meant to bring the student up to date. I feel sure that much of the future in social psychology is contained or foreshadowed in these thirty-eight selections.

The book is organized simply. Chapters 1 and 2 introduce the student to social psychology, while emphasizing theory and methodology. In Chapter 2 methods are illustrated, when possible, with one or more classic studies in the field. Thus both Chapters 1 and 2 teach the student the history of the field. Chapter 3 covers communication as the cornerstone of social interaction, and Chapter 4 discusses the person as an individual. Chapters 5 through 8 cover topics that are generally thought of in terms of interaction between two or more people: attitudes and attitude change, prejudice and discrimination, social influence, and aggression. Chapters 9 and 10 are also individual interaction chapters, but they cover the more positive behaviors of attraction and love, and altruism. Group behavior is covered in Chapter 11, and the two final chapters reflect a developing trend in social psychology—environmental and applied psychology.

Attribution theory presents a special organizational challenge. It touches on many aspects of social psychology and is itself a highly significant subject. Because of the diversity and complexity of the topics it addresses, I have chosen to deal with it at greater length than the usual one chapter's worth. The theory is introduced in Chapter 1, and then its applications to certain other topics are discussed in those chapters where these topics are themselves covered, that is in Chapters 3, 4, 7, 9, 10, and 13. The total coverage of attribution theory amounts to approximately a chapter, but I hope that this organizational scheme will make its contributions to the field more obvious to the student.

It is a distinct pleasure to acknowledge the many debts of gratitude I owe a large number of people who assisted in the preparation of this book. I want, first, to express my appreciation to those people who reviewed parts of the manuscript:

Dr. Anthony N. Doob—*University of Toronto,* Dr. Dwight Harshbarger—*West Virginia University,* Dr. Linda Jones—*Ithaca College,* Dr. Dale O. Jorgenson—*California State University, Long Beach,* Dr. David Kipnis—*Temple University,* Dr. Stephen G. West—*Florida State University,* and Dr. Ladd Wheeler—*University of Rochester.*

Three individuals read the manuscript in its entirety: Russel G. Geen of the University of Missouri, Arthur G. Miller of Miami University and Brendan G. Rule of the University of Alberta. I owe them a debt of gratitude for the many perceptive suggestions they offered and for the charitable way in which these were phrased.

Clark G. Baxter, Macmillan's psychology editor, deserves a special note of commendation and thanks. His unflagging enthusiasm, his carefully phrased reminders of responsibility, and his willingness to invest his time in a variety of tasks are all greatly appreciated and have contributed greatly to the quality of the finished product. There are many others at Macmillan who have made my job easier and the book a better one. Three deserve special mention: Hurd Hutchins, the production editor, who was always available, cheerful, and helpful and handled the book with a high level of professionalism; L. D. Clepper who was instrumental in developing and implementing the survey of social psychologists that helped me make decisions about the topics to be covered, and, finally, Frances Long who copyedited the manuscript with an unwavering devotion to clarity and correctness of English expression.

J. L.

Contents

ix

Social Psychology— The Theoretical Approach

1

The door closes and you are now twelve. For better or worse you now are a group with an important function. You are to decide an individual's fate and to be responsible to society for that decision. You must reach a decision, for not to reach a decision is to reach one. You are part of a jury, isolated from the rest of the world for whatever

1

Many activities take place in courthouses, but none as fascinating as the events that transpire in the courtroom: many dramas unfold here.

minutes, hours, or days it takes to reach a verdict. You will select a foreperson, deliberate the issues, sometimes argue, disagree, but your job is to decide.

This scene is re-enacted many times each year throughout countries that use the jury system to decide both civil and criminal cases. In Canada criminal cases are often decided by juries although civil cases except in Ontario are no longer decided by jury trials (Moore, 1973). In the United States, juries are still used to decide some civil and some criminal cases. Because the events that transpire in a jury room illuminate many of the issues we will be studying in social psychology, I would like to use this experience to help you understand the topic.

Consider the following case:

John Edwards is charged with the crime of breaking and entering (technically this is burglary) with attempted rape. Opening statements by the prosecution listed the crime. Defense's opening remarks contradicted those facts with an alibi to be presented by the defendant's wife.

The witness for the state, victim Anne Johnson, described her apartment's layout and her activities on the crucial night. She reported being awakened at 4:00 A.M. by an intruder with a sharp object at her throat. The words "I want you" elicited screams from the victim, which caused the intruder to flee and also aroused the landlady. A description was given to the police. Later in the week, the victim saw her attacker coming into the building and realized he lived in the apartment below. In court, the victim pointed out the defendant, who stood. The defense's cross-examination attacked the identification on the basis of the distance he was from her and the poor lighting. The defense also maintained that the "X-rated" movie the victim had attended that night could have affected her suggestibility to thinking the crime occurred. The prosecution's objection was over-ruled.

The defense witness, Paulette Edwards, was the defendant's wife. Her testimony centered on a party given that night which lasted into the early morning. She mentioned that her husband was sleeping at the time the crime occurred. Because of the position of their bed, any movement would have disturbed her sleep. That is, their bed was placed in a corner with the head and one side against a wall. Since she slept on the outer side, he would have had to climb out over her or out the foot of the bed to get out of bed. The prosecution's cross-examination dwelt on her role as hostess and the fact that she may have missed some of the finer details. Further, he challenged Mrs. Edwards' certainty of time. Redirect examination established the proximity of the two apartments and the fact that John Edwards, since he lived in the same building, would not have needed to wear a heavy, down jacket to get to the victim's apartment, an element in the description of her attacker given by Anne Jackson.

Closing statements for the defense re-emphasized the lurid nature of the movie the victim had attended and attacked the in-court identification as inaccurate. Prosecution's summation stressed the positive identification due to the length of time the victim had to observe her assailant. The crime's charges were stressed as was their seriousness.

After the case has been presented, the Judge charges you, the jury in the following way.

Ladies and gentlemen of the Jury, at this time it is the duty of the Court to instruct you as to the law in this case.

1. The indictment in this case charges the defendant with burglary and that he is alleged to have entered the apartment of Anne Johnson on December 15, 1974 with intent to commit a crime, to wit: rape.
2. In order to convict the defendant of burglary there must be proof beyond a reasonable doubt that the defendant did enter the apartment of Anne Johnson with intent to force Anne Johnson to engage in sexual intercourse with the defendant by forceful compulsion or the threat of forceful compulsion that would prevent resistance by a person of reasonable resolution.
3. The burden of establishing the guilt of the defendant beyond a reasonable doubt rests upon the Commonwealth throughout the entire case, and the defendant is not required to prove his innocence.
4. The indictment against the defendant is no evidence of guilt and carries with it no presumption of guilt.
5. The defendant has absolute right, founded on Constitution, not to testify.
6. If upon consideration of all the evidence, the Jury is of the opinion that the evidence is equally balanced, the verdict must be that of not guilty.
7. The Commonwealth's witness, Anne Johnson, has identified the defendant as the one who committed the crime. However, a mistake can be made in identifying a person by a witness attempting to be truthful.

8. In determining whether or not to accept as accurate the identification testimony of Anne Johnson using caution for the reason I just mentioned, you must also take into consideration the following: (a) Whether the testimony of the identification witness is generally believable; (b) Whether her opportunity to observe was sufficient to allow her to make an accurate identification; (c) All the circumstances indicating whether or not the identification was accurate.

9. Although the Commonwealth has the burden of proving that the defendant is guilty, this does not mean that the Commonwealth must prove its case beyond all doubt to a mathematical certainty, nor must it demonstrate the complete impossibility of innocence. A reasonable doubt is a doubt that would cause a reasonably careful and sensible person to hesitate before acting upon a matter of importance in his own affairs. A reasonable doubt must fairly arise out of the evidence that was presented or out of the lack of evidence presented with respect to some element of the crime. A reasonable doubt must be a real doubt; it may not be an imagined one, nor may it be a doubt manufactured to avoid carrying out an unpleasant duty.

10. Do not concern yourselves with deciding on a penalty.

11. So, to summarize, you may not find the defendant guilty based on a mere suspicion of guilt. The Commonwealth has the burden of proving the defendant guilty beyond a reasonable doubt. If it meets that burden, then the defendant is no longer presumed innocent and you should find him guilty. On the other hand, if the Commonwealth does not meet its burden, then you must find him not guilty.

Ladies and gentlemen, you may now retire to the Jury Room to decide on your verdict.

The immediate reaction of many people is that there isn't enough evidence upon which to make a decision. This is the objection of most jurors I have talked to about a case. Remember, most cases that have enough evidence to make them clear-cut never come to trial. If there is little or no evidence, the prosecution does not proceed; if the evidence is overwhelming, the defendant often pleads guilty in an attempt to obtain a lesser sentence. Therefore jurors mostly hear cases that are somewhat ambiguous.

On the basis of the evidence presented, how would you decide the case? Would you vote guilty or not guilty? Possibly you wouldn't know how to vote and would like to consider the views of the other eleven jurors. How do you think you would act in the jury room? If six people favored guilty and six not guilty, would you change your view? What if the other eleven jurors all disagreed with you? Would you then change your view? If during the course of the trial you had become friends with two other jurors, would their opinions influence your decision more than a juror you hardly knew?

There are many more questions such as these that I could ask, but these serve the purpose. Each question I've asked relates to topics of interest to social psychologists, and several of them pertain to subjects that have a chapter in this book devoted to them. This should not be surprising because social psychology studies the interaction of the individual and the environment. The environment can be the physical environment, the psychological environment, which includes other people, or some combination of the two. But let's be more precise about defining *social psychology*.

Defining Social Psychology

Social psychology is a broad field populated by such an assortment of individual-ists that it is difficult to make any definitional umbrella large enough to encompass all of it. Possibly Gordon Allport (1968, p. 3) did as good a job as any of defining social psychology when in the *Handbook of Social Psychology* he described the discipline "as an attempt to understand how the thought, feeling, or behavior of individuals are

SOMETHING ABOUT SOCIAL PSYCHOLOGISTS

Social psychology is primarily a twentieth-century phenomenon. The emphasis upon social behavior and how individuals affect each other's behavior is, in a scientific sense, quite new. As you will note throughout this book, the problems that social psychologists address are intertwined with societal problems. Therefore, if you assumed that social psychologists are personally and professionally concerned with social behavior and the problems it raises, you would be correct.

Another fact about social psychologists is that they write about many things. Recently a visiting social psychologist noted that she had been asked to be a young woman's mentor, and that the two of them were going to write about it. There is an excitement about being in a field that is involved in attempting to help clarify many of the problems faced by society. Consequently our ventures into social areas are oftentimes part of our work; thus work and community service, social involvement, and so forth overlap.

Social psychologists tend to write for both popular newspapers and magazines as well as scholarly journals. A recent study by Endler, Rushton, and Roediger (1978) pointed out an important aspect of publications by social psychologists. Endler et al. did not do a simple count of who published the most; rather they reviewed who was cited the most and who published the most in 1975. Their source was the *Social Science Citation Index*. This index lists all the publications in the major and many of the minor social science journals. However, the index lists citations of books, chapters in books, and convention papers as well as journal articles.

Citations are seen as a more meaningful way of determining the impact an author has on the field. For example, an article may be published and make virtually no impact on the field; i.e., few people read it and even fewer cite it in an article themselves. On the other hand, many people may read it and not cite it or many may read it and virtually all of them cite it. An important article generally will be cited more frequently than an unimportant one and thus citations are a valid index of the impact an article has on the field. By the same reasoning, the more an individual is cited, the more important a contribution he or she has made to the field.

Elder et al. (1978) listed the most cited psychologists in Canada, Great Britain, and the United States. This list was for all areas of psychology, not just social psychology. Of the individuals in this list, 22 percent listed social psychology as their major field. It is hard to determine just how many social psychologists there are, but it is quite probably well under 10 percent of psychologists. Therefore, social psychologists not only publish a lot, but their work is cited a lot also. Even though there are many references in this book to articles on social psychology, I have been quite selective in citing them. The articles that social psychologists produce are impressive both in quality and quantity.

Reference

Endler, N. S., J. P. Rushton, & H. L. Roediger. Productivity and scholarly impact (citations) of British, Canadian, and U.S. departments of psychology (1975). *American Psychologist*, 1978, *33*, 1064–1082.

influenced by the actual, imagined or implied presence of others." Now that definition may not make a lot of sense to you until some concrete examples are added to it. For example, what is the difference between a thought and a feeling, or a behavior, for that matter? How do the imagined and implied presence of others differ from each other? And a few thousand other questions.

One of the things you are going to discover as you read this book is that there is a great deal of disagreement about social psychology: what it is, where it has been, and most importantly, where it is going. In this chapter I will focus on what it is and will give you a short preview of where it appears to be going in the next few years. Most of all, however, I hope to impart to you some of the excitement the field holds for those of us who are working in it. Part of that excitement is its diversity; part is the fact that the field deals with some very difficult and vexing problems.

Theory

Current social psychology—possibly like early social psychology—looks with suspicion upon unitary theories designed to explain large segments of behavior. Recently a colleague whose speciality is learning was reading a good deal of social psychology remarked, "But there's no theory in social psychology." In the sense of the grand theories of learning or of personality, the statement is quite accurate. Social psychologists have an aversion to theories that are intended to account for more than small bits and pieces of behavior. The argument is often made that the social interactions of individuals are too complex for us to develop a comprehensive theory from them at this time, and so many minitheories are proposed. As Allport (1968, p. 9) puts it: "Few modern writers focus on a single motive or mechanism and claim it to be an all-sufficient explanation of social behavior. Yet even today we find authors who favor some one predominant factor to the *relative* neglect of others. Among them are such favorites as *conditioning, reinforcement, anxiety, sexuality, guilt, frustration, cognitive, role,* and *social class.*"

Scientific Theories

Each one of us has ideas, guesses, and conjectures about how things work. Sometimes our theories are very simple: sometimes quite complex. Gamblers probably have more theories, and more complex ones, than most other people. Their theories can be exceedingly elaborate, considering many variables and interweaving them in unique and highly creative ways. Their theories also are distinguished by their inaccuracy, because in casinos, lotteries, and almost all other forms of legal and illegal gambling, someone skims the cream off the top, so most gamblers will lose in the long run. Precisely because the odds are so bad, gambling theories aren't very successful.

There are two types of scientific theories. Those of one type, the informal theories, are a lot like any other type of theory, except that they differ from the outcome of a gambler's theory because there isn't a "house" to skim off the cream. In many other

Gamblers use many aids in developing their theories. Here are three aids available at a corner newsstand.

respects, however, informal scientific theories are ideas, guesses, or conjectures about how things work. These theories differ from the even less formal theories we have been talking about in two major ways. For a scientific theory to get very far, it should be both public and falsifiable (subject to being tested and disproved). Most gambler's theories do not become public. If they fail, the theorist is rather embarrassed to talk about it and if they are successful, it is even more important to keep them secret.

An informal scientific theory, on the other hand, if it is to gain acceptance must be made known to other scientists and subjected to their thoughts, comments, and empirical tests. In short, an informal scientific theory must be made public and put to the test. The way theories are developed, made public, and put to the test is the heart of science, and is very fascinating.

Formal scientific theories are quite a different matter. At the least, they should have a construct (a complex idea formed from a number of simpler ideas) system having a clearly stated syntax (structure of word order in a language), and a set of semantic (meaningful) links to observables. As you can see, even the minimal demands of a formal scientific theory are great. Few theories in social psychology meet these standards. The reason for this is that a formal theory must have a set of complex ideas with the relationship between the ideas and behavior clearly stated. Because we are not yet as sophisticated in predicting behavior as we would like, the breakdown in formal theories most often occurs in linking ideas to observables. Examples of social psychological theories that meet the minimal criteria here discussed are balance theory (see Chapters 5 and 9), Zajonc's theory of social facilitation (see Chapter 11) and the reinforcement-affect theory of attraction (see Chapter 9).

Many of the theories of social psychology are really hypotheses (very similar to informal scientific theories).

SOCIAL PSYCHOLOGY AND HISTORY

Many people, students, professors, and individuals not in academic pursuits, face the thought of history with less than positive emotions. Our culture has somehow come to view history as dry and boring. Throughout this chapter you will note several references to the history of social psychology and the history of ideas. These ideas are both helpful and provocative.

In a recent article Sampson (1978) has argued that the scientist in general and the social scientist in particular must deal with what he terms the "sociohistorical standpoint." This simply means that scientific "truth" is embedded in a social and historical context and the social and historical context affects our knowledge. In a discipline such as social psychology it almost seems unnecessary to emphasize such a point. Except for two reasons, it would be unnecessary. There are those, of course, who would ignore the social and historical context and attempt to find truth that transcends such variables. The other extreme argues that the social and historical context are so important and changeable that we cannot ascertain behavioral laws.

Sampson argues that social psychology developed in a sociohistorical ethos that was favorable to individualism, capitalism, male-dominance, and the middle class. If these sociohistorical variables affect our view of social psychology, then you can expect to see in these pages an emphasis on competition, the need to achieve, materialistic societies, the importance of the male, and prejudice. These issues are important and constitute a large portion of this book. Thus, it seems that there is little doubt that the social and historical nature of North American culture have influenced social psychology. If that society were altruistic, nonaggressive, unprejudiced and emphasized living in harmony with nature, Chap-

ters 6, 8, 10, and 12 in this book would be quite different from what they are.

Rosnow (1978) has proposed that the ideas of an eighteenth-century social philosopher, Giambattista Vico, have meaning for social psychology today. Vico argued that human nature and society are constantly changing. He did not, however, agree that this constant change must result in social-psychological chaos. Rather he felt that the changes are cyclical in nature. In fact, Vico argued that there were several stages of social evolution. First, there was a stage characterized by people of strength preying on the weak. Next was a stage in which the ruling class formed protective alliances for their own enhancement and serfs were at the bottom of the social order. Third, the serfs succeeded in gaining social reforms and rights previously denied them. This Vico saw as the age of reason, conscience, and duty.

Rosnow proposes that the cyclical nature of social change is a potent tool in studying social psychology. It should be possible, argues Rosnow, to incorporate new methods of studying social behavior to account for the changes that occur, but are themselves predictable. For one such application, look at McClelland's work on need achievement, which is discussed in Chapter 4.

References

Rosnow, R. L. The prophetic vision of Giambattista Vico: Implications for the state of social psychological theory. *Journal of Personality and Social Psychology,* 1978, *36,* 1322–1331.

Sampson, E. E. Scientific paradigms and social values: Wanted—A scientific revolution. *Journal of Personality and Social Psychology,* 1978, *36,* 1332–1343.

You might wonder why I don't just make a distinction between hypotheses and theories and leave it at that. Unfortunately, many hypotheses are labeled theories in the literature of social psychology and you should be able to distinguish between the two for yourself.

Theory Development

Proving a theory is impossible. Over the years scientific theories come to be accepted, but no one can guarantee that a better explanation (theory) will not come along in a few years to supplant the current one.

To reach a decision in the case of John Edwards, you had to develop a theory. The theory may be simple or it may be complex; but you must decide whether John Edwards is guilty. Your theory may be based on the assumption that Paulette Edwards lied to protect her husband; or it may be based on the assumption that Anne Johnson was mistaken in her identification of John. In research on jury decision making using this case, we have had jurors who adamantly argued one or the other of these points of view (plus many others).

The theory a juror develops has much more in common with a scientific theory than does one developed by a gambler. The juror and the scientist must take limited evidence and reach a series of decisions. Neither one ever knows that the theory is accurate. For example, the defendant may be convicted, but he is convicted by the fact that twelve people believe him guilty *beyond a reasonable doubt*. The scientist always knows that no matter how many experiments he runs that do not falsify the theory, someday the theory may prove inadequate.

The Role of Theory in Social Psychology— Monistic Theories

Monistic theories are theories that attempt to explain the world with one basic concept. A description of a few monistic theories might be helpful to you; most of these were philosophical in origin.

Hedonism

Hedonism, which began in Greek times and reached its high point with Jeremy Bentham (1748–1832), is a much maligned monistic theory. Probably because it has been associated with the quote "eat, drink and be merry, for tomorrow we die," it has been looked at with suspicion. Not that we don't enjoy the "eat, drink and be merry" part, but there is enough of the Puritan in all of us that we feel a little guilty about enjoying it. As we will see later, hedonism is much more than its popular image.

Allport (1968) advises us to consider the difference between hedonism of the past, the present, and the future. Hedonism of the past emphasizes that we do that (and only that?) which we have found pleasurable in the past. Certainly, there is evidence for the idea that when we are confronted with a situation that has in the past resulted in a pleasurable outcome, we welcome it. By the same token, we tend to avoid situations that have previously resulted in unpleasant consequences. Few, if any, people live strictly for pleasure in the present. We save money, we go to the dentist, wash dishes, and forego other pleasures. The more immature an individual, the more immediate gratification is practiced. However, this hedonism of the present, which most clearly fits the "eat, drink, and be merry" label, is clearly not a viable way of life for social animals.

The hedonism of the future, which is the view of the classical hedonists, is another matter. This view asserts that we behave in a manner that we expect to be most pleasurable. These expectations may come from previous experience, our own thoughts about what will happen, or a combination of the two. Some, including Allport, have agrued that it is hard to see how future pleasure can motivate present behavior. I have never had a problem with such an idea, in that we do save our money for future pleasure, we do forego immediate pleasure for anticipated future pleasure, and so forth. Humans can and do expect pleasure and they can think about pleasure and possibly experience it abstractly. The expectation of pleasure comes in many forms; for some it is physical, for others spiritual, for still others how they will be viewed historically. If we think of hedonism only as an abandoned seeking after physical pleasure, then it is not a very satisfactory explanation of motivation. If, however, we realize that the expected pleasures of hedonism of the future can take quite diverse forms for a species with as developed a cognitive capacity as humans, then it has many possibilities as a motivational construct.

Another monistic theory is that of power, which has received growing attention from social psychologists in recent years (cf. Kipnis, 1976). Thomas Hobbes (1588–1679) postulated a special form of hedonism, egoism, which inferred that the pleasure humanity sought was power. Allport (1968, p. 16) calls these theories *irrational* and suggests that an irrational theory must have two features: "(1) It must claim that the prime determinants of human behavior are emotion, drive, instinct or some form of blind will. (2) It must also square these motives with the apparently peaceful and logical structure of group living." Rational theories, on the other hand, emphasize the use of the mind and accept reason as the supreme authority. Thus, for our purposes, a rational theory of social behavior is one which asserts that rational processes guide our behavior. As will become apparent shortly, humans are probably too complex to divide into nice categories of irrational or rational; sometimes we are one and sometimes the other.

Hedonism is the basis for several important theoretical approaches in psychology. I will mention but two. The law of effect, which is generally associated with learning theory, says that a response will be strengthened when it produces an event that is satisfying to the organism. For example, if you are hungry, any response you make that produces food will be strengthened. That is, the next time you are hungry you are more likely to make the response that previously resulted in food. Hedonism has also been at the heart of the so-called "affect" theories of motivation such as that of McClelland (see Chapter 4). Both of these examples invoke hedonism of the future. It is apparent that hedonism is new neither in the world of ideas or in psychology.

The Faculties of the Mind

Beginning with Plato, and certainly within the few short decades of social psychology, three basic positions have been utilized in developing social psychological theories. Plato felt that the mind is constituted of three faculties, the affective or feeling, the conative or striving, and the cognitive or thought processes. Modern psychologists may stress either the affective, conative, or cognitive realms. Affect we may view as feelings or emotions, conation as striving, and cognition as thought.

AFFECT

Allport (1968) equates affect with sympathy, but it is apparent that affect or feelings or emotions are a basic component of the hedonistic doctrine, which we discussed earlier. In hedonism affect is directed toward oneself rather than toward another. For many years there has been a tension among philosophers, psychologists, and most other people concerning the appropriate reaction to oneself and to others. On the one hand, there have been strong social pressures (most often religious) to deny oneself and to be kind to others. In the Christian religion this pressure has resulted in extreme denials of self among certain of the clergy and other religious orders by taking vows of celibacy and poverty, with lesser requirements of self-denial for lay persons. We use the Christian religion only as an example; there are other traditions, religious and secular, East and West, that could serve as our illustration.

It is not surprising, then, that Allport would equate sympathy with affect. It is interesting to note, however, that the founder of the Christian religion seemed to have more insight into human nature than many present-day psychologists when he said, "Love your neighbor as yourself." In fact, Carl Rogers (1959) has developed a personality theory that is based on the self-concept. More specifically, Rogers says that the greater the difference in what a person is and what that person wants to be, the more maladjusted that person is. Social psychology has been very concerned with self-concept and in more recent years with altruism. As we shall see in later chapters, there is still basic argument among social psychologists concerning the effect of self-concept on social interactions, and the motivation behind altruistic actions.

It may be apparent to you by now that I am basically taking the position that hedonism and sympathy are not necessarily incompatible. In fact, if we listen to such diverse thinkers as Jesus Christ and Carl Rogers, it may be impossible to have the latter without the former.

Another element of sympathy that is often overlooked, but is receiving much more attention as research in the area of altruism progresses, is that it may indeed be pleasurable to help other people. If that is the case, then the barrier between what Allport views as sympathy and hedonism is further eroded. As we said in the beginning and will say again, the complexity of human behavior is enormous. That complexity causes both the fascination and the frustration of studying it.

IMITATION

The conative faculty described by Plato is probably best termed *imitation* (Allport, 1968). There is overwhelming social conformity in the world. Children grow up and act like their parents, who act like their parents before them, and so on. The howling, rooting, completely self-centered newborn grows up to become a member of society and except for those we label deviates, conforms to the demands of that society. This process, known as socialization, is one that has fascinated personality theorists, developmental psychologists, and many others. Bandura, a behaviorist (1971; 1973; 1974; Bandura and Jeffery, 1973), has developed the most general and viable view of imitation. Bandura points out that some years ago Reichard (1938) noted that in many languages the word for *teach* is the same as the word for *show,* indicating the importance of imitation, or what Bandura prefers to call modeling. Bandura (1973) points out that there are several reasons why modeling influences play a paramount role in learning in everyday life. First, when mistakes are costly, or even dangerous, modeling reduces them, thus allowing for a greater percentage of us to survive our formative years. This would not occur if, for example, we did not have the opportunity to view models crossing the street properly, avoiding vicious dogs, or learning to stay clear of the mean and sadistic bully down the block. In addition, some complex behaviors would never occur if they were not learned through modeling. Human speech is virtually impossible to learn without hearing it, as is exemplified by the enormous amount of time and effort it takes to teach a deaf child to speak. Finally, even in situations where it is possible for the individual to learn without viewing a model, the speed of learning can be considerably enhanced by viewing a model (Bandura and McDonald, 1963; Luchins and Luchins, 1961).

Bandura emphasizes three effects of modeling, the first of which we have already discussed, the acquisition of new patterns of behavior through observation. Second,

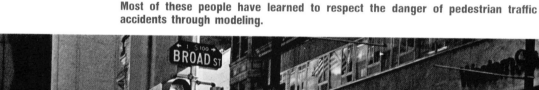

Most of these people have learned to respect the danger of pedestrian traffic accidents through modeling.

modeling can strengthen or weaken inhibitions of behavior that observers have previously learned. This weakening occurs through observing the effects of an action as they occur to a model. Just as a child can learn to cross the street in a crosswalk by observing others do it, seeing someone struck by a car while crossing in the middle of the block can have strongly inhibiting effects on the child. Finally, observing the actions of others serves as a social prompt that can facilitate similar behaviors in an observer. This response facilitation is distinguished from observational learning and disinhibition by "the fact that no new responses are acquired, and the appearance of analogous actions is not attributable to weakening of inhibitions because the behavior is socially acceptable and hence unencumbered by restraints (Bandura, 1973, p. 69)."

Gestalt psychologists meanwhile doubted the behavioristic interpretation of imitation and almost everything else. Asch (1952) argues that learning through imitation is possible "only when the observer has understood the sense of the action he has followed and when he has noted its relevance to the given conditions" (p. 390). Imitation for the Gestaltists is an intelligent process and the task of the observer is to learn what is to be imitated. Thus, for Asch, imitation is a process of discovering what it is that is to be imitated. He illustrates this point by referring to a parlor game that requires each participant to pass an object to the next person in exactly the same way it was received. The object of the game is to determine what it is that must be imitated—in this particular game it is whether the person who passed the object to you had his or her legs crossed or uncrossed. It is a very difficult game to master and makes Asch's point beautifully: that imitation is possible only when the observer has understood the action to be imitated.

COGNITION

When psychologists talk about cognitive psychology, what is typically meant is anything that has to do with thinking. This is a broad field, but it is made even broader by the fact that you may feel emotion or affect, but it is rarely in such a pure form that you do not think about it. Certainly we have all heard or possibly even felt an emotion so strongly that we reacted without thought. Stark terror in which a person freezes or performs superhuman feats of strength do occur. But basically, most emotions are mixed, to a lesser or greater degree, with thoughts or cognitions. Asch's description of imitation can in no way be understood without understanding the cognitive element in it.

For that matter, except for radical Skinnerians, of whom few are left, reinforcement theories in personality and in social psychology are becoming more and more cognitive (Mischel, 1968; Mahoney and Thorensen, 1974; Meichenbaum, 1972). Few people argue today that humans do not think about the reinforcements they receive, and there are more animal learning theorists who are following in Tolman's (1932) cognitive footsteps (cf. Bindra, 1976; Bolles, 1967; Capaldi, 1967). There are a few dyed-in-the-wool radical behaviorists today, but unfortunately most assertions that reinforcement is not a cognitive process come from detractors of the behaviorists position who attempt to set up "straw men" to knock down, with their assertions that reinforcement has no cognitive elements. Even the Skinnerians do not deny the existence of cognitive elements, just the profitability of studying them given our present state of knowledge.

Pluralistic Theories

Precisely because of the difficulty in accounting for social behavior with monistic theories, psychologists moved away from them to pluralistic theories. I will not discuss all the pluralistic theories offered, just some of them. For convenience sake, I will divide the discussion of seven pluralistic theories into three rough divisions; sociological, behavioral, and cognitive theories. Many of my colleagues will undoubtedly argue with my division, and like any organizational scheme it is arbitrary—it represents the world as I see it.

Sociological Theories

It is probably safe to say that sociologists and psychologists view the world somewhat differently. Sociologists are more concerned with the societal aspects of social psychology, whereas psychologists are more concerned with the individual aspects. The first two theories we will deal with are theories that are more concerned with the group than with the individual, so we have labeled them sociological in nature.

SOCIAL CLASS

In some countries, social classes are strictly adhered to by a caste system in which an individual may not change the caste into which he or she was born. This, of course, is social class taken to extreme limits and is not the real focus of our discussion. In less structured societies, classes arise and are typically based on heredity (as with kings and nobility), wisdom (as in Plato's Philosopher Kings), or more often wealth.

In Canada and the United States social class is not nearly so pervasive as it is in other countries. For example, Goyder and Curtis (1977) found that in Canada the correlation between father's and son's occupation is quite modest (about 0.38). This is quite close to the correlation found in the United States. Furthermore, Goyder and Curtis found that the relationship in Canada between occupations of grandfathers and grandsons and great-grandfathers and great-grandsons to be so small that they added only trivially to predicting future generations' occupations. They concluded that Canada, like the United States, was a country in which social class was not strong enough to deter individuals from achieving a higher (or lower) social class than their parents or grandparents had.

There is at least one occupation, however, in which social class plays a strong role in both Canada and the United States. Forcese and DeVries (1977) report that in the 1974 Canadian Parliamentary election, high-status occupations were overrepresented, relative to labor force statistics, particularly in the Liberal and Progressive Conservative parties. Only in the Social Credit party was there a numerical majority of lower-status candidates. Regardless of party affiliation, however, a high-status candidate had almost twice as high a probability of being elected as a low-status candidate. In both Canada and the United States, even though occupational mobility is high, high-status individuals are elected to govern the country.

Social class has had its most successful impact as a theory where it has aided in predicting behavior. That is, in certain areas, members of a specific social class are more likely to behave or perform in a certain way, thus allowing us to predict that behavior more accurately. For example, social class theory, even in the United States, where it is relatively informal, allows us to make certain predictions about behavior. Being a sociological theory, it is intended to predict how the class will behave and not how the individual will behave. Thus it has its greatest impact when social classes are the units of interest rather than individuals.

ROLE THEORY

Role theory also emphasizes the social nature of social psychology, rather than the individual. Role theory fits quite well with social class theory, because it emphasizes the role or roles that individuals fill, and these roles are, at least to some extent, a function of the social class a person is in. Note how well the definition of *role* fits with social class, since it is usually thought of as "a set of behaviors or functions which are appropriate to the position a person holds within a particular social context" (Biddle and Thomas, 1966; Shaw and Costanzo, 1970). For example, when you are acting as a student there are certain behaviors that are appropriate to your role as a student. When you go home, however, you may be a daughter, son, wife, mother, husband, roommate, and so on. In whatever role you occupy at home, there are certain behaviors that are appropriate to that role and you perform those behaviors.

Role theory is predictively at its best when hypotheses about a class of people—those occupying a specific role—are concerned. Role theory is not as concerned with the prediction of the behavior of one person, although such an interest does appear when role conflict occurs. Role conflict occurs when a person holds several positions that are incompatible with each other. If you are the mother of small children, role conflict occurs each evening when you need to sit down and study and your children are quite convinced that your more appropriate role is that of mother and you should read to or play with them. Thus, there is role conflict and both roles cannot be met simultaneously.

Behavioral Theories

In 1913 Watson published his now famous, or depending on your point of view, infamous, paper entitled "Psychology as a behaviorist views it." Behaviorism was to encompass American and Canadian psychology and hold sway for many years. Until Watson the major philosophical ancestors of psychology such as Locke and Berkeley argued that consciousness was the proper element for study. Early psychologists such as Wundt and Titchner were in total agreement about studying consciousness. Watson disagreed and argued that behavior was the proper element of study for psychology. Behaviorism came upon the scene and began to dominate that scene. Watson argued that he could shape a dozen healthy, well-formed infants and he could mold them into any type of specialist (Watson, 1930). This emphasis upon the importance of the environment in determining how far an individual could rise rather than being locked in to some predetermined "place in life" by heredity suited the temper of the times in early twentieth-century North America. In social psychology, two minitheories that are direct imports from behaviorism will be considered.

CONDITIONING

Conditioning, as it is usually used in social psychology, is taken from the learning process generally referred to as classical conditioning. By this time in your psychological studies you have probably been introduced to the basic elements of classical conditioning which were intensively studied by Pavlov (1927). To refresh your memory, a neutral stimulus is paired with a stimulus that will produce the response being studied. After many pairings, the formally neutral stimulus alone will produce the response. For example, Pavlov utilized salivation as a response to study. He found that hungry dogs would not salivate when a light was turned on, but would salivate when they were given meat powder. After several pairings of the light and the meat powder, the dogs would salivate as soon as the light came on. Stated more technically, the light was the conditioned stimulus (CS), the meat powder was the unconditioned stimulus (UCS), while salivation was the response being studied. When the response occurs because of the meat powder, it is called the unconditioned response (UCR); it is called the conditioned response (CR) when it occurs when the light is turned on by itself. Figure 1–1 is a schematic illustration of classical conditioning.

Many stimuli and responses other than lights, meat powder, and salivation have been studied, and certain social psychologists have developed classical conditioning models for social phenomena. One example of such a model is Byrne and Clore's (1970) model of interpersonal attraction.

According to Byrne and Clore, attraction occurs when a CS is paired with a UCS. Usually, the CS is a person, but in a series of unique studies, it has been shown that pairing a UCS with inanimate objects increases the positiveness of the individual's feelings toward the inanimate object (Griffitt and Guay, 1969; Sachs and Byrne, 1970). The UCS is usually an attitude, value, or evaluation, and if it is a positive

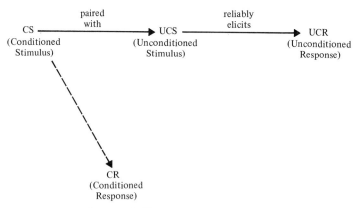

Figure 1–1 **Schematic illustration of classical conditioning.**

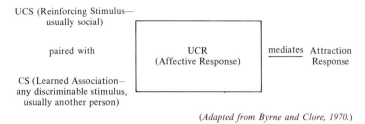

UCS (Reinforcing Stimulus—
usually social)

paired with

UCR
(Affective Response)

mediates Attraction
Response

CS (Learned Association—
any discriminable stimulus,
usually another person)

(*Adapted from Byrne and Clore, 1970.*)

Figure 1–2 **Schematic diagram of classical conditioning model of attraction.**

stimulus it leads to attraction whereas a negative UCS will tend to lead to dislike of the other person. The response that is made is an affective one which mediates the basic attraction response of liking or disliking the other person. Figure 1–2 shows the relationship schematically.

A classical conditioning model of attraction or any other social behavior (for example, see Staats and Staats, 1957, and Staats and Staats, 1958, for models that deal with the classical conditioning of meaning and attitudes) is enticing because of its simplicity and straightforward approach. It is also probably too simple an explanation for most social phenomena. Byrne (1971) utilizes not only classical conditioning, but instrumental conditioning, motivational constructs, information processing, and a whole host of other concepts in attempting to develop a predictive theory of interpersonal attraction. The essence of complex human interactions will probably need a number of explanatory and predictive models to be understood.

REINFORCEMENT

A closely aligned minitheoretical approach is reinforcement theory. Like classical conditioning, reinforcement theory is translated by analogy from learning psychology to account for social behavior. Usually, when a social psychologist labels his or her theory as a reinforcement one, the theory follows the instrumental learning paradigm. Instrumental learning occurs when a person's response produces some change in the environment. If the response produces a positive change, the probability of that response occurring again is increased, whereas a response that produces a negative change in the environment will decrease the probability of the recurrence of the response. The positive change in the environment, whatever it is, is called a positive reinforcer; the negative change is a punisher. Now, let us illustrate what we have just said using a common example from learning. If we put a hungry rat in a runway and put food at the end of the runway, the rat can change the environment positively by running down the runway (a response) and eating the food. On the other hand, if we put painful electric shock at the end of the runway, the rat negatively changes the environment by running to the end of the runway. The food is a positive reinforcer and the shock is a punisher. Common sense would tell us that the rat is going to run down the runway more often when there is food than when there is shock. This is what we mean when we say that the probability of a response will be increased by a positive reinforcer and decreased by a punisher.

Cognitive is derived from the noun *cognition,* which is defined as "the act or process of knowing; perception." This dictionary definition of cognitive is certainly in accord with Zimbardo's (1969, p. 11) statement: "If cognitions represent 'knowledge, opinion or belief about the environment, about oneself or one's behavior' (Festinger, 1957), then cognitive organization represents the psychological ordering and structuring of prior information processing and becomes a predictor of future motivational, attitudinal, and behavioral effects." This approach is also consistent with Zajonc's (1967) definition: "By *cognitive structure* or *cognitive organization* we shall mean any form of interdependence among cognitive elements, whatever their definitions, which has motivational, affective, attitudinal, behavioral, or cognitive consequences" (1967, p. 321.)

Unfortunately, such definitions are so broad as to include virtually everything and exclude nothing. Thus, whether a theory is viewed as a cognitive theory or not is a matter of emphasis and personal preference on the part of the theorist. This leads to at least a plausible deduction, namely that those who are behaviorists and those who are cognitive theorists are studying the same thing and using a different vocabulary to describe it. At one level, this is obviously the case. Both groups study behavior. At this level, the obviousness of this statement makes it absurd.

There is, however, another level at which the similarities between behavioristic and cognitive theories are such that it may be fruitful to view them as complementary rather than opposing views. I am, however, ahead of my story. First, a few words about specific cognitive theories are in order.

GESTALT THEORY

Gestalt is a German word, which is not easily translated into English although "figure," "form," or "pattern" probably comes closest to its meaning. The basic statement of Gestalt theory is that "the whole is greater than the sum of its parts." Gestalt psychologists have been active in many fields, studying such diverse psychological processes as perception, problem solving, psychotherapy, impression formation, and conformity. Probably its most important disciple in social psychology was Solomon Asch. Gestalt psychology and behaviorism are seen as opposing traditions, but interestingly enough, they both began about the same time and both were reactions against Wundt and Titchner (Boring, 1950). They did, however, react against Wundt and Titchner for quite different reasons. Gestaltists protested against the analysis of consciousness into elements and the exclusion of values from the data of consciousness. Behaviorism reacted against the inclusion of the data of consciousness in psychology.

Gestalt psychology cannot be understood without understanding a few of the basic principles of the theory. The most basic of the basic principles are the "laws of form." There are numerous laws of form (Boring reports 114 of them) but most are reducible to a few basics. Because Gestalt psychology arose as an experimental psychology most of its laws of form applied to visual perception. Two or three examples will give you a "flavor" of the movement: (1) A perceptual field tends to become organized, taking on form with each smaller part becoming connected to larger parts to form structures. (2) A structure may be simple or complex and the more complex a figure is the more *articulate* it is. (3) A good form is a well-articulated one, which tends to impress itself upon the observer.

Perhaps an example or two will be helpful. If we view the figure [ ], we tend to see a square, not two vertical lines with horizontal cross lines that are not connected. This principle is known as *closure,* because we tend to finish an incomplete figure. *Proximity* (closeness) is another organizing principle that we use. For example, if we see eight circles arranged in the following manner

$$0 \quad 0 \qquad 0 \quad 0 \qquad 0 \quad 0 \qquad 0 \quad 0$$

we tend to see four pairs of circles rather than eight separate circles. These are just two examples of many possible ones that point out Gestalt ideas.

The three laws of form, together with many other Gestalt ideas, were incorporated by Solomon Asch in studying a variety of social phenomena. Asch (1952, p. 52) started with the assumption (which he attributed to Von Ehrenfels, 1890) that "Many of the most obvious qualities we perceive are those which reside in an entire object and not in its parts." Stated another way, Asch was saying that *the whole is not the sum of its parts*—it is far more.

One of Asch's (1946) famous demonstrations of this Gestalt idea was in the area of impression formation. Two groups of subjects heard character descriptions of two individuals, which were identical except for one word.

Group A heard the individual described as intelligent—skillful—industrious—*warm*—determined—practical—cautious.

Group B heard the individual described as intelligent—skillful—industrious—*cold*—determined—practical—cautious.

A check list of trait adjectives, mostly opposites, was prepared, and after hearing the description of the individual the groups differed dramatically in other characteristics they attributed to the person precisely because they had heard him described as warm or cold. For example, of the group that had heard the individual described as warm, 91 percent said he was generous, 65 percent said he was wise, 90 percent said he was happy, 94 percent said he was good-natured and 77 percent said he was humorous. The group that had heard the individual described as cold responded quite differently with 8 percent saying he was generous, 25 percent wise, 34 percent happy, 34 percent good-natured and 17 percent said he was humorous. There were other traits that were not affected by the warm-cold description. These included honest, strong, serious, and persistent.

Asch argues that this experiment demonstrates that the change in one quality (warm vs. cold) produces a fundamental change in the entire impression of the person. Furthermore, as not all traits were equally affected, the results are not an indiscriminate one, that is, there was not a "halo effect." We will discuss Asch's work on impression formation in greater detail in Chapter 3. This, however, should give you the flavor of Gestalt theory as it applies to social psychology.

FIELD THEORY
Kurt Lewin developed field theory, which is essentially a cognitive approach. A person lives in his or her *life*-space, which is the immediate environment *as perceived*

by the individual. Lewin felt that a full understanding of the total field in which an individual exists involves a description (the *how* of that existence) and an explanation (the *why* of the existence). The person moves around—to get places, to get hold of things, to get rid of things. Desires are called *valences* in Lewin's system and something an individual wants has a positive valence and something the individual does not want, wants to be rid of, or avoid has a negative valence. Positive valences are *vectors,* a term which indicates a force pushing the individual toward the desired object. An object with a negative valence pushes the person away. Thus, if the life-space of an individual is known and the vector-valences of the objects in it are known, it is possible to predict with some degree of accuracy the result of the forces on the individual, or, more simply, what the individual will do.

The difficulty with Lewin's approach, which is taken from mathematics, is that people live in psychological space as well as physical space. What is important to an individual is not space as it actually exists, but space as the individual perceives it. In psychological space, distance may be greatly distorted in relation to physical space. Lewin met this difficulty by introducing the basic concept of topology—space that has in it only order, not direction or distance. In topological life-space, distance from point A to point B is only the number of intervening events.

E. C. Tolman, a cognitive animal learning theorist, felt very much at home with Lewin's approach. According to Boring (1950, p. 126), this was so because both men believed that "if you can describe motive and purpose in deterministic terms, you will have explained them and have obtained the predictive psychology of human nature that so many have sought." This is a rather strange alliance (at least from the viewpoint of modern social psychologists)—Lewin, who is a most important figure in the history of cognitive social psychology being aligned with an animal learning theorist—but an alliance that is not so far-fetched if the suggestion alluded to on page 18 is accurate.

OTHER COGNITIVE THEORIES

There is something slightly demeaning about being thrown into the "other" category. I do not mean to demean any of the theories mentioned here, but I would rather mention them than ignore them altogether. Most of these theories were developed to account for data of a specific sort. For example, cognitive dissonance (Festinger, 1957) and innoculation theory (McGuire, 1964) were developed mainly within the context of research on attitude change. Balance theory (Heider, 1946; 1958; Newcomb, 1953; 1959) was first developed to account for attitude change, but has been utilized in theorizing about interpersonal attraction (Newcomb, 1968). Social comparison theory (Festinger, 1954) and information integration theory (Anderson, 1968) were formulated for or have been expanded to account for research data concerning multiple social phenomena, but we must delay discussion of these theories until later in the book.

COMMENT

What are we to say about cognitive theories in general? Basically, it seems safe to assume that social behavior is influenced, mediated, or even controlled by some cognitive element. The major point of contention with cognitive theory *per se* is that the typical definition of *cognitive* in social psychology (see p. 18) is all-inclusive. Virtually every theory that depends to one degree or another on the ability to think or reason is a cognitive theory. That is precisely why there have been so many variations of cognitive theory, because it so adequately handles the how of human behavior (human reasoning ability). But it has been much less successful in answering the question why, although Festinger's social comparison and dissonance theories and, to a lesser extent balance theory, have wrestled with the problem. Gestalt and field theories were more attuned to the question of how humans interact with their environment than to the why of such interactions.

Attribution Theory

In what is undoubtedly a change from relying on minitheories, the 1970s have become the age of a single theory that attempts to account for much of human behavior. Ironically, the theory is built upon the individual's perception of the situation and has been termed by its founder, Fritz Heider (1958), "naïve psychology." If all of this sounds a bit simple, it is, at least in one manner of viewing the situation. Nevertheless, the complexities and scope of the theory also need recognition, and so another name has been given to the theory, *attribution* theory. In its broadest sense, attribution theory is concerned with the attempts of ordinary people to understand the causes and the implications of the events they witness and experience. For example, if you are a juror in the case of John Edwards, the attribution theorist is concerned with how you interpret what you have seen and heard in the courtroom and he reaches some conclusion about how it affects your vote of either guilty or not guilty.

One of the enormously important things that Fritz Heider first called to the attention of psychologists over thirty-five years ago was the simple fact that your actions are controlled by how you perceive an event more than by what actually happened. Furthermore, if for some reason or another you do not perceive something, it will have no effect on your behavior. For example, if you meet a man at a party who is strongly antiabortion and you are strongly in favor of abortion, you may leave the party convinced that he is a very narrow and bigoted person. This may occur in spite of the fact that he is far from that, being very sensitive to the pain and suffering of others in quite diverse situations. You, however, have not had the opportunity to perceive his opinions in other areas and so make your judgment of him on the basis of the information you have.

Heider's view of attribution was influenced by his early desire to become a painter. He argues that drawing and painting allow an individual directly to experience and interact with the phenomenon of interest. In turn, the individual becomes aware of the many ways in which the phenomenon can be perceived and interpreted. To be more exact, Heider sees attribution as a bridge between ourselves and things that are distant about which we need information. For example, if you are given a book in a foreign language you do not read, the information is there but you cannot bridge the gap between information and the knowledge the book contains. It is this

CAUSE OR REASON?

In a recent comment on attribution theory, Buss (1978) argued that attribution theorists have not adequately distinguished between cause and reason. Remember, the attribution theorist is very interested in the causes people attribute to events in their own lives and in the lives of others. If causes and reasons differ—and they do—then it is important for attribution theorists to keep the distinctions firmly in mind. Buss argued that this has not been done and it is vital for the theory for the distinction to be kept clear.

Buss points out that causes and reasons are logically different categories used to explain different aspects of behavior. Causes are the events, either external or internal, that serve to bring about a change. Reasons, on the other hand, are those things for which a change is brought about. These may include goals and purposes. For example, in a game of pool the cause of a ball starting to move and to drop in a pocket is that it was struck by the cue ball you just hit. The reason for that ball dropping is so that you may win the game.

The fourth point Buss makes concerns behavior that happens to a person. Behavior that is nonintentional and that a person "suffers" is an *occurrence,* but it is explained by that person and by observers with causes. Behavior that is done *by* a person, that is, behavior that has a goal or purpose, and is intended, is an action. This sort of behavior is explained by the actor with reasons, while the observer may use cause and/or reasons for explaining the action. That is when you, the actor, do something that has a goal or purpose, you know what that goal or purpose is and attribute your action to that reason. Someone observing you may attribute that action to a reason, which may, or may not, be the same goal or purpose you had in mind, or they may attribute that action to a cause.

The kinds of attributions made depend upon what kind of behavior is to be explained and who is doing the explaining. Recall that the two kinds of behavior to be explained are occurrences (i.e., behavior that happens to people) and actions (behavior that is done by a person). The person explaining the behavior may be actor or observer. Occurrences are explained by both actor and observer with causes. Actions are explained by the actor with reasons and by the observer with causes and/or reasons.

What does this critique of attribution theory by Buss mean? Basically, it means that the academic scientist must be more precise in the use of the words cause and reason than the intuitive scientist is. If attribution theory is to advance, according to Buss, the theorist must clearly distinguish between those behaviors that are causal in nature and those that are purposive. For example, if someone's house catches on fire because of faulty wiring, the fire happens to that person and should be explained causally. If, on the other hand, the individual sets his or her house on fire to collect insurance, the action has a goal and should be explained by referring to that reason.

Buss argues that this important distinction will go a long way toward clarifying attribution theory.

Reference

Buss, A. R. Causes and reasons in attribution theory: A conceptual critique. *Journal of Personality and Social Psychology,* 1978, *36,* 1311–1321.

step, bridging the gap between information out there and what it means to the individual, that is at the heart of attribution theory.

Correspondent Inference Theory

Jones and Davis (1965) developed an attributional theory that emphasized the fact that people will attempt to achieve desirable consequences by their behavior.

Look carefully at this picture. Try to infer what is happening. Can you see anything burning? If not, why are the firemen there?

Therefore, when actors have behavioral freedom, their intentions should be discernible from the consequences or effects of their behavior. The ideal perceiver is an information processor, but this individual considers what the actor might have done as well as what he did do. Further elaboration of the theory has been carried out by Jones and McGillis (1976).

All choices have consequences, even the choice to do nothing. The actor must have knowledge of the consequences, the ability to perform certain actions, and behavioral freedom. Each action, whether chosen or not, has multiple consequences. Some of these consequences are the same and are known as *common effects.* Common effects are not helpful in attribution, because they do not tell us why a certain action was chosen. *Noncommon effects* are the elements that are attributionally important.

In any choice there are common and noncommon effects. For example, assume you must decide whether to spend this coming weekend writing a term paper, which is due later this semester, or recreating. There may be many noncommon effects to these two choices, but let us concentrate on some positive and negative ones. If you write the term paper you will have to work hard and you will spend most of the weekend alone. However, you will be ahead in your assignments. If you choose to recreate, you will be with friends and be rested and relaxed next week, but you will still be no further along on your term paper. Whichever you choose, the perceiver will be able to attribute the cause of your behavior to one or more of these noncommon effects.

Consider the case in which you decide to recreate and you decide to go to a hockey game instead of a party. The common and noncommon effects now change radically. No longer is the effect on your assignments a noncommon element, it is a common one. The perceiver must now shift to other reasons to understand your

Note the weeds growing in the middle of the burned out structure. It is obvious that the house is not burning. But why are the firemen there? This house had been burned many months before and presumably the fire was set by someone in the debris that had not been cleaned up around the house. We do not know what the motives of the individual who set the fire were—to call attention to a substandard area, vandalism or something in between. This is a problem in attribution.

behavior. The noncommon effects now revolve around your feelings about hockey and parties, who will attend the party, how interesting the hockey game is, and so forth. As you can see, the perceiver must process different information.

Together with the desirability of the effects, common and noncommon effects can tell a lot about the actor's personal dispositions. For example, when there are many noncommon effects in a choice between two behaviors, it is very difficult to pinpoint one or even a few of these effects as causes of behavior. Therefore, the cause(s) of the actor's behavior is (are) ambiguous. If there are only a few noncommon effects and the effects are of high desirability, the actor's behavior is understood, but that understanding is trivial. For example, if an actor is going to buy a widget and store A has it for two dollars less than store B, then we may know why the actor bought it at store A, but the knowledge is trivial. Most people will buy an item at the best price available.

When the noncommon effects are few and the desirability of that effect or effects is low, Jones and Davis refer to this as *correspondence of inference.* Because the actor's noncommon effects are limited and the desirability low, the perceiver has the best chance of accurately perceiving the cause of the behavior. In other words, the perceiver has the best chance of actually discerning some underlying personal disposition that causes the behavior. High correspondence of inference is a measure of the perceiver's certainty about the role of causality and is obtainable most frequently when the actor's behavior is different from what most people would have done in that situation (Jones, Davis, and Gergen, 1961).

25

Attribution Theory

The analysis by Jones and his associates is, however, primarily concerned with the actor. Another attributional hypothesis, which emphasizes both the actor and the situation, has been proposed by Kelley.

Kelley's Attributional Analysis

Kelley's model of attribution also borrows heavily from Heider. Kelley emphasizes the distinction between attribution to the actor and attribution to the environment. Kelley's ideal perceiver is much like a social scientist conducting a series of experiments, because the ideal perceiver attributes causality to either the actor or the environment and tries to determine to which one it should be attributed. Suppose you attend a school dance with an attractive date immediately after an important sports victory by your team. Can the good time you have be attributed to your date, to the victory, to the social event, or to the interaction of the three? In making such decisions Kelley (1967) asserts that there are three attributional criteria to be considered.

The three criteria are distinctiveness, consensus, and consistency. Distinctiveness refers to whether the individual responds uniquely to different stimuli. The individual, either the self or another person, who responds uniquely to stimuli would be distinctive. For example, the Prime Minister who marries a much younger woman, enjoys night life and other pursuits normally thought to be the activities of the young and carefree, is distinctive.

Consensus refers to how other people respond to the same stimuli. High consensus implies that a great many people respond in the same way. For example, the cry of "fire" in a crowded building causes most people to flee. Low consensus is a stimulus to which people respond in different ways, or to which the target person responds differently than the majority of people. For example, Kelly would classify nonfleeing behavior when the cry of fire is sounded as a low-consensus behavior.

Consistency refers to two concepts, time and modality. Consistency over time refers to the individual responding to the same stimulus in the same way when it reoccurs over time. The consistency of modality refers to whether the individual responds to the same stimulus similarly regardless of the situation. For example, reacting with anxiety when a snake is encountered in its natural habitat over and over is consistency over time. Reacting with anxiety when a snake is encountered in its natural habitat, in a zoo, or even when shown in a movie is consistency over modality.

Kelley has emphasized the interaction of these three variables in self and other attribution. Distinctiveness is seen as the major determinant of causal attribution. The more distinctive the response to different stimuli, the more the response is stimulus influenced. For example, in predicting the behavior of an individual who responds uniquely to each of five stimuli, the most important element to know is the characteristics of the stimulus. On the other hand, an individual who responds in basically the same way to five different stimuli, creates a different prediction problem. In this case, knowledge about the individual's characteristic mode of behavior is vital. Consistency and consensus tell us about the stability and replicability of the effects being considered. The more inconsistent the behavior and the less consensus there is in it, the greater the distinctiveness must be to influence attribution. For example, if a person is in a situation in which there is little consensus and great inconsistency, distinctiveness becomes an even more important variable in attribution.

McArthur (1972) tested the implications of Kelley's analysis and found, in general, that the ideas concerning distinctiveness, consistency, and consensus were accurate. An example from McArthur's work would be helpful. Subjects read a sixteen-item questionnaire, with each of the sixteen items reporting the occurrence of some response by another person. For distinctiveness two items read as follows (McArthur, 1972, p. 174):

a. John does not laugh at almost any other comedian—(high).
b. John also laughs at almost every other comedian—(low).

Consistency information was conveyed by the following form:
a. In the past John has almost always laughed at the same comedian (high).
b. In the past John has almost never laughed at the same comedian (low).

Consensus information was transmitted in the following way:
a. Almost everyone who hears the comedian laughs at him (high).
b. Hardly anyone who hears the comedian laughs at him (low).

The cause of John's laughter was attributed to specific characteristics of John (person attribution) when there was low distinctiveness, low consensus, and high consistency. That is, when this combination of statements was presented,

John also laughs at almost every other comedian. Hardly anyone who hears the comedian laughs at him. In the past John has almost always laughed at the same comedian. [McArthur, 1972, p. 174.]

the cause of the laughter was attributed to John.

However, when this pattern of statements was presented,

John does not laugh at almost any other comedian. Almost everyone who hears the comedian laughs at him. In the past John has almost always laughed at the same comedian. [McArthur, 1972, p. 174.]

the cause of the laughter was attributed to the stimulus (the comedian).

DISCOUNTING AND AUGMENTATION

Kelley (1971) has also emphasized two attributional "rules," discounting and augmentation. These rules apply when there are single observations instead of multiple ones. Discounting refers to the fact that the role of any one cause is lessened (discounted) if other plausible causes are also present. For example, if there is one and only one plausible cause to which behavior may be attributed, the probability that the behavior will be attributed to that cause is high. However, if there are several plausible causes, the cause of the behavior will probably be spread among the possible causes.

The augmentation principle asserts that if there are inhibitory causes present with facilitative cause(s), the role of the facilitative cause(s) will be judged greater than if the facilitative cause(s) are presented alone. This merely means that if there is a cause that is seen as helping the behavior, it is pinpointed more readily as the cause of the behavior if a hindering cause to the behavior is also present.

The Intuitive Scientist

One implication of attribution theory is that everyone is an intuitive scientist. Humans, according to attribution theorists, are intuitive psychologists because they seek to explain behavior and to draw inferences about the environment. Furthermore, either implicitly or explicitly, humans attempt to predict behavior. "What can I do to improve my son's future?" "If I go to college will it help me build a better life?" "If I am nice to my boss, will he be more inclined to give me a raise?" Even though these questions are not phrased in the jargon of the professional psychologist, they are all attempts to predict outcomes.

Like the academic psychologist, the intuitive psychologist is guided by a number of assumptions. People would rather engage in pleasurable activities than in unpleasurable ones. It is not too strange when a person gives in to peers who are pressuring him or her and it is more unusual to find someone who does not conform. The intuitive psychologist, like the academic one, relies on data, although data sources may differ. For example, the intuitive psychologist may put a great deal of faith in rumors, the media, folklore, and so forth. From a variety of sources, he or she must store information, develop a system for retrieving it when it is needed, and use it appropriately. The ability of the intuitive psychologist to cope with the environment depends, to a great degree, on (1) the sources of data, (2) the storage system, (3) the retrieval system, and (4) proper application of data to the problem at hand. If any one of these steps breaks down, the individual will not be able to cope with the environment adequately. We see many instances of individuals who do not cope with the environment very adequately, and any one or several of the systems mentioned above may be faulty.

There are, however, differences between the intuitive scientist and the social scientist that should be made clear. The social scientist differs from the intuitive scientist by way of more precise, public, and falsifiable theories. These theories must, by their very nature, specify conditions under which relations do or do not hold. The intuitive scientist generally attends to one attribution at a time and does not have to be as specific as the social scientist. Further, the social scientist must make systematic observations and relate them to the general theory that has been formulated. Whereas there are many similarities between the intuitive scientist and the social scientist, there are also many differences.

The broad outlines of contemporary attribution theory were begun by Heider (1944, 1958) and developed in greater detail by Jones and Davis (1965), Kelley (1967), and several colleagues (Jones, Kanouse, Kelley, Nisbett, Valins and Weiner, 1972; Weiner, 1974). These theorists have emphasized two major tasks confronting the social observer. The first of these tasks is causal judgment and the second is social inference.

CAUSAL JUDGMENT

Causal judgment refers to the type of judgment that results when the observer seeks to identify a cause or set of causes to which some action or outcome may be attributed. Much research in attribution has been concerned with the locus of the cause of an event (i.e., whether the cause is internal to the individual or from some external source). For example, when you do poorly on an exam do you attribute that poor showing to yourself ("I didn't study enough," and so on) or do you attribute it to someone or something else (unfair test, or such)? The first of these (not studying enough) is an internal cause, whereas the second is external.

Interestingly enough, research has shown some inaccurate perceptions on the part of many individuals. Wortman (1976) has pointed out the following:

> The studies reviewed in this chapter have suggested that people minimize the role of chance in producing various outcomes, exaggerate the relationship between their behavior and "uncontrollable" life events, and tend to be unaware of the extent to which their behavior is controlled by external factors. At this point, it seems appropriate to raise the following questions: Why do people make attributions in this manner? Are such attributions adaptive or maladaptive? [Wortman, 1976, p. 43.]

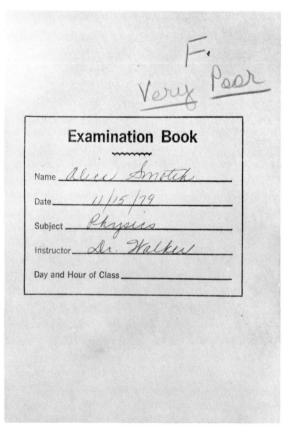

Receiving a test back from a professor with a poor grade on it is an unsettling experience. Is the grade attributable to internal or external events?

Learned Helplessness. Seligman (1974, 1975) has suggested that increasing your feelings of self-control is adaptive. According to Seligman it is the attribution of helplessness that creates problems for the individual. Wortman and Brehm (1975) have put the matter in perspective:

There is good reason to believe that exposure to uncontrollable outcomes can result in profound psychological upset. Many kinds of maladaptive behavior have been attributed to feelings of helplessness with respect to one's environment. For example, investigators have argued that the helplessness stemming from feelings of lack of control is an important factor in the development of such psychiatric disorders as depression and schizophrenia (Bateson, Jackson, Haley, & Weakland, 1956; Seligman, 1974, 1975). Cofer and Appley (1964), Janis (1958), and Janis and Leventhal (1968) have maintained that feelings of helplessness interfere with the ability to respond adaptively in stressful situations. Feelings of helplessness have also been proposed as a precursor of physical disease (Engle, 1968; Schmale, 1971). Some investigators (Greene, Goldstein, & Moss, 1972; Richter, 1957) have suggested that the perception of inability to exert control over one's environment can even result in sudden death from coronary disease or other factors. Feelings of lack of control have also been viewed as a cause of many types of antisocial behavior. [p. 278.]

Learned helplessness is the term Seligman and his associates have used to describe the results of learning to be unable to control events. In several animal studies, Seligman found that subjects who learned they were helpless could not function adequately when placed in a situation in which they were no longer helpless. Seligman and Maier (1967) exposed subjects to a number of shocks from which they could not escape. Later, when they were given the opportunity to escape from the shocks simply by jumping from one compartment of the experimental apparatus to another, they failed to learn this simple response. Animals who had never experienced the inescapable shocks easily learned to escape by jumping from one compartment to another which was "safe." Seligman attributed learned helplessness to the fact that the animals first learned that they would be shocked no matter what they did and that this punishment was inescapable. He reasoned that when they were put into a situation where their responses could have terminated the shock their motivation and cognitive functioning were reduced and this lowered their ability to learn to escape.

Similar effects have been demonstrated with humans as well. Hiroto and Seligman (1975) exposed subjects first to a set of soluble or insoluble problems and then gave them anagrams to solve. The group that had first worked on insoluble problems did much more poorly on the anagrams than did the group that worked on the soluble problems. Analogously to the animals who first learned they could not escape the punishment, the people seemed to learn that nothing worked. Therefore they gave up and made little effort to succeed. Other studies have replicated these results, and further established that the more experience subjects had with insoluble problems, the greater their feelings of helplessness and the lower their performance on later tasks (Roth and Kubal, 1975). We have many examples of this phenomenon in everyday life; a child who is forced to continue to try to develop a skill of which he or she is developmentally incapable will often refuse to attempt that activity later when it is possible to achieve.

Apparently, exposure to uncontrollable, positive events does not lead to learned helplessness (Benson and Kennelly, 1976). Only exposure to uncontrollable negative events seems to result in this negative outcome. On the other hand, exposure to controllable events can lead to increased performance (Eisenberger, Park, and Frank, 1976).

Abramson, Seigman, and Teasdale (1978) have specified the relationship between learned helplessness and attribution. Although agreeing with others (Weiner, 1974; Weiner, Frieze, Kukla, Reed, Rest, and Rosenbaum, 1971) that the dimension "stable-unstable" is independent of "internal-external" in attributing causes to self behavior, these authors argue for another dimension; global and specific. Remember internal-external refers to the source of the cause of the behavior. When it is internal, the cause is within the individual; external causes are outside the individual, such as luck or fate. Stable factors are thought of as long-lived or recurrent, while unstable factors are short-lived or intermittent. Many skills fall into these categories. For example, one's ability at math, baseball, or poetry is generally thought of as stable.

The addition of global and specific adds yet another important dimension to the attributional analysis of learned helplessness. Global factors affect a wide variety of outcomes, whereas specific ones do not. If an individual has learned to be helpless, it is a global characteristic if that helplessness generalizes to many situations; it is specific if it does not. Assume that an individual, through the luck of the draw, drew a particularly poor and vindictive math teacher in both the seventh and eighth grades. No matter how hard the individual studied or how much he or she knew, failure was always the outcome. This is a real-life equivalent to the learning phase of a learned helplessness experiment. Probably the individual will not work or be able to learn math in the ninth grade. However, if he or she also does poorly in English, French, science, and history, then we would say the characteristic is global rather than specific.

Thus Abramson et al. argue that there are eight possible outcomes of the three dimensions of internal-external, stable-unstable, and global-specific. These are shown in Table 1-1. As you can see from looking at the table, these possibilities all have different effects on future behavior. Particularly important is their effect on learned

Table 1–1 The eight possible causes of behavior when the internal-external, stable-unstable, and global-specific dimensions are considered

	Internal		External	
	Stable	*Unstable*	*Stable*	*Unstable*
Global	A recurring cause from within that generalizes to other situations	A nonrecurring cause from within that generalizes to other situations	A recurring cause from outside that generalizes to other situations	A nonrecurring cause from outside that generalizes to other situations
Specific	A recurring cause from within that does not generalize to other situations	A nonrecurring cause from within that does not generalize to other situations	A recurring cause from outside that does not generalize to other situations	A nonrecurring cause from outside that does not generalize to other situations

helplessness. When the specific combination of dimensions is known, prediction of future behavior is possible. For example, if a student has just failed a math test, the internal-stable-global combination will indicate that it is his fault, one that will recur and generalizes to many situations. A simpler way of stating this combination is that the student is saying "I am stupid." An internal-stable-specific combination would be stated "I am stupid in math." Note, however, that our predictions about how the individual would do in other situations varies with the combination of dimensions.

One important point needs to be added. We are dealing with the expectancy the individual has concerning his or her future behavior. As Abramson et al. say (1978, p. 59),

> In general, the properties of the attribution predict in what new situations and across what span of time the expectation of helplessness will be likely to recur. An attribution to global factors predicts that the expectation will recur even when the situation changes, whereas an attribution to specific factors predicts that the expectations need not recur when the situation changes. An attribution to stable factors predicts that the expectation will recur even after a lapse of time, whereas an attribution to unstable factors predicts that the expectation need not recur after a lapse of time. Whether or not the expectation recurs across situations and with elapsed time determines whether or not the helplessness deficits recur in the new situations or with elapsed time. Notice that the attribution merely *predicts* the recurrence of the expectations but the expectation *determines* the occurrence of the helplessness deficits.

The emphasis on expectancy is an important one and you should keep it firmly in mind. The construct goes well beyond the learned helplessness concept. In fact, as you will soon see, expectancy is, I think, a construct under which all of attribution is subsumed and is an important element in the total motivation picture.

Learned helplessness would be a problem of major proportions even if it were restricted to decrements in performance in the area in which the uncontrollable event occurred. However, its effects appear to be more widespread. Seligman (1975) has observed that when people cannot control their environment, a sense of sadness and hopelessness occurs. These, in turn, may be related to psychological depression, and according to Klein, Fencil—Morse, and Seligman (1976), may underlie such reactions. The inability to control your life is apparently a powerful negative stimulus.

Person Perception. Heider (1958) defined the attribution process as the organization of information from someone else's behavior into meaningful units. His emphasis was on the fact that an observer responds to the meaning of another person's actions, not to their overt behavior. These meaningful units, then, constitute the input of perception to the causal inference process. Other attribution theorists have emphasized a different element in the process of person perception. For example, Kelley (1967) does not emphasize the direct perception of causal entities in the perceptual field as Heider did. Rather, he emphasizes the combination of successive perceptual entities into stable sets of causal beliefs. This difference is an important one, at least in theoretical terms. If the object of perception is viewed as being the source of what is being perceived, two different persons perceiving the same other person will have similar perceptions. However, if the perceptions are combined in some way and that combination is the basic unit of person perception, two people might view the same other person quite differently.

To illustrate the point concretely, suppose you and a friend are watching a third person. What is important? Is it what the person you are watching actually does? Or is it the way you organize the perception? If it is the former, then the perceptions of you and your friend are likely to be rather similar, but if it is the latter, the two perceptions may be quite different.

Newtson (1976) has argued that the person being perceived generates some causal information. The nature and extent of this information is, as yet, unclear. However, this seems to indicate that Heider's proposition is the more accurate one and that perceptions of another are influenced by what the person actually does. If all of this seems rather commonsensical, it is. However, consider the unreliability of eyewitnesses to a crime. Or after an event involving another person both you and a friend have seen, ask the friend to describe it and see how closely your friend's attribution of causality agrees with yours. In other words, do you and your friend both think the other person acted the way he or she did *for the same reason?*

SOCIAL INFERENCE

Social inference refers to the formation of inferences about the attributes of relevant dispositions of actors or the property of situations to which those actors have responded. Undoubtedly, social inference is closely related to causal judgment, but now the intuitive scientist is concerned with making inferences about an event, not determining causes for that event. For example, if you are told that Beth has donated money to a charity, the task is to infer what that act means. It may mean that the act

To what may one attribute the behavior of the man wearing the sign? Do his actions constitute a meaningful unit?

reflected some personal disposition of Beth's. On the other hand it may mean that there was some situational pressure (social, economic, or such) on Beth to make the contribution. The aim of social inference research in attribution is to determine which disposition or combination of dispositions led to the behavior of interest.

The intuitive psychologist often underestimates the impact of social and situational influences and overestimates the role of personal dispositions in making assumptions about the causes that underlie behavior. Heider (1958) first made such an observation, and subsequent research has confirmed this (e.g., Bern, 1967; Jones and Davis, 1965; Jones and Nisbett, 1971). Why should this be the case? There seemingly is a greater willingness to attribute responsibility to another person's dispositions than to the situation. For example, in the United States there are constant outcries against welfare cheats, and from those who argue that if a person does not work, he or she should not eat. However, the majority of people who receive assistance from governmental sources either (1) have young, dependent children; (2) are disabled; or (3) are unable to find work. Whereas there are undoubtedly those who can work but don't, the majority cannot. This does not alter the fact that people are ready to attribute dispositional (don't want to work) rather than situational causes (can't work) to their need for assistance.

SELF-PERCEPTION

It is almost a truism that people know more about themselves and why they behave in certain ways than they know about others. Certainly we are more knowledgable about our own thoughts, feelings, and motives than we are about those of other people. Therefore, it follows that we should be more accurate about ourselves than we are about others. Whereas this is undoubtedly true, there is quite a bit of evidence that our self-perceptions are, in part, based on situational determinants.

Probably the most impressive demonstrations of situational cues on our perceptions of ourselves have been conducted by Schachter and his associates (Nisbett and Schachter, 1966; Schachter and Singer, 1962; Schachter and Wheeler, 1962). In one of these studies, which are discussed in greater detail in Chapter 9, subjects were injected with adrenaline, which causes short-term flushing, hand tremors, and accelerated heart rate. Then the subjects were divided into three groups; one was told exactly what to expect, one was told to expect side-effects but was misinformed about what those side-effects would be, and one was told there were no side effects. Then subjects waited in another room with a confederate who had been instructed to act either euphoric or angry. The euphoric confederate played with a hula hoop, made and sailed paper airplanes, and threw scraps of paper at a wastebasket as if playing basketball. Subjects who did not know why they were aroused were more influenced by the confederate than were subjects who knew what to expect from the adrenaline. Thus it seems that how we perceive what we are feeling and our behavior is influenced by situational determinants.

Certainly, our behavior has long been thought to be under some control of others with whom we associate. We do not lightly disagree with popular or powerful persons. We do not oppose the will of the majority unless we are willing to be "left out" of the group. Most of us, however, like to think that our thoughts and feelings are our own even if our behavior is influenced by others. The work of Schachter and others suggests that situational influences are powerful determinants of our feelings, and of thoughts as well.

OBJECTIVE SELF-AWARENESS

Duval and Wicklund (1972) have proposed a model of self-evaluation that emphasizes the relationship among states of consciousness. Specifically they argue that negative self-evaluation will occur only when consciousness is in an objective rather than a subjective state. Consciousness is seen by these psychologists as containing these two different subsystems; objective and subjective. Objective consciousness occurs when attention is focused on external stimuli, orienting toward a stimulus, or to viewing the self as an object for comparison. Subjective consciousness occurs when the individual's attention is turned inward.

Let us see what Duval and Wicklund propose when we turn our attention about ourselves inward. Note, now, that even though our attention is turned inward, we are still dealing with objective consciousness because we are viewing ourselves as an object for comparison. When we view ourselves objectively, we are comparing ourselves with what we want to be. Since for many of us our standards are quite high, we see ourselves not measuring up to our ideals. In a few instances, particularly when we have experienced a successful outcome, we may exceed our ideals.

Wicklund (1975) emphasizes the motivational properties of both the positive and negative feelings we have about ourselves when we objectively view ourselves. If the feelings aroused are negative (because we have failed to live up to our ideals) we seek to avoid whatever stimuli caused us to turn our view inward. If we cannot avoid such stimuli we try to distract ourselves from this state of objective self-awareness. For example, a student who is doing poorly in high school is forced to compare his or her ideals to reality every time a test is returned or a grade assigned. The student can avoid such stimuli by dropping out, or by deciding that the evaluations teachers give don't mean very much anyway.

If, on the other hand, the feelings generated by objective self-analysis are positive, we may actually seek out such experiences again. For example, if a young man attends his first dance and finds that the young women present are willing, even eager, to dance with him, the chances are quite high that he will want to return to another dance. In this instance, the forced look inward was quite pleasant and he would want to repeat the process.

How do researchers get subjects to focus upon themselves? There are several ways including listening to tape recordings of your own voice or viewing video tapes of yourself. However, possibly the most ingenious device is getting subjects to look in a mirror. Ickes, Wicklund, and Ferris (1973) had subjects take a test that supposedly measured a particular personality trait. They were then given bogus feedback; half of them received positive and half negative feedback. Half of each group were then given a mirror to look into. Exposure to the mirror lowered the self-esteem of those given negative feedback and raised the self-esteem of those given positive feedback.

It is obvious that objective self-awareness is a self-perception construct. That is, the inward searching necessary for objective self-awareness to occur is a perceptual aspect of knowledge of ourselves. Since self-perception is a special case of person perception, it fits nicely in attribution theory. Duval and Hensley (1976) have

One ingenious way to study objective self-awareness is to look at oneself in a mirror. In one way or another, however, the image in the mirror is distorted.

demonstrated that the subsystems of consciousness, of which objective self-awareness is one, contribute perceptual dimensions to objects and events. These, in turn, influence which of several possible causal attributions is actually viewed as the cause of a given effect. Here, then, we have come full circle in our analysis of objective self-awareness and find many of the same considerations of interest as in other aspects of attribution theory.

Comment

Even though the connections between attribution processes and behavior have been implied throughout our discussion, they need to be spelled out more clearly. This can be done in two ways. First, attribution can be seen as a second-order process subsumed under the idea of expectancy. Recall that much of the attributional work and research are tied very closely to expectancy. Expectancy colors what the perceiver perceives, and it is an important aspect in determining common and noncommon effects (Jones and Davis) and distinctiveness, consensus, and consistency (Kelley). Thus expectancy is vital to attribution. Expectancy is also important in other theories we have discussed (e.g., hedonism, reinforcement, and balance). Shortly, I will reiterate what might best be termed a hedonistic-rationalistic argument for behavior in general, one that is also subsumed under an expectancy construct. The second way in which attribution can be tied to behavior is through an attributional analysis of specific behaviors. In Chapters 3, 4, 7, 9, 10, and 13, there are sections that directly relate to specific behaviors.

Attribution theory is, at this stage of its development, not a cohesive theory of

35

behavior. It is, however, a theory that encompasses much of social behavior with which we are concerned. If it seems a bit difficult to grasp, that is probably because it has not as yet been adequately researched. Nevertheless, it is a process in which you frequently engage. As an example of what attribution theory is attempting to explicate, let us return to the jury that must decide the fate of John Edwards.

First the jury must decide whether they believe John Edwards did, indeed, enter Anne Johnson's apartment with intent to rape. This process is one that is quite complex in attributing causal attributes. The jury must decide if Anne Johnson's identification of John is accurate or if Paulette Edwards' testimony that her husband could not have been there is accurate. The jury, if it accepts Anne Johnson's testimony, is asserting that Paulette Edwards is mistaken or lying. Thus, there is a causal judgment made. Paulette Edwards made a mistake or lied to protect her husband. If, however, the jury accepts the testimony of Paulette Edwards, its members are asserting that Anne Johnson was incorrect in her assertion.

Note, however, that the attribution process is not at an end when the members of the jury decide that they do believe Anne Johnson. In that case, some determination must be made by the jurors concerning the responsibility of John Edwards for his actions. There was no evidence presented in this case to indicate that Edwards was unable to tell right from wrong, but this determination is not always so easily achieved. In a most celebrated case of the mid-1970s, Patricia Hearst was convicted of bank robbery after being kidnapped by the Symboniese Liberation Army. The jury had to determine whether her actions were caused by internal effects (she had "gone over" to her kidnapper's position) or to situational influences (she was forced to rob the bank by her captors). The jury attributed her actions to an internal belief and convicted her.

Even though we all engage in attributions of causality, the jury is probably the group that is most called upon to make causal inferences. Generally depending on secondhand sources, jurors must listen to the evidence, then attribute causality to the individual or the situation. This formalization of what we all do informally is one reason that juries are so fascinating.

Social Psychological Theory— Emerging Directions

After a rather detailed look at some of the major theories in social psychology, the question may be asked whether anything has been solved by all of this. At least one social psychologist (Gergen, 1973) has answered that question negatively, arguing that as social conditions change through history so does social behavior. At best, according to this view, any answers we develop will be outdated in fifty or a hundred years, so social psychology has relevance only as history. Gergen's comments unleashed a tidal wave of support, attacks, counterattacks, and more support (Buss, 1975; Cronbach, 1975; Elms, 1975; Gergen, 1976; Godow, 1976; Greenwald, 1976; Harris, 1976; Hendrick, 1976; Manis, 1975; 1976a; 1976b; Schlenker, 1974; 1976;

Secord, 1976; Smith, 1976; Thorngate, 1976). Some would argue that where there is so much smoke there must be fire, but another way of viewing the situation is that this is a difficult time in social psychology when a number of cherished theories and methods have fallen on hard times. The history of social psychology is important, but for other reasons. Plato enumerated a number of problems in *The Republic* that have not yet been solved. The fact that they sound and are familiar today should warn you that social problems do not seem to be tied to specific periods in history. McDougall back in 1908 anticipated such arguments when he said (1908, p. 17),

> If this view, that human nature has everywhere at all times this common native foundation, can be established, it will afford a much-needed basis for speculation on the history of the development of human societies and human institutions. For so long as it is possible to assume, as has often been done, that these innate tendencies of the human mind have varied greatly from age to age and from race to race, all such speculation is founded on quicksand and we cannot hope to reach views of a reasonable degree of certainty.

Today we do not accept McDougall's emphasis on instincts, but his logic makes a great deal of sense.

Actually, a lot has happened since Plato. One very large accomplishment is that we are now framing the questions of social psychology scientifically. That is, the questions are being asked in such a way that it is possible to answer them empirically rather than with someone's best guess. This, as you will see throughout the pages of this book, is a giant step forward. That the questions have not all been satisfactorily answered seems to be Gergen's major objection.

"But," you ask, "haven't you answered any of the questions?" And I would answer "Yes, a few: But there is still a long way to go." The fact that I have devoted the opening chapter to theory in social psychology and the fact that theory in the area is in such a state of disarray must give all of us pause.

Integrating Social Psychological Theories

It does not look as if anyone is adequately going to integrate social psychological theories at this time, first because our fund of knowledge is not yet adequate to the job, but even more so because, as implied earlier, certain theorists seem to prefer one form of theorizing and other theorists prefer another. Unfortunately, this state of affairs is quite unlike your liking to golf for relaxation while your neighbor prefers tennis. Under those circumstances one golfs and one plays tennis. Instead of such a logical arrangement, scientists feel it is, so to speak, not only necessary to play golf but to attack those who play tennis (or vice versa). Therefore, over the years, there has been a great deal of heat generated about theorizing in social psychology, instead of each of us doing his or her own thing and letting history decide which game was more important. In view of our combative history, I make the following suggestions only with some fear and trepidation.

It does seem to me that, even though meaningful theoretical integration is not yet possible for both objective and subjective reasons, we can critically examine theories that have been proposed to account for social behavior, both monistic and pluralistic, and point some directions that can be profitably followed.

Basically, two questions must be answered by a theory of social behavior, How and Why? Let us take the easier question first, How? A quick look at social behavior up and down the phylogenetic scale shows us that as animals increase in complexity, there is an increase in the complexity of social behavior. The outstanding feature of human beings is their brain, particularly the most recently developed part, the cerebral cortex, which is the center of thought as we know it, and in all probability the reason for more complex human social behavior. Human social behavior is based on humans' exceptional cognitive abilities. To put it another way, there will be no adequate social psychological theory that does not firmly ground itself in cognitive factors.

How? is the easy question. To say that humans think about what they are doing and that somehow these thought processes control human social behavior does not go nearly far enough. Why? is much more difficult. As this is being written, Gary Gilmore is much in the news. By the time you read this he may well be forgotten, so let us review the story. It is 1977 and no one has been executed in the United States since 1967. Gary Gilmore has been convicted of murder in Utah and sentenced to death. As Utah allows a choice of how this will be done, he chose to be shot rather than hanged. He also waived his rights of appeal and said he wanted to be shot immediately rather than spend the rest of his life in jail. Appeals were filed on his behalf, but against his wishes, by his mother and the American Civil Liberties Union (ACLU) (who are also concerned with several hundred other men on death row who do not want to be executed, as well as with Gary Gilmore). Gilmore took an overdose of sleeping pills and was rushed to the hospital where expert medical science saved his life so that it can be taken *properly* by the state in front of the firing squad. After the appeals of Gilmore's mother and the ACLU were disallowed, the judge, on December 18, 1976, set Gilmore's execution for January 17, 1977. Gilmore, despondent over the delay, again took an overdose of pills and again was saved by medical science in order to face the firing squad. The warden of the penitentiary where Gilmore was to be executed has been besieged with requests to be on the firing squad. On January 17, 1977, after more appeals in his behalf were disallowed, Gilmore was properly executed by the firing squad. This one incident shows how difficult the question of "Why?" is.

Yet the why of human social behavior may well have a rather simple, though partially complex answer. In observing human behavior many have been struck with the idea that given a choice, no matter how horrible that choice, people do what they expect will be the more pleasurable to them under the circumstances. Gary Gilmore would rather die than spend the rest of his life in prison, so in this case maybe he expects dying to be more pleasurable. In fact, it was reported that friends had supplied him with a lethal dose of drugs to use in case one of the appeals on his behalf was successful. This idea of doing what the individual expects will be most pleasurable is a form of hedonism, which we discussed earlier. One of the arguments against hedonism has been that we have many cases in which people have denied themselves and even given up their lives for a friend. How is this pleasurable? In Chapter 10 we will discuss altruism, and recent research in the area has indicated that altruism may very well be rewarding or pleasurable.

Taking a simple dictum, "Humans do what they expect is most pleasurable" and translating it into a science of social behavior is devilishly difficult. The theory, if it is to be testable and falsifiable, must be put in a more specific form than stated here. One must be able to predict what will be pleasurable to an individual, a group, even a nation, if this hedonic approach is to have credence as a scientific theory. Throughout the pages of this book, I think you will see embryonic developments leading in that direction.

Earlier we said the "How?" question was the easy one, but that was only partially true. To say that human social behavior is complex because humans have complex brains is to say very little. The hard part comes when we try to amalgamate the cognitive capacity of humans with the hedonic principle, which we have already discussed. Because of humans' enormous cognitive capacity, it is necessary to allow for many more types of pleasure and many more ways of arriving at that pleasure than the early hedonists even thought about: In short, if that is correct, there are an almost infinite number of variations on a theme. We may learn much from the behavior of animals lower on the phylogenetic scale, but they do not tell us the whole story. Although it is probably safe to say that a hungry person will seek food just as a hungry rat does, there are many more ways for the hungry human to find food because of cognitive complexity. On the other hand, Gary Gilmore went on a twenty-five-day hunger strike *because his execution had been temporarily stayed.* We know of few "lower" animals that have staged hunger strikes, and none that have aimed at facilitating their own execution.

What I am suggesting at this point is that human social behavior is based upon the hedonic principle of the expectation of pleasure, that there are general laws of what is pleasurable that will improve our predictive capacity, but because of the enormous cognitive capacity of humans there are many exceptions to these laws. To state the case in another way, I am saying that the behaviorists have been right up to a point and the cognitive theorists have been right up to a point. In fact, it seems to me that both have been studying the same phenomena, but their terminology is sufficiently different so that the two have been seen as opposite ways of approaching the problem.

Historically, behaviorists have concentrated on the environmental conditions (stimuli) that cause a person to behave in a given manner (response). Although not denying consciousness, the radical behaviorism of Watson and Skinner chose to ignore it. Behaviorism's critics have chosen to ignore the fact that many present-day behaviorists have chosen to ignore Watson and Skinner's advice to ignore consciousness. On the other hand, many cognitive theorists have chosen to emphasize consciousness and in their reaction against behaviorism have failed to capitalize on the hedonic assumption that behaviorism has espoused. It should be noted that many behaviorists have chosen to ignore the fact that certain cognitive theorists (cf. Festinger, 1957; Heider, 1946; 1958; Newcomb, 1959; 1968) have emphasized either a reduction of tension or the importance of a balanced state, both of which are hedonic in nature.

My modest proposal is that cognitive and behavioral theorists join together in attempting to understand human social behavior. If that is too much to ask, then at the very least I would hope that each side would quit attacking the other and let the search for understanding proceed in peace. I suspect, however, that a hundred years from now, whether we have scientific peace or war in the interim, any general theory of human social behavior will have a lot of what we now know as cognitive elements and a lot of what we know as behavioristic elements in it.

SUMMARY

1 Social psychology is an attempt to understand how the thought, feeling and behavior of individuals are influenced by the actual, imagined, or implied presence of others.

2 Scientific theories are ideas, guesses, and conjectures about how things work. Scientific theories differ from other theories in that they must be both public and falsifiable. Proving a theory is not possible, but over the years, as evidence mounts, many scientific theories are accepted unless and until a better one emerges.

3 Hedonism and the Faculties of the Mind, which include affect, imitation, and cognition, are monistic theories. Each has been used to explain behavior.

4 Pluralistic theories, illustrated by sociological, behavioral, and cognitive theories have also been used to explain behavior. Sociological theories include social class and role theory, behavioral theories include conditioning and reinforcement, and cognitive theories include Gestalt and Field theories.

5 Attribution theory is concerned with the attempts of ordinary people to understand the causes and implications of the events they witness and experience. The theory recognizes the fact that individuals' actions are controlled more by how they perceive an event than by what actually happened. Everyone is an intuitive scientist in that each person seeks to explain behavior and to draw inferences about the environment.

6 Causal judgment (the fact that an observer seeks to identify a cause to which some action may be attributed) is mainly concerned with the locus of the cause of an event. Learned helplessness describes the condition that results when you learn that you are unable to control events.

7 Heider defined the attribution process as the organization of information from someone else's behavior into meaningful units. Other theorists emphasize correspondent inferences and the interaction of actor and situation. Person perception is extremely important for attribution theory.

8 Social inference is closely related to causal judgment, but is concerned with the inferences made about an event, not with determining the causes of that event. The intuitive scientist often underestimates the importance of social and situational influences and overestimates the role of personal dispositions in making assumptions about the causes that underlie behavior.

9 Social psychology still faces many of the problems it did when it was in its infancy, but it has made progress, particularly in the area of framing questions scientifically. It is proposed that behavioral and cognitive theories be integrated to advance the discipline most rapidly.

Affect Feeling or emotion.

Attribution Theory The theory that stresses the cognitive processes through which perceivers interpret their own and other people's behavior.

Behavioral Theories Theories that emphasize observable behavior.

Behaviorism The approach to psychology that explains behavior mainly in terms of observable stimuli and responses.

Burglary The act of breaking and entering the building of another with intent to commit a felony.

Causal Judgment The act of seeking to identify a cause or set of causes to which some action or outcome may be attributed.

Classical Conditioning A procedure to study the associative processes in learning by pairing a neutral stimulus with one which will reliably evoke a response.

Cognition The act or process of knowing.

Common Effects Consequences of two or more behaviors that are the same.

Conative Striving after a goal.

Consensus Other people's responses to the same stimuli.

Consistency The sameness of an individual's response to the same stimulus over time or regardless of the situation.

Construct A complex idea formed from a number of simpler ideas.

Distinctiveness Unique responses to different stimuli.

Falsifiable Subject to being tested and disproved.

Field Theory The general theory of motivation that emphasizes the total field of personal desires and environmental factors as determinants of behavior.

Gestalt Theory An approach to behavior that emphasizes an organized perceptual whole or unit.

Hedonism A monistic theory that pleasure or happiness is the highest good.

Hypothesis An assumption or guess.

Instrumental Conditioning A method of studying learning in which the emphasis is upon changes in the environment produced by the individual's response.

Interpersonal Attraction The feeling of liking a person.

Irrational Theories Theories that are based on emotion, drive, instinct, or some other form of nonrational behavior.

Law of Effect The idea that a response will be strengthened when it produces an event that is satisfying to the organism.

Learned Helplessness The results of learning to be unable to control events.

Monistic Theories Theories that attempt to explain the world with one basic concept.

Noncommon Effects Consequences of two or more behaviors that are different.

Pluralistic Theories Theories that attempt to explain the world with more than two basic concepts.

Reinforcement The presentation of positive or negative stimuli.

Semantics The study of meaning.

Social Inference The formation of inferences about the attributes of relevant dispositions of actors or the property of situations to which those actors have responded.

Social Psychology An attempt to understand how the thought, feeling, or behavior of individuals are influenced by the actual, imagined or implied presence of others.

Syntax The study of the structure of word order in a language.

Valence Desires.

REFERENCES

Abramson, L. Y., M. E. P. Seligman, and J. D. Teasdale. Learned helplessness in humans: Critique and reformulation. *Journal of Abnormal Psychology,* 1978, *87,* 49–74.

Allport, G. W. The historical background of modern social psychology. In G. Lindzey and E. Aronson (Eds.), *Handbook of Social Psychology.* Vol. I (2nd Edition). Reading, Mass.: Addison-Wesley Publishing Co., Inc., 1968. Pp. 1–70.

Anderson, N. H. A simple model for information integration. In R. P. Abelson, E. Aronson, W. J. McGuire, T. M. Newcomb, M. J. Rosenberg, and P. H. Tannenbaum (Eds.), *Theories of Cognitive Consistency: A Sourcebook.* Chicago: Rand McNally & Company, 1968.

Asch, S. Forming impressions of personality. *Journal of Abnormal and Social Psychology,* 1946, *41,* 258–90.

———. *Social Psychology.* New York: Prentice-Hall, Inc., 1952.

Bandura, A. (Ed.). *Psychological Modeling.* Chicago: Aldine Publishing Company, 1971.

———. *Aggression: A Social Learning Analysis.* Englewood Cliffs, N.J.: Prentice-Hall, Inc., 1973.

———. Analysis of modeling processes. In A. Bandura (Ed.), *Modeling: Conflicting Theories.* New York: Lieber-Atherton, 1974.

——— and R. W. Jeffery. Role of symbolic coding and rehearsal processes in observational learning. *Journal of Personality and Social Psychology,* 1973, *13,* 173–99.

——— and F. J. McDonald. The influence of social reinforcement and the behavior of models in shaping children's moral judgments. *Journal of Abnormal and Social Psychology,* 1963, *67,* 274–81.

Benson, J. S., and K. J. Kennelly. Learned helplessness: The result of uncontrollable aversive stimuli? *Journal of Personality and Social Psychology,* 1976, *34,* 138–45.

Bern, D. J. Self-perception: An alternative interpretation of cognitive dissonance phenomena. *Psychological Review,* 1967, *74,* 183–200.

Biddle, B. J., and E. J. Thomas (Eds.), *Role Theory: Concepts and Research.* New York: John Wiley & Sons, 1966.

Bindra, D. *A Theory of Intelligent Behavior.* New York: John Wiley & Sons, 1976.

Bolles, R. C. *Theory of Motivation.* New York: Harper & Row, Publishers, 1967.

Boring, E. G. *A History of Experimental Psychology* (2nd Edition). New York: Appleton-Century-Crofts, 1950.

Buss, A. R. The emerging field of the sociology of psychological knowledge. *American Psychologist,* 1975, *30,* 988–1002.

Byrne, D. *The Attraction Paradigm.* New York: Academic Press, Inc., 1971.

——— and G. L. Clore. A reinforcement model of evaluative responses. *Personality: An International Journal,* 1970, *1,* 103–28.

Capaldi, E. J. A sequential hypothesis of instrumental learning. In K. W. Spence and J. T. Spence (Eds.) *The Psychology of Learning and Motivation: Advances in Research and Theory.* Vol 1. New York: Academic Press, Inc., 1967, pp. 67–156.

Cronbach, L. J. Beyond the two disciplines of scientific psychology. *American Psychologist,* 1975, *30,* 116–27.

Duval, S., and V. Hensley. Extensions of objective self-awareness theory: The focus of attention-causal attribution, hypothesis. In J. H. Harvey, W. J. Ickes, and R. F. Kidd (Eds.), *New Directions in Attribution Research.* Vol. 1. Hillsdale, N.J.: Earlbaum, 1976.

——— and R. A. Wicklund. A theory of objective self-awareness. New York: Academic Press, Inc., 1972.

Eisenberg, R., D. C. Park, and M. Frank. Learned industriousness and social reinforcement. *Journal of Personality and Social Psychology,* 1976, *33,* 227–32.

Elms, A. C. The crisis in confidence in social psychology, *American Psychologist,* 1975, *30,* 967–76.

Festinger, L. A theory of social comparison processes. *Human Relations,* 1954, *7,* 117–40.

———. *A Theory of Cognitive Dissonance.* Evanston, Ill.: Row, Peterson (Currently New York: Harper & Row, Publishers), 1957.

Forcese, D., and J. DeVries. Occupation and electoral success in Canada: The 1974 federal election. *Canadian Review of Sociology and Anthropology,* 1977, *14,* 331–40.

Gergen, K. J. Social psychology as history. *Journal of Personality and Social Psychology,* 1973, *26,* 309–20.

———. Social psychology, science and history. *Personality and Social Psychology Bulletin,* 1976, *2,* 373–83.

Godow, R. A. Social psychology as both science and history. *Personality and Social Psychology Bulletin,* 1976, *2,* 421–27.

Goyder, J. C., and J. E. Curtis. Occupational mobility in Canada over four generations. *Canadian Review of Sociology and Anthropology,* 1977, *14,* 303–19.

Greenwald, A. G. Transhistorical lawfulness of behavior: A comment on two papers. *Personality and Social Psychology Bulletin,* 1976, *2,* 391.

Griffitt, W., and P. Guay. "Object" evaluation and conditioned affect. *Journal of Experimental Research in Personality,* 1969, *4,* 1–8.

Harris, R. J. Two factors contributing to the perception of the theoretical intractability of social psychology. *Personality and Social Psychology Bulletin,* 1976, *2,* 411–17.

Heider, F. Social perception and phenomenal causality. *Psychological Review,* 1944, *51,* 358–73.

———. Attitudes and organization. *Journal of Psychology,* 1946, *21,* 107–12.

———. *The psychology of interpersonal relationships.* New York: John Wiley & Sons, Inc., 1958.

Hendrick, C. Social psychology as history and as traditional science: An appraisal. *Personality and Social Psychology Bulletin,* 1976, *2,* 392–403.

Hiroto, D. S., and M. E. P. Seligman. Generality of learned helplessness in man. *Journal of Personality and Social Psychology,* 1975, *31,* 311–27.

Ickes, W. J., R. A. Wicklund, and C. B. Ferris. Objective self-awareness, and self-esteem. *Journal of Experimental Social Psychology,* 1973, *9,* 202–19.

Jones, E. E., and K. Davis. From acts to dispositions: The attribution process in person perception. In L. Berkowitz (Ed.), *Advances in Experimental Social Psychology.* Vol. 2. New York: Academic Press, Inc., 1965.

———, K. E. Davis, and K. J. Gergen. Role playing variations and their informational value for person perception. *Journal of Abnormal and Social Psychology,* 1961, *63,* 302–10.

———, D. E. Kanouse, H. H. Kelley, R. E. Nisbett, S. Valine, and B. Weiner. *Attribution: Perceiving the Causes of Behavior,* Morristown, N.J.: General Learning Press, 1972.

———, and D. McGillis. Correspondent inferences and the attribution cube: A comparative reappraisal. In J. H. Harvey, W. J. Ickes, and R. F. Kidd (Eds.), *New Directions in Attribution Research.* Vol. 1. Hillsdale, N.J.: Earlbaum, 1976.

————— and R. E. Nisbett. *The Actor and the Observer: Divergent Perceptions of the Causes of Behavior.* Morristown, N.J.: General Learning Press, 1971.

—————. Attribution theory in social psychology. In D. Levine (Ed.), *Nebraska Symposium on Motivation.* Vol. 15. Lincoln: University of Nebraska Press, 1967.

—————. *Attribution in Social Interaction.* Morristown, N.J.: General Learning Press, 1971.

Kipnis, D. *The Power Holders.* Chicago: University of Chicago Press, 1976.

Klein, D. C., E. Fencil-Morse, and M. E. P. Seligman. Learned helplessness, depression and the attribution of failure. *Journal of Personality and Social Psychology,* 1976, *33,* 508–16.

Lewin, K. *Field Theory in Social Science.* New York: Harper & Row, Publishers, 1951.

Luchins, A. S., and E. H. Luchins. Imitation by rote and by understanding, *Journal of Social Psychology,* 1961, *54,* 175–97.

Mahoney, M. J., and C. E. Thoresen. *Self Control: Power to the Person.* Monterey, Calif.: Brooks/Cole, 1974.

Manis, M. Comment on Gergen's "Social psychology as history." *Personality and Social Psychology Bulletin,* 1975, *1,* 450–55.

—————, Social psychology and history: A symposium. *Personality and Social Psychology Bulletin,* 1976, *2,* 371–72. (a)

—————. Is social psychology really different? *Personality and Social Psychology Bulletin,* 1976, *2,* 428–37. (b)

McArthur, L. A. The how and what of why: Some determinants and consistencies of causal attribution. *Journal of Personality and Social Psychology,* 1972, *22,* 171–93.

McDougall, W. *Introduction to Social Psychology.* London: Methuem, 1908.

McGuire, W. Inducing resistance to persuasion. In L. Berkowitz (Ed.), *Advances in Experimental Social Psychology.* Vol. 1. New York: Academic Press, Inc., 1964, pp. 191–229.

Meichenbaum, D. Cognitive modification of test anxious college students. *Journal of Consulting and Clinical Psychology,* 1972, *39,* 370–80.

Mischel, W. *Personality and Assessment.* New York: John Wiley & Sons, Inc., 1968.

Newcomb, T. An approach to the study of communicative acts. *Psychological Review,* 1953, *60,* 393–404.

—————. Individual systems of orientation. In S. Koch (Ed.), *Psychology: A Study of a Science.* Vol. 3. New York: McGraw-Hill Book Company, 1959. Pp. 384–422.

—————. Interpersonal balance. In R. P. Abelson, E. Aronson, W. J. McGuire, T. M. Newcomb, M. J. Rosenberg, and P. H. Tannenbaum (Eds.), *Theories of Cognitive Consistency: A Sourcebook.* Chicago: Rand McNally & Company, 1968. Pp. 28–50.

Newtson, D. Foundations of attribution: The perception of ongoing behavior. In J. H. Harvey, W. J. Ickes, R. F. Kidd (Eds.), *New Directions in Attribution Research.* Vol. 1. Hillsdale, N.J.: Earlbaum, 1976.

Nisbett, R. E., and S. Schachter. Cognitive manipulation of pain. *Journal of Experimental Social Psychology,* 1966, *2,* 227–36.

Pavlov, I. P. *Conditioned Reflexes.* Trans. by G. V. Anrop. London: Oxford University Press, 1927.

Plato. The republic. *Great Dialogues of Plato.* Trans. by W. H. D. Rouse, New York: Mentor Books, 1956.

Reichard, G. A. Social life. In F. Boas (Ed.), *General Anthropology.* Lexington, Mass.: D.C. Heath & Company, 1938. Pp. 409–86.

Rogers, C. R. A theory of therapy, personality, and interpersonal relationships, as developed in the client-centered framework. In S. Koch (Ed.), *Psychology: A Study of a Science.* Vol. 3. New York: McGraw-Hill Book Company, 1959.

Roth, S., and L. Kubal. Effects of noncontingent reinforcement on tasks of differing importance: Facilitation and learned helplessness. *Journal of Personality and Social Psychology,* 1975, *32,* 680–91.

Sachs, D. H., and D. Byrne. Differential conditioning of evaluative responses to neutral stimuli through association with attitude statements. *Journal of Experimental Research in Personality,* 1970, *4,* 181–85.

Schachter, S., and J. Singer. Cognitive, social, and physiological determinants of emotional state. *Psychological Review,* 1962, *69,* 379–99.

———— and L. Wheeler. Epinephrine, chlorpromazine and amusement. *Journal of Abnormal and Social Psychology,* 1962, *65,* 121–28.

Schlenker, B. R. Social psychology and science. *Journal of Personality and Social Psychology,* 1974, *29,* 1–15.

————. Social psychology and science: Another look. *Personality and Social Psychology Bulletin,* 1976, *2,* 384–90.

Secord, P. F. Transhistorical and transcultural theory. *Personality and Social Psychology Bulletin,* 1976, *2,* 418–20.

Seligman, M. E. P. Depression and learned helplessness. In R. J. Friedman and M. M. Katz (Eds.), *The Psychology of Depression: Contemporary Theory and Research.* Washington, D.C.: Winston-Wiley, 1974.

————. *Helplessness.* San Francisco: Freeman, 1975.

———— and S. Maier. Failure to escape traumatic shock. *Journal of Experimental Psychology,* 1967, *74,* 1–9.

Shaw, M. E., and P. R. Costanzo. *Theories of Social Psychology.* New York: McGraw-Hill Book Co., 1970.

Smith, M. B. Social psychology, science and history: So what? *Personality and Social Psychology Bulletin,* 1976, *2,* 438–44.

Staats, A. W., and C. K. Staats. Attitudes established by classical conditioning. *Journal of Abnormal and Social Psychology,* 1958, *57,* 37–40.

Staats, C. K., and A. W. Staats. Meaning established by classical conditioning. *Journal of Experimental Psychology,* 1957, *54,* 74–80.

Thorngate, W. "In general" vs. "It depends": Some comments on the Gergen–Schlenker debate. *Personality and Social Psychology Bulletin,* 1976, *2,* 404–10.

Tolman, E. C. *Purposive Behavior in Rats and Men.* New York: Appleton-Century-Crofts, 1932.

Von Ehrenfels, C. "Ueber Gestaltqualitäten," *Vierteljahrsch. Wissenschaft Philosophie,* 1890, *14,* 249–92.

Watson, J. B. *Behaviorism* (2nd Edition). New York: W. W. Norton & Company, Inc., 1930.

————. Psychology as a behaviorist views it. *Psychological Review,* 1913, *20,* 158–77.

Weiner, B. *Achievement Motivation and Attribution Theory.* Morristown, N.J.: General Learning Press, 1974.

Weiner, B., I. Frieze, A. Kukla, L. Reed, S. Rest, and R. M. Rosenbaum. *Perceiving the Causes of Success and Failure.* Morristown, N.J.: General Learning Press, 1971.

Wicklund, R. A. Objective self awareness. In L. Berkowitz (Ed.), *Advances in Experimental Social Psychology.* Vol. 8. New York: Academic Press, Inc., 1975.

2

Social Psychology Methodology

Probably one of the most chilling words for a student is *methodology*. In popularity methodology often ranks right up there with fractions for Lucy (the Peanuts character), math for most people, and statistics for psychology majors. Methodology is, however, a much-maligned concern and an important one. Just as Lucy could probably learn that two halves, three thirds, and four fourths all make a whole, methodology can also be understood rather painlessly, I think, if it is explained simply. In this chapter, I want to try to do that, as well as to help you understand why each method is used. I will try to tell you what particular problem was faced by a researcher when he or she used a particular method and, to the best of our present knowledge, I'll give you a little history about the introduction of the method into the discipline. Most importantly, for your understanding, for each method discussed I will describe a representative study in social psychology in some detail to help you grasp its significance more fully. Where possible, I will use studies that have become classics.

The first problem I face is in delimiting exactly which methods should be discussed, since there is not total agreement about which are most appropriate. Basically, I will develop a threefold division of methodologies based upon the major emphasis of each one. Case studies emphasize an individual and are uniquely "in-depth" researches, whereas surveys study more individuals in less depth. Finally, experiments are concerned with maximizing control over extraneous variables, with cause-and-effect relationships being the ultimate goal. Some of the major divisions are sufficiently complex so that it will be necessary to subdivide them further.

Before proceeding further in our discussion of methodology, it is appropriate to discuss its importance. In science, methodology is the tool or set of tools that allows the researcher to move beyond speculation about what is going to happen in a specific situation. In natural science, it has long been accepted that a rock and a feather will fall at the same rate of speed *in a vacuum.* Social scientists are attempting to understand how and why humans behave as they do. The why of human behavior is basically a theoretical question, but one that cannot be answered without the How. As far as research in social psychology is concerned, methodology is the basic method of answering How. It allows the social scientist to put his or her speculations (theories) to the test, and therefore is the basic tool that allows us to distinguish between scientific and nonscientific endeavors. Put in another way, scientific theories must be testable, or they are not scientific. Since we social psychologists think of ourselves as scientists, we place a great emphasis upon testing our theories.

Putting Methodology in Perspective

There is no doubt that there is a relationship between the theoretical position of an investigator and the methodology he or she adopts. For example, a radical behaviorist who adheres to Skinner's position will adopt a methodology that allows for the categorization of overt behavior. Observable behavior will be measured, whereas there will be no attempt to measure cognitive functioning. On the other hand, a cognitive social psychologist will generally use measures that allow inferences about cognitive functioning to occur. Undoubtedly the person who ignores cognitive

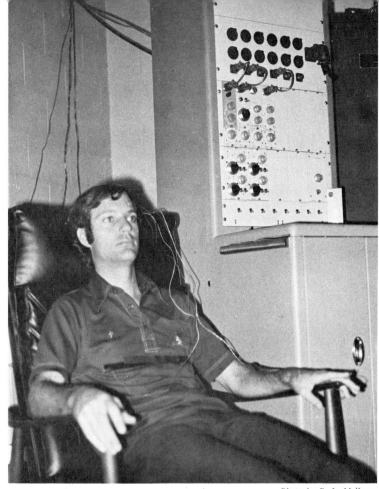

The individual pictured here is having physiological measurements taken. Might the electrodes and wires influence the individual's measurements?

Photo by R. L. Mellgren.

functioning will miss a lot of important data, as will the person who ignores observable behavior to draw inferences about cognition. As far as I know there is no methodology that allows us to measure everything at once. Thus, the assumption that we will learn more and attain our goal of predicting human social behavior more quickly if several theoretical positions proceed to "do their own thing" inevitably applies to methodology as well. Theories and methods are almost inevitably tied together.

Possibly the relationship between theory and method is most clear when the issue of what measures are acceptable is raised. Let us consider anxiety. What measure of anxiety shall we use? We could ask an individual if she or he is anxious. Many would argue that self-report measures are the best measures to use, because who can tell better that an individual is feeling anxious than the individual? On the other hand, it could be argued that anxiety is not a very acceptable emotion and the individual will not be truthful. Or it could be argued that the scientist must observe the individual's behavior (physiological measures such as heart rate, palmar sweating, and so on) to determine anxiety. However, since anxiety itself is not observable, some would argue that it is not a proper variable to study. Thus, depending on the individual psychologist's theoretical point of view, anxiety may be studied using self-report measures or physiological measures, or may not be studied at all.

Another point that needs to be stressed is that social psychology has traditionally relied almost exclusively on the experimental method. This chapter will cover that area; it also includes material on case studies and surveys. Do not be misled! Even though almost a third of this chapter is alloted to these two methods, they have not been nearly that important in social psychology to date. Case studies and the survey method have been included for three reasons. First, since you will not encounter them in the literature of social psychology very often, it is important that you understand their strengths, weaknesses, and difficulties when you do. Second, these methods, particularly survey research, are being utilized more often in social psychological research. Therefore it is important that students be introduced to these other methods of research. Finally, when students are assigned a research project in social psychology, either in this course or in a more advanced one, surveys tend to be popular choices. It sounds easy to go out and do a survey. But it is not easy to do a *good* survey, and I therefore want to spend some time discussing the area.

Case Studies

Gordon Allport (1961) has been one of the strongest proponents of case studies in social psychology. Allport was a leading advocate of the uniqueness of the individual and thus of the need to study individuals in depth. It is instructive to repeat Allport's definition and description of a case study.

A case study, of course, is a comprehensive framework into which all relevant and significant data pertaining to a single life are compiled and arranged. It is a device for avoiding an embarrassing mass of test scores, items of past history, and unrelated fragments of information. It has the advantage also of keeping attention riveted upon a single concrete life—where the psychologist's attention should be riveted more often than it is. When many cases are in hand various comparisons may be made (e.g., concerning the differences in personality among members of social classes or among people with contrasting national, racial, or developmental backgrounds). [Allport, 1961, p. 408]

As you can readily see, until the very last sentence of his description of case studies, Allport's description of them quite effectively excludes them from the realm of social psychology, because they refer only to one person. This, of course, has been the criticism of case studies by social psychologists and their relative unpopularity in the discipline. As, by definition, social psychology works with and studies individuals as they behave in the presence of others, case studies are somewhat limited.

Increasing Emphasis Upon the Individual

Allport's argument, however, was that you could not truly understand an individual without an in-depth probe of his or her basic characteristics. All too often, the "realness" of the person is lost if only one aspect is taken into consideration. Social psychologists are beginning to take more seriously the need to understand more about the individual who behaves in a specific way. Whether social psychologists will or should go to the extreme that Allport espoused is questionable. It is instructive, however, to illustrate how a *movement toward* more in-depth study of the individual within a social psychological context occurs.

The Acquaintance Process

One of the most ambitious research projects in the history of social psychology occurred at the University of Michigan in 1954 and 1955. It was a study of attraction, or as its author titled it, *The Acquaintance Process* (Newcomb, 1961). It may come as a surprise to many of my colleagues and to Professor Newcomb himself to find his monumental research effort described as a case study or more accurately, a series of case studies. Newcomb refers to his study as an experimental one, and that it was, albeit a specific type of experimental study. You will find it described here because, probably more than any other social psychological research effort, it collected in-depth data on a number of individuals and made comparisons among them. It therefore stands as a classic study in many ways, but particularly in developing and utilizing the case study method in social psychology.

Newcomb's study was one of attraction and how it develops. To study this important phenomenon he brought two different sets of 17 males to a house in Ann Arbor, Michigan. The first set came on September 12, 1954, and lived there throughout the fall semester. The second set arrived the next fall and spent a semester together. In exchange for up to five hours of their time each week, the men were allowed to live rent free in the house. Thus Newcomb was able to collect data from each of the 34 men for up to 75 hours and he collected an immense amount of information about each man.

As Newcomb was primarily interested in attraction, his major measuring device was one of attraction made by each man toward the 16 other men in the house, usually once a week. Attitudes about house policies, university practices, public affairs, racial and ethnic relations, religion, sex and family, and interpersonal relationships were assessed repeatedly throughout the term. During the second year of the study values were also assessed.

Personality variables were also obtained by Newcomb, and since they traditionally compromise the "heart" of the case study method in psychology, it is instructive to quote his comments about them.

Our basic proposition did not include personality variables as distinct from attitudinal ones. We were aware, nevertheless, that individuals almost certainly differ in several ways relevant to the operation of individual systems of orientation. Our subjects might well differ, for example, with respect to threshholds for tolerating strain, or in characteristic manner of attempting to minimize it. Quite apart from these considerations, moreover, the more or less persisting personal properties that our subjects brought to the research setting were surely among the crucial determinants of the kinds of interpersonal relationships that developed among them.

With the advantages of hindsight, we believe that our personality data should have been more complete, and more systematically obtained, in spite of our understandable reluctance to take time from an overcrowded schedule of data-gathering to obtain information the possible uses for which we could only guess at. [Newcomb, 1961, p. 43, italics added.]

The personality characteristics that Newcomb did obtain were authoritarianism, conformity, projection, need achievement, and need affiliation. All are standard personality tests and were administered once during the course of the semester.

You have now been given a flavor of the research that Newcomb conducted and an overview of the measures he used in developing in-depth profiles of each individual. What results did he obtain? Basically, Newcomb found "that the stronger an individual's attraction to another person, the greater the likelihood that he will perceive agreement with that other person concerning objects important and relevant to him" (1961, p. 70). In addition, he found that as two individuals became more attracted to each other, their agreement about the attractiveness of the other 15 men in the group also increased.

Newcomb noted some rather striking effects of the personality variables that he introduced in his study. For example, authoritarianism was found to be related to the phenomena that are crucial to the formation of interpersonal relationships. Equalitarians tend to be better able to estimate their fellow house members' actual attitudes, values, and orientations, even when these are in disagreement with their own. Authoritarians, on the other hand, tended to perceive more agreement than actually existed.

Obviously this brief overview can only give you a flavor of what is possible with the case study method when in-depth data are collected and then compared with in-depth data collected on a number of other individuals. The uniquely social psychological study by Newcomb shows the immense amount of information that can be collected as well as the theoretical advances that can be made utilizing this method.

Newcomb's method was, to say the least, elaborate and expensive. Few other researchers have been able to spend the time, effort, and money Newcomb did. There are, however, in other approaches, elements of the case study that are utilized to gain information. We now turn to a recent example.

SOCIAL EXCHANGE

Foa and Foa (1974, 1975) have developed a resource theory of social exchange. Like many social-psychological theories, it places its major emphasis upon a phenomenon, exchange, which is a theory that stresses the basic similarity of behavior among individuals. They have, however, begun to break down the all-inclusiveness of both the exchange system they use and of the reaction individuals have to the medium of exchange. To quote the Foas: (Foa and Foa, 1975, p. 2),

Spurred on by the relative success of economists in predicting and controlling behavior in the marketplace, social psychologists have attempted to apply the economic model to noneconomic exchanges, using the same rules for *all* types of transactions. The assumption that every transaction, both economic and emotional, follows the same rules caused disinterest in the problems of specifying and classifying exactly what is exchanged, and the only meaningful parameter in an event is the *amount* of the exchanged commodity.

Once theorists have assumed that different commodities follow different rules of exchange, it is a short step to assuming that different individuals value different commodities in different ways. The Foas (1974) have at least begun that activity by attempting to specify how individual characteristics may interact with the differential value placed upon different commodities. For example, a person who is low in self-esteem will react quite differently from a person who is high in self-esteem. If a person thinks he or she is unintelligent, unattractive, and generally unworthy, resources such as praise and honors that would be highly valued by a person high in self-esteem may extract a cost rather than provide a reward. Whereas this is obviously not a case study in the sense Allport described it, it is a move in the direction of understanding the individual more "in depth" than is done or espoused by most social psychologists. The movement toward the case study method utilized by the Foas is much more likely to occur than the elaborate data gathered by Newcomb in social psychology today.

COMMENT

The case study method when utilized properly offers social psychologists a superb tool for investigating social phenomena. It has been primarily the tool of the clinical psychologist, who uses it to assess maladaptive behavior. Since social psychologists are primarily interested in adaptive behavior and only secondarily in maladaptive behavior, the method has not been greatly utilized in social psychology. It does, as we have seen, have enormous potential in studying human behavior.

To repeat, the example we cited of Newcomb's work is generally viewed as an experimental study. It may be described as the case study method combined with the experimental method. It is also tremendously expensive! Newcomb needed rather a large amount of financial support to carry out his study. It is primarily this factor, expense, which makes this methodology so rare in social psychology.

Principles from the world of economics have been utilized to explain human social behavior. Can you see any relationship between the economic transactions conducted in this bank and social transactions?

The Survey Method

Crano and Brewer (1973, p. 20) define surveys as "all observations that occur in 'natural' settings with a minimum of interference over normal variations in behavior and choices." This sort of definition is general enough to allow for many types of investigations—and it does. Survey research differs from the use of case studies in at least three important respects. First, less information is generally obtained from the respondents, and, second, that information is usually more specific to the research aims involved. Finally, it is usual for more respondents to be used in survey research than in case study research.

Survey research has a wide area of applicability. All it requires is that the respondents be verbal (i.e., that they can or will communicate in some language) and that there is some reason to believe that they will be truthful. These requirements include all but the most extreme groups in our society, potentially excluding only preverbal infants, psychotics who are out of touch with reality, the senile, politicians, and the like. You should note, however, that I said "potentially excluding" only these groups. There is a major drawback to surveys that must always be kept in mind; namely, that the respondents will not be truthful. I will return to this particular drawback later in this section.

Surveys can be written, such as multiple choice questionnaires that are sent through the mail, or they can be oral, such as public opinion polls conducted by an interviewer which are asked of a selected group to determine generalized opinions about a specific issue. Each of these approaches has its advantages and its drawbacks, and I will try briefly to explain and discuss both methods.

It is not necessary to survey these people to find out what they want. They have come to a demonstration for more jobs. Not everyone is this vocal about what they think and surveys are useful tools in determining public opinion.

Written Surveys

Written surveys, or questionnaires, are probably used most often in social psychological research, because they have a beguiling simplicity and are inexpensive. It seems extremely reasonable to many individuals that the best way to collect information about a subject is to ask a few questions, distribute them in some way, and wait for the answers to roll in. In what I term "Pop Psychology," the written questionnaire is an important tool, and its results appear in such scientific publications as *Redbook, The Ladies Home Journal,* and *Playboy,* to name a few. It is an interesting aside on human nature that it is difficult to dissuade the uninitiated from believing anything published in surveys of this sort, whereas they suspect the accuracy of a scientifically developed survey because it sampled fewer people.

The key to the accuracy of any survey is the sample that is used. An enormous sample that is self-selected, as occurs when a magazine publishes a questionnaire, is often inaccurate because the people who fill out the questionnaire do so because they have a view they want to air. A scientific survey may select a small sample, but it is generally a sample that is representative of the group of people (population) whose views it is supposed to represent. There are a variety of different sampling techniques that can be used in social psychological research, but we will mention only two. The most used sampling technique is to draw a *random sample.* A random sample is a sample drawn in such a way that each individual in the defined population shall have an equal chance of being included in the sample and that the selection of one individual does not affect the likelihood of any other individual being included in the sample. Unless the population in which the researcher is interested is rather severely limited, practicality dictates that truly random samples are seldom drawn. In practice, however, the population of interest can be rather limited (to *a* university, *a* city or *a* state) and, generally speaking, be applied to other populations (universities, cities, or states).

Many of the statistical techniques that are used are based on the assumption that a random sample was used, and if there is some systematic bias in the sample, then erroneous conclusions will be reached. For this reason most magazine samples, even those with a hundred thousand respondents, are probably erroneous. The sample was self-selected and thus biased with people who had a particular interest in the survey being conducted. You can believe that the results are accurate representations for those people who chose to respond, but you cannot generalize beyond those individuals.

There is another type of sampling that is often used in survey research, known as stratified-random sampling. This sort of sampling is carried out when there is reason to assume that certain subgroups in the population would have specific views about an issue. This technique is most often used in public-opinion polling, particularly for political purposes. For example, if the poll is being taken to investigate public opinion about a specific piece of labor legislation, it is likely that people in the two major political parties would feel differently about the issue. It is also probable that people of different socioeconomic categories—unskilled workers, skilled workers, clerical and office workers, business, and professional—would systematically differ on the issue.

Other subgroups of the population might be expected to have systematically different views on the matter, male and female, urban and rural, and so forth. Having decided what variables are important in sampling, the researcher studies the population to see what proportion falls into each category. Any sample to be obtained should have a proportionate representation of all the subgroups that are deemed important. In other words, the population is stratified according to the important sampling variables and then within each subgroup (stratum) random sampling is carried out. This is, naturally, known as stratified-random sampling. As you can probably see, a much smaller sample allows for much greater precision of results if, and only if, the important subgroups are correctly identified. This sort of sampling technique, among other things, allows the political pollsters to be extremely accurate in their sampling of public opinion.

Not all questionnaire surveys are scientifically untenable. If proper sampling techniques are utilized, then the questionnaire that is filled out by the respondent can be extremely valuable. Sharpening up experimental hypotheses, testing instruments, and testing hypotheses are examples of the useful functions written surveys can serve. One excellent example of two of these functions was demonstrated by Fitzpatrick (1976).

Types of Interpersonal Communication. Fitzpatrick was interested in developing a typology of interpersonal communication between heterosexual couples who were either married or living together. She developed a questionnaire composed of more than 200 items that were based on a careful analysis of the work of Kantor and Lehr (1975). Nine hundred people who had lived with a heterosexual mate for at least six months prior to the study and who were living together at the time the survey was administered, responded. Careful attention was given to the demographic characteristics of the sample such as age, education, employment, number of children living at home, religion, and number of years living together. Since this was an instrument testing survey, these demographic characteristics were collated after giving the instrument rather than used as variables in stratifying the sample. This was done primarily because there were no a priori reasons to assume that any of these variables would affect interpersonal communication. They were, however, checked to allow the researcher to spot any unexpected systematic bias in the sample. The items on the questionnaire were then analyzed and an internally reliable instrument of 75 items was developed.

This instrument was then given to a sample of 136 people (68 couples), which was demographically quite similar to the original 900 respondents. The responses of these couples allowed Fitzpatrick to postulate three marital communicative types, which she labeled Independents, Separates, and Traditionals.

Independents are described by Fitzpatrick as reflecting an achievement of balance between autonomy and interdependence. She says of them (Fitzpatrick, 1976, p. 118), "Although they share many activities, engage in conflict when necessary, and freely violate the space of their mates, the Independents are relatively autonomous. They do not believe in traditional ideals but favor instead an ideology which stresses the uncertainty of life and value change." Separates accept both traditional and change-oriented values, they display no clearly defined ideology. The relationship involves a minimal amount of sharing between the partners and a high degree of conflict avoidance. The third type of relationship, the Traditionals, is committed to conventional values and is opposed to a change-oriented philosophy of life.

Oral Surveys

Fitzpatrick's work is an example of the quite impressive results that can be obtained with a written survey or questionnaire. The best-known survey research, which includes public opinion polls (especially political polls), is conducted via oral interviews. Probably the best known work of this sort done by a social scientist that was not political in nature was the research by A. C. Kinsey and his associates. This survey research concerned the sexual practices of Americans and began in the 1930s.

HUMAN SEXUAL BEHAVIOR

In the late 1930s Alfred C. Kinsey and his associates at Indiana University began a mammoth undertaking, which culminated in two books (Kinsey, Pomeroy, and Martin 1948; Kinsey, Pomeroy, Martin, and Gerbhard, 1953). These surveys were the first systematic study of the sexual behavior of males and females in the United States. In all, 16,392 persons were surveyed over a 15-year period usually by one of the four staff members who wrote the books. This was a pioneering effort dealing with a subject about which there was little knowledge and one that there was a strong social prohibition against talking about. In fact there were at that time strong sanctions against those who kissed (or did other things) and told, and society branded people who talked openly about their sexual activity as at best impolite and, at worst, liable to being prosecuted for deviant sexual behavior. Since society had and, to some extent, still has, a double standard for sexual behavior (it was all right for the male to make sexual conquests but no self-respecting man would knowingly marry a non-virgin) the second volume published by Kinsey and his associates was of much greater interest because it dealt with the sexual behavior of females.

Kinsey and his associates interviewed 7,789 females throughout the United States for their second report on human sexual behavior. A few of their observations about sampling and interviewing can probably portray more than anything the problems they faced and how they solved them.

Kinsey et al. (1953) recognized the advantages of probability sampling, and in particular stratified-random sampling, but for various reasons could not sample in that way. Remember, in stratified random sampling the researcher must know what proportion of the population fall into each stratum. As the strata in Kinsey's case were various sexual practices, he had no way to determine what proportion of the population fell into each subgrouping—that was one of the purposes of his study.

A second, even more persuasive, problem for Kinsey was the subject matter he wished to study. As he says (Kinsey et al. 1953, p. 25), "Our first and most decisive reason for not doing probability sampling on the present project has been the necessity for obtaining cooperation from the individuals who have served as subjects for the study. It has been necessary to convince each individual to give the time necessary for the interview, and to agree to answer questions on matters that many persons have never discussed with anyone, even including their spouses and their most intimate friends. We have asked for a record which was as frank and full and honest as memory would allow."

Kinsey et al. solved their problem by selecting groups from which they drew individuals. As they say (Kinsey et al., 1953, p. 26), "We have desired neither a representative sample of unreliable answers, nor a set of reliable answers from respondents who represented nobody but themselves. For this reason we have been compelled to substitute for probability sampling a method of group sampling through which we have tried to secure representatives of each component of the larger population in which we were interested." Basically, what Kinsey and his associates did was to gain the confidence of and access to various social units and thereby to individuals who were more inclined to discuss highly personal matters because of their allegiance to the group. Given the lack of information concerning the subject matter of interest and the delicacy of that subject matter, their sampling strategy was quite ingenious and successful.

Once the sampling procedure is decided upon, it is necessary to develop rapport with the respondents if truthful answers are to be received. This was a particular problem for Kinsey and his associates because of the subject matter of the study. This was done by assuring the respondents that the interviewer was objective, was not interested in passing judgment on any type of sexual behavior, was not interested in redirecting the respondent's behavior and most of all, the interviewer showed no emotion to any of the responses given. Elaborate identification, coding, and data-protection processes were developed and explained to all respondents, which helped ease the interviewing process. Furthermore, where necessary, questions were asked flexibly, taking into account the educational level, age, socio-economic background, and so forth of the respondent. As Kinsey et al. (1953, p. 61) say, "It is a mistake to believe that standard questions fed through diverse human machines can bring standard answers. The professionally trained subject may be offended at the use of anything but a precisely technical vocabulary for the anatomy and physiology of sex, but the poorly educated individual may have no sex vocabulary beyond the four-letter English vernacular."

For our present purposes, the essential points concerning the Kinsey studies have been made clear. It would be impossible to establish rapport, decide upon the exact phrasing of the questions, and explain the intricate measures that had been taken to insure confidentiality in a written survey. Thus Kinsey and his associates interviewed each respondent personally.

Why, you might ask, doesn't everyone interview respondents when they are doing survey research. The answer to that is that it is prohibitively costly. Kinsey and his associates spent between one and one half and two hours conducting each of the 16,392 interviews necessary for their study. That means that the team spent about 29,000 hours in the interviews alone. Since these were highly trained scientists carrying out the study, it is apparent that an enormous amount of financial support was necessary for the project, financial resources that are usually unavailable to researchers.

COMMENT

Among other things Kinsey found that females' sexual activity was about half that of males (when all forms of sexual activity are considered) and that males were more aroused by explicit sexual material, both literary and photographic, than were females. Kinsey's research began over 40 years ago and during that time things have changed rather dramatically. For one thing, females' sexual activity has increased, or at least their willingness to talk about it has increased.

Of most interest to us in a methodological chapter is the fact that when surveys are conducted (Abelson, Cohen, Heaton, and Suder, 1971), there still appears to be less interest in explicit sexual material among females than among males. However, different results are obtained in experimental research when laboratory research is conducted into (1) the physiology of sexual arousal (Masters and Johnson, 1966); (2) with individuals raised as males or females even though they were biologically of the opposite sex (Money, 1968); and (3) when males and females are shown or told the same erotic pictures and stories, the expected sex-differences do not appear (Byrne and Lamberth, 1971; Griffitt, May, and Veitch, 1974; Sigusch, Schmidt, Reinfeld, and Widemann-Sutor, 1970). That is, males and females are equally aroused by explicit sexual material. Why should this apparent contradiction occur? There may be a variety of perfectly reasonable answers to our question. The differential results between surveys and experiments may be caused by the passage of time or by the respondents' unwillingness to discuss a sensitive subject. On the other hand, the subject may not be as amenable to study using one or the other methodology. Sometimes surveys are our best research tool, but in other cases experiments are better suited to our needs.

Experiments

Experiments, broadly defined, are the heart of any science, and most scientific activity qualifies as experimental. For example, Crano and Brewer (1973, p. 20) define experiments thus: "Experiments (whether conducted in a laboratory or field setting) include all observations collected under conditions in which behavior choices are limited by the controlled manipulation of variables selected by the researcher." The dividing lines between all three of the categories in social psychological research is very thin and sometimes seemingly nonexistent. For example, the case study method involves the collection of in-depth data about individuals, but those data can be collected in a situation in which behavior choices are limited by the controlled manipulation of variables selected by the researcher. This was obviously the case in Newcomb's study—he manipulated certain variables (for example, he caused his 17 men to live in the same house), and rightly called his study an experiment, even though we have used it as an example of the case study method. By the same token, surveyors manipulate variables they are interested in when they call them to the respondent's attention by asking questions about them.

One of the recent trends in social psychology is in the area of moving from laboratory to field settings. The material in the body of the text points out the differences in these two types of research. It is, however, a much more difficult problem actually to move research from the carefully controlled laboratory setting to a field situation. Possibly the work reported recently by Edinger and Auerbach (1978) will illustrate.

Edinger and Auerbach were interested in predicting infractions in a prison population. Previous research in this area had emphasized one of two approaches, the trait or the situational. The trait approach emphasizes the characteristics of the individual, whereas the situational approach emphasizes environmental influences. Both have been shown to be limited in their predictive ability. That is, it must be noted that the individual is influenced by the situation and the individual makes up a portion of the situation. In addition, there is evidence that the interaction of situation and individual enhances predictability more than either situation, individual, or both viewed separately.

In addition, two important components of individual and situational aspects, response modes and stimulus/reward values are important in determining behavior. Response modes are the various ways individuals display an emotion or feeling. For example, some people cry when they are sad and laugh when they are happy. Others cry when they are happy and sad and still others neither cry when they are sad or laugh when they are happy. Stimulus/reward values are that of the perceived outcomes to the individual. To a child a lollipop can be a strong reward but to an adult it is generally not very potent in altering behavior.

Edinger and Auerbach were faced with what seemed an impossible task, predicting infractions in a federal correctional institution for 720 inmates in 16 different subsettings of the institution (e.g., inmate dormitories, commissary, work settings) when there were 63 different infractions that could be committed and 30 different punishments administered. Obviously their first job was to narrow down all of these categories.

First, they were able to use an instrument that categorized the vast majority of inmates into 3 groups on the basis of a personality test. Then they found that the inmates themselves categorized the 16 institutional subsettings into 2, highly supervised or with little supervision. Furthermore, the 63 infractions were classified into four groups by the inmates, verbal aggression, group defiance, evasive behavior, and pilfering. The 30 possible punishments were classified by the inmates as definitive punishment or pardon (getting off or nothing more severe than a reprimand). Thus the seemingly impossible task of predicting infractions seemed more manageable, but only empirical verification would allow an unambiguous test of the model.

The test of the model indicated that prisoners on the whole were more likely to commit verbal aggressive infractions in free time when they would more likely be pardoned than punished. One personality subgroup, however, actually engaged in more infractions when it was likely that they would be punished. Thus taking into account the four elements of the model increases the predictive power of correctional officials.

Reference

Edinger, J. D., and S. M. Auerbach. Development and validation of a multidimensional multivariate model for accounting for infractions in a correctional setting. *Journal of Personality and Social Psychology*, 1978, *36*, 1472–1489.

Why, then, don't we call all research experimental and be done with it? The major reason is that there seem to me to be important differences among the three. Any organizational scheme reflects the world in the way the individual organizing it sees things. There may be other perfectly valid ways in which to view reality, and with respect to methodology, most social psychologists don't agree on the best way to organize the research world. Because it is easier for you if there is some sort of organization and because this is the way I break things up in my own mind, I have chosen to differentiate broad categories into the type of data collected and/or the relative importance of the manipulation of variables by the researcher. To be consistent with the scheme I have chosen to follow, the organizing principle for the various different types of experiments described will be the amount of control of extraneous variables.

Correlational Research

Correlational research refers to the fact that the researcher is basically interested in how two (or more) variables relate to each other or correlate. In a correlational experiment, the experimenter exerts the least control over variables that are not of interest, and when the research project is finished, can say nothing about which variable caused an observed effect in the other variable. Let us see what this means in practice.

To begin with, correlation is a statistical tool, developed by Galton (1888) and elaborated by Pearson (1896), in which the relationship between two variables can be computed. For example, height and weight are variables that are correlated. Generally speaking, the taller a person is, the more he or she weighs. Obviously, this is not universally true because there are some short, heavy, people and some tall, light, ones. What Galton and Pearson developed was a mathematical way of describing the relationship. A correlation can be positive or negative and it can range from $+1.00$ to -1.00. A correlation of 1.00 (positive or negative) describes a perfect relationship. A positive relationship means that high scores on one variable go with high scores on the other variable, whereas a negative relationship means that high scores on one variable go with low scores on the other one. A zero correlation means that there is no relationship between the two variables. Figure 2–1 shows diagrams of positive, zero, and negative correlations. It should be noted that a correlation of $-.70$ and $+.70$ reflect the same strength of relationship, but the relationship is positive in one and negative in another. A perfect relationship ($+1.00$ or -1.00) means that the pairs of scores order themselves perfectly. For example, if the heaviest person in our sample was also the tallest, the second heaviest was the second tallest and so on to the lightest person being the shortest, then the correlation would be perfect ($+1.00$). If, by some chance occurrence we should find a sample of, say 10 or 12 people, in which the heaviest person was the shortest, the next heaviest person was the next shortest up to the last person who was both the lightest and tallest we would have a perfect negative (-1.00) correlation. Since height and weight are positively correlated, it is highly unlikely that we would find such an odd sample as we have just described, but not impossible.

With regard to the experimental use of correlation, it is important to understand that *causality cannot be inferred from correlation*. If we were attempting to say something about causality in the height and weight example described above, the question we would ask would be "Does height cause weight or does weight cause

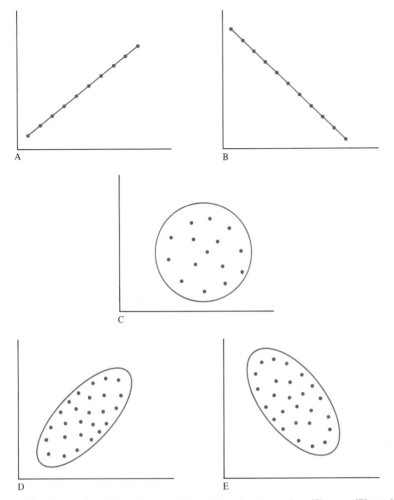

Figure 2-1 Correlation (A) perfect positive; (B) perfect negative; (C) zero; (D) moderately positive; (E) moderately negative.

height"? Or, consider the following example: There is a fairly high positive correlation between the number of crimes reported in cities and the number of churches in them. Now, do criminals go to church a lot or are churchgoers criminals? The answer is neither. In this particular instance a third variable is also highly correlated with the number of crimes and the number of churches in a city and that is the number of people in the city. The larger a city is the more crimes and churches it has. But the crimes do not cause the churches nor do the churches cause the crimes. They both are probably caused by the increased number of people in the city. We say "probably," because *correlation does not imply causality.*

Correlation research then, is research that is concerned with the relationship between two or more variables. Even though such research is more prevalent in personality psychology, it also is important and has a long history in social psychology. For example, F. H. Allport (1924, pp. 137–8) has this to say about correlational research:

A central problem in intercorrelation is the relation between intelligence and sociability. The correlation is seemingly positive, although the existence of highly intelligent criminals affords a striking exception. Dr. Webb (Webb, 1915), in collecting ratings of school and college students, found a correlative tendency, which he calls a 'general factor,' underlying character. Its presence is shown by a variety of virtues, and its absence by a variety of defects. Desirable traits correlate highly with one another; while undesirable traits also intercorrelate highly, and correlate inversely with desirable ones.

Thus we see that only 19 years after Pearson had established a mathematical formula for calculating Galton's co-relation coefficient, it was in use in social psychology. Probably in no other area was it used as extensively so early as in the study of interpersonal attraction.

SIMILARITY AND ATTRACTION: THE CORRELATIONAL APPROACH

"Birds of a feather flock together." "Opposites attract." These two mutually exclusive reasons to explain attraction have been and continue to be part of the folk wisdom of Canada and the United States. Starting in 1903, a series of correlational investigations utilized this then-new statistical technique to try to answer that question (Hunt, 1935; Kirkptrick and Stone, 1935; Morgan and Remmers, 1935; Newcomb and Svehla, 1937; Pearson and Lee, 1903; Schiller, 1932; Schooley, 1936; Schuster and Elderton, 1906) by comparing similarity between husbands and wives. Byrne (1971, pp. 25–37) gives an excellent historical account of these and other correlation studies which were designed to determine whether people who had made some sort of attraction response toward each other were more similar in beliefs, values, physical and psychological correlates, and so forth. The bulk of the data supported the idea that people who were shown to be attracted to each other by being married, or by establishing a friendship, were similar.

The problem arose in interpreting the data. Which came first, the similarity or the attraction? To put it another way, it is possible that two people are attracted to each other because they are similar. It is also possible that opposites attract—that there is some sort of "chemistry" that draws people together because they are different but that after a period of knowing each other, similarity develops. This view might well hold that the interpersonal relationship one builds with another overcomes the basic initial disagreement and turns it to similarity. Which is true?

With correlational research, it is impossible to answer the question, "Which came first; The attraction or the similarity?" All one can say is that at a given time in their relationship (after it has been formed) people who are attracted to each other are more similar to each other than are randomly paired couples. This limitation on the reply results, of course, because of the limitation we warned you about earlier—correlation does not imply causality. Another experimental method of determining which came first, attraction or similarity, must be used if we are to answer that question. It has been used, and the question answered, at least to the satisfaction of most social psychologists, but that story will have to wait for Chapter 9.

Correlational research involves collecting data and seeing if certain variables you are interested in correlate with each other. In other words, it gets its name from a statistical technique. It should be noted, however, that just because a psychologist computes a correlation coefficient on his or her data does not mean that the research is strictly correlational. We say that it is correlational when the major thrust of it revolves around the relationship of two or more variables. We are shifting gears slightly when we discuss field research, because now we are naming the type of research not by the statistical technique used, but by where it is done—in the field. Lest this sound like agricultural research, the referred to is not a corn, wheat, or oat field, but a behavioral one. What psychologists mean when they talk about field research is that they go out and observe behavior where it is occurring. We will differentiate two types of field experiments, the field study and the field experiment.

THE FIELD STUDY

The field study is observation of the behavior of people in their natural habitat. The intent of a field study is to gather data about how people behave in naturally occurring situations with a minimum of interference on the part of the researcher. It is this last requirement that makes the field study extremely difficult to do. In other sciences (e.g., physics) it has long been known that the mere act of measuring something will change that which you are measuring. This caution is even more important when the subject of study is the behavior of humans rather than the behavior of particles. We will illustrate field studies using two quite different approaches that are at two different ends of the continuum of altering behavior by observing or measuring it.

When Prophecy Fails. In the early 1950s Festinger, Riecken, and Schachter (1956) heard of a group of people who called themselves the "Seekers" and who believed that they were in contact with extraterrestial beings, the "Guardians." The "Guardians" had informed the leader of the "Seekers" that the northern hemisphere of the world was going to be inundated by a major flood. The "Seekers," of course, were going to be spirited away to safety prior to the flood. Although the group was not large, the belief in the prophecy was strong.

It is not unusual to hear of groups who prophecy the end of the world and their own miraculous deliverance from it. The most recent I am aware of is the people who felt that the comet Khahoutak would stop and let them climb aboard just in time to save them from the cataclysmic destruction of the world in the mid-1970s. What is common to all of these movements is their inaccuracy. What was uncommon to the "Seekers" movement was that they were infiltrated by Festinger and his associates solely for the purpose of studying their behavior. The researchers were particularly interested in the behavior of the "Seekers" when the prophecy that bound them together was disconfirmed.

Unfortunately for Festinger and his group, the "Seekers" did not seek out new members, and so it was necessary to fabricate stories that would gain them invitations to join the group. As Festinger et al. admit (1956, p. 24), "Unhappily, [the ruse] had been too successful, for, in our effort to tailor a story to fit the beliefs of the members of the group, and thus gain their approval for our observers, we had done too well.

We had unintentionally reinforced their beliefs that the "Guardians" were watching over humanity and 'sending' chosen people for special instruction about the cataclysm and the belief system."

Festinger and his group were well aware that the entry of four new people into a fairly small group within the space of a few days increased the assurance of the "Seekers" that the cataclysm would occur and they would be saved. As you can see, Festinger and his associates did alter the behavior they were studying in gaining admittance to the group. This, of course, is a problem in studying the behavior of all closed groups—does one upset or alter the behavior being studied by observing it? The answer, when the target of observation is a closed group is probably Yes.

Following their admission, Festinger and his group merely observed the behavior of the others, taking great pains to avoid influencing it by attempting to alter patterns of behavior. They even went so far as to avoid any coding of behavior, writing their account from memory. Again, though, two possible effects of this must be considered. The "Seekers" were a relatively small group, and the effect of four individuals who deliberately attempted not to influence behavior is unknown. Second, the fact that no coding system was devised means that more than the usual amount of observer bias could creep into the final interpretation of the behavior of the "Seekers."

A final point will be mentioned here and elaborated upon in a separate section of this chapter. From an ethical point of view did Festinger and his associates have a "right" to infiltrate the "Seekers"?

Law and Order. About fifteen years after Festinger and his associates infiltrated the "Seekers," Lawrence Wrightsman (1969) reported an ingenious field study in which we can say, with some confidence, that taking measurements did not affect his results. During the 1968 presidential election, law and order was a lively campaign issue. All three candidates advocated it, but Wallace was far more vocal about it than the other two candidates. Therefore, it seems reasonable to assume that people who supported Wallace were law-and-order advocates. In Nashville, Tennessee, just prior to the election, a law became effective requiring all cars in Nashville and Davidson County to display a Metro sticker, costing $15.00. Not to display a Metro sticker in Davidson County in early November, 1968, was a violation of the law.

Wrightsman's field study was relatively simple. He selected a sample of cars displaying political bumper stickers, either Humphrey, Nixon, or Wallace. Then he selected a group of control cars for each one; the first car parked to the left of the car with a political bumper sticker that did not have a bumper sticker for Humphrey, Nixon, or Wallace. Finally, a check was made to see if the car displayed a Metro sticker. Thus there were six groups: Humphrey, Nixon, and Wallace cars and a control group for each of the three candidates. Eighty-seven percent of the Humphrey cars had Metro stickers, whereas 77 percent of Humphrey controls had them; 87 percent of Nixon cars had them as did 81 percent of Nixon controls; 75 percent of Wallace cars had the stickers, whereas 84 percent of the Wallace controls had them. Cars with Wallace bumper stickers broke the law more often with regard to the Metro stickers than did any of the other five groups of cars. Wrightsman concluded that what people say about an issue does not necessarily alter their behavior.

Wrightsman's study, as you can see, had little impact upon the behavior of the people he was studying, and there is little or no reason to argue that in this field study the act of studying behavior had any significant effect upon that behavior.

The studies I have chosen to demonstrate field studies stand far apart on the issue of influencing the behavior they measure, but are quite similar in attempting to observe behavior as it occurs naturally. There was little or no *intent* to alter the process being observed or to influence it in any way. The fact that Festinger and his associates were not completely successful in their attempt only serves to show the inordinate amount of care a social psychologist must exercise successfully to complete his or her research.

FIELD EXPERIMENTS

Field experiments differ from field studies in one important respect. They either bring together groups of individuals who interact, or they introduce an experimental manipulation into the situation so that its effect upon behavior can be systematically studied.

The Robbers Cave. Robbers Cave is the rather prosaic name of a state park in Oklahoma where Muzafer Sherif and his associates carried out a field experiment that was concerned with the development, maintenance, and alteration of group norms. The experiment was the third in a series on group relations and involved the reduction of intergroup friction and conflict.

Twenty-two carefully selected boys about 11 years of age served as the subjects in the experiment. They were all from established, middle socioeconomic class, stable, Protestant families, and none of them was a problem in school, home, or neighborhood. Additionally, they were in the upper scholastic half of their classes, with above-average IQs, and were healthy, well-adjusted boys. Care was taken to select the subjects so that the results of the experiment could not be explained on the basis of social background differences, failure, excessive frustration, maladjustment, or scholastic or intellectual ineptitude.

The subjects were divided into two matched groups prior to the experiment, which was itself divided into three phases. Phase I was the formation of in-groups and this was accomplished by having each group interact with one another in appealing activities that required cooperation for their achievement. The practical way in which this was achieved was that for the first week of summer camp the two groups were kept apart and allowed to develop in group cohesiveness. By the end of the first week each group had adopted a name (the "Eagles" and "Rattlers"), appropriated a bunkhouse, hide-out, and swimming place of its own. Group cohesiveness was enhanced by supplying each group with a series of problems that required cooperative effort to achieve. For example, group members discovered canoes next to their respective bunkhouses and had to cooperate within their groups to carry them over rough terrain some distance away.

During Stage 1 the two groups were kept apart, and each group learned of the existence of the other only in the last days of Stage 1. In Stage 2, Sherif and his associates set out to test three hypotheses: (1)) when there are competition and frustrating relations between two groups, unfavorable stereotypes of the out-group will occur, (2) the competition will increase in-group solidarity, and (3) the pattern of in-group relationships will be changed because of the competition from the other group.

Stage 2 lasted for a week and consisted of a series of competitive and frustrating events. A tournament was announced and quickly resulted in mutual losses and retaliatory frustrating acts, such as burning or stealing each other's flags, name-calling, physical encounters, raids, and so on. The three hypotheses enumerated above were supported, which except for the third one, is probably not surprising. Those who rose to leadership positions in noncompetitive and nonfrustrating times were not always able to lead the groups when competition and frustrating situations arose and thus were replaced by other leaders.

Stage 3 was the most interesting phase, because Sherif and his associates set about to reduce intergroup conflicts and stereotypes, which is much more difficult to do than it is to create them. Stage 3 also lasted a week, and started with two days of contact while engaging in seven different pleasant activities. These contacts in no way reduced intergroup friction. Only when *superordinate* goals (goals that neither group alone could accomplish) were introduced did intergroup friction dissipate. A series of these goals such as (1) a broken water supply system when the groups were hot and thirsty and which could be fixed only by cooperative effort, (2) having to pool resources to rent a movie, and (3) a stalled truck that was needed to obtain food and

This group of young people just finished working together to collect marine specimens on a week long school field trip. Individuals who were previously unacquainted became close friends working on this and other superordinate goals throughout the week.

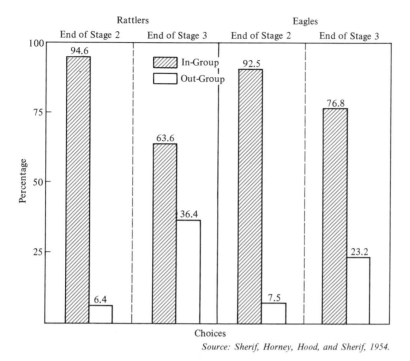

Source: Sherif, Horney, Hood, and Sherif, 1954.

Figure 2–2 Change in in-group and out-group choices for Rattlers and Eagles following intergroup conflict and frustration (Stage 2) and intergroup cooperation to solve superordinate goals (Stage 3).

could be started only by cooperative efforts of both groups, were introduced. One or two of these superordinate goals did not dissipate friction but a series of them did, and by the end of Stage 3 dramatic changes had taken place in the behavior of the groups. One measure, friendship choice, is shown in Figure 2–2. Whereas friendship choices were still predominantly for in-group members, Figure 2–2 shows the changes that took place in the short space of one week. These are truly remarkable.

COMMENT

Most field experiments are not so elaborate as the Robbers Cave Study and typically involve the introduction of some manipulation into an existing situation. This has been particularly true of experiments in altruism where the experimental manipulation may be as simple as introducing someone lying in the gutter on a busy street to find out how passers-by will react.

The designation of a study as a field experiment or a laboratory experiment, which is our next topic of discussion, may be rather narrow. Certainly Sherif and his associates controlled as many variables as they could in a three-week summer camp, but as you will see, in a laboratory experiment there is even greater control of extraneous variables.

Undoubtedly, the laboratory experiment has been the most popular approach to social psychological research in recent years, for a variety of reasons. Within the confines of the laboratory, as an experimenter is constantly available, it is possible to control more variables than it is even in a highly structured field experiment such as the Robbers Cave Study. The problems with laboratory research revolve around one central question, "Is such an artificial atmosphere provided that results obtained in a laboratory are not applicable outside of the laboratory?" In the Robbers Cave Experiment, the situation was sufficiently realistic that generalizations could be made concerning the behavior of the Eagles and the Rattlers to other groups in other types of situations.

Let us now consider two laboratory experiments, discussing them in the order of the amount of experimental control possible. First, we will consider simulation research and then what has been, for want of a better name, called a standard laboratory experiment.

SIMULATIONS

Simulation research is concerned with the problem of control of external variables, on the one hand, and the ability to generalize from laboratory research to more realistic settings, on the other. As we shall see, like any compromise, it, too, has its weaknesses. Abelson (1968, p. 275) said: "Simulation is the exercise of a flexible imitation of processes and outcomes for the purpose of clarifying or explaining the underlying mechanisms involved. . . Such an emphasis gives an important place to simulation as a theory-testing device, and it is precisely here that it can be important." Overly exaggerated claims about purporting to mimic real-world events have been made for simulations and such claims do a disservice to the technique.

There are several types of simulation. By far the most common type, and the only one we will discuss here, is the simulation of a real-life experience in which subjects are asked to play a role while their behaviors and actual reactions are closely watched. Much of the research is presented to the subject as a game, and in fact, such games as "Monopoly" and "Whodunit" are informal simulations in which each player takes a role that is foreign to his or her real-life occupation. Simulation researchers usually devise a game for the subjects to play and carefully control the options each player is given and study behavior under a prescribed set of circumstances. In what have now become classic studies Deutsch and Krauss (1960, 1962) studied the effects of threat on interpersonal bargaining.

Acme vs. Bolt. Subjects in a series of studies were asked to imagine that they were in charge of a trucking company that carried merchandise over a road to a destination. For each trip they completed, they would receive 60 cents minus expenses. Expenses mounted up at the rate of one cent for each second it took to reach their destination. Each player was either Acme or Bolt, and Figure 2–3 shows the road map shown to each player. The most direct route for both companies included a stretch of one-lane road, where only one truck could pass at a time. Additionally, there were gates, one controlled by Acme and one by Bolt. The alternate route for each player took an additional 10 seconds longer to traverse and thus automatically meant less profit.

FIELD RESEARCH YIELDS METHODOLOGICAL BENEFITS

The decade of the 70s has been the decade of attention to applied social psychology. The discipline in general has moved in the direction of studying new problems and in the process has opened up some new methodologies for the study of old problems. One of the most recent of these has been the study of juries.

Examples of these are Bray and Noble (1978) and Lamberth, Krieger, and Shay (1979). These studies and others like them focus on the deliberative process of the jury. Attention paid to this element of jury research can pay methodological returns in several areas. Included in these are group polarization, attitude change, and conformity.

Group polarization (see Chapter 11) is concerned with the effects of group decision making. The general finding has been that a group, after discussing the issue, will become more extreme in the direction the majority favored at the beginning. In a trial, this means that the jury will become more convinced of the verdict the majority initially held. Jury research is particularly well suited to this type of research because, in some jurisdictions, the law allows the judge to order a ballot of the jurors prior to the beginning of deliberations. With this knowledge and a post-deliberation ballot, the researcher can see exactly where each juror stood on the issue of the defendants' guilt both before and after the deliberations.

A second area of study within the jury decision-making literature is attitude change (see Chapter 5). When a jury goes into the jury room to deliberate, some individuals must change their attitudes towards the defendants' guilt if a unanimous verdict is to be reached. The use of a predeliberation ballot allows the researcher to know which jurors changed their minds. For example, both Bray and Noble and Lamberth et al. found that a personality characteristic is associated with the change in attitude toward the defendant's guild during deliberations. That is, high authoritarians are the ones who tend to change their attitude. Furthermore, Lamberth et al. pointed out that these people who changed were most influenced by egalitarian (low-authoritarian) jurors. Whereas there is much more research to be done in this area, the jury deliberation method seems aptly suited for the study of attitude change.

Finally conformity can be studied by close attention to the deliberative process. Many juries enter the jury room split fairly evenly for guilty or not guilty. As discussion proceeds, more and more people join the majority until there are 3, then 2, and finally 1 person opposing the majority. If you will read the section on conformity in Chapter 7, you will note that there has been a good deal of work on how individuals will react when they are in the minority and particularly where there is but one opposing a unanimous majority.

It should be emphasized that actual jury deliberations are secret and not open to study. Real cases can be reenacted and simulated juries run. There seems to be enough intrinsic interest in this process among citizens of both Canada and the United States to make jury deliberations an important methodological step forward.

References

Bray, R. M., and A. M. Noble. Authoritarianism and decisions of mock juries: Evidence of jury bias and group polarization. *Journal of Personality and Social Psychology,* 1978, *36,* 1424.

Lamberth, J., E. Krieger, and S. Shay. Juror decision making: A Case of attitude change mediated by authoritarianism. Unpublished manuscript, Temple University, 1979.

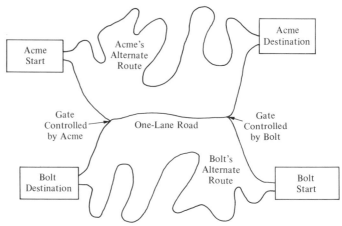

Adapted from Deutsch and Krauss, 1960.

Figure 2–3 **Map shown to players in interpersonal bargaining situation.**

The stage is now set to see how players cooperate and bargain when they either do or do not have a threat (gate) available to use against the other player. Deutsch and Krauss systematically varied threat by allowing (1) no threat (neither player could use the gate) (2) one company to have a threat, or (3) both companies to have a threat. Figure 2–4 shows the joint payoffs for both companies under the three varying threat conditions. It is obvious that when both players could utilize a threat, payoffs or profits fell dramatically. When only one had a threat, joint profits were below the situation in which neither had a threat. Interestingly enough, when only one had a gate, even that company suffered relative to the situation in which neither had a threat. But if only one company had a threat that company did better than the company without the threat.

In this situation, we can see the various and diverse types of questions that can be asked and answered in a simulation. It should be noted that subjects in the experi-

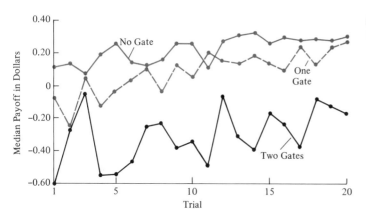

Figure 2-4 **Median joint payoff (Acme and Bolt) over trials.**

ment were role playing, i.e., they really had nothing to gain or lose by their action. There is, however, evidence to indicate that players in simulated games become extremely involved and that the more involved they become the more realistically they are likely to behave. Whereas the researcher can never be sure that given the same set of circumstances in a real-life situation the subjects would behave identically, the more involved and realistic the simulation is, the more likely are his or her results to be rather widely generalizable.

THE STANDARD LABORATORY EXPERIMENT

The title of this section is truly a misnomer because social psychological laboratories usually do not have an enormous amount of equipment that would be necessary in a physicist's or chemist's lab or even in the lab of many physiological psychologists. Although equipment is sometimes used in social psychology research, it is usually not so imposing that someone walking into the room realizes immediately that he or she is in a laboratory. Therefore laboratory research in social psychology refers more to the attempt by the experimenter to control as many extraneous variables as possible so that the subject will be concentrating on the variables of interest, than it does to a specific room or place.

The word *standard* is also a misnomer because there are not as many "standard" experiments in social psychology as there may be in other sciences. Frankly, the term is used for lack of a better one. The social psychologists laboratory, even though it may not look like whatever it is a laboratory is supposed to look like and it is not a place where standard experiments are run, is, nevertheless, an important aspect of social psychological research. Indeed, over the last several decades, laboratory experiments have been the cornerstone of social psychological research.

In the laboratory, the social psychologist, like any other scientist, is best able to manipulate *independent* variables, control *extraneous* variables, and measure *dependent* variables. These words should ring a bell for you who have had an introductory course in psychology. You will recall that an independent variable is one the experimenter controls; for example it may be group size, or order of presentation, or some other such variable. The dependent variable may be attitude change or conformity, or such, and is the entity the experimenter measures. Extraneous variables may be anything other than the independent variable that affects the dependent variables and thus alters the measurements taken.

If you think about it for a moment, you can readily see that case studies, field experiments, and simulations can have both independent and dependent variables. For example, the independent variable in Newcomb's attraction study might be said to be bringing 17 strangers together and letting them interact; in Sherif's Robbers Cave experiment it was the formation of groups. Two things should be noted, however. In Newcomb's study, the subjects might well have made friends through classes or some other social vehicle in a university rather than through the house in which they lived, and Sherif's groups might never have developed the in-group solidarity so important to the continuation of the experiment. Even more important, Newcomb's and Sherif's subjects had an enormous amount of time together when they were not being observed by the experimenter and thus all sorts of social activities could have occurred unknown to the experimenter. Which brings us to another important feature of standard laboratory experiments—the experimenter typically observes the subject throughout the experiment or has the capacity to do so for purposes of controlling extraneous variables.

As the standard laboratory experiment is so popular in social psychological research, we need here consider only one example, truly a classic in our discipline. You will come into contact with a great many others throughout the pages of this book.

Asch's Conformity Studies. Asch (1951; 1952; 1956) reported an ingenious and by now classic series of studies that might best be called, "Group Forces in the Modification and Distortion of Judgments" (Asch, 1952, p. 450). Asch was interested in some of the conditions that induce individuals to yield to group or social pressures or to remain independent when those pressures are contrary to fact. The experimental procedure was as follows (*Asch,* 1952, pp. 451–52):

A group of 7 to 9 individuals, all college students, are gathered in a classroom. The experimenter explains that they will be shown lines differing in length and that their task will be to match lines of equal length. The setting is that of a perceptual test. The experimenter places on the blackboard in front of the room two white cardboards on which are pasted vertical black lines. On the card at the left is a single line, the standard. The card at the right has three lines differing in length, one of which is equal to the standard line in the left. The task is to select from among the three lines the one equal in length to standard line as in Figure 2.5. . . .

The lines are vertical and their lower ends are at the same level. The comparison lines are numbered 1, 2, 3. Correctly matched lines are always at a distance of forty inches. In giving his judgment, each subject calls out, in accordance with the instruction, the member of the comparison line ("one," "two," "three") that he judges to be equal to the standards. When all the subjects have stated their judgments, the two cards are removed and replaced by a new pair of cards with new standard and comparison lines. There are twelve sets of standard and comparison lines in all.

For the first few trials, everything runs smoothly, with each person calling out the correct comparison since there is a large discrepancy in the incorrect lines and the standard line (ranging from $\frac{1}{4}$ inch to $1\frac{3}{4}$ inches when the length of the standard line ranges from $2\frac{1}{2}$ inches to 8 inches). After the first two trials a selected majority, who have been instructed by the experimenter, begin to select an incorrect line and they all select the same incorrect line. This leaves the real subject in a unique position. His eyes tell him one thing but six to eight other individuals all agree on another line as

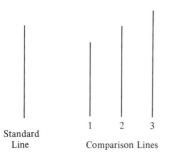

Standard
Line

1 2 3

Comparison Lines

Figure 2–5 A comparison to those used in Asch's conformity studies.

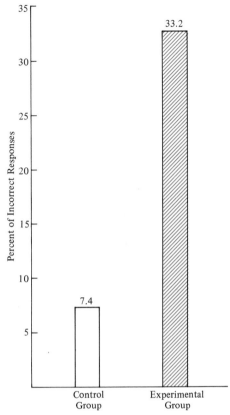

Figure 2–6 **Incorrect responses made by experimental and control subjects in Asch's conformity studies.**

Source: Asch, 1952.

being the same length as the standard line. The critical subject was always seated near the end, so that he would hear most of the other "subjects" call out their choice before he had to make his judgment.

The crucial question, of course was what effect the unanimous majority would have on the lone dissenter. Asch ran a total of 31 experimental subjects and 25 control subjects, who reported their judgments privately in writing. Figure 2–6 shows Asch's results. Two thirds of the time, experimental subjects resisted the majority but in 33.2 percent of the cases the experimental subjects yielded and selected the comparison line selected by the majority, whereas only 7.4 percent of the control subjects yielded. What is of crucial importance is that in a situation in which the lines were clearly discernible as being of different lengths, subjects yielded one third of the time. This classic study has been replicated a number of times and we will discuss it and variants on it at greater length in Chapter 7.

At this point you should note that the experiment was carried out in a classroom with only twelve sets of cards as equipment. Yet Asch had gained an enormous amount of control over the situation by enlisting other students to act as his majority, by assuring that the real subject sat near the end so his judgment would come after most other judgments, and so on. What is important about laboratory experimentation is not the setting but the control of extraneous variables that the experimenter has in the experiment.

COMMENT

Control of extraneous variables is a two-edged sword. If the laboratory experiment is so controlled that it or something akin to it never occurs in real life, does it tell us much? For example, how many times do any of us face a unanimous majority that is incorrect? The answer may be "More often than you think!" Nevertheless, Asch was too good a scientist not to investigate the effects of even one other person agreeing with the subject, and we will discuss that in Chapter 7. But the point is this: If a laboratory situation is too artificial and therefore does not generalize beyond the laboratory, is it of any use? The answer to this must be a qualified Yes. The control that is possible in the laboratory is important in isolating variables and studying them. The fact that they don't have the same cause-and-effect relationships outside of the lab may mean that they are not very important, but more probably it means that other variables interact with them to alter their effects.

Let us take an example from the natural sciences. A rock and a feather fall at the same rate *in a vacuum*. Scientists have known this for many years and developed theories to account for the effects of a vacuum even though humans did not encounter a naturally occurring vacuum until space exploration began in the 1960s.

Laboratory research in the social sciences has no similar clear-cut example to point to. Rather, we must guess as to whether our variables which are isolated and important in the controlled environments of the laboratory are sufficiently powerful to make themselves felt in the context of other variables. Fortunately with the variety of methods social psychologists have to study behavior, we can isolate variables and gain a better understanding of them in the laboratory and then test them in even more realistic settings. It is this moving back and forth from lab to more lifelike settings and back to the lab, and so on, which, I think, will be most beneficial to us as a research strategy in the future.

To assist in all of this, there are some tools, some pitfalls, and some general comments that need to be discussed in the last sections of our methodology chapter.

The Role of Data in Social Psychology

One statistical technique in social psychology—correlation—has already been discussed earlier in this chapter. By the time most students take social psychology they have had a course in statistics, or worse yet, they haven't, but the professor assumes they have. In this brief discussion, we will review a few statistical concepts, not with the aim of making you proficient in the subject, but to give you a conceptual view toward understanding the job of the scientist.

A scientist in any field wants to be able to understand and predict what will happen given certain sets of circumstances. For example, the chemist wants to understand what is going to happen when he mixes two volatile chemicals. After having done so once, and assuming that he survives the experiment, he now wants to be able to predict that result in advance. This rather flippantly serves to illustrate the difference between understanding and predicting. If the chemist is killed by the explosion he created, he may understand, just prior to death, the effects of mixing his two chemicals. If, on the other hand, he can predict what is going to happen, then he need not suffer the consequences of an unexpected physical explosion.

The social psychologist also wants to understand and predict human behavior, although the effects of psychological experiments normally do not culminate in an explosion. This is all by way of saying that the social psychologist, along with any other scientist, wants to be able to say that event A causes event B. Stated differently, the scientist wants to be able to imply and pinpoint causality. You will recall that correlation does not imply causality. Yet in experimental work, the psychologist is interested in implying causality, even more, in pinpointing causality. How do we go about doing just that?

Probabilities

Science is a discipline that must work by probabilities rather than absolutes, and statistics are the tools that tell us what our probabilities are in any given situation. For example, water boils at 212° Farenheit. Correct? Yes, at sea level, but if you're in the middle of the Rocky Mountains, the atmospheric pressure, which is one of the variables that control boiling, is different and therefore water does not boil at 212° Farenheit. A relatively small change in an experiment can change the results, even in the so-called hard sciences.

In psychology, and particularly in social psychology, we are dealing with more complex elements, human beings and their environment. If we wanted to be absolutely sure about a particular phenomenon we would have to test every individual under our experimental conditions. Since this is almost always impossible, we draw a sample of individuals, if possible, a random sample. This sample is tested and we make inferences to the population from which the sample was drawn on the basis of the behavior of the sample. This is a psychological experiment in its simplest form. There is, however, the necessity to assure ourselves that the mere passage of time or some variable other than our experimental manipulation did not affect the behavior of our sample. Thus, we use a second sample, called a control group, to use as a comparison for our experimental group. Possibly an illustration is in order.

Means and Variability

Let us assume that a certain social psychologist is interested in the effects on an individual's solitary behavior *when another person is present*. This, incidentally, is an area of great interest to social psychologists (according to Allport (1968) it was the *only* problem studied in the first three decades of social psychological experimentation) and today is known as social facilitation. A basic, simple design to study social facilitation would be to have a group of individuals perform a task, let us say, multiplication, alone and another group perform the task with another person present. Early experimentation by F. A. Allport (1924) showed that on a simple task, such as multiplication, the presence of another person facilitated performance. Thus,

The problem being worked on is very complex. Would you guess that the woman would be more likely to solve it working alone, or with someone else.

we might find that in a given time a group of people working alone would correctly do 10 multiplication problems whereas a group of individuals working with another person present would correctly do 14 multiplication problems. Does this mean that the group with another individual present works faster? Or to put it another way, is performance facilitated by the presence of another person? It is precisely at this point that the social psychologist uses statistics to help answer the question.

Recall that the group working alone (Group A) had a mean of 10 correct multiplication problems and the group working with another person present (Group B) had a mean of 14 correct responses. There are, however, several ways those two means could be arrived at. The mean, of course, is the arithmetical average arrived at by adding up the number of correct problems each individual in the group scored and dividing by the number of people in the group. One way to arrive at group means of 10 and 14 is for every person in Group A to get 10 correct and every person in Group B to get 14 correct. This almost never happens! What usually happens is that some individuals in the group score fewer correct than the mean and others score right at the mean or have more correct than the mean. This spread of scores around the mean is known as variability and enters into the answer to the question of whether Group B really did better than Group A. If there is very little variability about the mean, we can say that the probability is greater that the two means really do differ. Table 2–1 shows two hypothetical sets of data for Groups A and B. Both sets of data show that Group A has a mean of 10 and Group B has a mean of 14, but we come to quite different conclusions about the two groups in each set of data because of the variability. Figure 2–7 shows graphically two sets of data with high and low

76

Table 2-1 Two sets of hypothetical data for the number of correct multiplication problems for Groups A (alone) and Group B (with someone watching)

Low Variability		High Variability	
Group A	*Group B*	*Group A*	*Group B*
8	12	4	20
9	13	16	8
12	16	3	21
11	15	17	7
10	14	8	19
7	11	12	9
10	14	5	16
13	17	15	12
9	13	7	17
11	15	13	11
100	140	100	140
Mean = 10	14	10	14

variability. Whereas the means are identical the figure represents data from a much larger number of cases to show the curves more smoothly.

If we apply a statistical test to the data in Table 2–1, we find that in the set of data labeled Low Variability, the groups differ from each other to a statistically significant degree. That is because statistical tests are based upon the means of the two groups *and* the spread of variability of the scores around the group mean. Figure 2–7 shows the situation more clearly. In Panel 1, labeled Low Variability, there is almost no overlap between the two distributions of scores, whereas in Panel 2 labeled High Variability there is a great deal of overlap. Therefore, we cannot say that the samples' performance shows a statistically significant difference.

Even with the low-variability groups, we cannot say with certainty that the presence of another person facilitates performance. What we can say, and this is very important, is that *based upon the sample we have drawn we would expect the differences we obtained to occur less than 1 time in 1,000 by chance.* By convention, psychologists usually accept a finding as significant if it could have occurred by chance only 5 times out of a hundred. Of course, as this significance level decreases to 1 out of a hundred or 1 out of a thousand we are even more confident of our results. What must be remembered, however, is that we are dealing with probabilities and each of us knows that a significant finding may not be repeated (replicated) if the experiment is done again.

Contradictory Results

You will note as you progress through this book that there are quite a number of instances in which an experiment is not replicated. This may be because the original results were due to chance, but more often it is because of subtle changes in experimental procedure or some systematic bias in the results that occurs without intent.

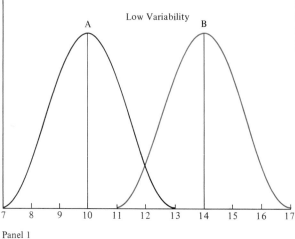

Figure 2-7 Schematic representations of curves with identical
means and low (Panel 1) and high
(Panel 2) variability.

Panel 1

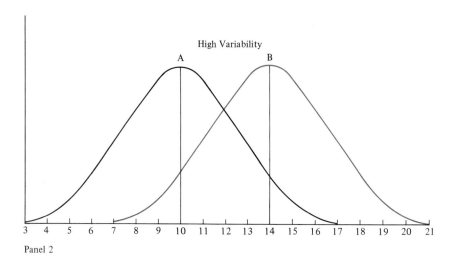

Panel 2

Unfortunately, it is impossible exactly to repeat a social psychological experiment
with human subjects. For one thing, times have changed; even a few days can have a
profound effect upon the subjects or subject matter of an experiment. Social psychologists are interested in topics that can fluctuate rather dramatically with the day's
news; attitudes, prejudice, interpersonal relationships, power, and so forth. Therefore,
it is impossible exactly to replicate an experiment. In addition, social psychologists
have not been as careful as they should in controlling all of the variables that are
controllable in the replication of a social psychological experiment. There is a built-in
urge to change this aspect of the study or that aspect of it. In a way that is virtually
unknown to the natural sciences "conceptual replications" in which the researcher
replicates an experiment but changes certain crucial aspects of the experiment are all
too common.

Part of the reason for this is that it is very difficult to get replications published in social psychological journals. Whereas it is true that the scientist who has originated an experimental technique or findings has probably made a greater contribution to science than someone who follows with a replication, it is even more true that someone who publishes nonreplicable results does inestimable damage to science. I should hasten to say that in the course of doing experimental work, results can occur by chance. Replication will never make us absolutely certain that the population will behave in a certain way under a specific set of circumstances, but if certain effects can be demonstrated more than once, it makes us more sure of the data.

Systematic Data Biasing

In their search for experimental bias, psychologists have been extremely diligent. Because of the fact that psychologists work with living organisms and social psychologists work primarily with people, it has long been suspected that experimental results are susceptible to artifacts—that is, results that are influenced in some way by the experimenter and are not the actual behavior patterns that would be displayed by individuals participating in experiments. The two most common of these, and the ones we will discuss, are experimenter expectancy effects and demand characteristics.

EXPERIMENTER EXPECTANCY EFFECTS

Rosenthal and his associates have been most vocal in calling attention to the possible biasing effects on experimental results that might occur because of the experimenter's expectancy. In one of the early studies of experimenter biasing effects (Rosenthal and Lawson, 1964) students enrolled in an experimental psychology class at Ohio State University served as experimenters. At the beginning of the semester the experimenters were assigned rats to work with in replicating seven standard operant conditioning studies utilizing a Skinner box. The experiments, which are often used to teach students in experimental psychology how to experiment with rats, included teaching them to press a bar, to press a bar only when a light was on, to chain a series of responses to obtain food, and so forth. Half of the experimenters were told that their rat was a Skinner Box–Bright rat and half were told that their rat was a Skinner Box–Dull rat. The two strains of rats were described as being selectively bred and it was said that those who had the bright rats could expect rather rapid results whereas those who had the dull rats were not to get discouraged, since even the dullest rats could, in time, learn the required responses.

In actuality, the rats did not differ in their breeding. They were randomly assigned to the student experimenters to test the effects of the student experimenters' expectations about the performance of their rats. The results of the study provided convincing evidence for the biasing effect of the experimenters' expectations, even on the behavior of rats. In almost every case the "Skinner Box–Bright" rats performed better than the "Skinner Box–Dull" rats.

If experimenter expectation can affect the performance of rats, what can it do to experiments when humans are the subjects? As you might have guessed by now, the answer is "A lot!"

Rosenthal and Fode (1963) selected ten students to serve as experimenters in a study that involved rating photographs. The subjects in the experiment were told to rate the pictures on the basis of whether the person in the picture was experiencing failure or success. The photographs were selected because they yielded neutral ratings, on the whole showing neither success or failure. The ten experimenters (who were really the subjects) were told they would be paid for their time and would be paid more "if your results come out properly—as expected." Five of the experimenters were told that they should expect the ratings of the photographs to be moderately successful while the other five experimenters were told that they should expect the ratings to be moderately on the failure side of the rating scale. When the experimenters expected successful ratings they got them more often than when they expected failure ratings, a result which has been replicated (Rosenthal, 1966, 1969).

The Pygmalion Effect. Probably the most dramatic and stringent test of Rosenthal's ideas about experimenter bias was performed at a school dubbed the "Oak School" and reported in Rosenthal and Jacobson (1968). In the spring of 1964 all children in the "Oak School" were given the Flanagan Tests of General Ability, a nonverbal intelligence test. The test was introduced to the teachers as the Harvard Test of Inflected Acquisition, a measure of intellectual "blooming," and that they could potentially expect 20 percent of the children to show increased intellectual development. Actually, the 20 percent of the children who were labeled "bloomers" were selected at random, and any differential ability existed in the teachers' minds.

The results of this study were indeed startling. The children were re-examined on the same test at the end of the one semester, one year, and two years. The results, shown in Figure 2–8, showed an overall gain in intelligence at all three measuring times, although the greatest absolute differences between the "bloomers" and the controls occurred at the end of the first year. Furthermore, the major and only significant differences occurred for first- and second-graders.

There have been a number of critical commentaries on the Rosenthal and Jacobson study (Elashoff and Snow, 1971; Flemming and Anttonen; 1971; Jensen, 1969; Snow, 1969), and a number of retorts. Expectancy effects of a systematic nature have been found in middle-class schools (Conn, Edwards, Rosenthal, and Crowne, 1968), with mentally retarded boys (Anderson and Rosenthal, 1968), and in an

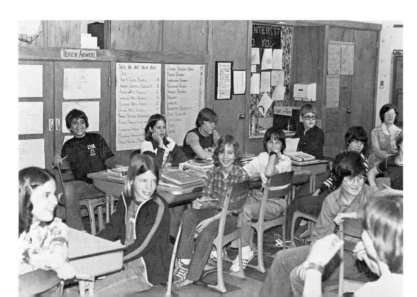

If their teachers knew their IQ scores, what effect would this have on these youngsters' performances?

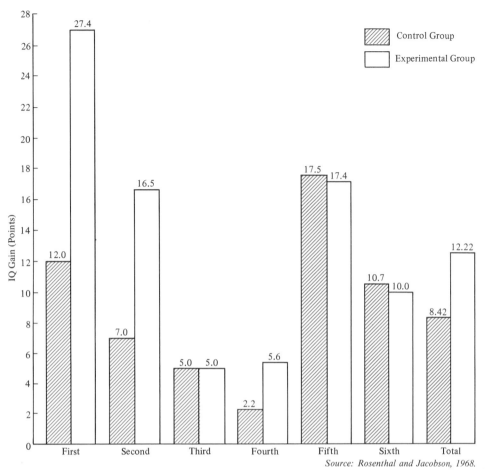

Source: Rosenthal and Jacobson, 1968.

Figure 2-8 Gains in IQs after one year by experimental and control groups for each of six grades and for the total school. The differences for first grade, second grade, and total school are significant.

Ontario training school for female offenders (Michenbaum, Bowers, and Ross, 1971). After the dust of the charges and countercharges has settled, or even before that has happened, serious social psychologists must admit the possibility of experimenter bias creeping into their research and take steps to avoid it.

As you will see in the chapters to come, there are ways to decrease or possibly even eliminate entirely the effects of experimenter bias. One of these is the simple expedient of keeping the experimenter who comes in contact with the subjects "blind" to what the experimental hypotheses are. Throughout this book you will see the attempts that are being made to eliminate this and all other sources of bias. Rosenthal, because of his pioneering efforts in calling our attention to experimenter bias, deserves a note of appreciation from all those interested in a viable science of social behavior.

Subject Effects

If experimenters are one source of bias in experimentation, subjects are also a very interesting potential source of biasing. First, a careful review of the social psychological literature indicates that possibly 70 percent or even more of the studies reported used college students as subjects (Higbee and Wells, 1972), confirming McNemar's ironic earlier quip (1946) "The existing science of human behavior is largely the science of the behavior of sophomores." To the extent that social psychological studies are carried out on college students, there is every indication that results are biased. In defense of the use of college students as subjects, it is possible to determine the differences between college students and the population in general. Additionally, the huge number of students going beyond high school to college makes that group more representative than it used to be, and many careful researchers replicate their studies with other groups of subjects (see Chapters 8, 9, 10 and 12, for examples). All these caveats are not intended to discount the seriousness of the overutilization of college students as subjects, rather they are meant to point out ways in which social psychologists are attempting to combat a potential bias in their data.

"Why," you may ask, "are college students used so much as subjects in social psychological experiments?" The answer is that they are available in large numbers at the places where most of this research takes place—universities. Your immediate response might well be, "But why doesn't the researcher get off his or her duff and go out into the community and find other subjects for research purposes?" The answer to that question is sometimes we do. Deutsch and Krauss's work, Festinger's, Fitzpatrick's, Kinsey's, Rosenthal and Jacobson's, and Sheriff's work, detailed earlier in this chapter, did just that. But, except for Fitzpatrick's study, there were already existing groups or some rather large inducement was added to obtain subjects. The real problem associated with obtaining other groups as subjects involves two or three dilemmas a researcher faces in attempting to find noncollege subjects. First, the general public faces with suspicion, if not downright horror, the psychologist who knocks at the door and says, "I'm a psychologist and I want to study your behavior." Latent fears of emotional maladjustment surface and the thought that goes through the head of the potential subject runs something like this, "Now even the people over at the university think I'm nuts!" No, this approach seldom works. A psychologist can advertise for subjects in the local newspaper and offer to pay subjects or ask them to volunteer. These two strategies have different but equally dangerous biasing effects. The psychologist who advertises for subjects faces biased results because usually only those who need money rather badly will be a research subject for the small amounts most research budgets allow.

Volunteer subjects have themselves been the subject of much research and generally speaking volunteers are "better educated, higher in status, more approval seeking, less authoritarian, more sociable and arousal seeking, brighter, and younger individuals (Rosenthal and Rosnow, 1975; Rosnow and Rosenthal, 1976). Thus, it seems that a researcher is faced with a major and important problem when research subjects are selected. That most have fallen back on the university student may not be as unfortunate as it first seems, because college students are probably the most representative group of individuals gathered together where research can be carried out. It is not enough, however, for the researcher to stop with college students. Careful analysis of the particular problem and careful cultivation of potential sources of subjects should, at the very least, allow the researcher to replicate the results found with college students on other populations.

Demand Characteristics. A rather long and very important series of experiments into what has been labeled demand characteristics has been carried out by Orne (1962, 1969). The basic contention of a demand characteristics explanation is that subjects in some way guess the experimental hypothesis and set out to "help" the experimenter by confirming it. The first step is to demonstrate the cooperative nature of subjects. To do this, Orne presented subjects with around 2,000 pages of random numbers with the instructions to sum each two adjacent numbers and continue this boring task until he returned. Orne found his subjects continuing 5 hours later. He then told them that as they finished a page they were to tear it into no less than 32 pieces and throw it in the wastebasket. Even these instructions had little effect on the persistence of subjects. Other experiments have confirmed the incredible degree of cooperativeness of subjects, and when asked about their behavior they reply that they thought the experimenter was interested in endurance and, therefore, their behavior was quite appropriate. Thus, to an amazing degree, Orne's contention that the demand characteristics of an experiment may influence the results seems valid.

How, you may ask, does a subject know what an experimenter wants, even assuming that subjects are compliant and willing to do what the experimenter wants? Even in Orne's own studies, subjects were wrong about what he was interested in. He actually was interested in how cooperative they were while they thought he was interested in endurance. It really makes little difference if the subjects guess the right or wrong hypothesis—if their behavior differs from what they would usually do in a given situation, then an artifact has entered into the research, usually biasing it beyond repair.

How have social psychologists faced the issue of demand characteristics? There are a number of ways, most of them involving attempts to keep subjects unaware of the real aims of the study. These deception experiments can sometimes be useful, but they are plagued by ethical questions (see the next section of this chapter) and the fact that even if the subjects are unaware of the real experimental hypothesis, if they guess an incorrect one, they can do equal damage to the research. Thus, it is necessary for experimenters to be extremely vigilant in attempting to ascertain demand characteristics in their experimental procedures. Sometimes other psychologists call attention to the demand characteristics of an experimental procedure and controversy erupts. One example of this is Page's claim (Page, 1969; Page and Lumia, 1968; Page and Scheidt, 1971) that the classical conditioning of meaning, attitudes, and stimulus-instigated aggression is unduly contaminated by demand characteristics. Investigators involved in those areas point out that Page's method of assessing demand characteristics is itself subject to the criticism of making subjects aware of the experimenter's hypothesis and allowing them to cooperate—that is, to demand characteristics (Berkowitz, 1973; Staats, 1969). Another example is a study which purported that when given an alternative, subjects will choose to look good rather than do what the experimenter wants (Sigall, Aronson, and Van Hoose, 1970). However, Adair and Schacter (1972) argued that the results obtained by Sigall et al. were a function of the instructions that were used. Rosnow, Goodstadt, Suls, Gitter, and George (1973), using a different task, confirmed the more obvious effects reported by Sigall et al. that subjects would rather look good than please the experimenter.

A more frontal assault on assessing the demand characteristics present in their experimental paradigm was carried out by Lamberth and Byrne (1971). Within the research paradigm for the study of interpersonal attraction developed by Byrne and his associates (see Chapter 9 for a fuller discussion of this methodology) subjects in one experiment were asked to state what the experimental hypothesis was. Only 18.5 percent were judged to be aware of the hypothesis by two independent judges. In a second experiment, subjects were divided into five groups which were (1) told that the more two people are alike the more they will like each other (the experimental hypothesis) and were asked to confirm the hypothesis; (2) told the experimental hypothesis but asked to behave in a manner they thought would be the opposite of the hypothesis; (3) told to guess the hypothesis and act to confirm it; (4) told to guess the hypothesis and act to disconfirm it; and (5) a control condition that was told nothing and was asked how attracted they were to the other person. In all five conditions, subjects validated the experimental hypothesis, which was that the more similar people are, the more they like each other. Another experiment in this research consisted of four groups. The first two were identical to groups 1 and 2 in the previous experiment and two new conditions were added. In these groups, subjects were given a false hypothesis, i.e., opposites attract, and half of them were asked to confirm the hypothesis and half to disconfirm it. Again, in all conditions, subjects were more attracted to the similar other and less attracted to the dissimilar other person.

Lamberth and Byrne concluded that demand characteristics play little discernible part in their research paradigm. These results have been replicated and elaborated by McGinley and Reiner (1976). These investigators looked more systematically at the small amount of demand characteristics that Lamberth and Byrne suggested might be in their data and were able to put a few more pieces of the puzzle together. This sort of work is extremely demanding and yet absolutely essential if demand characteristics are to be systematically investigated and either implicated or dismissed as a source of bias in a research area.

Comment. There are ways to mitigate experimenter and subject bias in research data. The examples given probably do more to reflect the real concern of social psychologists over these issues than anything else one might say. As you read this book, you will note that all sorts of controls have been instituted to ferret out and eliminate systematic bias in research. To be sure, no one seriously argues that such biasing factors have been eliminated—we can never be sure that we are aware of all or even most potential biasing factors. Researchers are alert to their potential effects and are attempting to eliminate them.

Experimental Bias: Fact or Artifact?

Kruglanski (1975) has argued that the considerable amount of concern about experimental bias is important but unnecessary. That is, it is important that the biasing effects of experimenters, demand characteristics, and volunteer subjects, among others, be studied, but that the evidence to date does not suggest that such potential artifacts have much effect on experimental results.

How, you might wonder, can Kruglanski argue that the sources of bias discussed in the preceding chapter do not affect experimental results? It is necessary to remember that the results of any experiment can be interpreted in several ways, depending upon the conceptual "set" of the experimenter. For example, the results of the Lamberth and Byrne (1971) study of demand characteristics in attraction research could have been interpreted as unimportant because no demand characteristic effects were discovered. This is precisely the way one anonymous reviewer interpreted the study.

On the other hand, it is virtually impossible to prove that demand characteristics, experimenter bias, volunteer artifacts, or some other experimental bias did not affect the results of an experiment. Instead of placing the burden of proof on the experimenter (to prove some sort of biasing did not occur) Kruglanski argues that it is the job of those who argue for the biasing effects of various artifacts to prove they do affect experimental results. When the problem is approached in this way there is much less evidence for experimental artifacts (see also Kruglanski, 1973).

Even though psychologists continue to attempt to control potential experimental biasing of data, it is possible that such measures are unnecessary. Until one position or the other is verified, however, it will be necessary to continue to control for artifacts.

Ethics in Social Psychological Research

Whenever research is being carried out with human beings as subjects, it is appropriate, if not mandatory, to consider the ethics of the situation. Scientists who worked on the atomic bomb found in the 1940s that once they had finished their work, it was too late to open a debate into the subtleties of how it would be used. By the same token, scientists who deal with human behavior cannot wait until some technique that is extremely effective and subject to misuse by others is perfected prior to considering the ethics of developing the technique. To date, psychologists do not even appear to be close to such a behavioral breakthrough. But if ethics are not of paramount importance in developing psychological knowledge, it is probably fair to say that ethical considerations will not be particularly important in how that knowledge is used.

Consider the case of Festinger and his associates who infiltrated the "Seekers" to study their behavior when the prophecy they believed failed. Does a scientist have a right to violate the privacy of such a group by duping them into believing that he and his associates were true believers? One must always consider the times when such things are done. Politicians could be more lax in their ethical codes prior to Watergate than after it. It does not make what they did any more ethical, but we are creatures of our environment. I doubt seriously that most social psychologists today would do what Festinger et al. did, because from our present vantage point on the eve of the 1980s we are much more attuned to personal privacy and personal rights. The year 1984 is imminent.

FIELD EXPERIMENTATION—SOME PITFALLS

In an interesting and important article, Schulz (1976) reported a field experiment in which institutionalized elderly people were the subjects. These people were randomly assigned to one of four groups. In one group the elderly could determine both the frequency and the duration of visits they received from college undergraduates. A second group was informed when the visits would occur and how long they would last. A third group was visited on a random schedule, while a fourth group was not visited at all. Predictable and controllable visits were the most effective in causing a positive impact on the well-being of the elderly people. That is, on measures of both physical and psychological well-being, those in the groups who could predict and control or who knew when the visitor was coming were clearly superior to those who were visited on a random schedule or not visited at all.

Schulz and Hanusa (1978) report a disturbing follow-up study of these elderly people. Twenty-four, 30, and 42 months after the initial study, the elderly subjects were again evaluated with respect to their physical and psychological well-being. These measures were two 9-point scales assessing health status and zest for life. The end points of the health status scale were labeled "in perfect health" and "extremely ill," whereas the end points of the zest-for-life scale were labeled "extremely enthusiastic about life" and "completely hopeless." The scales were filled out by the activities director of the nursing home in which the research was carried out. Since she had worked in the home for 11 years, she knew each of the residents personally. In addition, she was the one who had filled out these same scales for each resident when the initial study terminated two years earlier.

On both health and zest-for-life scales the two

groups that had been helped most by the visits (the predictable and controlled visits and the predictable visits) declined rapidly. At the first follow-up evaluation these two groups were below the random group and the no treatment group on both measures. The latter two groups had remained essentially stable on these measures since the termination of the study. The 30 and 42 month follow-up showed essentially the same results.

This study is highlighted here because it points out some of the ethical problems with field research. Few people would have suspected that the termination of visits by college students would have such an adverse effect on those it helped most. Seemingly, the situation was external, but unstable; that is, from the beginning, the residents knew the visits would continue for a limited amount of time. Thus residents who could predict the visits while they were occurring may have acquired a greater feeling of control over their environment. When this control was taken away from them by the cessation of visits, something akin to depression may have set in. This analysis is quite consistent with the analysis of learned helplessness discussed in Chapter 1.

Whatever the reasons for the results, field experimentation requires a great deal of sensitivity to potential ethical outcomes.

References

Schulz, R. The effect of control and predictability on the psychological and physical well-being of the institutionalized aged. *Journal of Personality and Social Psychology*, 1976, *33*, 563–573.

Schulz, R., and B. H. Hanusa. Long-term effects of control and predictability-enhancing interventions: Findings and ethical issues. *Journa of Personality and Social Psychology*, 1978, *36*, 1194–1201.

The history of social psychology has its good and its bad ethical moments. Mostly, psychologists are ethically concerned and aware, but like other professions, we have people who either don't care or don't think about what they are doing. The American Psychological Association has for a number of years had a code for conducting research with human subjects and it was most recently revised in 1973. The writing of the principles was itself a long and drawn-out process, which generated a considerable amount of disagreement and argument. Balancing the rights of individual participants with the need to know about certain psychological processes and the potential gain for humanity is no easy feat. Since deception is the issue that has been of most interest in social psychology, it will serve as an example of ethical problems.

Deception in Social Psychological Research

It is sometimes necessary for social psychologists to deceive subjects if they are to study certain phenomena in which they are interested. Let us consider the Asch study in conformity, which was discussed earlier. Asch deceived his subjects by enlisting the aid of the other people in the room to select the incorrect line and to do it unanimously so as to put as much social pressure as possible on the individual to distort his own perception. Was it ethical to do that? The answer to this question is quite involved, but let me develop a line of reasoning that I think every scientist should pursue before proceeding with the research.

First and foremost, how important is the problem being studied? In Asch's case, group pressure to conform is an important topic. As you will see in Chapter 7, social psychologists have studied it for some time and it does have many ramifications. Most social scientists would agree that Asch's problem was clearly important.

The next step in the process has to do with whether there is some way other than deception to study the problem at hand. Is it necessary to deceive subjects or can some other equally feasible method of study answer the experimental questions at hand? It seems obvious that Asch could not tell his subjects that the other people in the room had been instructed to select the incorrect line. Obviously there would have been no effect of a unanimous incorrect judgment if the subject was told that the other respondents were faking. Even though there is at least one hotly debated alternative to deception, namely role playing, which we shall discuss shortly, it seems clear that in Asch's study, deception was necessary.

The third stage in the decision to use deception involves the potential harm to the subject. Of course, this is a value judgment that is difficult to make and at times both the results of an experiment and the effects on subjects come as a distinct surprise to the researcher. Whereas it is probable that little or no harm was done to subjects in Asch's conformity studies, Milgram's (1963, 1964) studies of obedience, which will be discussed more fully in Chapter 7 are a different story. Basically, Milgram had subjects who thought they were delivering painful electric shock to another person continue to increase the level of shock to the point where it could easily be assumed that very real harm had been done to the person shocked. The first time this study was done, Milgram and the psychological world were surprised, even shocked, at the number of subjects who would continue to shock others beyond the point where it appeared they had done real physical harm to them. Equally shocking was the psychological stress subjects underwent who continued to administer what they thought was harmful shock. Milgram (1963, p. 377) himself described the stress subjects underwent, observing of one subject that.... "within 20 minutes he was reduced to a twitching, stuttering wreck, who was rapidly approaching a point of nervous collapse...." Baumrind (1964) criticized the research rather strongly and Milgram responded emphasizing the importance of the research and the fact that care was exercised in the experimental and postexperimental procedures to assure that subjects suffered no long-term psychological damage.

Because the results were unexpected, Milgram's defense seems quite appropriate. Once the detrimental effects on subjects have been understood, however, the picture is quite different. Should researchers continue doing the research when they know it will cause distress to their subjects?

This brings us to the final stage of a researcher's decision to use deception or, for that matter, to do any research, and that is the cost-benefit ratio. Again, we are dealing with subjective decisions and virtually every university now has committees that assist researchers who are dealing with human subjects to decide whether research should be done. Basically, researchers and ethics committees try to resolve the four problems I have been discussing and make a decision about whether the research should be conducted. Figure 2–9 presents the decision process schematically. The figure should call your attention to the fact that deception is not the only potentially harmful process in psychological research—far from it. It is the most often encountered one in social psychology and thus receives the most attention. Stress research and many other psychological research paradigms may be even more harmful than the worst of the deception studies. One alternative that has been proposed as a substitute for deception is role playing.

Role Playing

Role playing, in which the subject is instructed to act as if she or he were in the specific situation, has been proposed as an alternative to deception in social psycho-

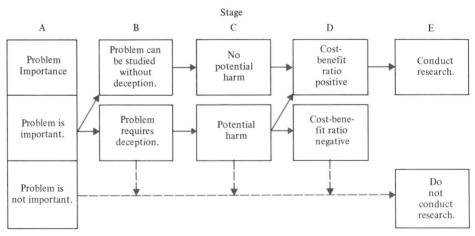

Figure 2–9 Schematic representation of decisions made in determining the ethical nature of research.

logical experiments. Kelman's (1967) article provided much of the impetus for the debate of the last decade over the use of deception. One of his suggestions was that new experimental methods, such as role playing or simulation, which call for a subject's informed participation, be used as a substitute for deception. Research almost immediately began into the applicability of role playing as an alternative to deception. Early results (Horowitz and Rothschild, 1970; Willis and Willis, 1970) indicated that while some of the more obvious experimental results could be duplicated by role playing, subtle interactions were not duplicated. Holmes and Bennett (1974) reported that role-playing subjects could duplicate self-report measures of stress but not the physiological ones of deceived subjects. It seems that role playing does not adequately duplicate the effects generated by deception in certain psychological studies. Thus, we are back to the problems and decisions presented in Figure 2–9.

Comment

This rather abbreviated discussion of ethics in social psychology could be carried out to much greater extremes with little extra effort, but our purpose has been served. Experimentation with human subjects is a serious business, and if ethical considerations are not given the highest priority in all phases of research planning and execution, harm to the subjects and potential harm to society can result. As should be evident by now, these are not matters that are easily resolved, but they are matters of paramount importance.

SUMMARY

1 Methodology in an important part of any science and there is an important relationship between theory and method.

2 Case studies are detailed compilations of relevant and significant data pertaining to one individual. The major study of attraction by Newcomb and the Foas' resource approach to exchange theory are used to illustrate the case study approach.

3 Surveys are observations that occur in natural settings with minimal interference in behavior and choice. Surveys can be written or oral, but the key to any survey is the adequacy of the sample it uses. Written surveys were illustrated by Fitzpatrick's work on types of communication. Kinsey's monumental study of male and female sexual activity illustrated oral surveys.

4 Experiments are at the heart of social psychology. Correlational research occurs when the researcher is interested in how two or more variables relate to each other. Because two variables are correlated does not imply that one causes the other. Thus when attraction researchers found that there was a correlation between similarity and attraction, it was impossible to say whether similar people were drawn to each other or whether people who were attracted to each other grew to be similar.

5 Field research occurs when the psychologist goes out to observe behavior in its natural setting. Field studies, such as the one detailed in *When Prophecy Fails,* and Wrightsman's study of attitudes and behavior are attempts to observe and not to change that behavior in any way. Field experiments, such as the Robbers Cave study, introduce experimental manipulations into a situation so that their effect on behavior can be measured.

6 Laboratory experiments have been the most popular approach to social psychological research in recent years. The major problem with laboratory experiments is to assure enough realism to allow generalization of results from one situation to another.

7 Simulations are concerned with the problem of control and realism. The most common form of simulation is the one in which subjects are asked to play a role while their behaviors and actual reactions are closely watched. Deutsch and Krauss' work on the effects of threat on interpersonal bargaining was used to illustrate simulations.

8 The standard laboratory experiment refers to the attempt to control as many extraneous variables as possible. In the laboratory, independent variables are manipulated and dependent variables are measured. Asch's conformity studies are an excellent example of laboratory research.

9 The social scientist wants to be able to infer and pinpoint causality. Statistical concepts and procedures, such as probabilities, means, and variability, help us to understand cause-and-effect relationships.

10 Systematic data biasing, such as experimenter expectancy effects, subject effects, and demand characteristics, have been carefully investigated in social psychology. There is disagreement concerning the magnitude of these effects on social psychological data.

11 Psychologists must be concerned with the effects on their subjects of their experimental manipulations as well as the effects on society of the results of their experiments. Deception in social psychological research is sometimes necessary, but should be used only when no other alternative is available *and* the problem under investigation is of great importance.

GLOSSARY

Case Studies   A comprehensive framework into which all relevant and significant data pertaining to a single life are compiled and arranged.

Conceptual Replication   Replications that change certain crucial aspects of the experiment.

Correlation   A statistical tool that allows for the computation of the relationship between two or more variables.

Demand Characteristics   Data biasing that occurs when subjects guess the experimental hypothesis and behave in a manner that confirms that hypothesis.

Dependent Variable(s)   The variable(s) the experimenter measures.

Experimenter Expectancy Effects   Experimental effects that are the result of the experimenter's expectations.

Experiments Scientific activity that includes observations collected under conditions in which behavior choices are limited by the controlled manipulation of variables selected by the researcher.

Extraneous Variable A variable the experimenter wishes to diminish in importance by controlling it.

Field Experiment Scientific activity that brings together groups of individuals who interact in nonlaboratory settings or that introduce an experimental manipulation in naturally occurring groups.

Field Research The systematic observation and classification of behavior where it actually occurs.

Field Study The observation of the behavior of people in their natural habitat.

Independent Variable(s) The variable(s) manipulated by the experimenter.

Independents Heterosexual couples who use a type of communication strategy that reflects a balance between autonomy and interdependence.

Laboratory Research The attempt to control as many extraneous variables as possible so that the subject will concentrate on the variable of interest.

Mean Group average.

Random Sample A sample drawn in such a way that each individual in the defined population has an equal chance of being included in the sample.

Replication The exact repetition of an experiment to verify its results.

Resource Theory of Social Exchange Social exchange theory that emphasizes the uniqueness of different resources.

Separates Heterosexual couples who use a type of communication strategy that involves a minimal amount of sharing and a high degree of conflict avoidance.

Simulation The exercise of a flexible imitation of processes and outcomes for the purpose of clarifying or explaining the underlying mechanisms involved.

Social Exchange A theory of social interaction in which individuals are assumed to weigh the costs and benefits of interpersonal relationships.

Stratified Random Sampling Sampling so that important subgroups are identified and these strata are then randomly sampled.

Superordinate Goals Goals that need the cooperation of more than one group of individuals to achieve.

Survey Observation that occurs in natural settings with a minimum of interference over normal variations in behavior and choices.

Traditional Heterosexual couples who use a type of communication strategy that indicates a commitment to conventional values and an opposition to a change-oriented philosophy of life.

Variability The spread of scores around the mean.

REFERENCES

Abelson, R. P. Computers, polls and public opinion—some puzzles and paradoxes, *Transaction,* 1968, *5,* 20–27.

Abelson, H., R., Cohen, E., Heaton, and C., Suder. National survey of public attitudes toward an experience with materials. In *Technical report of the Commission on Obscenity and*

Pornography. Vol. VI. Washington, D.C.; U.S. Government Printing Office, 1971. Pp. 1–137.

Adair, J. G., and B. S. Schachter. To cooperate or to look good? The subjects' and experimenters' perceptions of each other's intentions. *Journal of Experimental Social Psychology,* 1972, *8,* 74–85.

Allport, F. H. *Social psychology.* Boston: Houghton Mifflin Company, 1924.

Allport, G. W. *Pattern and growth in personality.* New York: Holt, Rinehart and Winston, 1961.

———. The historical background of modern social psychology. In G. Lindzey and E. Aronson (Eds.) *Handbook of Social Psychology.* Vol. I. (2nd Ed.) Reading, Mass.: Addison-Wesley Pub. Co., Inc., 1968, pp. 1–70.

American Psychological Association. Ethical principles in the conduct of research with human participants. *American Psychologist,* 1973, *28,* 79–80.

Anderson, D., and R. Rosenthal. Some effects of interpersonal expectancy on institutionalized retarded children. *Proceedings of the 76th Annual Convention of the American Psychological Association,* 1968, 479–80.

Asch, S. E. Effects of group pressure upon the modification and distortion of judgments in H. Guetzkow (Ed.). *Groups, Leadership and Man.* Pittsburgh: Carnegie Press, 1951.

———. *Social Psychology.* New York: Prentice-Hall, Inc., 1952.

———. Studies of independence and conformity: A minority of one against a unanimous majority. *Psychological Monographs,* 1956, *70,* (9, Whole No. 416).

Baumrind, D. Some thoughts on ethics of research: After reading Milgram's "Behavioral study of obedience." *American Psychologist,* 1964, *19,* 421–23.

Berkowitz, L. Words and symbols as stimuli to aggressive responses. In J. F. Knudsen (Ed.) *The Control of Aggression.* Chicago: Aldine Pub. Co., 1973.

Byrne, D. *The attraction paradigm.* New York: Academic Press, Inc., 1971.

———, and J. Lamberth. The effect of erotic stimuli on sex arousal, evaluative responses, and subsequent behavior. In *Technical reports of the Commission on Obscenity and Pornography,* Vol. VIII. Washington, D.C.: U.S. Government Printing Office, 1971, Pp. 41–67.

Conn, L. K., C. N. Edwards, R. Rosenthal, and J. Crowne. Perception of emotion and response to teachers' expectancy by elementary school children. *Psychological Reports,* 1968, *22,* 27–34.

Crano, W. D., and M. B. Brewer. *Principles of research in social psychology.* New York: McGraw-Hill Book Company, 1973.

Deutsch, M., and R. M. Krauss. The effect of threat on interpersonal bargaining. *Journal of Abnormal and Social Psychology,* 1960, *61,* 181–89.

——— and ———. Studies of interpersonal bargaining. *Journal of Conflict Resolution,* 1962, *6,* 52–76.

Elashoff, J. R., and R. E. Snow. *Pygmalion reconsidered.* Worthington, Ohio: Charles A. Jones, 1971.

Festinger, L., H. W. Riecken, and S. Schachter. *When prophecy fails.* Minneapolis: University of Minnesota Press, 1956.

Fitzpatrick, M. A. A typological approach to communication in relationships. Unpublished doctoral dissertation, Temple University, 1976.

Fleming, E. S., and R. G. Anttonen. Teacher expectancy as related to the academic and personal growth of primary-aged children. *Monograph of the Society for Research in Child Development,* No. 145, 1971, *36.*

Foa, U. G., and E. B. Foa. *Societal structures of the mind.* Charles C Thomas, Publishers, 1974.

——— and ———. *Resource theory of social exchange.* Morristown, N.J.: General Learning Press, 1975.

Galton, F. Co-relations and their measurement. *Proceedings of the Royal Society*, 1888, *45*, 135–45.

Griffitt, W., J. May, and R. Veitch. Sexual stimulation and interpersonal behavior: Heterosexual evaluative responses, visual behavior and physical proximity. *Journal of Personality and Social Psychology*, 1974, *30*, 367–77.

Higbee, K. L., and M. G. Wells. Some research trends in social psychology during the 1960's. *American Psychologist*, 1972, *27*, 963–66.

Holmes, D. S., and D. H. Bennett. Experiments to answer questions raised by the use of deception in psychological research. *Journal of Personality and Social Psychology*, 1974, *29*, 385–67.

Horowitz, I. A., and B. H. Rothschild. Conformity as a function of deception and role playing. *Journal of Personality and Social Psychology*, 1970, *14*, 224–26.

Hunt, A. McC. A study of the relative value of certain ideals. *Journal of Abnormal and Social Psychology*, 1935, *30*, 222–28.

Jensen, A. R. How much can we boost I.Q. and scholastic achievement? *Harvard Educational Review*, 1969, *39*, 1–123.

Kantor, D., and W. Lehr. *Inside the family: Toward a theory of family process*. San Francisco: Jossey-Bass, 1975.

Kelman, H. Human use of human subjects: The problem of deception in social psychological experiments. *Psychological Bulletin*, 1967, *67*, 1–11.

Kinsey, A. C., W. B. Pomeroy, and C. E. Martin. *Sexual behavior in the human male*. Philadelphia: W. B. Saunders Company, 1948.

————, ————, ————, and P. H. Gerbhard. *Sexual behavior in the human female*. Philadelphia: W. B. Saunders, Company, 1953.

Kirkpatrick, C., and S. Stone. Attitude measurement and the comparison of generations. *Journal of Applied Psychology*, 1935, *19*, 564–82.

Kruglanski, A. W. Much ado about the "volunteer-artifacts." *Journal of Personality and Social Psychology*, 1973, *28*, 348–54.

————. The human subject: Fact and artifact. In L. Berkowitz (Ed.). Advances in experimental social psychology, Vol. 8. New York: Academic Press, Inc., 1975. Pp. 101–47.

Lamberth, J., and D. Byrne. Similarity attraction or demand characteristics. *Personality*, 1971, *2*, 77–91.

Masters, W. H., and V. E. Johnson. *Human sexual response*. Boston: Little, Brown and Company, 1966.

McGinley, H., and M. Reiner. Reducing demand characteristics in the study of interpersonal attraction. Paper presented at the meeting of the Psychonomic Society, St. Louis, November 1976.

McNemar, Q. Opinion-attitude methodology. *Psychological Bulletin*, 1946, *43*, 289–374.

Mitchenbaum, D. H., K. S. Bowers, and R. R. Ross. A behavioral analysis of teacher expectancy effects. *Journal of Personality and Social Psychology*, 1971, *17*, 332–41.

Milgram, S. Behavioral studies of obedience. *Journal of Abnormal and Social Psychology*, 1963, *67*, 371–78.

————. Issues in the study of obedience: A reply to Baumrind. *American Psychologist*, 1964, *19*, 848–52.

Money, J. *Sex errors of the body*. Baltimore: The Johns Hopkins University Press, 1968.

Morgan, C. L., and H. H. Remmers. Liberalism and conservatism of college students as affected by the depression. *School and Society*, 1935, *41*, 780–84.

Newcomb, T. M. *The Acquaintance Process*. New York: Holt, Rinehart and Winston, 1961.

Newcomb, T., and G. Svehla. Intra-family relationships in attitudes. *Sociometry*, 1937, *1*, 180–205.

Orne, M. T. On the social psychology of the psychological experiment: with particular reference to demand characteristics and their implications. *American Psychologist,* 1962, *17,* 776–83.

————. Demand characteristics and the concept of quasi-controls. In R. Rosenthal and R. L. Rosnow (Eds). *Artifact in behavioral research.* New York: Academic Press, Inc., 1969, Pp. 143–79.

Page, M. M. Social psychology of classical conditioning of attitudes experiment. *Journal of Personality and Social Psychology,* 1969, *11,* 177–86.

————. and A. R. Lumia. Cooperation with demand characteristics and the bimodal distributioning of verbal conditioning data. *Psychonomic Science,* 1968, *12,* 243–44.

————. and R. Scheidt. The elusive weapons effect: Demand awareness, evaluation and slightly sophisticated subjects. *Journal of Personality and Social Psychology,* 1971, *20,* 304–18.

Pearson, K. Mathematical contributions to the theory of evolution: regression, heredity, and panmixia. *Philosophical Transactions,* 1896, *187A,* 253–318.

———— and A. Lee. On the laws of inheritance in man. I. Inheritance of physical characters. *Biometrik,* 1903, *2,* 357–462.

Rosenthal, R. *Experimenter effects in behavioral research.* New York: Appleton-Century-Crofts, 1966.

————. Interpersonal expectations: Effects of the experimenter's hypothesis. In R. Rosenthal and R. Rosnow (Eds.). *Artifacts in behavioral research.* New York: Academic Press, Inc., 1969, pp. 181–277.

———— and K. Fode. Three experiments in experimenter bias. *Psychological Reports, 12,* 1963, 183–89.

———— and L. Jacobson. *Pygmalion in the classroom:* Teacher expectation and pupils' intellectual development. New York: Holt, Rinehart and Winston, 1968.

———— and R. Lawson. A longitudinal study of the effects of experimenter bias on the operant learning of laboratory rats. *Journal of Psychiatric Research, 2,* 1964, 61–72.

———— and R. Rosnow. *Primer of methods for the behavioral sciences.* New York, John Wiley and Sons, Inc., 1975.

Rosnow, R. L., B. E. Goodstadt, J. M. Suls, and A. George Gitter. More on the social psychology of the experiment: When compliance turns to self-defense. *Journal of Personality and Social Psychology,* 1973, *27,* 337–43.

Rosnow, R., and R. Rosenthal. The volunteer subject revisited. *Australian Journal of Psychology,* 1976, *28,* 97–108.

Schiller, B. A quantitative analysis of marriage selection in small groups. *Journal of Social Psychology,* 1932, *3,* 297–319.

Schooley, M. Personality resemblances among married couples. *Journal of Abnormal and Social Psychology,* 1936, *31,* 340–47.

Schuster, E., and E. M. Elderton. The inheritance of physical character. *Biometrika,* 1906, *5,* 460–69.

Sherif, M., O. J. Horney, B. J. White, W. R. Hood, and C. W. Sherif. *Experimental study of positive and negative intergroup attitudes between experimentally produced groups.* Robbers Cave Study. Norman: University of Oklahoma, 1954 (multilithed).

Sigall, H., E. Aronson, and P. Van Hoose. The cooperative subject: Myth or reality? *Journal of Experimental Social Psychology,* 1970, *6,* 1–10.

Sigusch, V., G. Schmidt, A. Reinfeld, and I. Wiedemann-Sutor. Psychological stimulation: Sex differences. *Journal of Sex Research,* 1970, *6,* 10–24.

Snow, R. Unfinished pygmalion. *Contemporary Psychology,* 1969, *14,* 197–99.

Staats, A. W. Experimental demand characteristics and the classical conditioning of attitudes. *Journal of Personality and Social Psychology,* 1969, *11,* 187–192.

Webb, F. Character and intelligence. *British Journal of Psychology, Monographs,* No. 3, 1915, 1–99.

Willis, R. H., and V. A. Willis. Role playing versus deception: An experimental comparison. *Journal of Personality and Social Psychology,* 1970, *16,* 472–77.

Wrightsman, L. S. Wallace supporters and adherence to law and order. *Journal of Personality and Social Psychology,* 1969, *13,* 17–22.

3

Communication— The Basis of Social Interaction

The first two dictionary definitions of the word *communicate* are "to impart knowledges of" and "to make known." Now it would appear that communication per se plays little role in social psychology if the current crop of social psychology textbooks is to be taken as our guide. The books are full of nonverbal communication, persuasive communications, communicator credibility, and so forth. But they deal sparsely, if at all, with the basic notion of imparting knowledge of, or of making known. This is a bit surprising, because if you stop and think about the subject for a moment, you will realize that there would be no social interaction without communication. Think, if you can, about a society in which individuals are unable to communicate with each other.

All communication, of course, is not verbal. There are many ways to communicate when we don't say anything. Also, communication is more than sounds; we may communicate by looks, gestures, expressions, and a multitude of other ways. Animals (those other than humans) also communicate, and we will discuss the way they do so. A rather strong case can be made for the fact that communication is a necessary condition for the establishment of a society, that social behavior occurs within the context of some sort of society, and that it logically follows that communication is necessary for social behavior to occur. And what do we mean by *society?* For our purposes, the following definition of society seems best: *a closely integrated group of organisms held together by mutual dependence and exhibiting division of labor.*

The societies we will discuss range from relatively simple ones to the complex interactions of humans, but within a society there must be some form of communication if the members of the society are going to be able to depend on each other and if the labor that is necessary to the continuation of the society is to be divided. We will begin this chapter with some illustrations of social behavior among species other than *Homo sapiens.* Some of the ways in which other species communicate with each other are truly fascinating, although we are just beginning to understand these various forms of communication. A rather extensive review of the social behavior of honeybees, geese, and chimpanzees will give you a flavor of various types of communications in other species. Then, we will discuss the apex of communication, language, with specific emphasis on its development. One of the more exciting and interesting areas of research going on in communications today is the effort to teach chimpanzees to "speak" our language. Finally, we will come full circle and discuss what humans say when they don't say anything, otherwise known as *nonverbal communication.*

Animal Social Behavior

There is a long tradition in social psychology of "tipping our hats" to other species and realizing that they do have societies and social behavior. Roger Brown in his superb text *Social Psychology* (1965) devoted a chapter to the social behavior of animals and had this to say about animal society.

Which animal species live socially and which do not? Homo sapiens certainly does and so too do the social insects—the termites, wasps, and honeybees. These species live as aggregated populations throughout their life cycles. Individuals within the population perform different functions and these functions are integrated in the interest of the general welfare. In short there is a coordinated division of labor. There are also systems of communication; complex ones for both humans and honeybees. Most animal species do not live as lifelong aggregations with a high degree of interdependence among individuals and a well-developed system of communication, and so most species are somewhat less social than man and the honeybees. However, most species come together at some point in their life cycle and interact in a structural way and so almost all species are, in some degree, social. [Brown, 1965, p. 5].

The social interactions of different species range over a wide variety of patterns. Some live in nomadic, food-gathering bands, others come together to rest in large groups, even the larvae of barnacles attach themselves where other barnacles are. Most species come together in a social way only for purposes of reproduction. But consider the advantages to the species of sexual (vs. asexual) reproduction, which promotes genetic variability; since generally speaking, different males and females mate each time. This reshuffling of genes allows for the selection of adaptive forms, and this adaptation, in turn, helps the species to survive. There are innumerable advantages for a specific species of joining together in a society. These advantages vary with the species and the degree of social interaction.

The issue of the relationship between *Homo sapiens* and other species is one that has perplexed thinkers for thousands of years. Many early documents, particularly religious ones, were explicit about asserting the unique importance of humans (and especially males). Over the years, however, and particularly since the time of Darwin, ideas about other species have been modified. Somehow it is demeaning to some people to think that *Homo sapiens* evolved from other species that were or are "lower" than we. As we view the impact of the acts of humans on the environment and compare it with the manner in which other species treat the environment, certainly we must wonder about the supremacy of human beings.

Our topic, however, is communication, and more specifically the question of whether the communication of *Homo sapiens* and other species is the same sort of process or is a different process among humans. As we will shortly see, different species communicate in different ways and the language of humans is the most highly developed form of communication of which we are aware. Nevertheless, other species are imparting information to each other, and in some cases, an enormous amount of information. We cannot say that the differences in communication among species is a difference in kind, rather it is a difference in amount of communication. To the best of our knowledge, other species do not sit around and discuss the weather, the foibles of other people, or the latest styles in dress for hours on end, but quite possibly our doing so does not represent an advance in communication. In short, the communication of *Homo sapiens* and other species appears to be somehow the same in kind, though not in amount.

The Wynne-Edwards Model of Social Behavior

V. C. Wynne-Edwards (1962) has proposed a general model for animal social behavior. Each animal species has certain requirements for food, shelter, weather conditions, and so forth. These requirements define the potential *habitat* (place to live) of the species and within the native habitat of a species the requirements (food, water, and so on) will vary in abundance. Species tend to reproduce themselves in numbers sufficient to fill up the habitat but not in numbers that will overcrowd it. Not surprisingly, the species is more abundant in the habitat in which its requirements exist in greater abundance. The survival of the species is dependent upon the population's being regulated so as not to overtax the resources of the habitat and so as to assure dispersion of the species over the habitat in order that the needs of each individual be met. The Wynne-Edwards theory is that all elementary forms of social organization have evolved within a species because they allow the species to stabilize with ideal numbers and dispersion.

The Wynne-Edwards position is that species other than *Homo sapiens* have evolved instinctive social processes to cope with the problems of population. *Homo sapiens* have evolved a number of different mechanisms; cultural, biological, deliberate, or accidental, which have not always been adaptive and sometimes have threatened catastrophe. Some of these mechanisms (prejudice, discrimination, altruism, aggression, and so forth) will be discussed in later chapters. Wynne-Edwards' theory, however, does not have to deal with humans, only with other species.

Basically, the theory is a *homeostatic* one, which means it is based on the idea that a system will maintain internal stability by returning to the optimal state anytime there is a fluctuation away from such a state. A thermostat is a good familiar example of a homeostatic system. Its job is to keep the temperature of a given area at a specific level. When the temperature drops below or rises above a certain level the thermostat turns on a heating or cooling system to bring the temperature back to that level.

Wynne-Edwards' theory is that instinctive social behavior keeps a species at an optimal level for the habitat in which it exists. When the habitat becomes overcrowded or undercrowded, certain mechanisms are brought into play which bring the population back to a given level. For example, if the number of members of certain species (the flour beetles, guppies, sheep blowflies, and so forth) falls below an optimal level, numbers of eggs laid, the size of litters, the number of pregnancies, or the number of offspring that survive increase. On the other hand, among certain species (beetles, guppies, mice, and rats) when there is overpopulation, adults reduce fertility, lay fewer eggs and eat the eggs, larvae, or offspring that are produced (Brown, 1965). Another instinctive technique for population control is migration, at least among species that have the mobility to migrate to another habitat.

Whatever the technique, there must be some communication among the individuals of a species to allow for a determination of when the system is not balanced. Wynne-Edwards argues that many types of communal activity of a species—roosting together, spawning swarms, the evening rise to the surface of freshwater fish, and the synchronized morning songs of birds, have evolved because they allow the communication of a piece of vital information—the density of the population! Each individual has been involved in hunting for food during the day, so the amount available is known. When the amount of food is compared to the density of the population, Wynne-Edwards argues, the necessary information is available to increase or decrease that density and bring the system back into balance. This is a most basic and extraordinary form of communication. But there are other, even more fascinating ones.

The Dance of the Honeybees

Honeybees are a highly social species. They have a high degree of division of labor and are very dependent upon each other. Through the pioneering work of K. von Frisch (1965; 1968), we know that honeybees communicate the direction and the distance to a food source to their fellow hive members by means of a special dance.

There are specific ways in which the bee communicates. Probably the simplest is when the food source is close to the hive. The bee then performs a round dance on the comb, with no information about direction. The other members of the hive become aroused and search around the hive in all directions for food. When the food is more than 229 feet (70 meters) away from the hive the bee does a waggle dance. In this dance she wags her abdomen as she runs straight for a short distance and accentuates this wagging-distance indicator by producing a rasping sound with her wings. She then turns to one side and returns to her starting position and repeats the dance, this time turning to the opposite side. This dance continues and other bees in the hive become excited by the dance. They can perceive the odor of the blossoms the dancing bee foraged and the dance tells them the direction and distance to the food. If the food is close to the hive, then the waggle dance is short. Actually, it is probably more accurate to say that the distance of the wagging run reflects the distance to the food, the wind velocity, and whether the food is up a steep slope. So the distance of the wagging run of the bee is an indicator of the amount of energy it will be necessary to expend to get the food. The sound the bee makes with her wings is also important. Esch (1967) observed 15,000 of these dances and in no instance did a silent dance lead other bees to the food source.

The direction to the food source is given with reference to the sun. Rarely, a bee will dance in front of the hive and can be observed. The straight-line portion of the wagging dance runs at the same angle to the sun that the bee had flown on a straight-line course to the food. For example, if the bee flew directly into the sun or away from the sun, the wagging run is toward or away from the sun. If the bee flew with the sun 40° to its left to reach the food, then that is the direction of the straight part of the wagging dance.

But bees normally dance in the dark hive on combs that are vertical. In these cases the wagging dance communicates direction by translating the angle of the sun into an angle with respect to gravity. If the bee is to fly to the food source directly into the sun, the direction of the wagging run is straight up; it is straight down if the food source is away from the sun. By using this translation, the bee can indicate almost exactly where the food is.

Even more amazing is the fact that the bees take the changing angle to the sun into account. The sun's angle changes in a lawful manner, of course, and even though it is not understood how the bees do it, they are able to compensate for the changing angle of the sun. They must have experienced this change themselves, but only a few afternoons of experience with the shifting angle of the sun's rays is sufficient for a bee to learn to make the compensation.

Dancing is innate in bees, and there appear to be different dialects. The Egyptian honeybee will begin dancing when the food source is only 32.808 feet (10 meters), whereas the Kranier honeybee dances only when the food source is 164.04 to 328.08 feet (50 to 100 meters) away (Eibl-Eibesfeldt, 1975).

The dance of the honeybees communicates information to other honeybees that is important to the survival and well-being of the bees in the hive. According to Eibl-Eibesfeldt (1975, pp. 170–71),

The dance language shows some similarities to human language. It is a means of communication between conspecifics, and relations between things are communicated. However, in contrast to human language the system is a stereotyped, innate coding system. *Human language* is also based on an inborn potential for specific sound production and perhaps on the drive to speak, but the language symbols are individually learned and passed on by tradition. Individual experiences can be described by words and passed on, and abstract thinking permits communication about relationships between relationships. The bee dance is similar to human language in so far as it is also a symbolic language by which inexperienced individuals acquire knowledge without the object in question being present. The transfer of knowledge, however, is only made by animals that experienced the location of the feeding place in a previous flight. No bee will communicate a message just received from another bee to a third unless it has itself visited the feeding place. This language is "rumorproof" in a manner of speaking (Wickler, 1967).

As Eibl-Eibesfeldt has pointed out, the dance of the honeybees does communicate important information, but it is a far cry from human language. It does show, however, the importance of communication in the society of an organism as simple as the honeybee.

The Graylag Goose

A most fascinating example of the animal world is the graylag goose, because of some of its characteristics. We will deal with a number of aspects of the graylag goose, because it exhibits fairly unique patterns of behavior for an infrahuman species. For example, graylag geese are monogamous and seem to adhere to an incest taboo. The species is quite social and its members have a number of ways of communicating with each other.

GREETING BEHAVIOR

For example, when graylag geese greet each other cackling occurs. This occurs in very young chicks who have been separated from their mothers. Upon refinding the mother, the chick utters a tiny one- or many-syllabled "wee." As the intensity of the cackling increases, the gosling stretches out its neck. When adult graylag geese greet

**Geese are social animals
and mate for life.**

each other they emit a contact call without stretching out the neck and a loud cackling with stretching of the neck. According to Eibl-Eibesfeldt (1975), the contact call and the cackling are the same behavior at different levels of intensity. The "wee" sound of the gosling and the contact call and cackling of the mature goose are all released at the sight of a *conspecific* (a member of the same species).

There are other forms of communication between graylag geese, specifically a mother goose and her goslings. A young gosling will give a two-syllable "wi-wi" call occasionally, even when it is asleep under its mother. The call is answered by the mother and if it is not, it grows in intensity and urgency. Eibl-Eibesfeldt (1975) and Peiper (1951) have suggested that human infants do the same thing. The nighttime restlessness of infants comes from an old evolutionary need to be reassured by the presence of the mother, and it is still a very real need. To be left alone signifies danger to the infant because it cannot obtain food for itself. Today children are placed in beds, often in different rooms, but there is still a need to be reassured that the mother is present, and the crying at night is an attempt to gain this reassurance.

Interestingly enough, there are common elements in the greeting gestures of the graylag goose and in aggressive gestures. As Lorenz (1963) has pointed out, redirected threat movements may become signs of a bond being made by a pair of mating geese. The "triumph ceremony" of the graylag goose plays a special role during the formation of pairs. At first, the male makes sham attacks at objects that normally are avoided. Following such an attack, he returns to his intended mate and makes threatening gestures (stretching of the neck) beyond her. If she joins the male in this triumph ceremony, then the two have formed a defensive alliance. This alliance and the protection of the young from harm is necessary to raise a brood successfully.

Group bonds are formed among graylag geese, as well as other species. For example, graylag geese allow contact by their mates and their young, but attack strange adults or even strange young geese (Tinbergen, 1963). Wickler and Seibt (1972) speak of this sort of behavior as a bonding drive, and it can be established and strengthened through aggression. A pair of graylag geese are bonded together as a combat unit and according to Lorenz (1963) their greeting rituals stem from aggressive threat.

Learning in the Graylag Goose

Learning is, of course, extremely important for the survival of any species. In the graylag goose, unlike some other species, the young learn their migratory path south from their parents. Without this guidance, they stay where they were raised (Eibl-Eibesfeldt, 1975). Other sorts of behaviors are learned and are tenaciously adhered to once learned. This has a certain survival value, because tried and tested behaviors are superior to new ones, at least in certain respects. Such things as rank in a social order and territory are also learned. Lorenz (1963) has raised a number of graylag geese in his home. One of these geese had become used to a certain detour, walking past the bottom of the staircase toward a window in the hallway before returning to the stairs to ascend them. Once Lorenz did not let the goose in at the usual time; as a matter of fact, it was beginning to get dark when she was allowed in. She ran directly to the stairs when the door was opened. Here is how Lorenz describes what happened:

Upon this something shattering happened: Arrived at the fifth step, she suddenly stopped, made a long neck, in geese a sign of fear and spread her wings as for flight. Then she uttered a cry and very nearly took off. Now she hesitated a moment, turned around, ran hurriedly down the five steps and set forth resolutely, like someone on a very important mission, on her original path to the window and back. This time she mounted the steps according to her former custom from the left side. On the fifth step she stopped again, looked around, shook herself, and performed a greeting display behavior regularly seen in graylags when anxious tension has given place to relief. I hardly believed my eyes. To me there is no doubt about the interpretation of this occurrence: the habit had become a custom which the goose could not break without being stricken by fear. [Lorenz, 1963, p. 112.]

As with humans, habits become very ingrained and are difficult to break. When a habit has become ingrained and is broken as with the goose, superstitious behavior occurs.

Imprinting. Imprinting is genetically programmed learning so that during sensitive periods of their lifetimes members of certain species are able to learn certain activities. If this period is restricted to a relatively short developmental period, it is then referred to as a *critical period.* When critical periods end, if the animal has not learned the appropriate response, it will never learn it. Shortly after hatching, rythmic calls and extremely diverse moving objects will be imprinted upon by the graylag goose. It will follow another goose, a box, or a man. There seems to be a certain amount of survival value involved in this form of imprinting. In most situations the gosling will see and hear its mother and thus imprint on her. Once the gosling has followed a person, however, it cannot be induced to follow its mother (Lorenz, 1935). Imprinting differs from associative learning in at least two important respects. Imprinting takes place only during sensitive periods, whereas associative learning can occur at any time and following it forgetting can occur (Hess, 1959; 1973).

Imprinting also has a value in reproduction. Individual members of a species who have imprinted on a member of their species regard that object as the proper one for sexual activity. This has the advantage of sexual reproduction being maintained within the species rather than across species lines, particularly where the species are closely related.

Imprinting frequently occurs in a very restricted time period; a matter of a few hours. If the animal imprints on some object other than its own species, then it will follow that object. On the other hand, if the animal is kept in isolation for that period of time, it will not imprint on anything. Thus the process plays an important part in the recognition of the very young for its own species, for later sexual reproduction of the species, and in general the welfare and survival of the species. It is an innate, very fundamental form of communication, but an important one.

Chimpanzees

A species much closer to *Homo sapiens* on the phylogenetic scale is the chimpanzee, which is a highly intelligent anthropoid ape. Many are familiar with chimpanzees, having seen them in zoos or in movies. Chimpanzees are very social animals, greeting each other in several ways. They embrace and kiss with a touching of lips when they meet someone they know (v. Lawick-Goodall, 1965; 1968). They shake hands the way people do. The lower-ranking animal reaches toward the higher-ranking one with palm up, and in response to this the higher ranking animal gives his hand, which calms the other chimp. In this way lower-ranking animals solicit approval from higher-ranking ones (Eibl-Eiberfeldt, 1975). They also bow when greeting others (Goodall, 1965; v. Lawick-Goodall, 1968).

With this variety of greeting gestures, it is not surprising to find a well-developed social structure among chimps. In the wild, chimpanzees live in large, loose groups of animals that know one another well. Subgroups are formed by females with their young, and a newborn infant is introduced to other members of the group. After the young are several weeks old, their siblings are allowed to hold them (Goodall, 1963; 1965; v. Lawick-Goodall, 1965). A rank order exists among the adults, and males frequently threaten other group members. Occasional temper tantrums occur during which males will not only attack subordinate males but females as well. Apparently, these displays are displays of dominance.

Among chimpanzees there is no fighting for possession of a female in estrus, because she will peacefully mate with all males present (v. Lawick-Goodall, 1971). Jane van Lawick-Goodall has studied extensively chimpanzees in the wild and reports that they have a very complex social behavior. She says (1971, p. 116):

> The members who comprise it move about it constantly changing associations and yet, though the society seems to be organized in such a casual manner, each individual knows his place in the social structure—knows his status in relation to any other chimpanzee he may chance upon during the day. Small wonder there is such a wide range of greeting gestures—and that most chimpanzees do greet each other when they meet after a separation.

Chimpanzees are social animals and enjoy play. Here Lucy tickles her human friend.

Photo by R. L. Mellgren

The use of tools was at one time thought to be an ability possessed only by humans. Chimpanzees, however, have been observed using tools to perform a variety of tasks. The use of tools implies intelligent behavior because it demonstrates the capacity to solve relations between objects in a context not encountered before. That is, when a tool is used to perform a task that could not otherwise be achieved, we may think of that behavior as intelligent.

Jane v. Lawick-Goodall (1968; 1970) gives a number of remarkable examples of chimpanzees using tools in the wild. By our standards, they are primative tools. The dictionary defines a tool as an implement for doing work. The free-ranging chimpanzees Lawick-Goodall observed used thin twigs or grass stems as a tool to get termites for food. They opened the tunnel the termites use for swarming and pushed the twig or blade of grass into the tunnel and pulled it out with termites clinging to it. This behavior was repeated over and over. Chimpanzees also use leaves to soak up water in trees that they cannot reach with their lips. Then they use the leaves to clean themselves. These observations made in the wild merely substantiate work done earlier with captive chimpanzees.

Kohler's (1921) experiments with chimpanzees have become famous. He presented his chimpanzees with the following problem: They were in a cage with two sticks and a banana outside the cage. Neither stick by itself was long enough to reach the banana. Only after giving up and playing with the sticks for a period of time did the chimps realize they could put the sticks together (one fitted into a hole in the end of the other) and reach the banana. It was during play that the discovery was made that later proved useful in obtaining the banana. This use of tools and insightful behavior shows the high intelligence level of chimpanzees.

SOCIAL GROOMING BEHAVIOR

Certain animals shy away from bodily contact, whereas others use contact as a social device. Chimpanzees are contact animals and put their arms around each other, and even a higher-ranking animal will clasp a lower-ranking one for reassurance when frightened. Bodily contact has a calming effect and in contact animals social grooming is both widespread and plays an important part in the society. Through it animals can keep in communication with each other. Since there seems to be a strong motivation for grooming, it reinforces the relationships of those in the society.

Comment

The social groupings of animals other than *Homo sapiens* is, as you can see by our short discussion, quite diverse and yet very important to the well-being and survival of individuals and the species. Equally diverse and important is the way in which animals communicate with each other. As you will remember, animals communicate such diverse information as the population density, fear, greeting, and aggression by their social behavior. There is, however, one form of communication that, until recently, was assumed to be the exclusive province of humans—language. We turn now to language and language development in humans.

One of *the* things, if not the only thing, that differentiates human achievement from the achievement of other species is the fact that we have a language and it is so readily communicable. Even as we recognize that fact we must take great care not to get mixed up in a morass of claims and counterclaims about language that have been raging for years—but with special intensity since Noam Chomsky (1957) proposed his *generative-transformational grammar.* What Chomsky proposed was that there is a definite, freely explicit formal system to describe any particular language. What many people believe is that children learn whatever language they are to speak through imitation. This is a perfectly reasonable assumption as children whose parents speak French generally learn French first, children whose parents speak English generally speak English first, and so forth. We must say "generally," not because anyone has ever heard of a case where a child with English-speaking parents startles and mystifies his or her parents by learning to speak French, but because some children of English-speaking parents are brought up by an individual who speaks French as some children of French-speaking parents are brought up by a person who speaks English. These children do not necessarily learn their parents' language. But imitation fails for some children because they do not seem to be able to extract certain rules.

The basic question, of course, is what is language? Linguistics is the science of language and within linguistics it is probably fair to say that everyone agrees that language is a set of rules for the creation of infinitely numerous sentences.

First-Language Acquisition

One of the effects of Chomsky's (1957) book was to inspire research into the area of a child's language learning. The studies took their basic data from spontaneous speech by children. Even though many individuals doing linguistic research considered this course of knowledge quite hopeless (Lees, 1964; Chomsky, 1964), it seems that some very important data have come from three separate sources. Starting in the early 1960s Braine (1963), Brown (Brown and Fraser, 1963; Brown and Bellugi, 1964) and Ervin and Miller (Ervin, 1961; Miller and Ervin, 1964) began the systematic study of the first utterances of small children and these "gems" have been painstakingly recorded and transcribed. Now serious social scientists as well as harried mothers were listening to such profound utterances as "Hit ball," "More ball," and "That doggie." By 1971 this was being done in some thirty languages, and there seems to be a universal sequence of language development in the human species.

Brown (1973) has reported that there are five stages of early language development for American English. He labels and describes the first of these five stages as the basic semantic and grammatical roles. In this stage the utterances are short, having a mean length of one to two words, and are exemplified by such phrases as "All gone ball," "Adam hit," and "Adam hit ball." Stage 2 is called "the modulation of meaning," with utterances that have a mean length of 2 to 2.5 words and include "I walking," "There it is" and "That is going" as examples. The third stage, which

Brown labels "Modalities of the simple sentence," has a mean utterance length of 2.5 to 3 and includes "Does Eve like it?" "Yes he can," and "He does want to go." The fourth stage, with slightly longer utterances, is called "Embedding one simple sentence with another." Examples are, "You got a pencil in your bag," and "I want her to do it." The final stage, "Conjunction of one simple sentence with another" is exemplified by "I did this and I did that too" or "He's flying and swinging."

These stages are almost invariant for learning the English language and Stage 1 seems to be invariant for learning any language. But why do children learn language in this way? And, a question that must be answered even prior to that, how do they learn to progress through these stages? Brown (1973) considered several social-interaction variables as possible ways of accounting for the stages the child passes through. The frequency with which a child hears certain utterances, selective approval of correct utterances, and disapproval of incorrect utterances, or a kind of correction of the child's utterances, but these do not seem to account for the stages of language acquisition. There is, of course, one social-interaction variable that does affect language acquisition, and that is the language the child hears spoken. There is a very suggestive element in the stages Brown had developed, and that is the structural complexity of the forms themselves.

For now, we can take the easy way out and say that language is acquired, although the complexities of how that occurs are not understood. It is beyond the scope of this book to go any more deeply into the subject, and the references cited will keep even the most inquisitive of you thinking for some time.

There is a sidelight to language and language acquisition that bears some discussion, not because a language (if it is that) has been learned, but because of the individuals who have learned it. This is, after all, a chapter on communication and until a few pages ago we were discussing communication among nonhuman species. Here the individuals who are learning the language are not humans, but chimpanzees, thus the possibilities for learning more about the effects of language on social behavior are enormous.

Talking Chimpanzees

Actually chimpanzees can't talk, and this fact was the source of some satisfaction to a number of people who are overly zealous about the *primary* status of species *Homo-sapiens.* To a certain extent this may be understandable in a person who has accepted a strongly literalistic interpretation of the Old and/or New Testaments of the Bible. The idea of the pre-eminence of humans is a matter of faith for them and one of the things that certainly sets an objective criterion for differentiating humans from other species is language. It is, however, slightly surprising to find scientists making statements that would do credit to the most zealous guardian of a literalistic interpretation of the Bible, even though their reasons were quite different.

Roger Brown in his own special style had this to say about the matter (Brown and Herrnstein, 1975, p. 481):

It is a novel and not especially pleasant feeling for man to sense that another species is gaining on him. In the study of language, one begins to feel the hot breath of chimpanzee. Until the late 1960s, there had been just five attempts to teach chimpanzees to talk (Kellogg,

1968). All had been gratifyingly unsuccessful. . . Improvements of adaptation could only come by way of the slow process of biological evolution; the very much faster process of cultural evolution depends on the ability to transmit knowledge, which depends in turn on language and only man seemed capable of language.

Species *hubris* was everywhere evident. Noam Chomsky wrote: "Anyone concerned with the study of human capacities must somehow come to grips with the fact that all normal humans acquire language whereas acquisition of even its barest rudiments is quite beyond the capacities of an otherwise intelligent ape." (1968, p. 59.) Eric Lenneberg wrote: "There is no evidence that any nonhuman form has the capacity to acquire even the most primitive stages of language development" (1964, p. 67). Roger Brown is rather glad he kept his mouth shut.

The reason Roger Brown is glad he kept his mouth shut is because of three beguiling females named Washoe, Sarah, and Lana, who learned at least the rudiments of a language during the 1960s and 70s. We will use Washoe as an example, because for our purposes, her type of language is most interesting, since it readily allows for interchimp communication. Gardner and Gardner (1969) made a research breakthrough that, in retrospect, seems simple, but obviously was not. Of course, chimpanzees can't talk; their vocal anatomy is different from ours, and they can't easily produce the sounds necessary for a spoken language. But one thing they do in abundance is gesture. The Gardners' approach to the problem of chimpanzee language was to teach Washoe to speak with gestures using the American sign language (which is now called Amelsan). Although sign language had been little studied (except by McCall, 1965) there was the general impression that it contained at least the rudiments of language.

And so in June, 1966, Washoe, who was about 1 year old, was brought to Reno, Nevada, to learn sign language, and her accomplishment over the next 15 years amazed primatologists and linguists, but probably not other chimpanzees, since a number of them have also learned Amelsan. Under very controlled conditions Washoe had learned about 85 signs in three years and a year later she had a vocabulary of 160 signs. Even more important from a linguistic point of view, she was producing strings of up to five signs, which may or may not be sentences. Whether they are sentences or not is a problem to be solved by the linguists, but a cautionary note is in order here. As you can readily tell from the quotations above, certain linguists had already taken a rather strong stand about the linguistic capabilities of chimpanzees. As with all humans, and possibly chimpanzees too, linguists hate to admit that they were wrong. Thus, they may be more sure that Washoe's strings of signs are *not* sentences than a less involved observer. In addition, some of Washoe's signs were novel. That is, she created them herself. Finally, she instigated many conversations, making requests, asking questions, and making observations without prompting from her human companions. Amelsan was truly a means of communication between Washoe and her trainers. That is, she was not merely responding rotely to what she had been taught.

THINKING CHIMPANZEES?

Fouts and Mellgren (1976) point out that language is the result of cognition, but that it is not proper to infer that because a species does not have a language it does not think. There are several characteristics of language that presumably bear on the matter of whether chimpanzees think when they use sign language.

Bronowski and Bellugi (1970) pointed out that the early studies on sign language had not shown an important characteristic of language, *reconstitution*. Reconstitution is the ability to separate messages into smaller parts and to rearrange those parts to form other messages. Fouts and Mellgren argue that chimpanzees have taken information given to them, broken it into smaller parts, and rearranged these parts to form other messages. For example Lucy has called watermelon a "fruit drink," and a radish, after she had tasted it, was consistently referred to as "cry, hurt food."

Photos by R. L. Mellgren.

Lucy is signing. (Top, left) she has just completed the sign for "tickle" (the index finger extended and pulled across the back of the other hand). (Top, right) she is signing "fruit" to an apple stimulus (a loose fist pulled down the cheek from the ear to the chin). (Bottom, left) Lucy signs "leash," a sign that she invented. It consists of putting the curved index finger over her collar. (Bottom, right) she signs "flower."

(Mellgren, Fouts, and Lemmon, 1973.) Washoe has been observed to label a swan a "water bird" and a Brazil nut a "rock berry." This indicates that chimpanzees are able to combine signs in a novel fashion.

Another piece of evidence concerns chimpanzees' ability to comprehend novel commands. Chown (1974) taught a chimpanzee, Ally, to select one of five different items from a box and place it in one of three locations when given a command in sign language. For example, he was told to "put baby (doll) in box." After Ally had been trained, new commands, which were developed by adding new locations to place the object, as well as new objects, were given during the testing phase. During testing Ally was correct 38 percent of the time and he was correct on 31 percent of the novel commands. This is far above the chance level of 7 percent. Interestingly, Ally refused to place an object on a chair, which was a new location. He would stand in front of the chair and even sit in the chair while holding the object, but he would not place an object on the chair. Possibly Ally's conception of a chair did not include the function of holding an object.

Fouts and Mellgren also point out that chimpanzees refer to subjective states, much as humans do. When one is asked, "How are you?" socially acceptable answers include a short, concise reply although positive ones are highly preferable to negative ones. Even when we are regaled with a long list of ailments, we cannot be sure that the person in pain really "hurts." We must rely on his or her statement of subjective feelings. In the same way, chimpanzees have been observed to sign "hurt" when they have a cut or a sore and on one occasion, Washoe used the sign hurt to refer to her stomach when she had all the symptoms of intestinal flu.

Do chimpanzees lie? It has generally been assumed that only *Homo sapiens* lies and that other animals do not have this dubious capacity. To be sure, other animals can be sly, but they do not lie. Fouts and Mellgren however, present some interesting observations on Lucy, who was taught ownership of books; one was hers, one was Roger's, and one was Sue's. Roger taught Lucy which book was hers, which was his, and which was Sue's, but even in training Lucy would try to call Roger's book hers. When Sue came to test Lucy, not knowing which book belonged to her, which to Roger and which to Lucy, the chimpanzee correctly labeled Roger's book as his, but claimed ownership of the other two books. Thus when Roger was present, Lucy tried to preempt his book, but was willing to let the absent Sue's book be Sue's. However, when Sue was present, Lucy tried to claim her book and allowed Roger's to belong to Roger. It seems very possible that Lucy was lying.

There is still a great deal of controversy concerning subjective states of chimpanzees. That should not surprise us because there is still a great deal of mistrust of subjective states of humans. We are particularly reluctant to accept other people's statements concerning how they feel, what their emotions are, and so forth. This becomes obvious when psychologists are so reluctant to utilize self-reports of these emotions and feelings. However, it does seem that there has been enough work with chimpanzees to convince most of us that they may very well have language capabilities and that they think. There are, no doubt, many who would disagree with such a statement, but it is still exciting. The opportunity to communicate with another species opens new areas to us that are just being considered.

In 1970 Washoe was moved to the Institute for Primate Studies at the University of Oklahoma. Until that time she had lived in her own house trailer, but as chimpanzees grow older it becomes necessary to keep them in more secure places, and the Institute at Oklahoma had the facilities and welcomed Washoe. Dr. Roger Fouts, who had worked with the Gardners and with Washoe, also went to the Institute both to continue his work with Washoe and to begin teaching Amelsan to a number of other chimpanzees. One of the first questions that had to be answered about Washoe concerned her ability—was she some sort of chimpanzee genius? The answer is No, since a number of other chimpanzees at the Institute have also shown an ability for Amelsan that equals Washoe's. Lucy, Booee, and Bruno, to name only three chimps who talk, have all learned Amelsan. Since our interest is in the social function of language, we are especially concerned with chimpanzees' communication with each other. When Washoe moved to Oklahoma, she was, of course, the only chimp on the block who knew Amelsan, although she had spent the last four years of her life communicating only with humans in it. Much of the detail of chimp-to-chimp communication is still in an informal stage, and the basis for this section is found in Lamberth, McCullers, and Mellgren (1976). To quote them (p. 267),

For example, one day not too long after her arrival she was on an island at the Institute. Four other chimps were also on the island, and two of them began giving distress calls and running away. Washoe was playing with two younger male chimps. One of the male chimps ran when he heard the distress call of the other chimps. The other male failed to respond. Washoe had begun to move away from the danger, probably a snake, then stopped and signed to the unresponsive chimp, *come hug,* in an attempt to get him to safety.

Informal observations such as this one are fairly common, but an attempt is reported by Lamberth et al. to evaluate chimp-to-chimp communication in more detail. Booee and Bruno are both male chimps about 5 years old. Each had a vocabulary of approximately 35 signs at the time of the study. Bruno was given some fruit or a canteen of orange juice and Booee was observed to say "Give me, Bruno," "Give me drink, give me Bruno," or simply "Give me," on a number of occasions. Similarly Bruno would make the same demands of Booee when the situation was reversed. The problem in this situation was that there was no dialogue—only the unfortunate chimp talked without anything being "said" in response.

To further study chimp-to-chimp communication, Bruno and Booee were observed in a discipline situation. One chimp might be bad and punished by being sent to the corner of the room. Under these circumstances the chimps would use sign language to "comfort" each other. As an example, one might sign "come, hurry, come" to the other and the one being disciplined might sign "come, hug." At one time when Booee was on an island and Bruno was crossing the water in a boat, Booee signed "hurry, come." Games have provided the most natural and productive examples of chimp-to-chimp communication. The favorite game of the chimps is the tickle game, and it has resulted in numerous interchanges between the two chimps. In one such game, Booee signed "tickle Booee" a total of 14 times. Bruno has been observed using the more linguistically complex form "Booee tickle Bruno."

As Lamberth, McCullers and Mellgren (1976, p. 268) say,

Is the chimpanzee capable of language? Have we demonstrated this? It seems fair to say that for some people enough analogies have been established between the kinds of things people do and the things chimps do to warrant concluding chimpanzees have language abilities. On the other hand, there are people who would argue that the necessary experiments to show that the chimpanzees has true language abilities have not yet been done. The problem with answering the question of whether or not chimpanzees have the capacity for language is that there is no universally accepted definition for what constitutes language.

One of the crucial functions of language is to be able to communicate across generations, and thus the news that Washoe is pregnant was greeted with unbridled interest and enthusiasm. The questions were both numerous and important.

Nonverbal Communication

People have long been interested in what people are saying when they don't say anything; or what it is they are really saying when they do say something. Does all of this sound a little mystical? It's really not, for no matter what we say we communicate a great deal not by the words we speak, but in the facial expression, gestures, or tone of voice we use when we say them. The very same words said in two distinct ways with two different sets of facial expressions mean quite different things to us.

The irony of the whole field of communication is great. If you will remember, one of the focal points of this chapter is that humans have a distinct advantage over nonhuman species beause we have an extremely efficient way of communicating with each other, language. Furthermore, since that language is verbal, we need not see each other to communicate. Now we are coming full circle and saying that we do communicate in ways other than speaking or writing. Actually, what has happened over the years is that language has become our primary tool of communicating with

Look closely at this picture and see how many forms of nonverbal communication are taking place in this group. Come back to the picture after you've finished reading this section and look again.

each other, but because there are other ways to communicate, the subtleties of communication have grown by adding the nonverbal element to the verbal one.

Are Nonverbal Cues Innate?

One of the first questions to ask about nonverbal communication, as we did about verbal communication, is whether it is innate or not. The first piece of evidence comes from those who note the commonality of expressive features and mimic expressions among people from different cultures. For example, Asch (1952, p. 195) says,

> The accounts of ethnologists are in agreement that there is a fund of expressions that occur in human societies without exception. Crying in pain and weeping in sorrow are universal; fear gives rise generally to trembling and pallor. Laughter and smiling are general expressions of joy and happiness. It is probable that the identities cover a wider region, including reactions of surprise, boredom and puzzlement. We may therefore speak of certain invariants in emotional expression, though they have not been adequately described.

Fridjda (1965, p. 376) quoted in Eibl-Eibesfeldt (1974, p. 455), agrees.

> As far as the accuracy of the data allows, the mimic expressions and pantomime, which correspond to the described states, seem to appear in each people and race in a similar context or with the same meaning (perhaps one laughs without joy, but also because of it). It is true that important cultural differences exist in expressive behavior, but this in no way detracts from the constancy of these primary expressions.

On the other hand, others disagree. Eibl-Eibesfeldt (1975, p. 455) quotes Gehlen (1956) as follows:

> Inborn, instinctive behavior patterns are actually only demonstrable in very small children where they can hardly be distinguished from reflexes, such as sucking, grasping, and holding-on movements. Otherwise and quite generally human motor patterns are bare of all instincts . . . they are learned in their totality and concreteness in the way they are performed, they are built up individually through the integration of external stimuli and experiences.

LaBarre (1947) also feels that facial expressions are not universal and thus not innate. For example, he says (1947, p. 52),

> Smiling, indeed, I have found may almost be mapped after the fashion of any other culture trait; and laughter is in some sense a geographic variable. On a map of the Southwest Pacific one could perhaps even draw lines between areas of "Papuan hilarity" and others where a Cobuan, Melanesian dourness reigned. In Africa, Gorer noted that laughter is used by the Negro to express surprise, wonder, embarrassment, and even discomfiture; it is not necessarily, or even often a sign of amusement; the significance given to black laughter is due to a mistake of supposing that similar symbols have identical meanings. Thus it is that even if the physiological behavior be present, its cultural and emotional functions may differ. Indeed, even within the same culture, the laughter of adolescent girls and the laughter of corporation presidents can be functionally different things. . . .

Finally Birdwhistell (1963, 1968, 1970) agrees that no expressive movement has any universal meaning; that is, all expressive movements are learned within a culture and not inborn.

Eibl-Eibesfeldt (1975) disagrees and marshals an enormous amount of data to support his conclusions. The work of Eibl-Eibesfeldt and his approach are sufficiently interesting and important to spend some time considering his arguments. He is an ethologist, which is a science defined by Eibl-Eibesfeldt (1975, p. 9) in this way: "Ethology can best be defined as 'the biology of behavior.' In trying to understand *why* an animal behaves the way it does, ethologists search for the functions of the observed behavior patterns in order to learn what selection pressures have shaped their evolution." Eibl-Eibesfeldt feels that human ethology is emerging as a field and nonverbal communication is one aspect of that emerging field.

An Ethologist's View of Nonverbal Communication

Eibl-Eibesfeldt notes that beyond the anecdotal remarks of Gehlen, LaBarre, and Birdwhistell, which we quoted or mentioned earlier, he has failed to find any references supporting the view that facial expressions, gestures, and so forth are not innate. He says that LaBarre does not offer all correlations of Paupan or Melanesian laughter, or collect numerous incidents of laughter so that they could be studied. In fact, Eibl-Eibesfeldt decries the lack of systematic study of nonverbal communication. There are only a few isolated studies of descriptive-analytic investigations of human facial expression. Further, until recently, there was no way that one scientist could study the work of other scientists. As he says (Eibl-Eibesfeldt, 1975, p. 457), "As unbelievable as it may seem, the ethogram (the precise catalogue of all the behavior patterns of an animal) of man has not yet been documented and recorded in a way that would permit one scientist to examine the data of another which are not colored by the interpretations of the observer."

One of the major problems associated with the development of an ethogram of humans is that it is virtually essential to capture the gestures, expressions, and so forth on film for a permanent record that can be studied by other scientists. As soon as a camera is aimed at most people they do not act naturally, rather they try to make themselves look as good as possible for the camera. This often results in very stilted, sometimes even absurd looking pictures, but it does not allow for observation of behavior as it occurs naturally.

An ingenious method of photographing people in naturalistic poses was developed by Hass and tested in various parts of the world (Eibl-Eibesfeldt and Hass, 1966, 1967; Hass, 1968). The method is simple and consists of a movie camera with an attachment mounted in front of the normal lens of the camera containing a mirror prism that allows photographing to the side rather than in front of the camera. Figure 3–1 shows a schematic drawing of the camera. People, of course, realize that filming is going on, but they assume that the subject being photographed is in front of the camera. In fact, people in quite natural poses and actions are being photographed to the side of the camera. From these films a thorough study of nonverbal communication can be made and other scientists have a precise record of the subjects.

The methodology used by Eibl-Eibesfeldt is quite rigorous. When he wants to analyze facial expressions and gestures he films the unaware subject in slow motion, keeping a record of what occurred just prior to the filming. There is an effort to understand the behavior in the context of the situation and sequence in which it takes

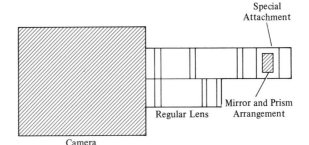

Figure 3-1 Schematic drawing of camera that allows people at the side rather than in front of the camera to be photographed.

place. Here is what Eibl-Eibesfeldt has to say about the results of this particular methodology (Eibl-Eibelsfeldt, 1975, pp. 465–66):

Although the work is still in progress, we have filmed enough to say that some of the more complex human expressions can be traced back to the superposition of a few fixed action patterns which do not seem to be culturally determined. To give just one example, we found agreement in the smallest detail in the flirting behavior of girls from Samoa, Papua, France, Japan, Africa (Turcana and other Nilotshamite tribes, Himba, Bushmen) and South American Indians (Waika, Orinoko). The flirting girl at first smiles at her partner and lifts her eyebrows with a quick, jerky movement upward so that the eye slit is briefly enlarged. The most probably inborn greeting with the eyes is quite typical. Flirting men show the same movement of the eye-brow, which also can be observed during a friendly greeting between members of the same sex. After this initial, obvious turning toward the person, in the flirt there follows a turning away. The head is turned to the side, sometimes bent toward the ground, the gaze is lowered, and the eyelids are dropped. Frequently, but not always, the girl may cover her face with a hand and she may laugh or smile in embarrassment. She continues to look at the partner out of the corners of her eyes and sometimes vascillates between that and an embarrassed looking away. . . .

Here we find that the superposition of a few invariable components (intention movements of turning toward someone, responsiveness, and turning away) yields a relatively complex and varible expression. The assertion of R. L. Birdwhistell (1963, 1968) that there is no expressive behavior independent of culture and that everything is learned is disproved by these results. In particular the principle of using antithetical movements in combination is a universal one.

Another nonverbal signal that Eibl-Eibersfeldt feels is universal and stereotyped is a friendly greeting that he calls the eyebrow flash. The flash is transmitted with smiling, headtossing, and nodding and while it is universal in the cultures Eibl-Eibesfeldt has studied, there are differences in the readiness with which the eyebrow flash is used (Eibl-Eibesfeldt, 1968; 1971; 1972; 1975). The flash seems to be utilized with reserve in Japan, whereas the Samoans regularly greet everyone with an eyebrow flash. Europeans use it not only in greeting but also in thanking, flirting, joking with children, and emphasizing a fact.

COMMENT

As an ethologist, Eibl-Eibesfeldt relies heavily on innate interpretations of animal (including human) activity. Later in this book, when I discuss aggression, I shall have occasion to refer again to Eibl-Eibesfeldt and his fellow ethologists concerning their view of the innate nature of aggression. For the moment, it is sufficient to say that he has presented a strong case for the universality of certain nonverbal communication signs and thus a strong case for their innate nature.

Of course, the ethologists were not the first to argue that certain nonverbal signs of communication were innate. Charles Darwin (1872) may not have been the first to do it either, but the fame he achieved for originating the concept of evolution has virtually obscured the fact that he believed facial expressions were innately deter-

MORE ABOUT FACIAL EXPRESSIONS

Work is progressing on many fronts to unravel the mysteries of what we see and what we learn from facial expressions. One theory that has been proposed is the preparedness theory. This theory, originally proposed by Martin E. P. Seligman, argues that stimulus situations differ in their associability with a variety of responses. This difference in associability comes about because a given species has an evolutionary determined readiness to associate easily some events but not others with facial expressions. For example, fear should be more easily associated with an angry facial expression than a happy one. This supposedly occurs because humans have learned to prepare for negative events when they view an angry face.

Öhman and Dimberg (1978) tested this theory by pairing faces with happy or angry expressions with electric shock. They reasoned that electric shock paired with an angry face should arouse subjects more than electric shock paired with a face with a happy expression. Further, they reasoned that when the shock was terminated and only the faces were shown to the subject, faces with angry expressions should continue to arouse subjects more than faces with happy expressions. This procedure, the termination of reward or punishment, is called extinction.

Subjects were brought into an experimental room and their left hands were attached to electrodes to measure galvanic skin response (palmar sweating). As many of you can attest, when you are nervous or aroused, your palms sweat. This palmar sweating is a good and often-used measure of arousal. Electrodes to deliver shock were attached to the right hand. The shock was adjusted for each subject so that it was annoying but not painful. All the subjects were shown a face with an angry expression on 8 trials and the same face with a happy expression on 8 trials. For half the subjects the angry face was accompanied by an electric shock and no shock was given when the happy face was given. The other half of the subjects received shock when the happy face was shown with no shock accompanying the angry face.

During the shock phase both groups evidenced more arousal when shocked than when not shocked. During extinction, however, arousal continued higher to the angry face than to the happy one. The researchers had run 4 trials prior to the shock showing the angry and happy faces by themselves. At that time there were no differences in arousal (galvanic skin responses) to the pictures. Thus the greater resistance to extinction (higher continued arousal) to the angry face than to the happy face argues for the preparedness theory. That is, it may well be that humans are more prepared to respond with arousal to an angry face although they don't actually do it until the angry face is paired with a negative stimulus (shock). After this has been done, however, and after the shock has terminated, the angry face continues to be more arousing to subjects.

Reference

Öhman, A., and V. Dimberg. Facial expressions as conditioned stimuli for electrodermal responses: A case of "preparedness"? *Journal of Personality and Social Psychology,* 1978, *36,* 1251–1258.

mined. However, Paul Ekman and his associates have re-emphasized Darwin's ideas and in the process added ammunition to the innate side of the debate. Briefly, Darwin's conclusions about the innate character of facial expressions led to two predictions: Since they are largely inherited, similar facial expressions should be shown by people in different cultures when they experience the same emotion. Second, because these expressions are universal, they should be recognized as indicating a particular emotional state. As you can see, these predictions are closely aligned with the work of Eibl-Eibesfeldt, which we have been discussing. Ekman and his associates (Ekman, 1972; Ekman and Friesen, 1975; Ekman, Friesen, and Ellsworth, 1972) have provided support for Darwin's predictions in two ways. First, Ekman videotaped the faces of individuals from widely varying cultures as they watched stress-inducing films. Subjects from diverse cultures generally showed very similar facial expressions in response to the stress-inducing film. Second, if facial expressions are universal, they should be recognized for what they are by individuals from many different cultures. Ekman has provided us with evidence that people in the United States, Brazil, Chile, Argentina, Japan, and New Guinea agree about the emotion being shown when they see pictures of an individual showing fear, disgust, happiness, and anger. Figure 3–2 shows the results graphically. It should be noted that the individuals from New Guinea were from culturally isolated groups and their high degree of agreement with other peoples' interpretation presents even more and impressive evidence for the universality of facial expressions of emotion.

The Forms of Nonverbal Communication

The work of Eibl-Eiberfeldt and Ekman has been discussed without bothering to define the term *nonverbal communiction*. There is a reason for waiting until now to define the term; Eibl-Eiberfeldt and Ekman were proposing that facial expressions are innate and although this is an important issue in nonverbal communication, we need not infer that this is all there is to nonverbal communication, or even the most important element. As Mehrabian (1972, p. 1) says, "In its narrow and more accurate sense, 'nonverbal behavior' refers to actions as distinct from speech. It thus includes facial expressions, hand and arm gestures, postures, positions, and various movements of the body or the legs and feet." Mehrabian goes on to say, however, that the concept has been used in a broader context and a variety of subtle aspects of speech frequently have been included in the discussion of nonverbal communication (frequency and intensity range, speech errors, pauses, rate, and duration). Finally, complex nonverbal communication phenomena such as sarcasm (in which inconsistent combinations of verbal and nonverbal behavior convey subtle feelings) have also been studied (Argyle, Salter, Nicholson, Williams, and Burgess, 1970; Mehrabian, 1970).

It is, then, more than nonverbal qualities that make up the content of nonverbal communication. As Mehrabian (1972, p. 2) says,

It is more the subtlety, then, of a communication form than its verbal versus nonverbal quality which determines its considerations within the nonverbal literature. Nonverbal behaviors *per se* form the backbone of this literature. Their subtlety can be attributed to the

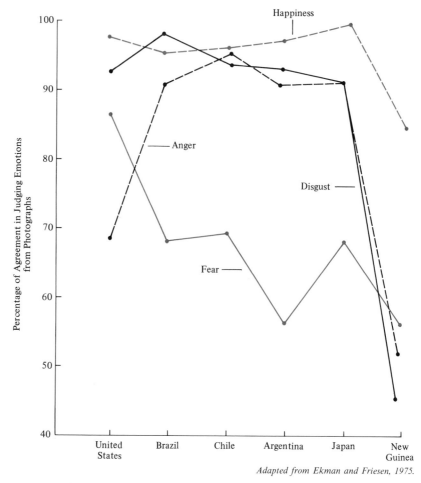

Adapted from Ekman and Friesen, 1975.

Figure 3–2 **Percentages of individuals in six countries who correctly identified the emotion shown in a photograph.**

lack of explicit coding rules for these behaviors in most cultures. Whereas verbal cues are definable by an explicit dictionary and by rules of syntax, there are only vague and informal explanations of the significance of various nonverbal behaviors. Similarly, there are no explicit rules for encoding or decoding paralinguistic phenomena or the more complex combinations of verbal and nonverbal behavior in which the nonverbal elements contribute heavily to the significance of a message.

Argyle (1972) views nonverbal communication as useful for humans in three different ways: to manage the immediate social situation, to support verbal communication, and to replace verbal communication. Argyle maintains that different researchers in the area have different conceptions about the essence of nonverbal communication. For example, some feel that it is itself a kind of language, whereas others have been concerned with the rules that govern verbal and nonverbal behavior in different situations. Finally, there is the conceptualization of nonverbal communication as a kind of adjunct to verbal communication, a position taken by both Argyle and Mehrabian and one that seems most reasonable for us to pursue.

Ekman and Friesen (1969) proposed five major categories that illustrate the functions of nonverbal behavior. The first of these, *emblem,* refers to a small class of nonverbal acts or gestures that can be accurately translated into words (shaking a fist at someone, a smile, a frown, or various obscene gestures that are readily recognizable). *Illustrators* are very much a part of speech and function as emphasizers (head and hand movements). Affect *display* refers to gestures or expressions that show emotion (see Figure 3–2). *Regulators* are used to help conversations proceed, conveying to participants in a social situation that they keep talking, clarify, and finish talking. Finally *adaptors* are acts that are related to bodily needs such as scratching, moving into a more comfortable position, and so forth.

Ten Major Nonverbal Signals

Argyle (1972) has classified the different kinds of nonverbal communication used by humans into ten different categories. The classification may be somewhat arbitrary, as any classification system is, but it should give you some idea about the different types of nonverbal signs that humans use. Do not feel that the ten categories related by Argyle are a further breakdown of the classification system Ekman and Friesen used. On the contrary, Ekman and Friesen's categorization is based on the function the particular form of communication serves, whereas Argyle's grouping is on the basis of similarity of the form the nonverbal communication takes.

Bodily Contact. Bodily contact may take the form of pushing, hitting, stroking, and so on, involving a number of different body areas. Cultures differ rather dramatically in the extent to which bodily contact is acceptable. Among Africans and Arabs there is a lot of bodily contact, whereas the British and Japanese are quite restrained in it. For example, in Britain the most common bodily contact that occurs is involved in greetings and farewells. Not surprisingly, bodily contact is much more common within the family unit, between husbands and wives and parents and children. Even in the family there are relatively prescribed areas of the body that can be touched by others. For example, Jouard (1966) found that male American white students were touched by their fathers primarily on the hands (when shaking hands) but that they were touched much more extensively by friends, particularly by friends of the opposite sex.

Proximity. One of the virtues of proximity is that it is relatively easy to measure how close people sit or stand. However, a great deal of research has yielded rather meager results. People do tend to stand somewhat closer to a person they like (and to someone whose eyes are closed) although the distances involved are small, on the order of 2 to 3 inches. This is compounded by the fact that there are much greater cross-cultural differences. Latin Americans and Arabs stand very close, while Swedes, Scots, or English, stand much farther apart. These cross-cultural differences carry over into our own experiences. I am not a Swede, Scot, or Englishman, but I have on occasion found myself in a conversation with a person who normally stands closer to the person with whom he is speaking than I do. The first few conversations we held, I found myself slowly retreating across the room, with him following to maintain his optimal distance, until I was backed against a wall. This occurred, even though neither one of us was conscious of the movement until it had been called to our attention.

There are individual differences in how close people stand to each other, but the only one that seems to show a consistent relationship is that maladjusted people tend to stand farther from others (Lott, Clark, and Altman, 1969). Changes in proximity communicate a desire to initiate or terminate an encounter. For example, if one person wishes to start an encounter with another person, he or she will move closer, although this must be accompanied with the appropriate gazes and conversation to be meaningfully communicated.

Hall (1963) concluded that culture was the primary determinant of the distance a person keeps from others. This portable "bubble," which has been referred to as personal space, is also influenced by age, sex, body image, leadership role, and possibly even more variables (Engebretson and Fullmer, 1970; Heshka and Nelson, 1972; Roger, 1976; Roger and Mjoli, 1976; Roger and Schalekamp, 1976). Personal space and proximity are obviously closely allied, but not identical. The work on proximity has stressed how close an individual stands to others he likes or dislikes and other variables that affect the distance between two people. Personal space is concerned with the buffer zones individuals keep around themselves in various situations and roles.

Bond, in a series of studies, has studied nonverbal communication, and more specifically proximity in Japan (Bond and Iwata 1976; Bond and Komai, 1976; Bond and Shiraishi, 1974). He has been interested in the effects of intrusion into personal space in Japan, an Asian country that is more crowded than many Western countries. Bond's work indicates that even in a crowded country like Japan, intrusion into personal space is disruptive. As he says, "The blunting of responses to crowding in the Orient is probably situation-specific. In a room 10 by 20 an interviewer who sits less than half a meter away was clearly behaving beyond the requirements of the situation. Under these circumstances subjects responded strongly to the intrusion (Bond and Iwata, 1976, pp. 124–25).

Orientation. The angle at which people sit or stand in relation to each other can vary from head-on to side-by-side. Orientation varies with the nature of the situation, culture, and sex. Those who are in a cooperative situation or who are close friends tend to adopt a side-by-side position, whereas people in a bargaining position tend to choose head-on positions. For other situations among persons from the United States and England the 90° position is most prevalent (Sommer, 1965; Cook, 1970). Arabs prefer the head-on position (Watson and Graves, 1966), whereas Swedes tend to avoid the 90° position (Ingham, 1971). Byrne, Baskett, and Hodges (1971) found that females sat next to a person they liked (in a side-by-side position), whereas males sat across from persons they liked.

Appearance. Many aspects of personal appearance are under voluntary control and others are partly so. Dress, hair styles, beards and mustaches on men, physique, and bodily condition all communicate something about the individual. It is, however, necessary to know the social class and cultural mores that the individual is adhering to or refusing to adhere to if the communication is to be adequately perceived. For example, an executive in a Wall Street brokerage firm may dress much differently than a student at a university (who may some day be an executive in a Wall Street brokerage firm). Hair styles change dramatically—long hair and unkept beards were a sign of extreme rebellion in the mid-1960s, whereas they were perfectly acceptable 10 years later. There is so much change going on in modern cultures that it is necessary to remain up to date if you are to understand what an individual is communicating by his or her appearance.

Posture and Position. There are many ways an individual can posture or position his or her body. A forward lean rather than a reclining position and an orientation of the torso toward rather than away from the addressee indicate a more positive attitude toward that person. There is a second set of postural cues that have to do with the status of the communicator and the addressee. For example, asymmetrical placement of the limbs, a sideways lean or a reclining position by a seated communicator and relaxation of the hands or neck, fall into this category. In general, a more relaxed position is assumed with a lower-status addressee (Mehrabian, 1972). Posture varies with emotional state and is less well controlled than facial expression (Argyle, 1972). There may be more meaningful nonverbal communication delivered by posture than by facial expression.

Goffman (1956) noted that in medical staff meetings, doctors often sat in undignified but comfortable positions whereas nurses, residents and social workers sat with a more dignified posture. Cohen (1972) found that in leaderless student groups, those students who were more dominant by a number of other indices also practiced careless posture. Thus posture in two quite different sorts of groupings seems to denote status.

Head Nods. A simple, frequent nonverbal signal is the head nod. It may seem to be minor, but it plays a very important role in connection with speech. One of its more usual functions is a reinforcer. If you are speaking and someone is nodding his or her head, the behavior that is followed by the head nod tends to increase. For example, there are innumerable anecdotal elaborations of classes deciding to nod their heads whenever the professor performs a given behavior; for example walking away from the podium and his or her notes until he or she is in the uncomfortable position of not knowing what to say next. There is a certain power to a head nod; if you are speaking and one person in the group consistently nods his or her head, you will, in all probability, speak more directly to that person. Head nods also help the flow of conversation, because they give permission to the individual to continue speaking. Rapid head nods, however, indicate that the nodder wishes to speak (Argyle, 1972).

Facial Expression. The face is one of the more useful communication areas and is used by nonhuman primates to communicate attitudes and emotions. Much facial expression, as we said in the last section of this chapter, appears to be culturally universal and unlearned. However, society places considerable restraints on the expression of negative attitudes or emotions, so that spontaneous facial expressions may be under careful control. Some aspects of facial expression are very difficult to control (for example, pupil size and perspiration during anxiety). Facial expressions also serve as helpful additions to conversation—a listener provides continuous commentary on the speech of another by the facial expressions exhibited. At the same time, a speaker accompanies his or her utterances with appropriate facial expressions

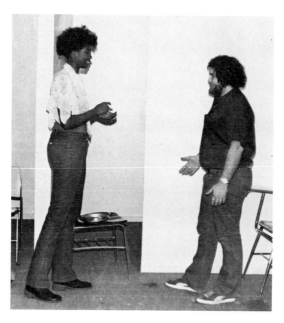

These two individuals are both gesturing. Do you see any other forms of nonverbal communication?

that indicate whether what is being said is supposed to be funny, important, serious, or whatever. (Vine, 1971).

Gesture. The hands are very expressive appendages, and although the head, feet, and other parts of the body are expressive, they are much less useful than the hands. There appear to be two classes of hand gestures that express emotional states. One class of gestures indicates general emotional arousal, whereas the other class expresses a specific emotional state; for example, clenching the fists in anger. As with other forms of nonverbal communication, gestures may be coordinated with speech to illustrate what is being said or to specify the shapes and sizes of objects. In extreme cases, gestures can replace spoken language in the deaf, for those who do not wish to call attention to themselves by making sounds, or, as we have seen, for chimpanzees.

Looking. During conversations people look at each other for periods of 1–10 seconds. This occurs for about 25 to 75 percent of the time. Periods of mutual gaze (that is, when both persons are looking at each other) are shorter and referred to as eye contact. People look about twice as much when they are listening as when they are talking. Looking plays an important role in communication. The act of looking at the speaker rather than at something or someone else indicates that a certain amount of interest is being shown in what is being said. Together with facial expression, rather specific interest or uninterest can be signaled by looking. Interestingly enough, people look more when the other person is more distant, which suggests that looking and proximity can substitute for each other as signals of intimacy. Figure 3–3 shows the effects of distance upon looking and eye contact. As you can readily see from the figure, people look (gaze) more often than they engage in eye contact and they increase both as the distance between them increases.

CIVIL INATTENTION

In 1963 Goffman proposed that the rule of civil inattention was perhaps the most constant of polite interpersonal rituals. As Goffman stated it, the rule concerns looking behavior when entering mutual copresence with another person; in that case "one gives to another enough visual notice to demonstrate that one appreciates that the other is present (and that one openly admits to having seen him), while at the next moment withdrawing one's attention so as to express that he does not constitute a target of special curiosity or design" (Goffman, 1963, p. 84). Until recently, Goffman's rule of civil inattention has been accepted, possibly because it makes sense to most of us and seems to be what we do.

Cray (1978) set out to test the rule of civil inattention in pedestrian passing. The original description of civil inattention asserted that when passing persons can eye one another up to approximately 8 feet, but then must drop their eyes or look away during the pass. Forty-eight pairs of passers were filmed as they passed each other on a busy, two-lane street. If Goffman's hypothesis is correct, we would expect that people would lower their heads as they approached a distance of 8 feet from each other. There was no evidence among these 48 pairs for downward gazing as people pass. This unexpected result led to the next study. Even though there was no evidence that people lowered their heads as they passed, they could have lowered or averted their eyes as part of the civil inattention system.

The second study that Cray performed involved filming 48 persons as they were passing another person. They were filmed from such an angle that it could be determined whether they lowered or averted their eyes as they passed the other person. Three pictures were taken, one when the passers were approximately 16 to 22 feet apart, one when they were approximately 8 to 11 feet apart and one when they were approximately 1.5 to 3 feet apart. There was no evidence of civil inattention; persons do not lower their heads or eyes when passing, nor do they look at a passer more from a distance than they do when they are close.

Further studies by Cray, which included subjects' rating slides of people's gazes as they approached and confederates purposefully staring or not staring at passers, also failed to confirm the civil inattention hypothesis. For example, raters found the direct and constant stare, and the sudden stare after no looking, the most polite, friendly, and natural.

It seems that although people do not look at a passer and then look away, they do not openly stare at everyone they pass. Generally speaking, people seem to look straight ahead along the sidewalk as they pass others. This is modified by sex; men tend to look at women passers and women tend to look at men passers more than they do same-sex passers. This may simply reflect a well understood phenomenon in our culture, men and women tend to be interested in each other.

Cray suggests it may be that college students do not conform to the civil inattention hypothesis, that civil inattention is conveyed through some subtle cues not picked up in his studies or that norms have changed in the 15 years elapsing between Goffman's hypothesis and his research. For whatever reasons, Cray was unable to find evidence for civil inattention.

References

Goffman, E. *Behavior in Public Places.* New York: Free Press, 1963.

Cray, M. S. Does civil inattention exist in pedestrian passing? *Journal of Personality and Social Psychology,* 1978, *36,* 1185–1193.

People tend to look at people more if they like them (Exline and Winters, 1965); however, the facial expression that accompanies looking can signal quite different emotions (aggression, sexual attraction, or clinical interest).

Another aspect of looking behavior is the stare. Ellsworth, Carlsmith, and Henson

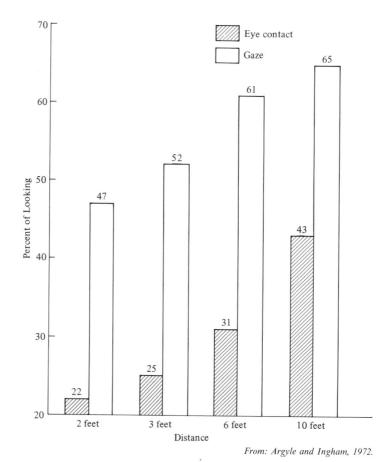

From: Argyle and Ingham, 1972.

Figure 3-3 Amounts of gaze and eye contact at different distances.

(1972) studied the effects of an unbroken stare on the behavior of people at a traffic signal. Put yourself in the subject's position for a moment. Suppose you have just stopped at a traffic light and an old motor scooter pulls up beside you. You look at the rider and he stares at you and continues to stare at you without any change in expression even when you've caught him at it. You're the one who looks away and when the light changes what do you do? If you are like the subjects in this experiment you get out of there fast. Subjects in the experiment crossed the intersection significantly faster than control subjects.

Possibly the subjects thought the starers wanted a drag race. Therefore, they had the starer stand on the street corner. No drag race, but the subjects left just as fast. In nonhuman primates the stare is a threat gesture. Does it serve the same function in humans? Neither this experiment nor the other research to date can answer that question, but it certainly suggests that we view a stare as a threat.

Implicit Aspects of Verbalization. An important communication technique is the tone of voice, pitch, stress, and timing. This difference can do much to convey the meaning of the speaker. The same words said in a friendly manner or in a sarcastic one can go a long way toward letting the other person know what the speaker is actually feeling. People are better able to communicate variations in negative affect than variations in positive affect (Zaidel and Mehrabien, 1969) whether facial or verbal channels are used. Seemingly negative affect is less often explicitly stated, and thus implicit statement through voice inflection or facial expression is easier. There are also implicit communications being made by a person who is being deceitful. Deceitful persons are more immediate in the cues they give and responses they make than are truthful ones (Mehrabian, 1971).

Doctors in medical staff meetings interrupt others without apology more than do nurses, residents, or social workers (Goffman, 1956). Interrupting others without apology is also characteristic of the more dominant members of leaderless student groups studied by Cohen (1972). It seems that unapologetic interruptions indicate dominance just as careless posture does. Thus, it seems that there are a number of nonverbal aspects of verbal communication that convey messages quite adequately.

COMMENT

Interest in human nonverbal communication is relatively new in the social sciences, having a tremendous upsurge starting in the early 1960s (Argyle, 1972). The fact that it is new and that it is very important for interpersonal communication means that the study of it will undoubtedly change many opinions about what is important and what various signs mean. As more knowledge is accumulated about nonverbal communication, social scientists may well understand more fully what people are actually communicating. In a society that is as mobile and as heterogeneous as the one we have in Canada and the United States, nonverbal aspects of communication are very important. For example, since much communication be-

In this advertisement for a medical school, the status of the doctor is communicated nonverbally.

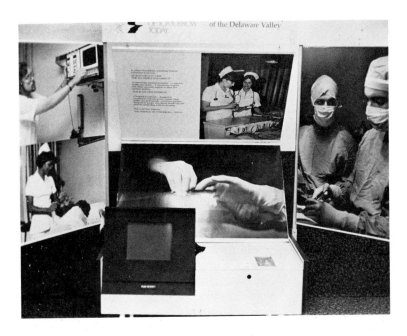

tween individuals seems to be nonverbal, it is very important for an individual to understand the cues given by others. If these differ appreciably from region to region or in ethnic groupings (e.g., French Quebec), then a more thorough understanding of the nuances of meaning of nonverbal communication is very important.

First Impressions

In setting the stage for social interaction among human beings communication is vitally important. Now, how do we start the process? For every person we know there was a first impression. "What did you think of me when we first met?" is an intriguing question. What is it that you notice about other people? Why do you pick out one person in a crowd? Because of physical attractiveness, facial expression, posture, conversation, or some other attribute? Communication begins to play its important role in social interaction as we begin to develop impressions of others.

The formation of impressions of others is highly dependent upon attributions the observer makes. For example, if someone you have never met walks into a room, stumbles on the doorsill, and spills his drink on an unsuspecting bystander, there are several conclusions that can be reached. One may be that he is a "klutz;" another is that he has had too much to drink or that he had an unfortunate accident, which is unlikely to recur. The last explanation is many times the correct one, but it is one that is seldom chosen. Why?

Information Processing: An Adventure in Attribution

When we first meet or see a person we start with a relatively "clean slate." That is, unless we have heard something or know something about the individual, we view that person's appearance, actions, and words as all there is to know about the individual. If our first encounter with the person is negative, we may never give the person another chance. Thus, first impressions are vitally important.

As soon as we meet another person, we begin to be bombarded with information about him or her. Physical appearance, attractiveness, posture, eye contact, accent, conversation, and his or her circle of acquaintances are just a few of the bits of information that shower us. How to process this information?

Basically, two approaches to processing information about another person have been suggested. The first of these, the *additive model,* is based on the assumption that people merely sum all of the information they have about another person and that forms their impression. When the man walked into the room, stumbled, and spilled his drink on a bystander, the information you have about him is "he looks clumsy" and his physical appearance. Since none of us look our best while stumbling and showering an unsuspecting bystander with our drink, probably both pieces of information are negative and you conclude he is a klutz.

In other situations, however, we may have both positive and negative information. The additive model implies that we would merely add up the negative and positive characteristics and come out with a negative or positive impression. But its not quite as simple as that. In Chapter 1 we discussed Solomon Asch's (1946) work on impression formation and pointed out that the characteristic "warm" versus "cold" had a great impact on what people thought of another person. Therefore, it seems obvious that some sort of weight must be given to each characteristic. Having green eyes is not so important to most people as being a warm individual. Therefore, the number of characteristics cannot simply be added together, each one must be given a weight. For example, let us assume that intelligence is given a weight of $+2$, warmth a weight of $+4$, coldness a weight of -4 and stinginess a weight of -3. A person who is intelligent, warm, and stingy would come out with a positive impression ($+2$, $+4$, $-3 = +3$), whereas a person who is intelligent, cold, and stingy would be viewed negatively ($+2$, -4, $-3 = -5$).

There are, however, situations in which an additive model does not seem to make sense. Consider a situation in which a woman has a majority of positive characteristics and you get to know her quite well. Because she has a majority of positive characteristics, it seems reasonable that your impression of her is favorable and continues to become more favorable. However, finding out that she is generous after knowing her for some time and having a positive impression will probably not alter your impression of her as much as it would have if you had discovered it early in the relationship.

There is another approach, called the averaging model. This model (Anderson, 1968, 1974; Kaplan, 1975) is based on the assumption that people average the information they receive about another instead of adding it. For example, if an individual is first characterized as intelligent, the total impression would be $+2$ as in the additive model. With the next characteristic, however, instead of simply adding it, it is averaged. Let us assume that warmth is the next characteristic; with the averaging model we would assume that the total impression would be $+3$ ($2 + 4 \div 2 = +3$) instead of 6. Table 3-1 gives an example that compares an individual using the two models. As you can see, in many instances the models do not agree about the strength of an impression toward another.

There is, however, a variation on the averaging model that seems to be most accurate. This model takes each piece of information, with its weight and averages it in to form the final impression (just as is done in Table 3-1). In addition to this, however, is the initial disposition of the individual to evaluate others in a positive or

Table 3-1 A comparison of the final impression of people using the additive and averaging models. Assume that good-looking = 3, warm = 4, brusque = −1, arrogant = −3, and unkind = −4.

	Additive Model	Averaging Model
She is good-looking, warm, and arrogant.	+4	+1.5
He is unkind, but good-looking.	−1	−.5
She is brusque and arrogant.	−4	−2
He is good-looking and arrogant.	0	0

negative manner. Some people seem to like everyone, whereas others dislike, or at least, are suspicious of, everyone. In addition, the importance of this initial disposition is also considered. That is, some people strongly feel they should like everyone, or they are afraid of everyone. Kaplan (1976) has devised a simple measure of an individual's disposition to feel positively or negatively toward others. Subjects are asked to select a list of 12 characteristics they would be most likely to use from a list of 36 such characteristics. Twelve of the traits are high likability, 12 are medium likability and 12 are low likability. Their pattern of choices reveals their own disposition to evaluate others positively or negatively. That is, individuals differ in their predisposition to use high, medium, or low likability characteristics.

This weighted average model previously discussed seems to predict the final impression of an individual much more accurately than either a simple additive or averaging model. This should not be surprising in that it is interactive in nature. That is, the model allows for the unique dispositions of each individual, both perceiver and perceived, and the characteristics of the situation. To be more explicit about this latter point, the credibility of the source from which information is received is important (Rosenbaum and Levin, 1968, 1969) and we tend to weight negative information more heavily than positive information (Hamilton and Zanna, 1972).

A highly credible source is more likely to be believed than a source of low credibility. For example, we would be more likely to listen to a doctor's estimates of a prospective medical student's abilities than we would to those of a plumber. On the other hand, a plumber's recommendation of an aspiring plumber would probably carry more weight than would a doctor's. Second, probably because we hear so little negative information about an individual we have never met, we tend to give it additional weight. For example, letters of recommendation typically say only good things about the person being recommended. What is significant in a letter of recommendation is what is not said. Reading such letters is an art; deciding what the individual truly means is not an easy task. Hamilton and Zanna (1972) found that, generally speaking, more weight is assigned to information regarding negative characteristics than to information regarding positive ones.

SUMMARY

1 To communicate is to impart knowledge of or to make known. Communication is necessary for society to function, although it need not be verbal communication. Other species communicate with each other in various ways.

2 Wynne-Edwards has proposed a model of animal social behavior that is homeostatic in nature. He argues that instinctive social behavior keeps a species at an optimal level for the habitat in which it exists.

3 Honeybees are a highly social species that have developed a high degree of division of labor. Honeybees communicate the direction and distance to a food source to their fellow hive members by means of a special dance.

4 Graylag geese are monogamous and appear to adhere to the incest taboo. They

also communicate with each other and exhibit the imprinting phenomenon that certain other species show.

5 Chimpanzees, anthropoid apes, have a well-developed social structure, and they have been discovered to use rudimentary tools.

6 A suitable definition of language has not yet been developed. First-language acquisition appears to progress through several invariant stages and to be most heavily dependent on the language the child hears.

7 Chimpanzees have learned what some scientists think is a language, Amelsan. Washoe was the first chimpanzee to learn Amelsan and others have followed, which has opened new possibilities in the areas of cognitive processes and in teaching communication.

8 Some scientists argue that nonverbal communication is innate and others disagree. Ethologists study a species in its natural habitat and argue that nonverbal communication is innate.

9 Facial expressions have been pointed to as a universal form of nonverbal communication. People in various cultures seem to use the same facial expressions to show specific emotions, and people from other cultures can look at a picture of an individual and detect which emotion is being shown.

10 Nonverbal communication is useful for humans in managing the immediate social situation, supporting verbal communication, and replacing verbal communication.

11 Ten major nonverbal signals have been studied: bodily contact, proximity, orientation, appearance, posture and position, head nods, facial expression, gestures, looking, and implicit aspects of verbalization.

12 Impression formation sets the stage for further social contact. Probably people average characteristics of others in arriving at a final impression.

GLOSSARY

Adaptors Acts that are related to bodily needs.

Additive Model A model of impression formation that is based on the assumption that people merely sum all information they have about another person to reach an impression.

Amelsan American sign language.

Asymmetrical Not identical on both sides of a central line.

Averaging Model A model of impression formation based on the assumption that people average the information they receive about another person.

Communicate To impart knowledge of or to make known.

Conspecific Characterized by membership in the same species.

Critical Period A short developmental period in which genetically programmed learning must occur if it is to occur at all.

Emblem A class of nonverbal acts or gestures that can be accurately translated into words.

Ethnogram The precise catalogue of all the behavior patterns of an animal.

Ethology The biology of behavior.

Eye Contact Mutual gaze.

Habitat The native environment of an animal or plant.

Homeostatic Characterized by the tendency, as of a system, to maintain internal stability by returning to the optimal state any time there is fluctuation away from such a state.

Illustrators Nonverbal forms of communication that function as emphasizers.

Imprinting Genetically programmed learning so that during sensitive periods of their lives members of certain species are able to learn certain activities.

Monogomous Having only one spouse.

Nonverbal Communication Communication that is contained in expressions, gestures, postures, implicit aspects of verbalization, and so forth.

Orientation The angle at which people sit or stand in relation to each other.

Proximity Nearness in place or time.

Reconstitution The ability to separate messages into smaller parts and to rearrange those parts to form other messages.

Regulators Nonverbal forms of communication used to help conversations proceed.

Society A closely integrated group of organisms held together by mutual dependence and exhibiting division of labor.

REFERENCES

Anderson, N. H. Application of a linear-serial model to a personality impression task using serial presentation. *Journal of Personality and Social Psychology,* 1968, *10,* 354–62.

———. Cognitive algebra: Integration theory applied to social attribution. In L. Berkowitz (Ed.), *Advances in Experimental Social Psychology,* Vol. 7. New York: Academic Press, Inc., 1974.

Argyle, M. Non-verbal communication in human social interaction. In R. A. Hinde (Ed.), *Non-Verbal Communication.* Cambridge, Eng.: Cambridge University Press, 1972.

——— and R. Ingham, Gaze, mutual gaze and proximity. *Semiotica,* 1972.

———, V. Salter, H. Nicholson, M. Williams, and P. Burgess. The communication of inferior and superior attitudes by verbal and non-verbal signals. *British Journal of Social and Clinical Psychology,* 1970, *9,* 222–31.

Asch, S. *Social Psychology.* New York: Prentice-Hall, Inc., 1952.

Asch, S. E. Forming impressions of personality. *Journal of Abnormal and Social Psychology,* 1946, *41,* 258–90.

Birdwhistell, R. L. The kinesis level in the investigation of the emotions. In P. H. Knapp (Ed.), *Expressions of the Emotions of Man.* New York: International University Press, 1963.

———. Communication without words. In P. Alexandre (Ed.), *L'Adventure humaine,* Encyclopedia Science de l Hamme. Paris, 1968, *5,*

———. *Kinesis and context.* Philadelphia: University of Pennsylvania Press, 1970.

Bond, M. H., and Y. Iwata. Proximics and observation anxiety in Japan: Non-verbal and cognitive responses. *Psychologia,* 1976, *19,* 119–26.

———. and H. Komai. Targets of gazing and eye contact during interviews: Effects on Japanese non-verbal behavior. *Journal of Personality and Social Psychology,* 1976, *34,* 1276–84.

———. and D. Shiraishi. The effect of body lean and status of an interviewer on the non-verbal behavior of Japanese interviewees. *International Journal of Psychology,* 1974, *2,* 117–28.

Braine, M. D. S. The ontogeny of English phrase structure: The first phrase. *Language,* 1963, *39,* 1–13.

Bronowksi, J., and U. Bellugi. Language name and concept. *Science,* 1970, *168,* 669–73.

Brown, R. *Social Psychology.* New York: The Free Press, 1965.

———. *A First Language: The Early Stages.* Cambridge, Mass.: Harvard University Press, 1973.

———. and V. Bellugi. Three processes in the child's acquisition of syntax. *Harvard Educational Review,* 1964, *34,* 133–51.

———. and C. Fraser. The acquisition of syntax. In C. N. Cofer and B. S. Musgrave (Eds.), *Verbal Behavior and Learning: Problems and Processes.* New York: McGraw-Hill Book Co., Inc., 1963.

———. and R. J. Herrnstein. *Psychology.* Boston: Little, Brown and Company, 1975.

Byrne, D., G. D. Baskett, and L. Hodges. Behavior indicators of interpersonal attraction. *Journal of Applied Social Psychology,* 1971, *1,* 137–49.

Chomsky, N. *Syntactic Structures.* The Hague: Mouton, 1957.

———. Formal discussion of W. Miller and W. Ervins "The development of grammar in child speech." In U. Bellugi and R. Brown (Eds.). The acquisition of language. *Monographs of the Society for Research in Child Development,* 1964, *29,* 35–39.

———. *Language and Mind.* New York: Harcourt Brace Jovanovich, Inc., 1968.

Chown, W. Productive competence in a chimpanzee's comprehension of commands. Unpublished master's thesis. University of Oklahoma, 1974.

Cohen, S. P. Varieties of interpersonal relationships in small groups. Unpublished doctoral dissertation. Harvard University, 1972.

Cook, M. Experiments on orientation and proxemics. *Human Relations,* 1970, *23,* 61–76.

Darwin, C. *The expression of emotion in man and animals.* London: John Murray, 1872.

Eibl-Eibesfeldt, I. Zur ethologie der menschlichen GruBvahaltens. I. Beohachtungen an Balinese, Papuas and Samoanan nebst vergleichenden Bemerkungen. *Z Tierpsychol.* 1968, *25,* 727–44.

———. Zur ethologie menschlichen GruBverhatlens II. Das GruBvaltern und einige andere Muster freundlicher Kontaktaufnahme derWaika-Indianer (Yanoama). *Z Tierpsychol.* 1971, *29,* 196–213.

———. *Love and Hate: The Natural History of Behavior Patterns.* New York: Holt, Rinehart and Winston, 1972.

———. *Ethology: The Biology of Behavior* (2nd Edition). New York: Holt, Rinehart and Winston, 1975.

———. and H. Hass. Zum projest einer ethologisch orientiertem. Untersuchung menschlichen Verbaltens. Mitt. *Max-Planck-Ges,* 1966, *6,* 383–96.

———. and H. Hass. Neve mege der humanethologie. *Homo,* 1967, *18,* 13–23.

Ekman, P. *Darwin and the Human Face.* New York: Academic Press, Inc., 1972.

——— and W. V. Friesen. The repertoire of nonverbal behavior: Categories, origins, usage, and coding. *Semiotica.* 1969, *1,* 49–98.

———W. V. Friesen, and P. Ellsworth. *Emotion in the Human Face: Guidelines for Research.* New York: Pergamon Press, Inc., 1972.

———, W. V. Friesen. *Unmasking The Face.* Englewood Cliffs, N.J.: Prentice-Hall, Inc., 1975.

———. Changes with age in the verbal determinants of word-association. *American Journal of Psychology,* 1961, *64,* 361–372.

Ellsworth, P. C., J. M. Carlsmith, and A. Henson. The stare as a stimulus to flight in human subjects: A series of field experiments. *Journal of Personality and Social Psychology,* 1972, *21,* 302–11.

Engebertson, D., and D. Fullmer. Cross-cultural differences in territoriality: Interaction distances of Native Japanese, Hawaiian Japanese, and American Caucasians. *Journal of Cross-Cultural Psychology,* 1970, *1,* 261–69.

Erwin, S. M. Changes with age in the verbal determinants of word-association. *American Journal of Psychology,* 1961, *74,* 361–72.

Esch, H. The evolution of bee language. *Scientific American,* 1967, *216,* 97–104.

Exline, R. V., and L. C. Winters. Affective relations and mutual gaze in dyads. In S. Tompkins and C. Izzard (Eds.), *Affect, Cognition, and Personality.* New York: Springer Publishing Co., Inc., 1965.

Fouts, R. S., and R. L. Mellgren. Language, signs, and cognition in the chimpanzee. *Sign Language Studies,* 1976, *13,* 319–46.

Frijda, N. H. *Mimik and pantomimik.* In A. Kirchoff (Ed.). Handbook of d. Psychologische, Ausdruckspsychol., 1965, 351–421.

Frisch, K. v. *Die tanzsprache und orientierung der bienen.* Berlin: Springer, 1965.

———. Honeybees: Do they use direction and distance information provided by their dancers? *Science,* 1968, *158,* 1072–76.

Gardner, R. A., and B. T. Gardner. Teaching sign language to a chimpanzee. *Science,* 1969, *165,* 664–72.

Gehlen, A. *Urmensch and Spätkultur.* Bonn, 1956.

Goffman, E. The nature of deference and demeanor. *American Anthropologist,* 1956, *58,* 473–502.

Goodall, J. My life among the wild chimpanzee. *National Geographic Magazine,* 1963, *125,* 272–308.

———. Chimpanzees of the Gombe stream reserve. In DeVore, I. (Ed.), *Primate Behavior.* New York: Holt, Rinehart and Winston, 1965, 425–73.

Hall, E. T. A system for the notation of proxemic behavior. *American Anthropologist,* 1963, *65,* 1003–26.

Hamilton, D. L., and M. P. Zanna. Differential weighting of favorable and unfavorable attributes in impressions of personality. *Journal of Experimental Research in Personality,* 1972, *6,* 204–212.

Hass, H. *Wir Menschen.* Wien: Molden, 1968.

Heshka, S., and V. Nelson. Interpersonal speaking distance as a function of age, sex, and relationship. *Sociometry,* 1972, *35,* 491–98.

Hess, E. H. Imprinting: An affect of early experience. *Science,* 1959, *130,* 133–41.

———. *Imprinting: Early Experience and the Developmental Psychobiology of Attachment.* New York: D. Van Nostrand Company, 1973.

Ingham, R. Cultural differences in social behavior. Doctor of Philosophy thesis. Oxford University, 1971.

Jouard, S. M. An exploratory study of body-accessibility. *British Journal of Social and Clinical Psychology,* 1966, *5,* 221–31.

Kaplan, M. F. Information integration in social judgment: Interaction of judge and informational components. In M. Kaplan & S. Schwartz (Eds.), *Human Judgment and Decision Processes.* New York: Academic Press, 1975.

———. Measurement and generality of response dispositions in person perception. *Journal of Personality,* 1976.

Kellogg, W. N. Communication and language in the home-raised chimpanzee. *Science,* 1968, *162,* 423–27.

Köhler, W. *Intelligensprüfungen an Menschenaffen.* Berlin, 1921.

LaBarre, W. The cultural basis of emotions and gestures. *Journal of Personality,* 1947, *16,* 49–68.

Lamberth, J., J. C. McCullers, and R. L. Mellgren. *Foundations of Psychology.* New York: Harper & Row, Publishers, 1976.

Lawick-Goodall, J. van. New discoveries among Africa's chimpanzees. *National Geographic Magazine,* 1965, *128,* 802–831.

Lawick-Goodall, J. van. The behaviour of free-living chimpanzees in the Gombe stream reserve. *Animal Behavior Monographs.* 1968, *1*(3), 161–311.

————. Tool-using in primates and other vertebrates. In D. S. Lehrman, R. A. Hinde, and E. Shaw (Eds.), *Advances in the Study of Behavior. New York; Academic Press, Inc.,* 1970, 195–249.

————. *In the Shadow of Man.* Boston: Houghton Mifflin Company, 1971.

Lees, R. Formal discussion of R. Brown and C. Fraser's "The acquisition of syntax" and of R. Brown, C. Fraser, and U. Bellugi's "Explorations in grammar evaluation." In U. Bellugi and R. Brown (Eds.), The acquisition of language. *Monographs of the Society for Research in Child Development,* 1964, *29,* 92–98.

Lennenberg, E. H. A biological perspective of language. In E. H. Lennenberg (Ed.), *New Directions in the Study of Language.* Cambridge, Mass.: M.I.T. Press, 1964.

Lorenz, K. Der Kimpan in der Umwelt des Vogels. *Journal of Ornithology,* 1963, *83:* 137–413.

————. *Das sogenannte Bose.* Vienna: Borotha-Schoeler, 1963.

Lott, E. E., W. Clark, and I. Altman. A propositional inventory of research on interpersonal space. *Naval Medical Research Institute Research Report,* 1969.

McCall, E. A. A generative grammar of sign. Unpublished master's thesis, University of Iowa, 1965.

Mehrabian, A. When are feelings communicated inconsistently? *Journal of Experimental Research in Personality.* 1970, *4,* 198–212.

————. Nonverbal betrayal of feeling. *Journal of Experimental Research in Personality,* 1971, *5,* 64–73.

————. *Nonverbal Communication.* Chicago: Aldine Publishing Co., Inc., 1972.

Mellgren, R., R. Fouts, and W. Lemmon. American sign language in chimpanzee: Semantic and conceptual functions of signs. Paper presented at Midwestern Psychological Association, Chicago, May 1973.

Miller, W., and S. Ervin. The development of grammar in child speech. In U. Bellugi & R. Brown (Eds.). The acquisition of language. *Monographs of the Society for Research in Child Development,* 1964, *29,* 9–34.

Peiper, A. Instinkt und angeborenes schema bein saügling. *Z. Tierpsychol.,* 1951, *8,* 449–56.

Roger, D. B. Personal space, body image, and leadership. An exploratory study. *Perceptual and Motor Skills,* 1976, *43,* 25–26.

———— and Q. T. Mjoli. Personal space and acculturation. *The Journal of Social Psychology,* 1976, *100,* 3–10.

———— and E. E. Schalekamp. Body-buffer zone and violence: A cross-cultural study. *The Journal of Social Psychology,* 1976, *98,* 153–58.

Rosenbaum, M. E., and I. P. Levin. Impression formation as a function of source credibility and order of presentation of contradictory information. *Journal of Personality and Social Psychology,* 1968, *10,* 167–74.

Rosenbaum, M. E., and I. P. Levin. Impression formation as a function of source credibility and the polarity of information. *Journal of Personality and Social Psychology,* 1969, *12,* 34–37.

Sommer, R. Further studies of small group ecology. *Sociometry,* 1965, *28,* 337–48.

Tinbergen, N. *The Herring Gull's World.* New York: Basic Books, Inc., Publishers, 1963.

Vine, I. Communication by facial-visual signals. In J. H. Crook (Ed.), *Social Behaviour in Animals and Man.* New York: Academic Press, Inc., 1971.

Watson, O. M., and T. D. Granes. Quantitative research in proxemic behavior. *American Anthropologist, 68,* 971–85.

Wickler, W. and V. Seibt. Ueber den Zusammenhang des Paarsitzens mit anderen Verhaltensweisen bei *Hymenocera picta* Dana. *Z. Tierpsychologia,* 1972, *31,* 163–70.

Wynne-Edwards, V. *Animal Dispersion in Relation to Social Behavior.* New York: Hafner Press, 1962.

Zaidel, S. F., and A. Mehrabian. The ability to communicate and infer positive and negative attitudes facially and vocally. *Journal of Experimental Research in Personality,* 1969, *3,* 233–41.

The Developing Person

Social interactions are carried out by individuals who were once no more than a single ovum and a single sperm. Our understanding of how an ovum and a sperm combine to develop into a person, much less how one particular sperm from among many is the one that fertilizes a specific ovum, is limited. We can say, with certainty, that which sperm fertilizes the ovum is dramatically important to the individual who results. How much of his or her physical characteristics, abilities, and personality are determined or mainly influenced, for better or worse, at the time of conception is

135

unknown, although most psychologists would agree that heredity plays an important role in the resulting person.

For our purposes it is adequate to begin our discussion of how a sperm and an egg ultimately become a member of society at the birth of the individual. Enormous growth and many changes occur between the time of conception and birth, but that is more clearly within the province of another area of psychology, which is called, appropriately enough, *developmental psychology*. In this chapter we will deal with two basic developmental themes that are important for social psychology. Before we can seriously consider the interaction of two or more human beings, which is the basis of social psychology, those individuals must change from squalling, egocentric, newborns to socially functioning people. This process is known as *socialization*. Another phase of development that occurs is the development of personality, and that is of paramount importance for social interaction, since the person is vitally important in his or her interaction with situations.

Socialization

"Socialization is the process by which the individual acquires those behavior patterns, beliefs, standards, and motives that are valued by, and appropriate in, his own cultural group and family." (Mussen, Conger, and Kagan, 1974, p. 365). To a certain extent the culture into which the child is born and in which she or he grows up determines both the *content* of socialization and its *methods*. We will confine our discussion of socialization, except for an example here and there, to Canada and the United States. Whereas there are differences between socialization practices between the two countries, on the whole there are probably greater differences within each country than there are between the two. Finally, it is impossible to cover everything that falls into the general category of socialization; rather, one must pick and choose from a rather long list of topics. I have chosen to include three that are particularly important for social psychology but will not be covered in another chapter: motives, with special emphasis upon sexual motives and curiosity; dependency; and moral development.

A motive and a behavior are two different things. How the two differ should be firmly grounded in everyone's mind. A motive is an unobservable mediating variable or construct that refers to a specific goal. When we discuss motives, it must usually be in the specific context of the goal, which may be a sought-after goal or one to be avoided. For example, most students have a goal in their educational careers, the most prominent one being to obtain a degree. I have met, however, students whose goal is not so much to obtain a degree as it is to get away from their parents; to them college seemed the most accessible and socially acceptable way to do so. More realistically, there may be rather large numbers of you who want an education, but getting away from parents (or children) is not an unpleasant prospect.

Behavior is observable, and it is from behavior that we infer motives. As with all inferences, the motives we infer may, in some way, be faulty or inaccurate. For example, we can infer several motives from the same behavior, such as athletic accomplishment. A boy who excels at athletics may do so because he wants to win, he wants approval from an athletic father, or he wants to avoid failure at another activity, such as his schoolwork. I call your attention to these facts not out of a perverse desire to confuse you but to point out the multifaceted possibilities of interpreting motivation from behavior.

Sexual Motives

If it is difficult to determine motives from behavior, when we approach sexual motives, the picture becomes even more clouded. Sexual motives include many kinds of pleasurable wishes that are usually related to genital sensations. It is surprising to many people to learn that very young children engage in masturbation and sex play and that these erotic stimulations increase and become more intense during the preschool period. It is not at all unusual for children to engage in some modified form of masturbation, such as touching and/or manipulating the genitals, at a very young age. We infer from this behavior that the sensations produced are pleasant and that pleasure is the motive behind such sex play. Preschool children are also often placed in a position where they can notice the difference between the genitals of children of the opposite sex, of adults and themselves. This brings about curiosity concerning genitals and oftentimes loud questions that prove embarrassing to adults, particularly if they are asked in a public place. According to Hattendorf (1932) these differences and curiosity elicit questions about sex, with a particular emphasis on questions about babies and where they come from. Judging from the time Hattendorf's study was published, children have been asking such questions for a long time.

In Western culture sexual activities have been subjects seldom spoken of in polite society, and even more seldom done. Most of us in Canada and the United States have grown up with strong misconceptions about sex because our major sources of information were equally ill-informed peers. Our own socialization has, for the most part, been to suppress sexual feelings, comments, and actions. Whereas most of us would agree that overt sexual behavior is an activity best engaged in privately, it is apparent that until recently sex was too much of a taboo. Most people who grew up in the 50s and early 60s can tell rather vivid stories of sexual misinformation that they heard from peers. Because of this sexual "taboo" many parents felt that they should suppress this natural interest in sexual activity by children. Many parents do not even

What motivates a swimmer to spend the long hours of practice necessary to master and excel at a stroke as difficult as the butterfly?

remember that they, as children, engaged in such sexual activity and were themselves extremely curious about sex. Oftentimes middle-class Western parents spank or scold their children if they discover them running around naked or playing with their genitals (Sears, Maccoby, and Levin, 1957). If this occurs, then the genitals may become the focus of conflict between the pleasant sensations caused by continued masturbation and the disapproval of their parents. There are more permissive cultures, for example that of the Trobiand Islands, where sexual exploration and play are not restricted or punished. There preschool children are highly active in genital play; in fact, a large proportion of their play is sexually oriented (Malinowski, 1927).

There is general agreement among such diverse theoretical points of view as Freud's (1972), Watson's (1919) and Kinsey's (1948) that sex is an innate motive in humans. Freud was among the first writers to suggest the existence of sexuality in infants and young children, and he based much of his personality theory on sexual energy or *libido*. Even though most psychologists do not attach as much importance to sexual motivation as did Freud, and at least one long-time adherent, Jung, broke with Freud over his emphasis upon sexuality as the most important motive in personality, it is an important motive.

No wonder that the child, who is struggling to understand and follow the rules placed upon him or her by society is perplexed. Sexual activity is pleasurable, and yet it is often punished, with no real explanation given. Why wouldn't a child play with his or her genitals? Primarily because society, through the parents, says No. Thus the child is forced to forego a source of unique pleasure, incur the wrath of parents, or engage in such activity in a secretive fashion. As Mussen, Conger, and Kagan (1974, p. 370) say;

> Punishment of early sexual activity or curiosity may be a major source of adolescent and adult anxiety about sex, misunderstandings, and handicapping attitudes about sex. Such adverse effects could be avoided if parents would handle their child's sexual curiosity frankly and realistically, acting neither embarrassed nor secretive about questions or, on the other hand, overwhelming the child with too much information.

Fortunately, the climate is changing and parents are becoming aware of the importance of a child's sexual self-exploration and the potential hazards of suppressing such feelings. It is still a difficult journey for the child to develop healthy attitudes and values about sex, which will be vitally important in the social interactions that come with adolescence and adulthood. With adolescence, tremendous hormonal forces are unleashed in the individual causing increased sexual drive. This sexual drive becomes more diffuse and ambiguous (Douvan and Adelson, 1966; Mussen, Conger, and Kagan, 1974) than the early emphasis upon the genitals. Virtually all available data, however, agree that sexual interests and behavior increase for both sexes in a dramatic fashion. There are sex differences between males and females, with males being more aggressive in sexual behavior, particularly masturbation (Kinsey et al., 1948; Kinsey et al., 1953; Reeny, 1961) and females displaying a more conservative attitude toward such sexual matters as premarital intercourse and pornography (Wilson, 1971; Zubin and Money, 1973).

It is beyond the scope of the present chapter to do more than call attention to the importance of the sexual motive in socialization. Adequate navigation through sexual waters allows an individual to interact with other persons in society in ways that are important for social psychology. This section is merely intended to call your attention to the problems. For a more thorough treatment of the development of sexual motivation you are advised to refer to the references or ask your instructor for more extensive material.

Sex-Role Identity

Men are men and women are women! At least that seems to be the conventional wisdom of the ages. Traditionally there has been a masculine role and a feminine one, and these have been seen as complementary positive attributes. By this I mean that there are certain positive characteristics that are needed in society. Some are masculine and some are feminine and together they complete the needs of society. Different theorists have used different labels for these domains. Parsons and Bales (1955) referred to masculinity as an instrumental orientation, which is a cognitive emphasis on getting the problem solved or the job done. Femininity was associated with an expressive orientation, which is an affective concern for the welfare of others and the harmony of the group. Bakan (1966) divided masculinity and femininity into an "agentic" or "communal" orientation. The masculine, agentic orientation is a concern for oneself as an individual, whereas the feminine, communal orientation stresses a concern for the relationship between oneself and others.

For many years the idea that masculinity and femininity were opposite ends of a continuum was accepted by most people. Men had their roles and women had theirs. In Canada and the United States, the traditional role for men was that of the breadwinner, while women bore and brought up children and cared for the home. Whereas there were instances where women worked outside of the home and men helped in the duties in the home, they were the exception rather than the rule. Not

The Amish have rejected social and technological advances, and farm their land without electricity, machines or chemical fertilizers. Sex-roles among the Amish are characteristic of sex-roles in the 18th century as exemplified by this woman waiting for her husband to return.

surprisingly, children learned to do what their parents did and the pattern continued through several generations.

As with many liberation movements (see Chapter 6) it is not clear just when things started to change. The women's liberation movement has called attention to the inequities that women have lived with for many years and it has made attempts to alter the situation. Of course, the women's movement is not an entity in itself, but rather a group of women loosely aligned to achieve a given purpose. One of the consequences of alterations in a woman's role is that sex-role identities are going to change. If women are going to work outside of the home more, there are inevitable consequences. The consequences we are interested in here are those that affect men and women now and the type of model children see.

If women work more outside of the home there are ramifications for them, their families, and their fellow workers. Each woman must adjust her life style and fulfill a new role as well as continue certain aspects of the traditional feminine role. A woman who works outside of the home cannot spend as much time fulfilling the traditional role of wife, mother, and homemaker. In addition, she will be forced into more situations in which traditional masculine characteristics are rewarded. While this is going on, if she is married her husband will probably be involved in activities that are more traditionally associated with the feminine role. This mixture of roles will, on the one hand, make sex-role models less distinct but may reflect a more accurate state of masculinity-femininity.

Psychological Androgyny

The possibility that a single individual can exhibit both masculine and feminine traits has been suggested by several writers (Bakan, 1966; Jung, 1953). More recently, the concept of *androgyny* (having both male and female characteristics) has had several advocates in the psychological literature (Berzins and Welling, 1974; Block, 1973; Spence, Helmreich and Stapp, 1975). Sandra Bem (1974, 1975, in press, a, b; Bem and Lenney, 1976) has been particularly active in investigating psychological androgyny. She says;

And yet, although I believe that it is *possible* for people to be both masculine and feminine, I also believe that *traditional* roles prevent this possibility from ever becoming a reality for many individuals. Over the last few years, the Women's Liberation Movement has made us all aware of the many ways that we, both men and women, have become locked into our respective sex roles. As women, we have become aware of the fact that we are afraid to express our anger, to assert our preferences, to trust our judgment, to take control of situations. As men, we have become aware of the fact that we are afraid to cry, to touch one another, to own up to our fears and weaknesses.

But there has been very little data within psychology to give legitimacy to these experimential truths. In many ways, my goal over the last few years has been to gather some of that legitimizing data, to try to demonstrate that traditional sex roles do restrict behavior in important human ways. [Bem, in press (b), p. 2.]

Bem points out that there is evidence that high levels of sex-typing may not be desirable. High femininity in girls has been consistently associated with high anxiety, low self-esteem, and low social acceptance (Cosentino and Heilbrun, 1964; Gall,

1969; Gray, 1957; Sears, 1970; Wehl, 1963). High masculinity in males has been correlated with better psychological adjustment during adolescence (Mussen, 1962), but during adulthood it has been correlated with high anxiety, high neuroticism, and low self-acceptance (Harford et al., 1967; Mussen, 1962). Additionally, greater intellectual development has been consistently correlated with cross sex-typing (i.e., with femininity in boys and masculinity in girls). Maccoby (1966) found boys and girls who are more sex-typed to have lower overall intelligence, lower spatial ability, and lower creativity.

Masculinity and femininity are both fundamental domains. An adult must be able to look out for himself or herself but also must relate to others' needs and to be sensitive. Limiting a person's capacity to respond in either of these two domains seems to be potentially destructive to individuals.

One domain, untempered by the other, would also be detrimental to the individual. Extreme femininity, without the complementary effects of self-concern may produce dependency and self-denial. Extreme masculinity, without a sufficient concern for the needs of others, may produce arrogance and exploitation. Thus, according to Bem, the very best personality would be the one that contains the most positive elements of both masculinity and femininity.

MEASURING PSYCHOLOGICAL ANDROGYNY

With this model in mind, Bem set out to measure androgyny and to test its effects. First, she constructed the Bem Sex-Role Inventory, which, unlike most other masculinity-femininity scales treats the two dimensions as independent characteristics. Earlier masculinity-femininity scales viewed the two as dependent, and femininity was often seen as the absence of masculinity. Bem not only views the two as independent dimensions, but she also views both as positive domains of behavior. The inventory consists of twenty masculine personality characteristics (e.g., ambitious, self-reliant, independent, assertive) and twenty feminine characteristics (e.g., affectionate, gentle, understanding, sensitive to the needs of others). In two studies Bem carefully tested the behavior of college students. Approximately one third of them had been classified masculine, one third feminine, and one third androgynous. The first of these (Bem and Lenney, 1976) attempted to determine whether masculine men and feminine women actively avoid activities that are stereotyped as more appropriate for the other sex. That is, will masculine men avoid feminine tasks (ironing cloth napkins and mixing baby formula) and will feminine women avoid masculine tasks (nailing two boards together or oiling squeaky hinges on a metal box)? The answer is Yes, but androgynous individuals move back and forth between these stereotyped roles with apparent ease. Next Bem (1975) tested the assumption that masculine individuals would be more independent and feminine individuals more nurturant. This turned out to be true, but of even more interest was the fact that androgynous individuals were capable of being both nurturant and independent.

With some justification Bem (in press) argues that androgynous individuals have the best of both possible worlds. When it is appropriate, they can be independent, but they can also be nurturant when that behavior is appropriate. Thus stereotyped, restrictive roles seem not to be the most fulfilling ones that we, as individuals, can undertake.

Many psychologists have argued that the individual's sex role is the most salient of the many social roles played. Lott (1978) investigated three related but independent questions concerning sex roles. First, she was concerned with the differences and similarities in the behavior of 4-year-old boys and girls. Secondly, she wanted to know how well observations of behavior match adult expectations of gender differences. Finally, she wanted to know whether children who behave less in accord with sex-role expectations can be distinguished from those who behave more in accord with sex-role expectations on the basis of situations in which they play, their fluency with ideas, and parents scores on sex typing.

Two samples of New Zealand 4-year-old kindergarten children were closely observed and their behavior noted. Furthermore, adults, both teachers and parents, rated either the children who had been observed or "most girls" and "most boys." In addition parents of the observed children completed a sex-typing scale for their child.

Direct observation revealed that girls played in more places than boys, related to adults more than twice as much as they did to boys and played indoors more than outdoors. Furthermore, the girls played at solitary activities more than boys did. Lott suggests that this latter result may occur because women are expected to be "loners," staying at home and observing the social activity of husbands and children from a distance. It is interesting to note, however, that even though there were differences between the behavior of boys and girls, there were far more similarities.

When adults were surveyed concerning their expectations of how most boys and most girls of this age acted, there were 18 areas of behavior in which adults expected boys and girls to differ. For example, adults expected boys more than girls to disobey adults, show off with both peers and adults, and argue with peers. Girls, on the other hand, were expected to cling to adults, ask help from adults, and show affection to peers more than boys. It is interesting to note, however, that actual behavioral differences appeared on only 5 of the 18 predicted behaviors. Boys and girls don't act as differently as adults expect them to.

The children's behavior was then compared to the adult's ideology about how they would behave. This resulted in girls and boys who behaved as expected and those who did not. Then the children were compared on a test of creativity, the Uses Test. Each child was shown six common objects and asked what they could be used for and then encouraged to give more uses until they could think of no more. The number of uses provided for a common object has been used as a measure of creativity that is independent of intelligence.

The children who behaved in more gender-inappropriate ways scored higher on the test of creativity than did those who behaved more in accordance with sex-role expectations. This probably occurs because they have experienced a greater range of situations than do children who are confined to sex-role stereotyped situations. This, of course, is consistent with Bem's work on psychological androgyny.

Reference

Lott, B. Behavioral concordance with sex-role ideology related to play areas, creativity, and parental sex typing of children. *Journal of Personality and Social Psychology,* 1978, *36,* 1087–110.

THE DEVELOPMENT OF SEX-ROLE IDENTITY

Possibly I have reversed the order of things by discussing Bem's work before I discuss how individuals arrive at a masculine or feminine role. However, since it seems that androgynous individuals may live fuller, more productive lives, I wanted you to keep Bem's research in mind as we discussed the development of sex-role identity.

There are certain biological differences between men and women; body build, sexual characteristics, and hormonal differences are probably the most important ones. Some researchers (Breverman, Klaiber, Kobayaski, and Vogel, 1968) suggest that men and women differ in certain cognitive abilities because of these physiological and hormonal differences. However, the majority of evidence does not support such an interpretation (Maccoby and Jacklin, 1974; Nisbett and Temoshok, 1976; Parlee, 1972). The evidence that has accumulated so far lends far more support to the idea that girls and boys are socialized differently and behave differently because they have been taught to behave differently.

Learning Sex Roles

In Canada and the United States, girls learn different behaviors are acceptable than boys do. Traditionally girls have learned to be nurturant, obedient, and passive, whereas boys are taught to be achievement-oriented, self-reliant, and aggressive. Undoubtedly things are changing. The Canadian Bill of Rights, the U.S. Civil Rights Act of 1964, and Title IX of the U.S. Education Act Amendments of 1972 have given legal status to the women's movement. Prior and subsequent to such legal activities, however, have been agitation on the part of women to be treated fairly and equally. Whether there is a desire on the part of both women and men to be treated *identically* is another question. Ultimately the question of how women are treated is undoubtedly intertwined with the socialization process. The roles girls learn to fill and the roles boys learn to fill will have a lasting impact on how women and men are treated as adults.

There are several viewpoints about how sex-roles are learned. Social learning theory, however, is probably the most viable theory to explain sex-role identity and the one I will emphasize. Whereas some sex-role identity will be learned by the child because parents reinforce specific behaviors, imitation is a far more important variable. (See Chapter 1.) According to Bandura (1971, 1974) and Mischel (1966, 1968), children learn appropriate sex-role behavior by watching others. For example, if a girl sees her mother fulfilling a role that emphasizes nurturance, obedience, and passiveness, the girl will learn the same traits. It is not necessary to reward the child for these behaviors, the child will learn them by observation.

If this viewpoint is correct, and there is strong evidence that it is, then the changing roles women adopt will change the socialization of future generations of children. The mere observance of the mother working outside of the home, being involved in the decision making, and being an equal partner with the father will change the roles girls learn. By the same reasoning, boys will more often see a father who is not the sole breadwinner and dominant force in the family, who is involved in nurturing the children, and so forth, and will learn these roles by observation. Draper (in press) has provided evidence for an analogous shift in sex roles among desert people in South Africa. The group has recently shifted from a nomadic existence, in which men and women shared equally in small-game hunting and food gathering, to a more agrarian way of life. Duties are now divided between men and women, with the men raising crops and caring for cattle while the women take care of immediate

This teacher models many roles in these first graders' lives; one of them is helping the children learn sex-role identity.

food and shelter needs. There are now different socialization pressures on girls and boys.

Sex and Attribution

Deaux (1976) has pointed out that sex-role attribution is important in three areas. First sex is important as a characteristic of the object being evaluated. When an observer is called upon to interpret or causally attribute the behavior of an actor, two types of information are important; the observed behavior itself and the expectancies that the observer has for that behavior.

Sex-role stereotype research has clearly isolated two distinct clusters of traits that are seen as distinguishing men from women. The first cluster contains traits that reflect competence, such as independence, competitiveness, objectiveness, dominance, and so forth. Men are seen as having these traits whereas women are not. The second cluster of traits emphasizes warmth and expressiveness, such as tactfulness, gentleness, and the ability to express tender feelings. Women are seen as possessing these characteristics whereas men are not.

If performance by an actor is consistent with the expectations for that actor, such behavior will be attributed to a stable cause. In most performance situations the stable attribution will be to ability or skill. Performance by an actor that is inconsistent with the expectations for that actor will be attributed to a temporary cause, many times to luck. Thus, the woman who is successful in a field demanding masculine stereotype characteristics will be considered lucky by many observers.

Second, sex is also an important variable of the person making the attribution. Attributions made by male and female actors generally show distinct differences, with females holding lower expectations for their performance than do males. These lower expectations serve as a self-stereotype. In attributing success to skill or luck, it would

THE TIMES—THEY ARE A-CHANGING?

We know we live in a time of social change that sometimes bewilders us. No one seems to uphold the valued ideas of the past, while some of the more detrimental attitudes never seem to go away. For example, honesty, pride in craftsmanship, and concern for others seem to be declining. Graft, corruption in high places, and deteriorating pride in an individual's work are becoming more characteristic of American and Canadian societies.

One area of social change that has been particularly perplexing has been the roles of women and, more particularly, how they are evaluated. What has been extremely distressing to women has been that even other women see the skills that women have developed to be less demanding than masculine skills. Goldberg (1968, p. 30) goes even further and says: "Women seem to think that men are better at everything—including elementary school teaching and dialectics!" Work published subsequent to Goldberg's experiment, which found that female college students gave more favorable ratings to articles purportedly written by males than by females, has not been unanimous about this conclusion.

Levenson, Burford, Bonno, and Davis (1975) found that women did not rate an article written by a male more favorably than one written by a female. When they rated political science essays rather than articles, females assigned significantly higher grades to essays written by women.

Moore (1978) analyzed men and women's evaluations of men and women authors in a real-life setting. *Contemporary Psychology* is a journal of book reviews and is, therefore, a naturally occurring place where men and women reviewers evaluate men and women authors. One hundred eighty book reviews were analyzed. Half of the books had been reviewed by male reviewers and half by female reviewers. Within each of these two groups one third of the books had been written by females, one third by males, and one third were multiple-authored books with at least one male and one female author. Several measures were taken, but we will concern ourselves with only one, the positive things said about the book by the reviewer.

Men were more positive toward male-authored books than they were toward female-authored ones, with the mixed-sex-authored books falling in between the male and female ones. If Goldberg was correct and continues to be correct 10 years later, we would also expect females to see more positive elements in male-authored books when compared to female-authored ones. However, this is not what Moore found. Female reviewers saw more positive elements in the female-authored books and less positive elements in the male-authored books with the mixed-authored ones falling in an intermediate position. Simply stated, male reviewers preferred male-authored books and female reviewers preferred female-authored books.

Females need to view their roles as demanding as male roles and to see themselves as capable as males in all roles before the subtle elements of sex-discrimination are abolished. As long as females see themselves as inferior in role or ability to males, it will be difficult or impossible to achieve equal rights for women. Moore's study seems to indicate that at least in one profession, psychology, women are viewing the work of other women in a more positive light. This is but a halting first step to sexual equality.

References

Goldberg, P. Are some women prejudiced against women? *Trans-Action*, 1968, *5*, (5), 28–30.

Levenson, H., B. Burford, B. Bonno, and L. Davis. Are women still prejudiced against women? A replication and extension of Goldberg's study. *Journal of Psychology*, 1975, *89*, 67–71.

Moore, M. Discrimination or favoritism? Sex bias in book reviews. *American Psychologist*, 1978, *33*, 936–938.

seem that women would expect success less often of themselves than men do and be more likely to attribute it to luck. As Deaux points out, this assumption has generally been borne out in research. Thus other people tend to attribute success by women in "masculine" areas to luck and women do the same thing to themselves.

The third area in which sex-role attribution is important is the sex linkage of a task. Bem has noted that the androgynous individual is comfortable with both masculine and feminine tasks. However, the general perception of sex-linked tasks is that those labeled feminine are easier than those labeled masculine (Taynor and Deaux, 1975). Thus, as Deaux points out, if feminine tasks are viewed as easier, they should also take less ability, and research indicates that such tasks are perceived as encompassing less skill.

This short discussion of attribution in sex-role questions points out that women are quite likely to be viewed as less able than men. If a woman succeeds at a masculine task, generally her success will be attributed to luck rather than skill. Not only is this attribution made by men, but by women whose self-stereotype is one of lower expectation. Finally, tasks in which women excel are seen as easier than those in which men excel. Thus, the deck seems to be stacked against women. Only as sex-role stereotypes are changed, by both men and women, can women's achievement, or more precisely the perception of women's achievement, equal that of men. We will have occasion to return to the subject of women and achievement later in this chapter.

Comment

We are living in an era of social change, and such times are exciting. Traditional roles are being set aside and people are being treated more equally. It is true that women are still discriminated against and there are gross inadequacies in Canada and the United States in the way women are treated. Changes are occurring, however primarily because women have demanded that they occur. To be sure, there are some men who have encouraged the movement toward equality of the sexes, but it is safe to say that they have not been in the majority. If women are paid equal wages for equal work and have the same opportunities for advancement, then many men fear the added competition for wages and prestigious positions. And yet a society that uses its full potential, rather than placing severe restrictions on one or both sexes, is more likely to be a productive, stable, and long-lasting society.

Another way of approaching the possible benefits to society is to consider the possibilities of the infusion of traditional male roles with traditional female characteristics, and vice versa. For example, if the nurturant characteristic of females was introduced into business, politics, and so forth, there would be profound effects for the better, I believe, in these areas. If, on the other hand, the male characteristic of self-reliance were introduced into the areas that are traditionally female, there would be equally beneficial results. But, of course, this is basically Bem's argument when she says that psychologically androgynous persons are more fulfilled than masculine or feminine persons. Bem's argument differs from the type of social order many people have been advocating by emphasizing the need for these characteristics, both male and female, in individuals.

Dependency has typically been seen as a motive that encompasses a number of desires—to be nurtured, comforted, protected, or aided by others or to be emotionally close to or accepted by others. Generally speaking, the dependency motive has a rather small target class of people; parents, teachers, or friends. A very young child may be quite specific in his or her dependency, wanting to be comforted by mother, but not by an older brother or sister, a playmate, or a nursery school teacher. Dependent behavior comes in numerous forms; seeking approval, assistance, attention, contact, recognition, or reassurance, resisting separation from or soliciting affection and support from adults. There is no direct relationship between the dependency motive and dependency behavior.

Within Western societies and more specifically within Canada and the United States, dependency is not a straightforward motivational situation. A young boy may very well be pushed toward independence by his parents while he is still desirous of being dependent. On the other hand, a young girl whose dependency motive is not so strong will be encouraged to continue to be dependent. Of course, such views among parents are undergoing change, but they have not changed entirely. Conflict can arise when the child's dependency motive clashes with his or her parents' desires.

A newborn child is exceptionally dependent when compared with the newborns of other species. Parents in Western cultures, usually begin the socialization process of teaching the child to be autonomous during the second year. Obviously, the child is still highly dependent upon his or her parents and the first target of the child's dependency is the mother, whose absence is frequently upsetting to the child.

For example, when they are with their mothers, children one year old, or slightly older, explore and play freely. If a stranger enters the room while the mother is present, the child is not terribly upset, although he or she may play somewhat nearer to the mother and explore less freely. If the mother leaves, however, dependency behavior increases. Maccoby and Masters (1970, p. 102) point out: "The amount of exploratory and play behavior was considerably greater, and the amount of crying considerably less when the mother was present than when the child was either alone or with the stranger."

A process of what Mussen, Conger, and Kagan (1974) call "spontaneous progressive detachment" begins after the first year. For those of you who have not had a developmental psychology course, it may be of some interest to briefly describe a careful short-term longitudinal study of children, so that you may have a better understanding of how psychologists can make statements such as the one in the last sentence.

Maccoby and Feldman (1972) observed children at the ages of 2, $2\frac{1}{2}$, and 3. The observations were made in an unfamiliar room, in the pressence of a stranger, and in a reunion with their mother. When the mother left the room, intensity of the child's protest decreased between the ages of 2 and 3, with the 3-year-olds being much less likely to cry when their mother's left. In addition, the 3-year-old's crying was much more likely to abate when they were soothed by a stranger than was the crying of a younger child similarly treated. The proportion of 3-year-olds who asked for their mother after she left and when they were with a stranger was also lower for the older children. Finally, in the unfamiliar room, remaining near the mother and touching her decreased with age. You should not, however, think of three-year-olds as terribly independent, because even they retreated toward their mothers when a stranger entered the room. At two the children interacted with the stranger primarily when the mother was present. By three years of age, the child did not need to have his or her mother present to maintain interaction with a stranger.

The preceding study may be interpreted to mean that the child's dependency on his or her mother is decreasing, but there is evidence to suggest that the child's dependency is changing its target. Heathers (1955) reports that two-year-olds are more likely to be dependent upon the teacher in a nursery school, whereas by four years of age, it is more common for the child to be dependent on peers. In addition, the form that dependency takes may change with age. A comparison of 2-, 4-, and 5-years-olds by Hartup (1963) indicates that 2-year-olds seek reassurance and positive attention from adults more frequently. Thus, it may be inferred from such studies that seeking reassurance and positive attention are more mature behaviors than clinging and seeking affection.

Dependency itself is a fairly stable characteristic, but it may be apparent that situational factors affect it rather dramatically. I have already noted that the target of dependent behaviors changes from parent or teacher to peers. In addition to the target of dependency changing, stress situations and isolation from social contact, or reduced social contact, can increase dependency behavior or the type of such behavior. More specifically when children were in an anxiety situation, more immature forms of dependency behavior increased (Rosenthal, 1967a, b). Relative social isolation tends to increase dependency behavior (Gewirtz, 1956; Sears, 1963). Obviously, from a social psychological point of view, the importance of situational factors should not be minimized. Again and again we come upon the recurring theme that social psychology studies the individual interacting with the environment. Here, at a very early age, the importance of situational factors upon a motive and behaviors that are primarily considered as intrapersonal variables is apparent.

The development of independence is, according to Mussen, Conger, and Kagan (1974, p. 557) "central to any discussion of the tasks of adolescence... An Adolescent's failure to resolve the conflict between a continuing dependence and the newer demands (and privileges) of independence will lead to difficulties in most other areas as well." It is seldom simple to establish true independence from parents because it is likely that the motivations and rewards for both dependence and independence are strong, which leads to conflict. On the one hand, parents very much want their children to be able "to stand on their own two feet" but feel hurt, ignored, or neglected when they are not consulted about or allowed to make important decisions for the child. The child, on the other hand, very much wants to make his or her own decisions, but may not want to forego the monetary or emotional support that dependence affords. To complicate the whole matter, even very independent children need emotional support from parents, particularly in times of crises.

The problem of independence is greatly compounded by society in Canada and the United States. The individual is expected to make enormous strides toward independence between the onset of puberty and adulthood. This, of course, occurs during the time that there are great hormonal changes occurring in the individual and great conflict over and around sexual behavior. Many primitive societies had *rites of passage* in which a child performed some act, or some ceremony was carried out that marked the change from childhood to adulthood. If adolescents look to the formalized codes of our societies, they are likely to be even more confused. Different states and provinces have different laws concerning the legal age to drink, drive a car, or vote. In the United States until the early 70s it was possible for a young man to be called upon to fight a war while he was considered too young to vote for or against the persons who authorized that war.

And yet most individuals do achieve a measure of independence. Obviously some achieve more whereas others achieve less, and their measure of independence influences their social interactions. A person who is highly independent of his or her parents will act quite differently than one who, even at an advanced age, requires parental approval for most of his or her actions. Most of societal interactions are based upon relatively independent status with regard to parents, but a rather large variation in the amount of dependence on peers. Remember the Asch study on conformity described in Chapter 2? One of the elements Asch (1952) discusses is that some of the subjects remained completely independent; that is, on none of the trials did they go along with the incorrect majority. At the other extreme, some of the subjects went with the majority on every judgment. I can make no comment or even speculations about the individuals who did or did not conform with respect to the specifics of their dependency motive. It is, however, interesting to note that a process of socialization, such as dependency, may have such a profound effect on conformity.

Moral Development

Probably the most important socialization process from society's point of view is moral development. Psychoanalytic theory refers to it as the development of the superego; other theorists and conventional wisdom have labeled it *conscience development*. Whatever it is called, the process by which the child acquires standards and beliefs about moral behavior is vital to a smoothly functioning society. Whereas it is true that different societies have different moral standards, it is necessary for people in a society to agree upon acceptable norms of conduct with respect to what is right and what is wrong. The reason for a basic agreement concerning moral behavior within a society is a practical one. If most people in a society accept most of the society's standards and obey them, then society can function. However, if a majority of the people don't accept the standards and disobey them, society comes to a grinding halt. For example, consider the problem of policing our laws, which are basically a codification of our society's moral standards. In other words, society has agreed, among other things, that individuals should not kill, rob, or do physical harm to each other. The vast majority of the citizens of Canada and United States agree and willingly obey the laws. The police are necessary to do two things: first to put some teeth into the accepted norms, and second, to apprehend those who violate the norms. Imagine the chaos that would result in society if most of the people in that society disagreed with these three norms and went around killing, robbing, or hurting others. Society would cease to function and we would have a completely different life style than we now have. This section is concerned with how the child develops the moral behavior that is the cornerstone of society.

According to Parke (1969, p. 507),

Discussions of moral development can be conveniently divided into three parts, behavioral, affective, and cognitive aspects of morality. The behavioral aspect has generally referred to the child's ability to resist temptation in the absence of external surveillance. The affective aspect focuses on the emotional reaction of the child to transgression. The existence of internalized norms is inferred from emotional reactions such as guilt which may follow violation of these standards. Much of the research in this area has been influenced by psychoanalytic theory. The third approach to moral development has been judgmental or cognitive; the stress has been on tracing developmentally children's use and interpretation of rules of judging the correctness of behavior in various situations involving moral conflict. Piaget's pioneering studies are the main inspiration for research into the judgmental aspects of morality.

LEARNING AND MORAL DEVELOPMENT

A number of researchers have reported that variables which effect learning have an influence on moral development. For example, Walters, Parke, and Crane (1965) report that punishment can influence children's resistance to temptation, but the timing of the punishment is crucial. Punishment delivered after a deviant response sequence is less effective in controlling behavior than punishment delivered at the initiation of the sequence. Aronfreed (1965) reported a study similar to Walters et al. (1965) in which he provided a verbal explanation for not handling a taboo toy at the same time the offenders were punished. This cognitive explanation increased response inhibition in the children and, more importantly, increased the effectiveness of the punishment that was delivered after the deviant response sequence. Thus, we see an example of a cognitive variable added to a behavioral one that increases the effectiveness of the behavioral variable. This is entirely consistent and to be expected if, as suggested at the end of Chapter 1, the most fruitful theoretical course seems to be one that takes both cognitive and learning variables into account. Field studies have supported the general observation that the combination of cognitive and learning variables is important. For example Gleuck and Gleuck (1950) reported that there is a positive correlation between the maternal use of reasoning and the development of conscience in children.

Mischel (1958, 1961, 1966, 1974) has studied an individual differences variable, the willingness to delay gratification, as a determinant of resistance to temptation for more than two decades. This variable, which incorporates cognitive, learning, and an individual differences approach to the study of moral development, is both intriguing and an excellent model for studying a difficult process. Mischel (1976) summarizes the variety of complex behaviors that are related to delay of gratification. For example, children who choose to wait for their rewards tended to exhibit higher social responsibility, cheat less, to be slower in yielding to temptation, and to a lesser degree to be somewhat brighter and more concerned about achievement. Not surprisingly, Mischel reports that delay of gratification differs radically across cultures and increases with age.

Mischel has long advocated considering the interaction of the individual and the situation, which is certainly not a new view. Hartshorne and May (1928) were among the first investigators to give explicit recognition to situational factors in the development of moral behavior. They argued that different situations elicit differing proportions of individuals yielding to temptations and that consistencies in demand behavior across situations were due mainly to the similarity of external cues in the situations. Certainly such factors as the risk of detection and the attractiveness of the incentives (situational factors) are important, but they do not seem to account for all differences in resisting temptation. Mischel has also emphasized the personal characteristics of the individual, a necessary element in the equation.

PSYCHOANALYTIC APPROACH TO MORAL DEVELOPMENT

Traditionally, the same end product—development of a conscience or superego—has been important in the study of resistance to temptation and the response to transgression. High resistance to temptation was expected from a person with a well-developed conscience, and when transgression did occur, severe guilt was expected to occur. However, more recent research has shown that these two indices, resistance to temptation and guilt following transgression have different antecedents and are not highly correlated (Parke, 1969).

For example, Hoffman and Saltzstein (1967) compared three different parental disciplinary practices that are associated with a highly developed guilt reaction following transgression. The three types of parental discipline were (1) power-assertative discipline, in which parents use punishment and withdrawal of material things; (2) love withdrawal, whereby the parent gives direct but nonphysical expression of disapproval; and (3) induction, in which the parent focuses upon the painful consequences of the child's act for parents and others. The use of induction as a disciplinary device was highly related to the presence of guilt following a violation as well as to other standards of moral development, such as internalized moral judgments, acceptance of responsibility, confession, and consideration for other children. Power assertion, however, appeared to be negatively related to indices of moral development, whereas love withdrawal produced few significant relationships.

This approach of assessing the impact of parental disciplinary procedures is, of course, quite compatible with the psychoanalytic focus upon the virtual immutability of early childhood experiences. According to this view, the early childhood years and the experiences contained in them are potent, if not absolute, determiners of adult behavior. Altering behavior at a later date is extremely difficult and is done only by long and extensive analysis. With respect to moral development, once the superego has developed, only by great effort is it possible to change it.

COGNITIVE MORAL DEVELOPMENT

The third approach to moral development has been on the judgmental or cognitive aspects of morality. The work of Jean Piaget into cognitive development has been an impetus to the study of developmental psychology in general. In fact, Piaget's concept of the stages of cognitive development is one of the major forces in developmental psychology, if not the major force with respect to moral development. Piaget's (1948) *The Moral Judgment of the Child* has been responsible for much of the research into morality. According to Piaget, there are two clear-cut stages of moral development, the heteronomous and the autonomous stages. In the heteronomous stage the child's understanding of moral rules is limited because of two defects in cognitive functioning. First, the child is unable to distinguish between subjective and objective phenomena and therefore views adult rules as fixed *external* realities. Second, the child confuses his or her own perspective with that of other persons. The first of these defects Piaget labels "realism" and the second "egocentrism," and together they result in a failure to regard moral rules as relative to various individuals and purposes. Until about seven years of age, the approximate dividing line between the two stages, the heteronomous child judges the severity of an act in terms of the amount of physical damage, rather than in terms of the intentionality of the act. Only in the autonomous stage does intentionality replace the consequences of the act as a basis for judgment. For example, a child in the heteronomous stage considers the accidental breaking of 15 cups as deserving with greater punishment than the intentional breaking of one cup, whereas the reverse is true in the autonomous stage. Research that has stemmed from Piaget's theory of moral stages has produced only limited support for Piaget's two stages theory (Kohlberg 1963b), and Kohlberg (1958, 1963a) has postulated six stages that are based on children's reasoning responses to hypothetical moral conflicts.

Kohlberg's Theory of Moral Stages. Kohlberg differs from Piaget in viewing moral development as an extended and complex process rather than a single step from heteronomous to autonomous morality. Additionally, Kohlberg's analysis assumes that the passage from one stage to another involves a change in the modes of thought that were associated with an earlier stage.

Kohlberg's six stages of moral development, which are actually three levels of morality, with each level composed of two types are these: "(1) Punishment and obedience orientation, (2) naïve instrumental hedonism (3) Good-boy morality of maintaining good relations, approval of others (4) Authority-maintaining morality (5) Morality of contract and democratically accepted law and (6) Morality of individual principles of conscience" (Kohlberg, 1963a, pp. 13–14).

Table 4–1 recapitulates each of the six stages and adds a good deal of explanation to the specific stages. Kohlberg felt that his stages define the actual sequence normally followed by an individual and that it was invariant. By this he means that attainment of a higher mode of thought depends upon attaining the previous one; that is, a person cannot skip from Stage 1 to Stage 4 or even from Stage 2 to Stage 4. Attainment of a next higher stage of thought requires a reorganization of the preceding stages' mode of thought.

Kohlberg determines a person's developmental stage by using nine hypothetical conflict stories and corresponding sets of probing questions (Kohlberg, 1958). The following is an example:

In Europe, a woman was near death from a special kind of cancer. There was one drug that the doctors thought might save her. It was a form of radium that a druggist in the same town had recently discovered. The drug was expensive to make, but the druggist was charging ten times what the drug cost him to make. He paid $200 for the radium and charged $2,000 for a small dose of the drug. The sick woman's husband, Heinz, went to everyone he knew to borrow the money, but he could only get about $1,000, which is half of what it cost. He told

Level 1. Premoral (or Preconventional)

Stage 1. Punishment and obedience orientation. The dominant motivation in this stage is to avoid punishment and to defer to power. Rules of conduct, which derive force from those who support them, are concrete and mainly prohibitory and apply to some but not all people. This stage is much like Piaget's heteronomous stage in which the seriousness of a violation depends on the amount of damage done.

Stage 2. Naïve instrumental hedonism. The motivation in this stage is to satisfy one's own desires and the desires of other persons the individual likes or loves. Much of the concern for others is involved with reciprocity; "You scratch my back and I'll scratch yours." To some extent, although not a very great one, intentions are considered in determining the seriousness of a violation (as in Piaget's autonomous stage).

Level 2. Morality of Conventional Rule Conformity

Stage 3. Good-boy (or good-girl) morality of maintaining good relations, approval of others. The motivation in Stage 3 is to win the approval of others and this is done primarily by doing what helps them. Actions are primarily judged by intention and the goal is to be thought of as a nice person.

Stage 4. Authority—maintaining morality. The motivation of this stage is to established authority and its rules, usually the law. The social order is more important than an individual's egoistic desires and must be maintained.

Level 3. Morality of Self-accepted Moral Principles

Stage 5. Morality of contract and democratically accepted law. There are values and principles that are valid beyond the authority of the persons or groups holding them. In a sense, society's values are right, but there is a further understanding that society can err and there are ways to change society's values within the system (election, and so on).

Stage 6. Morality of individual principles of conscience. In this stage the self-chosen ethical principles of one's own conscience guide the individual. Proscriptive concrete rules, like the Ten Commandments, are not the order of the day, rather a general universal value, such as "Love your neighbor as yourself" guides conduct. Although the conscience is the guide, this level of moral development must be carefully considered and be based on principles upon which everyone can act, and which are logical and comprehensive. Far from being an easy stage to reach, this stage is exceedingly difficult to attain. Examples of this sort of moral thinking are found in Lehmann's (1963) contextual ethics, which emphasizes the freedom and responsibilities of love, and in Rawls' (1971) principle that goodness is the greatest personal liberty that is compatible with equal liberty for others.

the druggist that his wife was dying and asked him to sell cheaper or let him pay later. But the druggist said: "No, I discovered the drug and I'm going to make money from it." So Heinz got desperate and broke into the man's store to steal the drug for his wife. Should the husband have done that?

Remember, Kohlberg maintains that it is necessary to pass through each prior stage before the next one can be reached, that is, that stages cannot be skipped. Turiel (1966) provided an interesting experimental test of Kohlberg's hypothesis. First he determined the stage of moral development that was presently dominant for each of his subjects. Then he divided them into three experimental groups and a control group. The experimental groups were exposed to moral reasoning in individual role-playing situations with an adult experimenter. One group was exposed to moral reasoning one stage below their own, one was exposed to moral reasoning one stage above their own, while the moral reasoning the third group was exposed to was two stages above their own.

The results of Turiel's study basically supported Kohlberg's position. As Turiel (1966, p. 6) said,

> The findings support Kohlberg's scheme of stages as representing a developmental continuum, in which each individual passes through the stages in a prescribed sequence. If the stages do form a developmental sequence, then it should be easier for subjects to understand and utilize concepts that are directly above the dominant stage than concepts that are two stages above.
>
> The Developmental interpretation is also strengthened by the finding that subjects assimilated the next higher stage more readily than the lower stage, even though they could understand the concepts of the lower stage as well as, if not better than, those of the higher stage. Hence, we have an indication that the attainment of a stage of thought involves a reorganization of the preceding modes of thought, with an integration of each previous stage with, rather than an addition to, new elements of the later stages.

These results and others (for example, see Tapp and Levine, 1972) combined with Kohlberg's own work, lend impressive support to a cognitively based theory of moral development. Turiel's results, which indicate that a child can better understand the next higher stage of development than the next lower one makes clear that when a higher stage of development is reached, the stage(s) which has been passed through is less available to the child than is the next higher stage, because it is necessary for the individual to reorganize his or her thoughts to deal with each succeeding stage of development. Thus, going back to a previous stage may be abhorrent to the individual because the present stage, in effect, rejects the rules, precepts, and ways of reasoning that were necessary in an earlier stage. Kohlberg's stages, although they are invariant in the sense that one must pass through each of them, are not invariant in the same sense that, say, mathematics, is. You need not reject the idea that $2 + 2 = 4$. Moral development is somewhat different from other sorts of development.

Comment

Socialization is an important process in understanding the individual in the social psychological equation—that the interaction of the individual and his or her environment are of paramount importance in understanding social behavior. The role of society in socialization should also not be ignored. Note that society is the entity that helps determine which sorts of socializing behaviors will be taught to or instilled in the child. What the child learns about sexual behavior, dependency, and morals is very much a function of what society dictates. It is only in the rarefied atmosphere of Kohlberg's fifth and sixth stages of moral development that society's right to dictate behavior is even questioned. In keeping with the spirit of our discussion; "Do you think that's right?"

The children are first graders
and are approaching, or in, a
critical period of moral development. The second graders
are further along in their moral
development, and the sixth
graders are moving into other
stages of development.

Personality

With respect to the social interactions an individual has and will have, personality is one of the basic determiners of (1) the types of people with which he or she will interact, (2) the quality of such interactions and, (3) to a great extent the quality of life the individual lives. It is, however, somewhat easier to enumerate the effects of personality than it is to tell you exactly what personality is, that is, to define it. However, for our purposes, I think the following serves well (Lamberth, Rappaport, and Rappaport, 1978, p. 6). "Personality is made up of those characteristics each person possesses which determine his or her cognitive, emotional and overt behavior." To what extent does this definition narrow our view of the individual? The answer is "very little," and it may even expand it, because cognitive, emotional, and overt behavior covers just about everything you do; whether it be thinking, acting (rationally, or irrationally), or feeling. The definition of personality I have chosen to emphasize is broad, because the field of personality is itself broad. This section of the book will treat personality primarily as it relates to social behavior, which is, after all, what this book is all about.

Personality Theory

Personality theory is in the grand tradition of the study of personality. Probably because of the influence of Freud, who developed an elegant, full-blown personality theory, theorists in this area until recently have felt it necessary to develop theories on a rather grand scale—theories that attempt to explain all of human behavior. It is possible to differentiate theories on the basis of those whose major aim is to explain behavior rather than to predict it, and most personality theories are those that attempt to explain rather than predict. That is, most personality theories explain a behavior after it has occurred a whole lot better than they can predict what someone will do in a given situation. It is, of course, scientifically more desirable to predict than to explain, and typically, predictive theories are developed hand-in-glove with empirical research into the area. Many of the best-known theories of personality were developed not in a research context, but in a clinical setting. For example, Freud's psychoanalytic theory was developed in the context of seeing patients in private practice in Vienna. Even though he was not depending solely on his rational powers, which were awesome in their own right, the observations he made and the data he collected were selected more to support his theory than to test it. In fact, it was not Freud himself who put psychoanalysis to the empirical test, but his followers, and there are many who would argue that this particular theory has not met the empirical test very well.

Fortunately, we need not deal with all the personality theorists or even a representative group of them. There are a number of books which do that quite adequately (Bishoff, 1970; Hall and Lindzey, 1978).

Because psychologists are working with a variety of constructs, most of which are unobservable, the problem of measurement is of crucial importance and psychologists have used a number of measurement techniques. To return to an earlier example, there are well-defined and accepted standards for measurement of such physical characteristics as height and weight. But, how do you measure aggression, or attraction, or altruism? There have been a number of ways worked out and throughout the course of this book you will see different techniques for such measurement. But consider the problem faced by the psychologist who wants to know how aggressive an individual is. One way to determine an individual's aggressiveness is to observe how often he or she performs an aggressive act toward someone else. For example, you might follow a person (let us assume a male for our example) and determine his aggressiveness by observing how many times he hits someone else. Although this may be a reasonable way to proceed, except for the fact that it takes an enormous amount of time, you might also misclassify certain actions. What would you do if he pats someone on the back? Such an action falls under the classification of hitting, but it may also be a friendly act. Or what of the times the individual doesn't hit someone, but merely shouts a long string of obscenities at the other person? As you can begin to see, the problem of personality assessment is a thorny one.

Psychologists have developed a number of assessment devices, and for ease of classifying them, they may be divided into categories on the basis of the directness of measurement. As usual, this book will stress those that are most used by, and most useful to, social psychologists.

PROJECTIVE TECHNIQUES

Projective techniques are the least direct measuring devices that psychologists use, because they attempt to tap elements of the unconscious mind. By definition, the unconscious mind is unknown to the individual: It is the repository for things forgotten or things that make the individual sufficiently uncomfortable so that they are relegated to the unconscious mind. This may be done through repression, reaction formation, denial, or some other defense mechanism (cf. Page, 1975, for an excellent discussion of these defense mechanisms). Projective techniques were developed to tap the unconscious mind, and the two most popular of these are the Rorschach Inkblots and the Thematic Apperception Test (TAT) (Murray, 1943). These tests are called projective because they are attempts to get the individual to reveal or project what is going on deep inside his or her mind.

As an example, the TAT consists of a series of ambiguous pictures, and the individual is told to tell or write a story about each picture. This theoretically allows the elements of the unconscious mind to surface in the series of stories the individual produces, and a skilled examiner supposedly can determine what is occurring in the individual's unconscious mind.

To say the least, projective techniques are the subject of great disagreement. They are not very reliable. And the word *reliable* is used here in a special, technical sense as applied to a test. In psychological measurement, a test is *reliable* if it gives a stable, fairly dependable measure. Typically, this is ascertained by testing an individual once and then testing the same person at some future time. For example, if I gave you the TAT today and then gave it to you again next month, and found that in both instances the test labeled you as an achievement-oriented person, I would have some evidence that the test was giving a stable, dependable measure and thus was reliable. If, on the other hand, the test labeled you as an aggressive person on one administration, and a passive one on the next administration, there would be evidence that it was unreliable. After many individuals are tested and retested it is possible to obtain a precise estimate of a test's reliability; and projective tests are not highly reliable. This should really come as no surprise, since they were developed to tap the unconscious mind, which is typically unknown even to the individual being tested. Therefore, projective techniques are more useful in clinical settings in which they can be combined with other sorts of measuring instruments.

OBJECTIVE MEASURES

Objective personality tests are in appearance much like objective quizzes you take in your classes, except that they attempt to determine your personality characteristics, not how much you know. They are tests that have typically been carefully developed by starting with a definition of the characteristic or set of characteristics of interest. Some, like the Taylor Manifest Anxiety Scale (Taylor, 1953), measure just one trait, whereas others, like the Edwards Personal Preference Schedule (Edwards, 1959), measure a whole battery of needs. Some (for example the MMPI (Hathaway and McKinley, 1943) were developed to assess abnormal personality functioning, whereas others (cf. the 16PF; Cattell, Eber, and Tatsuoka, 1970) were developed to assess the functioning of normally behaving individuals. Each test, and there are thousands, vary in both their reliability and validity. *Validity* is another technical term that determines whether a test measures what it purports to measure. For example, if a test supposedly measures anxiety but in fact measures aggression (or any other characteristic), it is not a valid test. To be valid, a test must measure what it is supposed to measure.

Generally speaking, objective tests are more reliable and valid than projective techniques. The reliability aspect should be rather clear to you. A test that is attempting to measure something objectively is more direct in its measurement, and since it need not cut through the subjective nature of the unconscious, it will be,

Taking a test. There are signs of both concentration and anxiety.

generally speaking, more reliable than a projective test. If a characteristic or trait is stable, and most test constructors assume a rather large amount of stability for the traits they are attempting to measure, then an unreliable test cannot be valid. Think about it for a moment. If the trait being measured is stable—meaning that if you've got it today you'll probably have it next week—an unreliable test cannot be valid. Why? Because if the trait is still there but on the second testing the test does not pick it up (which is what happens with an unreliable test) then the test isn't valid.

Objective tests, then, attempt to ask rather directly about the typical ways in which you behave. Because the test constructor is aware of how a great many other people behave who exhibit the trait or traits he or she is interested in, this direct method of asking about how you think, feel and/or act allows a relatively accurate personality description of the individual being tested. It is not perfect, because people sometimes lie, they sometimes bend or stretch the truth a bit, or they simply do not know how they would act or feel in a given situation. There are pitfalls in objective psychological testing, although they are not as severe as those in projective testing. These pitfalls have however, been serious enough to lead to the most direct form of personality measurement.

Behavioral Measures

Behavioral measures of behavior are the most direct form of measurement available, and it is probably safe to say that they are the most reliable and valid measurements. They also are the most costly in terms of time and money and if not carefully done they are subject to great error. The impetus for behavioral measures in personality has come from social learning theorists. These individuals were concerned with the lack of reliability and validity of both projective and objective measures, but even more important, they were convinced that traditional approaches to personality centered too much on the individual and not enough upon the effects of the situation on the individual's behavior. There were a number of persons in this movement including Dollard and Miller (1950), Rotter (1954, 1972), Bandura (1969, 1971), Wolpe (1958), and Krasner and Ullman (1973), but probably the most influential single book was Mischel's (1968) thoughtful analysis of the concept of traits, the way they had been conceived, and his assertion that personality theorists had ignored for too long the vast importance of the situational influences upon behavior.

It is easy to see that such an orientation would emphasize behavioral measures, or at least measures that assess the trait or characteristic in the context of different situations. One of the comments which Mischel makes is that tests of cognitive ability seem to be better predictors of future behavior than are tests of personality traits. One of the reasons for this may be that certain cognitive type tests are, either intentionally or inadvertently, given within the context of the behavior they are ultimately to predict. For example, IQ tests predict school achievement rather well. Note, however, that IQ tests are given in the context of a testing situation and much of school achievement is based upon how well the student does on tests.

Behavioral measures are, in their simplest forms, samples of the behavior being studied or predicted. In the case of intelligence and school achievement, the tests are a sample of test-taking ability. Other behaviors require different sorts of measurement procedures, some of them rather complex. Because it is virtually impossible for a psychologist to follow an individual around observing all of his or her behavior, behavior is often sampled by a variety of persons specifically trained to do so—teachers, family, friends, or the individuals themselves. Of course the information is only as valid and reliable as the observers are in noting the behavior and as the interpreter of the behavior is in interpreting that behavior.

Comment. Assessment or the measurement of behavioral charcteristics is a difficult and tricky business. It is not easy to get an accurate reading on an individual's behavior, yet it is essential if psychological research and treatment are to be successful. In this book we are much more concerned with psychological research than with treatment, thus we are specifically interested in how individual differences on certain personality variables affect social behavior. The remaining pages of this chapter will review three personality characteristics or traits that do influence our social behavior.

Self-concept

One of the more important personality characteristics in social psychology is self-concept. There are several reasons for this state of affairs, of which two warrant comment.

First, and probably foremost, it is necessary for an individual to hold herself or himself in high esteem if she or he is to treat other individuals in a manner that indicates esteem for the other person. To put it another way, it may well be impossible to treat other people any better than we treat ourselves or to hold anyone else in any higher esteem than we hold ourselves. I have no strong empirical evidence for such a view, yet it is one with a long, though at times ignored, history. Jesus Christ made a statement, the first half of which has been greatly publicized and the second half greatly ignored, when he said, "Love your neighbor as yourself." For some reason, religious groups have emphasized the virtue of denying oneself for others. In Chapter 10 we will discuss altruism in some detail and suggest that even the noblest of human actions may hold rewards of its own. I would like to suggest that one reason for the importance of self-concept in social psychology is that a society of people who have a low self-concept may not be a society at all, or may at least be dysfunctional.

The second reason for the use of self-concept in social psychology may, at first glance, seem incredibly mundane. That is, self-esteem is an important personality variable in social psychology because we have a method of measuring it. This may seem mundane, but it decidedly is not. To make use of an unobserved construct, which self-concept obviously is, a psychologist must have a method of pinning it down by measuring it. For example, if you wanted to classify people on the basis of height or weight, you would measure them with a ruler or weigh them on a scale. You wouldn't just say that that person looks kind of tall or that one looks kind of heavy. When working with unobservable variables, such as self-concept, it is even more important to be able to measure the construct. For example, the ludicrousness of looking at someone and deciding that the person is kind of high or kind of low in self-esteem should be obvious to you.

An example of the importance of measurement in dealing with personality constructs is to compare the utility of Freud's three elements of personality structure, with self-concept. Freud's id, ego, and superego are constructs that have been used in an explanatory fashion and are not measurable. They have, therefore, not been nearly so useful as predictive constructs as has self-concept, another unobservable, but this time measurable, construct.

THE DEVELOPMENT OF SELF-CONCEPT

Rogers (1964) emphasized that a healthy personality must develop as the person really is, and yet the demands of socialization do not allow such unbridled development. Basically, the story of the development of self-concept is the story of the resolution of the tension between these two forces.

The first evidence of the tension between the real desires of the individual and the demands of society generally comes with the parents. The parents' own self-concepts and the way they treat their children should influence the child's self-concept. College students who are themselves high in self-acceptance perceived their parents as more loving and less rejecting than did those who were less self-accepting (Medinnus, 1965), and in general, children of mothers who were high in self-concept were themselves higher in self-concept than were children of mothers who were low in self-concept (Samuels, 1970; Schwartz, 1967). As early as secondary school, there is evidence that a student's self-concept is influenced by the teacher's image of the student (Grierson, 1961; Richardson, 1965; Schultz, 1967). Evidence such as this gives strong support to the contention of self-concept theorists that early influence on the child, first by parents, followed by influence from peers, plays an important role in the development of self-concept. One very striking study was carried out by Piers (1972), who selected a group of children who were in therapy and a control group who were not in therapy. As would be expected, the therapy group was lower in self-concept than the nontherapy group, but Piers then had the parents of each child fill out a measure of self-concept *as the parents thought the child would respond*. The parent's perception of the self-concept of the children in therapy was lower than the parent's perception of the self-concept of the nontherapy group. Again, we see the importance of the parents in the self-concept of the child.

The fact that each child typically has two parents represents another potential pitfall for the child in developing positive self-esteem. The parents may have two sets of expectations towards and desires for the child, expectations which are quite different. If the desires of the parents differ, the child is faced with an impossible dilemma; he or she can never be successful in attaining the esteem of both parents. Wyer (1965), utilizing several hundred college students and their parents, found that the more the parents disagreed about their child's effectiveness and their desires for the child, the less effective the child was in coping with the academic requirements of college.

Changing Self-concept

We have briefly discussed the development of self-concept. A question that might be asked is whether self-conception can be changed and if so, how? Obviously now, we are discussing people who are low in self-concept. It seems unnessary to change the self-concept of those who are already high in it.

There have been a number of studies aimed at answering the question of changing self-concept, and the results are mixed. Some of the earliest of these studies were reported by Rogers and Dymond (1954), who studied the effectiveness of therapy in changing self-concept. Rogers developed a specific therapy, which was called "client-centered" or "non-directive." Consistent with his theory, the therapy was based on the assumption that only the individual involved could really know what his or her real self was. The task of the therapist was not to determine what was best for the client, but to act as an enabler in allowing the client to understand his or her real self. For the therapist to tell the client how to act might only compound the problem by forcing the client into behavior patterns that were even more removed from the real self.

In specific, experimental tests, Rogers and his associates (Rogers, 1967; Rogers and Dymond, 1954) studied the effectiveness of client-centered therapy with both neurotic and psychotic clients. The results showed that client-centered therapy was basically rather effective with neurotic clients in that they reduced the gap between actual and ideal self over the course of therapy. With psychotics, more specifically schizophrenics, the results were not very encouraging. The therapy group did show a *slightly* higher release rate and were better able to maintain themselves when released. What was of more interest in this study was that the therapists themselves were greater sources of help and/or harm to the client than was the type of therapy. Empathetic, genuine, and understanding therapists were better able to lead clients into self-exploration and improvement on the schizophrenic scale of the MMPI. Consistent with previous research (Satz and Baraff, 1962), Rogers found that clients with the least understanding therapists were actually worse after therapy than before. Truax and Mitchell (1971) report that in two out of three cases the therapist is wasting time, or worse, being harmful to the client.

One of the basic techniques used by parents and society in general is to reward or reinforce desired behavior, to ignore or punish undesired behavior, or a combination of the two. Sometimes material reinforcers such as money or food are used, but more often, social reinforcers are utilized in social interactions. For example, smiles, compliments, love, and other such reinforcers are powerful determiners of behavior, particularly if the basic biologic needs have been met. As we shall see in Chapter 9, two of the most important of social reinforcers are being agreed with concerning important issues and being evaluated positively by someone else, particularly someone you care about or respect. The effectiveness of agreement and positive evaluations depends on the self-concept of the individual, that is, agreement and positive evaluations are effective if the individual being evaluated or agreed with is basically in agreement with the conclusions expressed.

To simplify things, let us just consider evaluations. If you positively evaluate a person who is high in self-concept you do two things simultaneously—you provide a socially desirable bit of praise *and* you agree with the individual's evaluation of himself or herself. These two variables are confounded and it is not possible to unravel them with high self-concept people. It is possible to separate the two with low self-concept persons. Generally speaking, a compliment does not agree with the self-evaluation of a person low in self-concept.

Padd (1974) investigated the problem of what is reinforcing to low self-concept persons by using positive evaluations that subjects had previously indicated were unlike themselves. For example, one of the statements Padd used was "I have initiative," a statement most persons low in self-concept would say was unlike them. Then Padd gave them either agreement or disagreement on the statement for performing a simple task and measured the speed of their performance. Additionally, he measured the subject's attraction to the person who had purportedly rendered the evaluation they received. As might be expected, a clear-cut picture of which is more important to persons who were low in self-concept, a socially desirable compliment or agreement, was not readily apparent, because they seemed to respond to both. Careful analysis of Padd's study indicates that low self-concept people seem to be initially reinforced by positive evaluations, even though these evaluations disagree with their analysis of themselves. Prolonged use of these type of reinforcers, because of suspicion or some as yet unspecified other variable, seems to inhibit their effectiveness. Thus, changing self-concept seems to be an especially difficult task.

Social psychology is a science that emphasizes behavior, and the relationship between changing self-concept and behavior is important. A person who is low in self-concept feels that he or she is not very worthy in some or many areas. If a person feels unreliable, unattractive, unintelligent, weak, and so forth the implications for behavior are obvious. That person will probably be unsuccessful and lead an unhappy life. However, if it is possible to change the individual's self-concept, then there is the possibility that behavior will change also. Instead of assuming that all efforts will result in failure, the individual may begin to think about succeeding. Thinking about success may well lead to placing oneself in a situation where it is possible to succeed.

It is important to emphasize that self-concept may have important implications for behavior, but that specific areas of self-concept will probably affect certain behaviors. For example, if an individual's feeling about how attractive he or she is is enhanced, the individual's social life may improve, but academic achievement may not. If, on the other hand, the individual's intellectual self-concept is increased, we may well see better academic performance. That is, raising self-concept must be seen as enhancing an individual's perception of self-worth in specific areas and a corresponding change in behavior in those areas. This again emphasizes the importance of the situation in determining an individual's behavior. Social psychology is the interaction of individual and environment and both must be considered.

COMMENT

Self-concept is an important personality variable for social psychology. One disquieting course of research has been the attempt experimentally to manipulate self-esteem by giving subjects false information intended to raise or lower their self-esteem. This experimental approach theoretically has much to recommend it. As you will remember from Chapter 2, experimental manipulation of a variable allows the researcher to determine cause-and-effect relationships. Thus, by manipulating self-esteem, the researcher can make more determinations about the behaviors it causes. There is, however, a very serious drawback to this sort of approach. As I have pointed out, self-concept is rather stubbornly resistant to change and an experimental investigation, which, as is usually the case, lasts a few hours or days, is unlikely to have much effect on stable patterns of thought or behavior. Add to this the fact that a low self-esteem manipulation involves deceiving a subject about a number of rather important issues and telling him or her some unflattering (and patently untrue) things, the whole approach is fraught with difficulties. As indicated in Chapter 2, a decision about the research must be made in congruence with ethical principles, and to date most of the research that has manipulated self-concept seems to fall into a highly "doubtful" category. At the very least, a researcher should take extra precautions before proceeding with a manipulation of self-esteem.

Need for Achievement

A personality variable of some importance with respect to social phenomena is the need to achieve. Achievement is highly valued in virtually all societies, although the achievement itself may take different forms. In industrialized societies such as those in Canada and the United States, achievement is highly prized. The need to achieve (*n*-Ach) was originally defined as "The desire or tendency to do things as rapidly and/or as well as possible" (Murray, 1938, p. 164). It is evident that the two, doing things as rapidly and as well as possible, may be incompatible, but this is a relatively minor matter. The history of the development of the concept of *n*-Ach, and its measurement is highly involved, but adequate overviews of it are contained in Byrne (1974) and Lamberth et al. (1978). Our interest here is in some of the effects of *n*-Ach.

One preliminary comment seems to be in order. Most of the research on *n*-Ach has been conducted with males as subjects. McClelland et. al, (1953) reported that the achievement arousal conditions used in the construction of the test had no effect on TAT stories of female subjects. Research has indicated that females may respond to different cues for achievement than do males. That is, males respond to cues that stress intelligence and leadership, whereas females respond to cues that emphasize social acceptability (Field, 1951). Stein and Bailey (1973) have suggested that females do strive to achieve, but that their achievement is concentrated in different areas than is male achievement. In general, women may find it important to achieve in homemaking, child rearing, and the more traditional female roles of nurse and elementary teacher.

Horner (1972) has suggested that women have learned to fear success. A girl who is more intelligent or capable in masculine activities than males may be considered unfeminine. Many young girls have been warned to act less intelligent than their date and at all costs not to beat him in an athletic contest. This fear of success may cause anxiety when a woman is achieving and thus thwart the achievement.

There is evidence, however, that fear of success is not a generalized characteristic among women but is tied to specific situations. Women indicate more fear of success when the role or occupation they are concerned with is traditionally a masculine one. However, when the occupation being considered is a traditionally feminine one (nursing), fear of success stories are much less frequent (Alper, 1974). Conversely, when a male is described as ranking at the top of a traditionally female occupation, there is much more fear of success indicated for the male (Cherry and Deaux, 1975).

Thus fear of success is probably a reaction that is tied to specific situations rather than a general motive.

Since *n*-Ach in females is still a puzzling problem, the remainder of our discussion will be concerned only with males.

As with self-concept, *n*-Ach is learned, and it has certain motivational properties. A variety of studies have indicated that specific patterns of behavior develop with specific modes of child-rearing. As an example, Teevan and McGhee (1972) conducted an investigation into certain subelements of *n*-Ach, the desire to succeed and the fear of failure. When someone achieves, that person may be motivated by either of these elements, a desire to suceed or a fear of failure. Fear of failure develops in children when mothers punish unsatisfactory behavior and are neutral to satisfactory behavior. The desire to succeed develops when mothers treat unsatisfactory behavior neutrally but reward satisfactory behavior. This, of course, should not be particularly surprising. If a child is punished for unsatisfactory behavior while satisfactory behavior is ignored, anxiety and fear may develop around all activities. The child knows that he or she will receive no payoff when what is done is right, just punishment when he or she does something wrong. The opposite side of the coin, nothing happens when behavior is unsatisfactory but reward comes with satisfactory performance, should encourage the child to go out and give things a try.

Any measure of *n*-Ach is going to be highly influenced by the society in which it is developed. Since the major measure of this need was developed in the United States and refined in Australia and Canada which are all industrialized countries, it seems logical to expect that the measure will be highly influenced by the predominant elements within such societies. There does seem to be more *n*-Ach in middle-class than in lower-class families. In a particularly interesting study into socioeconomic class and *n*-Ach, Turner (1970) proposed that class itself was not the variable that differentiated between those children who would develop a high degree of *n*-Ach and those who would not.

Turner's reasoning was clear and straightforward. He felt that fathers who worked with people in a more autonomous and less supervised way would stress achievement, independence, and self-reliance in their children at home. Turner formed a dichotomy of the father's occupations for purposes of his study, calling those who assumed risk and management in business entrepreneurs and those who did not nonentrepreneurs. He further divided the fathers by socioeconomic class. Managers of bureaucracies and owners of large businesses were labeled white-collar entrepreneurs, and industry or factory managers or owners of small businesses were classified as blue-collar entrepreneurs. Whereas there were more entrepreneurs from the middle class, Turner found that sons of entrepreneurs did not differ in *n*-Ach regardless of class, and that they were higher in *n*-Ach than sons of nonentrepreneurs, regardless of class. Figure 4–1 depicts Turner's results graphically. As you can readily see, sons of entrepreneurs, whether white-collar or blue-collar, score higher on *n*-Ach than do sons of nonentrepreneurs. There is a slight tendency for sons of white-collar fathers to be higher in *n*-Ach than sons of blue-collar fathers, but it is obvious that the entrepreneurial variable is more important than the class variable.

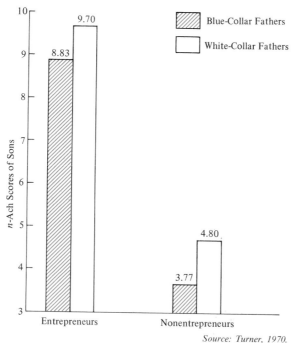

Figure 4–1 A comparison of *n*-Ach in sons of entrepreneurial, nonentrepreneurial, blue- and white-collar fathers.

Source: Turner, 1970.

The Achieving Society. Need for achievement has a special interest for social psychologists, because it is possible to study achievement in society, and in past societies as well as contemporary ones. The reason for this is that since *n*-Ach relies on written material for scoring, it is possible to select representative material from any society and determine the amount of *n*-Ach contained therein. For example, McClelland (1961) sampled *n*-Ach in the literature of countries at a specific time in their history. He found high correlations between *n*-Ach and actual achievement in Greece from 900 B.C. to 100 B.C., in Spain from A.D. 1200 to A.D. 1730 and in England at the time of the Industrial Revolution.

An example of a specific and intriguing relationship between *n*-Ach and actual achievement was reported by de Charms and Moeller (1962) who were interested in the long-term correlation between achievement imagery and actual achievement. To assure as large a part of the populace as possible being exposed to the literature in question, they chose children's readers in the United States from 1800 to 1950. At least four books for every 20-year period were chosen and scored for achievement. They developed an ingenious measure for achievement, the patent index, which is the number of patents issued per 100,000 inhabitants. Since patents are granted to protect an individual from having his or her invention stolen, patents are a well-documented measure of individual achievement. The comparison of *n*-Ach in children's readers and the patent index is shown in Figure 4–2. The relationship is truly startling. Since adults typically are the ones who apply for patents, if achievement imagery in children's readers is a predictor of what is to come, it seems likely that the patent index would trail the movements of *n*-Ach in the readers by about a generation. This

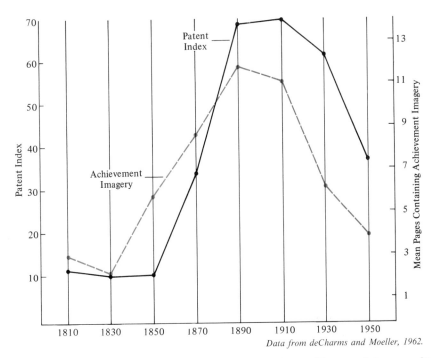

Data from deCharms and Moeller, 1962.

Figure 4-2 Number of pages (out of 25) containing achievement imagery in fourth-grade readers and the patent index (1810–1950).

is almost exactly what happened, and as Figure 4–2 shows, indicates that *n*-Ach can be profitably studied in societies.

The research in *n*-Ach is quite extensive and impressive, but there is still a nagging question that remains unanswered: "Why do some individuals, and thus groups and societies, achieve and others don't?" Part of the answer obviously lies in the definition of achievement that is used, the circumstances in which an individual, group, or society finds itself, natural resources, and a whole host of other potential variables. Richard de Charms (1968, 1972), whose work has just been discussed, argues that when a person feels that he or she is the originator of behavior or controller of his or her fate, the individual will act quite differently than when some external force is seen as the controller. In essence, de Charms adds another dimension to the work on *n*-Ach, suggesting that the highly motivated person sees himself or herself in control and as responsible for achievement. The person who is a low achiever views the situation as being in the control of someone or something outside of himself or herself and this is the reason why the individual does not achieve well. De Charms has brought us nicely to our next personality variable, locus of control.

Locus of Control

Locus of control is the name given to an area of research that was spawned by Rotter (Rotter, 1966; Rotter, Seeman, and Liverance, 1962), who defined it as the *degree to which the individual accepts personal responsibility for what happens to him or*

An oil refinery; a symbol of the achieving society.

her. Locus of control has been viewed as a dichotomy of internals and externals. *Internals* feel that the responsibility for events that happen lies within themselves, whereas *externals* feel that responsibility for such events resides in some external source, whether it is another person, society, or the fates. Thus an external perceives positive and negative events as being unrelated to his or her own behavior.

Rotter (1966) developed an objective, self-report scale of measurement for locus of control, called the Internal–External (I–E) Scale. The 23-item scale is arranged so that each item is scored either internal or external. As mentioned earlier, locus of control was originally conceived of as a dichotomy, and the I–E Scale has undergone a great degree of measurement research. The technique used to determine the characteristics of the I–E scale is factor analysis, which is a sophisticated statistical technique that can determine the number of factors in a scale by a close and thorough analysis of the way each item on the scale correlates with every other item. If the I–E scale is measuring a dichotomy, there should be one factor present when the scale is factor analyzed—that is, the presence of that particular factor could indicate an external orientation and its absence an internal one (or vice-versa).

There is, to say the least, conflicting evidence on the matter of the number of factors present in the scale. Walk and Hardy (1975) found one; others (Minton, 1972; Mirels, 1970; Reid and Ware, 1973) found two, and Reid and Ware (1974) found three. Should we go with the majority? The answer is obviously not. Even though the I–E Scale has been around for some time, it is a long and time-consuming job to study measuring scales adequately. The matter of how many factors are present in the I–E Scale is still open to question and will be, I suspect, for some time. Further evidence of this sort of laissez faire attitude of scientists is found in the fact that in one study Reid and Ware (1973) found two factors in the scale and in another (1974) they found three. There is still much work to be done before there is a definitive answer about the I–E Scale.

Behavioral Characteristics of Internals and Externals

The whole area of locus of control is a relatively new one, at least as far as having a measuring instrument of some precision to use. There have, of course, been references to our destiny being controlled by the fates, or luck, or some other such external force, throughout history. The importance of this personality variable, which cuts across other dimensions and on which individuals differ, is potentially of great importance. It is, however, too early to fit all of the pieces together to see what the final outcome will be. I–E research is relatively new, having had a measuring instrument for less than two decades, and so our discussion of it may not fit together as neatly as would be expected in an area of study with a longer history.

Rotter (1966) reported that males and females in the samples he drew (from the United States) did not differ on the I–E Scale. Two relatively recent research efforts have indicated that there may be differences between the sexes on the I–E Scale. Two large, independent cross-cultural studies found that females are more external than males when the samples are large and not differentiated by country (McGinnes, Nordholm, Ward, and Bhanthunnanin, 1974; Parsons and Schneider, 1974). Interestingly enough, these results do not contradict Rotter's results, because there were no differences found between males and females in the United States, where Rotter had standardized the scale. The overall difference is accounted for by the fact that females in other countries, specifically Australia, Israel, and Sweden are significantly more external than males. In addition to the McGinnes et al. and the Parsons and Schneider studies, Garza and Ames (1974) have compared individuals in other countries on the I–E Scale and the results have been quite consistent. People in Sweden are the most external, with Japanese being significantly lower than Swedes but higher than all of the other nations in which studies have been carried out (Australia, Canada, France, India, Israel, Italy, New Zealand, United States, and West Germany). Another consistent finding is that people in India are more internal than people in any other culture and significantly more internal than people in Sweden, Japan, France, and Canada. Figure 4–3 shows male and female I–E scores from 11 countries.

A particularly interesting study (Garza and Ames, 1974) shows how variables can interact to support our stereotypes of other cultures. Mexico is known as the land of "mañana," and Mexican-Americans have been stereotyped as externals, believing

Locus of control as measured by Rotter's Internal–External (I–E) scale has proven to be an important personality variable. Recall that locus of control refers to an individual's feelings concerning by whom or what his or her life is controlled. Internals feel that they control their own lives, whereas externals feel that their lives are more strongly controlled by forces outside of themselves.

There is another distinction that needs to be made. Everyone experiences both positive and negative events. That is, sometimes life deals us happy or positive experience and sometimes they (the experiences) are not so nice. It is entirely possible that individuals view positive and negative events differently, at least with regard to who or what is controlling them. We have all met people who are willing to take full credit for all the positive things that happen to them, but find many circumstances to blame when an unpleasant event occurs.

Gregory (1978) points out that there have been no studies designed expressly to test whether the Rotter Internal–External Scale can distinguish between internals and externals in both positive and negative outcome situations. He developed a test of whether Internals and Externals differ in the way they react to positive and negative outcomes.

Subjects were 107 students who participated in an angle-matching task. Half the subjects were told that they would be rewarded for succeeding at the angle-matching task whereas the other half were told they would be punished for failing at the angle-matching task. In addition, bogus feedback was delivered to the subjects. Half of each group were told they had done well while the other half was told they had done poorly. Finally, the subjects were divided on the basis of whether they were internals, moderates, or externals.

The major variable to be measured was the amount of time each subject took to make a decision under the various experimental conditions. The reasoning behind such a measurement is simple; if your fate is controlled by someone or something else, it makes little sense to ponder over a problem for a long time. If, on the other hand, you control your own fate, it makes sense to spend time on a difficult problem.

There were no differences in the amount of time internals, moderates, and externals took on the angle-matching task when they were to be rewarded for success. However, when they were to be punished for failing, internals took more time at the angle-matching task than did moderates, who took more time than externals. Under negative outcome conditions, internals and externals behaved as expected, but they did not differ under positive outcome conditions.

It seems, then, that the Rotter I–E Scale is predictive of behavior in negative situations, but not in positive ones. That this is the case is probably not too surprising, given human nature. All of us like to take credit for good things, and few of us want to be credited with the negative things in life. Recently a friend and I were discussing the different way good and bad news is delivered. If at all possible, bad news is delivered by mail, while a telephone call is used to deliver good news. It seems that most of us want to take credit for positive events. However, when something negative happens, externals prefer to let others take the blame.

Reference

Gregory, W. L. Locus of control for positive and negative outcomes. *Journal of Personality and Social Psychology,* 1978, 36, 840–849.

that the fates control their destiny. When Garza and Ames controlled socioeconomic status by matching Mexican-American and Anglo-American students on this variable, they found the Mexican-American students to be more internal than the Anglo-American students. Evidently, socioeconomic status was the variable that controlled an individual's perception of his or her fate. The fact that many Mexican-Americans are of a low socioeconomic class has allowed them to be stereotyped.

Locus of Control and Psychological Defenses. A psychological defense system is one that allows an individual to ignore or discount information or events that would be harmful to him or her. A number of studies have shown that externals appear to use fewer defenses, or more accurately, to use those defenses less often than do internals. This, of course, makes a certain sense. An internal, remember, feels that he or she is responsible for what happens, whereas an external feels that some other person or object is in control. As what happens to the external is not of his or her doing anyway, there should be less need on the part of external to rely on other defenses.

Evidence for this reasoning comes from several sources. Externals forget fewer failures than do internals (Efran, 1963), recall more negative information about personalities, devalue intelligence tests they had failed on more, and blamed the environment more in dealing with failures than do internals (Phares, Ritchie, and Davis, 1968; Phares, 1971; Phares, Wilson and Klymer, 1971). As you can see, all these results are consistent with the notion that externals have their own built-in defense system and it is not necessary for them to call on other defenses.

Locus of Control and Suicide. Suicidal individuals are characterized by feelings of hopelessness probably because they feel unable to alter unfavorable life circumstances. Boor (1976a) reasoned that suicidal behavior should be related to scores on the I–E Scale, because it assesses the extent to which a person perceives his or her life

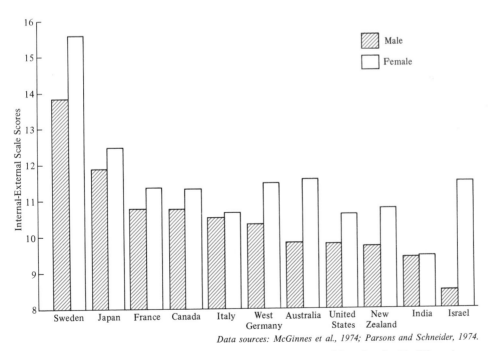

Data sources: McGinnes et al., 1974; Parsons and Schneider, 1974.

Figure 4–3 Internal-External Scale scores for males and females in 11 different countries. *Note:* The higher the score, the more external the person is.

as being under his or her own control or the control of some other person or object. Boor's reasoning seems simple and straightforward: those individuals who do not feel that they are in control of their own fate or destiny have more feelings of hopelessness, and maladjustment is related to I–E Scale scores (Joe, 1971). Utilizing Schneider's (1971) data on I–E scores obtained during 1966, 1967, 1969, and 1970, plus his own data from 1972 and 1973, Boor compared changes in the suicide rate per 100,000 population for the total population of the United States. He found that increases in externality on the I–E Scale correlated with increases in the suicide rate quite highly ($r = .88$, df $= 4$, $p < .02$). In other words over the years from 1966 to 1973 the mean I–E Scale scores increased from 7.5 to 10.7, and the suicide rate increased from 10.9 per 100,000 population to 12.0 per 100,000 population. Further, Schneider's and Boor's data came mainly from college students, and the suicide rate increase was greatest among young people, increasing from 6.4 to 10.6 among those 15 to 24 years of age and from 12.3 to 14.9 among those from 25 to 34 years of age. There was a slight increase in the 35–44 age group, and an actual drop in the suicide rate among all older age groups.

As indicated in Chapter 2, correlation does not imply causality, and certainly it would be difficult to argue that increases in I-E scores caused increased suicides or vice-versa. It is probably fairly safe to say that during the years 1966 to 1973 some other variable or variables were responsible for the increased suicide rate. Boor (1976a, p. 797), suggests that perhaps increased externality and suicide can be attributed "to such experiences as the Vietnam War and military conscription during the middle and late 1960s and to the Watergate scandal and high unemployment in the early 1970s."

Boor (1976b) also reports a study that compared the I-E scores obtained by McGinnes et al. (1974) and Parsons and Schneider (1974), discussed earlier in connection with the suicide rate in those countries. Evidence of a relationship between externality on the I–E scale and suicide in other countries would add more evidence to the idea that similar factors influence both the internal–external dimension and suicide. What is of interest here is the potentiality of the I–E Scale being used as a predictor of suicide. That, of course, would be a use for the scale which, if ever realized, would be far in the future.

Boor (1976b) found a significant correlation between externality on the I-E Scale and suicide rates ($r = .68$, df $= 8$, $p < .05$). Thus cultures that foster higher feelings of externality also tend to have higher suicide rates. Figure 4–4 shows the results graphically.

Comment. Rotter is one who might best be termed a cognitive social learning theorist, and it is interesting for our purposes to note that the amalgamation of learning theory and cognitive theory is evident in his work on locus of control. As with the other personality variables, locus of control is conceived of as a learned need or characteristic. It is also a cognitive variable, because of the necessity to make judgments about who or what controls the individual's fate.

Interestingly enough, cognitive social learning theorists have been active in the realm of personality study for some time now. It is only in social psychology that two camps have grown up, cognitive theorists and learning theorists. Why this occurred is something we will probably never know for sure, although we might trace it to a

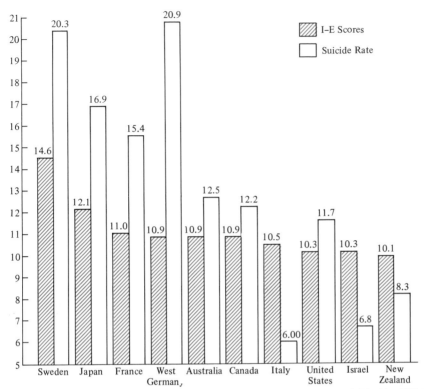

Sources: *Boor, 1976a, 1976b; McGinnes et al., 1974; Parsons and Schneider, 1974.*

Figure 4–4 Comparison of I-E Scale scores and suicide rates for 10 countries. *Note:* Higher I-E scores indicate greater externality; India is omitted because suicide data were not available.

reaction against radical behaviorism among social psychologists—a reaction that, I think, became an overreaction. The area of personality has shown us that what are two opposing camps in social psychology, learning and cognitive theories, are quite successful collaborators in personality to the benefit of both.

SUMMARY

1 Socialization is the process by which an individual acquires the behavior patterns, beliefs, standards, and values of society. Socialization occurs by a variety of methods, and the socialization of sexual motives is particularly interesting.
2 Sex-role identity is the development of a male or female orientation and is highly culture-specific. Bem has argued that the most fulfilled people are those who are androgynous in character, that is, who have the characteristics that are traditionally male and female. Sex-role identity is a learned characteristic with observational learning probably playing the most significant role in its development.

3 Dependency is the motive to be comforted, nurtured, protected, or aided by others. After the first year of life, when children are very dependent, a process of spontaneous progressive detachment begins. In adolescence, the child must learn to be independent, a process that is difficult and is made more difficult by societies that are not certain about when a child should be independent.

4 There are several views concerning moral development, with all agreeing that morals are learned. The most pervasive view of moral development is the cognitive one as exemplified by Kohlberg's stage theory. According to Kohlberg, there are six stages of moral development, with the sixth and highest stage attained by only a few people.

5 Personality is important for social psychology because it emphasizes what the individual brings to the situation. The assessment of personality is often done with tests, which may be projective, objective, or behavioral. Three personality variables that are important for social psychology are considered.

6 Self-concept is the feeling of worthiness or unworthiness an individual has. Self-concept develops in the tension of what the child would like to be and what society will allow the child to be, that is, how the child is socialized. Self-concept is difficult to change and yet, because it has been learned, it can probably be relearned.

7 Need for achievement (*n*-Ach) is the desire to do things well or as quickly as possible. Most *n*-Ach research has been carried out with males; increasing amounts of research with females has created a controversy over fear of success. McClelland has argued that there are some societies that achieve more than others and that this variable can be predicted from the literature of a society.

8 Locus of control is the feeling an individual has about the source of control of his or her life. Internals feel that control of events in their lives resides within themselves, whereas externals feel it resides in some external source. Internals and externals have been shown to differ on several important behavioral dimensions.

GLOSSARY

Agentic The masculine orientation that stresses a concern for oneself as an individual.

Androgyny State of having both male and female characteristics.

Assessment The measurement of a quality, charateristic, or construct.

Autonomous Stage In this stage, according to Piaget, intentionality replaces the consequences of an act as the basis of moral judgment.

Bem Sex-Role Inventory A measure of masculinity and femininity that treats the two dimensions as independent characteristics.

Communal Having the feminine orientation that stresses a concern for the relationship between oneself and others.

Complementary Completing something else or making it perfect.

Defense A psychological system that allows an individual to ignore or discount information that would be harmful to him or her.

Dependency The need to be nurtured, comforted, protected, or aided by others.

Egocentrism The inability of the child to distinguish between his or her perspective and that of others.

Expressive Orientation Parson and Bale's label for femininity that emphasized an affective concern for the welfare of others and the harmony of the group.

Externals Individuals who feel that responsibility for what happens to them resides in some external force.

Heteronomous Stage The state in which, until about seven years of age, the child's understanding of moral rules is limited because of realism and egocentrism.

Instrumental Orientation Parson and Bale's label for masculinity that emphasizes getting the problem solved or the job done.

Internals Individuals who feel that the responsibility for what happens to them lies within themselves.

Libido Freud's term for the biologically based sex instinct.

Locus of Control The degree to which an individual accepts responsibility for what happens to him or her.

Moral Development The process by which a child acquires beliefs and standards about moral behavior.

Motive An unobservable mediating variable or construct that refers to a specific goal.

Need for Achievement The desire or tendency to do things as rapidly or as well as possible.

Personality Those characteristics each person possesses that determine his or her cognitive, emotional, and overt behavior.

Projective Techniques Assessment techniques that attempt to tap the unconscious mind.

Realism Piaget's label for the child's inability to distinguish between subjective and objective phenomena, whereby he views adult rules as fixed external realities.

Realiability The measure of whether a test gives a stable, dependable assessment each time it is used.

Rite of Passage An act or ceremony marking the change from childhood to adulthood.

Self-Concept The esteem or value that an individual ascribes to himself or herself.

Sex-Role Identity The masculine or feminine roles that children learn as they are socialized.

Socialization The process by which the individual acquires those behavior patterns, beliefs, standards, and motives that are valued by or appropriate in, his own cultural group and family.

Validity An assessment of whether a test measures what it purports to measure.

REFERENCES

Alper, T. G. Achievement motivation in college women. A now-you-see-it-now-you-don't phenomenon. *American Psychologist*, 1974, *29*, 194–203.

Aronfreed, J. Punishment learning and internalization: Some parameters of reinforcement and cognition. Paper presented at the Biennial Meeting of the Society for Research in Child Development, Minneapolis, March 1965.

Asch, S. E. *Social Psychology.* New York: Prentice-Hall, Inc., 1952.

Bakan, D. *The Duality of Human Existence.* Chicago: Rand McNally Company, 1966.

Bandura, A. *Principles of Behavior Modification.* New York: Holt, Rinehart and Winston, 1969.

———. *Social Learning Theory.* Morristown, N.J.: General Learning Press, 1971.

———. (Ed.), *Psychological Modeling.* Chicago: Aldine Publishing Company, 1971.

———. Analysis of modeling processes. In A. Bandura (Ed.), *Modeling: Conflicting theories.* New York: Lieber-Atherton, 1974.

Bem, S. L. The measurement of psychological androgyny. *Journal of Consulting and Clinical Psychology,* 1974, *42,* 155–62.

———. Sex role adaptability: One consequence of psychological androgyny. *Journal of Personality and Social Psychology,* 1975 *31,* 634–43.

———. On the utility of alternative procedures for assessing psychological androgyny. *Journal of Consulting and Clinical Psychology,* 1977, *45,* 196–205.

———. Some presumptous prescriptions for a liberated sexual identity. In J. Sherman and F. Denmark (Eds.), *The Future of Women: Issues in Psychology.* New York: Psychological Dimensions, in press (b).

———, and E. Lenney. Sex typing and the avoidance of cross-sex behavior. *Journal of Personality and Social Psychology,* 1976, *33,* 48–54.

Berzins, J. I., and M. A. Welling. The PRE ANDRO Scale: A measure of psychological androgyny derived from the Personality Research Form. Unpublished manuscript, University of Kentucky, 1974.

Bishoff, L. J. *Interpreting Personality Theories.* New York: Harper and Row, Publishers, 1970.

Block, J. H. Conceptions of sex role: Some cross-cultural and longitudinal perspectives. *American Psychologist,* 1973, *28,* 512–26.

Boor, M. Relationship of internal-external control and United States suicide rate, 1966–1973. *Journal of Clinical Psychology,* 1976a, *32,* 795–97.

———. Relationship of internal-external and national suicide rates. *The Journal of Social Psychology,* 1976b, *100,* 143–44.

Braine, M. D. S. The entogeny of English phrase structure: The first phase. *Language,* 1963, *39,* 1–13.

Broverman, D. M., E. L. Klaiber, Y. Kobayashi, and W. Vogel. Roles of activation and inhibition in sex differences in cognitive abilities. *Psychological Review,* 1968, *75,* 23–50.

Brown, R., and U. Bellugi. Three processes in the child's acquisition of syntax. *Harvard Educational Review,* 1964, *34,* 133–51.

———, and C. Fraser. The acquisition of syntax. In C. N. Cofer and B. S. Musgrave (Eds.), *Verbal Behavior and Learning: Problems and Processes.* New York: McGraw-Hill Book Company. Pp. 158–97.

Byrne, D. *An Introduction to Personality* (2nd Edition) Englewood Cliffs, N.J.: Prentice-Hall, Inc., 1974.

Cattell, R. B., H. W. Eber, and M. M. Tatsuoka. *Handbook for the Sixteen Personality Factors Questionnaire.* Champaign, Ill.: Institute for Personality and Ability Testing, 1970.

Cherry, F., and K. Deaux. "Fear of success vs. fear of gender-in-consistent behavior: A sex similarity." Paper presented at the meeting of the Midwestern Psychological Association, Chicago, May, 1975.

Cosentino, F., and A. B. Heilbrun. Anxiety correlates of sex-role identity in college students. *Psychological Reports,* 1964, *14,* 729–30.

de Charms, R. *Personal Causation.* New York: Academic Press, Inc., 1968.

————. Personal-causation training in schools. *Journal of Applied Social Psychology,* 1972, *2,* 95–113.

————, and G. H. Moeller. Values expressed in American children's readers: 1800–1950. *Journal of Abnormal and Social Psychology,* 1962, *64,* 135–42.

Deaux, K. Sex: A perspective on the attribution process. In J. H. Harvey, W. J. Ickes, R. F. Kidd (Eds.), *New Directions in Attribution Research.* Vol. 1. New York: John Wiley & Sons, Inc., 1976.

Dollard, J., and N. E. Miller. *Personality and Psychotherapy.* New York: McGraw-Hill Book Company, 1950.

Douvan, E., and J. Adelsen. *The Adolescent Experience.* New York: John Wiley & Sons, Inc., 1966.

Draper, P. Kung women: Constrasts in sex egalitarianism in the foraging and sedentary contexts. In R. Reiter (Ed.), *Toward an Anthopology of Women.* New York: Monthly Review Press, in press.

Edwards, A. L. *Edwards Personal Preference Schedule.* New York: Psychological Corp., 1959.

Efran, J. Some personality determinants of memory for success and failure. Unpublished doctoral dissertation. Ohio State University, 1963.

Field, W. F. The effects on thematic apperception of certain experimentally aroused needs. Unpublished doctoral dissertation, University of Maryland, 1951.

Freud, S. Infantile sexuality. In W. Dennis (Ed.), *Historical Readings in Developmental Psychology.* New York: Appleton-Century-Crofts, 1972. Pp. 201–207.

Gall, M. O. The relationship between masculinity-feminity and manifest anxiety. *Journal of Clinical Psychology,* 1969, *25,* 294–95.

Garza, R. T., and R. E. Ames, Jr. A comparison of Anglo- and Mexican-American College students on locus of control. *Journal of Consulting and Clinical Psychology,* 1974, *42,* 919.

Gerwitz, J. L. A factor analysis of some attention-seeking behaviors of young children. *Child Development,* 1956, *27,* 17–36.

Gleuck, S., and E. Gleuck. *Unravelling Juvenile Delinquency.* Cambridge, Mass. Harvard University Press, 1950.

Gray, S. W. Masculinity-femininity in relation to anxiety and social acceptance. *Child Development,* 1957, *28,* 203–214.

Grierson, K. A study of the self-concepts of a group of adolescent students and the relationship between these self-concepts and behavioral ratings. *Dissertation Abstracts,* 1961, *21,* 2588.

Hall, C. S., and G. Lindzey. *Theories of Personality.* New York: John Wiley & Sons, Inc., 1978.

Hartshorne, H., and M. A. May. *Studies in the Nature of Character.* Vol. I. *Studies in Deceit.* New York: Macmillan Publishing Co., Inc., 1928.

Hartup, W. W. Dependence and independence. In H. W. Stevenson (Ed.), *Child Psychology* (62nd Yearbook of the National Society for the Study of Education). Chicago: University of Chicago Press, 1963. Pp. 333–63.

Hathaway, S. R., and J. C. McKinley. *MMPI Manual.* New York: Psychological Corp., 1943.

Hattendorf, K. W. A study of the questions of young children concerning sex: A phase of an experimental approach to parental education. *Journal of Social Psychology,* 1932, *3,* 37–65.

Heathers, G. Emotional dependence and independence in nursery-school play. *Journal of Genetic Psychology,* 1955, *87,* 37–58.

Hoffman, M. L., and H. D. Saltzstein. Parent discipline and the child's moral development. *Journal of Personality and Social Psychology,* 1967, *5,* 45–47.

Horner, M. The motive to avoid success and changing aspirations of college women. In J. M. Bardwick (Ed.), *Readings on the Psychology of Women.* New York: Harper & Row, Publishers, 1972. Pp. 62–67.

Joe, V. C. A review of the internal-external control construct as a personality variable. *Psychological reports,* 1971, *28,* 619–40.

Jung, C. G. *The Structure of the Unconscious.* In collected works. Vol 7. Princeton University Press, 1953.

Kinsey, A. C., W. B. Pomeroy, and C. E. Martin. *Sexual Behavior in the Human Male.* Philadelphia: W. B. Saunders Company, 1948.

Kinsey, A. C., W. B. Pomeroy, C. E. Martin, and P. H. Gebhard. *Sexual Behavior in the Human Female.* Philadelphia: W. B. Saunders Company, 1953.

Kohlberg, L. The development of modes of moral thinking in the years ten to sixteen. Unpublished doctoral dissertation. University of Chicago, 1958.

————. The development of children's orientations toward a moral order. I. Sequence in the development of moral thought. *Vita Humana,* 1963, *6,* 11–33 (b).

Kohlberg, S. L. Moral development and identification. In H. Stevenson (Ed.), *Child Psychology, 72nd Yearbook of the National Society for the Study of Education,* Chicago: University of Chicago Press, 1963 (a), pp. 277–332.

Krasner, L., and L. P. Ullmann. *Behavior Influence and Personality: The Social Matrix of Human Action.* New York: Holt, Rinehart and Winston, 1973.

Lamberth, J., H. Rappaport, and M. Rappaport. *Introduction to Personality.* New York: Alfred A. Knopf, Inc., 1978.

Lehmann, P. *Ethics in a Christian Context.* New York: Harper & Row, Publishers, 1963.

Maccoby, E. E. Sex differences in intellectual functioning. In E. E. Maccoby (Ed.), *The Development of Sex Differences.* Stanford, Calif.: Stanford University Press, 1966.

————, and S. Feldman. Mother-attachment and stranger-reactions in the third year of life. *Monographs of the Society for Research in Child Development,* 1972, *37*(1).

————, and J. C. Masters. Attachment and dependency. In P. H. Mussen (Ed.), Carmichael's Manual of Child Psychology, (3rd Edition). Vol. 2. New York: John Wiley & Sons, Inc., 1970. Pp. 75–157.

Malinowski, B. Prenuptial intercourse between the sexes in the Trabian Islands, N.W. Melanesia: *Psychoanalytic Review,* 1927, *14,* 20–36.

McClelland, D. C. *The Achieving Society.* New York: The Free Press, 1961.

————, J. W. Atkinson, R. A. Clark, and E. L. Lowell. *The Achievement Motive.* New York: Appleton-Century-Crofts, 1953.

McGinnes, E., L. A. Nordholm, C. A. Ward, and D. L. Bhanthumnanin. Sex and cultural differences in perceived locus of control among students in five countries. *Journal of Consulting and Clinical Psychology,* 1974, *42,* 451–55.

Medinnus, G. Adolescents' self-acceptance and perceptions of their parents. *Journal of Consulting Psychology,* 1965, *29,* 150–54.

Minton, H. L. Internal-external control and the distinction between personal control and system modifiability. Paper presented at Midwestern Psychological Association, 1972.

Mirels, H. L. Dimensions of internal versus external control. *Journal of Consulting and Clinical Psychology,* 1970, *34,* 226–28.

Mischel, W. A social learning view of sex differences in behavior. In E. E. Maccoby (Ed.), *The Development of Sex Differences.* Stanford, Calif.: Stanford University Press, 1966. Pp. 56–81.

Mischel, W. Preference for delayed reinforcement: An experimental study of a cultural observation. *Journal of Abnormal and Social Psychology,* 1958, *56,* 57–61.

————. Preference for delayed reinforcement and social responsibility. *Journal of Abnormal and Social Psychology,* 1961, *62,* 1–7.

————. Theory and research on the antecedents of self-imposed delay of reward. In B. A.

Maher (Ed.), *Progress in Personality Research* vol. 3. New York: Academic Press, Inc. 1966. Pp. 85–132.

———. *Personality and Assessment.* New York: John Wiley & Sons, Inc., 1968.

———. Processes in delay of gratification. In L. Berkowitz (Ed.), *Advances in Experimental Social Psychology.* Vol. 7. New York: Academic Press, Inc., 1974.

———. *Introduction to Personality.* New York: Holt, Rinehart and Winston, 1976.

Murray, H. A. *Thematic Apperception Test.* Cambridge, Mass.: Harvard University Press, 1943.

———. *Explorations in Personality* (1938). New York: Science Editions, 1962.

Mussen, P. H. Some antecedents and consequents of masculine sex-typing in adolescent boys. *Psychological Monographs,* 1961, *75,* 506.

———. Long-term consequents of masculinity of interests in adolescence. *Journal of Consulting Psychology,* 1962, *26,* 435–40.

———, J. J. Conger, and J. Kagan. *Child Development and Personality.* New York: Harper & Row, Publishers (4th Edition), 1974.

Nisbett, R. E., and L. Temoshok. Is there an "external" cognitive style? *Journal of Personality and Social Psychology,* 1976, *33,* 36–47.

Padd, W. Interpersonal attraction and reinforcing effects of self-attitudes on high and low self-esteem. Unpublished doctoral dissertation, University of Oklahoma, 1974.

Page, J. *Psychopathology: The Science of Understanding Deviance.* Chicago: Aldine, 1975.

Parke, R. D. (Ed.) *Readings in social development.* New York: Holt, Rinehart and Winston, Publishers, 1969.

Parlee, M. B. Comments on D. M. Broverman, E. L. Klaiber, Y. Kobayaski, and W. Vogel: Roles of activation and inhibition in sex differences in cognitive abilities. *Psychological Review,* 1972, *79,* 180–84.

Parsons, T., and R. F. Bales. *Family, Socialization, and Interaction Process.* New York: The Free Press, 1955.

Parsons, D. A., and J. M. Schneider. Locus of control in university students from eastern and western societies. *Journal of Consulting and Clinical Psychology,* 1974, *42,* 456–61.

Phares, E. J., D. E. Ritchie, and W. L. Davis. Internal-external control and reaction to threat. *Journal of Personality and Social Psychology,* 1968, *10,* 402–405.

———. Internal-external control and the reduction of reinforcement value after failing. *Journal of Consulting and Clinical Psychology,* 1971, *37,* 386–90.

Phares, E. J., R. G. Wilson, and N. W. Klymer. Internal-external control and the attribution of blame under neutral and distractive conditions. *Journal of Personality and Social Psychology,* 1971, *18,* 285–88.

Piaget, J. *The Moral Judgment of the Child.* New York. The Free Press, 1948. (First published in French, 1932.)

Piers, E. V. Parent prediction of children's self-concepts. *Journal of Consulting and Clinical Psychology,* 1972, *38,* 428–33.

Rawls, J. *A Theory of Justice.* Cambridge, Mass.: The Belknap Press of Harvard University, 1971.

Reeny, W. R. Adolescent sexuality. In A. Ellis and A. Aberband (Eds.), *The Encyclopedia of Sexual Behavior.* Vol. I. New York: Hawthorn Books, Inc., 1961. Pp. 52–68.

Reid, D. W., and E. E. Ware, Multidimensionality of internal-external control: Implications for past and future research. *Canadian Journal of Behavioral Science,* 1973, *5,* 264–71.

——— and ———. Multidimensionality of internal versus external control: Addition of a third dimension and nondistinction of self versus others. *Canadian Journal of Behavioral Science,* 1974, *6,* 131–42.

Richardson, M. Discrepancy measurements relating student self-concept of mental ability with mental health stability: An empirical study of ninth grades. Dissertation Abstracts, 1965, 26, 2592.

Rogers, C. *Psychotherapy and Personality Change.* Chicago: University of Chicago Press, 1954.

————. Toward a science of the person. In T. W. Wann (Ed.), *Behaviorism and Phenomenology.* Chicago: University of Chicago Press, 1964.

Rogers, C. R. *The Therapeutic Relationship and Its Impact: A Study of Psychotherapy with Schizophrenics.* Madison: University of Wisconsin Press, 1967.

————, and R. F. Dymond (Eds.), *Psychotherapy and Personality Change.* Chicago: University of Chicago Press, 1954.

Rosenthal, M. K. The effect of naval situation and anxiety on two groups of dependency behavior. *British Journal of Psychology,* 1967, *58,* 357–64 (a).

————. The generalization of dependency behavior from mother to stranger. *Journal of Child Psychology and Psychiatry,* 1967, *8,* 117–33 (b).

Rotter, J. B. *Social Learning and Clinical Psychology.* Englewood Cliffs, N.J.: Prentice-Hall, Inc., 1954.

————. Generalized expectancies for internal versus external control of reinforcement. *Psychological Monographs,* 1966, *80* (1, Whole No. 609).

————. Beliefs social attitudes, and behavior: A social learning analysis. In J. B. Rotter, J. E. Chance, and E. J. Phares (Eds.), *Applications of a Social Learning Theory of Personality.* New York: Holt, Rinehart and Winston, 1972.

————, M. Seeman, and S. Liverance. Internal versus external control of reinforcements: A major variable in behavior theory. In N. F. Washburne (Ed.), *Decisions, Values, and Groups.* Vol. 2. London: Pergamon Press, 1962.

Samuels, S. An investigation into some factors related to the self-concepts in early childhood from middle and lower class homes. *Dissertation Abstracts,* 1970, *30B,* 4366.

Satz, P., and A. S. Baraff. Changes in the relation between self-concepts and ideal concepts of psychotics consequent upon therapy. *Journal of General Psychology,* 1962, *67,* 291–98.

Schneider, J. M. College students' belief in personal control, 1966–1970. *Journal of Individual Psychology,* 1971, *27,* 188.

Schultz, J. A cross-sectional study of the development dimensionality and correlates of the self-concept in school age boys. *Dissertation Abstracts,* 1967, *27A,* 2898.

Schwartz, S. Parent-child interaction as it relates to the ego functioning and self-concepts of the pre-school child. Dissertation Abstracts, 1967, *27A,* 1898.

————. Relation of early socialization experiences to self-concepts and gender role in middle childhood. *Child Development,* 1970, *41,* 267–89.

Sears, R. R., E. E. Maccoby, and H. Levin. *Patterns of Child Rearing.* New York: Harper & Row, Publishers, 1957.

Sears, R. R. Dependency motivation. In M. Jones (Ed.), *Nebraska Symposium on Motivation.* Lincoln: University of Nebraska Press, 1963. Pp. 25–64.

Spence, J. T., R. Helmreich, and J. Stapp. Ratings of self and peers on sex role attributes and their relation to self-esteem and conceptions of masculinity and femininity. *Journal of Personality and Social Psychology,* 1975, *32,* 29–39.

Stein, A. H., and M. M. Bailey. The socialization of achievement orientation in females. *Psychological Bulletin,* 1973, *80,* 345–66.

Stephenson, W. *The Study of Behavior: Q-Technique and Its Methodology.* Chicago: University of Chicago Press, 1953.

Tapp, J. L., and F. J. Levine. Compliance from kindergarten to college. A speculative research note. *Journal of Youth and Adolescence,* 1972, *1,* 233–49.

Taylor, J. A. A personality scale of manifest anxiety. *Journal of Abnormal and Social Psychology,* 1953, *48,* 285–90.

Taynor, J., and K. Deaux. Equity and perceived sex differences: Role behavior as defined by the task, the mode, and the actor. *Journal of Personality and Social Psychology,* 1975, *32,* 381–90.

Teevan, R. C., and P. E. McGhee. Childhood Development of fear of failure motivation. *Journal of Personality and Social Psychology,* 1972, *21,* 345–48.

Truax, C. B., and K. M. Mitchell. Research on certain therapist interpersonal skills in relation to process and outcome. In R. E. Bergin and S. L. Garfield (Eds.), *Handbook of Psychotherapy and Behavior Change.* New York: John Wiley & Sons, Inc., 1971, 299–344.

Turiel, E. An experimental test of the sequentially of developmental stages in the child's moral judgments. *Journal of Personality and Social Psychology,* 1966, *3,* 611–18.

Turner, J. H. Entrepreneurial environments and the emergence of achievement motivation in adolescent males. *Sociometry,* 1970, *33,* 147–65.

Walk, S., and R. C. Hardy. The identifiability and consistency of the factor structure of locus of control. *The Journal of Psychology,* 1975, *89,* 149–58.

Walters, R. H., R. D. Parke, and V. A. Crane. Timing of punishment and the observation of consequences to others as determinants of response inhibition. *Journal of Experimental Child Psychology,* 1965, *2,* 10–30.

Watson, B. *Psychology from the Standpoint of a Behaviorist.* Philadelphia: J. B. Lippincott Company, 1919.

Wilson, W. C. (Ed.). Technical report of the commission on obscenity and pornography. Vol. VI. *National Survey.* Washington, D.C.: U.S. Government Printing Office, 1971.

Wolpe, J. *Psychotherapy by Reciprocal Inhibition.* Stanford, Calif.: Stanford University Press, 1958.

Wyer, R. S. Self-acceptance, discrepancy between parents' perceptions of their children, and goal seeking effectiveness. *Journal of Personality and Social Psychology,* 1965, *2,* 311–16.

Zubin, J., and J. Money (Eds.). *Contemporary Sexual Behavior: Critical Issues in the 1970's.* Baltimore: The Johns Hopkins University Press, 1973.

5

Attitudes and Attitude Change

If social facilitation was the major process studied during the first three decades of the formal history of social psychology, then it is probably accurate to say that attitudes and attitude change were the major focus of social psychological research in its second three decades. Gordon Allport (1935) published a relatively early treatment of the subject and 33 years later had this to say (Allport, 1968, pp. 59–60).

This concept (attitude) is probably the most distinctive and indispensable concept in contemporary American social psychology. No other term appears more frequently in experimental and theoretical literature. Its popularity is not difficult to explain. It has come into favor, first of all, because it is not the property of any one psychological school of thought, and therefore serves admirably the purposes of eclectic writers. Furthermore, it is a concept which escapes the controversy concerning the relative influence of heredity and environment. Since an attitude may combine both instinct and habit in any proportion, it avoids the extreme commitments of both the instinct theory and environmentalism. The term likewise is elastic enough to apply either to the dispositions of single, isolated individuals or to broad patterns of culture (*common* attitudes). Psychologists and sociologists therefore find in it a meeting point for discussion and research. This useful, one might almost say peaceful, concept has been so widely adopted that it has virtually established itself as the keystone in the edifice of American social psychology.

It is probably only fair to tell you at the outset that the "keystone" in the edifice of American social psychology has some cracks in it. In the decade of the 70s attitudes and attitude change have relinquished their pre-eminent status to other concerns. Just 8 to 10 years ago, it would have been virtually unthinkable to write a text in social psychology without including at least two chapters on attitudes, one on their nature and formation and one on attitude change. The unthinkable has been thought and done, signaling perhaps an end to the dominant position of attitudes in social psychology. Why has this come about? Such questions are easy to ask, but difficult to answer. Realistically this whole chapter will be an attempt to answer that question.

If there are those who read this chapter and disagree with the conclusion I have reached, I draw your attention to the graph for Chapter 5 for articles published in the professional journals found on the inside of the front cover. No other area in social psychology was as popular in the research literature as attitudes, reaching a high point in 1970 when about 1 out of 5 articles published in the *Journal of Personality and Social Psychology* was concerned with attitudes. By 1977, that figure had dropped to about 1 in 50 articles. In a very short period of time a very popular research area had lost much of its popularity.

I speak of the current neglect of attitudes and attitude change with some fear and trepidation because there may be a startling new research approach out there that will revolutionize the area. For you see, the neglect of attitudes and particularly attitude change in recent years has not come about because the problems have been solved; quite the contrary. People have lost interest in the area because it has proved to be so intractable. After 30 years or more of intensive research, there is still little consensus about why people change their attitudes and even fewer empirical demonstrations of actual change. This does not mean, however, that there will not be resurgence of interest because, as you will soon see, it is a vitally important topic.

Attitudes—Their Nature and Formation

We're back at square one and definition again. Before we can adequately understand attitudes, we should know what they are. Allport (1968, p. 60) says: "'Attitude' connotes a neuropsychic state of readiness for mental and physical activity." Murphy, Murphy, and Newcomb (1937, p. 889) say: "Attitude is primarily a way of being 'set' toward or against certain things." Katz and Stotland (1959, p. 428) say that "an attitude is a tendency or disposition to evaluate an object or the symbol of that object in a certain way." Notice that Allport's definition (which he had first stated in similar form in 1935) and that of Murphy, Murphy, and Newcomb seem to imply that behavior, either physical or mental, is a necessary condition of holding an attitude. The later definition tends to concentrate on the evaluative nature of an attitude and does not imply any overt behavior. Chapter 2 discussed Wrightsman's (1968) study, in which he compared law-and-order attitudes as exemplified by political stickers and adherence to the law. Wrightsman's study makes an important point, which has been a thorn in the side of attitude researchers. That is, attitudes do not necessarily involve overt behavior and the later definition of Katz and Stotland indicates that this lesson was learned through being brought up short by some experimental realities (also see Wicker, 1971). According to Insko (1967, p. 2) "more recent definitions focus on the affective tendency to favorably or unfavorably evaluate objects and entirely discard the notion that any overt behavior is implied. The most common contemporary usage seems to follow this example, thus regarding the evaluative dimension as the single defining dimension for attitudes."

Even though recent definitions of attitudes have stressed their evaluative nature and not their behavioral consequences, it is still almost a statement of faith among attitude researchers that attitudes affect behavior. How they affect it and what the exact relationship between the two is, is still a matter of conjecture.

To recapitulate, attitudes have three components, cognitive, affective, and behavioral. That is, an attitude has a cognitive element of belief about an object, an affective element that controls how much the person likes or dislikes the object, and thirdly how the person behaves on the basis of his or her cognitive and affective set. Consistent with more recent research on attitudes, we will deemphasize the behavioral aspect of attitudes. It is interesting to note, however, that there is probably a closer correspondence between the behavioral element of attitudes and attitude change, because to change an attitude requires behavior, at the very least cognitive behavior. It is also these two components of attitudes, their behavioral correlates and their change, that have proved most intractable to research.

We have mentioned several definitions of attitudes. But for our purposes, let us use this one: An attitude *is a relatively stable evaluative response toward an object that has cognitive, affective, and probably behavioral components or consequences.* Now how do we differentiate attitudes from opinions and values? In social psychology, attitudes are generally thought of as beliefs or cognitions about reality or some aspect of reality. Values, on the other hand, are typically placed in a category that is more ethical in nature. Thus a value would be thought of as a quality or object that is desirable as a means or as an end in itself. Another way of looking at values, one that has a slightly more artistic flavor, would be to describe values as ideals or customs that arouse an emotional response in persons in a society. However opinions and values are defined, they have not held the interest of psychologists that attitudes have held.

Fishbein and Ajzen (1975) have proposed a model to account for how a person processes information about an attitude. Their model is quite consistent with the three components of attitudes already discussed: cognitive, affective, and behavioral. There are, however, two important differences in the Fishbein and Ajzen model. Their information-processing approach translates the three attitudinal components into operational definitions that can easily be measured. Second, they subdivide the behavioral component of attitudes.

If an attitude is an evaluative response, then the strength of this evaluation (belief) can be measured by determining the *subjective probability* that the attitude object actually possesses the characteristic in question. One individual who believes in a supreme being may differ from another person who believes in a supreme being in terms of the probability that such a being exists. If one person believes that there are 5 chances in 10 a supreme being exists and another person believes there are 9 chances in 10 a supreme being exists, both might answer identically the question "Do you believe in a supreme being?" And yet they differ markedly in how certain they are that such a being exists. These differences in belief strength allow us to distinguish between the two individuals. It is not only possible to scale a person's belief strength, it is possible to scale the importance of an attitude. If an individual is certain that there is a supreme being but it is unimportant, the consequences for this person may differ from the consequences of another person, who is not so certain a supreme being exists but believes it vitally important. That is, Fishbein and Ajzen argue that it is the combination of the subjective probability that the attitude object actually possesses the characteristic in question and the importance of the characteristic that determines the strength of the attitude.

The second contribution made by Fishbein and Ajzen is the introduction of the concept of behavioral intention. An individual may believe certain things about a number of attitude objects, but have no intention of putting any of these beliefs into action. For example, an individual may believe strongly in law and order, but have no intention of following laws that are considered unimportant. Thus, the people who displayed Wallace bumper stickers in Wrightsman's study (see Chapter 2) may have believed in law and order but had no intention of obeying that particular law. We shall return to the issue of attitudes and behavior again in this chapter.

THE IMPORTANCE OF ATTITUDES

Why are attitudes important? Possibly, because of the state of affairs with respect to research in the area you've come to the conclusion that attitudes are not really important after all. Nothing could be further from the truth. People's attitudes have far-reaching and important ramifications—for an individual, a group, or a society. Let us consider the potential of attitudes for all three categories.

Consider yourself and your best friend, or if you have several friends you like about equally, select one of them. Do not select a friend with whom you are involved in a romantic relationship.

Think carefully about the attitudes you hold and then select the five attitudes you hold that are most important to you. Next compare these five attitudes of yours with your friend's attitudes about the same five topics. If you do not know what your friend feels about one of the attitudes you have selected discard it and select another one that is important to you. It is important that you are certain you know what your friend thinks about each topic. Do not make assumptions that he or she must feel this way (probably it's the way you feel anyhow). My guess is that you will find that you and your friend are in basic agreement about issues that you find important. Attitudes, and particularly similarity of attitudes, do seem to play a function in the people to whom we are attracted. (see Chapter 9).

Think now about groups, and for the moment specifically about minority groups.

Some people's attitudes about blacks include the idea that ghettos are for blacks and some ghettos are populated by blacks. Even though the advertising in this ghetto is "especially for blacks," none of us would choose to live in substandard housing.

To be even more specific, think about blacks and your attitude towards blacks. One obvious determinant of how you feel about blacks is whether you are black yourself. Another determinant about blacks for you is what you have been taught to believe about blacks, how much or how little contact you've had with blacks, which may be determined by where you were brought up, and so forth. We have attitudes about other groups and they may be accurate or inaccurate. (We refer to inaccurate attitudes as prejudice.) The point is, however, that we have attitudes about whole groups of people that can range from the grossest stereotypes to as sensitive an understanding of the other group as possible without actually being part of that group. Here again, attitudes are important, and when they are prejudiced or in other ways inaccurate, they can lead to enormous group tensions. The ramifications for the way we live are enormous.

Consider the attitudes of the population of the United States and Canada during World War II and the war in Vietnam. In the late 1930s and early 40s there were innumerable young men who were virtually beating down the door to enlist to fight in defense of their country. During the 1960s and early 1970s, there were thousands of young men who left the United States to reside in Canada and other countries to avoid being drafted. These individuals' attitudes about the war were obviously quite negative, but of more interest to us, the citizens of Canada's attitudes about the war were such that the Canadian government felt free to allow those who refused to fight in the war to live in peace in Canada. The attitudes of the people of the United States changed over the years, and whereas these young men were viewed with disdain by a large part of the population in the United States in the mid-1960s, they were all given amnesty on January 21, 1977, the first full day Jimmy Carter was President of the United States. Even more striking is the fact that Carter had said during the presidential campaign that he intended to do precisely what he did. Here, then, is a case of the powerful influence the collective attitudes of a society can have.

We have had three illustrations of the ways in which attitudes can have a strong and lasting impact on individuals, groups, and societies. You can quite probably think of an enormous number of other examples of the importance of attitudes. They are important; they are just quite difficult to deal with in a scientific manner.

The Formation of Attitudes

One of the reasons Allport advanced for the popularity of attitudes in social psychological research is that it escapes the environmentalists'—hereditarian controversy because it is possible to mix hereditarian and environmental explanations in about any proportion desired. Most attitude theorists today prefer their mix to be quite heavy on the learned aspect of attitudes and very light with respect to genes. Even though McGuire (1969) suggests the possibility that physiological and genetic characteristics may contribute to attitude formation, there is very little serious consideration given to the formation of attitudes except as they are learned. People learn to like or dislike all sorts of diverse things. For example, it would be rather unreasonable to assume that someone likes the Beatles more than Beethoven because of genetic factors, although there may be an interaction of genetic components with learning that cause an individual to have, say, a more positive attitude toward music than toward sports. A person who lacks physical coordination and prowess because of his or her genetic endowments may be drawn to less physical and more mental or aesthetic pursuits. Music, drama, or intellectual activities may be perferred by such an individual because of certain genetic characteristics. Furthermore, such physiological attributes as the ability to hear (pitch) accurately may help determine an individual's attitude toward music. Outside of such basic potential genetic effects on attitudes, a person learns his or her attitudes.

How Are Attitudes Learned?

Granting that attitudes are learned, we may well ask how it is done. Here we will discuss only three kinds of learning with respect to attitudes, and the basic fundamentals of these three mechanisms have already been covered in Chapter 1. The three basic ways in which attitudes are learned are classical conditioning, instrumental conditioning, and imitation.

Classical Conditioning. Arthur Staats and his associates (Staats, 1970; Staats and Staats, 1958; Staats, Higa, and Reid, 1970; 1972; Staats, Minke, Martin, and Higa, 1972) have developed a theory and a methodology for explaining attitude formation in classical conditioning terms. It is important to discuss the implications of Staats' work, but we should also note that others, notably Page (1971; 1972; 1973; 1974), have argued that the Staats' results are consistent with a demand characteristics explanation rather than a conditioning explanation. Not surprisingly, Staats remains unconvinced. The argument between Staats and Page is an important one, but it is also quite technical and is beyond the scope of this book to resolve. (And so far seems to be beyond the scope of the social psychological journals to resolve.) The controversy is mentioned here only so that you may be aware of it. Staats' approach serves as an excellent example of the use of classical conditioning principles in attitude formation. The substance of Page's argument concerns whether Staats' laboratory experiments may be explained via some experimental confound, not whether the principles of classical conditioning are a reasonable explanation for attitude formation in real life. An outline of one of Staats' experiments will give you an idea of how classical conditioning procedures can be utilized to explain attitude formation.

Lohr and Staats (1973) employed the behavioral theory of attitude formation: "that is, a stimulus that is paired with an event eliciting an attitude (emotional response) will also come to elicit the attitude" (p. 196). Remember, in classical conditioning, a previously neutral stimulus (CS) paired with a negative or positive stimulus (UCS) will in time come to elicit the emotional response (CR) by itself. The basic procedure Staats and his associates have used it to take positively rated words and negatively rated words and pair with neutral nonsense syllables (consisting of a consonant, vowel, consonant that have no meaning, such as CEF, LAJ, PID, or VOT). In this particular experiment native Japanese, Korean, and Cantonese speakers were used as subjects. Previous studies had indicated that the conditioning procedure was effective in English and Indo-European languages, so the generality of the conditioning effect was being researched by Lohr and Staats. Eighteen positive words and eighteen negative words were selected to be paired with the nonsense syllables. For any subject only positive or neutral words were paired with a specific nonsense syllable and negative or neutral words were paired with another nonsense syllable. Following multiple-conditioning trials, the nonsense syllables were rated by the subjects on a pleasant-unpleasant dimension. In all three languages the nonsense syllables that had been paired with positive words were rated as being more pleasant than the nonsense syllables that had been paired with the negative words. As the nonsense syllables were themselves originally picked because of their neutrality, Lohr and Staats (1973, p. 198) say, "The present study provides evidence that attitudes can be established in Sino-Tibetan languages employing the language conditioning procedure."

It is a long way from conditioning pleasant and unpleasant associations to nonsense syllables to learning attitudes by associating positive and negative affect with them. Yet in real life it is probably true that we hold certain of our attitudes because they were at one time associated with positive affect. For example, it is quite possible that parents hold certain attitudes and their children ascribe to the same position even though the parents have not specifically tried to teach the attitude to the child. These attitudes are, quite possibly, learned by being associated with pleasant things that occur in families. This, of course, is a naturally occurring form of classical conditioning.

Bandura (1965) has argued that classical conditioning can occur vicariously, that is, by imagined participation in the experience of others. It is not necessary, in this view, for the individual actually to experience the conditioning process. Rather, because someone else has experienced the process, an individual can learn the association by observation. Possibly an example will be of help. Most people do not need to be struck by a car to learn not to cross a busy street without exercising caution. Observing another person being injured by a car or even being told about someone who was injured serves to make us cautious. In the same manner, we may adopt attitudes held by our parents or other people close to us because we see how important that attitude is to the individual or how the individual has benefited from it. Thus children may understand little of political parties but they strongly agree with the position of the political party preferred by their parents.

Instrumental Conditioning. Another way in which attitudes are learned is by instrumental conditioning. In instrumental conditioning, remember, something is learned because it is reinforced. To be more technical, instrumental learning occurs when some desired behavior is reinforced and/or some undesired behavior is punished. With respect to attitudes, it is difficult to conceptualize experiments that would test the assumptions of attitude formation via instrumental conditioning precisely because so much instrumental conditioning occurs in "real life" that a few minutes or even hours in a laboratory will not make significant alterations in the pattern of attitudes formed. You might immediately argue that the same thing can be said about classical conditioning, and it can. Remember, however, that laboratory classical conditioning studies of attitude formation utilize neutral stimuli such as nonsense syllables. One basic difference between classical and instrumental conditioning is that in classical conditioning the originally neutral stimulus (CS) and the positive (or negative) stimulus (UCS) will be paired regardless of what the subject does. In instrumental conditioning the reinforcement (positive stimulus) is delivered only if the subject emits a response. Since, by definition, the neutral stimuli are neutral, there is little or no incentive for the subject to respond. This, no doubt, accounts for the more frequent use of a classical conditioning paradigm rather than an instrumental conditioning paradigm in experimental social psychology.

Many people who voted for Mr. Smith may have done so because he was a Democrat, but they may have learned to be Democrats via vicarious conditioning.

There have been some studies that have demonstrated attitude formation utilizing instrumental conditioning techniques. Let us consider two that were not laboratory experiments because there has been a good deal of criticism leveled at laboratory experiments (cf. Page, 1972); the criticism is that demand characteristics account for any observed effects. As demand characteristics are most applicable to laboratory research, we will again sidestep the controversy, this time by concentrating on nonlaboratory studies. This is done not to denigrate the controversy, but because the technicality of the arguments, pro and con, are beyond the scope of this book.

Hildum and Brown (1956) contacted subjects by telephone and asked them 15 redundant questions concerning their attitudes toward the general education requirements at Harvard University. Half of the subjects were reinforced for pro attitudes and half were reinforced for con attitudes. Two verbal reinforcers were used, "good" and "mm-hmm." Since "mm-hmm" had no effects, I will consider only those subjects reinforced by using the word *good* when they expressed the appropriate response for their (pro or con) experimental group. In this case, *good* produced more attitudes consonant with the attitudes expressed just prior to its utterance by the interviewer. In other words, when a subject was reinforced for taking a particular position, he expressed more attitudes consonant with that position.

Insko (1965) telephoned subjects and interviewed them about having a Springtime Aloha Week (a festival held each Fall) at the University of Hawaii. Half of the subjects were reinforced for positive statements about the idea and half for negative statements about it. One week later a questionnaire was passed out in a course all respondents were in, and one question about a Springtime Aloha Week was included among several others. Verbal reinforcement over the phone carried over to the written responses on the questionnaire a week later. This study in connection with the Hildum and Brown experiment lends support to the idea that instrumental reinforcement does influence the formation of attitudes.

Attitude formation in "real life" situations undoubtedly has an instrumental component involved in it. Children learn their parents' attitudes with an amazing frequency and it is relatively easy to see how this happens. Particularly with respect to those attitudes that are important to the parents, children are rewarded for adopting their parents' attitudes, and at times, punished for adopting attitudes that are different from their parents'. For example, most parents believe it is right to be truthful (at least most of the time) and expect their children to do the same (all of the time). Children are quite often reinforced for being truthful by social and material rewards. On the other side of this coin, children are often punished for not telling the truth. Obviously in real life children are not always rewarded for telling the truth or punished for lying, but it happens with sufficient regularity that children learn to tell some semblance of the truth.

At this point in our discussion you may be thinking about a distinction made earlier, and that is the distinction between attitudes and behavior. Is telling the truth an attitude or a behavior? Obviously the act of being truthful is a behavior, whereas the evaluative process about the concept of truth is an attitude. It is highly possible that most of the people who lie would support the concept that one ought to be truthful. It just so happens that in the complexities of modern life the attitude of truthfulness may come into conflict with, say, an attitude toward politeness. Many people whose attitudes include one favoring truthfulness lie quite often because they wish to be polite when asked to comment on a possession recently purchased by a friend. We have seen earlier that attitudes and behavior do not correspond exactly or even very closely. It may be that a good part of the reason for this lack of correspondence occurs because of two or more attitudes whose behavioral components conflict with each other.

Imitation. The third way in which people learn attitudes is through imitation, and this way is even more closely tied to behavior than is learning via instrumental conditioning. Probably the most prolific researcher in the area of imitation, or modeling, is Albert Bandura (1971a, 1971b, 1973; Bandura and Jefferey, 1973), who argues that an enormous amount is learned by observation of others. It is not necessary for a behavior to be reinforced for it to be learned, although reinforcement plays a large part in determining when the observer will perform the behavior. Behavior, and through behavior, attitudes can be learned by watching a model. If you give that thought some serious consideration, the potentialities are truly enormous.

Consider an example of behavior that occurs in American and Canadian homes with a great degree of frequency. A child has misbehaved and been caught. The child is punished by being spanked. What does the child learn from such an encounter besides the fact that it hurts to sit down? One way to look at the situation is to view it through the eyes of the child. In the first place the child has observed a model being aggressive (hitting) toward him or her. Second, the person who did the aggressing was a lot bigger than the target of the aggression. Putting these two things together, the child has learned that it is acceptable to hit others and it is also acceptable to hit others smaller than himself or herself. This may not be at all what the parents wished to convey with the punishment, but since punishment itself is notoriously unreliable in its effects, the child is more likely to learn that it is all right to aggress against littler people than not to misbehave. At any rate, in an instance such as this, behavior and attitudes may translate back and forth more readily.

Attitudes and Behavior

Inherent in our discussion of attitude formation in particular, but also true of attitudes in general, is the feeling on the part of psychologists that attitudes and behavior should show more consistency than they do. You will remember that early definitions of attitudes emphasized their behavioral component, but through bitter experience, later attitude theorists either omitted any reference to behavior or limited it to mental behavior.

During the time that attitude theorists were admitting that there is little reliable correspondence between attitudes and behavior, personality theorists were questioning the relationship between traits and behaviors. In personality, a trait is conceived of as an enduring, relatively stable, disposition to behave in a certain way. For example, a person who is aggressive is thought to be aggressive in most situations and over long periods of time. Many personality theorists have come to the conclusion that things are not quite that simple and that situational determinants of behavior are much stronger than previously assumed.

If attitude is substituted for trait, a situation basically similar to that existing in personality exists in social psychology today. Thus, borrowing from personality may be of some interest and may point in a research direction that could prove to be useful in better understanding the relationship between attitudes and behavior. One recent research area may well prove fruitful.

Reformulations in the trait-vs.-situation controversy in personality theory suggest that people differ in the extent to which situational factors, on the one hand, and dispositional factors, on the other, influence their behavior (Bem and Allen, 1974; Snyder and Monson, 1975). These differences have been conceptualized as a social psychological construct called *self-monitoring* (Snyder, 1974). The formulation is

---

ATTITUDES AND BEHAVIOR—ABORTION

In the 1970s abortion has become an issue over which many battles have been fought. In an interesting study of attitudes and behavior, Werner (1978) studied the correlation between activism on abortion issues and attitudes towards abortion. This research was primarily concerned with the amount of pro- or anti-abortion behavior that would be evidenced by a group of people who either favored or opposed abortion. The issue is one to which enormous amounts of publicity are given and, if there is a correlation between attitudes and behavior, it should show most clearly in an emotionally charged issue.

Four hundred and forty-eight subjects (266 female and 182 male) participated in the study. They were drawn from the San Francisco Bay area and the mean age was the mid-thirties. A 58-item measure of behavior was used, asking the respondents such things as whether they had tried to convince a friend about abortion, whether they had wired the President of the United States about the issue or whether they had worn a button favoring one side or the other in the issue. Attitudes towards abortion were measured in three ways; by open-ended essays, an abortion acceptability questionnaire, and an abortion attitude scale. Measuring the attitudes in three different ways allowed for the most stable determination of the individual's attitudes.

The first question to be answered was whether there was a directional consistency between attitudes and activism. That is, did those individuals who favored abortion support abortion in their activism? The answer is yes! Ninety two and one-half percent of the women and 93 percent of

the males were active in a pattern consistent with their attitudes.

The correlations between attitudes and activism were generally quite high. For females, the correlation between attitudes and activism was $+0.75$ for those opposed to abortion and $+0.56$ for those favoring abortion; for males the correlations were $+0.65$ and $+0.16$ respectively. The surprising low correlation for males who favored abortion is somewhat mystifying. In general, abortion is a somewhat more female-oriented issue; however males who opposed it showed a rather high correlation between attitudes and behavior.

The correlations reported by Werner are higher than those generally reported between attitudes and behavior. It should be noted, however, that Werner used a particularly salient attitude, was careful to measure it in several ways and used a self-report measure of activism. That is, the activism measure asked how many times individuals had engaged in a behavior. Any errors in reporting would probably be expected to be in the direction of agreement with the attitudes expressed. Even though the correlations between attitudes and behavior are higher than usually reported, all of these factors taken together still indicate a rather large discrepancy between attitudes and behavior.

Reference

Werner, P. D. Personality and attitude-activism correspondence. *Journal of Personality and Social Psychology,* 1978, *36,* 1375–1390.

based on the assumption that an individual in a social setting attempts to construct a pattern of social behavior that is appropriate to the particular context he or she is in. Two basic sources of information, among others, are available to the individual; cues about the situation and knowledge about inner states. Individuals differ in the extent to which they rely on either source of information. Those who heed situational cues (high self-motivating individuals) demonstrate considerable situation-to-situation fluctuations in behavior, whereas those who rely on inner states show less situation-to-situation fluctuation. Individual differences in self-monitoring are measured by the Self-Monitoring Scale whose psychometric properties have been subjected to detailed scrutiny (Snyder, 1972; 1974; 1976; Snyder and Monson, 1975).

High self-monitoring persons are aware that what they do and what they believe are discrepant, at least in certain instances. Low self-monitoring people, on the other hand, report that their behavior is under the guidance of relevant attitudes, that their behavior is a true and credible guide to inferring their attitudes, and that there is a considerable amount of correspondence between what they do and what they are. To be more specific, high self-monitoring persons endorse such statements as "I am not always the person I appear to be" or "I may deceive people by being friendly when I really dislike them" (Snyder, 1974, p. 531). Low self-monitoring individuals endorse such statements as "My behavior is usually an expression of my true inner feelings, attitudes, and beliefs" and "I can only argue for ideas that I already believe" (Snyder, 1974, p. 531).

Snyder and Tanke (1976) report a study in which high and low self-monitoring individuals were given the opportunity to write an essay that was basically in opposition to their initial position, or in agreement with it. In both instances there was greater correspondence between the written position (behavior) and the attitudes of low self-monitoring individuals than those of high self-monitoring persons. That is, after writing an essay favoring a specific position, whether they had initially agreed with the position or not, low self-monitoring individuals showed more congruence between the positions espoused in their essay (behavior) and their final attitudes than did high self-monitoring individuals.

Of course, there is a big difference between writing an essay in a laboratory and agreeing with the positions espoused in it to believing in law and order and obeying the law (see Wrightsman's field study discussed in Chapter 2). It is encouraging, however, to have researchers uncovering individual differences variables that are closely tied to situational variables. For decades, social psychologists have argued that the interaction of the situation and the individual must be studied, but then they promptly overemphasized the situation and underemphasized the individual. On the other hand, personality psychology has overemphasized the person and underemphasized the situation. It is intriguing and encouraging to see the two emphases being given equal or nearly equal weight in social psychology. It is, interestingly enough, also happening in a field of personality that has been called *cognitive social learning* (cf. Lamberth, Rappaport, and Rappaport, 1978, for a discussion).

Personality Traits and Attitudes

One of the intriguing similarities between personality traits and attitudes is that psychologists generally measure them in the same way. Most personality tests and attitude surveys are self-report measures. That is, the individual is asked how he or she would act or what is believed. Many, if not most, psychologists who study personality now believe that personality traits predict behavior in certain situations (Endler, 1973; Endler and Magnusson, 1975; Mischel, 1975). That is, it may be possible to predict behavior when a trait is known if the situation is sufficiently specific. For example, a general measure of anxiety does not predict academic achievement very well, but a measure of test anxiety predicts performance on tests quite well. The necessity to specify the personality trait and the situation is helping to develop more precise relationships between the two.

It may be that there will be a necessity to be more specific in determining attitudes and how they affect behavior in certain situations. Even though you may believe in certain ideals (hold certain attitudes), you may not express them or behave in accordance with them in specific situations. For example, if you strongly believe that there is nothing wrong with smoking pot, the situation in which you find yourself will probably influence what you say and do about it. Among your like-minded peers you may talk and act one way, but quite another when you are with your parents, grandparents, or at a convention of law-enforcement officials. Research is needed to determine if the weak link between attitudes and behavior is based upon the same mechanism as the weak link between personality traits and behavior.

The Measurement of Attitudes

In the early chapters of this book I have alluded to the measurement problem, but have not stated it explicitly. A scientist cannot study what he or she cannot measure. This statement seems almost too obvious to mention, but after perusing the history of social psychology, I feel compelled to mention it. And a second law of science is that the better the measurement, the better the science. To study an area adequately, it is necessary to develop measuring techniques that are accurate and, we hope, relatively easy to use. The next few pages will hit the high spots with regard to attitude measurement. It may also be appropriate to note that one of the reasons attitudes became the keystone of social psychology is that, at least on the surface, attitudes are relatively easy to measure.

Self-report Measures

One of the distinctive characteristics of humans is that we have the capacity to communicate with each other using spoken, written, gestural, or some other form of language. One of the distinctive characteristics of psychologists seems to be that they don't believe anything anyone writes, speaks, or gestures to them. Although ignoring gestures may simply be a form of protecting the psychologist's self-esteem, there appears to be every reason to take seriously what people say and write to you, and until there is evidence to the contrary, to entertain the thought that such communications may be accurate. Psychologists in general, and social psychologists in particular, have seemingly been unwilling to believe what they are told. Parenthetically, I must say that from my completely subjective, unscientific, biased frame of reference, I do think that clinical psychologists disbelieve more communications than do social psychologists, but that may well be a function of the fact that they work with more -paths (psycho, socio, and so on) than we do. This whole polemic is intended to assert that one of the best ways to find out what someone thinks about a given topic is to ask him (or her). True, care must be exercised to assure that the question is not asked in such a way as to determine the answer. For example, if your boss asks how you like her new dress, the chances are she will not receive a completely accurate answer. The degree of inaccuracy will be a function of what you actually think of the dress, how well your boss accepts criticism, how well you like your job, and a variety of other considerations. However, careful considerations of the factors that might bias an individual's self-report of his or her attitudes can go a long way toward assuring fairly accurate attitude measurement.

There are many ways to ask a person what he or she believes, but the four most popular in measuring attitudes are the Likert type, the psychophysical approach (Thurstone and Chave, 1929), the method of successive hurdles (Bogardus, 1925; Guttman, 1944; 1947) and the semantic differential (Osgood, Suci, and Tannenbaun, 1957).

The Likert-type attitude scale is probably the most used measure of attitudes and is based upon presenting the respondent with a series of statements concerning a particular issue and allowing the person to indicate which variation of the statement most closely approximates his or her attitude. There are usually 6 alternatives, 3 pro and 3 con, but sometimes a seventh category (neutral) is added. For example, instead of asking "Do you believe in a supreme being," a Likert-type scale would look something like this:

I strongly believe there is a supreme being.
I believe there is a supreme being.
I believe to a slight extent that there is a supreme being.
I neither believe nor disbelieve in a supreme being. (*May be omitted.*)
I believe to a slight extent that there is no supreme being.
I believe there is no supreme being.
I strongly believe there is no supreme being.

As you can see, there are gradations of belief in the topic and when several attitudes which cluster together are measured, the responses may be scored from -3 to $+3$ and summed to achieve an individual's attitude score about a cluster of related attitudes. Under those conditions, this approach is known as the *method of summated ratings.*

Thurstone's psychophysical approach is also based on assessing the evaluative feelings an individual has about a topic. It differs from the Likert-type scale in that a group of independent judges evaluate a series of statements about an attitude on the basis of how "pro" or "con" they are. These evaluations are then summarized to give a "scale value" to each statement. The individual then indicates which items he or she agrees or disagrees with as well as which items are neutral. A person is expected to disagree with items that are too extreme for him or her. The median or average value of the items the individual endorses is then used as an index of his or her attitudes. For example, the following items with their scale values are a few items taken from Thurstone (1931) about attitudes towards blacks.

*Scale
Value*   *Item*

10.3 I believe that the Negro deserves the same social privileges as the white man.

10.3 The Negro should be considered as equal to the white man and be given the white man's advantages.

7.7 The Negro is perfectly capable of taking care of himself if the white man would let him alone.

5.4 I am not at all interested in how the Negro rates socially.

2.7 Under no circumstances should Negro children be allowed to attend the same schools as white children.

0.9 The Negro will always remain as he is—a little higher than the animals.

0.9 The Negro should be considered in the lowest class among human beings.

The individual responding would mark those statements he or she agreed with and the median or mean of the scale values of those items would represent his or her attitudes towards blacks. Thurstone's statements about the racial issue show you what kinds of questions were being used in assessing attitudes about the topic roughly 50 years ago. More will be said on the subject in Chapter 6.

The method of successive hurdles is exemplified by Bogardus' Social Distance Scale in which the individual is asked to rate whether he or she would engage in general activities with specific (usually ethnic) groups. Each step indicates a willingness to engage in less intimate relationships. The scale from Bogardus (1933, p. 269) was as follows.

1. Would marry.

2. Would have as a regular friend.

3. Would work beside in an office.

4. Would have several families in my neighborhood.

5. Would have merely as speaking acquaintances.

6. Would have live outside my neighborhood.

7. Would have live outside my country.

The final self-report measure to consider is the semantic differential, which was developed by Osgood, Suci, and Tannenbaum (1957). The idea behind this approach is that individuals can determine degrees of feeling about a specific issue and one way of getting at that evaluative meaning is to use bipolar adjectives. An example of the semantic differential would be as follows. The individual is asked to check the space that most closely approximates his or her feelings about a specific issue. On an actual semantic differential, the numbers are omitted, just the blank spaces to check are provided.

Blacks

Warm	(7	6	5	4	3	2	1)	Cold
Sad	(1	2	3	4	5	6	7)	Cold
Nice	(7	6	5	4	3	2	1)	Awful

The scale is scored as indicated above, with low scores for the unpleasant dimension and high scores for the pleasant. A sum or an average can be taken to give an overall attitude. There is no one semantic differential; rather the topic and the bipolar adjectives make up a variety of such scales. As such, it is a flexible and useful tool of measurement.

Physiological Measures

There was a time, not too many years ago, when some social psychologists felt that physiological measures were better than any other measures, probably because it was assumed that the individual could not fake his or her blood pressure, heart rate, galvanic skin response, and the like. Here we are concerned with our subjects lying to us again. Physiological measures were rather simple but expensive to take, but it was assumed that we were really getting at what the individual felt. This view was greatly advanced by some startling research (Miller and Banuayizi, 1968) which indicated that supposedly involuntary responses such as heart rate and intestinal contractions were under voluntary control. This stimulated a great deal of research into voluntary control of supposedly involuntary responses (commonly called biofeedback), which indicates that these responses are under some form of voluntary control. Ironically enough, Miller and Dworkin (1973) reported difficulties in replicating the original experiments, but by that time biofeedback was so firmly established that it is really not very credible to contend that humans cannot voluntarily control at least some "involuntary" responses. Possibly rats can or cannot control such involuntary responses, but humans appear quite able to do so. Therefore, whereas it may be harder for individuals to fake their attitudes when physiologically measured, it is not impossible.

Another, more serious, drawback to the physiological measurement of attitudes is that such measures record arousal and an individual may become aroused either because of agreement or disagreement. Thus, just because an individual's heart rate or galvanic skin response changes when an attitude is communicated to him or her, it is impossible to say whether the individual agrees or disagrees with the position communicated.

For a variety of reasons, the physiological measurement of attitudes is fraught with difficulties and is rather seldom employed.

Unobtrusive Measures

Nothing warms the cockles of a social psychologist's heart in quite the way that an unobtrusive measure does, unless, of course, it is a nonobvious finding. The basic reason for this is that, properly used, unobtrusive measures are not subject to the falsification of more open measures. Unobtrusive measures fall into many categories, and some of them are fun because they are deductions made from data that should have no bearing on the activity being studied. For example, Mabley (1963) used water pressure rather than Nielson ratings to ascertain how many people were watching television. He found that water pressure in Chicago had been on a fairly even plateau throughout a tense Rose Bowl game, at the end of which it plummeted. Mabley concluded that many people were watching the game and rushed to drink or use the toilet at its conclusion. Obviously, this is not as accurate a record of TV viewing as can be obtained by asking people if they are watching TV, and it cannot be as accurate in determining which program was being watched, but it is an ingenious unobtrusive measure.

Kalven and Zeisel (1966) report a study in which an unobtrusive measure of jury behavior was used, a hidden microphone. A good deal of data was collected about jury deliberations and in response a law was passed prohibiting the recording of jury deliberations. This particular unobtrusive measure has resulted in a great deal of added difficulty in studying jury deliberations.

This section on unobtrusive measures began with a negative tone for a specific reason. Unobtrusive measures are fun, sufficiently so that they need to be carefully considered prior to being utilized. A properly used, ethical unobtrusive measure, whether it be observational, archival, or any other kind can be extremely valuable. Zajonc and Markus (1975) have shown how data collected for another purpose can be ingeniously used to understand a quite different problem. Used in this way, unobtrusive measures are vitally important and can add much to what has, indeed, become an overreliance on self-report measures. They do, however, contain the great danger of being misused. The misuse of such measures falls into two categories.

First, and foremost, there is the matter of ethics. A hidden microphone or camera, personal information retained in archives or data banks, academic records, and the like are all unobtrusive measures of something, but unless some restraint is used to assure that all persons who are involved won't be harmed by taking such measures, they should not be used. Only after serious thought is given to the ramifications of listening in, looking at, or observing people in their activities, then unobtrusive measures may be a useful device for studying attitudes.

Another problem of unobtrusive measures is their interpretability. Once an unobtrusive measure is taken, with how much certainty can a social psychologist draw conclusions? Take, for example, Mabley's measure of TV viewing, the drop in water pressure at the end of the Rose Bowl game. Quite frankly, there are a number of explanations for the water pressure drop. First, there could have been another, equally interesting, television program that ended at the same time the Rose Bowl did. Second, the Rose Bowl was being played in California with a two-hour time difference from Chicago. It may have ended at about the time thousands of people in Chicago started to prepare dinner. What was the weather like on that New Year's

Day? If it was pleasant, thousands of people could have come back inside as darkness was falling after a day outdoors and made use of a lot of water. One could go on, but to do so would belabor the point. Unobtrusive measures should give the scientist some rather unequivocal interpretation of the data, and if they don't, they are more fun than useful.

Unobtrusive measures can be vital measures to assessing attitudes. Wrightsman (1968) (see Chapter 2) gained a great deal of data quite ethically and was able to come to some rather straightforward conclusions by using unobtrusive measures—and it was fun to read about and, in all probability, to do. We need to approach them with caution because something that is fun sometimes is done whether it adds to our scientific knowledge or not.

Comment

The ready accessibility of attitude-measuring devices is one reason that attitudes became such an integral part of social psychology for so many years. This section on attitudinal measurement contains no treatment of behavioral measures of attitude. That, of course, is one of the problems of attitude measurement that is more real than apparent. You will recall that the preceding section made clear the lack of concurrence between attitudes and behavior. Behavioral measure of attitudes, which merely means observing behavior and inferring attitudes from behavior, is fraught with the same perils that occur when one tries to infer behavior from attitudes. I need not belabor the point now, except to say that the section on attitudes and behavior could easily have been included in the section on attitude measurement. The organization of this chapter calls attention to the fact that psychologists have vacillated about the behavioral component of attitudes. But even more important, it makes this next point. Social psychologists have, ironically, joined personality psychologists with respect to attitudes and behavior. That is, they have emphasized the interaction of person and situation for years, while overemphasizing the person and ignoring the situation. If an attitude is an evaluative predisposition toward an individual or object, why must attitudes be displayed in behavior? If we take seriously the idea that the environment has a great deal of impact on our behavior, then I can only say that it is not at all surprising that there is not more concurrence between attitudes and behavior. For example, a person may hate his or her boss, but need the job. The individual's attitude toward the boss may be very negative, whereas his or her behavior is at least neutral if not positive. More work like that of Snyder (Snyder, 1972; 1974; 1976; Snyder and Monson, 1975; Snyder and Tanke, 1976) may help us to sort out the relative influence of the individual and the situation.

Changing Attitudes

Most, if not all, of the reason that attitudes were predominant in social psychology for so many years was the golden ring of attitude change. If attitudes were of interest in social psychology, changing attitudes was infinitely more interesting, and profitable, for that matter. Even with the relatively primitive state of the art of changing attitudes, it is a multibillion dollar business. Madison Avenue has become synonymous with advertising agencies and these agencies are fondly desirous of changing your attitude about Brand X or Y or Z. If they can change enough people's attitudes, sales will zoom, and the agency will keep the account. Politicians periodically intensify their ongoing attempts at attitude change. In this instance they want to change attitudes that will influence voting behavior. To be quite honest about it, I suspect that most politicians would forego the change of attitude if the vote were available in some other way. Governments are constantly trying to change the attitudes of people in other countries about their government, their actions, and so forth. In this instance it is called propaganda.

You get the idea about the enormity of efforts toward attitude change and what is involved. There is no doubt that the whole idea of being able to change another person's attitudes is intriguing. How many times have we all thought "If so and so could just see how things really are;" or "If I could just convince her that this is the course of action we should really take." The scale is not quite so grand as Madison Avenue or propaganda, but the intent is the same—to change attitudes. It is, probably the intrinsically intriguing nature of the problem, added to the substantial

We are constantly bombarded with ads trying to make us change our attitudes.

monetary or patriotic benefits, that has had an important impact on attempts to change attitudes and on theories to account for that change.

Theories of Attitude Change

There have been an enormous number of theories of attitude change proposed, many more than we will have time to deal with here. Whole books have been written about it (Cohen, 1964; Fishbein and Ajzen, 1975; Insko, 1967; Triandis, 1971, to name a few) and undoubtedly more will come. The subject is extremely important and yet it has proven very difficult to develop theories of attitude change and even more difficult to successfully change attitudes. As indicated earlier, it is not the subject matter itself that has led to the decline in interest in attitude-change research, but the intractability of that subject matter to research solutions. Maybe it's just not possible to systematically change attitudes or maybe we social scientists have been following the wrong paths. Whatever the answer, let's take a little time to review three popular, but unsuccessful, theories of attitude change.

REINFORCEMENT THEORY OF ATTITUDE CHANGE

The reinforcement theory of attitude change is really a misnomer. There are a number of different reinforcement theories, but for explanatory purposes we may consider the theory set forth by Hovland, Janis, and Kelley (1953). The theory draws upon Hullian learning theory and in many ways is similar to the analogy of Hullian learning theory made to personality by Dollard and Miller (1950). Consistent with Hullian theory, the essence of this attitude-change theory is that the change results from learning produced by reinforcement.

Hovland, Janis, and Kelley differentiate between opinions and attitudes, with opinions being interpretations, expectations, or anticipations. Consistent with the distinction between opinions and attitudes given earlier in this chapter, opinions do not have the strong evaluative component that attitudes do. Both opinions and attitudes are viewed by Hovland, Janis, and Kelley as intervening variables that interact with each other. For example, you may hold the opinion that a politician is honest and have a favorable attitude toward him. When he pleads guilty to extortion, your opinion about his honesty will probably change and your attitude also may change to the unfavorable side of the scale. One of the most important elements in attitude change is the change in opinion that precedes it, and opinions are viewed as habits that have been built up over time by being reinforced. When an opinion changes, there is the *possibility* that an attitude or attitudes that are mediated by that opinion will also be subject to change. One way in which opinions can be changed is through persuasive communications. *A persuasive communication is viewed as a compound stimulus that raises a question and suggests an answer.* It is also assumed that the individual will provide his or her own answer to the questions. Few persuasive communications are as persuasive as the politician's guilty plea mentioned earlier. Most are much less dramatic and rely on three elements to change opinions.

The first of these variables that is important in opinion change is attention. If a person does not attend to a persuasive communication, it will have no effect upon

A sleeper effect in attitude-change research is defined as an increase in attitude change some time after an event has occurred to cause that change in attitudes. More specifically the sleeper effect initially referred to an increase in attitude change over time due to a persuasive communication delivered in association with a discounting cue because the communication and the cue became dissociated from each other. A discounting cue may be any cue which causes the subject to discount or devalue the communication. For example, let us assume that a group receives a communication from an auto assembly-line worker on the value of a balanced diet. Because the assembly-line worker has no background in nutrition, it is assumed that this would be a low credibility source and would not cause a great deal of attitude change. However, the sleeper effect would predict that over time the message and the source of the message would become dissociated; that is, the message would be remembered and the source forgotton. If that occurred, then after time had elapsed there would be a change in attitude.

The sleeper effect was first proposed by Hovland and his associates in their work on the reinforcement model of attitude change. For many years the effect was a widely accepted, though seldom-demonstrated phenomenon. It appeared that the effect was so intuitively appealing that a lack of empirical demonstration did it little harm.

Gillig and Greenwald (1974) reviewed the literature and found little evidence for a true sleeper effect (i.e., an increase in attitude change over time because of a disassociation of a persuasive communication from a discounting cue such as a low-credibility source). Furthermore, in seven attempts to demonstrate a sleeper effect, they were unable to do so, and therefore suggested that the sleeper effect should be "laid to rest."

Gruder, Cook, Hennigan, Flay, and Halamaj (1978) felt that the obituary for the sleeper effect was premature. They point out that a sleeper effect can be shown only if a discounting cue dissociates rapidly from the persuasive communication and if there is little delay in attitude change in the group that receives the message only (without the discounting cue). These researchers argue that those conditions have not always been met and that if they are, the sleeper effect may occur. In a series of studies, Gruder et al. demonstrated that the sleeper effect can be reliably elicited and measured. They conclude that the effect does occur and should be taken seriously.

What are we to conclude about the sleeper effect in attitude change? First, it seems obvious that it can be demonstrated in the laboratory. Whether it has any practical significance is an open question. As Gruder et al. point out, there is no way to know whether discounting cues dissociate rapidly from the persuasive communication. Therefore, only time will tell whether the sleeper effect is of theoretical importance only, or also of practical significance.

References

Gillig, P. M., and A. G. Greenwald. Is it time to lay the sleeper effect to rest? *Journal of Personality and Social Psychology*, 1974, *29*, 132–139.

Gruder, C. L., T. D. Cook, K. M. Hennigan, B. R. Flay, C. Alessis, and J. Halamaj. Empirical tests of the absolute sleeper effect predicted from the discounting cue hypothesis. *Journal of Personality and Social Psychology*, 1978, *36*, 1061–1074.

changing that person's opinion. A communication that is dull, or is about a topic that is totally unfamiliar to the individual, may not be attended to and thus will not lead to opinion change. If the person attends to the communication, then it must be comprehended. Communications that are beyond the ability of the hearer to understand will result in no opinion change.

If the communication is attended to and comprehended, then the final step in

The Bulletin

Sunday

West Edition

★ ★ ★   Sunday, February 25, 1979   ZXC

Section **A**

50 CENTS

Eilberg pleads guilty, avoids jail

Rep. Joshua Eilberg
... *won't go to jail*

By ROBERT W. KOTZBAUER
Of The Bulletin Staff

Former Philadelphia Congressman Joshua Eilberg yesterday entered a surprise guilty plea to misusing his public trust then was placed on five years probation, barred from seeking federal office ever again and fined $10,000.

Eilberg, 58, avoided a jail term with his plea bargain, but U.S. District Court Raymond J. Broderick's sentence also stipulated that he not seek state office during the term of probation and that he spend at least six hours a week in public service work.

"I regret very much I don't have the opportunity to run again," Eilberg, hands clasped behind his back, told Broderick. "That is very important to me."

The ban against holding "any office of honor, trust, or profit under the United States" is mandatory under the law, Broderick explained to Eilberg.

Eilberg is required "to devote six hours a week, without compensation, performing service for the community. . .in some place or institution where your talents will prove beneficial to the community." The place where he performs this service will be arranged by the federal probation service. The fine must be paid within 30 days.

The once-powerful Northeast Philadelphia Democrat pleaded guilty to one count of conflict of interest, abruptly ending his week-long trial before a word of testimony or a single document had been entered in evidence.

The charge, specifically, was that Eilberg had knowingly accepted private compensation, in addition to his salary as congressman, for services rendered before a government agency, the U.S. Community Services Administration (CSA) in 1975 and 1976.

Prosecutor Alan M. Lieberman, special assistant to U.S. Attorney Peter F. Vaira, told the seven-man, five-woman jury in his opening argument Friday:

Eilberg accepted at least $20,000 in fees, paid to his former law firm by Hahnemann Medical College and Hospital, to help the hospital get a $14.5-million grant from CSA.

This was clearly a violation of conflict-of-in-

terest laws designed to prevent "special interests" from getting special attention from the government, said Lieberman.

If convicted by the jury, Eilberg could have been sentenced to up to two years in prison, plus ordered to pay a $10,000 fine.

The plea agreement was worked out yesterday morning by Lieberman, Vaira and Assistant U.S. Attorney Frank H. Sherman at the request, according to Lieberman, of defense counsel John Rogers Carroll and Thomas Colas Carroll.

"We were ready to go to trial," Vaira said following Eilberg's plea.

But he added that the government, including his superiors in the U.S. Justice Department in

Please Turn to Page 3

Our faith in a politician is usually shaken when he or she pleads guilty to a criminal charge to avoid jail.

changing opinions (which mediate attitude change) is acceptance. It is at this stage that reinforcement becomes most important. There are several ways in which a persuasive communication can provide reinforcement for acceptance and start the process of attitude change. Hovland, Janis, and Kelley highlight three ways in which acceptance of the communication can be reinforcing. The first has to do with the expectation of being right or wrong. Being right is a reward, in many instances a powerful reward. For example, if an individual is right about the stock he or she buys, the rewards can be huge, whereas the punishment for being wrong about the stock market can be loss of money, or in extreme cases, financial ruin. This leads to a corollary statement about persuasive communications, that they should be more persuasive if they are espoused by an expert, primarily because experts are associated with being right. The second aspect of accepting a persuasive communication has to do with the intent of the communicator. If the communicator has something to gain by persuading you, then through experience with such situations in the past you will have learned that the change of attitude advocated by such a person may not be as rewarding as a change of attitude associated with a person who has nothing to gain. The final rewarding situation is the possibility of social approval or disapproval. Social approval is rewarding and social disapproval is punishing. For example, a prestigious person is more likely to denote social approval than a nonprestigious one,

203

and as such is more likely to be influential. Thus, these three reward variables combine to influence attitude change.

The reinforcement theory of Hovland, Janis, and Kelley is one that takes several possible sources of reinforcement into account and attempts to predict their effect by understanding the impact of each on the individual. As some of the variables may be said to be person variables (strength of desire to be correct or social desirability) and some are situational, the model is concerned with the interaction between person and situation. It does emphasize persuasive communications as a medium of opinion change that leads to attitude change. This is done because persuasive communications in political speeches, in advertisements, in editorials, in news stories, and in everyday conversation are the most prevalent devices used to attempt to change attitudes.

Research. There has been an enormous amount of research in the area of reinforcement and attitude change. Instead of trying to serve you a smorgasboard where you never get quite enough of anything but finish the meal feeling as if you've had too much of everything, let me briefly mention some of the work on reward for *counterattitudinal advocacy* (arguing for a point of view that is different from your own). Counterattitudinal advocacy occurs in debates, when someone is in the mood for an argument and takes whichever side of a discussion someone else has not already expounded, but probably occurs most frequently in attitude research.

A reinforcement orientation would lead to the expectation that when someone does engage in counterattitudinal advocacy, the more reward that is available for the position taken, the more attitude change there will be. Scott (1957, 1959) found that individuals who were reinforced by group approval or by cash prizes for counteratti- tudinal advocacy changed their attitudes more toward the position they previously had not favored than did those individuals who did not receive social approval or cash prizes for their counterattitudinal advocacy. Students who were given As for their counterattitudinal advocacy showed more attitude change than did students who received Ds (Bostrom, Vlaudis, and Rosenbaum, 1961), whereas students who were rewarded for counterattitudinal advocacy by being told that either the argu- ments they presented or the way they presented those arguments was extremely powerful also changed their attitudes (Wallace, 1966).

These studies seem to demonstrate convincingly that reinforcement plays a large role in attitude change, at least when counterattitudinal advocacy is used as the medium of attitude change. That point of view was shortly to be challenged by proponents of dissonance theory when it came upon the scene. As a matter of fact, in one of the studies cited above (Wallace, 1966), there was more attitude change when individuals were praised for having delivered superior speeches rather than having superior content in their speeches. Wallace interpreted this finding by saying there was greater dissonance raised between behavior and attitude when the subjects were told their presentations were superior than when they were told the content of their arguments was superior. Another way of looking at the situation is to conclude that it is more reinforcing to present an argument in a debate well than to present a good argument. But here we are getting ahead of ourselves into an intense controversy that developed later between dissonance theory and reinforcement theory.

COMMENT
Reinforcement theory of attitude change, if we relate it to the monistic theories covered in Chapter 1, is a hedonic theory and if we look at our list of pluralistic theories, it is, not surprisingly, a reinforcement theory.

BALANCE THEORY

Heider (1946, 1958) and Newcomb (1953, 1959) independently developed balance theories. Like reinforcement theory, balance theory is much more general than its application to attitude change. The general idea behind balance theory is that people seek balance in their cognitive structure and that attitude change comes about when the system is not balanced. A balanced state for Heider is a state in which everything fits together "harmoniously" without stress. Lack of balance results in stress and pressure to relieve the stress. Heider uses a series of symbols that refer to the person (*p*), another person (*o*) and an object (*x*). To explain the system, it is probably best to use illustrations of balanced and imbalanced situations. For example if *p* likes *o* and *x* is an attitude, then the system is balanced if both *p* and *o* feel the same way about the attitude, but it is not balanced if *p* feels positively toward *x* whereas *o* feels negatively toward *x*. Figure 5–1 shows schematic drawings of balanced and imbal-

Figure 5–1 Schematic drawings of balanced and imbalanced relationships. With respect to attitude change the drawing relates *p* (a person) to *o* (another person) to *x* (an object), which, in this instance, is an attitude.

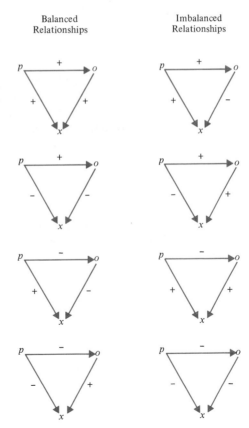

anced relationships. Note that both *p* and *o* do not have to feel positively toward *x* for the system to be balanced, they can both have a negative opinion toward *x*.

Heider's approach is Gestaltlike in its emphasis; that is, if relationships are balanced they provide a good Gestalt. Thus, if all three entities are positive, or if two are negative and one is positive, balance occurs. The system is imbalanced if one or three of the entities are negative. One shortcoming of Heider's model is that an element is either positive or negative, but the degree of feeling cannot be stipulated. When the system is not balanced, tension results, which forces the system back toward balance. This can be accomplished by several means, but the most crucial aspect for attitude change results when *x* is an attitude and *p* likes *o* but does not agree with *o* about *x*. In this instance the relationship can be changed by *p* by either deciding to dislike *o* or to change his or her attitude.

Newcomb's balance theory is much like that of Heider's except that he stresses balance as it applies to communication among people. Newcomb postulates a strain toward symmetry, which, in turn, influences communication between the two people so as to bring their attitude(s) into congruence. In Newcomb's study of attraction, discussed in more detail in Chapter 2, there was a tendency for those who were attracted to each other to agree with each other on many matters, and more importantly for our present discussion, these similarities, real as well as perceived, seemed to increase over time. This would indicate that those who were attracted to each other were attempting to bring their relationship into a more balanced state.

Research. A great deal of research has been carried out to investigate balance theory. Jordan (1953) presented subjects with 64 different triadic situations, half of which were balanced and half of which were not. In general, he found that balanced situations were rated more positively than imbalanced ones. However, in balanced situations that were in balance because *p* disliked *o* (and thus *o* disliked *x*, which *p* liked, or *o* liked *x*, which *p* disliked) there was about the same amount of unpleasantness as there was in imbalanced situations. Cartright and Harary (1956) point out that relationships between people and things differ. Heider had distinguished between sentiment relationships (ones that involve liking, admiring, loving, and so forth) and unit relationships (such as possession, cause, similarity, and the like). The opposite of liking is disliking, but the opposite of a bond built on a unit relationship is not necessarily the absence of the basic element of the relationship. To reiterate, liking people and things may well differ. With this in mind look carefully at Figure 5–2, which graphically presents the expressed pleasantness of balanced and imbalanced relationships reported by Jordan. As you can readily see, the greater pleasantness of balanced situations comes when sentiment relationships are positive, not when they are negative. In fact balanced relationships that are balanced because *p* dislikes *o* are as unpleasant as are imbalanced relationships. The data do not, however, allow us to say that the pleasantness of a situation is determined by positive relationships, because imbalanced situations with positive sentiment relationships are also perceived as unpleasant. Thus the type of relationship and the balanced or imbalanced nature of the relationship interact to determine pleasantness.

Price, Harburg, and Newcomb (1966) reported a study in which individuals were asked to rate hypothetical interpersonal situations on an uneasy to pleasant scale. Of interest to us are the balanced situations that would be analogous to the four

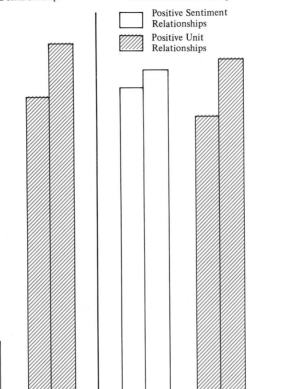

Balanced Relationships   Imbalanced Relationships

□ Positive Sentiment Relationships
▨ Positive Unit Relationships

Pleasantness

Figure 5–2   **Pleasantness of balanced and imbalanced sentiment and unit relationships. (Data from Jordan, 1953.) Low score indicates higher degrees of pleasantness.**

relationships represented in the left-hand panel of Figure 5-2. As in the Jordan study, the balanced positive sentiment relationships were pleasant. However, the balanced negative sentiment relationships were not more pleasant, thus confirming the results reported by Jordan.

Burdick and Burnes (1958) investigated the tension aspect of balance theory. Remember, an imbalanced state is conceived of as tension arousing, and thus unpleasant. Burdick and Burnes measured galvanic skin response (GSR) while the individual was being agreed with or disagreed with by an individual most of the subjects felt they would like. There was greater GSR deflections (indicating greater arousal) when subjects were disagreed with than when they were agreed with. This, of course, supports the notion that imbalanced states are arousing.

COMMENT

One of the basic arguments against balance theory is that it is vague and that experiments meant to support it may be interpreted in a completely different way. For example, the results in the Burdick and Burnes study can be explained more simply by saying that disagreement itself is arousing (for example see Clore and Gormley, 1969; Lamberth, Gouaux, and Padd, 1973; Davis and Lamberth, 1974). As Suedfeld (1971, pp. 7–8) says,

> While the basic idea was persuasive, the theory was vague and incomplete. For example, the three-entity relationship did not take into account the fact that liking and disliking usually flow in two directions... Though in many situations there are both positive and negative feelings toward a person or object, and though affects vary greatly in intensity (both "like" and "adore" are positive, but they hardly are equivalent), there was no way to assess the relative or absolute strength of sentiments. Furthermore, as Insko (1967) points out, experimenters have inferred imbalance when a subject rates himself as feeling uneasy, tense, or unpleasant on a scale from pleasant to unpleasant; but a stable-unstable rating of the relationship would seem more relevant to the theory and certainly to attitude change. Unfortunately, such ratings of stability may not be very reliable, and (a major flaw) there are no unequivocal behavioral measures of imbalance. But other consistency theories have not even tried to develop an independent measure of the hypothetical state; honor is due at least for the recognition of the problem.

Another criticism of balance theory seems appropriate. A balanced relationship may not always be a happy one. For example, you have a boyfriend and a girlfriend. According to balance theory, the relationship would be balanced if they liked each other. If, however, you discover the two in a loving embrace, their attraction to each other is evident and the balanced relationship should be highly pleasing. That is true unless your interest in one of them is also romantic. Then the balanced relationship would be highly uncomfortable.

With respect to the classification of theories discussed in Chapter 1, balance theory is a cognitive, hedonic theory.

COGNITIVE-DISSONANCE THEORY

In 1957, Leon Festinger proposed a theory that he termed *cognitive dissonance*, and which was to become the most popular theory of attitude change for the next fifteen or so years. The theory itself has never been stated as precisely as many wished and that is one of its weaknesses. I will, however, try to spell out both what it says and some of its implications.

The basic elements of dissonance theory are *cognitive elements*, which, according to Festinger (1957) are beliefs, opinions, and attitudes about various objects, facts, circumstances, behaviors, and so forth. Two cognitive elements may have relevant or irrelevant relations between them. An irrelevant relationship occurs when there are two cognitive elements completely unrelated. For example, an individual may know that the winter of 1976/77 was a cold one and that he or she was born on a given date.

For most of us, the two events have an irrelevant relationship. Relevant events, on the other hand are either dissonant or consonant. As Festinger (1957, p. 13) stated it, *"two elements are in a dissonant relation if, considering these two alone, the obverse of one element would follow from the other."* Two crucial words in this definition are only loosely spelled out by Festinger. "Follow from" may mean that the two elements have a strictly logical relationship, or one element may follow from another because of cultural mores, past experiences, and so forth. For example, a lung surgeon who smokes heavily would be in a dissonance-arousing situation because of past experience—he or she has seen what lung cancer can do and yet continues to smoke. Consonant relations imply that one cognitive element does follow from another, and in some sense are the opposite of dissonant relations.

The magnitude of dissonance is a function of the importance of the cognitive elements and the proportion of relevant elements that are dissonant. For example, if you find yourself in a situation where you are shortchanged, the amount of money involved will probably play a large part in determining how much dissonance is aroused. If your purchase was $4.99 and you gave the clerk a $5.00 bill, not getting any change would not be too upsetting. On the other hand, if you had given a clerk a $20.00 bill, not receiving any change would be quite upsetting. In one instance the importance of the cognitive elements is much greater than in the other. The other aspect that determines the magnitude of dissonance is the proportion of cognitive elements that are dissonant. Smoking is a good example of this. On one side those people who smoke have a cognition "I smoke." Over the last 20 years or so, medical researchers have been adding a large number of cognitive elements to produce a dissonant relation: cigarettes can cause cancer, emphysema, and heart disease, to name only three. As more is learned about cigarette smoking, more elements that argue against it are being added to the list and the proportion of relevant elements that are dissonant is changing in favor of not smoking.

In Festinger's model, cognitive inconsistency gives rise to a pressure or tension to reduce the dissonant state. The amount of pressure is a function of the magnitude of dissonance. There are three ways in which dissonance can be reduced. The first of these is changing a behavioral cognitive element—the smoker stops smoking. Second, dissonance can be reduced by changing an environmental cognitive element. For example, many kids while walking on a sidewalk learned the old rhyme that went something like this: "Whoever steps on a crack breaks his (her) mother's back." Obviously, people don't really believe that when they become adults, but watch and see how many people avoid tempting fate by assuring that their stride conforms to the configuration of cracks in a sidewalk. Finally, dissonance can be reduced by adding new cognitive elements that are consonant with one or the other of the elements in a dissonant relationship. For example, the cigarette smoker may read all the information tobacco companies publish trying to refute the Surgeon General's warning that cigarettes are hazardous to your health.

According to Festinger, dissonance has implications for a number of specific situations. One of these has to do with decisions. Prior to making a decision, the person is in a conflict situation. For example, shall I buy car A or car B. After the car has been purchased, the conflict is resolved, but dissonance is aroused. The cognitive elements that made the individual consider car B are still there and they are dissonant with the cognition that car A was purchased. Conflict occurs before a decision, dissonance comes after it is made. The magnitude of dissonance in this situation is a function of the importance of the decision, the *relative* attractiveness of both the chosen and unchosen alternatives and the amount of cognitive overlap between the two choices. In choosing an automobile, for example, if the final decision was between two colors of the same car there would be a lot of cognitive overlap and little dissonance. If, on the other hand, the choice was between a smaller, fuel-saving car and a much larger, more comfortable "gas guzzler" there would be less cognitive overlap, and thus more dissonance.

Dissonance aroused in such a "free choice" situation can be reduced in four ways; revoking the decision, increasing the attractiveness of the chosen alternative, decreasing the attractiveness of the alternative that was rejected, or increasing the cognitive overlap between the two choices. Revoking the decision, of course, throws the individual back into the predecisional conflict stage and the whole process must be done again. The more usual way of reducing the dissonance aroused by a decision is by increasing the attractiveness of the chosen alternative or decreasing the attractiveness of the rejected alternative.

Another situation in which dissonance can result is what Festinger referred to as forced compliance, which is compliance to public pressure without or prior to change in private opinion. Forced compliance can be elicited by the offer of a reward for compliance or by the threat of punishment for noncompliance. Dissonance results once forced compliance has occurred, because the cognitive elements about the individual's belief and behavior are in a dissonant relationship. The amount of reward and punishment offered to induce the behavior and the importance of the opinion or behavior involved combine to determine the magnitude of dissonance in a forced compliance situation. For example, if an adult is forced to endorse a position that is opposed to his or her own (endorse an opposing political candidate) then a large amount of dissonance is raised if the inducement to do so is, for example, $10.00. However if the inducement is $10,000.00, then there would be more justification and less dissonance. On the other hand, whereas $10,000.00 may be sufficient

Which car shall I choose? The more expensive gas guzzler on the left or the less comfortable one on the right? A decision of this sort may arouse quite a lot of dissonance.

justification for changing political candidates, it may be a paltry sum if one is bribed to betray his or her country. In this instance the $10,000.00 is the same, but the action is so much more important that a great deal of dissonance would be aroused.

Research. Dissonance theory has generated an enormous amount of research and through the decade of the 60s was the most popular theoretical explanation for attitude change (Insko, 1967; Suedfeld, 1971). The literature on dissonance theory and research leaves us in somewhat of a dilemma as to how to treat it. Even with one-sentence references to studies, which make your task as a student virtually impossible, there is not enough space to do justice to all of the research Festinger's theory generated. It is also true that in the late 1970s there are few dissonance-related studies being reported. So although it was at one time an enormously popular theory of attitude change, it is now virtually extinct. I will try to give the flavor of some of the dissonance research by selecting a couple of studies to report in detail, and will then report some of the research that led to the loss of popularity for dissonance.

Festinger and Carlsmith (1959) tested the idea that forced compliance produced by a small reward results in more dissonance-produced attitude change than does forced compliance for a large reward. Male subjects spent one hour at a boring task and were then told that the experiment was over but the experimenter would like to hire them to introduce the next subject to the experiment. It was explained that the assistant who usually did the job had not shown up. The assistant's job was to act like a subject who had just finished the experiment and to tell the next subject that it was fun and enjoyable. As an incentive, some of the subjects were offered $1.00 and some $20.00. The payment was for acting as an assistant at that time and also for being on call to help out later. After the subjects had complied and told the next "subject" (who was actually a female accomplice), the subjects were interviewed and during the course of the interview were asked to rate the enjoyability of the experiment. The predictions from dissonance theory are clear. The subject thinks, "The task is boring, but I'm telling her it is fun and enjoyable." Thus two cognitive elements are in a dissonant relationship. However, some of the individuals had $20.00 to compensate for their "white lie," whereas some only had $1.00. These latter subjects should have more dissonance aroused and one way to reduce that dissonance is to inflate the perceived enjoyment in the task. Figure 5–3 presents the results graphically. As can be seen by a brief inspection of Figure 5–3, the subjects who received only $1.00 liked the task much more than the subjects who received $20.00, who liked the task more than the control group, who simply rated the task without telling anyone that it was enjoyable. The control group may be seen as a baseline group for how enjoyable the task actually was. These results seem to support the dissonance point of view. As we shall soon see, there are other interpretations of this study, but I will postpone that discussion until I have discussed a study that utilized forced compliance and punishment.

Aronson and Mills (1959) hypothesized that the attraction toward a group is a function of the severity of the initiation procedures used to gain admission to that group. The more punishing the initiation the more the resulting dissonance aroused is reduced by liking the group. Assuming the individual joins the group, there is less justification for being in the group if the initiation is severe, unless the group is attractive. College women who had volunteered for participation in a series of group

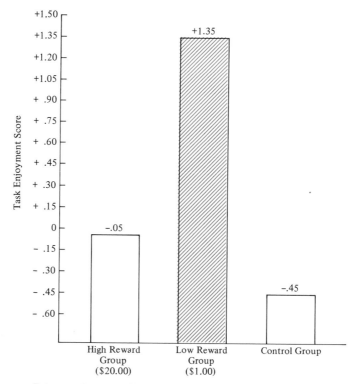

Figure 5–3 Enjoyment scores for subjects in three groups in the Festinger and Carlsmith (1959) study.

discussions on the psychology of sex served as subjects. When the subjects showed up for the discussion group the experimenter told them that to prevent embarrassment the participants would not actually see each other but would communicate via microphones and headphones. There were three conditions, severe initiation, mild initiation, and control. The initiation groups were required to take an "embarrassment" test, with the severe group reading 12 obscene words and two vivid descriptions of sexual activity in the presence of a male experimenter, whereas the mild initiation group read 5 sexual, but not obscene, words. The control condition had no embarrassment test at all. After the initiation the women were told that since the discussion group had already started and they had done no preparation for this session, they should just listen and not say anything. The group discussion the women heard was about the secondary sexual behavior of animals and had purposely been made dull and boring. After the discussion, the women filled out a questionnaire evaluating the discussion. The results indicated that the women in the severe initiation condition liked the discussion group more than the women in the mild initiation condition, who liked it slightly more than the women in the control condition.

Two studies cannot possibly do more than give you a flavor of dissonance research. Taking only these two studies as here described, you might wonder why dissonance theory had been eclipsed. These studies certainly seem to confirm it. But as you were warned earlier, there are many criticisms of dissonance theory, and we will turn to them now.

   Comment. According to Insko (1967 p. 282),

... from an internal point of view the most glaring weakness of the theory has to do with the vague way in which dissonance is defined. The net result of all of this is that we are left, not with a precise definition of dissonance, but with an intuitive feeling. Two cognitive elements are in a dissonant relationship if they are somehow or other "unreasonably" related.

   This particular vagueness has been one of the major criticisms of dissonance. It is difficult to specify when a dissonant relationship occurs and dissonance researchers have argued that only researchers who have obtained a dissonance relationship are fully qualified to disconfirm it (Brehm, 1965). This argument, of course, has some merit; any researcher should understand the phenomenon being researched adequately to do research on it properly. Science, however, is public, and one of its hallmarks is that a result in one laboratory must be confirmable in any other laboratory unless significant variables are not being controlled or the scientist is purposely attempting to find disconfirming results. Actually as Suedfeld (1971, p. 27) says "The argument (Brehm's) has a kernel of merit: a grasp of the problem should be demonstrated by critic and supporter alike. However, it is a fallacious prescription in the light of what we know about experimental artifacts. From this point of view, the criterion is the opposite: confirmation should come from researchers who have previously obtained negative results."

   Collins (Carlsmith, Collins, and Helmrich, 1966) is one who has previously obtained positive results. So, even the "dissonancers" should allow that he is capable of understanding the phenomenon. Let us turn to what he says. Collins, Ashmore, Hornbeck, and Whitney (1970, p. 11) report . . .

... six separate experiments which were conducted in an effort to produce a dissonance-predicted, negative relationship between financial inducements and attitude change. The first three were generally modeled after the Festinger and Carlsmith (1959) paradigm and found, if anything, a positive relationship. The last three, which closely follow Linder, Cooper, and Jones (1967), contains one replication, one non-replication, and one significant difference in the opposite direction. Although the existence of the dissonance-predicted, negative relationship is well established, its necessary prerequisites are not yet a matter of record.

   Collins and his associates were sympathetic to dissonance; in fact they say (Collins et al., 1970, pp. 21), "It should be stressed that the experimenters were seeking a dissonance effect; therefore, any experimenter bias on subtle points of the design should work in favor of the dissonance hypothesis." An even more disturbing aspect of the work of Collins et al. is the difficulty these researchers had in getting their results published. The publication of scientific information and the importance of outlets for results, even if they disagree with the "establishment" point of view is crucial to science. The 1960s were the "heyday" of dissonance theory and there is no way to estimate how many studies were done and remained unpublished because of this bias. Collins had his work published in the *Journal of Representative Research in Social Psychology,* which, has done an inestimable job for social psychology by allowing articles like this one to see the light of day. To quote Collins et al. (1970, p. 22),

> But the publically available, published versions of dissonance theory do not adequately specify the conditions for dissonance *arousal*. Furthermore, if our own experience in trying to publish anti-dissonance results is typical, the present studies are probably not unique in their failure to arouse dissonance. One editor even referred to the statistically significant, anti-dissonance, positive relationship of studies 1 through 3 as "negative results." The status of the dissonance-predicted, negative relationship as "well-established phenomenon" (which is inappropriate in our opinion) makes it almost impossible to publish failures to replicate.

Dissonance research has been criticized for other reasons, not the least of which is throwing out subjects, statistical methodologies which are open to question (see Insko, 1967 for a discussion of these criticisms) and the claim that shortcomings of the research are ignored in the discussion section of the papers themselves. (See Chapanis and Chapanis, 1964, and Suedfeld, 1971, for discussions of these criticisms.) For these and other reasons, dissonance has become almost a dead area. I have never done dissonance research nor been sympathetic to the view, but intuitively it seems to me that the theory has been well supplied with half of what it takes to understand a scientific theory. It has often been said that great scientists are both geniuses and plodders. At the very least, the creative genius necessary to conceptualize a theory and the dogged determination to test it empirically are necessary to theoretical growth. If both do not exist in one person, it is necessary for both to exist among those committed to a specific theoretical position. Festinger's ideas were brilliant and they still may receive experimental confirmation. At this time, however, they have not received that confirmation and so dissonance is disappearing from the theoretical scene.

To relate dissonance to balance and reinforcement theories, it is hedonic, as both of them are, and is obviously a cognitive theory.

Attitude Change: Present and Future

As you can see from the graph for Chapter 5 shown on the inside front cover, attitude and attitude-change research is not dead, although it is greatly reduced in popularity. Reviews of the area in the early 1970s were quite pessimistic about a variety of problems including the relationship between attitude change and behavior change, and definition and measurement (Abelson, 1972; Fishbein and Ajzen, 1972). It is difficult if not impossible at present to predict what directions attitude change research will take. About all one can do now is to describe some research that was aimed at attacking some of the problems associated with attitude-change research. This research was chosen because it was sufficiently interesting to at least one critic to draw his disagreement, and a subsequent rebuttal on the part of the original researcher. Since I am guessing about where attitude-change research will go in the future anyhow, it is probably best to select an approach that has generated enough interest to draw a critical reply.

Hendrick and Seyfried (1974) addressed the problem of the validity of attitude change produced in the laboratory. Combining attitude research and research on

ATTITUDE STABILITY AND BEHAVIOR

The stability of attitudes is an important factor underlying the attitude-behavior problem. Most definitions of attitudes stress their stability, but there is the realization that they change; (i.e., the attitude-change literature). One reason for the discouragingly small relationship between attitudes and behavior may be that attitudes change. As early as 1931, Thurstone suggested that the temporal instability in attitudes weakens the relation of attitudes to behavior. Although this is an obvious point; that if you change your attitude concerning an issue you will not behave in a manner consistent with your former attitude, there were no published reports that directly examined the point until Schwartz (1978) published such a study. In this study Schwartz tested several hypotheses: (a) the correlation of attitudes with behavior is stronger the shorter the time interval between attitude measurement and behavior; and (b) the correlation between attitudes and behavior is stronger the more stable the individual's attitudes across time.

Four groups of Israeli students at Hebrew University received a mailed appeal for volunteers to tutor blind children from the Jewish Institute for the Blind in Jerusalem. Three groups of subjects completed a questionnaire that contained an attitude item embedded in it that asked how much obligation each subject would feel to read to the blind if asked to do so. For one group, the questionnaire was completed 6 months before the request to help; another group filled it out 3 months prior to the appeal; a third group filled out the questionnaire both 6 and 3 months before the appeal was received; and a fourth (control) group did not fill out the questionnaire.

The first question to be answered by this research is how stable are attitudes. Recall that one group completed the questionnaire 6 and 3 months before receiving the appeal. The test-retest correlation for the item concerning reading to the blind was +0.58. This indicates quite a bit of stability but a good deal of change, also. In this sample there was attitude change over a six-month period.

The correlation between attitude and behavior was +0.47 in the group that had received the questionnaire 3 months earlier and only +0.13 in the group that had received the questionnaire 6 months earlier. For the group that received the questionnaire both 6 and 3 months earlier, the correlation between attitude and behavior was +0.13 at 6 months and +0.26 at three months. Thus, it is apparent that the first hypothesis (i.e., the shorter the time between attitude measurement and behavior, the stronger the relationship between the two would be) was confirmed.

The subjects who completed the attitude questionnaire at both 6 and 3 months prior to the behavioral request were divided into 3 stability groups on the basis of several attitudes about altruistic behavior; high, moderate, and low. Then the behavior for each of these 3 groups was correlated with their attitude toward reading to the blind. The more stable they were in their general attitudes toward altruism, the higher the correlation between their specific attitude toward reading to the blind and their actual behavior.

It is important to note that attitudes do change and these changes are bound to affect the relationship between attitudes and behavior. It is particularly important to measure attitudes as close to the time of the behavior as possible if the researcher is interested in the maximum relationship.

References

Schwartz, S. H. Temporal instability as a moderator of the attitude behavior relationship. *Journal of Personality and Social Psychology*, 1978, *36*, 715–724.

Thurstone, L. L. The measurement of attitudes. *Journal of Abnormal and Social Psychology*, 1931, *26*, 249–269.

interpersonal attraction (Chapter 9), the researchers found an ingenious way to assess the validity of attitude change. Subjects were matched on the basis of their attitudes and then one in each matched pair was assigned to an experimental condition and one to the control condition. Experimental subjects read a persuasive communication and then completed an attitude posttest, whereas the control group did not receive a persuasive communication. Subjects in both conditions then served in an interpersonal attraction experiment. As we will see in Chapter 9, individuals who share similar attitudes with other individuals are more attracted to those persons than to people with whom they disagree. Hendrick and Seyfried used this information to test for the validity of attitude change. After the experimental subjects had read a persuasive communication and filled out a second attitude questionnaire (presumably influenced by the communication) they were asked to indicate their attraction toward two individuals, one which espoused the attitudes the subject preferred before the communication and one which espoused the attitudes preferred by the subject after the communication. The control group, which was made up of individuals who were matched with the subjects in the experimental group on the basis of precommunication attitudes, also indicated their attraction toward the two strangers. The stranger whose attitudes reflected the precommunication attitudes of each pair was, of course, identical and should be the most liked unless the persuasive communication had really changed the attitudes of the experimental group. The results are presented in Figure 5–4, which shows that the control group most liked the stranger who had attitudes similar to their own at the start of the experiment. The experimental group, on the other hand, most liked the stranger who reflected their expressed attitudes

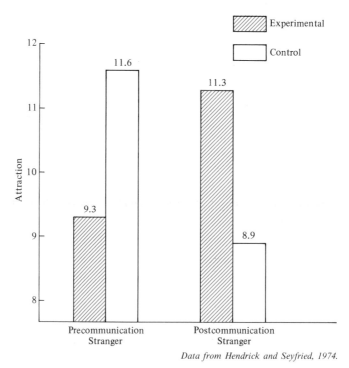

Data from Hendrick and Seyfried, 1974.

Figure 5–4 **Attraction toward strangers holding attitudes similar to those of the experimental groups' subjects prior to and after a persuasive communication.**

after they had read the persuasive communication. Hendrick and Seyfried concluded from these results that the attitude change expressed immediately after a persuasive communication carried over for 24 hours (to the next session) and was apparent when another measure of attitude change, attraction, was used.

Wells (1976a) argued that Hendrick and Seyfried's results were actually a result of demand characteristics in the experimental setting. Basically, Wells's argument was that when the experimental group received a posttest after the persuasive communication they "saw through" the experimental design and responded as they thought the experimenter wanted them to. Wells replicated Hendrick and Seyfried's study and added another group, one which received the persuasive communication but not a posttest on attitude change. This group did not differ on attraction responses from the control group, causing Wells to claim that demand characteristics accounted for Hendrick and Seyfried's results.

Hendrick and Bukoff (1976) countered with the argument that it is not viable to assume that Wells's third group (persuasive communication but no posttest) changed their attitudes in the same direction or to the same extent that the experimental group did. Since Wells did not take a posttest for his third group, it was essential that he make such an assumption. Hendrick and Bukoff then reported an experiment in which they presented evidence that supports the hypothesis that variability in the patterning (direction and extent) of attitude change among subjects accounted for Wells's attraction data; specifically for his third group. Hendrick and Bukoff essentially argue that it is not adequate to assume that attitude change in both of Wells's groups that receive a persuasive communication is the same. It is known from attraction research that subjects are exquisitely sensitive to even small differences in attitude patterns (Byrne, 1971).

Wells (1976b) remained unconvinced, but did not present empirical evidence in his rejoinder. Thus, for the time being, the argument has been delineated and we have probably not heard the last of it.

Conclusion

It is unfortunate that attitude and attitude-change research has fallen on hard times because it is an important topic. It is also not unusual for a research area to have a quiescent period following a particular exciting theory that does not live up (or at least has not lived up) to its early promise. I think we shall see a resurgence of interest in attitudes and attitude change in the future, but I am unwilling to even speculate as to when that will occur and what form it will take.

SUMMARY

An attitude is a relatively stable evaluative response toward an object that has cognitive, affective, and probably behavioral components or consequences. Fishbein and Ajzen have proposed a model of attitudes that emphasizes information processing. Attitudes are important and have far-reaching ramifications for the individual, group, and society.

2 Attitudes are learned, rather than inherited. The learning can occur via classical conditioning, including vicarious conditioning, instrumental conditioning, and imitation.

3 Attitudes and behavior do not show as much consistency as they should. At the same time that attitude theorists were questioning the predictive link between attitudes and behavior, personality theorists were questioning the predictive link between personality traits and behavior. Many personality theorists now believe personality traits predict behavior in specific situations, and it is suggested that attitudes may have predictive power in specific situations.

4 Attitudes may be measured by self-report measures, including Likert-type scales, the psychophysical approach, the method of successive approximations, and the semantic differential. Physiological measures of attitudes once seemed very promising, but more recent developments have indicated several difficulties with the approach. Unobtrusive measures of attitudes, when used properly and ethically, are excellent ways to measure attitudes, but the potential for misuse or error is great.

5 Changing attitudes is the intent of such diverse groups of people as advertisers, politicians, governments, and individuals. There are several theories of attitude change, including reinforcement theory, balance theory, and cognitive dissonance theory. None of the theories have been very successful in predicting attitude change.

6 Reinforcement theory of attitude change emphasizes that attitudes change because the individual is reinforced for changing the attitude. There has been an enormous amount of research in the area, with mixed results.

7 Balance theory asserts that people seek balance in their cognitive structure and that attitude change comes about when the system is not balanced. Balanced cognitions are more pleasurable than unbalanced ones and people seek to balance relationships. Research in the area, as with reinforcement theory, sometimes seems to support the theory and sometimes does not.

8 Cognitive dissonance theory is based on the assumption that inconsistent cognitions are unpleasant and that people try to reduce this unpleasant state of affairs by changing attitudes. As with the other theories of attitude change, cognitive dissonance research is mixed. Interest in the area has waned in recent years.

GLOSSARY

Attitude A relatively stable evaluative response toward an object that has cognitive, affective, and probably behavioral components or consequences.

Balance Theory A theory that emphasizes an individual's desires to keep cognitive elements harmonious.

Classical Conditioning A learning mechanism that emphasizes learning through association.

Cognitive Dissonance A theory that emphasizes the unpleasantness of two cognitions that are in disagreement and the individual's attempts to change one or the other.

Counterattitudinal Advocacy Arguing a position that is different from your own.

Imitation Learning that occurs by observing the behavior of others.

Instrumental Conditioning Learning that occurs because behavior is either reinforced or punished.

Likert-type Scale A specific attitude-measurement device.

Method of Successive Hurdles A measure of attitudes that asks whether an individual would be comfortable with a specific individual in increasingly intimate relationships.

Opinion A judgment based on insufficient evidence to imply certainty.

Persuasive Communication A compound stimulus that raises a question and suggests an answer.

Physiological Measurement Measures of blood pressure, heart rate, palmar sweating, and the like.

Reinforcement Theory of Attitude Change The theory that stresses reinforcement as the central mechanism in attitude change.

Self-monitoring A personality characteristic that indicates whether a person heeds situational cues or relies on inner states.

Self-report Measures Measures based on the statement of the individual.

Semantic Differential An attitude-measuring technique that uses bipolar adjectives to determine degrees of feeling.

Subjective Probability The strength of an individual's belief in some quality or construct.

Value A quality or object that is desirable as a means or end in itself.

Vicarious Conditioning Learning by imagined participation in the experience of others.

REFERENCES

Abelson, R. P. Are attitudes necessary? In B. T. King and E. McGinnes (Eds.). *Attitudes, Conflict and Social Change.* New York: Academic Press, Inc., 1972.

Allport, G. Attitudes. In C. Murchison (Ed.), *A Handbook of Social Psychology.* Worcester, Mass.: Clark University Press, 1935. Pp. 798–844.

———. The historical background of modern social psychology. In G. Lindzey and E. Aronson (Eds.). *Handbook of Social Psychology.* Boston: Addison-Wesley Publishing Co., Inc., 1968, Vol. I. Pp. 1–80.

Aronson, E., and J. Mills. The effects of severity of initiation on liking for a group. *Journal of Abnormal and Social Psychology,* 1959, *59,* 177–81.

Bandura, A. Vicarious processes: A case in no-trial learning. In L. Berkowitz (Ed.), *Advances in Experimental Social Psychology.* Vol II, New York: Academic Press, 1965. Pp. 1–55.

———. *Aggression: A Social Learning Analysis.* Englewood Cliffs, N.J.: Prentice-Hall, Inc., 1973.

———. *Social Learning Theory.* New York: General Learning Press, 1971a.

———. *Psychological Modeling.* Chicago: Aldine Publishing Company, 1971b.

————— and R. W. Jefferey. Role of symbolic coding and rehearsal processes in observational learning. *Journal of Personality and Social Psychology,* 1973, *26,* 122–30.

Bem, D. J., and A. Allen. On predicting some of the people some of the time: The search for cross-situational consistencies in behavior. *Psychological Review,* 1974, *81,* 506–520.

Bogardus, E. S. A social distance scale. *Sociological Social Research.* 1933, *17,* 265–71.

—————. Measuring social distance. *Journal of Applied Sociology,* 1925, *9,* 299–308.

Bostrom, R., J. Vlandis, and M. Rosenbaum. Grades as reinforcing contingencies and attitude change. *Journal of Educational Psychology,* 1961, *52,* 112–15.

Brehm, J. W. Comment on Counter-norm attitudes induced by consonant vs. dissonant conditions of role-playing. *Journal of Experimental Research in Personality,* 1965, *1,* 61–64.

Burdick, H., and A. Burnes. A test of "strain toward symmetry" theories. *Journal of Abnormal and Social Psychology,* 1958, *57,* 367–70.

Byrne, D. *The Attraction Paradigm.* New York: Academic Press, Inc. 1971.

Carlsmith, J. M., B. E. Collins, and R. L. Helmrich. Studies in forced compliance: I. The effect of pressure for compliance on attitude change produced by face-to-face role playing and anonymous essay writing. *Journal of Personality Social Psychology,* 1966, *4,* 1–13.

Cartwright, D., and F. Harary. Structural balance: A generalization of Heider's theory. *Psychological Review,* 1956, *63,* 277–93.

Chapanis, N. P., and A. Chapanis. Cognitive dissonance: Five years later. *Psychological Bulletin,* 1964, *61,* 1–22.

Clore, G. L., and J. B. Gormley. Attraction and physiological arousal in response to agreements and disagreements. Paper presented at the meeting of the Psychonomic Society. St. Louis, November 1969.

Cohen, A. R. *Attitude Change and Social Influence.* New York: Basic Books, Inc., Publishers, 1964.

Collins, B. E., R. D. Ashmore, F. W. Hornbeck, and R. Whitney. Studies in forced compliance: XIII and XV in search of a dissonance-producing forced compliance paradigm. *Journal of Representative Research in Social Psychology,* 1970, *1,* 11–23.

Davis, J., and J. Lamberth. Energization properties of positive and negative stimuli. *Journal of Experimental Psychology,* 1974, *103,* 196–200.

Dollard, Jr., and N. E. Miller. *Personality and Psychotherapy: An analysis in Terms of Learning, Thinking, and Culture.* New York: McGraw-Hill Book Company, 1950.

Endler, N. S. The person versus the situation—A pseudo issue? *Journal of Personality,* 1973, *41,* 287–303.

————— and D. Magnusson. (Eds.). *Interactional Psychology and Personality.* Washington, D.C. Hemisphere Publishing Corp., 1975.

Festinger, L. *A Theory of Cognitive Dissonance.* Stanford, Calif.: Stanford University Press, 1957.

————— and J. Carlsmith. Cognitive consequences of forced compliance. *Journal of Abnormal and Social Psychology,* 1959, *58,* 203–210.

Fishbein, M., and I. Ajzen. Attitudes and opinions. *Annual Review of Psychology,* 1972, *23,* 487–544.

————— and —————. *Belief, Attitude, Intention and Behavior: An Introduction to Theory and Research.* Reading, Mass.: Addison-Wesley Publishing Co., Inc., 1975.

Guttman, L. A basis for scaling qualitative data. *American Sociological Review,* 1944, *9,* 139–50.

—————. The Cornell technique for scale and intensity analysis. *Educational and Psychological Measurement,* 1947, *7,* 247–80.

Heider, F. Attitudes and cognitive organization. *Journal of Psychology,* 1946, *21,* 107–112.

—————. *The Psychology of Interpersonal Relations.* New York: John Wiley & Sons, Inc., 1958.

Hendrick, C., and A. Bukoff. Assessing the reassessment of the validity of laboratory-produced attitude change. *Journal of Personality and Social Psychology,* 1976, *34,* 1068–75.

———, and B. A. Seyfried. Assessing the validity of laboratory-produced attitude change. *Journal of Personality and Social Psychology,* 1974, *29,* 865–70.

Hildum, D., and R. Brown. Verbal reinforcement and interview bias. *Journal of Abnormal and Social Psychology,* 1956, *53,* 108–111.

Hovland, C., I. Janis, and H. Kelley. Communication and persuasion. New Haven: Yale University Press, 1953.

Insko, C. Verbal reinforcement of attitude. *Journal of Personality and Social Psychology,* 1965, *2,* 621–23.

———, C. A. *Theories of Attitude Change.* New York: Appleton-Century-Crofts, 1967.

Jordan, N. Behavioral forces that are a function of attitudes and of cognitive organization. *Human Relations,* 1953, *6,* 273–87.

Kalven, H., Jr., and H. Zeisel. *The American Jury.* Boston: Little, Brown and Company, 1966.

Katz, D., and E. Stotland. A preliminary statement to a theory of attitude structure and change. In S. Koch (Ed.), *Psychology: Study of a Science.* Vol. 3. New York: McGraw-Hill Book Company, 1959, Pp. 423–75.

Lamberth, J., H. Rappaport, and M. Rappaport. *Personality: An Introduction.* New York: Alfred A. Knopf, Inc., 1978.

———, C. Govaux, and W. Padd. The affect of eliciting and reducing properties of attraction stimuli. *Journal of Social Behavior and Personality,* 1973, *1,* 93–107.

Lehr, J. M., and A. W. Staats. Attitude conditioning in Sino-Tibetan languages. *Journal of Personality and Social Psychology,* 1973, *26,* 196–200.

Mabley, J. Mabley's report. Chicago *American,* Jan 22, 1963, 62–3.

McGuire, W. J. The nature of attitudes and attitude change. In G. Lindzey and E. Aronson (Eds.) *Handbook of Social Psychology* Vol. 3, (2nd ed.). Reading, Mass.: Addison-Wesley, 1969, Pp. 136–314.

Miller, N. E., and B. R. Dworking. Visceral learning: Recent difficulties with curarized rats and significant programs for human research. In P. A. Obrist Et al. (Eds.), *Current Trends in Cardiovascular Psychophysiology.* Chicago: Aldine Publishing Company, 1973.

———, and A. Banuazizi. Instrumental learning by curarized rats of a specific, visceral response, visceral or cardiac. *Journal of Comparative and Physiological Psychology,* 1968, *65,* 1–7.

Mischel, W. The interaction of person and situation. Paper presented at International Conference on Interactional Psychology, Saltsjökaden, Sweden, 1975.

Murphy, G., L. Murphy, and T. Newcomb. *Experimental Social Psychology.* New York: Harper & Row, Publishers, 1937.

Newcomb, T. An approach to the study of communicative acts. *Psychological Review,* 1953, *60,* 393–404.

———. Individual systems of orientation. In S. Koch (Ed.), *Psychology: A Study of a Science.* Vol. 3. New York: McGraw-Hill Book Company, 1959, Pp. 384–422.

Osgood, C. E., G. J. Suci, and P. H. Tannenbaum. *The Measurement of Meaning.* Urbana, Ill.: University of Illinois Press, 1957.

Page, M. M. Demand characteristics and the verbal operand conditioning experiment. *Journal of Personality and Social Psychology,* 1972, *23,* 372–78.

———. On detecting demand awareness by postexperimental questionnaire. *Journal of Social Psychology,* 1973, *91,* 305–323.

———. Demand characteristics and the classical conditioning of attitudes experiment. *Journal of Personality and Social Psychology,* 1974, *30,* 468–76.

————. Postexperimental assessment of awareness in attitude conditioning. *Educational and Psychological Measurement,* 1971, *31,* 891–906.

Price, R., E. Harburg, and T. Newcomb. Psychological balance in situations of negative interpersonal attitudes. *Journal of Personality and Social Psychology,* 1966, *3,* 265–70.

Scott, W. Attitude change through reward of verbal behavior. *Journal of Abnormal and Social Psychology,* 1957, *55,* 72–75.

————. Attitude change by response reinforcement: replication and extension. *Sociometry,* 1959, *22,* 328–35.

Snyder, M. Individual differences and the self-control of expressive behavior. Unpublished doctoral dissertation, Stanford University, 1972.

————. The self-monitoring of expressive behavior. *Journal of Personality and Social Psychology,* 1974, *30,* 526–37.

————. Attribution and behavior: Social perception and social causation. In J. H. Harvey, W. J. Ickes, and R. F. Kidd (Eds.), *New Directions in Attribution Research.* Hillsdale, N.J.: Earlbaum, 1976, Pp. 53–72.

———— and T. C. Monson. Persons, situations, and the control of social behavior. *Journal of Personality and Social Psychology,* 1975, *32,* 637–44.

———— and E. D. Tanke. Behavior and attitude: Some people are more consistent than others. *Journal of Personality,* 1976, *44,* 501–17.

Staats, A. W. A learning-behavior theory: A basis for unity in behavioral-social science. In A. R. Gilgen (Ed.), *Contemporary Scientific Psychology.* New York: Academic Press, Inc., 1970.

————, W. A. Higa, and I. E. Reid. *Names as Reinforcers: The Social Value of Verbal Stimuli* (Tech. Rep. No. 9, under Office of Naval Research Contract N00014-67-C-0387-0007) Honolulu: University of Hawaii, 1970.

———— K. A. Minke, C. H. Martin, and W. R. Higa. Deprivation-satiation and strength of attitude conditioning: A test of attitude-reinforcer-discriminative theory. *Journal of Personality and Social Psychology,* 1972, *24,* 178–85.

———— and C. K. Staats, Attitudes established by classical conditioning. *Journal of Abnormal and Social Psychology,* 1958, *57,* 37–40.

Suedfeld, P. Models of attitude change: Theories that pass in the night. In P. Suedfeld (Ed.), *Attitude Change: The Competing Views.* Chicago, Aldine Publishing Company, 1971.

Thurstone, L. L. *The Measurement of Social Attitudes.* Chicago: University Chicago Press, 1931.

———— and E. J. Chave. *The Measurement of Attitude.* Chicago: University of Chicago Press, 1929.

Triandis, H. C. *Attitude and Attitude Change.* New York: John Wiley & Sons, Inc., 1971.

Wallace, J. Role reward and dissonance reduction. *Journal of Personality and Social Psychology,* 1966, *3,* 305–312.

Wells, G. L. Reassessing the validity of laboratory-produced attitude change. *Journal of Personality and Social Psychology,* 1976a, *34,* 1062–67.

————. Attitude change validity: Reply to Hendrick and Berkoff. *Journal of Personality and Social Psychology,* 1976b, *34,* 1076–77.

Wicker, A. W. An examination of the "other variables" explanation of attitude-behavior inconsistency. *Journal of Personality and Social Psychology,* 1971, *19,* 18–30.

Wrightsman, L. S. Wallace supporters and adherence to law and order. *Journal of Personality and Social Psychology,* 1969, *13,* 17–22.

Zajonc, R. B., and G. B. Markus. Birth order and intellectual development. *Psychological Review,* 1975, *82,* 74–88.

Prejudice, Discrimination, and the Liberation Movements

6

Chapter 5 of this book dealt with a tradition in social psychology that has a long and honorable history. Much of what was said of a critical nature might be the reason for retiring an old horse that had run its last significant race. The comments made about the importance of the field might be suitable for engraving on a gold retirement watch. But now the deep and lasting significance of the effects of attitudes in just one area of social psychology must be high-lighted. The area involved is how we treat each other, or more specifically, how we mistreat each other.

Prejudice

Prejudice is an attitude; specifically an attitude toward a member of a racial, ethnic, minority, or majority group that results from the individual's membership in that group.

There is, however, another element to a prejudiced attitude that must be taken into account and is the basic element of prejudice; *the attitude is incorrect, or at the very least it is an inaccurate portrayal of the individual who holds membership in the group.* This aspect of the definition of prejudice needs to be stated because there has been such a reaction to prejudice that it has become almost impossible to differentiate between groups without being labeled prejudiced. A few examples seem to be in order.

It is not prejudiced to say that women have more estrogen than men, that the genitalia of men and women differ, and that the sexes differ in secondary sexual characteristics. It is not prejudiced to say that blacks' skin pigmentation differs from that of whites, that ethnic minorities have (recent?) ancestors who emigrated to the country in which they are a minority, and that homosexuals prefer sexual partners of the same sex. These statements are not prejudiced because they are correct.

It is prejudiced, however, to say that women cannot fill the same jobs men do, that blacks are unintelligent, that ethnic minorities are unclean, or that homosexuals are unhappy. These latter statements are statements that attribute to all individuals in a group certain characteristics with which their group has been labeled. On the whole, women are smaller in size than men and may not be able to do some of the more physically demanding jobs men do; but not all women are physically smaller or weaker than men. Some women are able to do the most physically demanding jobs that men do. It is true that as a group, blacks score lower on IQ tests than whites, but not all blacks score lower than whites, and as we shall soon see, the tests may not measure intelligence very accurately.

These few examples of accurate and inaccurate statements (and thus unprejudiced vs. prejudiced ones) are given as an example of how insidious prejudice is. As I looked for correct statements that could incorporate all of a group and thus be unprejudiced, I was hard-pressed to find them. As a matter of fact, you might think about the matter and see if you can find some differences that discriminate between black and white, minority and majority, or men and women that are true and that include every member of that group. This little exercise is intended as more than a

Is this street vendor black or white, Italian, Irish, Polish, German, or some other ethnic group? Your answer may give you a clue to your own prejudices.

futile one—I hope it will show you that most of the so-called differences among groups cannot stand up to the test of being unprejudiced. In short, most of the differences among groups that bring about such massive and often violent confrontations are not based on fact but on distortions of fact.

There is another aspect of prejudice that must be considered, and for want of a better term may be labeled "good" prejudice. That is the labeling of certain groups with attributes that are positive. "Jews are smart"; "blacks are natural athletes"; "Germans are industrious" are also prejudiced statements. These statements however are not derogatory, they are merely inaccurate. There are unintelligent Jews, blacks with two left feet, and lazy Germans. The heart of the matter lies within the root meaning of the word *prejudiced* which is to "pre-judge." It is just as inaccurate to attribute positive characteristics to a group as it is negative ones, and sometimes the effects are just as devastating to individuals within that group. As an example, consider a Jewish youngster who enters the class of a teacher who believes that all Jews are intelligent. If the child is average, the high expectations the teacher has will be dashed, and the child may well suffer.

An even more frightening aspect of good prejudice appears when it resides in the heads of policy makers. This type of approach could result, for instance, in an effort to channel Jews into professional occupations, Germans into business, and blacks into athletics. This sort of approach is detrimental to Jews, Germans, and blacks, as well as all other minority groups and the majority as well. To expect all individuals in a group to perform well in one area or another is not only totally inaccurate, it dehumanizes each individual in the group by not recognizing his or her uniqueness.

The Nature of Prejudice

If prejudice is not factual, and is inaccurate, why are we prejudiced? Why do people continue to mistrust others and hold negative images of them? Possibly the best place to start with an analysis of prejudice is with yourself. Are you prejudiced? Probably the immediate reaction from most of you is "Of course not!" Now, however, think about the groups of people around you; American Indians, blacks, Chicanos, gays, heterosexuals, Irish, Italians, men, Orientals, Polish, whites, women and, so forth. Are all of the things you think and feel about each of these groups accurate? Would you be willing to have a member of one of these groups as an acquaintance, friend, roommate, next-door neighbor, or spouse? If the answer to either of these questions about any group is No, then you must entertain the idea that you may be prejudiced against one of these groups. In a few instances there may be mitigating circumstances in which a negative answer to one of the questions does not mean prejudice. For example, if you are heterosexual you may well prefer to have a heterosexual spouse, but the exceptions are few. Also, those of you who may have decided that you are not prejudiced are probably kidding yourselves. Prejudice so pervades our society that it is a rare individual indeed who does not experience it. But where did prejudice come from?

THE HISTORICAL APPROACH

Historians remind us that prejudice has its roots in long years of conflict between groups. One of the most blatant and best documented cases of prejudice involves blacks in the United States. As this is being written "Roots" has just been shown on television to enormous audiences; an estimated 80 million Americans viewed the last episode of January 30, 1977 (Philadelphia *Inquirer,* February 2, 1977). This made "Roots" the most popular television show ever shown and of the first 10 places for the most-viewed show, "Roots" captured six. Remember, it is an 8-part series with 4 of the episodes being 1 hour and 4 of them 2 hours in length. My file of clippings about the show is enormous, and most of them are complimentary.

Whether the show was praised or not, it brought home to millions of Americans the indignities, the shame, the humiliation, and the horrors of slavery, because it is the story of one man's family, tracing it from the present to its origins in Africa. For years, Americans had believed or wanted to believe that slavery was as it was depicted in Harriet Beecher Stowe's, *Uncle Tom's Cabin,* or that the night riders depicted with such brutality in "Roots" had been correctly portrayed and glorified in the movie, *Gone With the Wind,* produced in 1938. The television drama "Roots" had an impact because it told the same story from a different point of view and it was difficult to recognize it from this vantage points. But "Roots" did more than change perspectives, it was told from a different point of view, and the black point of view is not only different, it is difficult for white Americans to accept.

Nevertheless, millions watched the drama and here are a few comments:

The scene at the bottom always differs from the view at the top. White people have been making movies about slavery from "Birth of a Nation" on past "Gone With the Wind." But surely so many of us never had such a stunning comprehension of what slavery must have felt like until we saw "Roots." [Winfrey, 1977.]

The visceral response to the televised version of Alex Haley's "Roots" reminds me of a friend's reaction some years ago to the movie "Exodus." "I went in vaguely anti-Semitic" he explained, "and came out a raving Zionist." [Yoder, 1977.]

If we are to truly understand the character-changing damage that slavery wrought on the soul of America we must keep in mind the acceptance of atrocity as a necessary part of the slave system. The fear of atrocities committed against the slave was one of the most influential means of slave control. Blacks who adjusted to slavery did so under the threat of extinction and not because "they loved Ole Massa," as so many historians of yesteryear indoctrinated their students and the public. [Jarret, 1977.]

At any rate, the story of slavery and the conflict between blacks and whites that has gone on for years in the United States has now begun to be more balanced in the telling. Allport (1954) points out that antiblack prejudice has its roots in slavery, in the slaveowners' deliberate separation of black families, in the exploitation of blacks by whites, and so forth. Those elements have taken on a new realism for millions who watched the episodes of "Roots."

There is, however, a rather glaring flaw in the reasoning cited above; namely that prejudice towards blacks occurs because of the way blacks were mistreated, subjugated, and exploited. This argument would certainly account for feelings of prejudice by blacks toward whites, but if it is to explain white prejudice toward blacks, some other mechanism must be invoked. That is, why should whites be prejudiced towards those they have subjugated because of that very subjugation unless they feel guilty or ashamed or in some other way sorry for those who have been mistreated? The fact of the matter is, the most prejudiced people seem to show these other mechanisms (such as guilt) to a lesser degree than do nonprejudiced ones.

A note should be added to the historical approach to prejudice. Blacks are not the only group who have felt the forces of prejudice against them. American Indians, ethnic minorities who have emigrated to the United States, French-speaking citizens of the province of Quebec in Canada, and women are other examples of groups who have felt the harshness of prejudice. In each instance, or so it seems to me, the historical explanation of prejudice is inadequate. It explains nicely the reasons why the exploited should dislike the exploiter, but prejudice goes in both directions and it does not explain why the exploiter should dislike the exploited.

SOCIAL AND CULTURAL PREJUDICE

Allport (1954, 1962) has argued that prejudice cannot be seen strictly as a social or cultural phenomenon, because society and culture are made up of individuals. In his own prose (Allport, 1962, pp. 129–30),

Let us summarize our discussion thus far. In order to improve relationships within the human family it is imperative to study causes. One valuable and valid approach lies in an analysis of social settings, situational forces, demographic and ecological variables, legal and economic trends. I have called these "societal" causes.

At the same time, none of these social forces accounts for all that happens—in technical terms—for all the variance in group relations. Deviant personalities, if they gain influence, can hasten, alter, or retard social forces. What is more, these forces, in and of themselves are of no avail unless they are channelized through the medium of conforming personalities. Hence to understand the full causal chain, we require a close study of habits, attitudes, perceptions and motivation.

Allport is pointing to the importance of both individual attitudes and societal attitudes as a basis for prejudice. Of course, we should never lose sight of the fact that societal attitudes would not exist if there were no individuals, whereas the reverse is not true. Individual attitudes exist without a society, but the fact that we live in a society greatly affects those of us in that society and more particularly our attitudes. (See the section on socialization in Chapter 4 for a more thorough discussion of the effects of society upon the individual.

But our question here is what effect do social and cultural attitudes have on prejudice? The question is one that must be answered in relation to the effects of individual attitudes upon attraction toward other individuals and groups (a topic we will explore in greater detail in Chapter 9). At this point in our discussion we can jump ahead enough to say that people basically are attracted to other people who are similar to themselves (see, for example, my discussion of Newcomb's work on pp. 50–52; Byrne, 1971; Rubin, 1973). This also seems to be true with respect to groups (Kidder and Stewart, 1975). As they say (pp. 26–27),

The effect of these real group differences on intergroup attraction and hostility has been demonstrated by several social psychologists and anthropologists. An extensive survey of thirty tribes in East Africa asked fifty respondents in each tribe to indicate whether they would be willing to work, visit, eat with or marry a person from each of thirteen other groups. In addition, the respondents were asked to indicate "which tribe is most similar to your own tribe" and "which tribe is least similar to your own tribe." Each tribe was then given a net similarity score in relation to each other by subtracting the number of times it was mentioned as least similar from the number of times it was named as most similar. The relationship between willingness to engage in social interaction and perceived similarity is positive and direct—the more similar the other tribe, the more willing persons were to work, visit, eat with and marry members from that group (Brewer, 1968; Campbell and LeVine, 1968). Tribes which share the same form of social organization (matrilineal [where the inheritance and name are passed from mother to daughter] versus patrilineal) [where inheritance and name are passed from father to son], the same linguistic origins, or a belief in a common ancestor are also more kindly disposed toward one another.

But there are an enormous number of ways in which individuals and societies differ from each other, and some are ignored, whereas others are closely attended to. Why, for example, should people attend to skin color or eye shape or language while not attending to equally different attributes such as hair color, height, or weight? It is true that people would attend to a green-haired, 8-foot, 700-pound man, but mainly because he would be an oddity. We do not normally react to hair color in the same way we do to skin color, to height in the same way we do eye shape, or to weight in the same way we do to language. As a matter of fact, language is one of the most visible differentiators among those who are discriminating and being discriminated against in Quebec.

Campbell (1967) has suggested that the greatest contrasts provide the strongest stimuli. As he says (p. 821),

The greater the real differences between groups on any particular custom, detail of physical appearance, or item of material culture, the more likely it is that that feature will appear in the stereotyped imagery each group has of the other.

Campbell further emphasizes the fact that if a group punishes its own members for some unacceptable characteristic, then this same characteristic or set of characteristics will also be used as a measuring rod to see how other groups stack up. That is, traits or characteristics that are important for maintaining in-group solidarity are also important for making judgments about other groups.

The importance of different characteristics among groups of individuals, whether they be social or cultural, is an important element in prejudice. There are, however, enough instances of groups living side by side in harmony even though they are different, to suggest that just differences between groups themselves will not bring about prejudice even though it may be a very important element in the process. At the very least, we must be able to make a clear specification about the specific differences that people will find adequate to cause prejudice.

I think an example from the history of Canada and the United States may be instructive. Both countries are part of the New World, and both were at one time colonies of the United Kingdom. In the mid 1770s, however, the United States felt that its differences with Britain were sufficient to start a revolution and become an independent nation. Canada remained a part of the Commonwealth until becoming an independent nation in a completely different way. The relations between the two countries are, however, excellent. In fact, the relationships among the three countries, Canada, Britain, and the United States, are all excellent.

In both Canada and the United States there has been an enormous "melting pot" effect. That is, people from various backgrounds and cultures have come together and instead of forming innumerable small groups that have consistently fought with each other, the groups have melded together to form one group. This is obviously an oversimplification, because in both countries there is still prejudice toward certain groups. Many ethnic groups, however, have come to both countries, have become assimilated, and are no longer the target of prejudice. How has this happened?

Kidder and Stewart (1975) suggest that one way this has come about is through conflict with an out-group that seems to make smaller in-group differences seem inconsequential. That is, comparison with an out-group heightens in-group solidarity, and the differences between the groups who are now banding together to face a mutual enemy are minimized. Indirect evidence for such a proposition comes from the behavior of citizens during war. During World War II, British hospitals fully expected an onslaught of patients with emotional disturbances because England was in the midst of life-disrupting, life-threatening, unpredictable air raids. But the rate of hospital admissions went down and not up as expected. Arthur (1971) reports essentially the same phenomenon in Norway, France, and Belgium.

The evidence suggests that conflict lowers the rate of emotional disturbances and enhances cohesiveness within a group. Experimental evidence for this exists, and probably the most impressive of that evidence is the work of Sherif and his associates, discussed in Chapter 2 as an illustration of a field experiment. In that work, it was found that it was possible to create in-groups and out-groups, to create a great deal of solidarity within a group, and most impressive of all to break down the barriers between two out-groups when superordinate goals called upon the individuals to put aside the differences that separated them in order to accomplish an important mission.

It seems, however, that in-group solidarity developed by a need to repel an out-group, as in a war, has two serious flaws as a way in which prejudice can be ameliorated. First, hostile feelings that were at first directed toward an out-group are merely redirected toward another out-group. Second, when the crisis is over, the prejudice may be shifted directly back to the group against which it was originally aimed. Sherif and his associates introduced superordinate goals that did not include a confrontation with another group, and this suggests that such confrontation is not necessary to break down barriers between groups. But we do not know if the introduction of positive superordinate goals will be adequate to maintain a relaxation in group hostilities once the goals are achieved. The specter of having continually to meet some crisis to reduce prejudice does not seem appealing.

COMMENT

It seems apparent that social and cultural differences do foster the type of antagonisms that can lead to prejudice. It is not clear, however, why some differences are seized upon and become salient factors in prejudice whereas other differences are not treated in the same way. It is apparent that old prejudices may be forgotten, at

There are those who argue that any contact between ethnic groups will reduce prejudice. As early as 1954, Gordon Allport argued that contact between ethnic groups is most likely to reduce prejudice when members of the majority encounter members of the minority who are equal or superior in status to themselves. The reason for this is relatively simple; people of the same ethnic group who differ in socioeconomic status are prejudiced toward one another. For example, middle-class blacks, Chicanos, Indians, whites, and so forth are prejudiced against poor people of the same group, and vice versa.

This argument makes the elimination of prejudice between majority and minority groups extremely difficult. In general, in Canada and the United States, whites are the majority group and are of a higher socioeconomic status than blacks, Chicanos, Indians, and so forth. If this argument is correct, it may explain why it has been so difficult to reduce prejudice by mixing ethnic groups without regard for social and economic status.

Clore et al. (1978) set out to test the proposition that prejudice could be reduced by contact between blacks and whites of the same social and economic status. Their laboratory was a summer camp where, for each of 5 weeks, approximately 20 blacks and 20 whites, children between 8 and 12, spent a week together. The children were mainly from economically deprived circumstances. The camp was arranged so that there were equal numbers of blacks and whites in positions of authority as helpers, counselors, and administration staff of the camp.

Several strategies were used to determine whether the camp changed children's interracial attitudes. First, they were asked at the beginning and end of camp how they felt toward children of the opposite race. Second, as soon as the campers arrived and just before they left, each child made three choices of other campers to play each of three games. Thus each camper could choose 9 other campers to play with and the number of cross-race choices was the variable measured. Finally, the campers were provided with cameras; half the campers were given the camera on the first day of camp and allowed to take 12 pictures and half were given the camera near the end of camp and allowed to take 12 pictures. The proportion of cross-race individuals in the pictures at the beginning and end of camp served as an unobtrusive measure of attraction.

The attitude, choice, and photographic measures all provided evidence that the camp experience produced significant changes in the reactions of similar socioeconomic class blacks and whites towards each other. The camp involved intimate, prolonged, rewarding contact in a situation that required cooperation on everyday tasks and a social structure in which blacks and whites were equal in numbers and authority. Under these conditions, it appears to be possible to increase cross-race attraction. Other studies have found similar results; substantial changes have been found in white coeds after a month of meeting 2 hours a day with a black coed, and other studies have found essentially the same results in a maximum-security state prison and among suburbanites. All of these results have occurred, however, when exposure was prolonged and the individuals were economically and socially equal.

These results are, of course, encouraging, but the problem of differences in socioeconomic status between majority and minority groups must first be dealt with if prolonged interaction is to be successful in reducing prejudice.

Reference

Clore, G. L., R. M. Bray, S. M. Itkin, and P. Murphy. Interracial attitudes and behavior at a summer camp. *Journal of Personality and Social Psychology*, 1978, *36*, 107–116.

least for a time, when superordinate goals are necessary. If the superordinate goal is war, however, the cure may be worse than the disease. Finally, it should be noted that one way prejudices die out is by the assimilation of those groups toward which the prejudices are aimed into the mainstream of society. Thus certain groups have been assimilated by the melting pots of Canada and the United States. There are, however, groups in both countries that are the target of prejudice who feel that the price of assimilation is too high for them to pay. It is, after all, the assimilated group that loses its identity, its culture, and its traditions in the assimilation process. We will have more to say about this matter later in this chapter.

THE INDIVIDUALISTIC ARGUMENT

Another possible source of prejudice is from within—that is, that individuals are predisposed to be prejudiced toward others for one reason or another. Part of this approach is labeled the *personality argument* by Allport (1962), who admits that there is impressive evidence to support the historical and sociocultural explanations of prejudice. However impressive the evidence for these approaches may be, he does not find them adequate. As Allport (1962, p. 123) says,

> But here is the nub of the matter. No man would say anything at all, nor do anything at all, unless he harbored within himself—in his own personality—the appropriate habits or expectancies or mental sets, or attitudes—call them what you will. Some inner dispositions are causing him both to talk like an angel and act like a devil, or to talk like a devil and act like an angel. What else than this did Myrdal mean by "the American dilemma?" It is not only possible, but usual, for Americans to have within their personalities contrasting and conflicting attitudinal dispositions. Our critics, it seems to me, are asking us to discard personality as a factor in prejudice on no other grounds than that personality is very complex. And whoever thought that it was not?

Allport argues very persuasively for a component of personality that is individualistic in nature; that is, that reflects the personality of the individual. And certainly there is impressive theoretical and empirical support for the proposition that individuals are predisposed to be prejudiced on the basis of their personality characteristics.

Allport first points to a conforming characteristic within individuals as an explanation of prejudice. The complexity of conformity, according to Allport, must be understood at three levels. The first of these is a common disposition to prefer what is familiar. Numerous anecdotal incidents and a good deal of systematic evidence substantiate the idea that people prefer what is familiar. However, this type of conformity is not strongly entrenched. As Allport (1962, p. 125) says: "This kind of conformity, be it noted, is not deeply set in the core of personality. It satisfies no basic needs. The preference for the familiar is merely skin deep."

A second type of conformity is based upon an emotional commitment to a way of life. It may involve prejudice, but it is not an isolated prejudice, rather one that is tied together with a set of values that runs deep within the person. If the disposition to prefer what is not familiar is not strongly entrenched in individuals, the emotional attachment to a way of life is. In numerous minority groups there is evident a love of the values, heritage, and culture that are unique to that group. In the United States many blacks do not want to be assimilated into the pervading culture. Rather, they want to retain many of the unique and valuable aspects of their heritage. This desire makes the issue of prejudice stand out in its boldest terms, because the insistence on retaining their unique cultural values assures that they will remain different and therefore more open to being targets of discrimination.

I wonder what would happen if blacks suddenly became the majority in an area. Would they be less prejudiced against minority groups because they understood the devastating effects of prejudice? Or would the anger and hostility that has built over the years come to the fore? There is a natural experiment presently going on in Canada in which a minority group now has power.

One of the most striking examples of commitment to a way of life and the prejudice, discrimination, and violence it can foster has been and continues in Quebec, Canada. The problem began in 1759 when the British captured Quebec and its 74,000 French inhabitants. These people, who were a small minority in Canada, refused to give up their language, their religion, and their culture. In the 200 years since then they have continued to hold on to these values. Unlike other minority groups, they did not want to become assimilated into the mainstream of Canada. Today, French-speaking Canadians make up about one fourth of Canada's 23 million inhabitants.

Yet their way of life is changing and there are stronger and stronger calls for the separation of Quebec from Canada. One of the reasons that there are louder calls for a separate Quebec is that the population of the province is increasing more slowly than that of any other Canadian province except Saskatchewan (Glazier, 1977). On November 15, 1976, Quebec elected a separatist government that has as its avowed intent the separation of Quebec from Canada and its establishment as a sovereign state. There are factors other than the separatist issue that led to the election of 71 members of the Parti Québecois (P.Q.) in the 110-member national assembly, factors such as inefficiencies and mismanagement by the Liberal government and high unemployment. But, in any event, a separatist government led by René Lévesque has been elected.

There is no doubt that French-Canadians have been discriminated against in a variety of ways because they are emotionally committed to a way of life. How are they to treat minorities now that they have power? As Glazier (1977, p. 178) says,

The real worry in Quebec today is not so much whether separatism becomes a geographic fact, but what is to become of the rights of the minorities who live in Quebec. Bill 22, the official language act, required the children of immigrants whose mother tongue was not English to attend French school; this provision was bitterly resented by those minority groups in Montreal who wanted their children to learn English first. . . .

Representatives of the P.Q., who talk so much about their rights as a French-Canadian minority in Canada, have not satisfied the minority in Quebec that they are any more concerned about their rights than the previous Liberal government. . . .

There is a new mood in Quebec, a new self-assurance on the part of the French-Canadians and a new uncertainty among all who are not part of this new French-Canadian nationalism. The shoe is on the other foot; instead of French-Canadians being dominated by the English the reverse is taking place.

Prejudice is a strange phenomenon, and all too often the ones who have had prejudice aimed at them do the same thing when roles are reversed. Quebec is one of the most startling examples and it will bear watching to see what happens. Will those who were the victims of prejudice treat others in the same way?

Allport's third type of conformity is based upon an insecurity that causes prejudice because the individual fears the consequences. What will happen if the suburban householder is friendly to the first black family on the block? Insecurity runs deep, and even though the suburbanite may want to be accepting, his or her fear of what the old neighbors will think is too powerful to allow such behavior. The status-seeking conformist will almost always reject groups he or she considers inferior and stay aligned with the "upper crust."

The Authoritarian Personality The concept of the authoritarian personality came to a scientific life in 1950 (Adorno, Frenkel-Brunswick, Levinson, and Sanford, 1950) and has generated an enormous number of supporters and critics (in almost equal numbers) since its appearance. Both the scope and the subtleties of the arguments are too time-consuming and inappropriate for my present endeavor. Suffice it to say that there are those who have damned the approach, those who have praised it, and those who have fallen somewhere in between (Byrne, 1974; Christie and Jahoda, 1954; Kirscht and Dillehay, 1967; Rokeach, 1960; Sniderman, 1975).

The scientific concept of the authoritarian personality germinated in the minds of Adorno et al. during the rise to power, the reign, and the fall of Fascism in Germany prior to and during World War II. The researchers were interested in the personality characteristics of those who were willing to obey orders, even up to and including the killing of millions of people because they were Jews.

Adorno et al. specified nine characteristics of the authoritarian personality that oftentimes cluster together. They are these:

1. A rigid adherence to values that are conventional and middle class. This characteristic was labeled *conventionalism*.
2. *Authoritarian submission* refers to the fact that authoritarians tend to yield uncritically to the idealized authority of those in power (the in-group).
3. Authoritarians tend to seek out for purposes of condemning, rejecting, and punishing people who violate those conventional values, a characteristic termed *authoritarian aggression*.
4. Tender feelings, subjective feelings, and the imaginative are distrusted, a view referred to by the researchers as *anti-intraception*.
5. *Superstition* and *stereotype* are part of the authoritarian's personality in that he or she tends to believe in the mystical determinants of the individual's fate and to think in rigid categories.
6. On the one hand, the authoritarian wants to be powerful but seeks to accomplish this end by associating with the in-group and deriving his or her *power and "toughness"* from that source.
7. *Destructiveness and cynicism*, which involves a generalized hostility toward and vilification of that which is human, is part of the syndrome.
8. The authoritarian has a predisposition to believe that wild and dangerous

things are going on "out there," a predisposition that comes from a *projection* of unconscious emotional impulses and results in a degree of paranoia.

9. The authoritarian is sure that wild things are going on out there and most of them have to do with *sex.*

The picture of the authoritarian that was drawn by Adorno et al. is one of a rigid person, fearful of power yet wanting it, fearful of plots, fearful of sex, and trying to espouse the right and eschew the wrong that is so clearly known. It is a rather pathetic picture and its major criticism, which has proved telling, is that it is too narrow. The authors of *The Authoritarian Personality* concentrated on the political right (or conservatism), whereas Rokeach (1954, 1956, 1960) has correctly pointed out that there can be authoritarians of all political persuasions—of the right, of the left, and in the center. He termed this grouping of characteristics *dogmatism,* and it did deal with the closed, rigid, fearful person regardless of his or her political persuasion.

And authoritarism, or dogmatism, is important in this section on prejudice, because rigidity leads to prejudice. There is, however, a difference in the form the prejudice takes for an authoritarian and a dogmatic.

The authoritarian is basically drawn to and identifies with the in-group. Almost by definition, minority groups or those who are a majority but do not hold power, are members of the out-group and all of the anti-out-group characteristics are trained on them. Thus blacks, chicanos, American Indians, Jews, ethnics, and other "undesirables" are to be treated with contempt, fear, and hostility. They are the objects of prejudice and it is a particularly virulent form of prejudice.

Now let us look at the other end of the political spectrum—the left. As Rokeach pointed out, "authoritarians of the left" are just as rigid as those of the right; but, in the United States they are part of the out-group themselves. Allport (1962, p. 128) says,

For one thing we now know of cases high in authoritarianism but displaying no hostility toward minority groups. On the contrary they are most favorably disposed. One man of this type denies that Negroes or Jews, Mexicans or Orientals have any faults at all. At the same time this man is insensitive, insightless, and insecure—scoring high on all authoritarian measures. In his case there is partiality toward, or love-prejudice for, out-groups.

This phenomenon was overlooked by the original authors of *The Authoritarian Personality,* but has been called to our attention by Rokeach who believes that there is considerable dogmatism among people harboring "liberal attitudes." Communists are of this type. We must therefore allow for "authoritarianism of the left." (Rokeach, 1956.)

This authoritarian of the left is, of course, not necessarily hostile to minority groups because he or she is also a member of a minority group—possibly not an ethnic, racial, or religious one, but a minority group all the same. The prejudice for this individual may be just as deep, but it is aimed at the in-group, and thus shows different behavioral manifestations. However, the individual is still predisposed to be prejudiced.

One of the more prevalent ideas concerning prejudice among the populace of both Canada and the United States is that prejudice is learned, not innate. Certainly the historical, social, and cultural, and individual explanations of prejudice are based on learning. People learn to be prejudiced against others in the historical approach, because those individuals are not equal to them in some way. By the same token, children are not born knowing that there are different social and cultural groupings—they must be taught that information. And no one argues that an authoritarian or dogmatic is born, he or she learns these characteristics. So why should we discuss prejudice as a learned phenomenon? To say that each of the approaches we have perviously discussed has a learned component is too general and in this section we need to consider how an individual learns to be prejudiced.

In the process of socialization, which we discussed in Chapter 4, children learn first from their parents, then from other adults, and as they grow older, increasingly from their peers. The whole process of socialization is one in which parents and peers pass along the values of the culture to the child. Thus, if the culture harbors prejudice against blacks, women, ethnic groups, or any other minority, the child will learn these ideas and translate them into his or her own value system.

In this day and age of mass communication, however, the effect of the media on prejudice must be considered. Television has become one of the major entertainment sources for young people in both Canada and the United States. Following the smashing success of *Sesame Street,* numerous television shows have been introduced both to entertain and, it is hoped, to educate children. To the extent that television reflects the culture's values, then we may consider it but another method of inculcating values of children. To the extent that this medium does not reflect the values of society, it must be considered another source of influencing children. So television, as well as other means of communication, must be included in the equation if we are to understand how prejudice is learned.

How do children learn to be prejudiced? One very obvious way is that they learn it through observation or modeling. This process (which is discussed more fully in Chapter 8) is one in which the child observes someone else doing something. If the child sees his parents or peers acting in a manner that is prejudiced toward another group then the child may very well learn that this sort of behavior is appropriate. In this type of learning it is not necessary for the child to act in a prejudiced manner to have learned prejudice; he or she may observe the action and file it away for future reference.

Another way in which children may learn prejudice is by direct reinforcement for prejudicial attitudes or punishment for nonprejudicial attitudes. These rewards and/or punishments may come from parents, peers, teachers, and other adults for holding the "proper" attitudes—ones that are prejudiced are rewarded and non-prejudiced ones are punished. Of course, it is difficult to find people who will admit that they are bringing up their children to be prejudiced, and to know that this behavior occurs we would have to be present while it was going on. Nevertheless, we can say with some assurance that some parents bring up prejudiced children by using direct reward and/or punishment.

Black dolls are more available in toy stores than they once were and black children are not forced to play with white dolls.

But what is learned by children who are in the group against whom the prejudice is directed? Clark and Clark (1947) used a unique and brilliant methodology to study the racial preferences of black children. Using both Southern and Northern male and female blacks, these investigators found that these children, who ranged in age from 3 to 7 overwhelmingly preferred a white doll to a black one. This finding, that black children prefer a white doll (or in some cases a photograph of a white person) has been noted by a number of other investigators (Lewis and Biber, 1951; Greenwald and Oppenheim, 1968; Morland, 1962, 1966; Porter, 1971). These investigations seemingly indicate that a child who grows up as a target for prejudice begins to deprecate his or her own racial or ethnic identity. Porter (1971) concluded that young children's doll or photograph choices may indicate an incipient racial attitude that can be accounted for by rejection or ambivalence toward their own race.

Interestingly, most of this research may have been influenced by several possible confounding elements. Porter (1971) suggests that some of the results may be explained by the fact that white experimenters were utilized in much of the work, and the children chose the white doll or photograph to please the experimenter. Second, and probably more important, when this research was started by the Clarks in the 1940s there were few if any black dolls available on the market. This state of affairs continued through the 50s and began to moderate only slowly toward the end of the 60s. Now, in the late 70s and early 80s, black dolls are no longer a curiosity, but they once were. Possibly children chose the more familiar toy (see Chapter 9 for a discussion of the effect of familiarity on preference).

The work also started before the "Black is beautiful" movement began, and the contribution of this movement to black self-identity, to black self-esteem, and to the development of self-worth as blacks in black children should not be underestimated.

We are living in a time when black self-esteem has gone through a period of violent rebellion and is growing in stature and popularity among the black community. Racial incidents that sometimes culminate in riots are now provoked more often by whites who fear the intrusion of blacks into what they have considered their territory—schools and neighborhoods.

But what has happened to the self-esteem of black children during this time? More recent investigators employing other methods have found an increase in self-esteem among black children (McCarthy and Yancy, 1973; Vershure, 1976). Additionally investigators using the same procedure as the Clarks found a reversal in preference among black children for a black doll (Harris and Brown, 1971; Hraba and Grant, 1970), while Moore (1976) using photographs of teachers found results consistent with those of Hraba and Grant. Figure 6–1 shows the striking reversal of black children's preference for a black doll between 1947 (Clark and Clark) and 1970 (Hraba and Grant). This reversal could have resulted from any of the reasons we stated above (black dolls are familiar, the "Black is beautiful" movement, the use of black experimenters, and so on), but most probably it has come from a combination of elements.

As the 1970s proceeded, it was apparent that blacks were being pictured in a more favorable light in the media. One example should suffice. Blacks are now shown in commercials having fun, using products, and involving themselves in life just as whites do. Some children's programs show blacks in the same way they do whites, having fun, laughing, being laughed at, and in general living life as white children do. This, too, might have had an effect on the self-esteem of blacks.

One of the negative concomitant results of the increase in black self-esteem may be a deprecation of whites. Whereas it is logically possible for black self-esteem to

Many whites fear black equality in housing and education. These issues, symbolized by the bussing controversy, have caused violent demonstrations in a number of cities in the United States.

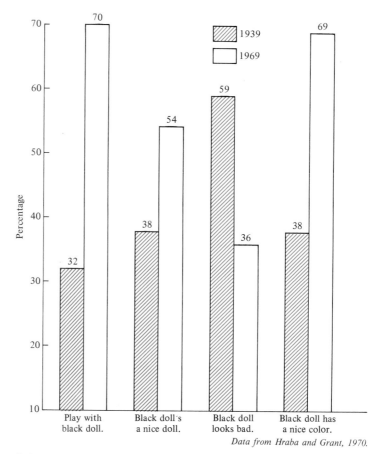

Figure from Hraba and Grant, 1970.

Figure 6-1 **Percentage of black children wanting to play with doll, feeling a doll is nice, that it looks bad, or has a nice color when offered a black doll in 1939 and in 1969.**

increase without a corresponding decrease in blacks' feelings about whites, it is not likely that this would occur, since many blacks view whites as the source of their frustrations. Thus it seems probable that an increase in problack feeling would be accompanied by an increase in antiwhite feelings. The empirical results concerning this supposition (that increased problack sentiments lead to increased antiwhite feelings) have been mixed. Banks (1970) and Paige (1970) found the problack and antiwhite feelings were positively related, but Caplan (1970) reviewed several riot situations and concluded that black militancy does not appear to be associated with hostility toward whites. Of course, the situations these researchers addressed are not comparable: Banks and Paige assessed individuals' feelings in a relatively calm atmosphere which differs greatly from the emotions generated in a confrontation.

Chang and Ritter (1976) reported research in which they compared responses by blacks in 1953 and 1974 on an Anti-White Scale and an Anti-Negro Scale developed

Blacks are portrayed in a favorable light in advertisements which were once reserved for whites.

by Steckler (1957). The 1953 sample was from Steckler's data, and the 1974 data was collected by Chang and Ritter. Over the 21 years between the two testings, antiwhite feelings increased dramatically, whereas anti-Negro feelings decreased. Thus, it seems that as black self-esteem increases, there is a corresponding increase in antiwhite feelings. Figure 6–2 presents the results graphically.

TELEVISED PREJUDICE

One of the interesting outgrowths of the alterations in programming on television is the treatment of prejudice and bigotry in more open ways, particularly in situation comedies. The first of these to gain wide audience acceptance and high ratings and to enjoy a long run on television was *All in the Family*. Archie Bunker was supposed to personify "Everyman" and was intended by Norman Lear, the producer, to be multidimensional, differentiated, and differentiable (Surlin and Bowden, 1976). Archie was intended to be a highly authoritarian, working-class husband and is generally so perceived. He is also highly prejudiced against a variety of minority groups, whom he describes in graphic terms, is terribly afraid of them, and in general displays most authoritarian characteristics.

239

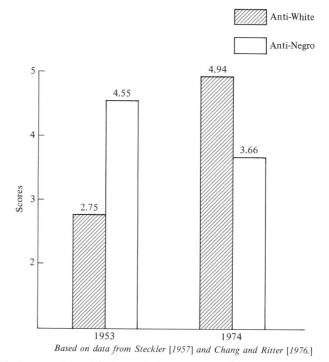

Based on data from Steckler [1957] and Chang and Ritter [1976.]

Figure 6–2. **Scores of black college students on antiwhite and anti-Negro scales in 1953 and in 1974.**

This program raised a storm of controversy almost from its inception as Surlin and Tate (1976, pp. 61–2) say,

> Research has dealt with the reaction of the viewing audience to the characterizations within the program and not with the humorous content *per se*. The most clear-cut finding to date is that highly bigoted viewers are more apt to agree with the point of view expressed by Archie Bunker than are less bigoted viewers (Brigham, 1975; Chapko & Lewis, 1975; Surlin, 1974; Tate & Surlin, 1976; Vidmar & Rokeach, 1974). Recently, respondents in agreement with Archie's point of view reported a greater degree of self-awareness concerning their beliefs and concurrent polarization in this belief system through continued viewing of "All in the Family."

Surlin and Tate (1976) specifically tested the assumption that more authoritarian individuals would view hostile humorous events in *All in the Family* as more humorous than would low-authoritarian individuals. Because of the complexity of the characters and the role played by Edith, Archie's wife, there was some reason for these investigators to suspect that sex would also play an important role in perceived humor. Finally, in an attempt to "tease out" cultural differences, even in two cultures that are closely related, a Canadian sample as well as an American one was drawn. Six humorous vignettes from *All in the Family* were presented to a sample of 245 individuals from Athens, Georgia, and 248 from Saskatoon, Saskatchewan. (Both are university towns located in a rural area.) As expected, U.S. viewers saw the vignettes

STEREOTYPES

Stereotypes are potentially one of the most damaging aspects of prejudicial behavior. Early research into the area of racial stereotypes found that both blacks and whites tended to assign one set of attributes (intelligent, industrious, progressive, and ambitious) to whites and another set (very religious, happy-go-lucky, musical, loud, and lazy) to blacks. Research in the 1950s showed that the stereotypes were more realistically class stereotypes, not racial ones. That is, upper-class whites and upper-class blacks were described with the same traits (intelligent, ambitious, progressive, and neat) whereas the same traits (happy-go-lucky, loud, physically dirty, and lazy) were used to describe lower-class whites and blacks.

Smedley and Bayton (1978) assessed the class and racial stereotypes of whites and blacks. They divided their subjects into groups that perceived themselves as above or below the average for their own race. That is, above- and below-average (socioeconomically) blacks and whites rated lower- and middle-class blacks and whites on a series of traits. Furthermore, each subject was instructed to rate the favorability of that trait rating as it was applied to that group. Thus, a trait could be assigned to one group as a favorable trait and to another group as an unfavorable one. For example, when whites characterized lower-class blacks as being rebellious, it was rated unfavorably. In contrast when lower-class blacks were labeled rebellious by blacks, the trait was rated favorably.

The research design used by Smedley and Bayton allowed the researchers to assign overall favorability ratings to each group rather than merely to list the traits that were used to describe that group. This method had the crucial advantage of letting one know not only what descriptive traits were used to characterize a group, but whether, from the subjects' point of view, these traits were positive or negative for that group.

As in past research, whites differentiated on the basis of class. Both groups of whites (those who perceived themselves as above and those who perceived themselves as below the socioeconomic average) viewed the middle class more favorably than they did the lower class. They did not differ in their view of blacks and whites. Blacks, on the other hand, differentiated on the basis of race. They viewed both lower- and middle-class blacks more favorably than they viewed either lower- or middle-class whites. In both groups the middle class was viewed more positively than the lower class of the same race.

In the 20 or so intervening years since research indicated that blacks and whites differentiated between groups on the basis of class (with upper class being viewed more favorably), things have changed for blacks. As Smedley and Bayton point out, racial stereotypes by the members of that race can be taken as a measure of racial self-concept. The early stereotype research indicated that both blacks and whites viewed blacks in a negative light. One of the efforts of the Black Movement has been to foster a higher self-concept for blacks. The black subjects in this research, who were college students, seem to have been influenced by this movement. Blacks see the black lower class in a more favorable light than they do the white middle class. The elimination of stereotypes has long been an aim of many people in a democratic society and the increase in black self-esteem is one step forward in this struggle.

Reference

Smedley, J. W., and J. A. Bayton. Evaluative race-class stereotypes by race and perceived class of subjects. *Journal of Personality and Social Psychology*, 1978, *36*, 530–535.

as more humorous than did the Canadian viewers, although, as Figure 6–3 shows, the differences were not large (although statistically significant). Males also saw the vignettes as more humorous than did females, and there was an interaction between

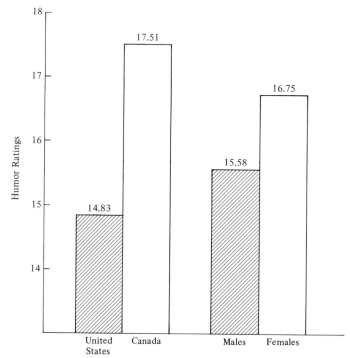

Adapted from data presented by Surlin and Tate, 1976.

Figure 6-3 Humor ratings for six vignettes from "All in the Family" for United States and Canadian audiences and for males and females. Low scores indicate more humor. Possible range of scores 6–30.

authoritarianism and sex, which is shown graphically in Figure 6-4. High-authoritarian males and low-authoritarian females saw the vignettes as more humorous than did the other subjects in this study.

The most serious aspect of the research on *All in the Family* to date is that viewing it leads to increased authoritarian thinking by high authoritarians and those who are from the lower social classes (Surlin and Bowden, 1976). It appears that viewers who are cognitively similar to Archie have their "beliefs raised to a level of consciousness and then reinforced. This can only lead to greater degrees of prejudice, closed-mindedness, and continued noncoping behavior in our pluralistic society" (Surlin and Bowden, 1976, p. 7). There is some evidence to suggest that possibly the same sort of reaction is occurring with regard to other shows that portray hostile humor. There is evidence that, as in viewing *All in the Family,* the more one views *Sanford and Son* and *The Jeffersons* the more entertaining they are perceived to be (Leckenby and Surlin, in press; Surlin and Cooper, 1976).

Thus, television appears to have an as yet unspecified effect on prejudice, in some ways positive and in other ways negative. Unfortunately, ratings and their companion, profits, appear to be more important considerations than anything else. This should not surprise us, as television has basically been viewed as a business run by

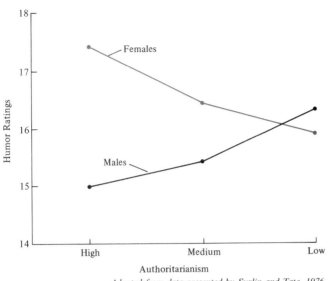

Adapted from data presented by Surlin and Tate, 1976.

Figure 6–4 **Interaction between authoritarianism and sex of viewers in humor ratings in six vignettes from "All in the Family." The lower the score, the more humorous. (Scores range 6–30).**

business. Surlin and Bowden (1971, p. 1) have summed up the present state of affairs nicely!

The electronic media have vastly changed the lives of modern men in a relatively short time. When television was first developed it was seen solely as an entertainment medium and left in the hands of businessmen. Recently, however, we have come to suspect that a television program that reaches millions of people in their own homes can have a greater effect on the thinking of its audience than a play or book, or even a movie. Most research and thinking has concerned news and public affairs programs and their effects, but lately, programs designed purely for entertainment have been studied.

In the past few years we have been dramatically shown what far-reaching effects the decisions of mass media executives, a relatively small number of people, can have on the entire country. We find that we must now begin to consider the "success" of a televised program as dependent on more than its economic results. We must consider how it will shape the thinking of television viewers.

As we become more aware of the ramifications of television content we are faced with the realization that we must be responsible for the good of society in our broadcasting decisions. This realization saddles mass media businessmen with a responsibility that they never asked for, that they are seldom equipped to handle, and that they now resist accepting.

Prejudice, as we have seen, is a pervasive element in society in Canada and the United States, and one of the striking aspects of the phenomenon is that in one way or another, prejudice is assumed to be learned. That is, the folk wisdom of our day says you have to teach a child to be prejudiced. But is that necessarily so?

I think prejudice in Canada and the United States is pervasive, yet there are students who would violently disagree with such a statement. There is no doubt that I cannot prove my argument, but let me cite a few facts that bolster it. First, prejudice can be aimed at many different groups. In the United States Blacks, chicanos, and Indians are probably the groups most discriminated against. In Canada, it appears that French-Canadians and Indians hold that dubious honor. We have discussed several of these groups already and will return to them. Ironically enough, this prejudice crosses national boundaries because, according to Cotnam (1977), French-Canadian literature, generally speaking, portrays the United States as a country full of people whose only values are materialistic. It was the task of the French-Canadians in general and their writers in particular to witness to the supremacy of their spiritual and intellectual values to the citizens of the United States.

We need not belabor the point that there is prejudice, pervasive prejudice, in both countries. This whole chapter is a catalogue of that prejudice and its effects. Because the United States has fought a civil war over its separatism and prejudice whereas Canada has not, my argument may have to be more fully justified to Canadian students. In 1967 the Hawthorn Report pointed out that 94 percent of Indian children drop out of school before the twelfth grade, that there is an average age-grade retardation of 2.5 years, and that only 57 Indian students out of 45,000 were attending universities across Canada in 1963. Bowd (1977) points out that little of substance has been done to alter the situation.

Blacks in Canada are a more diffused group than are blacks in the United States. Possibly it is this diffusion, or some other reason, but according to Winks (1971), blacks in Canada are less militant, less essentially separatist, than their counterparts in the United States. As Winks describes the situation in Nova Scotia,

... Indeed, Negroes in Nova Scotia were, until the spring of 1965, so reluctant to make "racial" demands upon the closed white leadership of their province, they continued to accept segregated schools, inadequate public transport, and the designation "coloured," and only agitation by "outsiders"—Negroes from the West Indies and the United States—began to move the Nova Scotia Negro away from his general reliance on prayer and passivism. [Winks, 1971, pp. 96–97.]

The equality of blacks in Canada is more apparent than real. There have been few blacks who have escaped the lower classes, and the lower class will settle for improvement rather than reform. In addition, black communities in Canada are seldom contiguous. There is no black belt as in the Southern United States and no large urban ghettos. Thus, a cohesiveness that would call attention to the inequalities that beset black Canadians has not emerged.

In a penetrating analysis of Canada's minority groups Elliott (1971) has this to say:

At first glance, it may not be apparent that minority groups are disadvantaged relative to the majority. It is commonly accepted by Canadians that their society is egalitarian. Immigrants have been drawn by this ideology to Canada's shores, seeking a higher standard of living as well as political and personal freedom. In spite of society's beliefs in fair play and the inherent worth and dignity of man, our society suffers from ethnic and social class prejudice and discrimination. [Elliott, 1971, p. 1.]

Untaught Prejudice

One of the most provocative ideas about prejudice that I have seen or heard in a long time is that we may be approaching the subject too naïvely. The reason I consider the idea provocative is that it is one that was generated by a colleague and myself in one of those long scholarly sessions professors involve themselves in (when anyone else has them we refer to them as bull sessions). We published this idea as sort of an aside in another book (Lamberth, McCullers, and Mellgren, 1976). Our provocative idea has yet to draw a response, but that will not deter me from expressing it again. It is speculative, and frankly I do not know how to operationalize research into the question. Thus, at the present time, it is a nontestable theory, but one that both makes some sense to me and has enormous implications for dealing with prejudice.

The idea developed from a discussion of research with monkeys, specifically, with monkeys reared in isolation. When given the choice, monkeys reared in isolation will choose to associate with other monkeys reared in isolation rather than with monkeys reared by a mother with other monkeys. The socially reared monkeys return the sentiment, but this is not surprising, since monkeys reared in isolation display grossly abnormal behavior patterns. To sum it up in a word, monkeys reared in isolation are "weird" monkeys.

When we combine this information with extensive research in interpersonal attraction (see Chapter 9 for a complete discussion of attraction), which indicates that, for the most part, people are drawn to other people who are similar to themselves (Byrne, 1971), then we can begin to make some sense out of the data that tell us that socially isolated monkeys choose to associate with other monkeys like themselves. There may be some reason for individuals to prefer similar others.

Our next thought had to do with the evolutionary survival value of associating with similar others. Let us take the example of an antelope. If an antelope, particularly a young one, freely associates with all other species available in the natural habitat, then there will be certain other species that do it no harm (for example, zebras). On the other hand, if an antelope develops a close relationship with a lion, the relationship might become closer than the antelope had in mind. Thus, there is a certain survival value in associating *only* with similar others, for antelopes and all other species including *Homo sapiens*. Certainly at one time, at the dawn of the age of our species, there was a survival value in associating only with other specimens of *Homo sapiens*. Even later in history, as *Roots* so dramatically pointed out, it was wise for a black man in Africa to avoid men whose skin was a different color because he might end up a slave in America.

Possibly, we thought, there is an evolutionary "holdover" that once served its purpose, survival, but like our appendix, is no longer necessary. When it becomes inflamed, either the unnecessary appendix or survival mechanism, it must be removed. No longer is it enough to say that if you don't teach your child to be prejudiced, he or she won't be. Possibly, we must take positive action to teach children not to distrust those who are different from themselves. If there is some validity to this position, then it would help explain why we have been so unsuccessful in eliminating prejudice.

These, of course, are speculative thoughts. Take them for that and see if they make any sense to you.

Comment

Prejudice is a very prevalent part of our lives—a part that has led to horrors beyond imagination and still leaves us with difficult social problems throughout Canada and the United States. Our review of why prejudice occurs is somewhat frustrating, because we can see the enormous effects and yet, seemingly, can do nothing about it. Which theory of the nature of prejudice is correct, or is there some element of truth in all of them?

But now, we turn to a closely allied subject, discrimination.

Discrimination

If prejudice is an attitude, then discrimination is action based on the prejudiced attitude or attitudes. In being consistent with the definition of prejudice given earlier in this chapter, *discrimination is action based on an incorrect or inaccurate attitude toward a member of a racial, ethnic, minority, or majority group that results from the individual's membership in that group.* Prejudice is an attitude (the way someone feels toward or what one thinks about another person); discrimination is action based on those feelings and thoughts.

Chapter 5 made the point that attitudes and the behavior based on those attitudes do not always coincide. In fact, one of the major difficulties in attitude research is that people may feel one way about an issue and act another. In a classic study LaPiere (1934) set out to determine the relationship between attitudes toward a minority group and actual behavior toward individuals in that group. He traveled for three months with a Chinese couple across the United States and up and down the West Coast. At that time, there were strong feelings of prejudice toward Orientals, but in spite of this fact in stopping at about 250 hotels and restaurants, they were refused service only once. Later LaPiere wrote to each of the places they had stopped and asked if Chinese patrons would be accepted. Only about half of the owners or managers replied, but of those who did, 90 percent said they would *not* accept Chinese patrons. Thus what restaurant and hotel owners did and what they said they would do varied greatly.

LaPiere's findings should not lead you to believe that there is no discrimination in the country, then or now. It may merely mean that there is a good deal of prejudice that never gets translated into discrimination. In many ways, some subtle and some not so subtle, there is an enormous amount of discrimination going on in Canada and the United States. One hardly knows where to begin in recounting the list of indignities that have been suffered by individuals and groups. It is sort of like an "Honor Roll" of the dead—most of us would rather be left off than to receive the honor.

247

Discrimination

The Effects of Discrimination

I cannot catalog all of the horrible effects of discrimination against all the groups in Canada and the United States who have received the dubious distinction of having prejudice against them acted out. For that matter, I must be selective in the groups I pick, because we have, for all of our cries about democracy and freedom in Canada and the United States, been terribly discriminatory toward many different groups. We share the distinction of both having been colonies of a great colonial power, Britain; but we have not improved upon Britain's unenviable record in discrimination. Such sweeping generalizations need some substantiation and I will now move to providing such information. I will discuss discrimination against women, blacks, and Indians, trying to do more than catalog discriminatory acts.

WOMEN

Those of the so-called "weaker sex" have had many indignities aimed at them, not the least of which are actions by men who felt that women *were* the "weaker sex." Women could not vote in the United States until they fought for the right and won it early in this century; they could not own property for many years, and women still have trouble getting credit, being paid an equal wage for equal work, and, in general, living in today's society.

But still a different indignity also exits for women in Canada and a number of women in the United States. The right to a trial by a jury of your peers is one of the most cherished rights in English common law, dating from the signing of the Magna Carta (1215). Until very recently, however, in the United States you could have a jury of your peers as long as you weren't female, because from the very beginning indentured servants, outlaws, and women were excluded from jury service. The United States added slaves to the list of those excluded (Cornish, 1968). With the passage of the Fourteenth Amendment to the Constitution of the United States, blacks won the right to serve on juries, at least in theory. Women were still excluded. It was not until 1957 that women won the right to sit on Federal juries, although some states had granted women that right much earlier. Utah was the first, in 1898, and many others followed when the Ninteenth Amendment to the constitution was passed (1920). As late as 1966, Alabama, Mississippi, and South Carolina still barred women from state juries (Nemeth, Endicott, and Wachtler, 1976). According to Nemeth et al.,

They now provide for women to serve but it should be noted that the 1972 code of South Carolina, while providing for the "alternate method of drawing and summoning jurors" with no restrictions based on sex, still allows for the original method by which the selection process involves only *male* electors, [1976, p. 293.]

Why were, and to a much lesser extent are, women excluded from jury service? The basic reason was that women were not thought to be intellectually capable of fulfilling the duties of a juror. Jury selection is filled with much folklore and inaccurate information, but some of the reasons women were felt to be incapable of jury duty were that they tended to be emotional, submissive, envious, and passive (Appleman, 1952; Darrow, 1936; Goldstein, 1935). These assertions were made in the absence of any strong (or even weak) experimental evidence to support them.

The experimental evidence that has accumulated in the last 25 years or so indicates that men and women do differ in the way they act when serving as jurors. However, there is apparently a complex interaction or series of interactions between the type of case being heard and the juror's sex. For example, Simon (1967) found that women in general were more sympathetic to a defendant in a house-breaking case. Housewives however, were more punitive than men toward a defendant accused of incest whereas women working outside the home were more in agreement with men in the incest case. Nagel and Weitzman (1972) found that each sex tends to favor its own sex in the amount of damages awarded in a civil case, whereas Rose and Prell (1955) found that each sex tends to be less punitive towards members of its own sex in criminal cases. Nemeth et al. (1976) found no differences between the sexes in terms of the verdicts rendered in both civil and criminal cases. Although the Nemeth et al. studies were carefully controlled, they were laboratory studies that used simulated cases and college students as jurors. As we shall see in Chapter 11, there may be problems in generalizations from simulated jury studies to actual ones.

The evidence from a variety of sources is strong that women serve well on juries and that there are no reasons to exclude them. The fact that women could not be tried by a jury of their peers in Federal courts until 1957 and in one state may still be unable to have a jury of their peers is a blatant form of discrimination.

BLACKS

Where do we start? First of all one must be selective here or all of our space will be filled with listing instances of discrimination. And we want to do more than that. We want to deal with an area that is uniquely psychological and has a continuing impact on blacks. The most obvious candidate as a topic for discussion is intelligence, or more precisely, intelligence testing. The first successful intelligence test was developed by Alfred Binet, a Frenchman, who with Theophile Simon published the Binet-Simon Scale in 1905. Others had tried and failed, but Binet succeeded because he was attempting to measure symbolic processes (thinking) and he had a specific task. Binet's task was to develop a test that would screen out the noneducable children in the Paris school system, a task that formerly took a year or two of the child's time sitting in class until his or her teacher realized the deficiency. Even though IQ tests were developed in France, they have had their most devoted adherents and disciples in the United States.

James M. Cattell and G. Stanley Hall were two of the most important psychologists in transporting the idea of intelligence testing to the United States. But Lewis Terman, who coined the term *intelligence quotient* (IQ), and Carl Brigham have probably had the most long-lasting and direct influence on intelligence testing, particularly as it applies to blacks and other ethnic minorities. This is primarily so because Terman developed the Stanford-Binet Intelligence Scale and Brigham developed the Scholastic Aptitude Test (SAT). The Stanford-Binet is the most popular and widely used individual intelligence test for children (the standard by

One of the major individual IQ tests is contained in this box, and it has the potential problems of discrimination discussed in the text.

which other tests are judged) and the SAT is used by most colleges as one major determiner of whether a student should be admitted.

Throughout the course of this book, where it seems appropriate, you have found and will continue to find sketches of the history of psychology in general and social psychology in particular. Such a sketch is in order here, primarily because what a test constructor has thought about the issues surrounding his or her area of expertise undoubtedly has had an effect on that person's work. As scientists we should not let personal beliefs interfere with our development of scientific knowledge, but we do. Here is what Terman (1916) had to say about a pair of Indian and Mexican children:

> Their dullness seems to be racial, or at least inherent in the family stocks from which they come. The fact that one meets this type with such extraordinary frequency among Indians, Mexicans and Negroes suggests quite forcibly that the whole question of racial differences in mental traits will have to be taken up anew . . . . children of this group should be segregated in special classes. . . . There is no possibility at present of convincing society that they should not be allowed to reproduce. . . . They constitute a grave problem because of their unusually prolific breeding.

Carl Brigham (1923) noted that individuals who had immigrated to the United States 16 to 20 years earlier showed about the same level of IQ as native-born Americans, but those tested within 5 years of their immigration appeared to be feeble-minded. As Brigham was convinced that IQ tests were measuring native or inborn intelligence (even for those who could not read or write), he was unable to conclude that these marked differences resulted from a language deficiency on the part of the later immigrants. The immigrants of 20 years earlier (1900–1910) had come from England, Germany, and Scandinavia. More recent immigrants (1915–1920) had come from southern and eastern Europe: Jews, Poles, Russians, and Italians. Thus Brigham concluded that the more "Nordic" blood, the more intelligent one was, whereas an increase in "Alpine" or "Mediterranean" blood indicated less native intelligence.

These were two of the important originators of the intelligence testing movement in the United States, and like many of the other early intelligence test researchers were members of the Eugenics Research Association. *Eugenics* is a science that attempts to improve the inborn or inherited qualities of a species, especially humans. There is little doubt that many of the early researchers in intelligence felt that IQ was primarily innate and not very amenable to change by environmental factors.

But what about today? Since 1969, when Arthur Jensen reopened a long-smoldering controversy by maintaining that IQ was largely innate and early intervention programs, such as Head Start, would not alter IQ, there has been an enormous controversy raging in the United States. On the one hand, there are those who, at one level or another, side with Jensen in claiming that black children have genetically limited intellectual potential (Jensen, 1973; Shockley, 1971, 1972). Others (Anastasi, 1976; Kamin, 1974; Scarr and Weinberg, 1976) take a different position, arguing that the environment plays a much more important role in the development of IQ than the hereditarians believe. It would be highly inaccurate to argue that there is complete agreement on either side of the issue among the individual psychologists, but these are the general positions.

What does this have to do with discrimination? There is general agreement that blacks score about 15 points lower on IQ tests than do whites. As you may have guessed by now, the argument between the hereditarians and the environmentalists is over the question of why blacks, as a group, score lower than whites. The hereditarians say that black children have a genetically limited intellectual capacity, whereas the environmentalists argue that several environmental factors, which have nothing to do with innate ability, combine to lower blacks' scores on the tests. These may be broken down into the following categories: (1) the tests are biased; (2) blacks are poorer and live in a different environment than whites; and (3) changes in that environment should alter IQ. Let us look at each one of these issues.

Biased Tests. Virtually everyone agrees that it is impossible to develop an IQ test that is not affected by the culture an individual belongs to. When language is a barrier, when different points of reference are important, or when a completely different life style is encountered by the testee than was envisioned by the test constructor, bias in the results will occur. This has been understood for years, but apparently among many IQ test constructors in the United States, it was adequate to aim for the majority, which meant the white, middle class in standardizing their tests. IQ tests are developed in such a way that the normalization sample is vitally important, because it is to the performance of this group that future testees will be compared. These groups, although containing blacks and other minority groups members, typically did not contain them in sufficient numbers materially to affect the group norms. Furthermore, it has been only in the last twenty years or so that there has been a large-scale realization that the culture a poor black child grows up in is

DESEGREGATION AND RACIAL ATTITUDES

Within the United States there has been a massive movement to desegregate public schools. The most visible, if not the most often-used, tool in this movement has been bussing to achieve a racial balance in the schools of an area. Bussing has been highly commended by some and just as highly condemned by others. Interestingly enough, even some of its former adherents now oppose it because it has brought violence to some cities and an exodus of many middle-class families in most cities where it has been used. Whereas bussing has been the visible symbol of a major social disagreement, there is a more basic issue that must be addressed; does desegregation change racial attitudes?

Stephan and Rosenfield (1978) pointed out that since 1954, 13 studies have focused on the effects of school desegregation on the racial attitudes of whites toward blacks. Predominately positive effects were found in four of the studies; seven found predominately negative effects and two found no effects. Many of these studies focused exclusively on entire ethnic groups as their unit of analysis. Stephan and Rosenfield argue that during desegregation within any ethnic group some individuals will change their attitudes in a positive direction and some will change in a negative direction. Therefore, they decided to study the correlates of individual changes in racial attitudes during school desegregation.

The design of the study was longitudinal, i.e., students' racial attitudes were examined while they were in segregated schools, or at most, naturally integrated schools, and again 2 years later after court-ordered desegregation. Sixty-two percent of the sample was white, 23 percent Mexican American, and 15 percent black. (The study took place in a city in the southwestern part of the United States.) Students' racial attitudes, self-esteem, and amount of interethnic contact were measured. In addition, parental punishment practices and attitudes toward integration and authoritarianism were assessed.

The advantage of this study over many others is that it measured the racial attitudes of the same school-age children both before and after court-ordered desegregation. The major variables that influenced racial attitudes were increases in self-esteem, increases in interethnic contact, parental punitiveness, and parental authoritarian child-rearing practices. These last two variables were negatively correlated with racial attitudes. That is, more punitive and authoritarian parents resulted in negative changes in racial attitudes. Increases in self-esteem and interethnic contact resulted in positive changes in racial attitudes.

The results reported by Stephan and Rosenfield are consistent with most of the previous research in this area with regard to racial attitudes and interethnic contact, self-esteem, and parental punishment and authoritarianism. It paints a rather complex picture of the potential effects of desegregation on racial attitudes. If there is high self-esteem among the children, increased interethnic contact and nonauthoritarian parents who don't normally punish them severely, racial attitudes will probably become more positive. If these elements are not present among the children in desegregated schools, we can probably expect more negative racial attitudes. Obviously, the issue of improving racial attitudes is a complex one and one that needs attention to several issues.

Reference

Stephan, W. G., and D. Rosenfield. Effects of desegregation on racial attitudes. *Journal of Personality and Social Psychology,* 1978, *36,* 795–804.

really a different culture from that of the suburban middle class. Cultures were tacitly assumed to be identical for those who lived in the United States. Now, we know that the experiences of poor people differ dramatically from those of people in the lower, middle, or upper socioeconomic classes of this country. Strangely enough, this very obvious fact was not given much consideration until recently. As Anastasi (1976, p. 59) says,

> Another more subtle way in which specific test content may spuriously affect performance is through the examinee's emotional, and attitudinal responses. Stories or pictures portraying typical suburban middle-class family scenes, for example, may alienate a child reared in a low-income inner-city home. Exclusive representation of the physical features of a single racial type in test illustrations may have a similar effect on members of an ethnic minority. In the same vein, women's organizations have objected to the perpetuation of sex stereotypes in test content, as in the portrayal of male doctors or executives and female nurses or secretaries. Certain words, too, may have acquired connotations that are offensive to minority groups. As one test publisher aptly expressed it, "Until fairly recently, most standardized tests were constructed by white middle-class people, who sometimes clumsily violate the feelings of the test-taker without even knowing it. In a way one could say we have been not so much culture biased as we have been 'culture blind' (Fitzgibbon, 1972, pp. 2–3)."

Whether culture-biased or culture-blind, the tests are still unfair.

Socioeconomic Class. We have already encountered this particular reason for blacks scoring lower on IQ tests than whites do, but here let us be more specific. Two general themes can be quickly developed. First, blacks have been second-class citizens, by law, until recent years and, in fact, since the founding of the United States. That long-overdue steps to alleviate this situation are slowly being taken does not alter the facts. Even if all of the indignities that accrue to a person with black skin were erased from this day forward, it would take many years for blacks to build their own traditions and life styles based on equal affluence with other Americans. Even then an IQ test should take into account the specific culture blacks would choose to build. But we are not anywhere close to these events occurring.

Second, because blacks are poorer than whites, it is possible, even probable, that decreased IQ scores of blacks are affected by elements that accompany poverty rather than genetics. For example, poor mothers eat less nutritious meals than do mothers who have more money to spend on food, and this difference in nutrition in turn affects the child from the time of conception to birth and beyond. After birth, the poor child is less well nourished than the more affluent, and the inferior diet affects development. The poor child may have fewer intellectually stimulating toys, attention, and experiences than the more affluent child because his or her parents spend a good deal of their time getting the necessities together. All of these things work against the poor child. As we have said, blacks as a group score about 15 points lower on IQ tests, but an almost-forgotten statistic is that regardless of race children whose fathers are laborers score about 20 points lower than children whose fathers are professional men. Socioeconomic class appears to have more of an effect than race.

Compensatory Programs. One of Jensen's (1969) major arguments was that compensatory education programs didn't work and the reason they didn't was the high heritability factor of intelligence. When massive compensatory education programs such as Head Start began, the early returns were superb. Very large increases in IQs appeared to result, but later testing indicated that these gains in IQ were transitory and disappeared shortly. Two different lines of research are pertinent to our analysis.

In which of these two environments would a child have a better chance to develop his or her full potential?

The first of these has been carried out by Scarr and Weinberg (1976), who investigated the effects of compensatory education taken to its logical extreme, interracial adoption. These investigators studied the effects upon IQ of black and interracial children adopted by advantaged white parents. Whereas the adopted children did not score as high as their adoptive parents or the natural children of those parents, they scored in the normal range for white children. The earlier a child was adopted, generally speaking, the higher his or her IQ was. For example, children adopted during the first year of life scored almost 4 points higher than those adopted later. Figure 6–5 shows the data graphically. This is not to suggest that adoption by white parents is a good way to increase the IQ scores of black children, rather that this study presents dramatic evidence for the alterability of IQ scores, suggesting that they are not determined as much by heritability as by environment.

Blacks generally score about 15 points below whites on IQ tests (Jensen, 1973; Loehlin, Lindzey, and Spuhler, 1975), and recent studies have indicated that low IQ scores predict poor school performance, regardless of race (Cleary, Humphrey, Kendrick and Wesman, 1975). The realization of these facts led to the development of early-intervention programs, such as Head Start, which were intended to intervene at an early age and increase IQs. However, it was precisely these programs that Jensen (1969) claimed had not done their job and could not do so because IQ was not environmentally determined. If, as Scarr and Weinberg (1976) contend, IQ can be altered by the environment, then why have compensatory education programs failed? There are two answers to that question, and we should take them in order.

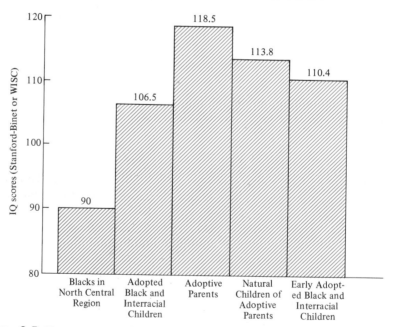

Figure 6–5 IQ scores of adoptive parents, their natural children, adopted blacks, and interracial children compared to the average black IQ for the North Central region of the United States.

First, why should they work? Under most of these programs a child is removed from the home environment for a few hours (usually 3 to 6) five days a week and then returned to the disadvantaged environment for the rest of the time. Even if such programs are adequately staffed (which they seldom are) and run by the most able and competent individuals, why should such a small amount of intervention, based on a type of intervention that is not fully understood, work? Although there has been some research that describes the immediate environment of lower-working and middle-class homes (Hess and Shipman, 1965; Kohn, 1959; White and Watts, 1973), there is still little understanding of how middle-class homes develop the environment that fosters increased IQ performance and concomitant improved school achievement. Until the environmental variables that govern the development of higher IQs are better understood, intervention programs such as Head Start will probably not be very successful. What is of importance in the Scarr and Weinberg study is that those environmental variables exist. Now, research must determine what they are and how they best work.

The second answer to our question of why early intervention programs don't work is that they do. There is increasing evidence, reported at the 1977 meeting of the American Association for the Advancement of Science, that the effects of early intervention programs do carry over into school performance (Warren, 1977). Dr. Francis Palmer, a psychologist at the State University of New York at Stonybrook had this to say (Warren, 1977, p. 8):

We have contended all along that you can't test the results of intervention until the children go to school. . . . Nevertheless, he said, many conclusions about compensatory education have been drawn without benefit of longitudinal data.

Palmer presented the bulk of the evidence on compensatory education from ten different studies involving more than 2,000 children in various experimental and control groups, most of whom were followed from pre-kindergarten age through the third grade and beyond.

The results indicate that children who had some sort of compensatory education scored about 10 points higher on IQ tests than did children who had not had such experiences, even after being out of the program for several years. A durable increase in reading ability was found for children who had been in a compensatory education program, and they were more likely to achieve their grade and not be held back. Finally, the earlier and longer the intervention, the better the results. Thus, it seems that evidence is accumulating which indicates that compensatory education programs, with all of their failings, do help. Furthermore, when these results are combined with the results of the Scarr and Weinberg study, evidence supporting the environmental effects on IQ scores becomes even more impressive.

We have dealt here with only one small area of discrimination against blacks, but as you can see, this area leads to many others: socioeconomic effects, environmental effects, the politics of education, test bias, and many more. This is not the only way blacks have been and are being discriminated against, but it may be illustrative of the way discrimination reaches its tentacles into many areas. This particular bit of discrimination influences school performance, placement in school, satisfaction with school, and continuing or dropping out during elementary and secondary school. It also pervades acceptance into and performance in college, which in turn is a determining factor in the type of employment a person receives, which helps determine socioeconomic class. In short, this one area of discrimination is both devastating and long-lasting.

INDIANS

This section begins with a misnomer based on ignorance. To refer to American Indians as Indians is as precise as referring to Italians, Norwegians, Germans, Spaniards, Swedes, and Russians as Europeans. There are over three hundred tribes of Indians in Canada and the United States with three hundred different culture bases and three hundred different languages. Before the white man came to their homeland they had made impressive contributions to agriculture, flint and stone work, art, and religion. It is beyond the scope of this section to do more than briefly discuss some of the amazing accomplishments of the Indians prior to the greatest disaster that occurred to them, the colonization of the New World. The Iroquois were the most highly organized and held the largest area among Eastern Indians stretching from Hudson Bay to the Carolinas. The Southeastern Indians, which included the Cherokee, Chickasaw, Choctaw, Caddo, and Seminole tribes had a highly developed culture organized around intense agriculture, complex political organizations, social grades, and so forth. The plains area Indians included the Arapaho, Blackfoot, Cheyenne, Comanche, and Kiowa tribes. They roamed the plains hunting buffalo and living a nomadic existence. They developed a highly individualized, geometric art. The Indians of the Southwestern area included Apache, Hopi, Mohave, Navaho, Pima, Taos, Yuma, and Zuni. Some of these were pueblo dwellers, who fashioned villages by building dwellings into the side of cliffs, and who also utilized agriculture, whereas others were more nomadic. The California area included more linguistic stocks and a greater number of tribes for its size than did other areas. Among the important linguistic stocks were the Athapascan, Karok, Shoshonean, and Yurok, each represented by one or more tribes. Art and basketry were highly developed, as were hunting and fishing. The North Pacific Coast Indians were accomplished canoeists, fishermen, and woodcarvers, and had highly developed social organization. Some of the tribes in this area were the Bannock, Kutenai, Snakes, Ney Percé, and Salishan. This one paragraph can hardly do justice to any large group, but does show the enormous diversity of Indians in North America.

The history of treatment of the Indian following the colonization of Canada and the United States is shocking and outrageous. Lands that belonged to Indians were taken by the white man, Indians were slaughtered by wars, disease, and decimation of the food supply. If settlers wanted land the Indians owned, the Indians were moved. In the 1800s many tribes were moved to Oklahoma because their lands were needed. One such incident involved the Cherokees, who were moved from the Southeastern United States in 1838 in the dead of winter. Seventeen thousand started the journey and less than six thousand finished it alive.

LaDonna Harris, a Comanche, said it far better than I could:

Indians are the highest and lowest of many things in the United States. We have the highest infant mortality, the lowest life expectancy, the highest suicide rate, the lowest income, the highest drop-out rate, the lowest educational level. We have the poorest housing and the poorest health. A higher percentage of us are in prison, and we have the longest sentences.

These sad facts are the result of long years of institutions—governmental, religious and educational—telling us every day of our lives that there is no value in our culture. It is no wonder that this is frequently translated into low self-esteem and self-hate, self-hate often took the form of high alcoholism and four times the national average in suicides, the ultimate in self-hate. [1974, pp. 10–11.]

One cannot begin to relate the discrimination perpetrated against Indians, but probably the most chilling aspect of it can be visualized in Figure 6–6, which graphs the Indian population in the United States. The population figures for 1200 and 1500 are, of course, estimates, but are the more conservative estimates—some scholars

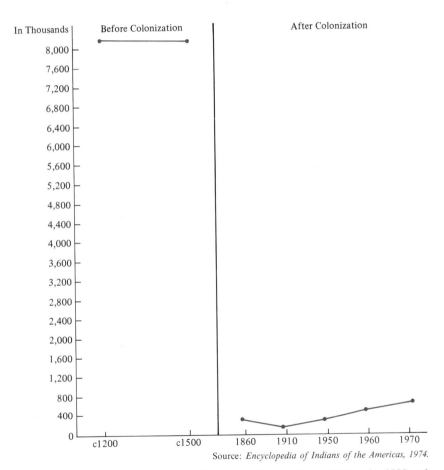

Source: *Encyclopedia of Indians of the Americas, 1974.*

Figure 6–6 Population of American Indians in the United States. Figures for 1200 and 1500 are the most conservative estimates (some estimates run seven times this number). The first census taken by the U.S. government was in 1860 and no data are available prior to that time. Indian population dipped to 220,000 in 1910 or ⅟₃₇th of the population in 1500.

have suggested that the population ran as high as 90 million, although that figure seems excessively high. At any rate, the 220,000 figure by 1910 indicates that Indians were just about extinct.

Increases in population since that time have occurred and the sharp increases in the last twenty or thirty years have been both an actual increase and an increase in the willingness of Indians to be counted as Indians. As Indian awareness, self-esteem, and pride continue to grow, these people who are descendants of so many diverse cultures may well be able to shake off the effects of discrimination and live with pride and freedom again in the United States.

Liberation Movements

Liberation implies that the state the individual or group is in must be changed; that freedom is being infringed upon. Even though a liberation movement can begin with one person, this discussion will concentrate on groups. There are an enormous number of liberation movements, both historical and current, which have demanded freedom from oppression—one notable one is the revolution of the thirteen colonies in the 1770s, which resulted in the United States. Later liberation movements tend to be more social in nature: The participants want to be free of trait identifications that have grown up and become accepted by society, and sometimes even by members of the group itself as innate. For example, blacks are not intelligent enough to care for themselves, Indians are drunks, women are weak and passive and must be protected (which may very well mean exploited). Through the years these traits have not only been associated with members of the group, but because the society rewards behavior that is consistent with the stereotype and punishes behavior that is not, these traits do continue to play a part in the behavior of such groups. The society is shocked when Indians rebel at Wounded Knee, women strongly support the Equal Rights Amendment to the United States Constitution, or blacks in long, bitter bussing controversies in Boston or Louisville return the violence meted out to them.

It is difficult to trace the history of liberation movements or even analyze them because by their very nature they tend to be clandestine. The literature of such movements tends to be privately circulated pamphlets, papers, and newsletters that are seldom kept by libraries. Often the rhetoric of a movement seems diffuse and vague to those outside the movement, primarily because the majority of the society does not even know the existing conditions that make it necessary for the movement to complain. And it is a breaking down of very serious barriers that cause the complaint in the first place.

Gordon Allport (1954, Chapter 9), writing primarily about blacks and Jews attributed the following possible personality characteristics to those who had been victimized by society: sensitivity, submission, fantasies of power, desire for protection, indirectness, ingratiation (flattering the more powerful person or group), revenge and sabotage, sympathy, self-hatred of one's own group, self- and group-aggrandizement (these last two alternate), display of flashy status symbols, compassion for the underprivileged, identification with the dominant group's norms, and passivity.

Freeman (1971), in reviewing the personality profiles of young girls drawn up at about the same time Allport was listing his characteristics of those victimized by society (Terman and Tyler, 1954), found some interesting parallels. Girls in 1954 were viewed as being sensitive, conforming to social pressures, responsive to the environment, ingratiating, sympathetic, as having low levels of aspiration, compassionate toward the underprivileged, and anxious. Girls' opinions of themselves grew worse as they grew older whereas boys' opinions of themselves grew better, despite the fact that girls do consistently better academically until well into high school.

Kidder and Stewart (1975, pp. 92–93) point out that

Freeman's line of argument implies, in effect, that in any group (be it women, blacks, American Indians or whatever) whose survival depends on the good will of a more powerful group, there will develop the necessary traits to ensure survival: for example, if you are black or female, you are traditionally not supposed to take the initiative in an interaction with a white male. Therefore, since you are not supposed to find out by direct inquiry what is in the mind of this more powerful other, you will understandably learn to be very sensitive to that person's nonverbal reactions. Yur survival might very well depend on interpreting correctly the real meaning of a raised eyebrow and acting accordingly—hence the so-called greater intuitiveness, sensitivity, and indirectness of both blacks and women. Similarly, the traits of ingratiation, submission, and conformity would be interpreted not as inherent traits that would inevitably appear in all blacks (or women, or Indians) at all times, but as sensible strategies for dealing with more powerful authorities in whose hand one's fate may ultimately lie. To be an uppity nigger or an aggressive woman (that is, to attempt independent action and achievement) may result in social disapproval and ostracism at the very least and, not infrequently, in actual physical harm at the hands of the dominant group. Lynchings of blacks on the flimsiest of pretexts and the burning of so-called witches in the past may be seen as an affirmation of the optimal survival strategy of the underdog: be unobstrusive; avoid at all costs offending the more powerful other, assure him of superiority; and learn to read his moods. In the language of the behaviorists, forthrightness, initiative, and independent achievement disappear from these oppressed groups because these traits are punished (Pascale & Kidder, 1973). The opposite behaviors, so aptly summarized by Allport, persist because they are rewarded, or positively reinforced—or at least because they are less apt to lead to punishment.

Freeman's (and Kidder and Stewart's) argument has some very interesting implications for society, some pleasant and some not so pleasant. The argument basically is that oppressed groups have "learned their place" in society and that the characteristics mentioned by Allport (1954), and by Terman and Tyler (1954) are not innate. If these characteristics are indeed learned, then they are amenable to change by changing the environment. There are no large-scale research projects that have attempted to alter the behavior of oppressed groups of which I am aware. Rather than seeking out such subjugated groups in Canada and the United States, we wait until they scream loudly enough to be heard. There are, however, several illustrative incidents that attest to the notion that the personality characteristics of individuals in low-status groups are learned and are thus reversible.

For many years Jews have been the "whipping boys" of various and assorted groups of tyrants, with Hitler being the most recent example in a long line of infamy.

However, since the founding of Israel as a nation, Jews have taken on a more militant stance. They have been attacked and have repelled the attacks. The stereotype of the Jew has changed from the docile old gray-bearded man being mistreated to the lean, hard-fighting man of the Israeli army. Shortly after the six-day Middle East War in 1967, a poster of a short, bearded, bespectacled Jewish man in a telephone booth changing into a Superman costume became popular among young American Jews. The symbolism is obvious. By a change in the situation, the creation of a nation, Jews learned that the subservience that had been forced on them when they lived in other countries was no longer necessary. They learned not to be submissive but to respond to their proud heritage.

On a Six Nations Indian Reserve in Canada, there is an Indian school totally staffed by Indians, whose graduation rate from high school has exceeded the Canadian national average. This is, of course, a direct contradiction to the stereotype of Indians—lazy, shiftless, and incapable of making it in the world. The superintendent of this school system maintains that the reason for his students' high graduation rate is that all teachers have a sense of their own "Indianness" and that they can relate the pride in their own heritage which demonstrates to the student that each one can make it without becoming a "White Indian." This superintendent seems to be striking the same chord that Ladonna Harris did. She expressed the problems of Indians in terms of a low self-esteem. Superintendent Hill (1970) of this Indian school has been able to instill a sense of self-worth in his students and has made them extremely successful.

The Goals of Liberation Movements

What is it that those in various liberation movements want? That question is not a simple one to answer both because the aims of different liberation movements and the aims of different individuals within a single movement may differ. There is a dizzying array of claims and demands from various groups, which seem almost contradictory. In 1954 in the United States, blacks wanted integrated schools, by the 1970s the more outspoken blacks either didn't seem to care if schools were integrated or actually wanted separate schools (Cleaver, 1969). In 1967, Canada's Native Alliance for Red Power demanded that the Indian Affairs Bureau be staffed by Indians at all levels and be responsible to the Indians of Canada. By 1970, Canada's Indians were demanding the abolition of the Indian Affairs Branch (Jack, 1970).

Many other examples can be cited, but these two suffice to show the basic principle—liberation movements want equality. In 1954, blacks had separate but unequal schools. In the 1970s many blacks want the freedom to choose whether they will have separate or integrated schools. Between 1967 and 1970 the Canadian Indians learned that Indians within the existing bureaucracy could be co-opted if the power and the freedom to make decisions continued to reside in the white populace.

Basically, liberation movements want freedom, just as people have wanted freedom for thousands of years. Different movements come to the fore at different times and Kidder and Stewart (1975) assert that there are three things that singly or together can contribute to a liberation struggle. First is the social context. For example, it is difficult to conceive of a women's liberation movement in the absence of reliable contraceptive technology that can be controlled by women. If a woman must choose between the risk of an unplanned pregnancy and a continuing relationship with a man, she is at a great disadvantage in competing with men in our society. There is a bitter truth to the old adage, "keep them barefoot and pregnant and down on the farm." But if a woman can plan pregnancies or choose not to bear children, she is in a position to compete. Thus the social context would not have supported a women's liberation movement without contraceptives.

Another element in liberation movements that can move them to cohesive action is a particularly salient event. Eldridge Cleaver refers to the Watts riot in 1965 as a particularly salient event in the black liberation movement, which escalated the black struggle. In 1955 Rosa Parks refused to give her seat on a bus to a white man and sparked the Montgomery bus boycott and subsequent years of civil rights demonstrations. It is interesting to note that blacks demonstrated in a primarily nonviolent way for a decade after Rosa Parks refused to give up her seat and then the next several years were marked by violence. The desire for freedom was great and every avenue to achieve it was tried.

The existence of one or more liberation movements sparks confidence in other oppressed groups. Chapter 1 dealt with imitation as a particularly efficient form of learning, and groups do learn from the success of other groups. It is futile to point a finger at any one movement and say others imitated them. Did women imitate blacks, or did blacks learn from the tactics of the "suffragettes" of several decades past? It is useless to try to find the first such group, but it is very useful to point out that when one group succeeds in gaining a greater measure of freedom, others will follow.

Comment

If there were no prejudice and no discrimination, there would be no need for liberation movements. But there is and there are. How long movements will exist is an open question answerable only by the decision of those in the liberation movements as to when a point of diminishing returns is reached. The history of humanity is that power is not given up without a fight. Those who hold power want to keep it and those who are subjected to that power want freedom. In the next chapter we will consider power, power-holders, and the effects of power more fully.

SUMMARY

1 Prejudice is an attitude toward a member of a racial, ethnic, minority, or majority group that results from the individual's membership in that group. Furthermore, the attitude is incorrect or at the very least is an inaccurate portrayal of the individual who holds membership in the group. Prejudice is usually negative although it can be positive.

2 The historical approach to prejudice emphasizes the long years of conflict among groups. The televising of "Roots" in the United States in early 1977 and again in

late 1978 presented to viewers a vivid illustration of the conflict among blacks and whites.

3 Prejudice also has its roots in social and cultural phenomena, with the most obvious differences between two groups usually being the characteristic most discussed in relation to prejudice.

4 For one reason or another, individuals are predisposed to be prejudiced. One of the characteristics that may be most susceptible to prejudice is conformity, particularly as it is manifested by the authoritarian personality.

5 Much of the thought about prejudice emphasizes that it is learned, not innate. One of the most pervasive ways children learn to be prejudiced is through modeling. The more open showing of televised prejudice appears to have both negative and positive effects on viewers' prejudice.

6 Discrimination is action based on a prejudiced attitude or attitudes. The relationship between prejudiced attitudes and discriminating behavior is not a perfect one.

7 Women, even though they are not a minority group, are discriminated against in a variety of ways. One of the most striking ways discrimination has affected women in the United States was their ineligibility to serve on juries until fairly recently.

8 Blacks have been discriminated against in a variety of ways, but probably no more pervasively than in the area of IQ testing. Early IQ tests were developed and refined by many individuals who felt minority groups were inferior to the white middle class, and still today a controversy rages over the innate intelligence of blacks.

9 Indians have been discriminated against by having their land taken, by being slaughtered in wars, and by the decimation of their food supply. By 1910, Indians were almost extinct in the United States, numbering about 220,000.

10 Liberation movements are based on the assumption that a group's freedom is being infringed upon. It is difficult to trace the history of such movements because they tend to be secretive. One of the latest of such movements is women's liberation, which has much in common with previous movements.

11 The specific goals of liberation movements vary, although in general it may be said that liberation movements want freedom.

GLOSSARY

Authoritarian Personality A personality marked by a cluster of nine characteristics that define a personality trait first described by Adorno, et al. and that is basically a closed conservative belief system.

Binet–Simon Scale The first successful intelligence test, developed in 1905.

Discrimination Action based on an inaccurate attitude toward a member of a racial, ethnic, minority, or majority group that results from the individual's membership in that group.

Dogmatism A closed belief system that is not conservative—an authoritarianism of the middle and left portions of the political spectrum.

Eugenics The science that attempts to improve the inborn or inherited qualities of a species, especially humans.

"Good" Prejudice Prejudice that is favorable to the group.

Historical Theory of Prejudice The theory that attempts to account for prejudice by emphasizing the long years of conflict between groups.

Individualistic Theory of Prejudice The theory that attempts to account for prejudice by emphasizing certain personality characteristics.

Liberation Movements Groups that want freedom; particularly freedom from stereotypes that have been accepted by society about the group.

Normalization Sample The group that is tested and upon whose performance norms for a test are developed.

Parti Québecois The party elected in Quebec in 1976 that has as its avowed policy a separation of Quebec from the rest of Canada.

Prejudice An incorrect attitude toward a member of a racial, ethnic, minority, or majority group that results from the individual's membership in that group.

Salient Prominent or conspicuous.

Social and Cultural Theory of Prejudice The theory that attempts to account for prejudice by emphasizing the differences in societies and cultures.

REFERENCES

Adorno, T. W., E. Frankel-Brunswick, D. Levinson, and R. N. Sanford. *The Authoritarian Personality,* New York: Harper & Row, Publishers, 1950.

Allport, G. W., *The Nature of Prejudice.* Reading, Mass.: Addison-Wesley Publishing Co., Inc., 1954.

————. Prejudice: Is it societal or personal? *Journal of Social Issues,* 1962, *18,* 120–34.

Anastasi, A. *Psychological Testing* (4th Edition). New York: Macmillan Publishing Co., Inc., 1976.

Appleman, J. A. *Successful Jury Trials: A Symposium.* Indianapolis: The Bobbs-Merrill Co., Inc., 1952.

Arthur, J. *An Introduction to Social Psychiatry.* Baltimore: Penguin, 1971.

Banks, W. M. The changing attitudes of black students. *Personnel and Guidance Journal,* 1970, *48,* 739–45.

Bowd, A. D. Ten years after the Hawthorn Report: Changing psychological implications for the education of Canadian native peoples. *Canadian Psychological Review,* 1977, *18,* 332–45.

Brewer, M. B. Determinants of social distance among east African tribal groups. *Journal of Personality and Social Psychology,* 1968, *10,* 279–89.

Brigham, C. C. *A study of American intelligence.* Princeton: Princeton U. P., 1923.

Brigham, J. C. Ethnic humor on television: Does it reduce/reinforce social prejudice? Paper presented at the American Psychological Association, Chicago, 1975.

Byrne, D. *The Attraction Paradigm.* New York: Academic Press, Inc. 1971.

————. *An Introduction to Personality: A Research Approach* (2nd Edition). Englewood Cliffs, N.J.: Prentice-Hall, Inc., 1974.

Campbell, D. T. Stereotypes and the perception of group differences. *American Psychologist.* 1967, *22,* 812–29.

———— and R. A. LeVine. Ethnocentrism and intergroup relations. In R. P. Ableson,

E. Aronson, W. J. McGuire, T. M. Newcomb, M. J. Rosenberg, and P. H. Tannenbaum (Eds.), *Theories of Cognitive Consistency: A Sourcebook.* Chicago: Rand McNally & Company, 1968.

Caplan, N. The new ghetto man: A review of recent empirical studies. *Journal of Social Issues,* 1970, *26,* 59–74.

Chang, E. C., and E. H. Ritter. Ethnocentrism in black college students. *The Journal of Social Psychology,* 1976, *100,* 89–98.

Chapko, M. K., and M. H. Lewis. Authoritarianism and "All in the Family." *Journal of Psychology,* 1975, *90,* 245–48.

Christie, R., and M. Jahoda (Eds.). *Studies in the Scope and Method of "The Authoritarian Personality."* New York: The Free Press, 1954.

Clark, K., and M. Clark. Racial identification and preference in Negro children. In T. Newcomb & E. Hartley (Eds.), *Readings in Social Psychology.* New York: Holt (Now Holt, Rinehart and Winston), 1947.

Cleary, T. A., L. G. Humphreys, S. A. Kendrick, and A. Wesman. Educational uses of tests with disadvantaged students. *American Psychologist,* 1975, *30,* 15–41.

Cleaver, E. Tears for the pigs. *The Humanist, 29,* 6–8, March–April, 1969.

Cornish, W. L. *The Jury.* London: Penguin Press, 1968.

Cotnam, J. Americans viewed through the eyes of French-Canadians. *Journal of Popular Culture,* Spring 1977, 784–96.

Darrow, C. Attorney for the defense. *Esquire,* 1936, 36–37 and 211–13.

Elliott, J. L. Minority groups: A Canadian perspective. In J. L. Elliott (Ed.), *Immigrant Groups.* Englewood Cliffs, N.J.: Prentice-Hall, Inc., 1971, 1–14.

Fitzgibbon, T. J. *The Use of Standardized Instruments with Urban and Minority-Group Pupils.* New York: Harcourt Brace, Jovanovich, Inc., 1972.

Freeman, J. The social construction of the second sex. In M. H. Garskoff (Ed.), *Roles Women Play.* Belmont, Calif.: Brooks-Cole, 1971.

Glazier, K. M. Separatism and Quebec. *Current History,* April, 1977, 154–57.

Goldstein, I. *Trial Technique.* Chicago: Callaghan and Co., 1935.

Greenwald, H., and D. Oppenheim. Reported magnitude of self-misidentification among Negro children—Artifact? *Journal of Personality and Social Psychology,* 1968, *8,* 49–52.

Haley, A. *Roots.* Garden City, N.Y.: Doubleday & Company, Inc. 1976.

Harris, L. Preface. In K. Irvine (Ed.), *Encyclopedia of Indians of the Americas.* St. Clair Shores, Mich.: Scholarly Press, 1974, 10–11.

Harris, S., and J. R. Brown. Self-esteem and racial preference in black children. *Proceedings of the 79th Annual Convention of the American Psychological Association,* 1971, *6,* 259–60 (Summary).

Hawthorn, H. B. (Ed.), *A Survey of the Contemporary Indians of Canada.* Vol. 2, Ottawa: Indian Affairs Branch, 1967.

Hess, R. D., and V. C. Shipman. Early experience and the socialization of cognitive modes in children. *Child Development,* 1965, *36,* 869–86.

Hill, J. *The London (Ontario) Free Press,* February 25, 1970, p. 12.

Hraba, J. and G. Grant. Black is beautiful: A re-examination of racial preferences and identification. *Journal of Personality and Social Psychology,* 1970, *16,* 398–402.

Irvine, K. (Ed.), *Encyclopedia of Indians of the Americas.* St. Clair Shores, Mich.: Scholarly Press, 1974.

Jack, H. Native alliance for red power. In Wabageshig (Ed.), *The Only Good Indian.* Toronto: New Press, 1970.

Jarrett, V. *Roots* has a lesson for blacks and whites. *Philadelphia Inquirer,* 2-1-77.

Jensen, A. R. How much can we boost IQ and scholastic achievement? *Harvard Educational Review,* 1969, *39,* 1–123.

———. *Educability and Group Differences.* New York: Basic Books Inc., Publishers, 1973.

Kamin, L. J. *The Science and Politics of I.Q.* New York: Halsted Press, 1974.

Kidder, L. H., and M. V. Stewart. *The Psychology of Intergroup Relations: Conflict and Consciousness.* New York: McGraw-Hill Book Company, 1975.

Kirscht, J. P., and R. C. Dillehay. *Dimensions of Authoritarianism.* Lexington, Ky. University of Kentucky Press, 1967.

Kohn, M. L. Social class and the exercise of parental authority. *American Sociological Review,* 1959, *34,* 352–66.

Lamberth, J., J. C. McCullers, and R. L. Mellgren. *Foundations of Psychology.* New York: Harper & Row, Publishers, 1976.

LaPiere, R. T. Attitudes vs. action. *Social Forces,* 1934, *13,* 230–37.

Leckenby, J. D., and S. H. Surlin. Incidental social learning from black or white oriental TV entertainment. *Journal of Broadcasting,* in press.

Lewis, C., and B. Biber. Reactions of negro children toward negro and white teachers. *Journal of Experimental Education,* 1951, *20,* 97–104.

Loehlin, J., G. Lindzey, and J. N. Spuhler. *Race Differences in Intelligence.* San Francisco, Calif.: W. H. Freeman and Company, Publishers, 1975.

McCarthy, J. D., and W. L. Yancey. Uncle Tom and Mr. Charlie: Methaphysical pathos in the study of racism and personal disorganization. In E. C. Epps (Ed.), *Race Relations: Current Perspectives.* Cambridge, Mass.: Winthrop, 1973.

Moore, C. L. The racial preference and attitutde of preschool black children. *Journal of Genetic Psychology,* 1976, *129,* 37–44.

Morland, J. Racial acceptance and preference of nursery school children in a southern city. *Merrill-Palmer Quarterly Behavior and Development,* 1962, *8,* 271–80.

———. A comparison of race awareness in Northern and Southern children. *American Journal of Orthopsychiatry,* 1966, *26,* 22–31.

Nagel, S., and L. Weitzman. Sex and the unbiased jury. *Judicature,* 1972, *56,* 108–111.

Nemeth, C., J. Endicott, and J. Wachtler. From the '50s to the '70s: Women in jury deliberations. *Sociometry,* 1976, *39,* 293–304.

Paige, J. M. Changing patterns of anti-white attitudes among blacks. *Journal of Social Issues,* 1970, *26,* 67–86.

Pascale, L., and L. Kidder. Penalties for role reversals: As seen in the popularity ratings for aggressive women and passive men. Paper presented at Eastern Psychological Association, April 1973.

Porter, J. D. *Black Child, White Child.* Cambridge, Mass.: Harvard University Press, 1971.

Rokeach, M. The nature and meaning of dogmatism. *Psychological Review,* 1954, *61,* 194–204.

———. Political and religious dogmatism: An alternative to the authoritarian personality. *Psychological Monographs: General and Applied,* 1956 (Whole No. 425), *70,* 1–43.

———. *The Open and Closed Mind.* New York: Basic Books, Inc., Publishers, 1960.

Rose, A., and A. Prell. Does the punishment fit the crime? A study in social valuation. *American Journal of Sociology,* 1955, *61,* 247–51.

Rubin, Z. *Liking and Loving.* New York: Holt, Rinehart and Winston, 1973.

Scarr, S., and R. A. Weinberg. IQ test performance of black children adopted by white families. *American Psychologist,* 1976, *31,* 726–39.

Shockley, W. Morals, mathematics, and the moral obligation to diagnose the origin of Negro IQ deficits. *Review of Educational Research,* 1971, *41,* 369–77.

———. Dysgenics, geneticity, raciology: A challenge to the intellectual responsibility of educators. *Phi Delta Kappan,* 1972, *53,* 297–307.

Simon, R. J. The Jury and the Defense of Insanity. Boston: Little, Brown and Co., 1967.

Sniderman, P. M. *Personality and Democratic Politics.* Berkeley: University of California Press, 1975.

Steckler, G. Authoritarian ideology in Negro college students. *Journal of Abnormal and Social Psychology,* 1957, *54,* 396–99.

Surlin, F. H. "All in the Family" as a mirror of contemporary American culture. *Family Process,* 1974, *13,* 297–315.

——— and E. Bowden. The psychological effect of the television characters: The case of Archie Bunker and authoritarian viewers. Paper presented at Association for Education in Journalism. College Park, Md., 1976.

——— and C. F. Cooper. The Jeffersons and their racially integrated neighbors: Who watches and who is offended. Paper presented at the Southern Speech Communication Association, San Antonio, 1976.

——— and E. D. Tate. "All in the Family": Is Archie funny? *Journal of Communication,* Autumn 1977, 61–68.

Tate, E. D., and H. F. Surlin. Agreement with opinionated television characters: A cross-cultural comparison. *Journal Quarterly,* 1976, *53,* 199–203.

Terman, L. M. *The Measurement of Intelligence.* Boston: Houghton Mifflin Company, 1916.

Terman, L. H., and L. E. Tyler. Psychological sex differences. In L. Carmichael (Ed.), *Manual of Child Psychology* (2nd Edition). New York: John Wiley & Sons, Inc., 1954.

Vershure, B. Black is beautiful: A re-examination of racial self-identification. *Perceptual and Motor Skills,* 1976, *43,* 482.

Vidmar, N., and W. Rokeach. Archie Bunker's bigotry: A study in selected perception and exposure. *Journal of Communication,* 1974, *24,* 36–47.

Warren, J. Found: Long-term gains from early intervention. *APA Monitor,* 1977, *8*(4), p. 8.

White, B. L., and J. C. Watts. *Experience and Environment.* Englewood Cliffs, N.J.: Prentice-Hall, Inc., 1973.

Winfrey, L. *Roots* deserved its wide audience. *Philadelphia Inquirer,* February, 1, 1977.

Winks, R. W. The Canadian Negro: The problem of identity. In J. L. Elliott (Ed.), *Immigrant groups.* Englewood Cliffs, N.J.: Prentice-Hall, Inc. 1971, 95–104.

Yoder, E. M., Jr., *Roots* as history and show business. *Today's Post,* King of Prussia, Pa. 2-8-77.

Social Influence-
Its Use and Effects

Social power, which is the ability of individuals to affect the behavior and beliefs of others, is a relatively unique concept in social psychology. The effects of power directed toward a person or group have long been studied and some of the true classics of social psychological research have been the result. Conformity, compliance, and obedience have been the products of power, and in most cases there has been an outcry against the excessive use of power in Canada, the United States, and the rest of the world. Surprisingly enough, for all of the emphasis upon the effects of power, there has been little study of those who hold and wield power: the political, economic, religious, and educational leaders who regularly make decisions that affect the behavior and beliefs of others.

This chapter will be divided into five sections, the first three of which deal with the effects of power when it has been wielded: conformity, compliance, and obedience. These three effects have rather specific meanings for social psychologists that will be discussed more fully in the appropriate section. The fourth section deals with power from the perspective of the powerholder. This perspective, which has been presented most forcefully and persuasively by David Kipnis, is one that is often overlooked in social psychology, yet one that is vitally important. The chapter concludes with a discussion of conflict and its resolution.

Social Influence

The use of power, or social influence if you prefer, has certain effects. I do want to change from using the word *power* now to the more generalized concept of social influence, because power implies that the influence is being exerted by an individual or a small group of individuals. There are other sources of social influence, and basically their efforts have been broken into three groupings—conformity, compliance, and obedience. It may seem to you initially that three words do not differ much, but you will see important differences in them as we progress through the rest of this chapter.

Conformity

In a very general sense, psychologists use the word *conformity* when they mean going along with group pressures. Kiesler (1969), however, identifies several ways in which an individual can conform. An individual may behave in a manner consistent with the group, or may change an attitude because of group pressure or may have a basic personality trait of conformity. Even though Kiesler differentiates forms of conformity, he is not changing the basic mechanism of conformity, which is yielding to group pressures. Conformity is an incredibly common occurrence. It is much like being caught up in the current of a fast-flowing river where it is much easier to go along than to swim against the current and not conform. It is easier to dress like everyone else does, to wear your hair the way they do, even to act like they do, rather than to fight current trends and do something different.

With the advent and popularity of the television show, "Happy Days" in the late

In many subtle and not so subtle ways this group of college students is conforming. Note dress, hair styles, beards, and so forth.

1970s, many of us who grew up in the 1950s were startled to see what we looked like, how we acted, the music we liked, and so forth. More than one chagrined mother was able to pull out clothes from long ago for her daughter to wear to a 1950s day at school. Many fathers had to admit that, "Yes, I wore my hair in duck tails with it flat on top and it did take a lot of grease to keep it in place." What hurt was not the fact that the young people of the 1970s were having these special days, but that they laughed about it so much.

People do conform, even though they might have to go to extremes to do it. The difficulty of the conformity is not what is important. It may have taken a generation of young girls hours to put on the "in" clothes and boys to get their hair looking just right. What would have been more difficult is to violate the accepted norms of the group and not conform.

Because of this phenomenon, conformity, and the enormous lengths people will go to achieve it, psychologists have long been intrigued by it. A fascinating study in its own right would be where each set of norms originated. Where did the ridiculous dress patterns of young people in the 1950s come from? Where did the dress patterns of today's young people originate? Why do men wear ties? (Even immediately following the Arab oil embargo of 1973–74 when air conditioning was severely curtailed, it was virtually impossible to get United States businessmen to leave their ties at home.) There are a fascinating number of customs that have developed, but that is not where social psychologists have expended their efforts. The origin of most customs and traditions is probably too deeply buried in history to dig them out. Psychologists have sought to show that social norms do exist because of pressure from the group, but unfortunately the fascinating development of specific norms will have to wait for some other time.

CONFORMITY VERSUS CONVENTIONALITY

Is it conforming when a person says "good morning" as you pass? Is it conformity when you end a telephone conversation with "good by"? Conformity refers to going along with group pressures and it is implicit in the way psychologists use the term that the individual, if left entirely alone, would behave in some other way. The line between conformity and conventionality is quite thin, but the best way to distinguish between the two is to consider the situation and the effect of the behavior on the individual. Conventions are generally agreed upon modes of behavior and many of them are of no great importance to individuals. To adhere to conventions that are unimportant is not the same thing as conforming. To adhere to important conventions with which you disagree, or to violate important conventions with which you agree, because of group pressure, is to conform. As with so many things in social psychology, it is not possible to distinguish between conventionality and conformity without knowing about the individual and the situation.

PRECONFORMITY RESEARCH

In total darkness, a stationary point of light appears to move about. This bit of information, called the autokinetic phenomenon, was discovered by the Army Air Corps when they flew night missions in close formation. On totally black nights when planes had but a stationary pinpoint of light on the fuselage, the pilots in the rear of the formation were sure the planes ahead were moving around. As you can well imagine, taking evasive action while flying in close formation is disastrous. Thus planes today have a flashing light on them, not a stationary one.

Muzafer Sherif (1935, 1936) used the autokinetic phenomenon to study conformity. He recruited subjects from Columbia University and New York University to participate, either individually, or in small groups of two or three. The room was totally dark, and a tiny point of light could be seen through a hole in a metal box. Sherif relied on the fact that the light would appear to move, even though it was stationary, and so told his subjects:

When the room is completely dark I shall give a signal, *Ready* and then show you a point of light. After a short time the light will start to move. As you see it move, press the key. A few seconds later the light will disappear. Tell me the distance it moved. Try to make your estimate as accurate as possible. [Sherif, 1936, p. 95.]

Sherif had a fascinating situation. The light was not moving, but he knew that it appeared to move. What would his subjects do? He found that individuals reacted in idiosyncratic ways, but there seemed to be a pattern. Some people perceived the light to be moving great distances, others small distances, and still others somewhere in between. Once each individual had developed a pattern of perception, she or he then fairly consistently perceived the light to be moving about that distance. So far, Sherif's contribution has nothing to do with conformity—it merely shows that people, in the absence of any other information, will establish their own norms.

What happens when a subject, having developed his or her own norms is faced with conflicting norms from other people? Sherif, having allowed individuals to develop their own norms now put three of them together in a group. Taking a dramatic example, Sherif brought together an individual who had estimated that the light moved about 7½ inches, one who judged it as moving slightly less than two inches, and the third who had guessed it as moving slightly less than 1 inch. Figure 7–1 shows graphically the startling results after three sessions—all three individuals were estimating that the light was moving slightly more than 2 inches. Thus one individual had reduced his estimates almost 5 inches whereas another had more than doubled his estimates. The third hardly changed his estimates at all. Although the effect was not nearly as startling for all subjects as Figure 7–1 depicts, it does show the general trend, which was the development of a group norm. In one case it meant a dramatic lowering of the estimate, in another an increasing of the estimate, whereas in a third little change was shown. The important point is that this group norm was developing and each individual was adjusting his estimate to conform to the group norm.

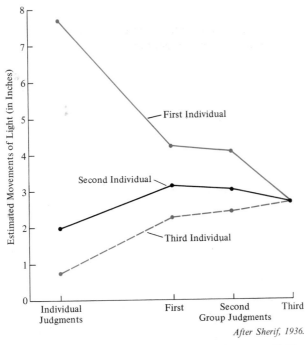

After Sherif, 1936.

Figure 7–1 Changes in individual perceptions of the distance a light moves when estimates are made individually and in groups.

This, of course, was a completely unstructured situation. Sherif's subjects were estimating how far a *stationary* light was moving, but the norms the group developed were strong. After group testing was completed, individuals were retested and instead of the judgments reverting to what they had been prior to the group sessions, they tended to cluster around the group norms. Thus it seems that the norms established by the group were more powerful than individual perceptions—in this particular situation. This paragraph started with an emphasis on the fact that this was an unstructured situation. There is some question as to whether Sherif's experiments should be labeled conformity experiments at all. Rather, the work concerns reaching a consensus concerning reality under conditions of extreme ambiguity. This section is therefore entitled "Preconformity Research," because the stimulus was so ambiguous that it may not have been conformity when a subject altered his or her judgments to agree more closely with the judgments of another. As the light wasn't moving anyhow, possibly this lack of a reference point for the subjects caused them to be easily influenced by the judgments of others, and once the influencing had occurred there was no overriding reason for the individual to return to his original, individual estimates.

Such a hypothesis is entirely plausible, and it was with the background of Sherif's studies that Solomon Asch began to study conformity. In Chapter 2, we discussed the methodology of Asch's conformity studies in some detail and it would be appropriate for you to turn back to those pages and refresh your memories about them. In the next section we deal primarily with Asch's results.

ASCH'S CONFORMITY STUDIES

Two of the most important elements of Asch's studies as contrasted to Sherif's were that there was a reference point for each individual and it was highly structured. There was little doubt about which line was the correct choice in Asch's studies. Therefore the choices that were to be made were clear-cut. However, in this structured situation, Asch found mistakes made in roughly one third of the cases. That is, individuals yielded to social influence one out of three times. Why should this occur? Asch presents three possible explanations, which he refers to as "Forms of Yielding." Furthermore, Asch was quite specific in how he defined *yielding:* "To yield under the given conditions is to subordinate one's authentic mental processes to those of others" (Asch, 1952, p. 468).

The first form of yielding Asch refers to, and the rarest, observed in only one of 31 subjects, was a reported change in the perception of the line. He yielded on every trial except one and said that the majority made him reconsider, that is to change his answer to the answer given by the consolidated group. This subject, however, insisted that he only did what he thought was right, that is he gave truthful answers. He is quoted as saying that to do otherwise would have been dishonest. Asch feels that the subject was telling the truth and that he reported what he thought he saw. That is, the effect on this subject was to distort his perception of the lines.

The second form of yielding reported by Asch is due to distortion of judgment. Most subjects who yielded did so for this reason, which may be summed up as "I am wrong and they are right." This particular judgment also affected a certain number of those who remained independent, but those men continued to deliver their judgments as they saw them in spite of the social influence of the group. The group that felt the majority was right and yielded saw their disagreement as a personal defect, according to Asch. Announcing their disagreement amounted to a public admission of this defect, and, Asch contends, they were unable to do this. One of the remarkable aspects of this group is that they yielded to the majority ostensibly for the sake of the experiment. Somehow they had convinced themselves that not yielding would "interfere" with the experiment even though they knew that one of the major aims of the experiment was to study independent judgment. When this contradiction was called to their attention, they did not dispute it, they only smiled sheepishly or helplessly.

The third form of yielding was due to distortion of action. Unlike the subjects in the two groups above, these individuals became relatively uninterested in the question of correctness, rather they exhibited one overriding need not to be different. This group was dominated by the thought that to deliver the correct answer would exclude them from the group and that this represented a serious, although unspecified, negative reflection on them. Thus, they wanted to appear like everyone else, and to do this they willingly submitted to the group judgment. According to Asch, this group was least affected by the perceptual confusions, for they were able to note the relationships between the lines quite accurately and did not even try to bring them into line with those of the majority. They simply supressed their own judgment to conform to the collective judgment of the group.

VARIATIONS ON A THEME

Asch varied his experimental situation in three distinct ways to ascertain what variables in his experiment were most important in influencing subjects to yield. First, he altered the stimulus lines to make the discrepancy between the standard line and the line chosen by the majority even greater (from 1 to 7 inches instead of from $\frac{1}{4}$ to $1\frac{3}{4}$ inches). Under these circumstances subjects concurred with the erroneous majority on 28 percent of the judgments. Thus, the stimulus does not seem to be the crucial variable.

Next, Asch reduced the size of the erring group to one and found that one naíve subject confronted with one individual who chose the incorrect line was virtually uninfluenced by the other person. Evidently, it is necessary for the subject to be faced with a *group* of people who disagee about the correct line to cause subjects to change their estimates.

The third alteration Asch made in his procedure was for the subject to be faced with a group in which one other person selected the correct answer. Recall that, in the basic experiment, the subject had been faced with a unanimous majority who disagreed with him. In this new setting, the partner was third to answer and so always answered prior to the subject; therefore the subject had some verification and support. Would the introduction of a partner alter the social influence exerted by the group? The answer is Yes. The majority effect was markedly weakened, with subjects yielding on only 13 percent of the estimates. Not only was the total amount of yielding weakened, the degree to which any single subject yielded was greatly diminished. No one made more than three errors whereas in the original study, when the majority was unanimous, 26 percent of the subjects made more than three errors.

These young people have formed a group with a specific goal. According to Asch, being a member of a group involves certain dynamics.

Introducing even one person into the group who agrees with the subject is enough to dramatically reduce, although not entirely eliminate, the group's influence.

Asch discusses the dynamics of consensus in this way:

. . . As soon as a person is in the midst of a group he is no longer indifferent to it. He may stand alone in a wholly unequivocal relation to an object when alone; but as soon as a group and its direction are present he ceases to be determined solely by his own coordinates. In some way he refers the group to himself and himself to the group. He might react to the group in many different ways: he might adopt its direction, compromise with it, or oppose it; he might even decide to disregard it. But even in the latter instance (which superficially seems to be an absence of group influence) there is a clear and determined reference to the group as fully as in the preceding cases. One can make a more specific assertion about this responsiveness to the group; if conditions permit, the individual moves toward the group. . . .

. . . The individual comes to experience a world that he shares with others. He perceives that the surroundings include him, as well as others. He notes that he, as well as others, is converging upon the same object and responding to its identical properties. Joint action and mutual understanding require this relation of intelligibility and structural simplicity. In these terms the "pull" toward the group becomes understandable. [Asch, 1952, pp. 483–84.]

CRUTCHFIELD'S STUDIES

Richard S. Crutchfield (1955) added both a methodological and a conceptual refinement to the study of conformity. He developed a series of five booths that were located side by side and screened from each other. Each booth was equipped with a panel, which had a row of numbered switches used by the subject to signal his or her judgment about the items that were projected on the wall in front of the group. The panel also contained a series of signal lights that indicated what judgments the other four subjects were giving to each item. The subjects responded in sequence and were not allowed to talk to each other while doing so. In actuality, the experimenter controlled the lights that appeared in all of the booths, so that each subject was misled and believed that the others in the experiment really responded in a specific pattern that was actually predetermined by the experimenter. Thus, the experimenter had control over the stimulus conditions each subject received. Under these experimental conditions there is no requirement that the experimenter have five or six confederates each time the experiment is run and five subjects rather than one can be run at a given time. Clearly, Crutchfield's approach represents a methodological advance over Asch's.

In addition to bringing group judgments at variance with the subjects' own judgment with five people at once, Crutchfield varied the stimulus material used. In a typical one-hour session, he was able to present both matters of fact and opinion, some easy and some difficult. Crutchfield (1954a, 1954b, 1958, 1959, 1962) utilized this standard technique with more than 600 people, all of whom were clearly above average in intelligence. Of special importance for our discussion is that the tasks upon which he induced agreement were more engrossing than the line-judging task Asch used. It is possible that subjects in Asch's experiments did not consider the line-judging task important enough to face the consequences of disagreeing with a unanimous majority.

Crutchfield's studies showed that individuals will yield to group pressure, even on opinion or attitude items that are of high social relevance to them. For example, in a sample of 50 military officers, when questioned privately, not one of them agreed with the statement, "I doubt whether I would make a good leader." However, under group pressure, 37 percent of the officers agreed with the statement. Crutchfield found that there was more yielding on difficult items (ones in which the individual is initially uncertain) than on easy ones, which confirms the necessity for Asch and Crutchfield to follow Sherif's experiments with more unequivocal stimuli. Crutchfield found, as did Asch, that there are extremely large individual differences in yielding; some few people yielded on all items and a few others yielded on none. Most people yielded on some of the items, but even among them, there were large individual differences in the amount of yielding encountered.

COMPARING THE ASCH AND CRUTCHFIELD STUDIES

Throughout this book I have been emphasizing the importance of the situation in determining behavior. Here is a superb example. Asch and Crutchfield were both studying conformity, both had several people gathered together and subjects in both experiments received feedback that unanimously contradicted their perception. But the two situations were not identical. Asch's subjects faced the majority and heard them reveal their judgments, whereas Crutchfield's subjects could not see the other individuals and received their judgments via a lighted panel. Could these small situational differences affect behavior? Many psychologists would expect even these small differences to affect behavior, because "face-to-face, hearing someone say it" should be more powerful than the relatively annonymous Crutchfield situation. Deutsch and Gerard (1955) and Levy (1960) have shown that when the types of items are identical, there is more yielding in the Asch situation than in the one developed by Crutchfield. The kind of yielding, however, and the psychological significance of it appear to be quite similar.

Thus, even small situational differences such as we have been discussing can affect the amount of yielding that occurs. When these relatively artificial situations are translated into real-life situations, it is probable that the amount of conformity shown will again be altered, but that the psychological significance of it may be similar. Seldom are we faced with unanimous majorities which disagree with us, although one that does occur with some regularity is in jury deliberations. We will say more about that in Chapter 11.

Explaining Conformity—Social Comparison and Attribution

There have been a number of attempts to explain conformity. Festinger (1954) proposed a social comparison theory which asserts that there is a basic drive within each of us to evaluate our own abilities and opinions. It is distressing to announce confidently the answer to a question posed in class and be wrong—or to challenge someone to a race and lose. The way that we avoid such mistakes is to compare ourselves to others and this process becomes vitally important to us. It is a process that we learn, one which becomes very important to us. We do not like to compare ourselves to a group and find we are deviant. This, of course is exactly what happened to the subjects in the Asch experiment. They were faced with a dilemma and the tension aroused by viewing the lines differently from their social comparison group caused some of them to adhere to the group's incorrect choice.

Ross, Bierbrauer, and Hoffman (1976) have contended that the Asch conformity situation presented subjects with an attribution crisis. That is, subjects in Asch's experiments were faced with two questions: "Why are my peers selecting a line that I view as obviously incorrect?" and "What would my disagreement imply about me and what I think of my peers?" Both of these are attribution questions. The first concerns the cause of the peers' behavior, and the second the cause of the subject's behavior. In an everyday situation most of us can attribute differences between ourselves and others to different payoffs. For example a defense attorney who disagrees with a prosecutor about capital punishment knows why he opposes it and why the prosecutor favors it. There is, however, no obvious difference in payoff that Asch's subjects could see. This argument that different payoffs would allow the subject to attribute peers' incorrect choices to a desire to increase their potential payoff was tested by Ross et al. (1976). As they predicted, conformity decreased when subjects knew that their peers were attempting to gain a larger payoff. Thus some, but not all, of the conformity observed by Asch seems to be explained by attribution theory.

Other possibilities have been raised in attempting to explain conformity. One of these is the individual's sex. It has been argued that females are more conforming than males. In an ingenious study by Sestrunk and McDavid (1971), however, this fallacy was exposed. These investigators reasoned that studies that had shown females to conform more than males had contained a subtle bit of sexism. That is, the tasks that had been selected for use in conformity studies were more familiar to males than to females. They picked some items that were masculine, some feminine, and

For many years it was assumed that women conformed more than men, although this idea has recently been questioned. Certainly, visual indicators of conformity do not seem more numerous in the women in this group.

some neutral. They found that males conformed more on the female items, females conformed more on the male items, and the two sexes conformed about equally on the neutral items.

Comment

How important is conformity? There is no doubt that there could not be a reasonable society in Canada or the United States if the members of that society did not conform to a certain degree. The socialization of children is a part of teaching the young members of society to conform. In this respect it should be emphasized that conformity is absolutely essential to the continuation of a social organization.

When, however, society demands that all people, in all places, at all times, conform, we may assume that conformity probably has gone too far. The ability to hold differing views that reflect differing approaches to problems is important. The difficult task is determining the dividing line between an appropriate amount of conformity and an inappropriate amount. Part of that determination is tied closely to an individual's motivation to conform. Even more important, however, is the balance that is struck by a society between pressures to conform and the freedom to deviate from group norms. The reason for this is quite simple; some of the most important advances, ethical, technological, interpersonal, and so forth, are contributed by people who deviate from social norms.

Society, it seems to me, may be compared to a lake. If it is a completely closed body of water into or out of which no water flows, it evaporates and becomes a dry lake bed. If water flows only into the lake but never out of it, the evaporation of water so condenses the chemicals and minerals that the lake becomes uninhabitable. If the water is constantly being changed by water flowing in and out, the lake has a chance to survive. Changing the water seems to be a necessary ingredient for a healthy lake.

Changing the norms of society also seems to be a necessary ingredient for a healthy society, but that change generally must come slowly and continuously or its impact will damage or ruin the society. That is, change is generally more helpful

277

when it evolves rather than occurs as the result of a revolution. Thus, conformity is important, in both a positive and negative way. It is necessary for a society, but too much of a good thing becomes a negative force.

Compliance

Another way in which an individual can respond to social influence is to comply. *Compliance occurs when a person is influenced by another because the complier hopes to achieve a favorable reaction from the other individual.* Note that compliance differs from conformity in at least two important ways. The complier is (1) generally responding to an implicit or explicit request from another person rather than to group pressures and (2) expects to gain some sort of reward for complying. Thus, compliance is usually seen as a type of reaction to social influence that is not as deeply felt by the individual nor likely to be as long lasting.

Herbert C. Kelman has long contributed to thought about social influence. He has developed a three-part classification scheme that emphasizes compliance and two other more deeply held responses to social influence, what he had termed identification and internalization. These latter processes deal primarily with the effects on the individual when he or she goes beyond the internal motivation to comply. We will not deal with these two in any greater depth, but it seems appropriate to give a few lines to Kelman's thoughts about them:

> Compliance can be said to occur when an individual accepts influence from another person or from a group in order to attain a favorable reaction from the other, that is, to gain a specific reward or avoid a specific punishment controlled by the other, or to gain approval or avoid disapproval from him. Identification can be said to occur when an individual accepts influence from another person or a group in order to establish or maintain a satisfying self-defining relationship to the other. In contrast to compliance, identification is not primarily concerned with producing a particular effect in the other. Rather, accepting influence through identification is a way of establishing or maintaining a desired relationship to the other, as well as the self-definition that is anchored in this relationship. By accepting influence, the person is able to see himself as similar to the other (as in classical identification) or to see himself as enacting a role reciprocal to that of the other. Finally, internalization can be said to occur when an individual accepts influence in order to maintain the congruence of his actions and beliefs with his value system. Here it is the content of the induced behavior and its relation to the person's value system that are intrinsically satisfying. [Kelman, 1963, p. 400.]

Even though there may seem to be some similarities between what Kelman called identification and conformity, he has made it very clear that he feels he is studying compliance in depth and that the stages of identification and internalization are primarily dealing with the motivational components of in-depth compliance (Kelman, 1974). Tedeschi (1974) points out that Kelman's categories, viewed from the perspective of the individual, are indeed social influence, but viewed from the perspective of society, they are social control. This points out a fine line, but a distinction that needs to be made in this chapter—conformity, compliance, and obedience can be either social influence or social control. Which it is depends upon which view is taken; from the view of the powerholder or system, it is social control, but it is social influence when viewed from the perspective of the individual.

This brief detour has been included to whet your appetite for a more thorough understanding of why people comply. We do not presently have more time to spend on Kelman's intriguing ideas, but you may pursue them yourself if you are so inclined. Particularly appropriate are two articles (Kelman, 1961; Kelman and Lawrence, 1972) even though his long-promised book has not yet appeared.

Each of us is faced each day with requests to comply with someone's request, for which we will receive something. Advertisers ask us to eat Brand X rather than Brand Y so that we will grow stronger, get slimmer, or be more healthy. Other advertisers promise us the reward of healthy teeth and relief from disgusting, embarrassing mouth odor if we will use their products. Friends ask for help in schoolwork, or in the neighborhood, or just ask us to listen to their problems. Family members want us to clean the house, fix up the house, serve a meal, or entertain them. At the same time, we are making similar requests of friends, neighbors, and family. Few times do we comply with a request for help entirely to help the other person—rather we expect something in return. If we help someone, we expect to be repaid for it. We are sometimes surprised if our friends and relatives treat us in the same way—expect a favor for a favor—but they usually do. The business of helping someone out implies that he or she will help us, and vice versa.

Much of the psychological research into compliance has been concerned with why people comply and an attempt to theorize about the nature of compliance. The other side of the compliance coin is how we get people to comply with our requests.

Why People Comply

Some of the research into compliance has been primarily aimed at understanding some of the phenomena that affect compliance. For example, Carlsmith and Gross (1969) studied the effects of guilt on compliance. The experiment involved learning and the subject was put in the position of being the teacher and correcting the subjects when they made a mistake. For some subjects, the correction consisted of sounding a buzzer on each trial in which the learner was incorrect, whereas other subjects were led to believe that they were shocking the learner with electricity each time an incorrect response was delivered. After the experiment, the learner mentioned to the subject that he was involved with an attempt to stop the construction of a freeway through a grove of redwoods in northern California and he needed volunteers to telephone requests to people to sign a petition. Only 25 percent of those who corrected the learner with a buzzer agreed to help, but 75 percent of those who thought they had shocked the learner agreed to do so. Thus, those who thought they had harmed the learner, presumably because they felt guilty, were more willing to comply with the request to help out a cause that was important to the learner.

Freedman and Fraser (1966) developed a technique they called the "foot-in-the-door" technique to achieve compliance. The basic idea is to get the person you want to comply with a large request to grant a small request. The name, of course, comes from door-to-door salesmen who feel that if they can get their foot in the door,

THE FINE ART OF LOW-BALLING

There are many sales techniques that have been utilized to obtain compliance from a customer. One that has been most associated with car sales is known as "low-balling." The particulars of the technique vary, but the general idea is to get a customer's commitment to buy a car at a low price; considerably lower than the salesperson intends to sell the car for. After a discussion with the "boss" the salesperson regretfully informs you that the boss won't allow the good deal and the actual cost of the car will be more. Often times this higher price is as high or even slightly higher than the price a competing dealer had quoted. The folklore of automobile sales says that low-balling is a more effective technique than trying to sell the car by telling the customer the actual price from the beginning of negotiations. Are we such irrational creatures that low-balling really works? Or is low-balling a myth?

Cialdini et al. (1978) decided to test the idea that low-balling is an effective way of obtaining compliance. Their experimental procedure was to contact potential subjects for a psychology experiment and use a low-ball procedure on half of them and tell half of them the bitter truth from the beginning. The 63 subjects were contacted by phone and asked to participate in a psychology experiment. The low-ball group was asked to indicate whether they would participate in the experiment. After the subject had agreed to participate, the low-ball strategy was employed: They were then told that the experiment was to be conducted at 7:00 A.M. Subjects in the control condition were told before being asked to commit themselves about participating that the experiment was at 7:00 A.M. As you know, most college students do not consider 7:00 A.M. to be a reasonable time to engage in any activity other than sleep. Thus, the effectiveness of the low-ball strategy could be assessed by determining the number of subjects who complied with the request in the two groups.

Fifty-six percent of the subjects in the low-ball condition agreed to participate in the experiment, whereas only 31 percent of the subjects in the control condition agreed to comply with the request. The low-ball procedure was even more effective when the number of subjects who actually showed up for the experiment at 7:00 A.M. is considered. Fifty-three percent of the low-ball subjects and only 24 percent of the control subjects appeared for the experiment. Additional experiments by Cialdini et al. found that the low-ball procedure differed from and was more effective than the foot-in-the-door technique discussed in this chapter, and is effective only when the individual has a high degree of choice in the original decision. That is, if you choose to buy the car at a lower price (are not forced to do so by some circumstance) the low-ball technique is quite effective. If the original decision was not your own choice for some reason (there is only one dealer in town, a parent or spouse forced you to choose the car, etc.) then low-balling is not as effective.

It does seem that low-balling is an effective sales technique. Think about it the next time you are offered a great deal on a car (or any other purchase) and then find that the irrational boss won't let the sympathetic salesperson carry through on the deal. If you buy the object, maybe you're the irrational one.

Reference

Cialdini, R. B., J. T. Cacioppo, R. Bassett, and J. A. Miller. Low-ball procedure for producing compliance: Commitment then cost. *Journal of Personality and Social Psychology*, 1978, *36*, 463–76.

they will eventually be able to get inside and make a sale. Freedman and Fraser first contacted housewives by telephone and asked them to answer a few questions about the soap they used, a small request. Next, they asked if each housewife would permit a survey team to come into her home and carry out a two-hour classification of the household products she used, a large request. They found that of those who had previously granted the small request, 53 percent later complied with the large request, whereas only 22 percent of those who had not been "softened-up" with the small request agreed to the large request. Freedman and Fraser also found that the technique is mose effective when the initial small request is similar to the subsequent large request, although even compliance with a very different small request leads to more compliance when the large request is presented. Freedman and Fraser based their explanation of the "foot-in-the-door" technique as one of self-perception; that is, when one has complied that person views himself or herself as one who cooperates with good causes or becomes involved in similar action. The Freedman and Fraser study has essentially been replicated by Pliner, Hart, Kohl, and Sarri (1974).

Demonstrations such as these two help us to understand why people comply, but they are limited in that they pertain only to a specific situation or a small set of situations. Different theorists have attempted to explain compliance in different ways. For example, Michner and Burt (1974) have commented upon legitimacy as a basis of social influence. Although their discussion is both detailed and enlightening, it deals primarily with organizational or instrumental legitimacy, and I would like to point us in the direction of two theories of social exchange that emphasize the interpersonal aspects of compliance.

EQUITY THEORY

Homans (1961) has developed a model called equity theory, which is built on Skinnerian operant-conditioning principles, and assumes that each individual feels that he or she is being treated fairly. Five basic propositions are developed by Homans which assert that (1) behavior that has been associated with reward is more easily elicited, especially if the reward is meaningful to the person; (2) the more often a person's activity is rewarded by another, the more often that activity will be repeated; (3) the more valuable the reward for an activity the more often it will be repeated; (4) the more often a person has received a rewarding activity from someone else, the less valuable another unit of the same reward becomes; and (5) unless a person views as equitable the costs and rewards in a relationship, he or she is not likely to continue the relationship.

Basically, Homans attempted to tie down the proposition that people expect to be rewarded for their actions and in turn to pay for what they receive in the social arena much as they do in the commercial one. If rewards outweigh costs or costs outweigh rewards, the resultant relationship will not be balanced and will lead to friction.

The concept of social exchange will be dealt with in Chapter 10, but the importance of it for compliance is fairly obvious. People comply because they expect to gain something for their compliance. Homans' theory goes one step beyond that and argues that the social system must be balanced just as the economic one is—that costs and rewards must be in some sort of balance for the system to work.

Foa and Foa (1974, 1975) go one enormous step further and specify the types of social resources that are available and point out that only certain classes of resources are effective payments for rewards given in that class. As Foa and Foa say,

Spurred on by the relative success of economists in predicting and controlling behavior in the marketplace, social psychologists have attempted to apply the economic model to noneconomic transactions. The assumption that every transaction, both economic and emotional, follows the same rules caused disinterest in the problems of specifying and classifying exactly *what* is exchanged. If one assumes the rules to be the same for every transaction, it becomes irrelevant to state what is exchanged, and the only meaningful parameter in an exchange is the *amount* of the exchanged commodity. Another interesting but unfortunate consequence of imitating the economic model is that negative exchanges have not been recognized as transactions. For some reason exchanges of the type "I shoplift—you pickpocket" have traditionally been of greater interest to lawyers than to economists. Similarly, interactions such as "I interfere with a pleasurable activity of yours—you express dislike for me" have often been called "frustration-aggression sequences": their transactional nature has been ignored. [Foa and Foa, 1975, p 2.]

The Foas have pointed out a crucial element in the compliance situation. It is not sufficient to say that an individual complies because he or she is rewarded. Rather, it is necessary to know what resource an individual is being asked to give and what resource he is being offered as a reward. For example, if you are offering love or friendship to another individual, the resource the person offers in return is much more effective if it, too, is love or friendship rather than money. In the world of economics, from which equity theory and exchange theory evolved, the medium of exchange does not take on the significance that it does in social exchange, in which there are multiple resources. The Foas have begun to classify the types of social resources available and which of them serve as appropriate compensation for each specific other resource. Later we will discuss their classification more fully. At this time it is sufficient to emphasize that when we come to deal with social rewards (or resources) the situation is greatly complicated; whereas an economic theory may serve a valuable function in sketching in the broad outlines of compliance, the specifics are much more subtle and have to be painstakingly developed. It would be too simple to say that in the economic world there is only one resource, money. On the other hand, some sort of monetary resource is involved in almost all economic exchanges. Even if an executive is really concerned with obtaining power in a given situation, money is often the medium of exchange used in the transaction. But even in this example, there is a question of whether we are not moving into the area of social exchange. It is to the subtleties in social exchange that the Foas have addressed themselves.

Comment

Compliance is a necessary ingredient for any society. As people are rarely able to depend upon themselves for all they need, it is essential for them to make requests of others and those requests, in turn, will be either accepted or rejected. The decision to accept or reject is based on what resources the other individual can offer to influence the person who, it is hoped, will comply. You will remember that the definition of compliance (being influenced by another in the hope of achieving a favorable reaction from that person) implies doing something in exchange for a reward. Typically this occurs when the powerholder does not have the resources required, or does not choose to use the resources required, to *force* the obedience. When the situation is such that the powerholder's resources are sufficient to force compliance, then the act of obeying is no longer referred to as compliance, but obedience.

Obedience

One of the most startling, disquieting, and by now, famous social psychological experiments was carried out by Stanley Milgram in the early 1960s, first at Yale University and then at other locations. The fact that the study has been replicated on numerous occasions and in a variety of countries greatly increases our confidence in the results. In Chapter 2, Milgram's work was mentioned in connection with ethical considerations. As you see the basic structure of the experiment, it will be possible for you to grasp more fully the difficulties of ethics in psychological experimentation.

Milgram's Studies of Obedience

Milgram (1963), after much deliberation and questioning of students, colleagues and "people on the street," developed an experimental methodology for the study of obedience. As he clearly stated, much of the impetus for his work evolved from the World War II:

> Obedience, as a determinant of behavior, is of particular relevance to our time. It has been reliably established that from 1933–1945 millions of innocent persons were systematically slaughtered on command. Gas chambers were built, death camps were guarded, daily quotas of corpses were produced with the same efficiency as the manufacture of appliances. These inhumane policies may have originated in the mind of a single person, but they could only be carried out on a massive scale if a very large number of persons obeyed orders.
>
> Obedience is the psychological mechanism that links individual action to political purpose. It is the dispositional cement that binds men to systems of authority. Facts of recent history and observation in daily life suggest that for many persons obedience may be a deeply ingrained behavior tendency, indeed, a prepotent impulse overriding training in ethics, sympathy, and moral conduct. [Milgram, 1963, p. 371.]

The study that Milgram developed and ran in response to some of the general questions that were raised in his mind about obedience is important enough to discuss in some detail. The procedure used was to order a naïve subject to shock a victim with electricity. A simulated shock generator was used, which had thirty clearly marked voltage levels ranging from 15 to 450 volts. Each group of four switches had the following designations indicated: Slight Shock (15–60 volts), Moderate Shock (75–120 volts), Strong Shock (135–180 volts), Very Strong Shock (195–240 volts); Intense Shock (255–300 volts); Extreme Intensity Shock (315–360 volts); Danger: Severe Shock (375–420 volts). The final two switches were simply marked with the designation *XXX*.

The orders to give shock to a victim were purportedly part of a study of learning, with specific emphasis upon the effects of punishment on memory. As the experiment proceeded, the subject (in early experiments only males were used as subjects) was ordered to shock the learner each time he had a mistake and to move the intensity of shock one level higher in preparation for the next mistake. Each subject had received a sample shock from the shock generator of 45 volts to further convince him of the authenticity of the shock procedure. Thus, from the subject's point of view, he knew

COMPLIANCE: THOUGHTFUL OR MINDLESS?

When someone asks you for the time or for directions, often you comply without thinking about it. Do you ever comply when someone asks you to do something that is illogical? Or do you ever comply when someone asks you to do him (or her) a favor, but gives a reason for needing the help that is meaningless? Langer, Blank, and Chanowitz (1978) investigated what they called the mindlessness of supposedly thoughtful action. These researchers were interested in finding out how closely individuals attend to what they do. Social psychology is replete with theories that assume that people think. But do we?

Langer et al. questioned how often people actually think about what they do. We have all had occasion to wonder why we did something after we have done it. Langer and her associates suggested that oftentimes we follow a "script" of how things should be and behave accordingly. For example, if someone asks a small favor of us, we will oftentimes grant it automatically. When a large favor is asked, we may be more inclined to need a good reason for complying.

Langer and her coworkers report an ingenious experiment that utilized as subjects people who were about to use a university copy machine. The subjects were approached by an experimenter who asked if he or she could use the machine first. Half of the subjects were told the experimenter had 5 pages to copy and half were told he or she had 20 pages to copy. These two groups were further subdivided by the use of three "reasons" for needing to copy ahead of the subject. The control group received no rationale; they were merely asked if the experimenter could copy first. The second group received a request to copy first with an irrational justification. These individuals were asked if the experimenter could copy first because he or she "had to make copies." The third group was told that the experimenter was in a rush. Once the request was made and either complied or not complied with, the experimenter unobtrusively counted the number of pages the subject copied. If the subject had more pages to copy than the experimenter, the request was considered a small favor; whereas it was considered a large favor if the subject had fewer pages to copy than the experimenter. This approach to determining whether the request was large or small seems logical since the amount of time the subject would have to spend depended on the number of pages he or she had to copy plus the number of pages the experimenter had to copy if the request were granted.

Recall that Langer and her associates had predicted that when the favor was small, subjects would "mindlessly" grant it. When the favor was large, however, they would think about it. The "mindless" test came from comparing the request to copy first "because I have copies to make" with the simple request and the request to copy first because "I'm in a rush." When the favor was small, 60 percent of the people allowed the experimenter to copy first when the simple request was made. When the redundant information "I have copies to make" was added, 93 percent of the subjects complied. When the excuse, "I'm in a rush" was added, the compliers increased only to 94 percent. When the favor was large, 24 percent of those who were simply asked complied and the same number complied when the excuse "I have to make copies" was added. However, for the large favor, 42 percent complied when they were told the experimenter was in a rush.

I seems, then, that when we are asked small favors, even a meaningless excuse increases compliance; but that doesn't happen when the favor is large. How much of our seemingly thoughtful compliance is really "mindless?"

Reference

Langer, E., A. Blank, and B. Chanowitz. The mindlessness of ostensibly thoughtful action: The role of "placebic" information in interpersonal interaction. *Journal of Personality and Social Psychology,* 1978, *36,* 635–42.

that he was to shock a learner each time the learner made a mistake, and to increase the intensity of shock after each mistake. Prior to the administration of any shock, the subject was to announce the voltage level of the shock to be administered.

The victim (learner) was a confederate of Milgram's and in all conditions gave a predetermined set of responses with approximately three incorrect responses for each correct one. No vocal response was heard from the victim until the shock level reached 300 volts (labeled Intense Shock), when pounding on the wall could be heard by the subject. This, of course, is the twentieth shock that has been delivered by the subject. At this point, subjects ordinarily asked the experimenter for guidance. The experimenter told the subject that the absence of a response was a wrong answer and the subject should be shocked as scheduled. The experimenter advised the subject to wait 5–10 seconds before considering no response a wrong answer and then to increase the shock level one step for each failure to respond just as he would do for any other wrong answer. The learner again pounded on the wall at the administration of the 315-volt shock, following which he was not heard from again nor did he respond to any of the questions.

At various points in the experiment, the subject turned to the experimenter for advice on whether he should continue to administer shocks, or in other cases the subject might indicate that he did not wish to continue. Milgram, feeling that it was important to have standardized responses to such inquiries had developed the following sequence of "prods" for the experimenters to use to keep their subjects responding.

Prod 1: Please continue or Please go on.
Prod 2: The experiment requires that you continue.
Prod 3: It is absolutely essential that you continue.
Prod 4: You have no other choice, you *must* go on.

The prods were used in sequence; that is, only if Prod 1 had been unsuccessful was Prod 2 used, and so forth. If a subject refused to obey after Prod 4, the experiment was terminated.

How many of you would shock the learner up to the 450-volt level? Upon asking that question in class, I typically get no responses. Milgram asked 14 Yale senior psychology majors to predict the behavior of 100 hypothesized subjects after they had been given a complete description of the experimental procedure. The most pessimistic respondent indicated that 3 percent would go all the way to the limit in delivering shocks and the average was that 1.2 percent of subjects would deliver 450 volts. Milgram informally polled a number of his colleagues and found essentially the same sort of responses, with the general prediction being that few, if any, of the subjects would go beyond the Very Strong Shock (195–240 volts) designation. The actual behavior of Milgram's subjects, who represented a wide range of ages (20–50) and occupations, are shown in Figure 7–2.

No subject quit before the victim pounded on the wall (after 20 shocks had been delivered) and then only 12.5 percent refused to go on. Another 10 percent of the subjects refused to go on after the second episode of wall pounding, but 65 percent of the subjects continued to deliver shock right up to the XXX designation. As no

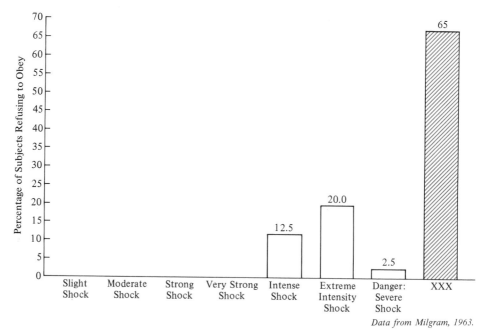

Data from Milgram, 1963.

Figure 7–2 Percentage of subjects refusing to obey instructions to continue shock-ing the learner. All who quit at Intense Shock did so when victim first pounded on the wall (300 volts) and half of those who quit during Extreme Intensity Shock did so when victim pounded on the wall the second time (315 volts).

further response was received from the subject after he pounded on the wall the second time, and he no longer attempted to answer the questions, it is reasonable to assume that the victim was in considerable trouble. Nevertheless, 65 percent of the subjects continued to deliver shock—*nine more times.*

The very first study in this series that Milgram (1961) carried out utilized Yale University undergraduate students, and a generalized explanation for their behavior was that they were a competitive lot who would step on anyone to achieve their own ends. This 1961 study was not published in the usual psychological journals; rather it was contained in a report to the National Science Foundation. Possibly even Milgram believed the competitive, undergraduate explanation, or more likely, he followed careful scientific procedures and replicated his work. At any rate, this criticism led to the first study published in the psychological literature, which has just been described in some detail (Milgram, 1963). These subjects were professionals, white-collar workers, industrial workers, and unemployed persons. One of the immediate reac-tions to this work was that it was carried out in a psychological laboratory at Yale, and the subjects were aware of the fact that a university of Yale's stature would not allow people to be seriously harmed. But since Milgram's first report, this experiment has been carried out at other universities, in settings that have no connection with a university, and in other countries, with essentially the same results. Explanations other than the one arrived at by Milgram—that people are extremely obedient—do not seem to be very credible at this time. There are, however, four distinct experimental variations that have had an influence on the number of subjects who obey completely.

287

Obedience

PROXIMITY

Milgram (1965a) describes a study in which four experimental conditions were utilized to bring the victim psychologically closer to the subject. Here is the way Milgram described each of the four conditions.

In the first condition (Remote Feedback) the victim was placed in another room and could not be heard or seen by the subjects, except that, at 300 volts, he pounded on the wall in protest. At 315 volts he no longer answered or was heard from.

The second condition (Voice Feedback) was identical to the first except that voice protests were introduced. As in the first condition the victim was placed in an adjacent room, but his complaints could be heard clearly through a door left slightly ajar, and through the walls of the laboratory.

The third experimental condition (Proximity) was similar to the second, except that the victim was now placed in the same room as the subject, and 1½ feet from him. Thus he was visible as well as audible, and voice cues were provided.

The fourth and final, condition of this series (Touch-Proximity) was identical to the third, with this exception: the victim received a shock only when his hand rested on a shock plate. At the 150-volt level the victim again demanded to be set free (a part of the voice protests introduced for conditions 2, 3 and 4) and, in this condition refused to place his hand on the shockplate. The experimenter ordered the naïve subject to force the victim's hand onto the plate. Thus obedience in this condition required that the subject have physical contact with the victim in order to give him punishment beyond the 150-volt level. [Milgram, 1965a, pp. 61–62.]

The results of this experiment were both startling and extremely interesting. Figure 7–3 depicts them graphically. The first thing to note is that in the remote condition, which basically replicated Milgram's first study, 66 percent of the subjects were completely obedient, as compared to 65 percent the first time. However, as the victim became more visible and close to the subject, complete obedience declined. Just hearing the victim had little effect; it caused only 3.5 percent more of the subjects to be less than completely obedient. But when the subject could see the victim, 22.5 percent more of the subjects defied the experimenter. Finally, when the subject had to force the victim's hand onto the shockplate to deliver the shock, another 10 percent defied the experimenter. This may sound as if great strides in humanitarianism were being made by making the victim visible to the subject and forcing his hand onto the shockplate. You should note, however, that almost 1 out of 3 subjects continued to shock the victim right up to the 450-volt limit, even when it was necessary to force his hand onto a shockplate.

There is another form of proximity that is important in the study of obedience—the proximity of the authority source to the subject. In another series of conditions, Milgram (1965a) varied the proximity of the experimenter (the source of authority) and the subject. In one condition, the experimenter sat within a few feet of the subject; in a second, the experimenter left the room after giving his initial

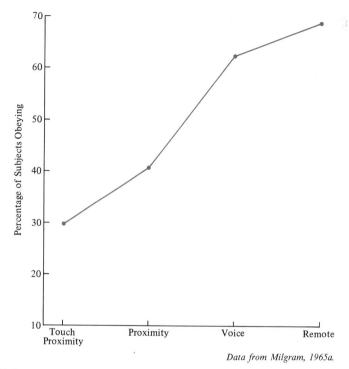

Data from Milgram, 1965a.

Figure 7–3 Percentage of subjects in each of four conditions obeying the experimenter's demands to continue shocking the learner up to 450 volts.

instructions and gave his remaining orders by telephone; in the third, instructions were provided by tape recording with the subject never being seen.

In the condition in which the experimenter was present, 65 percent of the subjects were fully obedient, whereas only 22.5 percent were fully obedient in the condition in which the experimenter delivered his initial instructions in person and then used the telephone for subsequent instructions. In addition, when the experimenter was out of the room, many subjects, although obeying the command to shock the victim, lowered the level of shock substantially. Even while assuring the experimenter over the phone that they were delivering the required intensity of shock, some subjects had lowered the shock generator to its lowest level. These subjects seemed to be able to handle the conflict inherent in the situation more easily by lowering the shock level than by defying the experimenter openly.

Other experiments were carried out in which the experimenter left the room, issued instructions by telephone, and then later returned to the room. Even when he had exhausted his authority over the subjects by telephone, he was, in many cases, able to reestablish it by his presence. Thus the presence of the authority figure seems to be an important variable in obedience, just as the presence of the victim seems to be an important variable in defiance of that authority.

Elms and Milgram (1966) interviewed 40 persons who had been subjects in the Milgram "Proximity Series" (1965a) study; 20 who had defied the experimenter's prods and 20 who had been fully obedient. They were administered two standard psychological tests, the Minnesota Multiphasic Personality Inventory (MMPI) (Hathaway and McKinley, 1951) and the California F-Scale (Adorno et al., 1950). There were no differences between the two groups on the MMPI, which is not highly surprising since it was developed as a screening device for psychotics. The California F-Scale however, did show differences between the two groups, even after the educational level of the two groups was controlled for. (This control was a necessary procedure since Christie (1954) noted that education and F-Scale scores are correlated.) On the California F-Scale obedient subjects were shown to be significantly more authoritarian than were defiant ones. In addition, an interview was carried out with each of these subjects, and Elms and Milgram report:

> Other similarities to findings reported in *The Authoritarian Personality* are found in obedient subjects' feelings of the father's lack of closeness when the subject was a child, and the relative glorification of the Experimenter and downgrading of the Learner. The authoritarian tendency toward stereotyped glorification of the father is not observed in obedients— quite the contrary,—but this may be partly the result of the interviewer's negative ratings of "stern" and other authoritarian adjectives describing the father, in the blind categorization of descriptions. Additionally, the generally older subjects in the present study may find it easier to express critical attitudes toward their fathers than the young adults who composed a large proportion of Adorno et al. samples.
>
> The reporting of less severe childhood punishment by obedients is also atypical of the "authoritarian personality". . . . [Elms and Milgram, 1966, pp. 286–87.]

It thus seems apparent that at least one personality variable, authoritarianism, does influence obedience. This is not particularly surprising since the California F-Scale, which measures authoritarianism, was developed during a massive research effort aimed at understanding how and why the atrocities committed during World War II could happen. At that time, individuals who committed the atrocities claimed that they were only obeying orders, which, of course, could ultimately be traced to Hitler. The same atrocities were part of the impetus for Milgram's study of obedience. Even though the research projects of Adorno et al. and Milgram were quite independent, it is not surprising that they should isolate the same sort of personality characteristics that seem to be displayed by those who are obedient.

SEX

For a variety of reasons, most of Milgram's studies of obedience used male subjects. Kilham and Mann (1974) described a study in which they varied both the responsibility and the sex of the subject. They had a transmitter condition in which the ". . . transmitter administered the paired associate test, monitored the responses, and passed orders on to the executant. . . . [The executant] had to administer the shock after seeing the responses flash up on the panel. The transmitter still communicated the order and indicated the correct shock level (1974, p. 698)." Male executants and transmitters were paired with male learners, and female executants and transmitters were paired with female learners. The results of the study are shown in Figure 7–4. As that figure shows, there was considerably more obedience in the transmitter conditions than in the executant ones, and males were much more obedient than females. The results for the transmitter and executant conditions are not terribly surprising because the transmitter is in a relatively safe psychological role. As Kilham and Mann put it,

. . . he (the transmitter) can disclaim responsibility for the orders and can argue that he had no part in their execution. The transmitter can argue that his highly specialized part in the act was only of a trivial, mechanical nature. For example, at his trial Adolf Eichmann claimed for himself a transmitter role in the extermination of Jews. He argued, "In actual fact I was merely a little cog in the machinery that carried out the directives of the German Reich." [Kilham & Mann, 1974, p. 697.]

The results of most interest in the Kilham and Mann study have to do with the fact that females were less obedient than males in both the transmitter and the executant conditions. Kilham and Mann do not accentuate this difference to any great degree, although they do speculate about it. It seems inconsistent with evidence that females conform more than males in a variety of experimental conditions in social psychology laboratories. But most studies of conformity are concerned with persuasibility and not obedience. Here is the extent to which Kilham and Mann reflect on this issue:

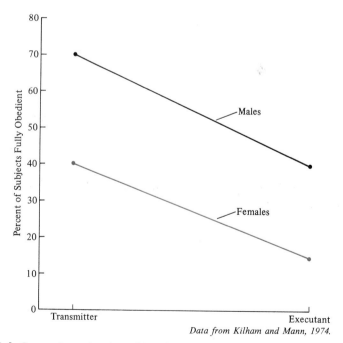

Data from Kilham and Mann, 1974.

Figure 7–4 Comparison of male and female transmitters' and executants' obedience.

It may be the case that when females are expected to conform in the realm of action, particularly aggressive action, against another female, they are more reactive. Female students may seek to form an alliance with the other female (the victim) in the situation in order to oppose the unreasonable demands of an aggressive male experimenter. Or female defiance may be due to a concern for the vulnerability of the female victim. A replication of the present study in which subjects are required to shock victims who are either the same or opposite sex would allow for a more informative discussion on this point. [Kilham and Mann, p. 702.]

In spite of the traditional caveat that more research is needed, there does appear to be rather substantial evidence that females are less obedient than males in this situation. Speculation as to why this is so must remain speculation at the moment. You should, however, recall that our discussion of prejudice against women in Chapter 6 dealt with the exclusion of women from juries because of their purported persuasibility. Data from Nemeth, Endicott, and Wachtler (1976) indicated that women were not more persuasible in jury situations; rather that there is a complex interaction between the crime the defendant is accused of, the sex of the juror, and the juror's behavior. Kilham and Mann's study, which compares women with men and finds them less obedient, questions even further some of the common stereotypes of females.

GROUP EFFECTS

Milgram (1964) made a very cogent and important point when he argued that social psychology must come to grips with the importance of the behavior contents on which it is focused. As Milgram put it,

But eventually social psychology must come to grips with significant behavior contents, contents that are of interest in their own right and are not simply trivial substitutes for psychologically meaningful forms of behavior. Guided by this consideration, a relatively potent form of action was selected for shaping by group pressure. We asked: Can a group induce a person to deliver punishment of increasing severity to a protesting individual? Whereas Asch and others have shown in what manner group pressure can cause a person to pronounce judgments that contradict his thinking, the present study examines whether group pressure causes a person to engage in acts at variance with his uninfluenced behavior. [1964, p. 138.]

In designs that drew upon Asch's conformity studies and his own previous obedience studies, Milgram (1964, 1965b) examined the effects of both negative and positive group pressure upon the individual. In the first of these studies Milgram was interested in the negative influence a group could assert upon an individual.

Using the basic experimental setting just described, Milgram instituted several significant changes in order to study the effect of a group on obedient behavior. In this study there were supposedly three teachers instead of one and the lowest shock level suggested by any of the three teachers was to be delivered. Two of the teachers were confederates, and the subject was the teacher who had the task of administering the shock to the learner. The shock level was the lowest suggested by any of the three teachers, and thus the subject could effectively control the level of shock. The other two teachers always suggested one step increase in the voltage each time the learner made a mistake. Thus, subjects were not faced with instructions to obey and raise the shock level one step for each mistake, but they were pressured to conform by the two other members of the group.

The learner also indicated verbally that the shock was uncomfortable in the following manner: (1) at 75, 90, and 105 volts the learner emits a slight grunt; (2) at 120 volts the learner shouts that the shocks are becoming painful; (3) painful groans are heard at 135-volt level; (4) at 150 volts the learner cries he wants to be released from the experiment, saying that he has a heart condition; (5) cries of this type continue until at 180 volts the learner cries, "I can't stand the pain"; (6) by 285 volts his response is an agonized scream; and (7) from 300 through 450 volts the learner shouts that he will no longer provide answers to the memory test.

A control condition was run in which there was but one teacher (the subject) who did not face any group pressure to increase the shock. This condition gives a baseline with which to compare the effects of group pressure. That is, the difference in the intensity of shock for each mistake between the control condition and the experimental condition can be viewed as a measure of the effects of the group on the learner. The effects of group pressure were marked. Figure 7–5 shows the percentage of subjects in each condition who delivered the various levels of shock. Also included in the figure are the data from Figure 7–2, which shows the percentage of obedient subjects (those who were instructed to continue increasing the shock level). It should be noted that in the terminology we have been using the experimental group is conforming and that the data from Figure 7–2 indicate obedience. Inspection of Figure 7–5 shows that most of the control subjects who had no pressure on them to obey or conform refused to go beyond the slight shock category, whereas most of the subjects who were instructed to do so (obedience) went all the way through the highest shock level. Subjects who were under group pressure fell midway between the two other groups with 52.5 percent refusing to go beyond the halfway point (Very Strong Shock—240 volts) and 47.5 percent continuing, with 17.5 percent going all the way to the 450-volt intensity. Thus, while group pressure exerted a strong influence on the level of shock a subject would deliver, it was not so effective as direct instructions from the experimenter. Subjects obeyed more than conformed.

There is, however, another aspect of group pressure, which is a less studied phenomenon. What are the positive aspects of group pressure, or as Milgram (1965b) phrases it, the liberating effects? In this study there again were three teachers, but now the two confederates who were teachers disobeyed the experimenter. One refused to continue after the 150-volt shock was administered and the second quit after the 210-volt shock. At this point, the subject was left alone to administer the shock, and in fact, was ordered to do so by the experimenter, who indicated that it essential that the experiment continue. Under these conditions 10 percent of the subjects quit at or before the shock intensity beyond which the first confederate refused to go. An additional 52.5 percent of the subjects quit at or before the 210-volt shock (where the second confederate quit), but 37.5 percent went beyond 210 volts, and 10 percent of the subjects delivered the 450-volt shock. It is obvious that there is a greatly increased incidence of disobedience when the group disobeys, but it does not affect the behavior of everyone.

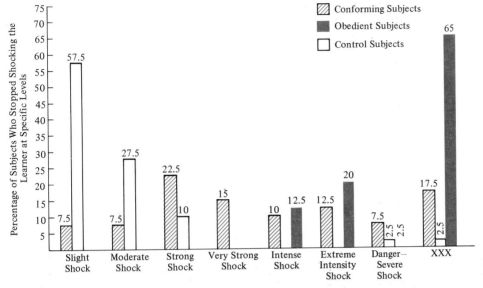

Figure 7–5 Percentage of conforming, obedient, and control subjects who continued to shock the learner in Milgram's (1963, 1964) studies.

Comment

Milgram's work has been criticized (see Baumrind, 1964), but the criticisms seem to be relatively minor compared to the contribution that has been made to our understanding of obedience. The most telling criticism of this area of research is the question of whether it should be continued or not. Milgram reports that his subjects displayed a great deal of tension and anxiety during the experiment, which was wholly unexpected. This, of course, was because the results (i.e., that so many subjects would deliver the high intensities of shock) were unexpected. The ethical issue raised is whether the research is important enough to continue after it was apparent that it would cause discomfort to subjects. Milgram argues, persuasively I believe, that in light of obedience in World War II by the Nazis, by Lieutenant Calley at My Lai in Viet Nam, and other such incidents, it is vitally important for us to understand the phenomenon. Moreover, in a recent article (Milgram, 1977) he has made explicit his belief that participants' reactions to experiments should be considered more seriously. The data reported by Milgram show that 84 percent of the subjects indicated they were glad to have been in the experiment, 15 percent indicated neutral feelings, and only 1 percent indicated unhappiness with being in the experiment.

The study of obedience implies a giver of orders who wishes to exercise power over the actor. What can we say about the order giver? We turn our attention now to that person, the powerholder.

The Powerholder

Kipnis (1974, 1976) has decried the lack of psychological theory to understand the actions of those who hold power. He points out that such an understanding must include (1) whom the person in power will influence; (2) the kind of demands that are made; and (3) what resources will be invoked to bolster power demands. As Kipnis so aptly puts it,

> ... Given that he has access to resources that are needed or valued by others, we are concerned with the circumstances that influence his use of such resources and how this use feeds back on his self-perceptions and his perceptions of others. The paper will focus mainly on the individual who has access to institutional resources, such as money, law, and military force. Access to these institutional resources may be a result of the person's role in an institution, his wealth, or special friendships that give him "behind the scenes" influence. Less attention will be paid to individuals whose resources are based upon personal qualities, such as beauty, strength, or intelligence. This is because access to institutional resources allows even the most ordinary of persons to extend their influence over others to a far greater degree than is true for the same person acting alone. Politicians control patronage; bankers, money; military officers, weapons; college professors, the baccalaureate degree. In all instances, access to these institutional resources increases the individual's potential for controlling the behavior of others and for shaping society. [1974, p. 83.]

Kipnis begins his discussion of the use of power by developing a model of the power act from the perspective of the powerholder. The model, which is an adaptation of a classification of the use of resources as it has been examined by various researchers, was first proposed as a classification scheme by Cartwright (1965).

One note of caution should be introduced here. The concept of power is extremely difficult to define. Tedeschi (1974) points out that in the eleven contributions to *Perspectives on Social Power,* there are at least five different ways of defining power. From Kipnis' perspective, which emphasizes the powerholder, power may best be defined as attempting to make a target do something he or she would not ordinarily do.

The Act of Power

The actual use or act of power may best be understood if the steps that lead to it are understood. Kipnis' model delimits seven steps, beginning with the motivation to power and continuing through the consequences of the power act for the power-holder.

POWER MOTIVATION

Why is power exercised? To be more specific why does someone in power (politician, banker, military officer, and so on) attempt to get an individual to do something he or she would not ordinarily do? The answer has its roots in the powerholder's dependency on others to facilitate events that are important for his or her policies, decisions, or goals. When the powerholder is both dependent on another person and he or she believes that the other person(s) is (are) willing to provide what is needed to fulfill important goals, then the powerholder experiences an inclination to influence others and thereby to gain satisfaction. Kipnis calls these inclinations *power motivations* and says: "*Power motivations arise when an individual experiences an aroused need state that can only be satisfied by inducing appropriate behavior in others* (1974, p. 84)." Kipnis even more explicitly places his model in the hedonic camp when he states that these "power motivations are reduced when the target person performs the desired behavior" (1974, p. 84).

Surprisingly enough, we are not dealing with a state that is foreign to most of us, because most of the conventional desires of modern humans are instances that involve the arousal of the power motive. The need for affection, material goods, status, as well as the need of the Prime Minister or President to influence large numbers of his countrymen, can be viewed as the arousal of the power motive. The desire for material goods, for example, fits nicely into the definition of getting a target (your employer) to do something he would not ordinarily do (give you money). The way this is achieved is by performing a valuable service—but by so doing, you are influencing his behavior.

The point made here must not be taken lightly; to one extent or another we all use power. When we think of power we think of it as a tool used to control our behavior, but the story is much more complicated than that. Each of us may not use power on so grand a scale as a head of state, but we do use it, and Kipnis' explication of the power motive takes this fact into account.

Power motivation has been viewed from several perspectives, with one of the

This labor headquarters demonstrates the position unions have assumed in an industrialized society: the union of workers has given them power.

more frequent explanations for it being an irrational impulse. In this view, power is both a means and an end; the powerholder derives enjoyment from its use (Christie and Geis, 1970; McClelland, 1969); or because it allows the powerholder to avoid feelings of weakness and the resultant loss of control (Veroff and Veroff, 1972). Another view of power motivation is that it is a role behavior, a duty to be fulfilled. The needs of the group, the organization or the country, demand that power be wielded, and the individual is caught in the dilemma of having to exercise power because of his or her role. In certain instances, the powerholder may be called upon to do things that he or she would not normally do, or, may find indeed the influencing act distasteful or painful (Milgram, 1963). Yet another way of viewing power motivation is as a universal drive. In this view, inducing certain behaviors in others can be decisive in obtaining rewards for yourself. When viewed this way, the emphasis is upon humans pursuing resources, which, in turn, only enhance the ability to influence others and thereby enjoy the good life. In this view, power very closely approximates an end in itself.

REQUEST FOR COMPLIANCE

Given the need for power, the next step is for the individual to request compliance, a step that is often omitted because it is doomed to failure. The criminal who politely asks for money, the shopper who requests that she be given a new item in a store, or the leader who politely requests that an army not invade his territory are most likely to be refused. At times compliance by simple request works, but not very often. To be successful in obtaining what he or she wants the powerholder most often must invoke resources.

RESOURCES

Resources may reside within the individual (personal) or be available because of the institutional role that individual occupies. Personal resources include strength, intelligence, and beauty, whereas institutional resources are much more varied in influence and depend upon the status of the institution and the status of the individual in the institution. Among these resources are access to money, military force,

The police car and its occupant symbolize the power of law.

is probably futile to attempt to develop a general classification scheme of such resources; rather a classification within each institution makes more sense.

If an individual has few or no resources to utilize in attempting to influence another person, the attempt will probably fail. If that occurs, then the individual may either accept an unfulfilled need or turn his or her attention to obtaining appropriate resources for influencing the target person successfully. Then the individual needs to be selective in determining the resources that will be helpful in achieving his or her aims. Goodstadt and Kipnis (1970) reported that when work supervisors had a choice between invoking personal and institutional resources to influence the behavior of their subordinates, they overwhelmingly chose institutional ones. Foa and Foa (1974) have developed a theory of resource exchange which presents evidence that particular needs can be met only by appropriate resources and not by just any resource. For example, an individual who is attempting to obtain liking and loving from another individual should invoke persuasive resources rather than economic or military ones.

One corollary of the gap between available resources and needs is important for society. Gurr (1970) has pointed out that as the gap between needs and the capability of satisfying those needs increases, the probability of violence increases. That is, as it becomes more and more apparent to the individual that his or her resources are pitifully inadequate to influence the behavior of others, the resource of violence is more seriously contemplated and then invoked.

REGION OF INHIBITION

What inhibits a powerholder from exercising power? Kipnis believes that there are two basic ways in which the use of available resources can be inhibited. First, the power motive may, in some way, be reduced. Kenneth B. Clark (1971) proposed that some sort of drug or "power pill" be developed that would eliminate, or at least reduce, the powerholder's desire to exercise his or her power. Second, the individual may have to use different resources or less extreme ones because of a variety of inhibiting factors. Some theorists view the region of inhibition as a cognitive area in which the costs of attempting to influence others are weighed against the benefits to be gained (Pollard and Mitchell, 1972, Tedeschi, Schlenker, and Lindskold, 1972). Other theorists feel that the use of power is inhibited, even though an individual might gain much more through its use than he or she would lose, because egalitarian motives override power motives (Leventhal and Lane, 1970; Pepitone, 1971; Walster, Bersheid, and Walster, 1970). There also appear to be stable individual difference variables that are related to the inhibition of using power (Christie and Geis, 1970; Megargee, 1971). Thus leaders who lacked self-confidence or who viewed themselves as being externally controlled (see Chapter 4) were reluctant to invoke personal resources as a means of inducing others to comply (Kipnis and Lane, 1962; Goodstadt and Kipnis, 1970). Finally, group norms—set up by institutions and societies to govern their actions, standards which may be in the form of customs or laws—inhibit the use of power. And these standards may vary with time or circumstances. For example, prior to the revelations of alleged corruption in high places during the Watergate scandal of the early 1970s in the United States, politicians were able to operate under a much more closed system. "Post-Watergate" behavior on the part of

As the gap between needs and the capability of satisfying those needs increases, the probability of violence increases. The gap referred to is illustrated by these two houses, both of which are located in the same metropolitan area.

the politicians has had to be more open and available to public scrutiny, and therefore of higher standards.

MEANS OF INFLUENCE

If the use of power is not restrained by an inhibitory factor, the powerholder's full resources may be invoked to obtain compliance. The problem now becomes one of how to present the available resources to the target in the form of a promise or a threat. One of the major determinants of the form of presentation of the resources is the nature of the resources themselves. Bombs and guns are, generally speaking, much more suitable to threat than are intelligence or knowledge. Money provides the powerholder with a broad range of alternatives, from extreme punishment to impressive promises. In those situations in which only threats are available to the powerholder, interpersonal relationships are basically hostile and destructive. For example, Berger (1972) found that in a simulated atmosphere in which managers were allowed only coercive means to influence their workers (i.e., to deduct pay) the managers generally believed that their workers disliked them, whether they actually invoked the coercion or not. In such a situation, managers directed most of their attention toward marginal workers as the most suitable group to influence.

THE TARGET'S RESPONSE TO THE INFLUENCE

Once the powerholder has invoked influence, how does the target respond? If the response is to comply, is the compliance given willingly or grudgingly? The more interesting case, of course, is the one in which the target ignores or refuses to comply with the powerholder's request. How does the powerholder respond? Kipnis suggests that when this happens the powerholder must recycle through earlier stages. What happens next is dependent upon the strength of the power motive, the unused available resources, and the strength of the restraining forces. The powerholder considers these facts and then decides whether to persist, to modify his or her original needs, to abandon the influence attempt, or to persist by invoking other resources. Usually, but not always, when other resources are invoked, they are harsher in nature than the original ones. There are instances, however, in which greater rewards rather than harsher punishments may be the resources invoked in a new attempt to influence the target. The crucial variable is the powerholder's ability to diagnose the cause of the target's resistance, and an incorrect diagnosis may cause more, not less, resistance.

CONSEQUENCES FOR THE POWERHOLDER

If the powerholder is successful and his or her needs are reduced, then the powerholder should experience satisfaction. If, on the other hand, the influence attempt is resisted, the powerholder's needs remain unfulfilled and frustration and self-doubt are experienced. The use or attempted use of resources to influence others may, in addition to fulfilling or frustrating the powerholder's needs, change that individual's view of his or her own worth and even his/her view of those less powerful persons, the targets. For example, the powerholder may be successful in influencing others, but may attribute that success to the wrong cause. A powerholder may feel that a successful attempt to influence a target occurred because of that powerholder's own persuasiveness, when in actuality it occurred because the target feared the economic consequences of resisting. In this case, the powerholder, alters his or her self-opinion by assuming he/she is more persuasive than is actually the fact. Further, the powerholder may be quite mistaken in not realizing that the target is hostile toward him/her on account of the use of a harsh resource (fear) when the powerholder thought the resource used was a more positive one (persuasiveness). This particular misconception may be compounded by the fact that the powerholder is the recipient of flattery from the target; flattery that is motivated by fear. The powerholder who does not recognize this fact may feel that he or she is quite special, both persuasive and the object of flattery, when in actuality he or she is the object of fear.

Changes in the powerholder's values and beliefs may occur as a result of attempts to hold and extend influence. For example, Galbraith (1967) has argued that managers in large business corporations are practically forced to make decisions and minimize risks for the corporation even if these decisions violate laws and are contrary to the general welfare of the public. Businesspersons who do business with city and state governments, and who find that corruption and political "kick-backs" are necessary to obtain and maintain business, participate in such behavior even though their values are such that the behavior is abhorrent to them. In these cases, the executive must "go along" or face the loss of power, job, business, and income with all of its myriad implications.

Finally, the use of power may well change the powerholder's view of the worth of less powerful persons. The less powerful may be devalued because the powerholder believes that the behavior of the target is not completely autonomous—is, in fact, partially controlled by the powerholder's orders and suggestions. Thus the target is not given the credit deserved, because the powerholder usurps it for himself or herself. In addition to devaluing the target, the powerholder often expresses a desire to maintain a certain social distance from the target, possibly because it is easier to influence others if little emotional involvement is allowed.

Kipnis's Summary

Kipnis summarizes power in this way:

From the point of view of the powerholder the power act is like a game. Each step flows from the previous one, and penalties blocking progress continually arise. The contingencies are such that without a need, influence is unlikely to be attempted. Without resources, influence is unlikely to be attempted. In the presence of strong inhibitions, influence is unlikely to be attempted. Without the proper means of influence, influence is unlikely to be attempted.

The initial sequences of the power act can be described in terms of an instrumentality view of motivation. The perception that others mediate desirable outcomes for the powerholder provides the incentive to take action. The expectancy of successful influence, the second major variable in instrumentality theories, is provided by the kind and amount of resources available. The more resources available, the higher the expectations of successful influence. As the individual proceeds from step to step in the power sequence, the expectancies of success and the incentives for influencing the target take on new values. Further, the region of inhibition adds negative values to the instrumentality model. Several other investigators (Pollard and Mitchell, 1972, Tedeschi, Schlenker and Lindskold, 1972) have also noted the usefulness of some form of instrumentality theory for explaining the power act. An added value of the present analysis is that it considers how the availability of resources can shape the initial expectations of the powerholder, [1974, p. 97.]

Comment

Kipnis has presented an especially incisive and cogent view of power from the powerholder's perspective. In doing so he has called our attention to the centrality of the powerholder in acts of influence, an element long disregarded in our concentration on the effects of a successful attempt to influence another, by securing compliance, conformity, or obedience. Kipnis' theory is a hedonic theory that is both behavioral and cognitive. As I have long argued for an amalgamation of these two theoretical approaches, I find Kipnis' work especially appealing. He has given us the most thoughtful and complete account of power analyzed from the powerholder's perspective.

Conflict and Its Resolution

At several points in this chapter we have approached the subject of conflict, but not quite got there. I could deal with conflict in Chapter 8 on aggression, but after discussing compliance conformity, obedience, and the use of power, and before discussing aggression, it seems an ideal time to introduce the subject of conflict. Not all conflicts are aggressive, although some of our best remembered ones were. White (1966) has argued that misperception played a large part in two particularly devastating conflicts, World Wars I and II. At the other extreme of violence, conflict plays a role in bargaining and negotiation. Chapter 2 discussed Deutsch and Krauss's now classic work on bargaining. What do such diverse events as war and interpersonal bargaining have in common?

Brickman (1974) proposes a definition for conflict that stresses the situational aspects of conflict. He says, ". . . conflict exists in situations in which parties must divide or share resources so that, to some degree, the more one party gets, the less the others can have" (Brickman, 1974, p. 1). This has led to the idea of expressing conflict in terms of payoff; that is, a situation is a conflict one when a high payoff for one individual will lead to a low payoff for the other. If you have reread the section on interpersonal bargaining in Chapter 2, you will note that different ways of responding can lead to different payoffs for the competitors.

Conflict Research

The study of conflict involves many ethical considerations. It is abundantly clear that a scientist cannot study violent conflict in the laboratory. There are ways, however, in which conflict can be studied by involving subjects in games. Generally speaking, the games are set up in such a way that payoffs can be based on the amount of competition or cooperation each subject uses in the game. There are several such games in use.

Zero-sum games in which the total payoff in a situation is constant. In a zero sum game the reward one individual receives comes from the possible rewards for the other person. Consider a poker game in which two players are involved. At the end of the game your winnings (or losses) added to your opponents winnings (or losses) equal zero. If there are more than two people in the game, the combination of winnings and losses sum to zero.

There are, however, few situations that are zero-sum games. Even hockey games and other athletic contests are not purely competitive. That is, it is not necessary for one team to lose a point every time the other team gains one. To assure fair competition, rules are generally followed, and there is cooperation as well as competition. Games with both competitive and cooperative aspects are known as mixed-motive games.

THE PRISONER'S DILEMMA GAME

The Prisoner's Dilemma Game (Luce and Raiffa, 1957) is one in which two individuals are put in a particularly difficult situation. As they describe it,

> Two subjects are taken into custody and separated. The district attorney is certain they are guilty of a specific crime, but he does not have adequate evidence to convict them at a trial. He points out to each prisoner that each has two alternatives: to confess to the crime the police are sure they have done or not to confess. If they both do not confess then the district attorney will book them on some very minor trumped-up charge . . . ; if they both confess, they will be prosecuted, (and) he will recommend (a rather severe) sentence; but if one confesses and the other does not, then the confessor will receive lenient treatment for turning state's evidence whereas the latter will get the "book" slapped at him. [Luce and Raiffa, 1957, p. 95.]

To say the least, the situation is a difficult one. If you were in that spot would you confess or refuse to confess? If you confessed, you might receive a light sentence (if your partner doesn't confess). If you don't confess you may have to face only the minor charge, assuming your partner also doesn't confess. As you can see, the situation clearly presents a dilemma. To make the dilemma more concrete let us assume that the minor trumped-up charge carries with it a three-month sentence, the lenient treatment is probation, a rather severe sentence is three years and "the book" slapped at him is 10 years. Figure 7–6 shows the alternatives for you and your partner.

A quick look at Figure 7–6 indicated that your best strategy would be to confess, *if your partner doesn't.* If you do and he does too, you stand to lose three years. However, if you don't confess, you stand to lose three months or 10 years. Thus to cooperate (with your partner) in not confessing, will be most advantageous to both of you. To confess (compete with your partner) carries with it potentially lesser as well as severe consequences. In short, the situation is quite a dilemma.

All of the choices in this particular illustration of the Prisoner's Dilemma game are negative, but this need not be the case. Researchers have changed the payoffs to money or points and used the general format of the game. Figure 7–7 shows the

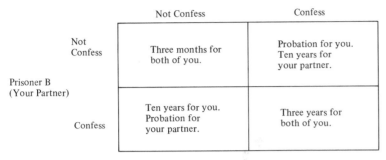

Figure 7-6 A schematic representation of the sentences that can be expected in the Prisoner's Dilemma game.

potential positive payoffs in the game. As you can see, you both gain the most if you cooperate, but you gain most if you are competitive while your partner is cooperative. If, on the other hand, you cooperate while your partner competes, your partner gains more than you do.

Several reviews of the literature (cf. Apfelbaum, 1974; Nemeth, 1972) have indicated that there are four general aspects of the situation that influence whether you cooperate or compete:

Structural Characteristics of the Game. The definition of the Prisoner's Dilemma game demands that the payoff for you when you compete and your partner cooperates be larger than the payoff for you when you both cooperate, which is larger than the payoff for you when you both compete, which is larger than the payoff for you when your partner competes and you cooperate. In Figure 7-7 this is shown as 8 is larger than 5, which is larger than 3, which is larger than 2. However, we could make these numbers minimally different; for example 4, 3, 2, and 1. On the other hand, we could increase the difference between the payoffs. Not surprisingly, the payoffs do influence the competitiveness or cooperativeness of players. This has been demonstrated primarily by comparison with other experimental games (Enzle, Hansen, and Lowe, 1975; Oskamp, 1972).

Why should a change in the relative size of the payoffs change the cooperativeness or competitiveness of individuals? Remember that at least two other people are observing you as you play the game, your partner and the experimenter. Because

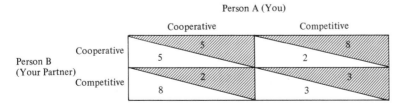

Figure 7-7 Positive payoffs in the Prisoner's Dilemma game. Payoffs in shaded area are yours and in the unshaded area are your partner's.

COOPERATORS AND COMPETITORS

Have you ever met a person who always seems to be competing with you and everyone else? Have you ever met a person who always seems to cooperate with you and everyone else? Kelley and Stahelski (1970) have argued that there are two stable types of individuals, cooperative and competitive personalities. These types of individuals have different views of what they can expect from others, competition or cooperation. Cooperators see the world as comprised of both cooperators and competitors whereas competitors view the world as being comprised mainly of competitors. Kelley and Stahelski reported evidence from a Prisoners Dilemma Game (PDG) supporting their idea. Miller and Holmes (1975) argued that the PDG was an impoverished atmosphere to test such an idea because of limited choices. That is, subjects can only cooperate or compete. Miller and Holmes expanded the choices to allow a subject who expected a competitive choice from the opponent to make a defensive (rather than competitive or cooperative choice) choice and receive a small positive outcome. The results from the expanded PDG showed that subjects expected their opponents to share their own goal orientation; that is competitors expected others to compete and cooperators expected others to cooperate.

Schlenker and Goldman (1978) report an experiment in which they attempted to sort out the elements in the argument just cited. Recall that with regard to competitive individuals there seems to be little argument to the idea that they view others as being competitive. What is in dispute is the orientation of the cooperative person. Kelley and Stahelski argue that cooperators see a wide range of potentially cooperative and competitive individuals whereas Miller and Holmes argue that cooperators expect other cooperators.

Schlenker and Goldman utilized cooperative and competitive subjects (males and females) in one of three PDG matrices. In one, the payoffs were such that cooperation was encouraged, another was one designed to encourage competition and one intermediate matrix. They found that, as Kelley and Stahelski predicted, competitive subjects expected most opponents to be competitive whereas cooperative opponents ex-

pected a wide range of cooperative and competitive opponents. In direct opposition to Miller and Holmes' suggestion, cooperative subjects expected about one third of the population to cooperate and two thirds to compete.

With regard to cooperative and competitive behavior, subjects were more cooperative when they played with the cooperative rather than competitive outcomes, when they had chosen a cooperative goal, and when they faced a cooperative opponent. There were, however, indications that the opponents' strategy had a greater influence on players, regardless of whether they were cooperators or competitors, than Kelley and Stahelski would predict.

In general, we can say that there are cooperators and competitors in the world and that they differ in how they view the world. Competitors are somewhat inflexible in that they see a malevolent world and mistake cooperators for competitors no matter what the context. Cooperators are more flexible in that they recognize the diversity of dispositions that exist in other people. They are influenced by their partner's behavior and are affected by the situation and the behavior of their opponent.

If these behavioral characteristics generalize to situations in everyday life, then there are some important ramifications for all of us. First, are you a cooperator or a competitor? If you are a competitor, you probably assume everyone is competing when some are not. If you are a cooperator, you may be more accurate in your judgment of others and respond more appropriately.

References

Kelley, H. H., and A. J. Stahelski. Social interaction basis of cooperators' and competitors' beliefs about others. *Journal of Personality and Social Psychology,* 1970, *16,* 66–91.

Miller, D. T., and J. G. Holmes. The role of situational restrictiveness on self-fulfilling prophecies: A theoretical and empirical extension of Kelley and Stahelski's triangle hypothesis. *Journal of Personality and Social Psychology,* 1975, *31,* 661–73.

Schlenker, B. R., and H. J. Goldman. Cooperators and competitors in conflict. *Journal of Conflict Resolution,* 1978, *22,* 393–410.

excessive competitiveness is not a socially desirable characteristic, many of us will not wish to appear overly competitive for small payoffs.

Characteristics of Players. Women tend to be more cooperative in the Prisoner's Dilemma game than do men. With the exception of this individual differences variable, there appear to be no other enduring personality variables that influence cooperation or competition in experimental games. On the other hand, self-expressed competitors expected their opponents to be competitive, whereas self-expressed cooperators expected their opponents to cooperate (Kelley and Stahelski, 1970). Motivating instructions also have a large effect on players; competitive instructions increase competition whereas cooperative instructions decrease competition (Deutsch, 1960).

Characteristics of Opponents. By now it should be clear that your opponent is quite important in the Prisoner's Dilemma game. A consistent opponent can give you a good idea of what the rewards or punishments will be for each decision you might make. There appear to be two specific opponent characteristics that bring out the competitiveness in most people. A study by Marlowe, Gergen and Doob (1966) indicates that people tend to be more competitive when their opponent is quite self-confident and there will be future interactions. Players are most competitive, however, against self-effacing opponents who will not be seen again. The moral of this study seems to be that to obtain cooperation you should seem neither too egotistical nor too weak.

Opponent's Tactics. In the Prisoner's Dilemma your opponent can adopt one of three tactics; unconditional cooperation, unconditional competition, or a combination of cooperative and competitive moves. An opponent's tactics are quite influential in the tactics you adopt. Seemingly, subjects are willing to exploit a cooperative opponent if they are sure that the opponent won't retaliate. Shure, Meeker, and Hansford (1965) found that subjects who played an avowed pacifist who refused to make competitive moves and who refused to use an unrelated punisher (electric shock) when he was being exploited, exploited him even more.

The combination of cooperative and competitive responses is known as the contingent strategy, because the experimenter programs the game so that the opponent's response is based on your immediately preceding response. Let us assume that the game runs for 20 trials. On the first trial you make a cooperative response. In the contingent strategy, your opponent will make a cooperative move on the second trial. The contingent strategy produces the highest level of cooperation across a variety of situations (Nemeth, 1972).

One major criticism of the Prisoner's Dilemma game is that it is unrealistic in that the players are not allowed to communicate with each other. In the Trucking Game discussed in Chapter 2, when neither player had a threat (competitive edge), the joint payoff of both companies was highest. When only one company had a threat, the joint payoff of the two compaines fell below the joint payoff when neither had a threat, although the company with the threat did better than the company without it. When both companies had a threat, the joint payoffs fell dramatically. The moral of the story seems to be that cooperation is more beneficial than competition, at least in the situations these games portray.

Comment

As the results of research on games proceed, it becomes clearer that cooperation seems more productive, at least in certain situations. Without a doubt, the societies in Canada and the United States are interdependent. By that I mean that I, for instance, must rely on others to provide food, shelter, transportation, and so forth. In return I provide parts of an educational opportunity for many individuals, knowledge gained from research, and so forth. It is obvious that things go more smoothly if I cooperate with those other individuals in society with whom I interact.

At the same time, however, business in capitalistic countries such as Canada and the United States is competitive. That is, Company A tries to sell its products to more consumers than Company B can, while Company B is doing the same thing. If the truth were known, I suspect that the top officers in both company A and Company B would be delighted if their competitor sold so little that it was forced to close its doors. When competitiveness is taken to the level of nations, one of the outcomes is war. That this state of affairs has been so predominant in human history is one of the great tragedies of mankind. On the other hand, the total lack of competitiveness, much like the total lack of aggression (see Chapter 8), also has unpleasant consequences. Cooperativeness seems a more productive strategy in many situations than competitiveness, but both appear necessary. The job of society is to find the optimal mix of the two to keep severe conflict at a minimum.

SUMMARY

1 Conformity generally means going along with group pressures. Conventionalism is distinguished from conformity by the importance of the situation and its meaning to the individual.

2 Preconformity research dealt with the change in people's estimates in an ambiguous situation when others disagreed with them.

3 Asch placed subjects in a situation in which very unambiguous choices had to be made, but others in the group made incorrect choices. Crutchfield expanded on Asch's studies, and people complied about 35 percent of the time. Social comparison theory, attribution theory, and the sex of the individual have been used to explain this important phenomenon.

4 Compliance occurs when a person is influenced by another because the complier hopes to achieve a favorable reaction from the other individual. Several explanations for why people comply have been suggested, including guilt and the effects of getting a "foot-in-the-door," and equity theory.

5 Milgram studied obedience in what is now a classic series of experiments. He found that people are willing to obey authority even when it seemingly means seriously hurting another person. The proximity of the subject and experimenter, certain personality characteristics, the sex of the subject, and group pressures all influence the amount of obedience shown.

6 Milgram's work has been criticized on ethical grounds, not because it was done but

because it was continued after experimenters knew that it caused great distress to subjects. Milgram contends that subjects did not wish they had not been in the experiment and that this is of great importance.

7 The exercise of power is attempting to make a target do something he or she would not ordinarily do. Powerholders have long been ignored in social psychology until Kipnis developed a theory that includes whom the powerholder will influence, the kinds of demands made, and what resources will be invoked to bolster power demands.

8 Kipnis views power as a motivation that arises when an individual experiences an aroused need state that can only be satisfied by inducing appropriate behavior in others and is reduced when this appropriate behavior is performed.

9 Conflict research has been carried out primarily in the context of experimental games. It appears that situational variables, the players' and the opponents' characteristics, and the opponents' tactics influence cooperation or competition in a player.

GLOSSARY

Authoritarians Individuals who show a pattern of personality traits that emphasize conformity and compliance.

Autokinetic Phenomenon A stationary point of light that appears to move in total darkness.

Compliance State of being influenced by another because the complier hopes to achieve a favorable reaction from the other person.

Conformity Going along with group pressure.

Conventions Generally agreed-upon modes of behavior.

Foot-in-the-door Technique The compliance strategy that precedes a large request with a small one to obtain cooperation.

Identification Accepting influence from another person or group in order to establish or maintain a satisfying self-defining relationship to the other.

Internalization Accepting influence in order to maintain the congruence of a person's actions and beliefs with his or her value system.

Obedience Behaving in conformity with orders given by an authority figure.

Power The ability to make a target do something he or she would not ordinarily do.

Region of Inhibition The inhibition of the power act by reduction of the power motive or group norms.

Social Comparison Theory A theory that asserts there is a drive within each one of us to evaluate our own abilities and potentials and that we make this evaluation by comparing ourselves to others.

Social Influence The pressure exerted on an individual or group to alter his or her attitudes or behavior.

Social Norms The attitudes, values, and opinions that are acceptable and therefore define acceptable behavior in a social group.

Social Power Social influence, with the pressure being exerted by one person or a small group of people.

Adorno, T. W., E. Frankel-Brunswick, D. Levinson, and R. Sanford. IV. *The Authoritarian Personality.* New York: Harper & Row, Publishers, 1950.

Apfelbaum, E. On conflicts and bargaining. In L. Berkowitz (Ed.), *Advances in experimental social psychology.* Vol. 7. New York: Academic Press, Inc., 1974. Pp. 103–156.

Asch, S. E. *Social Psychology.* New York: Prentice-Hall Inc., 1952.

Baumrind, D. Some thoughts on ethics of research: After reading Milgram's "Behavioral study of obedience." *American Psychologist,* 1964, *19,* 421–23.

Berger, L. S. Use of power, Machiavellianism, and involvement in a simulated industrial setting. Unpublished doctoral dissertation, Temple University, 1972.

Brickman, P. Role structures and conflict relationships. In P. Brickman (Ed.), *Social Conflict.* Lexington, Mass.: D. C. Heath & Co., 1974, 1–33.

Carlsmith, J. M., and A. E. Gross. Some effects of guilt on compliance. *Journal of Personality and Social Psychology,* 1969, *11,* 240–44.

Cartwright, D. Influence, leadership, and control. In J. G. March (Ed.), *Handbook of Organizations.* Chicago: Rand McNally & Company, 1965, pp. 1–47.

Christie, R. Authoritarianism re-examined. In R. Christie and M. Jahoda (Eds.), *Studies in the Scope and Method of "The Authoritarian Personality."* Glencoe, Ill.: The Free Press, 1954, 123–96.

——— and F. Geis. *Studies in Machiavellianism.* New York: Academic Press, Inc., 1970.

Clark, K. B. The pathos of power, *American Psychologist,* 1971, 26, 1047–1057.

Crutchfield, R. S. A new technique for measuring individual differences in conformity to group judgments. *Proceedings of the Invitational Conference on Testing Problems.* Princeton, N.J.: Educational Testing Service, 1954 (a), 69–74.

———. The measurement of individual conformity to group opinion among officer personnel. Institute of Personality Assessment and Research, University of California, Berkeley, *Research Bulletin,* 1954 (b).

———. Conformity and character. *American Psychologist,* 1955, *10,* 191–98.

———. Conformity and creative thinking. Paper delivered at Symposium on Creative Thinking. University of Colorado, 1958.

———. Personal and situational factors in conformity to group pressure. *Acta Psychologica,* 1959, *15,* 386–88.

———. Detrimental effects of conformity pressures on creative thinking. *Psychological Beiträge,* 1962, *6,* 463–71.

Deutsch, M. The effect of motivational orientation upon threat and suspicion. *Human Relations,* 1960, *13,* 122–39.

——— and H. Gerard. A study of normative and informational social influences upon individual judgment. *Journal of Abnormal and Social Psychology,* 1955, *51,* 629–36.

Elms, A. C., and S. Milgram. Personality characteristics associated with obedience and defiance toward authoritative command. *Journal of Experimental Research in Personality,* 1966, *1,* 282–89.

Enzle, M. E., R. D. Hansen, and C. A. Lowe. Causal attribution in the mixed-motive game. Effects of facilitory and inhibitory environmental forces. *Journal of Personality and Social Psychology,* 1967, *7,* 372–86.

Festinger, L. A theory of social comparison processes. *Human Relations,* 1954, *1,* 117–40.

Foa, U. G., and E. B. Foa. *Societal Structures of the Mind.* Charles C Thomas, Publisher, 1974.

——— and ———. *Resource Theory of Social Exchange.* Morristown, N.J.: General Learning Press, 1975.

Freedman, J. L., and S. C. Fraser. Compliance without pressure. The foot-in-the-door technique. *Journal of Personality and Social Psychology,* 1966, *4,* 195–202.

Galbraith, J. K. *The New Industrial State.* Boston: Houghton Mifflin Company, 1967.

Goodstadt, B., and D. Kipnis. Situational influences on the use of power. *Journal of Applied Psychology,* 1970, *54,* 201–207.

Gurr, T. R. *Why Men Rebel.* Princeton, N.J.: Princeton University Press, 1970.

Hathaway, S. R., and T. C. McKinley. *The Minnesota Multiphasic Personality Inventory Manual.* Revised. New York: The Psychological Corporation, 1951.

Homans, G. C. *Social Behavior: Its Elementary Forms.* New York: Harcourt Brace Jovanovich, Inc., 1961.

Kelley, H. H., and A. Stahleski. The inference of intention from moves in the prisoner's dilemma game. *Journal of Experimental Social Psychology,* 1970, *6,* 409–419.

Kelman, H. C. Process of opinion change. *Public Opinion Quarterly,* 1961, *25,* 57–78.

———. The role of the group in the induction of therapeutic change. *International Journal of Group Psychotherapy,* 1963, *13,* 399–432.

———. Further thoughts on the processes of compliance identification and internalization. In J. T. Tedeschi (Ed.), *Perspectives on Social Power.* Chicago, Aldine Publishing Company, 1974. Pp. 125–71.

——— and L. H. Lawrence. Assignment of responsibility in the case of Lt. Calley: preliminary report on a national survey. *Journal of Social Issues,* 1972, *28,* 177–212.

Kiesler, C. A. Group pressure and conformity. In J. Mills (Ed.), *Experimental Social Psychology.* New York: Macmillan Publishing Co., Inc., 1969. Pp. 233–306.

Kilham, W., and L. Mann. Level of destructive obedience as a function of transmitter and executant roles in the obedience paradigm. *Journal of Personality and Social Psychology,* 1974, *20,* 696–702.

Kipnis, D. The powerholders. In J. T. Tedeschi (Ed.), *Perspectives on Social Power.* Chicago: Aldine, 1974. Pp. 82–122.

———. *The powerholders,* Chicago, Ill.: The University of Chicago Press, 1976.

——— and W. P. Lane. Self-confidence and leadership. *Journal of Applied Psychology,* 1962, *46,* 291–95.

Leventhal, G. S., and D. W. Lane. Sex, age, and equity behavior. *Journal of Personality and Social Psychology,* 1970, *15,* 312–16.

Levy, L. Studies in conformity behavior. A methodological note. *Journal of Psychology,* 1960, *50,* 39–41.

Luce, R. D., and H. Raiffa. *Games and decisions.* New York: John Wiley & Sons, Inc., 1957.

McClelland, D. C. The two faces of power. *Journal of Interpersonal Affairs,* 1969, *24,* 141–54.

Marlowe, D., K. J. Gergen, and A. N. Doob. Opponent's personality expectation of social interaction and interpersonal bargaining. *Journal of Personality and Social Psychology,* 1966, *3,* 206–213.

Megargee, E. L. The role of inhibition in the assessment and understanding of violence. In J. L. Singer (Ed.). *The Control of Aggression and Violence.* New York: Academic Press, Inc., 1971.

Michener, H. A., and M. R. Burt. Legitimacy as a base of social influence. In J. T. Tedeschi (Ed.), *Perspectives on Social Power.* Chicago, Aldine Publishing Company, 1974. Pp. 310–48.

Milgram, S. Dynamics of obedience. Washington: National Science Foundation, January 25, 1961 (mimeo).

———. Behavioral studies in obedience. *Journal of Abnormal and Social Psychology,* 1963, *67,* 371–78.

————. Group pressure and action against a person. *Journal of Abnormal and Social Psychology,* 1964, *69,* 137–43.

————. Some conditions of obedience and disobedience to authority. *Human Relations,* 1965 (a), *18,* 57–76.

————. Liberating effects of group Pressure. *Journal of Personality and Social Psychology,* 1965 (b), *1,* 127–34.

————. The perils of obedience. *Harper's Magazine,* December 1973.

————. *Obedience to Authority.* New York: Harper & Row, Publishers, 1974.

————. Subject reaction: The neglected factor in the ethics of experimentation. Hasting Center Report, October 1977, 19–23.

Nemeth, C. A critical analysis of research utilizing the prisoner's dilemma paradigm for the study of bargaining. In L. Berkowitz (Ed.), *Advances in Experimental Social Psychology.* Vol. 6, New York: Academic Press, Inc., 1972. Pp. 203–234.

————, J. Endicott, and J. Wachtler. From the 50s to the 70s: Women in jury deliberations. *Sociometry,* 1976, *39,* 293–304.

Oskamp, S. Effects of programmed strategies on cooperation in the prisoner's dilemma and other mixed-motive games. In L. Wrightsman, J. O'Conner, and N. Baker (Eds.), Cooperation and competition: Readings on mixed-motive games. Monterey, Calif.: Brooks/Cole, 1972. Pp. 147–89.

Pepitone, A. The role of justice in independent decision-making. *Journal of Experimental Social Psychology,* 1971, *7,* 144–56.

Pliner, P., H. Hart, J. Kohl, and D. Saari. Compliance without pressure: Some further data on the foot-in-the-door technique. *Journal of Experimental Social Psychology,* 1974, *10,* 17–22.

Pollard, W. E., and T. R. Mitchell. A decision theory analysis of social power. *Psychological Bulletin,* 1972, *78,* 433–46.

Ross, L., G. Bierbrauer, and S. Hoffman. The role of attribution processes in conformity and dissent: Revisiting the Asch situation. *American Psychologist,* 1976, *31,* 148–57.

Sherif, M. An experimental study of stereotypes. *Journal of Abnormal and Social Psychology,* 1935, *29,* 371–75.

————. *The Psychology of Social Norms.* New York: Harper & Row, Publishers, 1936.

Shure, G. H., R. J. Meeker, and E. A. Hansford. The effectiveness of pacifist strategies in bargaining games. *Journal of Conflict Resolution,* 1965, *9,* 106–117.

Sistrunk, F., and J. W. McDavid. Sex variable in conforming behavior. *Journal of Personality and Social Psychology,* 1971, *17,* 200–207.

Tedeschi, J. T. Introduction and overview. In J. T. Tedeschi (Ed.), *Perspectives on Social Power.* Chicago, Aldine Publishing Company, 1974, pp. 1–15.

————, B. R. Schlenker, and S. Lindskold. The exercise of power and influence: The source of influence. In J. T. Tedeschi (Ed.), *The Social Influence Process.* Chicago: Aldine Publishing Company, 1972, pp. 287–345.

Veroff, J., and J. Veroff. Reconsideration of a measure of power motivation. *Psychological Bulletin,* 1972, *78,* 279–91.

Walster, E., E. Berscheid, and G. W. Walster. Reactions of an exploiter to the exploited: compensation justification, or self-punishment? In J. R. Macaulay and L. Berkowitz (Eds.), *Altruism and Helping Behavior.* New York: Academic Press, Inc., 1970.

White, R. K. Misperception as a cause of two world wars. *Journal of Social Issues,* 1966, *22,* 1–19.

8

Aggression and Violence

    When power fails, can aggression be far behind? This question is a pertinent one, and realistic in its recognition of how events take place. If power is used to attempt to make a target do something he or she would not ordinarily do, what is the next step when power fails? Do we aggress, or at the very least, contemplate aggression? And just what is meant by aggression? In contemporary usage the meaning of the word is imprecise. A salesman may be labeled aggressive for actively pursuing an order; a nation may be viewed as aggressive for actively pursuing the acquisition of another nation's territory; a woman may be thought of as aggressive for pursuing her right to an equal day's pay for an equal day's work. Even though popular usage may employ the same word to describe all these events, it seems very imprecise to label all three events aggression.

During the 1970s, part of the confusion surrounding *aggression* was alleviated by the introduction into popular books and the public mind of the concept of assertiveness. Prior to a distinction being made between being assertive and being aggressive, there was a tendency to consider any reaction to unjust treatment or any pursuit of one's own ends as aggressive. Psychologists had for many years defined aggression more narrowly than had popular usage, but nevertheless there was a great deal of confusion concerning the definition of aggression.

Psychological Definitions of Aggression

Even when we dispose of popular misconceptions, however, aggression is still not easy to define. How are we to delimit the meaning of the term in a meaningful way?

Dollard, Doob, Miller, Mowrer, and Sears (1939), whose theory of aggression occupies a prominent historical position in theorizing about aggression, define it as "any sequence of behavior, the goal response of which is the injury of the person toward whom it is directed." It is certainly not unusual to define aggression in terms of injurious intent, and most subsequent theorizing has emphasized this element (Berkowitz, 1962; Feshback, 1970; Sears, Maccoby, and Levin, 1957). Buss (1971), on the other hand, defines aggression as a response delivering noxious stimulation to another organism. Bandura (1973) argues that aggression is a complex event and defining it must take into consideration not only injurious intent but *social judgments* that determine which injurious acts are labeled as aggressive.

This brief look at the different ways in which aggression is defined is not meant to be exhaustive; it is meant to point out that psychologists have had still another disagreement about what they are studying. If aggression is action taken with injurious intent, then is a dentist being aggressive when he or she drills your tooth to fill a cavity? Is a doctor being aggressive when yanking your finger, which has been "jammed," back into place? Contemporary society considers these two to be helping, not hurting, professions, and the actions of dentists and doctors, as such, are not viewed as aggressive. If we define aggression as Buss has, that is the delivery of noxious stimulation to another organism, we face the same problems we did with the injurious intent definition and more. It is quite simple to deliver noxious stimulation to an organism without even knowing it or being aware of what you have done. For example, in a baseball game a hitter, while merely trying to get a hit, can hit a line drive that delivers quite serious noxious stimulation to the infielder it hits in the chest.

Some writers (Berkowitz, 1965; Feshback, 1970) have attempted to deal with the problem of aggression by dividing aggression into two categories, instrumental aggression and hostile aggression. Instrumental aggression is aimed at securing rewards other than the victim's suffering. Thus, terrorist activities, war, or any other act whose major purpose is something beyond the injury inflicted on individuals is viewed as instrumental aggression. For example, Hiroshima was largely demolished by the atom bomb in order to achieve a quick end to World War II, thus it would seem to be instrumental aggression. Hostile aggression is aimed solely at inflicting injury or harm on others. Apparently, the only difference in the two is whether the aggression is intended to achieve power, status, peace, and so forth, or whether it is intended only to achieve the suffering of another person.

"Terribly complicated" is the best way to describe this process of defining aggression. That is why no one has achieved a very satisfying definition by the process. It should be pointed out that aggression must not only be viewed from the victims' and the aggressors' points of view, but from society's vantage point as well. For example, what is the "bone-crushing" tackle that is delivered in a football game? Is it aggression? In certain instances it is more harmful to the recipient than a bullet that only delivers a flesh wound. Even though the 1975–76 season in the National Hockey League brought about some criminal charges and fines for violence in Toronto, the harm done to players in sporting contests has not generally been placed in the same category as shooting, cutting, or hitting another person in a fight outside of a sports arena. This very fact, however, points out still more of the difficulty in defining aggression.

Bandura (1973, p. 5) explains well:

For purposes of the present discussion, aggression is defined as behavior that results in personal injury and in destruction of property. The injury may be psychological (in the form of devaluation or degradation) as well as physical. Although this formulation delimits the phenomenon in a meaningful way, it should be made clear that aversive effects cannot serve as the sole defining characteristic of aggression. Individuals who hurt others while performing a socially sanctioned function . . . would not be considered as acting in an aggressive manner. Nor would bulldozer operators destroying condemned buildings to make way for new construction be charged with committing aggressive acts. Conversely, some forms of conduct would be judged aggressive even though no personal injury or property damage occurred. A person who attempted to hurt another individual by firing a gun at him or by striking him with a lethal object, but who happened to miss the unsuspecting victim would be judged as behaving violently. . . .

In social learning theory, aggression is treated as a complex event including behavior that produces injurious and destructive effects as well as social labelling processes. According to this view, a full explanation of aggression must consider both *injurious behavior* and *social judgments* that determine which injurious acts are labelled as aggressive.

Possibly it will be easier to understand what aggression is if we understand its source. That is, is aggression innate, learned, or a combination of the two? There is disagreement about this aspect of the phenomenon also, with some psychologists arguing that humans are instinctively aggressive and others arguing that aggression is learned.

Instinctual Theories of Aggression

Instinctual theories of aggression are firmly grounded in biological determinism, specifically the survival of the fittest. The argument goes something like this. In earlier evolutionary days, aggression had high survival value, and through natural selection the most aggressive individuals survived and passed these tendencies on to their offspring. Over the years, the environment has changed more rapidly than have humans' aggressive tendencies, and aggression has not retained its survival value. Quite the contrary, with the rapid increase in the technology of destruction, instinctive aggressive tendencies threaten the very existency of the human race. Instinctive aggression still exists, however, and for these theorists is a fact of life that must be dealt with.

Instinctual explanations of aggression are relatively numerous; however, two should suffice to give you the flavor of the approach.

Psychoanalytic Theory of Aggression

In his early discussions of aggression, Freud (1920) believed that aggression was a "primary response" to the thwarting of pain-avoiding or pleasure-seeking behavior. His view of aggression changed markedly, however, as he changed his instinctual theory of motivation (Freud, 1922, 1933). The major change in regard to aggression came when he postulated two opposing sets of instincts. Life instincts (Eros) were aimed at prolonging and enhancing life. Instincts such as the development of positive emotional ties between individuals, and other pleasurable motives, were part of the life instincts. Death instincts (Thanatos) constantly attempted to destroy life *within* the organism, and aggression is the turning of the death instincts outwards. This revision of motivating forces made aggression an inborn drive rather than a consequence of the thwarting of pleasurable intentions.

The social implications of such a change in emphasis are enormous. Humans are seen as the battleground between life instincts and death instincts, and even though the intensity and form of aggression can be altered, it is a condition of humanity that must be recognized. Freud reiterated his view that aggression is instinctual and the destructiveness associated with it cannot be eliminated in an exchange of letters with Einstein (Freud, 1950). In fact, to eliminate aggressiveness, in Freud's view, would be detrimental to the individual. This state of affairs comes about because if the energy in the death instinct is not turned outward, it will be utilized in self-destruction (Freud, 1933). The individual is the scene of a motivational battle, and if one does not aggress then one will be killed, not by others but by oneself.

This rather depressing picture of human nature is only one of the reasons that the idea of Thanatos was never taken too seriously by others, even by strongly partisan psychoanalysts. The notion that individuals harbor an instinct that is constantly trying to kill them and that it must be turned outward to protect the individual's life is neither appealing nor scientifically credible. Today, most psychoanalysts have compromised with Freud's viewpoint (Gillespie, 1971). They still treat aggression as an instinctual drive but reject the self-directed death instinct.

Ethological Theories of Aggression

Ethology is the study of instincts and action patterns common to all members of a species in their natural habitat, or more precisely "the biology of behavior" (Eibl-Eibesfeldt, 1975). Aggression, from at least two ethologists' points of view (Lorenz, 1966; Eibl-Eibesfeldt, 1975), is basically instinctual. Ethologists have spent the majority of their energies in the study of species other than humans, although "*Human* ethology (I. Eibl-Eibesfeldt and H. Hass, 1966) is emerging as a new field of research" (Eibl-Eibesfeldt, 1975, p. 8). Thus, much of the evidence cited by ethologists comes from studies of other species and their behavior.

Lorenz, like Freud, postulates an instinctual system of aggression. This system generates its own source of energy regardless of the external stimulation the organism receives. That is, the urge or drive to aggress builds up and is finally released by an appropriate fighting stimulus. If the urge toward aggression builds up to a certain level and no appropriate releasing stimulus is present, the organism will attack an inappropriate stimulus. For example, certain male tropical fish attack only male fish of the same species, leaving all other fish alone. This occurs because these fish compete with each other for mates and food. If all but one male is removed from the aquarium, the one male will now attack males of another species that he ordinarily would have ignored. In addition, if all fish except a female of his species are removed from the aquarium, the fish will eventually attack the female. Lorenz contends that the increase in the urge to aggress finally reaches the point where the fish will attack an inappropriate target.

Thus, since this fighting urge or drive continues to build up until it is relieved by a releasing stimulus, it is self-generating rather than reactive to external stimuli. This conclusion has certain implications for the study of aggression, not the least of which is a very pessimistic one—that is, that little can be done to alleviate aggression. Aggression, according to Lorenz, has very positive consequences in subhuman species. Fighting disperses populations widely over habitable areas, allowing for full and efficient use of the food supplies. It produces selective breeding of strong members of the species. Aggression in subhumans is seen by Lorenz as a beneficial urge, because there have also developed innate mechanisms within species to prevent them from destroying members of their own species. For example, Lorenz contends that defeated wolves turn their assailants off by exposing their necks to the victor, who then does not kill the defeated wolf. Additionally, animals aggress toward each other in highly ritualized ways that often determine the victor by endurance rather than by serious injury.

Lorenz argues that humans are endowed with the same fighting instinct as lower animals, but that there is a difference. In humans the innate urge to aggress is fully developed, but the corresponding innate inhibitions against killing members of the same species are absent. In the so-called lower animals, natural selection ensured that animals with potentially powerful destructive potential evolved strong aggression-inhibiting mechanisms to prevent extermination of the species. We may assume that those powerful species that did not develop such inhibitions did not survive because they killed each other off. However, because *Homo sapiens* was a harmless creature, without the physical ability to destroy large prey, inhibitory mechanisms never developed. Human intelligence, however, provided the species with most destructive weapons for which there are no innate predators. Thus, humans did develop the innate drive to aggress, but did not develop the innate inhibitory mechanisms that would preclude the destruction of the species. Therefore, human intelligence is seen as a potentially devastating element for the species.

CRITICISMS OF INNATE EXPLANATIONS OF AGGRESSION

Bandura (1973, p. 15) disagrees with this point of view when he observes, "The proverbial Martian, viewing the skeletons of dinosaurs in natural history museums and the masses of lively people inhabiting the earth, would undoubtedly leave unconvinced that intelligence and the capacity to learn through experience are necessarily life-shortening attributes."

Bandura and others argue that Lorenz's approach to aggression is too simple—

As Bandura points out, the skeletons of dinosaurs are not impressive proof of the life-shortening capacities of intelligence.

that an instinct to aggress is an inaccurate description and that aggression is learned. It is difficult to argue by analogy from subhuman animal behavior to human behavior. It does appear that Lorenz has made too many assumptions. For example, Barnett (1967) contends that animals do not possess innate signals for stopping attacks and that the stereotyped signals they do use have variable effects. That is, there is no consistent stopping of the attack when one of these signals is used. Schenkel (1967) argues that there is inaccuracy even in Lorenz's widely cited account of the behavior of defeated wolves mentioned earlier. What Lorenz interpreted as a submissive gesture by the vanquished was actually a challenging response by the victor prior to launching a dangerous attack.

Who is correct? One of the best statements I have seen on the matter comes from an ethologist and points out the difficulties of making assumptions about human behavior on the basis of animal behavior.

In man, anger and war, especially when physical damage to the individual results, are considered by psychologists to be aggressive. "Possessive" feelings on the other hand, do not usually have this connotation. For the student of animal behavior, however, not only all situations in which one animal kills or damages another (with, perhaps, the exception of the predator-prey relationships under certain conditions) but all in which threat of some kind or another takes place are considered aggressive. As one can expect, these differences in opinion have led to bitter controversy when comparisons between man and animals have been drawn. [Rasa, p. 214.]

Comment

Instinctual theories of aggression are not the major theoretical positions taken by psychologists today. There are many reasons for this state of affairs, but probably the most persuasive is that instincts tend to explain everything but predict little. By this I mean that it is easy to say that humans are aggressive because they have an instinct to be aggressive. This, however, does not say much about which nation will war on another nation, which child will injure another child, or which individual will point a gun at another person and pull the trigger. The eternal quest of science is the elusive goal of prediction, and instincts predict very little.

Learning Theories of Aggression

A generalized term such as *learning* may have many or few specific meanings. As used here, it is quite broad with many specific ramifications. One such ramification—and an obvious one at that—is that aggression is not innate, rather it is learned. The learning may come from many sources and take many forms, as you will readily see. The basic position, however, disavows the notion that aggression comes from some sort of inborn characteristic and asserts that through experience individuals come to aggress.

The frustration-aggression hypothesis was first proposed by Dollard, Doob, Miller, Mowrer, and Sears (1939) and two of their rather sweeping generalizations attracted considerable attention. They maintain that every frustration produces an instigation to aggression, and more surprisingly, every act of aggression can be traced back to frustration. Since *frustration* was defined as the blocking of an ongoing, goal-directed activity, all aggression must necessarily involve the thwarting of the attainment of a goal. The basic assumption of the hypothesis was that interference with goal-directed behavior evokes an aggressive drive, which, in turn, motivates individuals to aggress. Miller (1941) and Sears (1941) quickly amended the proposition to allow for the possibility that there were other responses to frustration than aggression, but basically the idea still maintained that frustration caused an instigation to aggression.

Berkowitz and his associates are the leading proponents of the frustration-aggression hypothesis although in modified form. Frustration results when a person is prevented from getting what he wants in a given situation. The anticipation of the pleasure in store for him is thwarted. There is a distinction made between frustration and deprivation. According to Berkowitz (1965, 1969) a person is not frustrated simply because he lacks something, (i.e., is deprived of something). The person must want the item and anticipate its pleasures to be frustrated when he does not obtain it. For example, if you really want a car and are thwarted by circumstances from obtaining one, then you are frustrated. However, if public transportation is quite convenient for you, you are concerned about the environment and the quality of air we breathe, and you do not really desire that car, frustration will not occur when you do not get it.

But Berkowitz points out that unavailable things are not the only bases for frustration. If one of your most important beliefs, opinions, or attitudes is challenged, that challenge may also cause frustration. To the extent that you want that cherished belief to be true, frustration may occur when doubt is cast on its validity. For example, some of the strongly held beliefs in the world among certain individuals are religious beliefs. Throughout history people have lived and continue to live celibate lives, have been imprisoned or even died for their religious beliefs. Others have been mocked and ridiculed because they have espoused their beliefs openly by preaching on street corners or chanting, dancing, and singing in unique costumes in public. In the late 1970s there has been an enormous rekindling of interest in religion in Canada and the United States. To the extent that the people involved strongly espouse whatever their religious belief may be, calling those beliefs into question can cause immense frustration.

ANGER

Berkowitz (1962) introduced anger as an intervening variable between frustration and aggression. Berkowitz first argued that anger was primarily released by specific external cues, but he later agreed (Berkowitz, 1969) with the notion that anger may elicit aggression in the absence of external aggressive cues. A number of studies have provided evidence supporting Berkowitz's contention that anger mediates aggression.

Cathedrals such as this one are symbols of the strong religious attitudes many people hold.

Berkowitz and his associates have been extremely active in experimentation on the problem and one of the latest reviews of the subject is found in Berkowitz, 1974.

An example of a typical experiment will be helpful in understanding Berkowitz's experimental approach. Geen and Berkowitz (1966) conducted an experiment in which subjects were angered by a confederate of the experimenter and then observed either a nonaggressive but exciting film, or an aggressive fight film. Subjects were then given the opportunity to deliver electric shocks to another confederate whose name was either the same as or different from the loser in the aggressive fight film. The greatest aggression (shock) was shown toward the confederate whose name was the same as that of the loser in the fight. Berkowitz's approach has been to emphasize the general arousal properties of anger that lead to aggression.

An important element in aggression, however, is the effect of viewing aggression upon potential aggressors. For example, it may be argued that the effects of aggression—injury, harm, blood, or gore—will be so offensive that aggressive tendencies will be reduced; these signs of suffering may serve to induce sympathy for the victim (Berger, 1962). On the other hand, these signs of aggression may enhance the frequency and intensity of such attacks (Feshback, 1964; Sears, 1958). It was precisely because two such different reactions to the same stimuli can occur that Berkowitz proposed anger as an intervening variable in the study of aggression. If the external stimuli present arouse anger, then aggression will likely increase, whereas it may not occur at all if the external stimuli arouse sympathy.

Baron (1971a, 1971b, 1974) demonstrated that exposure to a filmed or live aggressive model increases aggression in subjects who have already been angered.

Baron was primarily concerned with specifying the variables that reduce the effects of aggressive models, but in the process he has shown that angered subjects deliver high-intensity shocks to others when they have observed a model doing the same thing. Thus, his experiments support Berkowitz's contention that anger is an important mediator between frustration and aggression.

An elaboration of one of Baron's studies may be of great value to you in understanding this relatively complex situation. Baron first angered half of his subjects by having a confederate evaluate their proposed solution to the rising crime rate. To assure that anger was aroused, after the subject had proposed a solution to the problem, the confederate made his evaluation by either flashing a light or delivering a shock from 0 to 10 times, with more stimuli (light or shock indicating poorer work). It was explained to both subject and confederate that the confederate was free to use either the light or the shock—that the number of stimuli delivered was the important variable. Subjects who were in the angered condition received an unfavorable written response to their solution and nine shocks. Subjects in the nonangered condition received favorable written responses and one light flash. Subjects in the angered group were incensed by being shocked when they could have received the same information via light flashes, and reported significantly more anger immediately prior to the beginning of the second phase of the experiment.

The second phase of the experiment was conducted in such a way that the subject believed he had the opportunity to deliver shock to the confederate who had earlier evaluated his work. The design of the study was such that some subjects had no aggressive model to follow whereas others did, and some subjects received cues about the amount of pain being felt by the confederate receiving the shock whereas others did not. Shocks were purportedly delivered by the subject to the confederate by a modified Buss "aggression machine" (Buss, 1961), which has 10 switches that can be used by the subject, each successive switch delivering a higher level of shock. The subject was free to select any intensity of shock he desired and to hold the switch down for any duration (thus delivering the shock for the length of time) he chose. Pain cues were delivered by a psycho-autonomic pain meter, which ostensibly measured the amount of pain (e.g., none, mild, moderate, strong, and very strong) the confederate was experiencing, but which in actuality was controlled by the experimenter. Thus angry or nonangry subjects who had an aggressive model or did not have an aggressive model to follow and who either received feedback in the form of pain cues or did not receive feedback were allowed to aggress. Figure 8–1 shows Baron's experimental design.

Baron's results are interesting and straightforward. Subjects who had an aggressive model to follow aggressed more strongly themselves (as measured by both the intensity and duration of shocks delivered). In addition, nonangry subjects decreased their aggressiveness slightly when pain cues were present, whereas angry subjects exhibited slightly increased aggression when pain cues were present. The interaction between the two was significant, indicating that if a person is angered, pain cues given off by the victim tend to increase aggression, whereas if the person is not angered, pain cues from the victim tend to decrease the amount of aggression exhibited. This interaction is shown in Figure 8–2.

One note of caution is in order. As Rule and Nesdale (1976) have pointed out,

	Nonangry Subjects		Angry Subjects	
No Model	Subject did not receive pain cues as he shocked confederates.	Subject did receive pan cues as he shocked confederates.	Subject did not receive pain cues as he shocked confederates.	Subject did receive pain cues as he shocked confederates
Aggressive Model: No pain cues on psychoautonomic pain meter	Neither subject nor model received pain cues as subject shocked confederate.	Subject and model received pain cues as subject shocked confederate.	Neither subject nor model received pain cues as subject shocked confederate.	Subject and model received pain cues as subject shocked confederate.
Aggressive Model: Pain cues on the psychoautonomic pain meter	Neither subject nor model received pain cues as subject shocked confederate and pain cues were seen by S when model shocked confederate.	Subject and model received pain cues as subject shocked confederate and pain cues were seen by S when model shocked confederate.	Neither subject nor model received pain cues as subject shocked confederate and pain cues were seen by S when model shocked confederate.	Subject and model received pain cues as subject shocked confederate and pain cues were seen by S when model shocked confederate.

Figure 8-1 Diagram of Baron's (1974) experimental design.

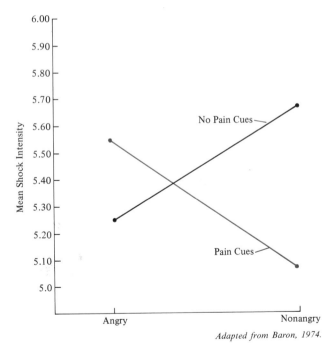

Adapted from Baron, 1974.

Figure 8-2 Mean shock intensity (on a 10-point scale) delivered by angry and nonangry subjects who had information about the amount of pain experienced by the victim (pain cues) or did not have that information (no pain cues).

anger can be expected to mediate aggression when that aggression is hostile; it would not play nearly so important a role in instrumental aggression. That is, when aggression is intended primarily to injure the victim, anger plays an important role. But conditions assumed to induce anger do not increase instrumental aggressive responses (Rule and Hewitt, 1971; Rule and Nesdale, 1974; Rule and Leger, 1976).

EMOTIONAL AROUSAL

In addition to frustration and anger, there are other emotional states of arousal possible. These have typically been referred to as general emotional arousal, and they apparently play an important, yet complex, role in aggression. One of these variables is the cognitive state of the individual, or more simply, to what the individual attributes his or her emotional arousal. According to Rule and Nesdale (1976) general arousal interacts with anger in quite specific ways to affect frustration.

First, angered subjects who are further aroused by nonaggressive stimuli are more aggressive than subjects who are merely angered. For example, Zillman and his associates (Zillman and Bryant, 1974; Zillman et al., 1972) used physical exercise as a source of general arousal and found that when it could be attributed to anger, this nonaggressive general arousal led to increased aggression. Zillman, Johnson, and Day (1974) found that subjects rated the physical exercise as unenjoyable, but this aversiveness was not itself adequate to increase aggressiveness until it was attributed to the anger.

To illustrate Zillman's procedure, Zillman and Bryant (1974) had subjects do one of two tasks immediately prior to the ostensible beginning of the experiment. Half the subjects performed a nonarousing disc-threading task while half the subjects performed strenuous exercise for one minute. During the experiment, which was a competitive game, subjects were told that they could deliver a noise to one earphone of their opponent that could vary from slight to intense and painful, or they could reduce a noise being delivered to the other ear. Immediately after the general arousal manipulation and during the first game, there were no differences between generally aroused (exercised) and nonaroused subjects. At the end of the first game, half the subjects in each group were exposed to an anger-provoking statement by their opponent and half were not. Thus two groups of subjects had experienced general arousal unassociated with the opponent and half of each group had been angered by the opponent. A second game was played and the main dependent measures of aggression were the frequency and intensity of sound delivered to the opponent. Figure 8–3 shows the frequency of delivery of the noxious stimulus. As can be seen in the figure, the aroused subjects were less aggressive toward the opponent when there was no anger provocation present, but in the provoked group the general arousal combined with the anger to make these subjects more aggressive than subjects who had not been aroused but were provoked. Again in this situation we see an interaction—one between general arousal and anger—in determining aggression. Other generally arousing stimuli have been found to interact with anger to produce aggression (Donnerstein, Donnerstein, and Evans, 1975; Konečni, 1975).

One very interesting and important source of emotional arousal and its effects on aggression is sexual arousal. Early research in the area yielded inconsistent results, but later work (Baron, 1976; Donnerstein, Donnerstein, and Evans, 1975) has

ATTACK AND AGGRESSION

Aggression continues to be one of the most fascinating and most important problems that social psychology addresses. It is fascinating because of the various ramifications of aggression. It is important because unbridled aggression is enormously destructive to any society.

Attack has been repeatedly demonstrated to be a potent instigator of aggressive behavior, whereas the reduction in attack leads to a corresponding reduction in aggression. It is not, however, clear why attack is so powerful in instigating aggression. Very possibly the relationship is a complex one and a function of several factors. Previous research has implicated anger and external rewards as diverse as social approval and money.

Dengerink, Schnedler, and Covey (1978) point out that the role of escape from or avoidance of attack has been suggested as a mediator of aggression, but little empirical work has been done in the area. They set out to assess the effects of the possibility of avoiding attack on aggressive behavior, both in response to and in the absence of attack. Attack and aggression were both operationally defined using electric shock. That is, when subjects were shocked, it was considered to be attack and they, in turn, could respond by shocking the person who had attacked them.

Subjects were male undergraduates who were divided into 4 groups. All groups were run with two subjects supposedly interacting. In one group (the control group), subjects received shock on half of 61 trials no matter whether they delivered shock or not. In another group, subjects received a high-intensity shock after delivering shock to the other person and a low-intensity shock after not delivering shock. Another group received shock at a moderate intensity after delivering shock and at a low intensity after not delivering it. The fourth group received a high-intensity shock after delivering shock and a moderate shock after not delivering shock.

After receiving shock, the subjects in the four groups just described did not differ in either the probability that they would shock the person who had attacked them or in the intensity of shock delivered. When no shock (attack) was delivered to the subject, he was more likely to aggress against the other person when the shock did not depend on his response (the group that received shock on half the trials). The other three groups were less likely to aggress after no attack than was this control group.

Another experiment investigated the effect of withdrawing attack after a highly intense aggressive response. In a two-person interaction, subjects were shocked and this shock was withdrawn only after the subject responded with the highest level of shock available to him. A control group was run in which subjects were yoked to the experimental group. (A yoked group's members receive the same treatment that the members of the experimental group receive, regardless of their behavior.) On attack trials there was no difference between the experimental and control groups on either probability or intensity of shock. On no-attack trials, the experimental group was more likely to deliver a higher intensity shock to the attacker.

It appears that aggressive tendencies are highly stimulus-controlled and that aggression in response to attack may be hard to modify. Even when a reduction in aggression would reduce the attack on them, subjects did not lower their aggression compared to controls. On no-attack trials, subjects did respond to the avoidance possibility. Thus, it seems that when we are attacked even the opportunity to avoid further attack does not reduce our own aggression.

Reference

Dengerink, H. A., R. W. Schnedler, and M. K. Covey. Role of avoidance in aggressive responses to attack and no attack. *Journal of Personality and Social Psychology,* 1978, *36,* 1044–1053.

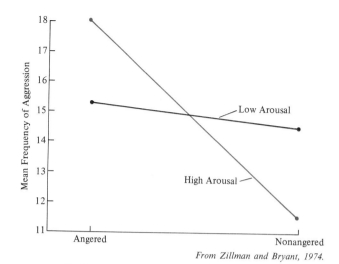

From Zillman and Bryant, 1974.

Figure 8-3 The effects of general arousal and anger on aggression.

indicated a very important relationship between the timing of sexual arousal, the degree of arousal, and aggression. Mildly erotic material (*Playboy* centerfolds) tends to reduce aggression when compared to highly erotic material (e.g., pictures of heterosexual intercourse). Donnerstein, et al. (1975) conclude that mildly erotic stimuli shift the subject's attention from the potential aggression target. Highly erotic stimuli do not reduce aggression and may even increase it. An increase in aggression occurs if the subject first views the highly erotic material and then is angered. If the subject is first angered and then views the highly erotic material, aggression is not affected. Thus, there is a complicated interaction between erotic material and aggression.

This interaction is, however, extremely important. With the increase in erotic explicitness and violence in the media, the relationship between the two takes on added significance. If the arousal associated with erotica is added to the arousal generated by violence to increase aggressive behavior, then the combination of the two may be doubly damaging. We will return to violence and the media later in this chapter.

A second effect of general arousal on aggression occurs when a person's cognitions about the cause of his or her arousal are shifted from the anger to the source of the general arousal. Under these conditions, aggression decreases. For example, Geen, Rakosky, and Pigg (1972) had subjects read a sexually exciting story as they were being shocked by a confederate. Additionally, some subjects were led to believe that their emotional arousal was caused by the shock, others were led to believe the emotional arousal resulted from the story, whereas still other subjects were led to believe their emotional arousal resulted from a drug. Subsequently, subjects who believed their arousal resulted from the drug or the story delivered less intense shocks (aggressed less) than subjects who believed their emotional arousal resulted from the shocks they had received. Furthermore, subjects who thought their arousal resulted from the shock reported more anger than the other subjects. Thus, to the extent that subjects believe their arousal is attributable to stimuli other than attack, their anger and aggression are reduced.

The effect of general arousal on anger and subsequent aggression is not a simple one. As Rule and Nesdale put it,

> In summary, the studies reviewed in the preceding four sections have indicated that in addition to the facilitative effect of general arousal, the specific arousal state of anger is an antecedent of aggressive behavior regardless of whether that anger is precipitated by goal blocking or insult. Moreover, studies have been reviewed which support the view that general arousal from a variety of sources increases a person's aggression if this arousal state is perceived as anger but decreases a person's aggression if his arousal state is attributed to a source other than to a source of anger. [1976, p. 859.]

COMMENT

The frustration-aggression hypothesis has gone through many changes in its explanations of aggression. This, of course, is in the best tradition of science: a theory is proposed and then logical or empirical problems within the theory are discovered. In the course of research into the topic, these disconfirmations of portions of the theory lead to alterations in the theory and its continued refinement. For example, with respect to aggression and the frustration-aggression hypothesis, there have been many refinements. Very early the idea that frustration always leads to aggression was proposed, but was subsequently altered to make the theory more general. The role of anger, however, because of its complex interaction with general arousal, has been harder to pin down. It has taken many different researchers sorting out the loose ends to arrive at our present level of understanding. Undoubtedly, there will be other refinements to the theory as more research is done in this vital area.

Social Learning Theories of Aggression

One thing that both instinctive theories and the frustration-aggression theory have in common is that they all explain aggression in terms of internal forces. Psychoanalytic theory and ethologists assert that there is an aggressive instinct, whereas the frustration-aggression hypothesis is dependent upon a drive state (frustration) to explain aggression. As we have seen, even though there has been a modification of the concept of frustration (from frustration to anger to general emotional arousal), these explanatory constructs all emphasize an internal drive state.

Bandura (1973) has been the most prominent of the social learning theorists who have argued that motivated behavior such as instincts and drives do, indeed, exist—but that they are not very adequate predictors of behavior. For example, it is easy to say that a sadistic murderer had an aggressive drive. How do we know he had an aggressive drive? Because he savagely murdered twelve people. However, the aim of science is to predict behavior not explain it. Bandura would be more interested (as would most of us) in predicting who the murderer was (before he murdered), when, why, and whom he would kill. Such predictive ability is a tall order and one that we are not likely to fill anytime soon.

Bandura argues, however, that we will never fill it if we do not shift the focus of causal analysis from hypothesized instincts and drives to a detailed examination of how the environment affects human functioning. Human behavior must be analyzed in terms of the stimulus events that evoke it and the reinforcing events that maintain it. To many people the whole idea that humans' actions are more externally controlled than previously thought conjures up visions of *1984* and *Brave New World* in which technicians manipulate people at will and all freedom is, at best, illusory.

One of the unfortunate consequences of this environmental approach, which began with Watson and flourishes today under the leadership of Skinner and his associates, is that in an attempt to avoid all "internal" explanations of human functioning, it neglected the cognitive capacity of both humans and other animals. There are today a large group of behaviorists who insist upon examining humans' cognitive contribution to behavior.

According to Bandura there are two ways in which behavior can be acquired: through direct experience or by observing the behavior of others. Direct experience is largely governed by rewarding and punishing outcomes. People are constantly confronted by different situations and act in different ways. If their actions result in pleasant outcomes, then they will probably repeat them. If, however, the outcome is quite unpleasant, it is highly likely that that behavior will not be repeated. For example, if you find yourself in a threatening situation (i.e., being mugged, robbed, or simply accosted by sinister-looking individuals) in the future you may avoid the place in which the unpleasant situation took place.

However, Bandura points out that it is not necessary actually to experience reward or punishment for us to learn; rather we can do it vicariously. Most cities have certain sections into which most of us will not venture alone and on foot at night. Most of us have never experienced an unpleasant event in that section of town—primarily because we have never been there alone and on foot at night—but we have heard about it. Bandura maintains that learning by experience is exceedingly laborious and often hazardous.

There are, according to Bandura, three regulatory functions that control all human social behavior, including aggression. These three are stimulus, reinforcement, and cognitive control.

STIMULUS CONTROL

Events can be rewarding or punishing and the same event can be rewarding to one person and punishing to another. In the earliest years of development, environmental events that are not inherently punishing probably exert little control on infants and young children. But later in development, children come to fear and avoid individuals or situations that are associated with pain or distress, while being attracted to individuals and situations that are associated with pleasure. Social characteristics are learned by subtle and complex mechanisms, many of them vicarious. Prejudice towards minority group members (and others) can occur even though one has never met or seen a member of that minority. For example, Nazis are still probably one of the most disliked groups of people in the world, but how many of you have met a Nazi? Finally, provocative thoughts can evoke certain types of social behavior, often aggressive. Many individuals have mistakenly thought that they were being discriminated against or harmed only to find out that such was not the case.

This is one of those sections of a city most of us would rather not be in after dark.

How many of you, when walking past a group that suddenly explodes with laughter as you arrive, do not seriously entertain the thought that you are the butt of the joke?

Basically, Bandura is arguing that stimuli can come to evoke a response on the part of an individual by being associated with response consequences (either positive or negative). The identical actions will result in markedly different consequences. For example, insulting a physically large or verbally adept aggressor will result in quite different consequences than the same insult aimed at a submissive person. Therefore, most of us pay close attention to cues that signify the probable consequences of our act and, to one degree or another, regulate our activity on the basis of such information.

The most ubiquitous stimulus cue is the action of others. People talk when others talk, leave social functions when others leave, drive above the speed limit in a pack of cars, and look upward when others do so. Modeling influences play an especially important role in the rapid contagion of aggression. If people laugh, talk, and break speeding laws when others do, why should they not aggress? In the summer of 1977, a massive blackout hit New York City and thousands looted, pillaged, and aggressed in other ways. They saw others aggressing and behaved as the models did. Why?

327

Motorists stuck in a pack; as soon as this jam opened up, all sped forward together and broke the speed limit.

Bandura argues that when behaving like others produces outcomes that are rewarding, stimulus cues from models become powerful determinants of behavior. On the other hand, when individuals see others punished for their behavior, dissimilar behavior becomes rewarding and individuals will imitate the dissimilar behavior. To return to the great blackout of 1977, when people saw looters making off with all forms of expensive goods, then it was reinforcing to join them in looting. However, when the police moved into an area and the negative aspects of looting were vicariously experienced by onlookers, the role of a law-abiding, nonlooting citizen took on rewarding characteristics.

Reinforcement Control

Reinforcement control refers to a feedback system that emphasizes reinforcing consequences. There are several reinforcement parameters that are important. For example, persons rewarded every time they perform a behavior (that is, who receive continuous reinforcement) are more likely to become discouraged and quit responding more quickly than those who are rewarded intermittently. If the reward is delayed for any appreciable period of time, it is not so effective in maintaining behavior. Even though many people think of reinforcement in terms of tangible rewards and punishments, much of human social activity is regulated by symbolic rewards. Evaluation (either positive or negative), attention, affection, rejection, and other similar social responses acquire a powerful role in regulating human activity. Particularly in a society in which basic physiological needs are met (food, shelter, clothes, and so on), social reinforcers play an enormous role in regulating behavior.

Even more symbolic, but no less important in regulating behavior, is vicarious reinforcement. It would be highly inefficient if each one of us had to experience the consequences of all possible acts. Fortunately, all of us can profit from the experiences of others. We do not have to experience quicksand, the venom of a poisonous snake, or the consequences of stepping in front of a moving car to learn to avoid these disasters. This ability to learn vicariously has, as you can see, immense survival value.

Another form of reinforcement control, and one that works at the highest level of psychological functioning, is self-reinforcement (Bandura, 1971; Mahoney and Thorensen, 1974; Meichenbaum, 1975a, 1975b). People set certain standards for themselves and respond to their behavior in self-satisfied or self-critical ways, depending upon their own self-imposed demands. For example, the reactions of the various individuals to whom a professor gives a grade of B display enormous variation. To some there seems to be no reaction one way or the other, and I suspect that their self-imposed demands deal with something other than grades. Some students, who seemingly have imposed a self-demand for a C, are elated whereas others (who probably expect only As) are depressed, hostile, or aggressive. The grade is the same, only the self-evaluation differs, and thus the reinforcement consequences differ correspondingly.

When a self-monitored reinforcement system has been established, a particular situation can produce two sets of consequences; external reward for an internally devalued behavior or internal reward for external punishment. For example, consider the case of an architect who has developed a highly ethical system which demands that her work be judged on the basis of merit alone. However, she works in a city where architects who obtain contracts with the local government are expected to "kick-back" a portion of their fee to the party in power. If she refuses to participate in the kick-back scheme, she will receive no contracts. If she does kick back part of her profits, she devalues her own ethical system.

On the other side of the coin are those who are punished for their beliefs. Many minority groups have had to break the law and be punished for their rights. If the external punishments are sufficiently severe, most individuals will refrain from the activities in which they believe. There are, however, individuals whose sense of self-worth is so strong that they will continue no matter what the risk. Thus, there are Martin Luther Kings in the history of every nation.

COGNITIVE CONTROL

Human behavior cannot be fully explained in terms of external inducements and response consequences. Humans' cognitive capacities greatly increase the information that can be derived from experiences and determine whether external events are interpreted accurately. Interestingly enough, what is of most importance in determining behavior oftentimes is not the actual events themselves, but how the individual interprets those events. Even more basic is the fact that a connection must be made between an event and a reinforcer for the reinforcer to be effective.

Popular portrayals of behavioral approaches emphasize an almost magical quality to the susceptibility of behavior to being controlled. In such a scenario, individuals are guided to act (manipulated) without being aware of what is happening to them. There is, however, little evidence to support the notion that meaningful behavior is altered when the cognitive connection between the behavior and the reinforcement is not made. Behavior is altered when the individual is aware of and values the reinforcement consequences associated with that behavior.

Donnerstein and Wilson (1976) report an experiment that reinforces our point about cognitive control quite nicely. Subjects were angered by another person and then given an opportunity to shock that individual using a modified Buss "aggression machine." The opportunity to shock the individual who had angered him was afforded the subject by a learning experience in which he was purportedly the teacher and the individual who had angered him was the learner. A second group was run in which the subject was not angered. Thus, there were an angered and a nonangered group of teachers as the learning task started. A second variable, noise, was introduced. Half of each group of subjects (teachers) received 1-second noise bursts through earphones approximately every four seconds as they were teaching the learner and delivering shocks for each incorrect response. Half of the noise subjects received high and half low intensity noise. The subject could select the intensity of shock he wished to deliver. Thus there were four groups; angered high-intensity noise, angered low-intensity noise, nonangered high-intensity noise, and nonangered low-intensity noise. The dependent variable was the intensity of shock delivered to the learner.

Angered subjects delivered more intense shocks than did nonangered subjects. Furthermore, noise intensity did not affect the level of shock delivered by nonangered subjects but greatly increased the intensity of shock delivered by angered subjects. Here again, there appears to be an increase in aggression caused by an irrelevant stimulus (noise). That is, the learner had angered the subject, but the learner was not responsible for the noise. Nevertheless, the level of aggression increased with increased noise.

Donnerstein and Wilson report a second experiment that is even more appropriate for our discussion of cognitive control. In this study subjects were subjected to the noise before they were angered and then three groups were formed. The first was a group that received high-intensity noise while performing a math test before they were angered. The second received noise during the experiment but were told they could control the noise if they so desired. That is, they were told they could shut off the noise, but were asked not to since the experimenter needed subjects who participated in the experiment with the noise on. None of the subjects terminated the noise. The third was a no-noise control group. The sequence of events in this experiment was noise while doing a math test (either no noise, high-intensity noise that could be controlled, or high-intensity noise that could not be controlled), anger arousal (either angered or not), and then the learning task in which the subject acts as teacher. As before, the dependent variable was the intensity of the shock delivered by the subject.

Angered subjects delivered a higher intensity of shock than did nonangered subjects. Noise did not affect nonangered subjects but it did affect angered subjects in a most interesting way. The angered subjects who did not have control over the noise delivered more intense shocks than did either of the other two angered groups (noise with control and no noise).

Recall, now that the angered subjects in the two noise groups (control and no control) both received the same amount and intensity of noise. The only difference was the control group knew they could terminate the noise, but they never did. Yet this bit of cognitive information—feeling that they controlled the noise—significantly reduced their level of aggression. The way an individual perceives a situation greatly influences his or her behavior in that situation.

COMMENT

The three regulatory functions that control behavior are closely intertwined. For example, even though self-reinforcement was discussed in the section on reinforcement control, it is equally important for cognitive control. The three together are needed to explain behavior from a social learning point of view.

One final comment is important. Bandura has pointed out a distinction that is very important—many behaviors are learned vicariously but not performed until situations arise that call for their performance.

Bandura (1965) had children view a model whose behavior included novel physical and verbal aggressive acts. In one condition, the model was punished for behaving aggressively; in the second, the model was rewarded for the aggression; and, in the third condition, the model was neither punished nor rewarded. Children who saw the model punished for aggression aggressed less than children who saw the model rewarded or receive no positive or negative consequences. In addition, boys reproduced substantially more of the aggressive behavior than girls did.

Following the performance, the children were offered rewards for each modeled aggressive response they could accurately reproduce. This was, of course, to determine how much aggressive behavior they had learned but not performed in the performance test. In every condition the children could perform more of the aggressive acts they had viewed than they did in the performance test, indicating that they had indeed learned more aggression than they displayed. The rewards completely eliminated the previous performance differences regardless of how the model had been treated and virtually eliminated the large differences between boys and girls. Figure 8-4 presents the results graphically. As can be readily seen, the children had learned many more of the modeled responses than they spontaneously reproduced.

Modeling and Aggression

The social transmission of aggression has been most clearly demonstrated in controlled experimental studies, and Bandura and his associates have both pioneered the efforts and continued to provide provocative research evidence. Bandura, Ross, and Ross (1961) had children observe models behaving in a physically and verbally aggressive manner toward a large inflated plastic figure. The aggressive acts modeled were rarely, if ever, displayed by children, who had no previous exposure to the modeled performances. Following exposure to the model, children were allowed to display what they had learned in a situation that contained a variety of materials they could use for either aggressive or nonaggressive activities. Learning was measured in one of two ways—either by observing the children's spontaneous behavior or by asking them to reproduce all the modeled aggressive actions and remarks they could recall (Bandura, 1965). Bandura (1973) argues that the latter is a better index of

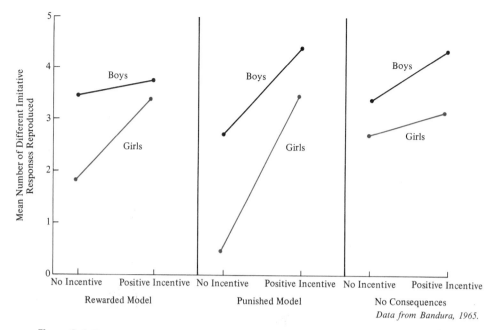

Data from Bandura, 1965.

Figure 8–4 More responses are learned than are performed unless steps are taken to draw out what is learned. In this case, children were rewarded (positive incentive) for each novel imitative response they could reproduce.

observational learning because people generally learn more then they spontaneously perform.

Both children and adults can acquire attitudes, emotional responses, and complex patterns of behavior through behavioral demonstrations, pictorial representation, and verbal description (Bandura and Mischel, 1965; Bandura, Ross, and Ross, 1963; Prentice, 1972). For equal learning to occur, it is necessary to assure that the different stimulus modes convey the same amount of information, that they are equally effective in commanding attention, and that the learners are equally adept in translating the information regardless of the mode of presentation. When some of these conditions are not met, observed actions are more effective in teaching aggression (Grusec, 1972). Thus, it appears that the media, most importantly television, are one source of potential violence that needs and has received investigation.

Bandura's basic position is that aggression is learned through modeling and the model can be presented live or symbolically (on film, in verbal reports, or in written reports) and that as long as the cognitive capacity of the individual viewing the model is adequate, the aggressive behavior is learned. It may not immediately be performed, but the learning has taken place. In another area of behavior, antismoking ads reflect Bandura's point. One such ad shows a man mowing the lawn with his little boy mowing right behind with his toy mower. The Dad washes the car while the boy washes his toy truck. Finally Dad sits back under a tree, relaxes, and lights up a cigarette. The little boy sits back under the tree, relaxes and *watches.* The point is obvious—even though he has not done it yet, the boy has learned to smoke.

This teacher is tall and imposing, yet he has been a model of cooperative rather than aggressive behavior. Not surprisingly, his students cooperate with him.

INSTIGATION OF AGGRESSION

Bandura argues that many of the events that evoke aggression are learned, not acquired from some genetic endowment. Because much of this learning takes place naturally at a very early age, experimentation into the exact origins of the instigation to aggress are somewhat difficult (in Chapter 9, we will encounter some of the same difficulties in attraction research). For example, if one questions the ancestry of a two-year-old it will not provoke aggression, but the same words uttered in a neighborhood bar late on Saturday night may well evoke violent reactions.

A number of studies with animals indicate that stimulus conditions can control aggression. For example, several experiments have been carried out in which a previously ineffective stimulus (such as a tone) is repeatedly paired with pain-elicited aggression in pairs of animals (Farris, Gideon, and Ulrich, 1970; Lyon and Ozolins, 1970; Vernon and Ulrich, 1966). After a number of pairings in which the tone precedes provoked assault, the appearance of the tone alone tends to produce aggression. By the same token, aggressive elicitors tend to lose their aggression-provoking abilities when they are presented without aggression (Farris, Fullmer, and Ulrich, 1970).

In a classic study, *Violent Men,* Toch (1969) examined the actions of chronic assaulters. One of the cases he studied had suffered a humiliating beating as a youngster at the hands of a large opponent. In the future this incident seemed to control his violent behavior; he would become violent at the slightest provocation by a large person. This real-life case history provides us with evidence that what happens in animal experiments can also happen with humans. The fact that it is ethically improper to place humans in experiments such as the one described above with animals makes us careful when we generalize to the instigation of aggression in

Aggression requires a target. One of the most often asked questions when aggression occurs is "how could he (she) do that to someone?" There are innumerable reasons, but an intriguing possibility suggested by Worchel and Andreoli (1978) is that we tend to deindividuate those against whom we aggress. *Deindividuation* is the depersonalizing of another individual. The suggestion here is that we depersonalize people against whom we aggress by recalling little unique information about them.

Worchel and Andreoli first developed a scale that allowed people to be classified along a individuation-deindividuation dimension. The most distinctive information was name, personality, physical characteristics, habits, background, and mottoes, whereas the least distinctive information was age, home town, race, present residence, political party, and religion.

Subjects were brought to the experiment with a confederate and were told that this was a learning experiment. They were to write an essay and it would be evaluated by the other subject (the confederate). This was done so that half the subjects could be angered by receiving a negative evaluation and half would receive a positive evaluation. The subjects were further divided by telling a third of each group that they would reward the person who had just evaluated them for correct answers, shock the person for incorrect answers, or merely record the confederate's answers. Thus there were angry and nonangry subjects who expected to be able to aggress, reward, or not respond to the person who had just evaluated them.

Angry subjects shocked the confederate more than nonangry subjects, and nonangry subjects rewarded the confederate more than angry subjects. These rather obvious results replicated much research on aggression. What was of particular interest in this study was a recall task. At the beginning of the experiment, subjects filled out a form that contained the six most and least distinctive characteristics previously mentioned. Midway through the experiment, subjects read the other person's form. At the end of the experiment, they were asked to recall all the information they could about the other individual.

Deindividuating (least distinctive) information was more readily recalled by angry subjects than by nonangry subjects, and subjects aggressing against the confederate also recalled more deindividuating information than did subjects rewarding the subject. The results for individuating (most distinctive) information were just the opposite. Nonangry subjects recalled more individuating information than did angry ones, and subjects rewarding the confederate recalled more individuating information than did those shocking the confederate.

It seems, then, that when we are angry with persons or about to aggress against them, we recall approximately the same amount of information about a given person as when we are not angry or about to reward him or her. The type of information, however, is quite different. We recall depersonalized information in negative situations and personal information in positive situations. Possibly we do not want to think of the individual as a person if we are angry or going to aggress, whereas we want to think about people's uniqueness when we are not angry or are going to reward them.

Reference

Worchel, S., and V. Andreoli. Facilitation of social interaction through deindividuation of the target. *Journal of Personality and Social Psychology*, 1978, *36*, 549–56.

humans. However, case histories such as the one provided by Toch make us more confident of the generalization.

Response contingencies also serve to control aggression. For example, animals can be trained to aggress in quite specific situations. Reynolds, Catania, and Skinner

(1963) reinforced hungry animals whenever they attacked another animal under blue light, but never rewarded the animals when they aggressed under green light. Under these conditions, animals often fought under blue light, but seldom under green light. In field studies of primates, past successes and failures in combat establish a well-defined dominance hierarchy that inhibits in-group fighting. If strangers are introduced into the society, it results in fighting that persists until a new dominance hierarchy is established (Southwick, 1967).

Like primates, humans often fight for dominance when new members are introduced into a society or, more often, when a formerly dominant member of a society departs. For example, when the president of a company or country suddenly dies, his death may very well set off a long series of aggressive encounters unless there is a well-established process for succession. Aggression is not, however, an inevitable consequence of social organization. There are societies in which the prevailing reinforcement system promotes nonaggressive qualities (Alland, 1972).

Comment

It is clear that instinctual theories of aggression differ markedly from Berkowitz's frustration-aggression hypothesis and Bandura's social learning approach. It is often difficult for students—and, frankly, for others, as well—to understand the differences between the frustration-aggression hypothesis and the social learning approach. The crux of the matter seems to be that Bandura and Berkowitz have been working toward the same goal from two slightly different perspectives and sometimes the distinctions that are so clear to a researcher in the field are sufficiently subtle to make it difficult to follow them. Let us contrast the two.

Berkowitz argues that goal-directed behavior that is blocked (frustration) may combine with other emotional arousal to determine the aggression focused on the individual. This impulsive emotional arousal component is greatly affected by situational cues and can even be regarded as conditioned responses to external cues (Berkowitz and Frodi, 1977). Thus, it appears that it is necessary for there to be some frustrating event that combines with impulsive emotional arousal to determine the level of aggression displayed. A number of studies by Berkowitz (1971, 1973, 1974) have demonstrated that the mere presence of objects or occurrences associated with aggression can strengthen that aggression.

Bandura argues that aversive experiences can lead to emotional arousal and that the individual considers another external cue, the consequences of the action, before determining which course of action to follow. That is, aggression may be one of the modes of behavior—even the most frequent one—if there occurs an aversive event that signals positive consequences for aggressing. However, it is not the only behavior possible. Figure 8-5 represents four different theoretical views, including those of Berkowitz and Bandura, schematically.

The basic differences between Berkowitz and Bandura seem to me to be differences in emphasis. The two emphases are traceable to a dispute in learning from

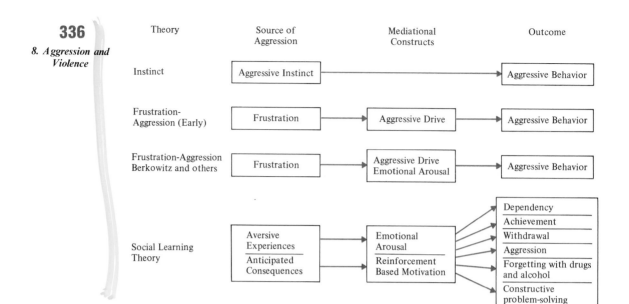

Figure 8–5 Schematic representation of various theories of aggression.

which the two draw their ideas. There are those individuals in learning who draw their basic approach from Clark L. Hull (1943, 1951), who emphasized the necessity of drive reduction if learning was to occur. His work was greatly advanced by Kenneth Spence (1960) and is still an important force today. During much of the time this drive explanation of learning was developing, B. F. Skinner (1938, 1953, 1974) was developing an approach to learning and behavior that he called radical behaviorism. His view was that psychologists should stick to studying those things that were most amenable to study. To him, this meant that those things that can be observed are easier to study and that the payoff in predicting human behavior would be much higher if psychologists stuck to observables. Internal states such as drive, frustration, and anger are not observable, but the external stimuli leading to an aversive event and the response (i.e., aggression) are. These observable events are what we should be studying. Note Skinner did not and does not say that the unobservable internal events do not occur. They do. According to Skinner we simply do not yet have the ability to study them adequately.

Berkowitz seems to approach the problem of aggression from the tradition that emphasizes drive, an internal state, whereas Bandura has emphasized external events (stimuli, cues, reinforcements, and responses). It is probably fair to say that Berkowitz leans toward the Hull–Spence tradition, whereas Bandura is Skinnerian in orientation.

Bandura, however, has emphasized the cognitive control of aggression, and cognitions are certainly internal states. One of the recent developments in social learning theory has been its emphasis on cognitive variables as the most stable of internal states and thus excellent candidates for study. These variables include, but are not restricted to, expectancy, cognitive complexity, creativity, and vicarious reinforcement and punishment. One of the early advocates of such a position was Julian B. Rotter (1954), but in the last fifteen years or so there has been a greatly increasing interest in cognitive social learning.

Much of this work has been carried out in the general area of personality (Bandura, 1969, 1977a, 1977b; Meichenbaum, 1975; Mischel, 1968, 1973; Mahoney, 1977; Mahoney and Thorenson, 1974), with emphasis upon the cognitive control of behavioral change. However, many of the same cognitive elements that are proving effective in behavior change in personality are also operative in aggression. Thus, while Berkowitz and Bandura often appear to be like "ships passing in the night" (it is frustratingly difficult to find an article in which Bandura compares and contrasts Berkowtiz's position to his own, or vice versa) it appears that both are studying the same phenomena with different emphases. Berkowitz is now more willing to discuss emotional arousal other than frustration than he once was and Bandura is concentrating more and more on internal variables. Possibly the ships passing in the night are coming closer to each other and before too much longer there will be more communication between the two. Our understanding of aggression will be enhanced when that occurs.

There are close ties between aggression and the work by Milgram on obedience (see Chapter 7) and Zimbardo's work on deindividuation (see Chapter 11). Certainly Milgram's subjects were aggressing, or thought they were, and the process of deindividuation oftentimes leads to aggression. Since these topics are covered at some length in other chapters, I wish only to draw your attention to them now and suggest that you read those sections and consider them in light of what is known about aggression.

Violence

Violence is as American as apple pie, permeating our lives in an ever-increasing crescendo. Crime statistics are on the way up and when they level off (as they did in 1976) or when they drop (as they did in the first half of 1977), we are told we must not relax our vigilance. It has always been assumed that there are certain areas of towns and cities into which it is unwise to venture unescorted after dark. Recently, however, it seems that those dangerous areas are expanding until virtually whole cities are dangerous. To escape the violence, innumerable individuals have fled to the suburbs only to find that violence is also a way of life there. People try to protect their homes with locks (one, two, three, and more per door) floodlights, dogs, and burglar alarms. People do not venture out into areas where they once walked freely—by day or night.

Those brought up in the 1940s or 1950s, who remember peaceful streets and schools, return for visits and are shocked to find unsafe streets and armed security guards patrolling the halls of schools. Violence abounds and violence increases, but what causes it? Is it really worse than it was 20 or 30 or 100 years ago?

There are probably several explanations for violence, but if Berkowitz, Bandura, and many others who have studied the topic closely are correct, then it seems to me that we must take seriously what was implicit in their early research and has been made explicit as their research has progressed. Both men (and many others as well) have pointed an accusing finger at the media, primarily television but also newspapers, movies, and magazines. The advent of television and its immedite acceptance by the public have made it one of the most prevalent media forces in existence. Virtually every home has a television set, and children, especially, watch it many hours per day. In 1972 a report was made to the Surgeon General of the United States Public Health Service by an advisory committee which concluded among other things, that (1) about eight violent episodes per hour occurred in what is the mostly heavily viewed time of day; (2) cartoons (meant for children) are the most violent; and (3) there is "a preliminary and tentative indication of a *causal* relationship between viewing violence and aggressive behavior. . . ." (1972, p. 11).

There is no doubt that violence predates television. To argue that all violence stems from that medium is ludicrous. It is not ludicrous, however, to discuss the effects of viewing violence on violent behavior. Television has made the viewing of violence more commonplace, and therefore its effects need to be carefully studied.

Because we are living in a world in which the first generation of children brought up on television is reaching maturity and because of the possible (probable?) deleterious effects of violence on individuals, it is worthwhile to concentrate on television violence and its possible effects for the remainder of this chapter. Both Berkowitz and Bandura have had much to say about the problem, and we will highlight their analyses of how televised violence can be harmful. Further, we will look at the latest evidence concerning violence on television and see if the picture has changed since the report to the Surgeon General in 1972.

There are many social problems in our world; some can be solved or at least ameliorated, whereas others are quite intactable. Which camp does aggression fall into? Maybe we will know more after our inquiry.

The Contagion of Violence

Berkowitz (1971) has approached the subject of televised violence squarely and he not only reached certain conclusions about its effects on children and adults, but has proposed a theory of why these effects occur. He cites a 1969 report on televised violence that highlights what will be a recurring theme in our discussion—the attitude of the networks towards their product.

Each year advertisers spend $2½ billion in the belief that television can influence human behavior. The television industry enthusiastically agrees with them, but nonetheless contends that its programs of violence do not have any such influence.

The preponderance of the available evidence strongly suggests, however, that violence in television programs can and does have adverse effects upon audiences—particularly child audiences. [Eisenhower et al., 1969, p. 5.]

Some ninety years ago the French sociologist Gabriel Tarde (1890) suggested that epidemics of crime follow the telegraph line. By this he meant that violence which is reported to the public may be reenacted by certain individuals. He pointed out that the after-effects of the Jack the Ripper murders inspired a series of female mutilations in the English provinces. And certainly Jack the Ripper was not the only infamous character to inspire others to violent acts.

To substantiate his claim that violence breeds violence, Berkowitz reports crime statistics obtained from the Federal Bureau of Investigation. The crimes sampled were aggressive in nature and covered the period from 1960 to 1966 for forty cities scattered across the country. During this time there were two particularly violent episodes that would be expected to increase the number of violent crimes if, indeed, Tarde and others were right. In late November, 1963, John F. Kennedy was assassinated and during the summer of 1966 Richard Speck murdered eight nurses and Charles Whitman went to the top of the "Tower" on the University of Texas campus with a veritable arsenal of weapons and shot 45 people before he was killed by police. Berkowitz reasoned that these episodes should have some effect on the commission of violent crimes across the country.

Berkowitz analyzed the violent crimes (murder, rape, aggravated assault, and robbery) and arrived at a mean number of violent crimes for the 84 months covered. He then computed the deviations from that means for each of the 84 months. All months in the years 1960–1963 were below the average, whereas all months in the years 1964–1966 were above the average. The jump from below average to above average occurred in January 1964, which recorded by far the greatest increase in crime of the 84 months. Another large increase in crime appeared during the summer of 1966. Thus, it is apparent that violent crimes increased most dramatically following the occurrence of, and widespread publicity accorded to, violent episodes.

A Classical-Conditioning Model

Berkowitz (1971) argues that the contagion of violence may be best explained by a classical-conditioning model. Classical conditioning is the learning of responses through association with stimuli that are rewarding or punishing (see Figure 1–2 and pp. 16–17 for a discussion of classical conditioning). Berkowitz's argument is that aggressive behavior seems to function like a conditioned response to situational stimuli. The observer reacts impulsively to particular stimuli in the environment, not because of the anticipation of pleasure or weakened inhibitions. Rather, the situational stimuli evoke the response the observer is already set to make. Berkowitz considers this aspect of aggression to be classically conditioned because pairings of the unconditioned stimulus (factors that arouse aggressive impulses) and the conditioned stimulus (situational cues that help elicit aggressive impulses), eventually lead to the evocation of the conditioned response by the conditioned stimulus.

It should be noted that Berkowitz suggests that there are two aspects to aggression, one intentional and the other involuntary. The intentional aspect of aggression is that an aggressor wants to injure his or her target. Anger may be the source of the aggression and so the individual lashes out, trying to hurt with all due deliberation. But, Berkowitz argues, at the same time involuntary, impulsive processes might operate to intensify the strength of the attack. It is this involuntary, impulsive component that Berkowitz feels can be profitably regarded as conditioned responses.

For example, let us say that a woman is angry at a friend and intends to do her harm. The anger is there, but situational cues that have been conditioned by repeated pairings with aggression may serve to increase the aggression. All of us have seen guns used in aggressive ways, in movies or television if not in real life. So if the aggressor happens to see a gun as she is about to commit her aggressive act, she may grab the gun and shoot her target instead of hitting or slapping her. The impulsive portion of aggression is the portion of the aggressive act that Berkowitz views as classically conditioned and the strength of the conditioned response can be altered by that conditioning.

A number of experiments have demonstrated that the mere presence of objects or occurrences that are associated with the idea of aggression can strengthen ongoing aggressive behavior (Berkowitz, 1971, 1973, 1974). An especially cogent demonstration of this phenomenon is the "weapons effect" (Berkowitz and LePage, 1967) in which subjects who were angered saw either a gun or a badminton racket as they were given the opportunity to aggress against the victim by delivering shock. The subjects who saw the weapon aggressed more than those who did not. This particular experimental effect has been the subject of some controversy. Some investigators (Buss, Booker, and Buss, 1972; Page and Scheidt, 1971) have failed to obtain the effect, whereas others (Frodi, 1975; Simons et. al., in press; Turner and Goldsmith, 1976) have found it. Turner and Simons (1974) suggest that the weapons effect occurs only when naïve subjects (naïve with respect to the experimental hypothesis), who have little or no concern about how they are evaluated by the experimenter, participate in the experiment. Since these conditions are peculiar only to the experimental situation and not to real-life aggressive situations, the conditions necessary for the weapons effect to occur in naturally occurring aggressive situations seem to be easily met.

Turner, Layton, and Simons (1975) extended laboratory research on the weapons effect to a naturalistic setting. They had a pickup truck with a gun rack in the rear window block traffic at a green traffic signal for 12 seconds. For some trials a rifle was in the gun rack and for others it was empty, and added to this a bumper with either the word "Friend" or "Vengeance" was visible. Thus drivers were blocked at an intersection by a pickup truck with a rifle present or not present and a bumper sticker that indicated aggressive or nonaggressive feelings. The presence of the rifle increased the number of the people who honked at the truck. Honking was the measure of aggression in this setting. Furthermore, the presence of the Vengeance bumper sticker increased honking over that observed when the bumper sticker read "Friend."

This demonstration of increased aggression when a gun is present in a naturalistic setting greatly increases our confidence in the effects of a weapon on aggression. The failure to establish the weapons effect in some laboratory studies does, indeed, seem to be tied to conditions that are peculiar to the experimental setting.

Thus, it does seem that situational cues pull aggression, or at least the intensity of the aggression, out of the individual. This effect appears in at least one study carried out in another country (Belgium), by Leyens and Parke (1975). Berkowitz does not completely exclude the internal arousal necessary for aggression to occur, but he does seem to be emphasizing the situational stimuli that intensify aggressive behavior. Thus, Berkowitz (1974) has proposed that an environmental detail can acquire the ability to pull out aggressive impulses by being associated with positive reinforcements for aggression. Furthermore, neutral stimuli that are merely paired with information about a tormentor's suffering can develop the ability to intensify later attacks on another target (Swart and Berkowitz, 1976).

This particular element of aggression, the ability of situational cues to act as conditioned stimuli to intensify the level of aggression, is of special importance in the contagion of violence. As individuals are rewarded for aggression, and as others hear about it, read about it, or see it, they too can become more aggressive because of the conditioning that has gone on previously (throughout their lives). As these conditioned responses are strengthened by continual pairing with reward for aggression (either actual or vicariously experienced), aggression can be intensified.

To the extent that the media, and particularly television, make violence and aggression a commodity that is experienced frequently, conditioning can and does occur; as the conditioning occurs, there is an ever greater chance that aggressive acts that are viewed will be reenacted by others. Thus, violence on television can be expected to have a cumulative effect; that is, violence should lead to ever-increasing violence. And that appears to be what is happening.

BANDURA'S APPROACH TO TELEVISED VIOLENCE

Bandura (1973) is in total agreement with the claim (really a rather obvious fact) that there is a great deal of violence on television (Gerbner, 1972a, 1972b). He points out, however, that evaluation of the impact of violence on individual and collective aggression may bring about censorship. Thus, according to Bandura, many social scientists claimed that televised influences were innocuous long before there were data to support or not support such a stand. Others have continued to defend the impotence of televised violence even in the face of growing evidence to the contrary.

Several lines of argument have been advanced by the proponents of the innocuous nature of televised violence. First, they say that television is a multidimensional problem and that to indict television as the only source of violence is unfair and is merely a way of finding a scapegoat. No behavior, so the argument goes, is ever completely controlled by a single determinant. Second, they admit that modeled aggression occurs, but claim it is not very important. In this view the impact of television is portrayed as relatively minor. Then, after it does not exist or it is minor, comes a third line of defense—it affects only disturbed people. This approach rests on the unsupported foundation that aggression is a sign of an emotional disorder. This approach has a circularity to it that is hard to break. If the person is aggressive, he or she is emotionally disturbed. How do we know that the person is emotionally disturbed? He or she is aggressive, isn't that so? But, as Bandura points out, aggression is not a sick behavior generated by internal pathology. As Bandura says,

A social system gets its members to aggress, whatever their personal makeup, by legitimizing, modeling, and sanctioning such behavior, not by inducing emotional disorders in them. For this reason, one would not contend that broadcasters make heavy use of violence because they are emotionally disturbed, have a weak sense of reality, or are homicidally predisposed. Aggression is typically used because it is successful in getting people what they want. Although the industry is quick to attribute aggressive modeling to defects in children and parents, it doubtless ascribes increases in consumer behavior to the power of the medium rather than to pathologies in the viewer. [1975, pp. 267–68).]

Another claim that is often made about televised violence is that although it may affect children, who are less able to foresee the effects of their aggressive acts, adults, who possess a greater reality sense are relatively immune to its influences. Bandura rejects this point of view by pointing out that there are innumerable experimental studies which show that otherwise considerate college students act more aggressively after viewing aggressive models than do students who have not seen such models, and that it is adults, not children, who commit crimes copied from television plots.

Yet another argument from the forces that wish to leave television unfettered is the claim that a warm, loving atmosphere for the child to grow up in is all that really matters. This approach states that if the family is a warm and loving one, then these positive emotions will overcome any negative aspects that television introduces into the home. Bandura dismisses this suggestion by pointing out that a warm, loving family has never been suggested as an antidote for contaminated water or milk that may have been delivered to the home. Indeed, any health officials who proposed such a solution would have been thought incompetent.

Finally, advocates of leaving television alone argue that violence has a cathartic effect, that is the releasing of pent-up socially undesirable emotions. In this view, aggression is seen as a drive that builds up within the individual. When the drive reaches a certain level, then it must be released. The argument is that viewing aggression can provide the cathartic effect that is necessary to reduce the drive level. Thus, it is better to have people releasing their aggressive drives vicariously as they view television rather than aggressing against each other. In this approach to the legitimacy of televised violence, television is an unsung hero that allows aggressive drives to be released all over the living room floor rather than allowing blood to flow in some argument. The vicarious cathartic effect has been studied quite intensively, however, and the evidence against it is overwhelming (Bandura, 1973; Berkowitz, 1971; Konečni and Doob, 1972).

For example, Goldstein, Rosnow, Raday, Silverman, and Gaskell (1975) reported a study in which adult males were interviewed either before or after seeing arousing and aggressive movies (e.g., *Clockwork Orange* and *Straw Dogs*), or arousing but nonaggressive movies (e.g., *The Decameron*) or nonarousing, nonaggressive movies (e.g., *Fiddler on the Roof* and *Living Free*). The study was carried out in Canada, England, Italy, and the United States, so it may be properly viewed as a cross-cultural field study. The viewers' level of punitiveness was used as an index of aggression and the researchers concluded that the aggressive films increased the viewers' level of aggression, whereas nonarousing, nonaggressive films decreased the viewers' level of aggression. Arousing, nonaggressive films did not alter the viewers' aggressiveness. Thus, far from supporting a cathartic interpretation of viewing aggression, Goldstein, et al., presented evidence that there appears to be just the opposite occurring—aggression is increased after viewing an aggressive film.

It has long been argued that there is one type of violent activity that has a cathartic effect on observers and that is viewing violent sporting events. Millions of people watch football, boxing, hockey, and other violent sports not, we are sure, to decrease their own aggression but because they enjoy it. However, the argument has been advanced that this is a healthy outlet for aggression. Goldstein and Arms (1971) measured male spectators' levels of hostility before and after a football game and, as a control, before and after a gymnastics competition. This nonaggressive sport was used as a control to assure that viewing any sport for several hours would not lead to an increase in aggressiveness. The football game was the 1969 Army-Navy game, and the gymnastics competition was between Army and Temple. There was a significant increase in hostility following the viewing of the football game, but not after viewing the gymnastics contest. Furthermore, there was more of an increase in hostility among fans who supported the winning team (Army) than among fans who supported the losing team (Navy). As Goldstein says,

. . . This finding lends support to the social learning and imitation theory of Bandura. The pro-Army fans saw Army players rewarded for their aggressiveness on the field, while the pro-Navy fans saw their team punished (by being beaten) for their aggression. Thus the vicarious reward served to heighten Army fans' aggressiveness and the vicarious punishment served to inhibit to some degree the aggressiveness of Navy fans (although the latter still showed a significant increase in hostility). [1975, p. 50.]

Even if there were cathartic effects of viewing violence, these would be greatly outweighed by the learning of new and unique ways to commit aggression that both children and adults observe on television. It is not enough to have violence portrayed by someone shooting another; drama demands new, ever more esoteric ways of aggressing lest the dramatic value of each method be lost through endless repetition. Thus, television has become a medium through which one can learn the latest and most esoteric forms of violence by passively watching.

Even the argument that parents can monitor the televised fare that enters their home is hollow. How would parents react if they were told that the water that came from the tap, or the milk from the dairy, had to be monitored for impurities? If not outraged, parents would then demand a means of testing for impurities. No such test, is provided however, for parents in the monitoring of television. If the television industry will not regulate itself in respect to violence, it seems that the least it could do would be to have published in the *T.V. Guide* a statement of how many acts of violence are committed in each program. A statement might contain the name of the show, the time and channel, and possibly the following sort of entry: "6 murders, 3 robberies, 2 rapes, and assorted minor violence."

Is it possible to have violence on television without the negative consequences that we have discussed? Bandura admits that if violence were presented as a morally reprehensible and costly way of achieving desired goals, viewers might be deterred from resorting to similar tactics when the temptation arises. But analyses of television shows indicate that violence is *not* presented as a devalued behavior; rather, it is condoned. Moreover, it is difficult to depict violence negatively rather than positively and hope in that way to suppress the tendency to violent behavior in the viewer. For example, depicting the punishment of perpetrators of violent acts is an undependable inhibitor of violence. Observing punishment of the violent person may suppress, but it cannot erase, what the viewer has learned from witnessing the acts of violence.

Even the punishment of violence, when punishment occurs, is overshadowed by dramatic requirements. For example, throughout a televised drama the perpetrators of violence amass rather large rewards, live more affluent lives than those who are not violent, and only in the end (if at all) are they punished. Their reward is immediate and lavish; their punishment is delayed and oftentimes weak or nonexistent. Television does not portray the injunction "the wages of sin is death," rather that the wages of violence are a hell of a lot better than the wages an ordinary person makes. Immediate reward is a more effective reinforcer than delayed punishment is a deterrent. When there is an ethical ending, it is often interrupted by commercials; when this happens young children fail to grasp the relationship between aggressive actions and unfavorable outcomes and are therefore not dissuaded from aggressive acts (Collins, 1973).

It seems that the idea of using television to show violence for its cathartic effect, or for its potetial inhibitory effect when violence is punished, is poor strategy. Here we are assuming, of course, that the aim of television should encompass the good of society. In fact, the aim of television is to make a profit, and if violence "sells" it will be shown unless and until there is a public outcry against it.

Bandura succinctly sums up the network attempt to have it both ways. On the one hand, network officials argue vociferously that their commercials are effective, while arguing equally vociferously that what is seen in their programming is ineffective in altering behavior. As Bandura puts it,

> The networks' unwavering uncertainty about the effect their programs have on people is captured in the story once told of a patient who consulted a psychiatrist concerning doubts over his wife's fidelity. During the next visit the patient reported seeing his wife accompany an amorous man into a hotel room, whereupon they promptly disrobed and jumped into bed. At that moment the lights were turned off, leaving the husband at the keyhole still feeling uncertain about his wife's infidelity. [1973, pp. 273–74.]

Alternatives to Violence

If violence breeds violence, then it seems possible to assume that viewing positive social behaviors may affect behavior positively. In a series of studies, Aletha Stein and Lynette Friedrich (Friedrich and Stein, 1973; Stein and Freidrich, 1972; Stein and Friedrich, 1975a, 1975b; Stein et al., 1973), also Vondracek et al. (1973), have studied the effects of prosocial behavior on children. Using edited tapes of the television program "Mr. Rogers' Neighborhood," these investigators have found that children can learn a variety of complex positive ideas from brief exposure to television. These include understanding feelings, sharing, helping, knowing that wishes do not make things happen, and appreciating the value of an individual as a unique person. More important, children seem to be able to generalize televised content to situations in their own lives. These prosocial ideas are more effectively picked up by children if there is some subsequent adult-assisted rehearsal of the prosocial behaviors.

Television Today

Our discussion of aggression and violence has indicated that televised violence leads to aggression and that there are alternatives. That is, prosocial behavior can be enhanced by viewing programs that portray positive social behaviors. But what is the

WHY IS TELEVISION VIOLENT?

As more people become aware of the potential dangers of televised violence, a recurring question asserts itself: Why is television violent? One instant answer to that question is that people like violent shows, watch them, and this results in good ratings for violent shows. The report to the Surgeon General (1972, p. 8) stated that ". . . violent material is popular." The evidence for the belief that violence is popular is weak, resting primarily on the popularity ratings of adventure shows. It should be noted that adventure shows may contain elements other than violence itself (e.g., plot, characters, and nonviolent adventure) that are popular. Many people enjoy adventure and involve themselves in it in nonviolent ways. Sky-diving, skiing, auto rallying, and many other activities are filled with adventure and are relatively nonviolent.

Diener and DeFour (1978) suggested that violent programs are laden with action, suspense, and interpersonal conflict. Possibly it is these factors, not violence, that have been responsible for the popularity of violent programs. Thirty male and female undergraduate students rated 71 different episodes of 12 adventure programs. They rated the shows for verbal and physical aggression, drama, action, and humor. The Nielson ratings for these shows were then correlated with the four rating categories. Interestingly enough, the most aggressive shows were not the most popular ones. There was a tendency for aggressive shows to be intermediate in popularity, with the less aggressive shows either very popular or not at all popular. Furthermore, less than a third of the households viewing television at the time adventure shows were aired were watching those shows. These data suggest that violence is not the most important element in a program's popularity.

To test further the role of violence in a program's popularity, 100 college students (48 females and 52 males) viewed either an uncut version of "Police Woman" or the same episode from which all violence had been edited. Half of the subjects viewed the unedited version, and half viewed the edited version (from which a thug beating up a man and forcing his hand into boiling water, a police officer being beaten, a loan shark releasing a car jack and allowing the car to fall on a mechanic, and a chase and shoot-out scene in which two criminals are shot, were cut). Subjects rated both versions on violence and likability.

The uncut version was perceived as considerably more violent than the edited version. There was a slight but nonsignificant tendency for the violent program to be liked more than the nonviolent one. The differences were so small, and the sample sizes so large that it is safe to say that for college students and this program, violence did not enhance the program's likability.

These two experiments taken together suggest that violence is not as popular as some have assumed. Recall that the low correlation between violence and the Nielson ratings suggested that most people were not watching the most violent shows; rather the most violent were intermediate in popularity. Showing subjects an edited or unedited version of an adventure show verified that subjects saw the unedited version as more violent than the edited one. They did not, however, like the violent version more. This research strongly suggests that the television networks could decrease the amount of violence shown without decreasing the popularity of a program. Whether this will be done or not remains to be seen.

Reference

Diener, E., and D. DeFour. Does television violence enhance progam popularity? *Journal of Personality and Social Psychology*, 1978, *36*, 333–41.

content of television programming today? Analyses of television programming always run somewhat behind—it takes time to view, code, and analyze hours and hours of television programming. But analyses of prime time and Saturday morning pro-

Children spend many hours in front of a television set. What are they learning?

gramming from 1967 to 1975 (Gerbner and Gross, 1976) indicated that about 80 percent of the plays contained at least one incident of violence and that the frequency of violent events (8 per hour) did not decline over the 9 years sampled. Programs directed at young children had the greatest incidence of violence, with cartoons having the highest frequency of violence. It should be noted that cartoons did reduce their violent events from about 22 incidents per hour in 1969 to "only" about 16 in 1975. This, of course, is still a violent incident occurring about every $3\frac{1}{2}$ minutes. Figure 8-6 shows the number of violent episodes per hour in each of three different viewing times.

Thus, to return to Bandura's analogy, television producers are still not sure about the wife's fidelity—or lack of it.

VIOLENT ACTS AND VIOLENT TIMES

Archer and Gartner (1976) have presented rather startling evidence concerning violent acts and violent times. The violent times these researchers refer to are probably the most violent—war. They note that during the Vietnam War the murder and nonnegligent homicide rate in the United States more than doubled, following a period of thirty years of steady decline. Although this sudden increase in violence is suggestive, obviously many more data are needed before any general determinations can be made about the relationship between war and violent crimes. Archer and Gartner set out to collect these data and to compare the data with various existing theories concerning the effects of wars on violence. They found seven theoretical models that addressed this subject.

Social Solidarity Model. The social solidarity model has been advanced by several researchers who have suggested that wars increase social solidarity, and thus reduce crime rates. As early as 1906, Summer argued in his classic *Folkways* that wars increase discipline and the strength of law. Mannheim (1941) agreed and referred to a 1914 article in the *Times* of London, which argued that the criminal, like the honest citizen, is impressed by the duty to create as little trouble as possible during war. The

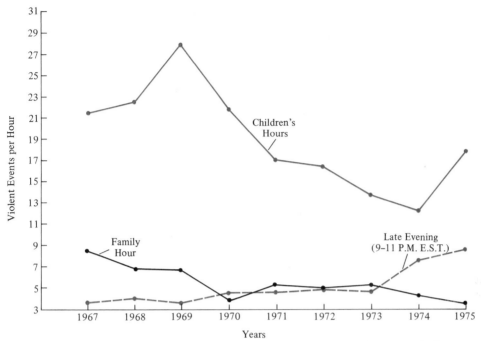

Source: G. Gerbner and L. Gross, *Living with television: The violence profile.* Journal of Communication, *Spring 1976, 173–99.*

Figure 8–6 Number of violent events portrayed on television for various time periods from 1967 to 1975.

social solidarity model predicts that crime during a war should decrease, but that it should return to its prewar rate when the crisis is past.

Social Organization Model. The primary use of the social disorganization model with regard to war is to describe the social and psychological changes in a defeated nation (Luden, 1963; Mannheim, 1965; Sutherland and Cressey, 1960). This model predicts that there should be crime-rate increases whenever war disrupts society, but that they should be more extensive in defeated countries, where the disorganization is greatest.

Economic Factors Model. The economic factors model is tied to the state of the economy of a warring nation both before and after the war. The model would predict a decrease in postwar crime if the postwar economy is in better shape than the prewar one, whereas it would predict an increase in postwar crime if the postwar economy were in worse shape than the prewar one.

Catharsis Model. The catharsis model reflects a persistent belief that wars substitute public violence for private violence. Because killing is legally sanctioned during a war, it provides an outlet for aggressive sentiments or instincts (Mannheim, 1941). This model predicts that violent crimes will decrease during a war, but the duration of the decrease following the war is dependent upon the duration of the cathartic effect. It is probably safe to say, however, that the countries which experience the most violence in a war would experience the most catharsis and would thus experience a postwar decline in violent crimes.

Violent Veteran Model. The violent veteran model is an old one. At least since the American Revolution people have speculated that war veterans would commit more violent crimes than other people. The basic idea of this model is that war has resocialized soldiers to be more accepting of violence. It has been suggested that war develops an appetite for violence (Hamon, 1918), or that the habit of violent solutions to problems becomes ingrained in veterans (Abbott, 1918). The potential problem surfaced again with reference to Vietnam veterans (Lifton, 1970; Mantell and Pilisuk, 1975).

Artifacts Model. The artifacts model should really not be referred to as a model since it encompasses many different events. Basically, the artifacts model asserts that changes in the wartime or postwar crime rates are due to various artifacts that have occurred because of the war. For example, one artifact that often occurs in a war is the depression of wartime crime rates because of the conscription of men in the crime-committing age and their subsequent wounding or deaths in the war itself.

Legitimation of Violence Model. The legitimation of violence model derives from the fact that killing and other forms of violence are officially sanctioned during war. This means that the society reverses its customary prohibitions against killing and, instead, honors acts of violence that would be severely punished during peacetime. Several researchers have suggested that this social approval of violence produces a lasting reduction in the inhibitory mechanisms that forbid murder (Engelbreicht, 1937; Sorokin, 1925).

Archer and Gartner (1976) proceeded to study the effect of war on violent crime by constructing an inventory of crime-rate data with both historical and comparative depth. A 110-nation Comparative Crime Data file was collected by these researchers. The essential aspects of the file were that it had time-series rates of various offenses for the period 1900–1970. The offenses that have been used to construct the inventory are homicide, assault, robbery, theft, and rape.

The next step was to compare postwar homicide rates with homicide rates prior to the war in various countries. Homicide was chosen because some of the other crimes in the Comparative Crime Data file appear to be highly under-reported in many countries. The prewar and postwar periods were arbitrarily set at 5 years to give stability to the data and because the twentieth century has not been characterized by long periods of peace. Even using a 5-year pre- and postwar period means that the Korean War must be excluded because the five years preceding it overlap the five-year period following World War II. Finally, nations were divided into combatant and control nations (nations that did not participate in the war).

Selecting 14 wars that occurred in the twentieth century and dividing nations into combatant and noncombatant countries for that war, the prewar homicide rate (homicides per 100,000 population) was compared to the postwar rate. Three categories were developed—a decrease in homicide rate, an unchanged rate, and an increased one. A nation had to have a decrease of at least 10 percent in its homicide rate to be classified in the first category, a rate that neither decreased or increased more than 10 percent to be classified unchanged, and a rate that increased more than 10 percent to be classified in the increased category.

Of the 50 combatant nations in the 14 wars surveyed, far fewer showed a decrease and far more showed an increase in postwar homicide rate than did the control nations. Figure 8–7 presents the results graphically.

Furthermore, combatant nations were classified by degree of participation; the nations were divided into nations that experienced more than 500 deaths per one million prewar population, and those that experienced fewer than 500 deaths per one million prewar population. If changes in homicide rate are a function of the level of a nation's participation in the war, then one would expect the nations with the largest losses to have the highest homicide rates. This is what has occurred following wars in the twentieth century. Nations with the highest losses in the war have had more frequent increases in postwar homicides than nations with lower losses in the war.

With these data in mind it is possible to examine each of the seven theories mentioned earlier and determine how well they predict the actual occurrences in wars in the twentieth century. When this is done, only the Legitimation of Violence Model accounts for all the data. As Archer and Gartner say,

However, the legitimation model is the only one of the seven discussed in this paper that is completely consistent with our finding of frequent and pervasive postwar homicide increases in combatant nations. [1976, p. 958.]

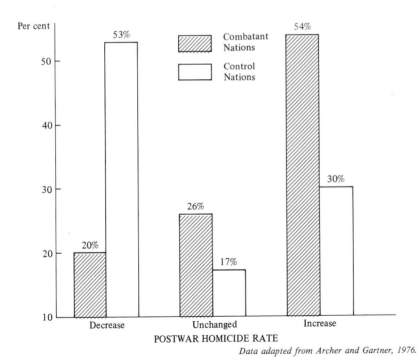

Data adapted from Archer and Gartner, 1976.

Figure 8–7 **Changes in postwar homicide rates for combatant and control nations following 14 twentieth-century wars.**

COMMENT

The work of Archer and Gartner (1976) may provide additional evidence for the notion that imitation is one of the major ways in which aggression is learned. The evidence concerning homicide rates following wars strongly implicates a mechanism that is very similar to imitation. If governments condone violence, violent acts are accepted, even glorified, and the civilian populace is encouraged to tolerate such violence, then this violence is imitated after the war. The fact that as more violence is experienced by a nation in a war, homicide rates show greater increase following that war is comparable to the idea that the more violence viewed by an individual the more violence the individual will tend to become involved in. Thus, this study, which is methodologically far removed from the laboratory studies conducted by Berkowitz and Bandura, supports their views concerning the contagion of violence.

Violence Breeding Violence

Even though there are still those who argue that violence on television is not harmful (Schneider, 1977), an increasing number of voices have been raising still more serious questions with regard to televised violence. Thomas, Horton, Lippincott, and Drabman (1977) were concerned with two of its potentially serious effects.

First, earlier research had suggested that repeated exposure to violence through this medium may result in a gradual blunting of emotional responses to subsequent displays of aggression both on television and in real life. Evidence from systematic desensitization therapy suggests that after a patient has had emotional reactions to a previously anxiety-provoking situation reduced, he or she can more easily engage in that behavior. That is, if a person who is afraid of heights learns to be unafraid of heights it is easier for the patient to ride in airplanes, climb up tall ladders, and the like. Thomas et al. are suggesting that repeated exposure to televised aggression may desensitize people to the anxiety they previously felt when viewing violence and make it easier for them to engage in violence.

Second, an individual's willingness to engage in helping behavior may be reduced by prolonged exposure to violence. There are many real-life examples of failure of bystanders to take action when someone is in trouble (see Chapter 10). Several explanations for this phenomenon have been advanced, but recent experimental studies by Thomas and Drabman (Drabman and Thomas, 1974; Thomas and Drabman, 1975) suggested that children who had witnessed televised violence prior to witnessing a fight between two younger children decreased their willingness to intervene.

Thomas et al. (1977) conducted a study in which children and adults viewed either televised violence or an exciting but not violent program and then were exposed to a view of real-life violence. Physiological measures indicated that the arousal level of those who had first viewed the violent television program were lower during the real-life violence than were those of the subjects who had viewed the exciting, nonviolent program first. This study presents strong evidence for the idea that exposure to violence blunts the emotional arousal associated with that violence.

Gerbner et al. (1977) have pointed out another, parallel aspect of viewing television. In preparing their yearly report on violence in television these investigators have shown that heavy television viewers tend to overestimate the amount of violence that occurs in real life when they are compared to light television viewers. Furthermore, heavy television viewers were more likely than light television viewers to be suspicious and to mistrust others. This was particularly true of children. For example, when asked "Do you think most people would try to take advantage of you if they got a chance or would they try to be fair?" 71 percent of heavy-viewing children and only 46 percent of light-viewing children said most people would try to take advantage of them.

The chilling implication of the work by Thomas and Gerbner is that television changes the behavioral and attitudinal characteristics of those who are exposed to it. The unfortunate aspect of this is that television probably could change these characteristics for better or worse, but the way its programming is now constituted it has a definite negative effect. Thus, if this view is correct, the violence on television appears to breed more violence and makes it acceptable by changing the attitudinal characteristics of those who view it.

SUMMARY

1 Aggression is a difficult concept to define, with most theorists emphasizing that aggression includes an intent to injure another person.

2 Instinctual theories of aggression are founded in biological determinism. Freud's psychoanalytic theory and ethological theories of aggression are instinctual theories. There is, however, much criticism of instinctual theories.

3 The frustration-aggression hypothesis asserts that the blocking of ongoing, goal-directed activity (frustration) can lead to aggression. Anger can be an intervening variable between frustration and aggression. General emotional arousal can interact with anger to increase aggression.

4 Bandura argues that aggression can be understood only by analyzing the stimulus events that provoke it and the reinforcing events that maintain it. Aggression can be learned by direct experience or by observing the behavior in others. According to Bandura, three regulatory functions control aggression; stimulus, reinforcement, and cognitive control.

5 Controlled experimental studies have shown rather conclusively that individuals can learn to aggress merely by seeing another person aggress. This observational learning is known as modeling.

6 Violence is a fact of life, and one that seems to be increasing. Violence seems to be contagious; an outbreak of it in one place is followed by violence elsewhere.

7 Berkowitz has developed a classical-conditioning model of violence in which aggressive behavior functions like a conditioned response to situational stimuli, which act like conditioned stimuli.

8 Televised violence may well be one of the most damaging components in the lives

of modern American and Canadian children. There is evidence to support the contention that viewing violence on television leads to increased aggression. There are, however, those who argue that televised violence is not harmful.

9 Some progress has been made in the modeling of prosocial behavior. After viewing televised programs that show helping, children can learn to be more helpful.

10 Television in the United States today is very violent; on the average one violent event occurs on television every 7.5 minutes.

11 Violent times lead to violent acts. Evidence indicates that violence increases during the most violent of times—war. Several theories are proposed to account for the increase in violent acts during wars (acts that are unrelated to military activity) and only the idea that war legitimatizes violence seems to explain the data.

GLOSSARY

Aggression Any behavior sequence that is intended to injure the person toward whom it is directed.

Catharsis The release of pent-up emotions.

Classical Conditioning The learning of responses through association with stimuli that are rewarding or punishing.

Cognitive Control The control exerted on behavior by cognitive functions.

Eros Life instincts in psychoanalytic theory.

Ethology The study of instincts and action patterns common to all members of a species in their natural habitat.

Frustration The blocking of ongoing, goal-directed activity.

Hostile Aggression Aggression aimed solely at inflicting injury or harm on others.

Instinctual Theories of Aggression Theories of aggression that emphasize the innate qualities of aggressive acts.

Instrumental Aggression Aggression aimed at securing rewards other than the victim's suffering.

Modeling The social transmission of behavior (learning) that is accomplished by viewing the behavior of others.

Physiological Measures Measures of physiological responses such as heart rate and blood pressure.

Prosocial Behavior Behavior that is positive and altruistic.

Reinforcement Control The feedback system that helps control behavior by emphasizing the positive or negative outcome of that behavior.

Self-reinforcement The rewarding or punishing effects of behavior that is imposed by the individual owing to his or her own standards.

Stimulus Control The role that external stimuli play in controlling behavior.

Thanatos Death instincts in psychoanalytic theory.

Vicarious Reinforcement Reinforcement experienced by others but affecting an individual because he or she has seen, read, or heard about its effects.

Abbott, E. Crime and the war. *Journal of Criminal Law and Criminology,* 1918, *9,* 32–45.

Alland, A., Jr. *The Human Imperative.* New York: Columbia University Press, 1972.

Archer, D., and R. Gartner. Violent acts and violent times: A comparative approach to postwar homicide rates. *American Sociological Review,* 1976, *41,* 937–63.

Bandura, A. Influence of models' reinforcement contingencies on the acquisition of imitative responses. *Journal of Personality and Social Psychology,* 1965, *1,* 589–95.

————. *Principles of Behavior Modification.* New York: Holt, Rinehart and Winston, 1969.

————. Vicarious and self-reinforcement processes. In R. Glaser (Ed.), *The Nature of Reinforcement.* New York: Academic Press, Inc., 1971. Pp. 228–78.

————. *Aggression: A Social Learning Analysis.* Englewood Cliffs, N.J.: Prentice-Hall, Inc., 1973.

————. Self-efficacy: Toward a unifying theory of behavioral change. *Psychological Review,* 1977 (a), *84,* 191–215.

————. *Social Learning Theory.* Englewood Cliffs, N.J.: Prentice-Hall, Inc., 1977 (b).

————, and W. Mischel. Modification of self-imposed delay of reward through exposure to live and symbolic models. *Journal of Personality and Social Psychology,* 1965, *2,* 698–705.

———— D. Ross, and S. A. Ross. Transmission of aggression through imitation of aggressive models. *Journal of Abnormal and Social Psychology,* 1961, *63,* 575–82.

————, ————, and ————. Imitation of film-mediated aggressive models. *Journal of Abnormal and Social Psychology,* 1963, *66,* 3–11.

Barnett, S. A. Attack and defense in animal societies. In C. D. Clemente and D. B. Lindsley (Eds.), *Aggression and Defense.* Los Angeles: University of California Press, 1967. Pp. 35–36.

Baron, R. A. Exposure to an aggressive model and apparent probability of retaliation from the victim as determinants of adult aggressive behavior. *Journal of Experimental Social Psychology,* 1971 (a), *7,* 343–55.

————. Reducing the influence of an aggressive model: The restraining effects of discrepant modeling cues. *Journal of Personality and Social Psychology,* 1971 (b), *20,* 240–45.

————. Aggression as a function of victims' pain cues, level of prior anger arousal, and exposure to an aggressive model. *Journal of Personality and Social Psychology,* 1974, *29,* 117–24.

————. Heightened sexual arousal and physical aggression. Paper presented at the meeting of the Midwestern Psychological Association, Chicago, 1976.

Berger, S. M. Conditioning through vicarious instigation. *Psychological Review,* 1962, *69,* 450–66.

Berkowitz, L. *Aggression: A Social-Psychological Analysis.* New York: McGraw-Hill Book Company, 1962.

————. The concept of aggressive drive: Some additional considerations. In L. Berkowitz (Ed.), *Advances in Experimental Social Psychology.* Vol. 2. New York: Academic Press, Inc., 1965. Pp. 301–329.

————. The frustration-aggression hypothesis revisited. In L. Berkowitz (Ed.), *Roots of Aggression.* New York: Atherton Press, 1969. Pp. 1–28.

————. The contagion of violence: An S-R mediational analysis of some effects of observed aggression. In W. Arnold and M. Page (Eds.), *Nebraska Symposium on Motivation.* 1971. Lincoln, Nebraska: University of Nebraska Press. Pp. 95–135.

————. Words and symbols as stimuli to aggressive responses. In J. F. Knutson (Ed.), Control of Aggression: *Implications from Basic Research.* 1973, Chicago: Aldine-Atherton. Pp. 113–43.

————. Some determinants of impulsive aggression: Role of mediated associations with reinforcements for aggression. *Psychological Review.* 1974, *81,* 165–76.

————, and A. Frodi. Stimulus characteristics that can enhance or decrease aggression: Associations with prior positive or negative reinforcements for aggression. *Aggressive Behavior,* 1977, *3,* 1–15.

————, and A. LePage. Weapons as aggression—eliciting stimuli. *Journal of Personality and Social Psychology,* 1967, *7,* 202–207.

Buss, A. H. *The Psychology of Aggression.* New York: John Wiley & Sons, Inc., 1961.

————. Aggression pays. In J. L. Singer (Ed.), *The Control of Aggression and Violence.* New York, Academic Press, Inc., 1971.

————, A. Booker, and E. Buss. Firing a weapon and aggression. *Journal of Personality and Social Psychology,* 1972, *22,* 296–302.

Collins, W. A. The effect of temporal separation between motivation, aggression and consequences: A developmental study. *Developmental Psychology,* 1973.

Dollard, J., L. W. Doob, N. E. Miller, O. H. Mowrer, and R. R. Sears. *Frustration and Aggression.* New Haven, Conn.: Yale University Press, 1939.

Donnerstein, E., M. Donnerstein, and R. Evans. Erotic stimuli and aggression: Facilitation or inhibition. *Journal of Personality and Social Psychology,* 1975, *32,* 237–44.

———— and D. W. Wilson. Effects of noise and perceived control on ongoing and subsequent aggressive behavior. *Journal of Personality and Social Psychology,* 1976, *34,* 774–81.

Drabman, R. S., and M. H. Thomas. Does media violence increase children's tolerance of real-life aggression? *Developmental Psychology,* 1974, *10,* 418–21.

Eibl-Eibesfeldt, I. *Ethology: The Biology of Behavior.* (2nd Edition).New York: Holt, Rinehart and Winston, 1975.

———— and H. Hass. *Zum projekt einer ethologisch orientierten. Untersuchung menschlichen Verbaltens. Milt. Max-Planck-Ges.* 1966, *6,* 383–96.

Eisenhower, M. S., et al. Commission statement on violence in television entertainment programs. Washington, D.C.: National Commission on the Causes and Prevention of Violence, 1969.

Engelbreicht, H. C. *Revolt Against War.* New York: Dodd, Mead & Company, 1937.

Farris, H. E., W. H. Fullmer, and R. E. Ulrich. Extinction of classically conditioned aggression: Results from two procedures. *Proceedings of the 78th Annual Convention of the American Psychological Association.* Washington, D.C. American Psychological Association, 1970. Pp. 775–76.

————, B. E. Gideon, and R. E. Ulrich. Classical conditioning of aggression: A development study. *Psychological Record,* 1970, *20,* 63–68.

Feshbach, S. The function of aggression and the regulation of aggressive drive. *Psychological Review,* 1964, *71,* 257–72.

————. Aggression. In P. H. Mussen (Ed.), *Carmichael's Manual of Child Psychology,* Vol. II, New York: John Wiley & Sons, Inc., 1970. Pp. 159–259.

Freud, S. *A General Introduction to Psycho-Analysis.* New York: Boni & Liveright (Now Liveright), 1920.

————. *Beyond the Pleasure Principle.* London: International Psychoanalytic Press, 1922.

————. *New Introductory Lectures on Psycho-Analysis.* New York: Norton, 1933.

————. Why war? In J. Strachey (Ed.), *Collected Papers.* Vol. V. London: Hogarth Press, 1950, Pp. 273–87.

Friedrich L. K., and A. H. Stein. Aggressive and prosocial television programs and the natural behavior of preschool children. *Monographs of the Society for Research in Child Development,* 1973, 38 (*4,* Serial No. 151).

Frodi, A. The effect of exposure to weapons on aggressive behavior from a cross-cultural perspective. *International Journal of Psychology,* 1975, *10,* 283–92.

Geen, R. G., and L. Berkowitz. Name-mediated aggressive cue properties. *Journal of Personality,* 1966, *34,* 456–65.

―――, J. J. Rakosky, and R. Pigg. Awareness of arousal and its relation to aggression. *British Journal of Social and Clinical Psychology,* 1972, *11,* 115–21.

Gerbner, G. Violence in television drama: Trends and symbolic functions. In G. A. Comstock and E. A. Rubinstein (Eds.), *Television and Social Behavior.* Vol. 1, *Content and Control.* Washington, D.C.: Government Printing Office, 1972 (a). Pp. 28–187.

―――. The violence index: A rating of various aspects of dramatic violence on prime-time network television 1967 through 1970. Unpublished manuscript, University of Pennsylvania Press, 1972 (b).

―――, and L. P. Gross. The violence profile v: Trends in network television, drama and viewer conceptions of reality. Unpublished manuscript, University of Pennsylvania, 1976.

―――, L. Gross, M. F. Eleey, M. Jackson-Beeck, S. Jeffries-Fox, and N. Signorielli. TV violence profile no. 8: The highlights. *Journal of Communication,* 1977, *27,* 2, 171–80.

Gillespie, W. H. Aggression and instinct theory. *International Journal of Psycho-analysis,* 1971, *52,* 155–60.

Goldstein, J. H. *Aggression and Crimes of Violence.* New York: Oxford University Press, Inc., 1975.

―――　and R. L. Arms. Effects of observing athletic contests on hostility. *Sociometry,* 1971, *34,* 83–90.

―――, R. L. Rosnow, T. Raday, I. Silverman, and G. D. Gaskell. Punitiveness in response to films varying in content: A cross national field study of aggression. *European Journal of Social Psychology,* 1975, *5.*

Grusec, J. E. Demand characteristics of the modelling experiment: Altruism as a function of age and aggression. *Journal of Personality and Social Psychology,* 1972, *22,* 139–48.

Hamon, A. *Lessons of the World War* (Trans. by B. Mall). London: Fisher Unwin, 1918.

Hull, C. L. *Principles of Behavior.* New York: Appleton-Century-Crofts, 1943.

―――. *Essentials of Behavior.* New Haven, Conn.: Yale University Press, 1951.

Konečni, V. J. The mediation of aggressive behavior: Arousal level versus anger and cognitive labeling. *Journal of Personality and Social Psychology,* 1975, *32,* 706–712.

―――　and A. N. Doob. Catharsis through displacement of aggression. *Journal of Personality and Social Psychology,* 1972, *23,* 379–87.

Leyens, J. P., and R. D. Parke. Aggressive slides can induce a weapons effect. *European Journal of Social Psychology,* 1975, *5,* 229–36.

Lifton, R. J. The veterans return. *New York Times,* November 8, 1970, p. 32.

Lorenz, K. *On Aggression.* New York: Harcourt Brace Jovanovich, Inc., 1966.

Luden, W. A. *War and Delinquency.* Ames, Iowa: The Art Press, 1963.

Lyon, D. O., and D. Ozolins. Pavlovian conditioning of shock-elicited aggression: A discrimination procedure. *Journal of Experimental Analysis of Behavior,* 1970, *13,* 325–31.

Mahoney, M., and C. Thorensen (Eds.), *Self-Control: Power to the Person.* Monterey, Calif.: Brooks/Cole, 1974.

Mahoney, M. J. Reflections on the cognitive-learning trend in psychotherapy. *American Psychologist,* 1977, *32,* 5–13.

Mannheim, H. *War and Crime.* London: Watts, 1941.

―――. *Comparative Criminology.* London: Routledge and Kegan Paul, 1965.

Mantell, D. M., and M. Pilisuk (Eds.). Soldiers in and after Vietnam. *Journal of Social Issues,* 1975, *31,* 1–195.

Meichenbaum, D. Self-instructional methods. In F. H. Kanfer and A. P. Goldstein (Eds.), *Helping People Change.* New York: Pergamon Press, Inc., 1975 (a). Pp. 357–92.

———. Theoretical and treatment implications of developmental research on verbal control of behavior. *Canadian Psychological Review,* 1975 (b). Pp. 22–27.

Miller, N. E. The frustration-aggression hypothesis. *Psychological Review,* 1941, *48,* 337–42.

Mischel, W. *Personality and Assessment.* New York: John Wiley & Sons, Inc., 1968.

———. Toward a cognitive social learning reconceptualization of personality. *Psychological Review,* 1973, *80,* 252–83.

Page, M. P., and R. J. Scheidt. The elusive weapons effect: Demand awareness, evaluation apprehension, and slightly sophisticated subjects. *Journal of Personality and Social Psychology,* 1971, *20,* 304–318.

Prentice, N. M. The influence of live and symbolic modeling on promoting moral judgments of adolescent delinquents. *Journal of Abnormal Psychology,* 1972.

Rasa, O. A. E. Aggression: Appetite or aversion? An ethologists point of view. *Aggressive Behavior,* 1976, *2,* 213–22.

Report to the Surgeon General, United States Public Health Service. *Television and Growing Up: The Impact of Televised Violence.* Washington, D.C. U.S. Department of Health, Education, and Welfare, 1972.

Reynolds, G. S., A. C. Catania, and B. F. Skinner. Conditioned and unconditioned aggression in pigeons. *Journal of the Experimental Analysis of Behavior,* 1963, *6,* 73–74.

Rotter, J. B. *Social Learning and Clinical Psychology.* Englewood Cliffs, N.J.: Prentice-Hall, 1954.

Rule, B. G., and L. S. Hewitt. Effects of thwarting on cardiac response and physical aggression. *Journal of Personality and Social Psychology,* 1971, *19,* 181–87.

——— and G. J. Leger. Pain cues and differing functions of aggression. *Canadian Journal of Behavioral Science,* 1976, *8,* 213–22.

——— and A. R. Nesdale. Differing functions of aggression. *Journal of Personality,* 1974, *42,* 467–81.

——— and A. R. Nesdale. Emotional arousal and aggressive behavior. *Psychological Bulletin,* 1976, *83,* 851–63.

Schenkel, R. Submission: Its features and functions in the wolf and dog. *American Zoologist,* 1967, *7,* 319–29.

Schneider, J. A. Networks hold the line. *Journal of Communication,* September/October 1977, 9–17.

Sears, R. R. Non-aggressive reactions to frustration. *Psychological Review,* 1941, *48,* 343–46.

———. Personality development in the family. In J. M. Seidman (Ed.), *The Child.* New York: Holt, Rinehart and Winston, 1958.

———, E. E. Maccoby, and H. Levin. *Patterns of child Rearing.* Evanston, Ill.: Row, Peterson (Now Harper & Row, Publishers, New York), 1957.

Simons, L. S., M. R. Fenn, J. F. Layton, and C. W. Turner. An investigation of behavior in an aggressive carnival game. In J. J. Kock (Ed.), *Der Feld Experiment in Der Sozial Psychologie,* in press.

Skinner, B. F. *The Behavior of Organisms: An Experimental Analysis,* New York: Appleton-Century-Crofts, 1938.

———. *Science and Human Behavior.* New York: Macmillan Publishing Co., Inc., 1953.

———. *About Behaviorism.* New York: Alfred A. Knopf, Inc., 1974.

Sorokin, P. *The Sociology of Revolution.* Philadelphia: J. B. Lippincourt Company, 1925.

Southwick, C. H. An experimental study of intragroup antagonistic behavior in rhesus monkeys

(Macaca mulatta). *Behaviour,* 1967, *28,* 182–209.

Spence, K. W. Behavior therapy and learning: Selected papers. Englewood Cliffs, N.J.: Prentice-Hall, Inc., 1960.

Stein, A. H., and L. K. Friedrich. Television content and young children's behavior. In J. P. Murray, E. A. Rubinstein, and G. A. Comstock (Eds.), *Television and Social Behavior.* Vol. 2. *Television and Social Learning.* Washington, D.C.: Government Printing Office, 1972. Pp. 202–317.

———— and L. K. Friedrich. The effects of television content on young children. In A. E. Pick (Ed.), *Minnesota Symposium on Child Psychology.* Vol. 9. Minneapolis, University of Minnesota Press, 1975 (a). Pp. 78–105.

———— and L. K. Friedrich. Impact of television on children and youth. In E. M. Heatherington (Ed.), *Review of Child Development Research* (Vol. 5). Chicago: University of Chicago Press, 1975 (b). Pp. 183–256.

————, ————, Deutsch, and C. Nydegger. The effects of aggressive and prosocial television on the social interaction of preschool children. Paper presented at the meeting of the Midwestern Psychological Association. Chicago, May 1973.

Sutherland, E., and D. Cressey. *Principles of Criminology.* Chicago: J. B. Lippincott Company, 1960.

Swart, C., and L. Berkowitz. The effect of a stimulus associated with a victim's pain on later aggression. *Journal of Personality and Social Psychology,* 1976, *33,* 623–31.

Tarde, G. *Penal Philosophy.* Boston: Little, Brown and Company, 1912. (French ed., 1890.)

Thomas, M. H., and R. S. Drabman. Toleration of real-life aggression as a function of exposure to televised violence and age of subject. *Merrill-Palmer Quarterly,* 1975, *21,* 227–32.

————, R. W. Horton, E. C. Lippincott, and R. S. Drabman. Desensitization to portrayals of real-life aggression as a function of exposure to television violence. *Journal of Personality and Social Psychology,* 1977, *35,* 450–58.

Toch, H. *Violent Men.* Chicago: Aldine Publishing Company, 1969.

Turner, C. W., and D. Goldsmith. Effects of toy guns and airplanes on children's antisocial free play behavior. *Journal of Experimental Child Psychology,* 1976.

————, J. F. Layton, and L. S. Simons. Naturalistic studies of aggressive behavior: Aggressive stimuli, victim visibility, and horn honking. *Journal of Personality and Social Psychology,* 1975, *31,* 1098–1107.

———— and L. S. Simons. Effects of subject sophistication and evaluation apprehension on aggressive responses to weapons. *Journal of Personality and Social Psychology,* 1974, *30,* 341–48.

Vernon, W., and R. Ulrich. Classical conditioning of pain-elicited aggression. *Science,* 1966, *152,* 668–69.

Vondracek, F. W., A. H. Stein, and L. K. Friedrich. A non-verbal technique for assessing frustration response in pre-school children. *Journal of Personality Assessment,* 1973, *37,* 355–62.

Zillman, D., and J. Bryant. Effect of residual excitation on the emotional response to provocation and delayed aggressive behavior. *Journal of Personality and Social Psychology,* 1974, *30,* 782–91.

————, R. C. Johnson, and K. D. Day. Attribution of apparent arousal and proficiency of recovery from sympathetic activation affecting excitation transfers to aggressive behavior. *Journal of Experimental Social Psychology,* 1974, *10,* 503–515.

————, A. H. Katcher, and B. Milansky. Excitation transfer from physical exercise to subsequent aggressive behavior. *Journal of Experimental Social Psychology,* 1972, *8,* 247–59.

9

Attraction and Love

Why do you like people? Who do people like you? How many people do you like? How many people do you love? These questions are some of the most important ones we ask and answer if we take interpersonal relationships seriously. Not only is it important to have friends and loved ones but it is important to know when someone who acts like a friend is really a friend. For thousands of years people have wondered whether an individual who is paying them a lot of attention really likes them, or is merely using them to gain some other resource they control (money, status, information, and so on).

Strangely enough, even though there has been an enormous amount of interest shown in attraction and love, there was, until about a quarter of a century ago, very little systematic study of the processes that govern liking and loving. Zick Rubin (1973) portrays the social psychologist's interest in attraction and love in terms of a guest at a party who arrives when the party is almost over. Prior to the arrival of the psychologists, the poets, playwrights, journalists, philosophers, and historians had had their say about why people like each other. Why was the psychologist so late to the party and what is there left to say?

Attraction and Love—The Folklore Approach

Robert Zajonc has compared the development of the scientific approach in other sciences to the development of science when it deals with interpersonal relationships. He says (Zajonc, 1966, pp. 2–3),

Around 250 B.C. the Greek astronomer Eratosthenes calculated the circumference of the Earth by comparing the angles of the moon seen in Alexandria and in Aswan, which lies directly to the south on the tropic of Cancer, and where on the day of the summer solstice the angle of the moon seen is exactly 90°. His results—among the first scientific observations recorded in history—differ from the present estimates by about 180 miles, or less than 1 percent.

The velocity of light was first measured in 1675 by the Danish astronomer Ole Römer, who compared the observed eclipses of Jupiter's moons with predictions based on precise theoretical calculations. His results also agree very closely with the present ones. . . .

The first experimental observation in social psychology was performed in 1897 by Triplett. It dealt with the effects of competition on human performance. Triplett measured the average time required to execute 150 winds of a fishing reel. His subjects performed the task while working alone and while competing in pairs against each other. Performance was found to improve when carried out in competition.

Why did the first scientific measurement precede the first social-psychological measurement by 2,100 years? Certainly it could not be argued that the equipment for Eratosthenes' measurement existed and therefore could be used whereas Triplett had to wait until fishing reels and clocks were invented. No, the reason social-psychological measurement was so late in arriving on the scene was that people already knew everything there was to know about social psychology, or thought they did, because people are the central figures in social-psychological measurement.

Recently a friend and I were discussing our research and he lamented the fact that he was a social psychologist and not a physicist. As he put it, "All the people I deal with think they know more about aggression than I do. They are the ones that are aggressive, aren't they? I wish I did research on quarks. Then no one would know what I was talking about."

The problem of dealing with issues that are already well understood by the general populace is a serious one. Undoubtedly there was no systematic research on a number of important areas in social psychology because the prevailing wisdom of generations was that we knew all there was to know about these areas. Doing research when all the answers are known is not a very popular endeavor. Probably no area of social psychology has been more beset with such difficulties than the area of attraction and love. On the one hand, certain people argue we know why people like and love each other, and even if we don't, scientists have no business snooping into such intimate relationships.

Likes Attract—Opposites Attract

A superb example of the folklore about attraction is that people like people who are like themselves. On the other hand, the idea that opposites attract is equally appealing to certain people, and this idea is also important folklore. Now which is it? Do people like people who are similar or do people like opposites? Somehow or other it seems to me that we can't have it both ways. Either people like people who are similar to them or they like people who are dissimilar to them, but we can't use both statements as a generalized rule. True, we could say that in certain situations people are drawn to people who are like themselves and in other situations they like opposites. But that isn't what the folklore says, and to specify when people like opposites and when they like likes is to study the subject scientifically. Therefore, even if you have an aversion to understanding more about why people like each other or why people love each other, these are important issues in our relationships with others.

Measuring Liking and Loving

It may be easy to say that you like someone, but what do you mean by that? You may like your best friend, a casual acquaintance, and your psychology professor, but for quite different reasons and in quite different ways. Love is even more difficult. Does one love parents in the same way he or she loves a spouse? Not really. Love of parents does not typically include the intimacy of sexual love involved between spouses. Other cultures were much more aware of these differences in meaning than we are. For example, ancient Greek had three words for love: *phileos,* which referred to the love of friendship, *eros,* which referred to sexual love, and *agape,* which meant unselfish, platonic love of one person for another. All three of these meanings have been subsumed under one word in English. No wonder we have difficulty in defining it.

It is this difficulty in defining liking and loving that haunts us when we try to measure the two. If, as is usual, it is difficult for you to be specific in telling us why you like or love someone, that makes it difficult for us to measure liking and loving. But we want to do more than say John likes Harold; we want to be able to say John likes Harold more than he likes Joe. Ideally, we would like to be able to say that John likes Harold twice as much as he likes Joe. Unfortunately, we are far from such an ideal. We are presently content with simply measuring liking and loving.

But still the question exists, "How do you measure liking and loving?" Basically, the only way to do it very accurately is to ask people. Some social psychologists have argued that unobtrusive measures of attraction are best. The idea is that if you ask people something, they won't know or won't tell the truth. If people don't know they like someone, then it seems to me that no matter how unobtrusive the measure, it will still be inaccurate. On the other hand, if they don't want to tell you, some unobtrusive measures may be helpful. For example, watching people as they interact, how they communicate nonverbally, with whom they spend time, and so forth, may tell you a lot about who likes whom. But it may not. One example should suffice. A person who wants very much to keep his or her job may smile when the boss is around, do everything the boss wants, give many nonverbal signs of liking, and nevertheless despise the boss.

When it comes to love, the problem is even more intricate. One measure of love that has long been used, at least in Canada and the United States, is marriage. Yet how many loveless, even hateful, marriages continue because of the children, religion, money, or some reason other than love. It is almost measuring the unmeasurable, but not quite.

These two people are interacting. Do you see any signs that might give you a clue as to whether they like each other?

What may be termed the first systematic and scientific study of attraction was carried out by Sir Francis Galton in 1870. He studied the marriage patterns of a group of eminent men and the families that produced them. He concluded that the marriages of illustrious men were with equivalent women. Karl Pearson (Pearson and Lee, 1903) quantified Galton's and other data before concluding that there is a selection of like by like between spouses. Thus, the first study of attraction supported the notion that likes attract.

Subsequent research was mainly correlational in nature. That is, the attitudes, opinions, values, tastes, and so forth of husbands and wives were correlated, and it was found that husbands and wives were more similar to each other than would be expected by chance (Kirkpatrick and Stone, 1935; Morgan and Remmers, 1935; Newcomb and Svehla, 1937; Schiller, 1932; Schuster and Elderton, 1906). For example, Schiller correlated several variables and found that the correlations between husbands and wives were higher than the correlations between randomly selected couples. Figure 9-1 shows the results. As can be readily seen, the husbands and wives are much more similar than are the randomly paired couples.

Another relationship that has been studied correlationally is friendship. For example, Winslow (1937) found that friends possess considerably more similarity of opinions than could be expected by chance. Richardson (1940) also found a higher correlation between friends on six values than between randomly matched pairs. Furthermore, Richardson found higher correlations between friends when the women he questioned were more mature adults than when they were younger undergraduate

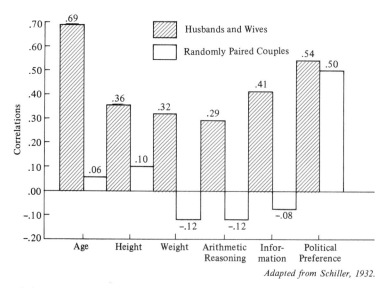

Adapted from Schiller, 1932.

Figure 9-1 Correlations between husbands and wives and randomly paired couples on six variables.

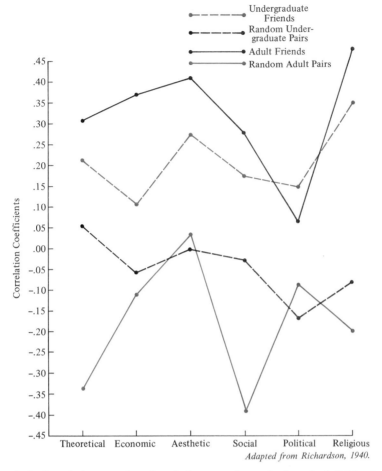

Figure 9–2 shows the correlations between the friends and the randomly paired couples on the six values.

Adapted from Richardson, 1940.

Figure 9–2 Correlations on six values between undergraduate and adult friends and undergraduates and adults randomly paired.

women. Figure 9-2 shows the correlations between the friends and the randomly paired couples on the six values.

Richardson (1939) concluded that attitudinal traits showed the most consistent result of similarity between husbands and wives and between friends. That same conclusion still holds true. Friends, engaged couples, spouses, and other individuals who have made some sort of explicit attraction response are more similar to each other in a variety of attitudes, physical characteristics, and so forth, but the strongest relationship occurs when attitudes are considered. Byrne (1971) has provided an excellent review of this early correlational literature.

As those who have been attracted to each other are more similar than would be expected by chance, the problem of which attracts—likes or opposites—is settled, isn't it? Not really, because if you think back to our discussion of correlation and causality in Chapter 2 you will remember that correlation does not imply causality. Here is a superb example of what is meant by that statement. We know that spouses are more similar to each other than are randomly selected pairs. What we don't know is whether the two were more similar before they met and similarity drew them together or whether something else caused them to like each other and they gradually changed until they became similar to each other. Unfortunately, correlational studies do not solve the problem for us. We still don't know whether likes attract or opposites attract and grow more similar over the years. I might add, however, that the whole process of friendship and marriage is a strange one if people are attracted to others because they are different from each other and then proceed to change and become more similar.

If a researcher is to state with some degree of certainty that a stimulus causes a response, it is necessary to control other variables that might influence the response of interest. In this case, the response is attraction. A gigantic step in this direction came in the 1950s when T. M. Newcomb studied attraction among college men. In Chapter 2, this research project was described in some detail and you should review that section before reading further.

The Acquaintance Process

Basically, Newcomb (1961) brought two groups of 17 men together for a semester and watched the attraction between and among them grow. He was careful to assure that none of the individuals had ever met prior to coming to live in his dormitory. Throughout the course of the semester that each group lived together, Newcomb and his associates measured the changing patterns of attraction. At first, Newcomb found that individuals were attracted to other persons whom they perceived to be similar to themselves in respect to attitudes that they considered important. As incorrect perceptions of others were altered, attraction towards individuals changed, but there was little change in the attitudes themselves. As Newcomb (1961, p. 254) says,

We found little change in individuals' attitudes during the four months of our data-gathering—or, more accurately, we found little change in those attitudes that were systematically related to attraction. We may have sampled too limited a range of attitudes, but there are good grounds for suspecting that most attitudes of sufficient importance to our subjects to influence their attraction toward others had already achieved such stability, before they met each other, that not much change was to be expected during so brief a period.

House members' orientations toward each other—that is to say, their attraction—had, however, no previous history and they changed a good deal from first to last. . . . That is, as individuals acquired more information about each other's attitudes, their high-attraction preferences tended to change in favor of individuals with whom they were more closely in agreement.

Now we know, likes attract. Attitudes didn't change but attraction did; that must be the answer. But, as Newcomb pointed out, possibly there were not enough of the relevant attitudes measured. Since these men were interacting daily and there were so many variables that Newcomb could neither measure or control, we can feel more certain that similarity leads to attraction, but we're not there yet.

Look at this group of people. Are there any you think you might like just from looking at them?

From Laboratory to Real Life

During the late 1950s a research program was begun by Donn Byrne at the University of Texas. This program has resulted in the publication of numerous articles, chapters, and papers dealing with attraction. The approach taken by Byrne and his associates was a careful controlling of variables that might influence attraction and a systematic investigation of each one of them. To some, such an approach seems wasteful of time and effort, but it is necessary if a researcher is to be able to say with some degree of certainty that a specific stimulus causes a response. As we have seen so far in our discussion of attraction, determining whether likes or opposites attract is no small chore.

INVESTIGATING ATTRACTION IN THE LABORATORY

Several steps needed to be taken to overcome some of the difficulties we referred to in earlier attraction research. The first step was to control rigidly the stimulus person to whom a subject would respond. To do this adequately, it was necessary to consider all of the possible attributes of an individual that might influence attraction—sex, appearance, manner, nonverbal forms of communication, accent, and so forth. As any one of these attributes might affect attraction and the researchers did not know which ones would, the first step was to eliminate the physical presence of the person the subject was to evaluate. Therefore, subjects were told that another individual had filled out an attitude survey and they (the subjects) were to respond to the individual on the basis of the attitudes held by the other individual.

The next step was to develop a measure of attraction. If you put your mind to the task, each one of you could probably think of many ways to measure attraction. Friendship, engagement, marriage, or some other such measures could be used. However, remember the decision had been made to keep the two individuals from meeting each other. Thus a paper and pencil scale was probably the only way to measure attraction in this situation. Therefore, The Interpersonal Judgment Scale (Byrne, 1961) was developed. On the scale subjects filled out four buffer items and then were asked how much they liked the stranger whose attitude survey they had just seen and how much they would like to work with the individual. These two items are summed to yield an attraction score that can range from 2 (very negative) to 14 (very positive).

You may be thinking about this time that such an artificial situation has little to do with deep, abiding friendships and the attraction that enters into a happy marriage. You may be right. But these first steps of controlling as many extraneous variables as possible are necessary if the base relationship between a stimulus and a response is to be understood. No doubt reading an attitude survey filled out by another person and then evaluating him or her on the basis of such limited information is artificial—but necessary. Once the relationship between attitudes and attraction is understood, then other variables can be added to the attitudes and their effect on attraction measured.

To make a long story short, in a number of studies people liked people who were similar to themselves and did not like people who were not similar to themselves (Byrne, 1961, 1962; Byrne and Nelson, 1964). As a matter of fact, attitude similarity and attraction provided such a stable relationship that it was possible to predict attraction with a high degree of accuracy if the proportion of similar attitudes was known (Byrne and Nelson, 1965a). Data from several different investigations were combined that included the responses of 790 subjects who had received one of 11 different proportions of attitude similarity. The data suggested that there was a linear relationship between attraction and proportion of similar attitudes. In other words, as attitude similarity increased, attraction increased along with it.

Extraneous Variables

As more control is introduced into the laboratory, then the possibility of extraneous variables entering into the relationship being studied is possible. Two such variables are experimenter effects (Rosenthal, 1966; 1969) and demand characteristics (Orne, 1962, 1969). Both of these issues were discussed in Chapter 2, so we will return to them only briefly here.

Experimenter effects refer to the biasing of subjects' responses by the experimenter. Even though these effects are generally unintentional, they can be quite strong. However, Byrne (1971) has argued that they are not a viable explanation for the attitude similarity-attraction relationship. A number of attraction studies have been run in groups in which subjects from several different conditions were present (Byrne, 1961, 1962; Byrne and Nelson, 1965a). In addition the experimenter did not know which condition any subject was in. Thus to influence subjects under these conditions the experimenter would simultaneously have to influence subjects to do different things when the experimenter does not know what any given subject should do to support the hypothesis. If this sounds like an impossible task, it is. In attraction experiments in which subjects have been run individually and thus could be influenced by the experimenter, the results have been substantially the same as when subjects are run in groups (Byrne, Lamberth, Palmer, and London, 1969; Gouaux, 1971; Lamberth, 1971). Thus it seems improbable if not impossible for experimenter bias to influence the attitude similarity–attraction relationship.

Demand characteristics could also account for the relationship between attitude similarity and attraction. They could, but they probably don't. In Chapter 2 we discussed a study by Lamberth and Byrne (1971) in which demand characteristics in attraction research were carefully investigated. In that study, groups of subjects were told to try to guess the experimental hypothesis and try to comply with it or do the exact opposite. Other groups were told the hypothesis, whereas still other groups were told a false hypothesis (i.e., opposites attract) and then told either to respond in such a way that the hypothesis would be supported or to do the exact opposite. Whatever instructions were received by the subjects did not influence their responses. The only significant results were the effect of attitude similarity on attraction. Figure 9–3 shows the results for the groups who were told to guess the hypothesis and those told the hypothesis. These, of course, are the crucial groups, since the basic idea of demand characteristics is that subjects will guess the correct hypothesis and then do what the experimenter wants. Therefore, it seems highly improbable that demand characteristics unduly influence the relationship.

THEORY BUILDING
Empirical relationships are better understood if they are described in theoretical terms. The importance of a theory that not only explains results but helps to guide research itself is inestimable. From the earliest period of the research program carried

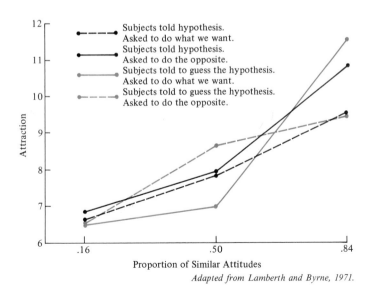

Adapted from Lamberth and Byrne, 1971.

Figure 9–3 Attraction responses by subjects told the experimental hypothesis or asked to guess it and requested to support the hypothesis or do the exact opposite.

out by Byrne and his associates, the stimuli were conceptualized as reinforcers. That is, attitudes were seen as reinforcers (similar ones) or punishers (dissimilar ones). It was well understood by these researchers that stimuli other than attitudes would affect attraction. However, if all stimuli that influenced attraction could be characterized as reinforcers, then a relationship among various classes of stimuli could be established. The intent of the researchers was to develop a theoretical approach that could encompass more than attitudes. Just as it was necessary to exclude the influence of sex, appearance, manner, nonverbal forms of communication, accent, and the like in the early research, it was a foregone conclusion that these variables ultimately would be introduced systematically into the research. However, instead of developing separate theories for attitudes and attraction, sex and attraction, appearance and attraction, it seemed better to develop a theory that encompassed a variety of stimuli. The problem is not unlike the old problem of adding apples and oranges. How many apples equal an orange? However, when a more general category, fruit, is used, both apples and oranges can be included.

Let us look carefully at research that shows how the seemingly impossible task of adding apples and oranges can be accomplished. Byrne and Rhamey (1965) investigated the effects of attitudes and personal evaluations. They assumed that if attitudes influenced attraction, evaluations such as "I think you're intelligent," "I think you're handsome," "I think you're capable" would have an even greater effect on attraction. This assumption is rather straightforward. If we like to be agreed with, we like to be complimented even more. Indeed, that is precisely what Byrne and Rhamey found. Furthermore, and of even greater importance to future research, they found that evaluations were three times as powerful as attitudes in determining attraction. In future studies it was possible to determine not only that a specific stimulus affected attraction, but to be precise in determining how much a specific stimulus would affect attraction.

THE BYRNE–CLORE REINFORCEMENT-AFFECT MODEL OF ATTRACTION

In 1970 Byrne and Clore proposed a reinforcement model of attraction and this was later altered to make more explicit the cognitive role of affect (feelings or emotions) in 1974 (Clore and Byrne, 1974). The model, which we used as an example in Chapter 1 (see Figure 1–3), assumes that a process very similar to classical conditioning occurs. That is, a previously neutral stimulus is paired with a stimulus that is either positive or negative. The positive stimulus leads to positive affect and the negative stimulus leads to negative affect. The affect mediates the attraction response and leads to liking or disliking.

For example, let us assume that you have just met Jim at a party. Jim is the neutral simulus. As soon as you begin to talk, Jim, who is a very intense fellow, begins to expound on his ideas concerning religion. If Jim's ideas concerning religion agree with yours, then Jim's ideas represent a positive stimulus; if they disagree, they represent a negative stimulus. The intensity of the stimulus is determined by how important you think religion is. This combination, then, leads to an affective response on your part which in turn leads to a feeling of "I like Jim," or "I don't like Jim." Of course, we have omitted a number of other factors—Jim's looks, dress, accent, and so forth—for the sake of simplicity. In actuality, each of these and many more stimuli would enter into the determination of your affect, which mediates attraction. Byrne and Clore assume that there are other stimuli having nothing to do with Jim that will combine with the affect directly associated with him in determining your attraction toward him. For example, if you have a headache, you're depressed, you're angry, or some other such thing, your liking of Jim will be decreased. If however, you feel good, your attraction toward Jim will be increased. Interestingly enough, several experiments have "turned things around" and associated positive or negative stimuli with inanimate objects and found that subjects' evaluations of random shapes, the experimental room, the experimental apparatus, and so forth increase as their positive affect increases (Byrne and Clore, 1970; Griffitt and Guay, 1969; Sachs and Byrne, 1970).

The argument made by Byrne and his associates is that conceptualizing attraction as a function of reinforcement and affect helps us to understand the process more readily. A stimulus is noticed and this stimulus then has an effect upon the affect that the individual is feeling currently. There may be incidents so dramatic in our lives that virtually no stimulus is capable of altering affect. For example, if someone you love very much has died, your generally negative feelings will probably not be altered much by similarity, positive evaluations, or any other positive stimulus. In fact, you may be so grief-stricken that no other stimuli are even noticed.

RESEARCH IN THE REAL WORLD

The research by Byrne and his associates was grounded in real-world correlations indicating similarity between those who were attracted to each other. To determine causality, however, strict controls were established and an artificial situation was utilized. After a more thorough understanding of attitude similarity and attraction was attained, it was possible to test some of the experimental findings in more realistic settings. You may ask, however, what was gained by moving the research to the laboratory. The answer to that is that a theory encompassing much more than attitude similarity and attraction had been developed. Indeed, the reinforcers in addition to attitudes and evaluations, that had been tested under laboratory conditions and had influenced attraction included physical attractiveness (Byrne, London, and Reeves, 1968) emotional disturbances (Byrne and Lamberth, 1971; Novak and Lerner, 1968), and race (Byrne and Wong, 1962). On the other hand, occupational prestige (Byrne, Griffitt, and Golightly, 1966), most personality characteristics (Byrne and Griffitt, 1969; Byrne, Griffitt, and Stefaniak, 1967; Griffitt, 1969; Palmer and Byrne, 1970) and economic information (Byrne, Clore, and Worchel, 1966) did not influence attraction. This, of course, is all in addition to the primary goal of establishing a causal relationship between similarity and attraction—a relationship that has now been expanded to encompass many different reinforcing stimuli.

Computer Dating. A study by Byrne, Ervin, and Lamberth (1970) investigated attraction in a less controlled, more realistic setting. In addition, a follow-up two to three months later assessed how long-lasting the effects were.

A 50-item questionnaire was constructed and 420 individuals were pretested on it. From this pool of people, 44 couples were selected. Twenty-four of the couples were matched because they were similar to each other (on their answers to the 50-item questionnaire), and 20 couples were matched because they were dissimilar from each other. The study was conceived of as a computer-dating study because the 24 similar couples were computer-matched for similarity, what *supposedly* occurs when you respond to a computer-dating service.

The couples were given a small amount of money and sent to the Student Union for a short "coke date." When they returned their proximity to each other was noted as they approached the experimental room. The distance could range from touching each other to standing as far apart as possible. The subjects were then separated and asked to evaluate their dates on the Interpersonal Judgment Scale and to assess the physical attractiveness of their date. Two to three months later, it was possible to locate 74 of the 88 original subjects who were questioned about their date.

People who have used computer dating services haven't ever been this mismatched. What are the characteristics of an ideal match?

Social psychologists are inevitably faced with concern for the applicability of the results of their work to real life. This is especially true when the research that has been carried out has been done in the laboratory. Because laboratory research involves the control of as many extraneous variables as possible, it departs most noticeably from real life. Researchers in interpersonal attraction have been aware of this problem and have faced it in several ways. By combining laboratory research, field experiments, and field studies, they have been able to conclude with some confidence that similarity on a variety of variables leads to attraction.

There is, however, an interesting study reported by Kandel (1978) that investigated attraction between pairs of high school students. A large sample of high school pairs (dyads) were tested on a variety of characteristics including socioeconomic status, leisure-time activity, the use of legal and illegal drugs, religiousness, and academic interest. Of the 1,879 dyads, 73 percent had friendships of 3 years or more, whereas only 11 percent had friendships of less than 1 year. Most (91 percent) of the students selected a best friend who was the same sex as themselves and this selection of best friend was the measure of attraction used.

Similarity in real friendship pairs varied greatly among the variables measured. Not surprisingly, grade in school, sex, race, and age were most highly correlated. These results are not surprising precisely because students are most closely associated in school with others who are the same age and in the same grade. Even in high school, best friends tend to be of the same sex. The importance of race is interesting in that even in schools that were racially mixed, best friends tended to be of the same race.

The next most important dimensions in friendship dyads were not attitudinal but behavioral. The highest similarity in behaviors were those associated with the use of drugs. The order of importance was marijuana, psychedelics, methedrine, and heroin, followed by the legal drugs—cigarettes and alcohol. Similarity among friends on these behaviors was higher than on academic interests (educational aspirations, overall grade average, classes cut, and so forth). Next in line of importance was participation in peer activities. The fact that the highest similarity of behavior had to do with drug usage as contrasted to more traditional adolescent behaviors suggests that deviant activities (such as drug usage) need the support of the peer group for both their initiation and continuation. These findings tie in closely with the results of conformity research (Chapter 7) and group behavior (Chapter 11).

Many studies of attraction have concentrated on attitude similarity. If there were a one-to-one correspondence between attitudes and behavior, then attitudes might be totally acceptable as indicators of behavior. As it has become increasingly apparent that attitudes and behavior are not that highly related, it becomes more important to include behavior in the study of attraction.

Whether illicit behaviors are more powerful indicators of behavior than licit ones is an open question. Possibly legal or traditional behaviors will not show such powerful effects as mediators of attraction.

Reference

Kandel, D. B. Similarity in real-life adolescent friendship pairs. *Journal of Personality and Social Psychology*, 1978, *36*, 306–312.

Couples who were similar to each other were more attracted to each other than were couples who had been matched on the basis of dissimilarity. Furthermore, the physical attractiveness of the date also affected attraction, with attractive dates being better liked than unattractive ones. Figure 9–4 shows the results graphically. Another measure of attraction that was taken was the proximity of the couples as they

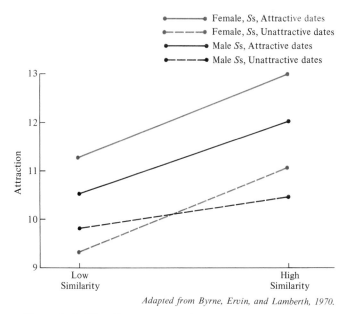

Adapted from Byrne, Ervin, and Lamberth, 1970.

Figure 9–4 Attraction responses in a computer dating study.

returned from their date. This measure also was influenced by similarity and attractiveness of the date.

In the follow-up investigation at the end of the semester, individuals with similar and attractive dates were more likely to remember correctly their date's name, to have talked to the individuals again, or to want to date them than were individuals with dissimilar and unattractive dates. People who had similar, unattractive or dissimilar, attractive dates fell in between the extremes of the individuals with similar-attractive and dissimilar-unattractive dates. Thus both similarity and physical attractiveness influenced attraction and interaction between dates some months later.

It is important to note that even though the couples were matched for similarity or dissimilarity they were not told what they were to discuss. The researchers had no way of knowing what information was exchanged during the course of the date or whether the pairs were actually similar or dissimilar on topics other than the fifty upon which they were matched. It is entirely possible that a couple which had been matched as similar discussed topics upon which they were dissimilar. Such circumstances would, of course, work against the results that were obtained. Thus, this study, carried out under conditions more nearly approaching those of real life, is an important one.

Ten Days in a Fall-Out Shelter. Griffitt and Veitch (1974) report an experiment that constituted a severe real life test of the similarity-attraction relationship. Thirteen male volunteers were paid to spend 10 days in a small, simulated fall-out shelter that was hot (86°) and humid (80 percent). Their diet was severely limited, consisting of 1.25 quarts of water a day and a few crackers and sugar candies. There was a toilet separated from the main room only by a cloth curtain. The total space available for each individual was 22.2 square feet. None of the individuals knew each other before they went into the shelter, so Griffitt and Veitch utilized these subjects to test the effects of attitude similarity on attraction.

Prior to the time they entered the shelter, the subjects filled out a 44-item attitude scale. At several times during their stay in the shelter they were asked to indicate which individuals they would like to have stay in the shelter and which ones they would like to have thrown out. Even though the relationship was not as strong as the attitude similarity-attraction relationship is under laboratory conditions, the first and second most-liked individuals were more similar to the subject than were the first and second most-disliked individuals.

It should come as no surprise that the relationship between similarity and attraction was not so strong in this situation as in a more carefully and controlled laboratory experiment. Considering the fact that each subject had less than a 4 × 6 ft piece of "territory" in a hot, humid room for 10 days, it is surprising that any similarity-attraction effect was evident. The intensity of emotions in such confined quarters, as well as the few topics assessed, could well have "washed-out" the effects of attitudes on attraction. That it did not is an indication of the robustness of this relationship.

Comment

The research program by Byrne and his associates is certainly not the only one or, some would say, the best example of how to conduct research. It is, however, the most extensive program of research in interpersonal attraction. Having been involved in the research on attraction, I am biased in favor of the approach taken. It is slow tedious work, but the final result is an understanding of attraction that is relatively unambiguous.

Other theoretical approaches have been suggested for explaining attraction, the most important one being balance theory, which was first proposed by Heider. We discussed the theory briefly in Chapter 5 and will review it here with particular emphasis upon its application to attraction. Following that we will briefly discuss a sort of minitheory of attraction known as gain-loss theory.

Balance Theory

In Chapter 5, balance theory (Heider, 1946, 1958; Newcomb 1953, 1959, 1971) was discussed with respect to attitude change. I said at that time that it was a much more general theory and particularly Newcomb has utilized the theory to explain interpersonal attraction. In his study of college men living in a dormitory together (Newcomb, 1961) balance theory was the theoretical concept used to explain his findings. That is, Newcomb argued that forming friendships with those who agree with you leads to a balanced situation. Early in the semester Newcomb found that the men formed friendships with those who, they perceived, agreed with them. As the semester progressed and they knew what others actually thought, they formed friendships with those they did agree with.

The basic formulation of balance theory is that if a person (p) likes another person (o), then when any other object of consideration (x) enters the picture, it is more harmonious if both like or dislike *x*. *X* may be an attitude, a person, a value, a piece of art, a movie, and so forth. On the other hand, if *p* likes *x* but *o* dislikes *x*, then there is an imbalanced state. If my friend's enemy is my friend, or if my enemy is my friend's friend, then an imbalanced situation occurs. According to balance theorists, balance is a cognitive state with a Gestaltlike emphasis. That is, a relationship that is in balance provides a good Gestalt.

You should review the discussion with respect to balance and attitude change in Chapter 5, with particular reference to Figures 5–1 and 5–2. Figure 5–1 merely illustrates balanced and imbalanced relationships. Figure 5–2 shows that balance can be achieved in two ways. In the first, a person likes another person and both like or dislike an object. These are referred to as positive sentiment relationships, ones that involve liking, admiring, loving, and so forth, and are the most satisfying of all relationships. Another way to achieve balance, however, is to have one person dislike another person and both of them like or dislike an object. These are referred to as positive unit relationships, such as possession, cause, similarity, and the like, and are about as unpleasant as imbalanced situations. For example, if you dislike another individual and you both like or both dislike an object, the relationship is balanced, but it is not very pleasant.

Newcomb's conceptualization of balance in attraction takes the results referred to in Figure 5–2 and others like them into account. According to Newcomb (1971) the most dissatisfying relationships occur when *p* likes *o* but they disagree about *x* (positive sentiment relationships that are imbalanced in Figure 5–2). These Newcomb refers to as *imbalanced* relationships. When *p* discovers that the relationship is imbalanced, he or she is motivated to do something about it and the way to do this is to alter the *p-o-x* relationship in order to restore balance. One way to do this is to change his or her own attitude about *x*. However, most of us don't react that way. Rather, *p* would tend to try to get *o* to change his attitude about *x*. How many times have you found yourself in a situation in which you attempt to get a friend to change his or her attitude about something on which you disagree?

Another way for *p* to restore balance to the relationship is to misperceive *o*'s position. Remember, Newcomb in his study of attraction pointed out that early in the semester the men liked those they perceived as similar, whether they actually were similar or not. The fourth way that *p* can change the situation into a balanced one is to alter his or her liking for *o*. Now however, the relationship is no longer a positive sentiment one, it is a positive unit relationship. Newcomb refers to these relationships as *nonbalanced*. According to Newcomb, balanced relationships are pleasant, imbalanced relationships are unpleasant, and nonbalanced relationships are accompanied by feeling of indifference. That is, if *p* cannot get *o* to change *o*'s view or views and will not change his or her own views, then the relationship suffers. If enough of these instances occur, then *p* may gradually decide that *o* is not as likable as he or she had thought, and the relationship disintegrates into one of nonbalance.

Newcomb argues that nonbalanced relationships generate indifference, but this is difficult to reconcile with the data presented in Figure 5–2. Nonbalanced relationships are the positive unit relationships in Figure 5–2, and it should be noted that these are as unpleasant as the imbalanced positive sentiment relationships (which are also Newcomb's imbalanced relationships). Price, Harburg, and Newcomb (1966) report a study in which all eight of the possible balanced, imbalanced, and non-balanced relationships were evaluated by subjects on an uneasy-pleasant scale. As expected, the balanced situations received a rating of pleasant and the imbalanced a rating of uneasy by a vast majority of the respondents. What is crucial to the nonbalanced situations is that they be viewed as neutral if they are, indeed, sources of indifference. These four situations did receive many more neutral responses than the balanced or imbalanced situations, but in no case did a majority of the respondents feel these nonbalanced situations were neutral.

Common sense indicates that nonbalanced situations in time become neutral. Old friendships or romances that have broken up because the people involved were spending more time arguing than agreeing will, in time, become hotbeds of indifference. As the relationship moves from a balanced to a nonbalanced one, it is initially very painful, and then indifference sets in. In all probability, Price, Harburg, and Newcomb would have found many more neutral responses to nonbalanced situations if they had asked their subjects to think about old, nonbalanced relationships.

Gain-Loss Theory of Attraction

Aronson and Linder (1965) proposed a somewhat different view of attraction, although it was based on balance theory. They argued that attraction is not just a function of the relationship among *p-o-x,* but that the sequence of behaviors toward one another may influence attraction. As they put it,

> Stated briefly, it is our contention that the feeling of gain or loss is extremely important—specifically, that a gain in esteem is a more potent reward than invariant esteem, and similarly, the loss of esteem is a more potent "punishment" than invariant negative esteem. Thus, if O's behavior toward P was initially negative but gradually became more positive, P would like O more than he would had O's behavior been uniformly positive. [Aronson and Linder, 1965, p. 156.]

The idea proposed by Aronson and Linder is that people would be more attracted to a person who was initially negative and then changed to positive in his or her evaluations of them than they would be to a person who was consistently positive toward them. Conversely, they argued that a person who initially evaluated a subject positively and then changed that evaluation to a negative one would be less liked than a person who evaluated the subject negatively all the time. The first of these effects they referred to as a gain in attraction because of the change from negative to positive evaluations, and the second was called loss because of the decrease in attraction from positive to negative.

The experiment was carried out at the University of Minnesota and utilized 80 women as subjects. Subjects overheard another person evaluate them on seven different occasions with the evaluations being all positive in the positive-positive condition, all negative in the negative-negative condition, beginning as negative and slowly changing to positive in the negative-positive condition, and beginning as positive and moving to totally negative in the positive-negative condition. The crucial comparisons were, of course, between the subjects' evaluations of the evaluator in the negative-positive and positive-positive conditions (gain) and in the subjects' evaluations of the evaluator in the positive-negative and negative-negative conditions (loss). The results are presented in Figure 9–5. As can be seen, the evaluations in the negative-positive condition were more positive than in the positive-positive condition and they were more negative in the positive-negative than in the negative-negative condition. However, this latter effect (the loss phenomenon) was not statistically significant.

The notion that someone is more attractive to the subject after changing from negative to positive evaluations of him or her is intriguing. Possibly because it is so intriguing, the idea has generated a good deal of research. Why should someone like you more if you are at first negative to him or her and then change to positive? Is it possible that the way to get someone to like you is first to respond negatively to that person and then respond positively? What does the notion of gain-loss have to say about long-term relationships? Is it possible that if a man constantly compliments his wife he will, in time, be part of the positive-positive syndrome? If so, a compliment from a new and unique source or from an old admirer who has rejected her will be more potent than will her husband's already expected compliment. Before we go too far in our assumptions about how things will work, possibly a look at the evidence is in order.

THE STABILITY OF THE GAIN-LOSS PHENOMENON

Because the gain-loss idea raised a variety of intriguing questions about attraction, a number of studies have pursued it. The most consistent finding is that, as in the Aronson and Linder study, loss does nor occur (Hewitt, 1972; Mettee, 1971a; 1971b; Sigall and Aronson, 1967; Taylor, Altman, and Sorrentino, 1969; Tognoli and Keisner, 1972). In addition, at least three studies (Hewitt, 1972; Mettee, 1971b; Tognoli and Keisner, 1972) have found neither loss nor gain results. Thus, it is clear that even though the idea is intriguing, it is an elusive one at best. Mettee and

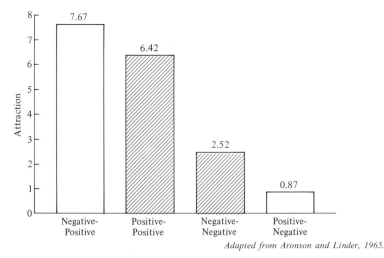

Adapted from Aronson and Linder, 1965.

Figure 9–5 Mean attraction responses following evaluations sequenced to be negative-positive, positive-positive, negative-negative, and positive-negative.

Aronson (1974) have carefully detailed the studies that have explored the phenomenon and argue that under the proper stimulus conditions gain will occur.

An interesting and practical study into one aspect of the phenomenon is reported by Berscheid, Brothen, and Graziano (1976). These investigators set out to test Aronson's ideas about gain and its effects on long-term interpersonal relationships. Aronson put it rather clearly and succinctly:

> Mr. and Mrs. Dating, who have been married for 10 years, are preparing to leave their house for a cocktail party. He compliments her—"Gee, honey, you look great!" She yawns. She already knows that her husband thinks she is attractive.
>
> Mr. and Mrs. Dating arrive at the cocktail party. A male stranger begins to talk to Mrs. Dating and after a while he says, with great sincerity, that he finds her very attractive. She does not yawn. The compliment increases her liking of the stranger.
>
> This little episode is an example of what some of my students have called Aronson's Law of Marital Infidelity. [Aronson, 1970, p. 48.]

Berscheid et al. (1976) suggests that possibly Aronson has been too quick to leap from laboratory findings to naturalistic situations without proper scientific care. In essence, they set up a situation in which a subject was first evaluated negatively and then positively or was consistently evaluated positively (just like the gain condition in the Aronson and Linder study). Then they devised a triangle in which the subject heard two people evaluate her. One of the evaluators was consistently positive, whereas the other one began negatively and proceeded to become more positive. In the situation in which each subject heard only one set of evaluations (positive-positive *or* negative-positive) the negative-positive evaluator was better liked than the positive-positive one. However, when subjects heard both a positive-positive and a negative-positive evaluator, the gain phenomenon did not occur. As a matter of fact, the positive-positive evaluator was liked significantly better than the negative-positive evaluator.

In addition to concluding that Aronson was premature in espousing his "law" of marital infidelity, Berscheid et al. make an excellent point. They suggest that social psychologists must be extremely careful in considering the stimulus context in which behavior occurs. For example, because subjects who hear all positive evaluations like the evaluator less than subjects who hear negative-positive evaluations, we must not conclude that subjects who hear both evaluators will also like the negative-positive evaluator more. As a matter of fact, they like that evaluator less.

Comment

I could not more fully agree with the conclusion arrived at by Berscheid et al. When the situation in which the individual finds himself or herself is not adequately considered, enormous difficulties can occur. Generalizing from one situation to another is extremely hazardous because, as Berscheid et al. so clearly illustrate, it can cause one to draw inaccurate conclusions. Not only were the conclusions that had been drawn inaccurate, but the results were completely reversed when the differences between the two situations were taken into account. A clear and steady appraisal of

Mental hospitals are disturbing to us. The condition of the sign in this photo is representative of how society views them.

the situation is required if we are to understand any variable in social psychology. It seems, however, that attraction is especially vulnerable to such a charge because there are complex, changing interactions going on at all times.

People like each other for varied and complex reasons. You may well like a person who agrees with you, but if you find out that the person who agrees with you is mentally disturbed, you won't like him or her as much (Byrne and Lamberth, 1971; Novak and Lerner, 1968). If someone agrees with you or compliments you excessively, you are more likely to believe it if you are poor and unattractive than if you are rich or attractive. Many people agree with and compliment beautiful or rich people, not because they really agree with them, but because they may be able to gain some personal or monetary favor from them. This thing called attraction is really quite complex.

Attribution and Attraction

One of the most natural links between two areas of social psychological research is the one between attribution theory (Chapter 1) and attraction. Attribution theorists have called our attention to the fact that how an individual perceives another is crucial to the perceiver's conclusions about the other. Several of these conclusions affect attraction directly. For example, if you observe another person and come to the conclusion that he is generous, kind, witty, intelligent, and handsome, your attraction toward that person will probably be pretty high. Unless, of course, you are both vying for the same girl's attention.

Interestingly enough, the perception of an individual may vary from perceiver to perceiver. If we all viewed other people identically, then the same people would tend to be the best liked in any situation. Even though this state of affairs may exist on elementary school playgrounds, as we grow older, different individuals are well liked by different groups. For example, in elementary school the biggest boys, who can run the fastest and play games most skillfully, are very popular. By the time people reach college there are still those who are attracted to sports heroes, but there are others who form their friendships among those who are politically active, or who emphasize

378

Young children often idolize sports heroes and select their friends from the most athletic. But as they grow older, other activities such as intellectual or artistic interests may form the basis of friendships.

intellectual pursuits, or who stress improving the lot of others, and so forth. Attraction is inextricably tied to our perception of others and through that to attribution.

INGRATIATION

One of the most interesting applications of the ingratiation concept comes when we think about who likes us and *why?* Stated another way, we are considering ingratiation, a tactic used by some people to make others like them. Basically, what the ingratiator is doing is trying to convince you that you are liked, generally to satisfy other motivations. The individual may want you to purchase a car, and treats you as if you were the most likable person in the world. People who are relatively wealthy are almost always besieged by individuals who "like" them and they must sort out those who like them from those who like their money.

Jones (1964) in an in-depth analysis of ingratiation has suggested that the potential ingratiator can use four sets of tactics to gain someone's liking. The first of these is outright flattery. Most people find it hard to resist liking others who think highly of them, and most of us are willing to believe almost anything said about us as long as it is positive. Of course, the ingratiator must be careful not to go too far, because the credibility of most of us can be strained. Another way an ingratiator can work is by using the knowledge that likes attract. Pointing out real or fabricated similarities between the ingratiator and the target, particularly on important topics, is an excellent tactic. An added touch is to disagree on some noncrucial or unimportant topics.

A third way an ingratiator can work is to present a favorable impression of himself or herself. Of course, care must be taken not to threaten the target with an overly favorable impression. Finally, Jones suggests that rendering favors is a reasonable tactic of ingratiation. This approach utilizes the principle that people like people who give them gifts. One note of caution concerning favors is applicable; the recipient should not feel a sense of social indebtedness, or the effects of the favor will be diminished.

At each stage of the ingratiation process, the important element is not what the ingratiator intends, but how the target perceives the actions. As long as the target accepts the compliments, agreements, self-presentation, or favors as real, ingratiation can occur. The basis for that ingratiation is that the target believes he or she is liked. The attraction is not real, but the target thinks it is and acts accordingly.

Comment

Attraction is a uniquely personal phenomenon. With virtually every variable we know influencing attraction (attractiveness, evaluations, similarity, and so forth), the important element is how the individual perceives the other person. For example, you may agree with another person (have similarity) on many attitudes, but if you do not know you agree, it will not influence your attraction toward that person. If another person really likes you but you don't know that, this information will also not affect your attraction toward him or her. On the other hand, if you believe the compliments, agreements, and so forth of an ingratiating salesman you may like him and buy his product, even though he detests you. The *perception* of the other person's behavior, intent, and motives is nowhere more important than in attraction. Simply stated, we are attracted to people we think agree with, like, and positively evaluate us. How they actually feel is important only insofar as it gives us accurate perceptions about their feelings.

This particular phenomenon, the importance of how we perceive others' feelings about us, explains the many instances of people who continue to think they are liked by a person who finds them very unlikable. Until the perceiver perceives that he or she is not liked, his or her behavior will continue to reflect the inaccurate state of his or her perceptions.

Characteristics Affecting Attraction

We have talked a lot about likes attracting, but mainly we have been concerned with two types of similarity—attitudes and evaluation. In the research that Byrne and his associates have done, in work carried out by Newcomb and others in balance theory, and in the gain-loss model of attraction, we have skipped back and forth between attitudes and evaluations. Most investigators agree that positive evaluations are a special case of similar attitudes and negative evaluations are a special case of dissimilar attitudes for most of the population. Why? Most people have a positive self-concept. We think we are basically worthy people. When others say we are intelligent, attractive, perceptive, thoughtful, and so forth, they are agreeing with us. Furthermore, they are agreeing with us about a very important issue—ourselves. Thus Byrne and his associates have argued that evaluations are three times as important in influencing attraction as are attitudes, and other researchers certainly feel evaluations strongly influence attraction.

What else affects attraction? The answers to that may be innumerable, but let us look quickly at just two.

PROPINQUITY

Propinquity, which means how close you are to another person, not surprisingly affects attraction. In spite of folklore adages such as "birds of a feather flock together" and "absence makes the heart grow fonder," the closer two people are to each other, the more likely they will become friends. In a series of investigations in the early 1950s Festinger, Schachter, and Back (1950) found that people learn to like people that they encounter often. Thus, just the fact that you live close to someone does not mean you will come to like that person; you must also encounter him or her. For example, Caplow and Foreman (1950) found that friendships were a function of the distance between apartments in a married-student housing complex. Among elderly residents of a housing project, most of the friendships formed are between individuals living on the same floor (Nahemow and Lawton, 1975).

So, what's so strange about people forming friendships with those they see often? On the other hand, why don't people *dislike* most of the people they see often? If you see your neighbor several times a week he or she is likely to do quite a number of things to upset or anger you. It would seem much easier to carry on a friendship with a person you don't have to encounter while carrying out daily chores like mowing the lawn, shoveling snow off the walk, or putting the garbage out. So the fact that we do like people we come in contact with is surprising—or isn't it?

One explanation for liking people we see often is that generally most people like others until they have a reason to dislike them. This makes a good deal of common sense. If we spent most of our time looking for people we didn't like, we could, undoubtedly, find them but that wouldn't be too pleasant. But if we expect to like people, then possibly we will like them, and so it seems that our expectations may play a large part in why people like others who are near.

Mere Exposure. Zajonc (1968) proposed that mere exposure to any stimulus results in increasingly positive evaluations of that stimulus. Additional work has indicated that repeated exposure to Turkish words (Zajonc and Rajecki, 1969), Japanese ideographs (Moreland and Zajonc, 1976), public figures (Harrison, 1969), and photographs of strangers (Wilson and Nakajo, 1965) lead to increased liking for these diverse stimuli. Brickman, Meyer, and Fredd (1975) have suggested that one reason

Would you expect people to like each other more in the apartments above or the single family dwellings below?

for the attitude-similarity effect on attraction is that we like whatever is familiar, including attitudes.

Saegert, Swap, and Zajonc (1973) exposed subjects to other people either 0, 1, 2, 5, or 10 times while they were tasting either pleasant or noxious substances. The more often a subject was exposed to another person, the more attracted she was to the other person, regardless of whether she was tasting a pleasant or noxious substance. Figure 9–6 shows the results. Brockner and Swap (1976) found that when subjects are exposed to similar and dissimilar others, the number of exposures and attitudinal similarity influence attraction. Thus repeated exposures to another person, even under noxious stimulus conditions or when that person is disagreeing with you seems to increase attraction. Of course, if the person becomes too obnoxious, it may be that you will purposely avoid associating with him or her. It is obvious that mere exposure by itself is not a sufficient condition to assure attraction, or we would like everyone with whom we associate and that obviously isn't true. Mere exposure, however, could well be the reason we come to like people we are exposed to frequently, and why propinquity influences attraction.

PHYSICAL ATTRACTIVENESS

For many years, people have attempted to improve on the physical attractiveness with which they were born. To be sure, different cultures admire different characteristics and the same culture may admire different characteristics at different times in history. An implicit assumption in our visits to beauty shops, hair stylists, fashionable clothing stores, and the like is that others will like us more if we are more attractive. Is this implicit assumption correct?

There is considerable evidence that physical attractiveness does influence liking and that it is advantageous to be good-looking (Berscheid and Walster, 1974; Byrne, London, and Reeves, 1968). Not only are attractive people liked more, but they are seen as having other favorable attributes just because they are good-looking (Miller, 1970; Dion, Berscheid, and Walster, 1972). As if that weren't enough for the majority

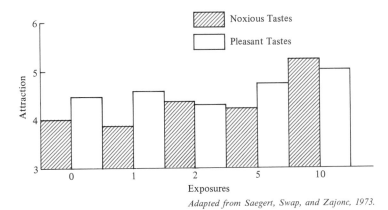

Adapted from Saegert, Swap, and Zajonc, 1973.

Figure 9–6 Attraction as a function of number of exposures to another person and tasting pleasant (Kool-Aid) or noxious (weak solutions of vinegar, quinine, or citric acid) substances.

The complexity of social relationships is great. There is little wonder that folklore has led us to believe that both opposites attract and likes attract. Consider for a moment the possibilities of variation in a relationship: casual acquaintance, friend, date, brother or sister, spouse, parent, child, and so forth. Do the same sorts of rules govern how we treat others in these various types of relationships? It would, indeed, be strange, if there were not different rules for different relationships.

Clark and Mills (1979) report a study in which they investigate one type of rule in two relationships. They broadly categorize relationships into communal and exchange relationships. Communal relationships are those in which the giving of a benefit in response to a need for that benefit is appropriate. Exchange relationships are those in which the giving of a benefit in response to the receipt of a benefit is appropriate. Clark and Mills suggest that family relationships are an example of a communal relationship and less intimate relationships, such as friendship or social or business contacts, are examples of exchange relationships.

The design of the experiment was as follows: Unmarried male college students served as subjects. Subjects worked at a performance task while a television monitor showed an attractive female working at a similar task. When the subject finished his task, he was awarded an extra point of course credit for finishing on time and was given the opportunity to send some of his materials to the female, who supposedly had a more difficult task. When she finished, she was awarded 4 extra points and sent a note to the subject thanking him for his aid (a no-benefit condition) or sent a note of thanks and gave him one of her extra points (benefit condition). To manipulate the type of relationship, the female was described as married or unmarried. It was assumed that when the female was married the subject would assume that the only type of rela-

tionship possible would be an exchange one. However, when the female was unmarried Clark and Mills assumed that subjects would at least consider the possibility of a communal relationship. To be more explicit, the researchers assume that we desire communal relationships with attractive others, but only if they are available for such a relationship (in this case unmarried).

The predictions concerning this experiment are rather straightforward when Clark and Mills' assumptions are met. In the exchange relationship, the female would be better liked if she provided a reciprocal benefit; that is, when she returned the note of thanks and the extra point. In the anticipated communal relationship, the female would be better liked when she returned just the note and not the extra point. This is exactly what happened.

You might wonder why communal and exchange relationships differ, when exchange theorists argue that exchange works even in marriage (Walster, Walster, and Berscheid, 1978). As more work is done on exchange theory in intimate relationships it is becoming apparent that couples sometimes see themselves as one couple, not two individuals. If this reasoning is true, then it may be that exchange will have to be conceptualized in terms of exchange not only between individuals, but exchange between communal units. This will, of course, add more complexity to an already complex situation, but it may describe human behavior more adequately.

References

Clark, M. S., and J. Mills. Interpersonal attraction in exchange and communal relationships. *Journal of Personality and Social Psychology,* 1979, *37,* 12–24.

Walster, E., G. W. Walster, and E. Berscheid. *Equity: Theory and Research.* Boston: Allyn & Bacon, Inc., 1978.

of people who are not extremely attractive, attractive people's work is viewed as superior (Landy and Sigall, 1974), they can be more persuasive (Mills and Aronson, 1965), their evaluations of others have more impact (Sigall and Aronson, 1969), and they are more sought after as dates (Walster, Aronson, Abrahams, and Rottman, 1966). So, it seems that it is better to be attractive than unattractive. There is, however, just so much we can do to improve upon what we were born with.

However, before speculating on possible improvements, there is one bit of evidence concerning attractiveness that is important. Different people see *different* other persons as being attractive. For example, in the computer dating study (Byrne, Ervin, and Lamberth, 1970) discussed earlier, both the experimenter and the subjects rated subjects on physical attractiveness. The correlations between the experimenter's rating of physical attractiveness and the subjects' ratings of their dates' attactiveness were significant (.59 for ratings of males and .39 for ratings of females), but still low enough to indicate a good deal of disagreement. This merely means that the boy or girl you find attractive may not be attractive to others. One reason for this seems to be that the personal characteristics attributed to an individual (e.g., friendly, helpful, energetic) can influence ratings of physical attractiveness. Gross and Crofton (1977) had subjects rate photographs as physically unattractive, average, or attractive after they had read a description of the individual that was unfavorable, average, or favorable. The degree to which the description was a favorable one, as well as the attractiveness of the individual in the photograph, had strong effects on the rated attractiveness of each individual pictured. Thus it seems that both the title of the article by Dion, Berscheid, and Walster (1974) "What is beautiful is good" and the title by Gross and Crofton (1977) "What is good is beautiful" have a kernel of truth in them.

Romantic Love

The scientific study of love is really quite new, although the topic is one that has been of immense interest for centuries. If we can say that poets, novelists, journalists, and so forth have been more concerned with liking than scientists have, then that goes, but even more so, for love. If attraction is difficult to study, love is even more difficult. Just because the subject is difficult, however, doesn't mean that it should be ignored. Fortunately, it has not been. Rubin (1970, 1973) has described his research on loving in a most delightful way. His first step was to distinguish between liking and loving, a very difficult task. Rubin argues that liking focuses on a favorable evaluation of the other person on task-related dimensions such as maturity, good judgment, and intelligence. Love, according to Rubin, is characterized by dimensions of attachment, caring, and intimacy.

Berscheid and Walster (1974) have argued that attraction and love are different phenomena and that love needs independent attention. They point out that many have despaired of understanding the nature of love. Those who have not despaired of understanding love have been quite definite about it. As Berscheid and Walster (1974, p. 356) say,

Other writers have tried to explicate *facets* of romantic love. . . . These analysts have often provided compelling—but unnervingly inconsistent—insights into the nature of passionate love.

To overcome this lack of knowledge in the area, Berscheid and Walster have proposed a theory of love and pointed out how it differs from attraction.

A Little Bit About Love

There are three important, rather elusive, considerations that differentiate attraction and love and must be carefully considered by the researcher who is interested in love. The first of these is fantasy. Almost everyone agrees that people are attracted to others who reward them, but lovers may love people who actually reward them or people who reward them in their fantasies. As Berscheid and Walster point out, an individual may have grandiose daydreams about a perfect and flawless creature who delivers unlimited reward. At the very least the individual anticipates unlimited reward. Compared to our fantasies the reward we receive in actual interactions may seem quite paltry. Interestingly, some of the most extreme passion is aroused by individuals we have never met, or know only slightly. As we get to know them, reality strikes home and our anticipations of unlimited pleasures and rewards begin to vanish.

A second difference between attraction and passionate love is in the part played by time. Homans (1961) argues that the more two people interact the more they will like each other. But passionate love is a fragile thing, caught in a fight against time. Williamson (1966), in a marriage and family text, warns that romantic love is temporary. Although passion may be necessary for marriage, it cannot be expected to last long. Reik (1944) is even more pessimistic, warning that the very best you can hope for after a few years of marriage is an "afterglow." What a comedown—from the hot, intense fires of passion to an afterglow. Berscheid and Walster point out that this dwindling to an afterglow ensues because the actual, not the fantasized, rewards enter the picture. No mortal can live up to the fantasized ideal that developed during the passionate stage of love.

Attraction seems to be a sensible phenomenon. We like those who reward us and dislike those who thwart our desires. Passionate love seems not to follow such sensible rules. Some people seem to manage to fall in love with beautiful, intelligent, considerate, and wealthy people. But others seem to fall as deeply in love with people who are almost guaranteed to hurt them. Possibly you have known someone who manages to fall in love with people who hurt him or her time after time. Passionate love seems to be controlled by an array of conflicting emotions.

A Theory of Passionate Love

Walster and Berscheid (1971) proposed a tentative theory of passionate love that followed Schachter's general theory of emotion (1964). The theory of romantic love required that individuals be aroused physiologically and that situational cues indicate that "passionate love" is the source of their intense feelings.

Schachter and Singer (1962) found a way to test the notion that physiological arousal and appropriate cognitions are separate and indispensable components of a true emotional experience. The investigators physiologically aroused their subjects by injecting them with epinephrine, a drug whose major effect is to arouse the individual. The arousal consists of palpitations, tremors, accelerated breathing, and sometimes flushing. These reactions are identical to the physiological reactions that accompany a number of natural arousal states. Subjects were unaware of what they were being injected with and half received a saline solution placebo. Then one third of each group of subjects was told exactly what to expect—that is physiological arousal. Another third was given no information, and the final third was misled as to what to expect; that is they were told the shot would probably make them feel numb. Finally, half of each group was participating in a happy, pleasant interaction when the shot took effect (15–20 minutes later) and half of each group was participating in a tense, angry situation.

Schachter and Singer predicted that subjects who received epinephrine and did not know what to expect from it should experience greater emotion (either happiness *or* anger depending on the situation they were in when the shot took effect) than those who received a placebo or who received epinephrine and knew what to expect from it. The data supported the predictions and additional support has been added by Schachter and Wheeler (1962) and Hohmann (1962).

Walster and Berscheid (1971) adopted the Schachter two-component theory of emotion to account for love. Their speculation centered on the apparent jumble of contradictions that don't seem to fit a reward model. For example, why are both intensely positive and intensely negative experiences conducive to love? A simple reward model would expect that intensely negative experiences should lead to less, not more, love. Yet lovers have quarreled, fought, endured intense discomfort for each other, separated and found they could not stand being apart and reunited since the dawn of recorded history. Berscheid and Walster (1974) suggest that what may be important in determining how the individual feels about a person who is generating these intense feelings is how the reactions are labeled. If these emotions, both positive and negative, can be attributed to passionate love, love should be the emotion experienced. As soon as these feelings, particularly the negative ones, can no longer be attributed to love, the love withers and dies.

Generating Physiological Arousal

Berscheid and Walster suggest that there is little direct evidence to support the contention that while physiologically aroused both positive and negative stimuli can increase passion, but they argue that there is indirect evidence. There is some evidence that fear, rejection, and frustration may enhance romantic passion.

Unpleasant Emotional Experiences

Brehm, Gatz, Geothals, McCrommon, and Ward (1970) tested the hypothesis that a man's attraction toward a young female college student would be enhanced by arousal, even if that arousal was from a negative source. Three groups of subjects were used. The first was told that they would receive three "pretty stiff" electrical shocks during the course of the experiment (threat subjects). The second group was told the same thing but then was told that the experimenter had made a mistake and they were actually in the control condition ("threat-relief" subjects). The third group was a control condition group that never heard about any shock being administered. Brehm and his coworkers hypothesized that both the threat subjects and the threat-relief subjects would be aroused (although for different reasons) and would like the young lady more than the control subjects did. This prediction was accurate. A frightening event may increase attraction.

Rejection is another negative emotion that, according to Berscheid and Walster, may heighten passionate love. Jacobs, Berscheid, and Walster (1971) report an experiment in which men were given positive or negative personality reports. Soon after receiving these reports half of each group met a female college student (actually a confederate) who responded to the man with a warm, affectionate, and accepting evaluation. The other half met the same girl, but she responded to them in a cool and rejecting way. The men who had received the negative personality evaluation were more attracted to the accepting girl than were the men who had received the positive personality evaluation. On the other hand, the men who had received the negative personality evaluation disliked the cool rejecting girl more than did the men who had received the positive personality evaluation. Thus, an arousing personality evaluation affected the way men responded to acceptance, and, more importantly, to rejection.

Frustration is another negative emotion which, Berscheid and Walster suggest, enhances passionate love. They report two sets of experimental data to support this view.

Hard-to-get girls are more desirable than easy-to-get girls, at least according to folklore. Walster, Walster, Piliavin, and Schmidt (1973) reported several experiments designed to show that a hard-to-get girl was, indeed, more attractive than an easy-to-get one. Despite advice from Socrates, Ovid, and even Dear Abby, the men in Walster et al.'s experiments did not opt for the hard-to-get girl. In both laboratory and field experiments it was found that boys had just as high an opinion of easy-to-get as of hard-to-get girls. Finally the researchers devised a way to present each subject with a girl who was selectively hard-to-get. She responded to five males and indicated that she was uninterested in the other four, but would really like to go out with the subject. The selectively hard-to-get girl was more liked than a generally hard-to-get or easy-to-get girl. Thus there seems to be little evidence that men choose to endure the frustration associated with pursuing the hard-to-get girl. Possibly the experimental manipulations of Walster et al. were not appropriate, because many people do seemingly chase hard-to-get individuals.

Driscoll, Davis, and Lipitz (1972) proposed that parental interference in a love relationship causes frustration and intensifies the feeling of the lovers. These investigators interviewed 91 married couples and 49 dating couples who were seriously committed to each other—most had been going together for about 8 months. The couples indicated how much parental interference they felt they had had in their marriages and courtships, and an assessment was also made of how much in love they were. Parental interference and romantic love correlated .50 for the unmarried sample and .24 for the married couples, indicating that the more parental interference there was, the more the couple felt they were in love. Six to ten months later, the authors again interviewed the couples and were able to determine whether the parents had become more or less interfering in the relationship and how these changes in parental interference affected love. Changes in parental interference correlated .30 with changes in romantic love, indicating that as interference increased, love also increased. Thus, parental interference in a relationship seems to intensify, not diminish romantic love. As Driscoll, et al. say,

As has been pointed out earlier, the predicted effect of parental interference intesifying romantic love is consistent with the operation of two rather well-supported psychological principles—goal frustration and reactance. But the application of these principles to the complex circumstances of romantic love is perhaps novel enough to justify a distinctive name—the Romeo and Juliet effect. [Driscoll, et al., 1972, p. 9.]

PLEASANT EMOTIONAL EXPERIENCES

The discussion of unplesant emotional experiences enhancing love is more crucial to Berscheid and Walster's hypothesis concerning passionate love, but we must not overlook the positive effects of emotional arousal that occur.

According to Berscheid and Walster, it may come as a surprise to religious advisers, school counselors, and psychoanalysts, but sexual gratification has probably done as much to enhance passionate love as sexual frustration has. Valins (1966) demonstrated that men who erroneously thought they had been aroused by a woman were more attracted to her than they were to a woman they thought had not aroused them. The men's heart rate was monitored and they were erroneously told that their heart rate altered markedly with some of the pictures, but not with others. They were much more attracted to the women they thought had caused their heart rate to alter than they were to women they thought had had no effect upon them.

Psychologists, poets, and novelists have tended to focus almost exclusively on the satisfaction of sexual needs in romantic love. There are, however, other needs that a love partner may meet and when an unfulfilled need is met, romantic love is intensified.

Finally, Berscheid and Walster point out that there is something exciting about danger. They argue that psychologists have stressed the negative aspects of danger too much. People seek out dangerous experiences; they seem to enjoy the excitement that accompanies them. Mountain climbing, sportscar racing, and parachuting all are dangerous and part of their appeal is the danger they provide. Berlyne (1960) has recognized that danger and delight often go together and has systematically explored the conditions under which novelty and excitement are attractive.

Labeling

The second part of the theory of passionate love that Berscheid and Walster have proposed is labeling. Once the person is aroused, it is imperative for the theory that the arousal be labeled love and not something else. How do we label arousal?

Children learn to label a vast array of stimuli that impinge upon them. Through parental guidance and experience, an individual learns cultural norms concerning categories of stimuli (situations) that are arousing. Even though the physiological signals may be identical for intense happiness and fear (e.g., pounding heart, sweaty palms, flushed face, and so on) we know from the context that one is pleasurable and one is not. For example, a couple kissing for the first time will be more likely to label the physiological changes they feel "happiness" than will a person accosted by a gun-wielding man in the subway.

But according to Berscheid and Walster some emotions are better articulated than others. Children have relatively clear perceptions as to what happiness, jealousy, hate, and embarrassment feel like, but may have little experience with bliss, contempt, or loathing. Passionate love is a poorly articulated emotion. Many parents assume that children are incapable of experiencing passionate love and thus do not help their children to articulate it. In addition, individuals sometimes experience mixed emotions. For example, you may have found yourself in situations that simultaneously make you feel happy and sad. Many people feel very mixed emotions when they have broken up a strong relationship that is no longer satisfying. The sense of freedom is pleasurable, but the feeling of having hurt someone is noxious.

Cultural norms specify some of the antecedents of whom it is reasonable to love. We have already discussed physical attractiveness as a determinant of attraction. It is, however, also a determinant of whom our culture says we are to love. Berscheid, Dion, Walster, and Walster (1971) found that the more attractive girls dated considerably more than did the less attractive girls. The more someone dates a person the more likely he or she is to fall in love with that person. Culture determines eligible candidates for love.

In essence, Berscheid and Walster argue that the labeling aspect of romantic love is very much a cultural phenomenon. They point out that many young adults use the term *romantic love* to describe relationships with the opposite sex that are strong and positive and still in progress. Strong, positive affective relationships that have been terminated are called *infatuation*.

Romantic Love—Misattribution or Drive Reduction?

The basic assumption of the formulation of romantic love by Berscheid and Walster is that certain forms of arousal are attributed to the wrong cause. This misattribution formulation, although fascinating, has been questioned. Kenrick and Cialdini (1977) have reinterpreted the studies utilized by Berscheid and Walster in the following way. The major emphasis, according to Kenrick and Cialdini, should be on negative reinforcement, not misattribution. *Negative reinforcement* is a technical term that refers to the cessation of a punishing stimulus. For example, if you are being shocked, negative reinforcement occurs when the shock is turned off. Chapter 1 dealt with positive reinforcement and noted that its presentation increases the probability of the response that produces it. By the same reasoning, the probability of the occurrence of the response that produces the cessation of a punisher is also increased. This is the phenomenon called *negative reinforcement*.

The basic idea Kenrick and Cialdini propose is that unpleasant events that occur in the course of passionate love are not associated with love through inappropriate labeling but through negative reinforcement. Berscheid and Walster point out that they were trying to account for the fact that intensely pleasurable and intensely unpleasurable events all get labeled *love*. Kenrick and Cialdini argue that the occurrence of pleasurable events and the cessation of unpleasurable ones lead to love. In other words, the continuation of pleasurable events is positively reinforcing and the cessation of unpleasurable ones is negatively reinforcing. Whether positive or negative, reinforcement accounts for passionate love. As Kenrick and Cialdini (1977, p. 385) say,

Lovers not only provide increases in arousal for one another, but they also provide reductions of that arousal, in the form of social acceptance, physical caresses, sexual release, etc. While it may be true that high levels of aversive arousal are often associated with high degrees of passionate love, it is our major hypothesis that it is more often the reduction of that arousal, rather than its labelling, that intensifies the relationship. Lovers are sometimes heard to report that a "lovers quarrel" was almost worth it because the making up was so much fun. While an attribution theorist would see the potentially relabelled arousal inherent in such a quarrel as the central mediator, it seems at least as likely that the making up after the heightened aversive arousal is responsible for strengthening the bond. Such an event can be seen to be especially rewarding, embodying both the removal of a noxious state and the substitution of a pleasant one.

Kenrick and Cialdini's argument makes a certain amount of sense. Furthermore, they are able to reinterpret much of the data Berscheid and Walster use in terms of positive and negative reinforcement. They do not argue that all stimuli are properly labeled. Rather, they think there is some misattribution occurring in romantic love, but that there is far less misattribution than Berscheid and Walster would have us believe. Which interpretation do you think is correct?

The Problem With Misattribution

Possibly passionate love is an exception, but social psychologists are less inclined these days to interpret behavior in terms of systematic mistakes people make. Even though behavior may not always seem rational to us, we are beginning to realize that though people differ in many ways, they also have many similarities. I have argued repeatedly in this book for the position that people do the things that they expect will be most pleasurable or least unpleasurable. A lovers' fight is unpleasant, but does the making up more than compensate for the unpleasantness? Is misattribution of the arousal a better way to account for passionate love continuing in spite of negative fights? Or is it more precise to attribute it to the pleasure of reconciliation?

Misattribution in general is based on the assumption that humans don't use their cognitive powers very well. Either side in such a debate could marshal an impressive array of incidents to prove its point. As sort of a statement of faith in humanity, I like to believe that there is less rather than more misattribution going on. This is to say that I think humans behave the way they do for good reasons. Granted, we do not yet know those reasons, but I think they are there.

Comment

Berscheid and Walster have presented an impressive array of theory and data to support their contention that arousal leads to passionate love—if it is labeled properly. Both the arousal and the labeling are important for romantic love to develop. Kenrick and Cialdini have argued that positive and negative reinforcement can account for passionate love and have come to this conclusion using the same data Berscheid and Walster use. Whichever side is correct, both must answer the question "What does passionate love lead to?"

One of the answers to this question is that romantic love leads to a long-standing, intimate relationship. Do the same sorts of mechanisms control these intimate relationships? Not surprisingly, Walster, Walster, and Berscheid (1978) argue that long-term intimate relationships, such as marriage, long-term friendships, and parent-child relationships are guided by mechanisms other than an increase in arousal and a labeling of that emotion. For example, the intensity of passionate love is sustained for only a short time in most relationships. The relationship may evolve into something more permanent, but the volatile nature of passion precludes its being the basis for a relationship of long standing. Let us see how Walster, Walster, and Berscheid account for the long-range outcome of romantic love—marriage.

Equity—The Key to Marital Happiness?

Equity theory, which asserts that people mentally calculate the value of the inputs and the rewards each individual gives or receives and try to equalize them, is the important mechanism in marriage, according to Walster, Walster, and Berscheid. Even though they realize that many people will draw the line with marital relationships and argue that equity is not an important variable, these investigators do not agree. As they say,

When Equity theorists contend that equity considerations apply not only in casual relationships, but perhaps even in close friendships as well, many readers can grudgingly agree. However when Equity theorists proceed one step further, and suggest that equity considerations shape romantic and marital relationships, many readers rebel. They insist that these are "special" relationships. [Walster, Walster, and Berscheid, 1978, p. 162.]

Mate Selection

The preceding section of this chapter dealt with mate selection—at least in situations where romantic love leads to marriage. There is evidence, however, that things change as relationships progress. For example, Morse, Reis, and Gruzen (1973) found that men were attracted to the most physically attractive woman early in a relationship. But as time passed, things changed. men with a high self-concept, who thus felt they had a lot to offer a woman, continued to express great interest in the highly physically attractive woman. Men with a low self-concept, who felt they didn't have that much to offer, began to express less interest in the physically attractive woman.

Silverman (1971) had observers rate the physical attractiveness of dating couples in bars, theater lobbies, and at social events. The couples were rated on a five-point scale of physical attractiveness with intervals of .5 points. A female observer rated the males and a male observer rated the females, so one person could not have arbitrarily

The social changes that have occurred in the last several years may have had an effect on whom we like and why. More specifically, it seems that the changing role of women in society will have an impact on how men and women respond to each other. In this era of changing roles there are men and women who feel that the traditional role for men and women is best. That is, men are expected to earn the living for the family and be in charge of the outside chores of the home. Women are expected to keep the house and raise the children. A newer way of viewing male and female roles is that there is more sharing of responsibilities. That is, women are more involved in working outside of the home and men are more involved in helping with household duties and raising children.

Grush and Yehl (1979) report an experiment in which they categorized people as being traditionals or nontraditionals in terms of their attitudes toward marital roles. A special questionnaire was developed for this study that included domestic, financial, social, familial, and career decisions. Pretesting the questionnaire on three groups of females (National Organization of Women, college students, and policemen's wives) who were expected to differ in their traditional versus nontraditional views indicated that the questionnaire showed these differences. In addition, two groups of males (college students and policemen) differed in their traditional versus nontraditional views. Thus, traditional and nontraditional men and women were to indicate their attraction toward a traditional or nontraditional other.

Attraction is a many-faceted emotion, however. We may be attracted to one sort of person for one role and another sort for another. For example, if you are in a military unit, you may very much want a large, mean individual whose bravery outweighs all other feelings when you are about to enter battle. You may, however, be disinclined to have this individual as a close friend.

Grush and Yehl reasoned that traditionals and nontraditionals may very much like a similar individual (with respect to sex-role considerations) as dating or marriage partner, but that this information may not influence their liking of the individual in another role. Thus, they assessed three forms of attraction: as a dating or marriage partner (personal role), as a debater or panelist (functional role), and how much the individual is liked in general. The only information the subjects had about the other person was their responses to the traditional-nontraditional questionnaire, and this information was either similar to or dissimilar from the subject's own. Thus traditional and nontraditional males and females evaluated similar or dissimilar others on three types of attraction: personal, functional, and general.

Traditional females and nontraditional males did not differentiate between individuals on the basis of similarity of sex roles on any of the three measures of attraction. Nontraditional females and traditional males liked the similar other more on the basis of personal and general attraction, but not on the basis of functional attraction. That is, nontraditional females and traditional males were more attracted to other individuals who held their views on sex roles when the measures were for personal (dating and marriage) or general attraction. They did not prefer one or the other in a functional role (debater).

It may be that nontraditional females and traditional males feel more threatened in a changing society than do traditional females and nontraditional males. Nontraditional females may be at the forefront of many social changes while traditional males are battling against the change. At any rate, these two groups do prefer similar others in personal and general attraction.

Reference

J. E. Grush and J. G. Yehl. Marital roles, sex differences, and interpersonal attraction. *Journal of Personality and Social Psychology*, 1979, 37, 116–23.

decided to rate couples similarly. Sixty percent of the couples were rated no more than a half point apart and fully 85 percent of the couples were separated by no more than one scale point. Even though different observers rated different individuals, they did see them together as couples and this could have affected the ratings. Murstein (1972) controlled for this variable by securing photographs of steadily dating or engaged couples. These individuals were far more similar in physical attractiveness than were randomly paired couples.

Earlier in this chapter we discussed the idea that married people are similar to each other. Equity theory rephrases some of these considerations by arguing that individuals trade resources. There is evidence that more attractive people are successful in marrying-up; that is, in attracting mates who are of a higher socioeconomic status (Elder, 1969). Berscheid, Walster, and Bohrnstedt (1973) found that if a relationship was inequitable in physical attractiveness, there was a tendency for the less attractive partner to be more loving and to expend more effort in the relationship. It seems possible that beauty can buy not only socioeconomic status but also love and sacrifice.

MISMATCHED MATCHES

Berschied, Walster, and Bohrnstedt (1973) posed an interesting question. What happens when, by chance, luck, or some other circumstance a relationship is mismatched? Is the "superior" partner miserable and the "inferior" one deliriously happy? Another way of looking at the same question is what would have happened to all those very normal boys who have dreamed of life with the reigning movie queen? Would they have been happy? Would a real-life Eliza Doolittle be happy with Henry Higgins as portrayed in *My Fair Lady?* Berscheid et al. predicted that the answer would be "No." It is obvious why the "superior" partner would be unhappy, but the "inferior" partner would always live in fear that the mate would find someone who offered more. Both partners in an inequitable relationship should feel uneasy.

Walster, Walster, and Traupmann (1977) interviewed 500 University of Wisconsin men and women who were dating "casually" or "steadily." They were asked to indicate how content, happy, angry, or guilty they felt. The results are shown in Figure 9–7. In general the more equitable a relationship is, the more content and happy a couple are and the less angry and guilty they are. There is a tendency shown in these data for people who are getting far more than they deserve to feel slightly more content, happier, and less angry than people who are getting much less than they deserve. People who are getting much less than they deserve, not surprisingly, do not feel as guilty as people getting far more than they deserve.

RESTORATION OF EQUITY

If there is a mismatch, how can equity be restored? Walster, Walster, and Berscheid (1978) suggest several ways in which this is possible, but admit that they are speculating. There are very few data that shed light on the subject and most of these are anecdotal and tangential. However, the theorists' speculations are of interest.

One way people can restore equity in a relationship is by instituting real changes in the relationship. If one partner is "superior" in one area, he or she may slip in other

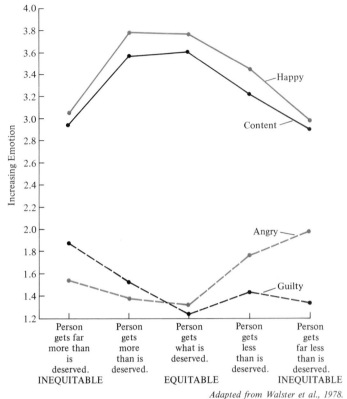

Figure 9-7 Happiness, contentment, anger, and guilt as a function of equitable and inequitable relationships.

ways. For example, if a woman brings a large amount of money into the family, she may feel that she can become careless about her dress, cleanliness, or weight. Or she may feel she is entitled to talk to her partner only when she feels in the mood for conversation. Alternatively, she may express her love less or make fewer sacrifices for the good of the relationship.

Another way of restoring equity to the relationship is to restore psychological equity. Basically this is done by changing one's mind about what is important, by ignoring the inequity, or by misperceiving it. For example, if a man becomes careless of his weight and his attention, his mate may assume that physical condition and memory deterioration are a natural part of the aging process. There are many ways in which a couple can restore psychological equity because marriage includes so many aspects of behavior and covers such a long time span. Walster, et al. say,

Probably, many couples then, when confronted with the fact that the balance of their marriage has changed, find it easiest to restore psychological equity to their relationship, and to convince themselves that these changes are not real changes, or that they are not really very important. [Walster, Walster, and Berscheid, 1978, p. 184.]

Walster, Berscheid, and Walster (1973) point out that if a couple's relationship becomes grossly inequitable, they should be tempted to end it, by divorce, separation, or annulment. A dating couple suffers when a relationship breaks up, but as Bohannan (1971) documents, married couples who divorce suffer even more. Their own investment in the relationship is sacrificed, their parents and friends may express shock and disapproval, they may lose rights to their children, their friends may drop them, and to top it all off, both partners usually have to alter their life style, since it is considerably more expensive to maintain two households as opposed to one. Divorce is costly, but equity theorists argue that if couples cannot find a better way, they pay the price and divorce.

Many Canadians and still more Americans marry, but many more Americans than Canadians choose to leave the field.

For example, in 1975 the Canadian marriage rate was 8.7 per 1,000 population (Glick and Norton, 1972). The United States rate was higher (9.9 in 1976) but not decidely so. Both countries' rates were exceeded by those of the U.S.S.R. (10.1) and Egypt (10.0). The United States has a much higher divorce rate than Canada. In 1976, the divorce rate was 5.0 per 1,000 population in the United States and less than half that in Canada (2.2 per 1,000 in 1975). Both countries have a high marriage rate, but Canada has a lower divorce rate, indicating less instability in family life. Even at a 2.2 per 1,000 divorce rate, Canadians have a high rate; approximately 25 percent of the marriage rate.

What these statistics mean is that about 2 out of 5 couples in the United States and 1 out of 5 couples in Canada feel that the suffering in their marriage is worse than their pain would be if they ended it. Consequently, the price is being paid by many Americans and Canadians.

Comment

Love and marriage may go together like a horse and carriage, but there may well be two mechanisms operating in them. Berscheid and the Walsters think passionate love is so emotion-packed that it differs from other forms of human interaction. There is a certain common-sense aspect in such an approach. When people are highly aroused, because of stress, fear, love, or any other emotion, their behavior is much harder to predict. Possibly lovers do respond to equity principles, but we just don't very well know how to assess the value of inputs and outcomes for an aroused person.

At any rate, once the fires of passion have settled down, it is clear, at least to Berscheid and the Walsters, that equity considerations control the behavior of marriage partners. Of course the complexity of the situation, coupled with an idealistic feeling that we should give more than we receive, makes many people recoil at the idea of equity in marriage. Yet most people do seem to be interested in how they are coming out in life. Few, if any, of us want to be at the bottom of the heap or get less than we deserve. That marriage should follow the same pattern should not surprise us when we consider all our other relationships. People want what's coming to them, and if equity theorists are correct, not a whole lot more, or a whole lot less.

397

Summary

SUMMARY

1 As early as 1870 it was discovered that people who like each other are similar. It is, however, not possible to assert from correlational data that likes attract.

2 In the 1950s and 60s systematic research began to aim at determining the relationship between similarity and attraction. A classic study by Newcomb lent support to the idea that likes attract.

3 Laboratory research by Byrne and his associates has given strong support to the idea that similarities attract. A reinforcement affect model was developed to explain the similarity-attraction phenomenon. The laboratory research findings have been supported and extended in several studies done in more "real-life" settings.

4 Variables that affect attraction, in addition to similarity are evaluations, emotional disturbance, and race.

5 Balance theory has also been used as an explanatory construct for attraction. According to this theory, attraction should be enhanced in balanced situations and decreased in imbalanced ones.

6 The gain-loss theory of attraction is built on the assumption that invariant positiveness from a person leads to less liking on the part of another than first negativeness and then positiveness (or the reverse of this, that positive-negative leads to more disliking than does invariant negativeness). The evidence for the theory is mixed, with the loss phenomenon being highly suspect and the gain phenomenon being replicable only part of the time.

7 Other variables that strongly influence attraction are propinquity, mere exposure, and physical attractiveness.

8 Romantic love has been conceptualized in a two-stage model that attempts to explain the contradictions in the behavior of people in love. The model suggests that the first stage is arousal and it makes no difference in love whether the arousal results from positive or negative stimuli. What is important is how the individuals in love label that arousal; if it is labeled *love* it will enhance the relationship.

9 Equity theory, which asserts that people mentally calculate the value of the inputs and rewards each individual gives or receives and try to equalize them, has been suggested as an important element in marriage. An intriguing idea generated by equity theory is that both the "superior" and the "inferior" partner in an inequitable relationship feel uneasy.

10 It is possible that equity can be restored in inequitable relationships by instituting real changes in the relationship or by restoring psychological equity. If equity cannot be achieved in a marriage, one way of resolving the situation is by leaving the field, i.e., divorcing.

Affect   Feelings or emotion.

Agape   Unselfish, platonic love.

Attraction   Liking or disliking of others.

Balance Theory   A theory of attraction that emphasizes the agreement or disagreement between two individuals in regard to a third person.

Equity Theory   A theory based on the assumption that people mentally calculate the value of the inputs and rewards each individual gives or receives and try to equalize them.

Eros   Sexual love.

Gain-loss Theory   A theory of attraction which asserts that negative-positive evaluations are more pleasurable than are invariant positive ones (gain), and that positive-negative evaluations are less pleasurable than invariant negative ones (loss).

Imbalanced Relationships   A situation in which two people like each other but disagree about a third person.

Ingratiation   A tactic used by some people to make others like them.

Interpersonal Judgment Scale   A paper-and-pencil measure of attraction used in many attraction experiments.

Misattribution   The cognitive process through which people misinerpret the source of their own and sometimes others emotions and/or behavior.

Negative Reinforcement   A process in which an aversive stimulus is terminated, thereby increasing the probability of the occurrence of the response that terminated the noxious stimulus.

Nonbalanced Relationship   A relationship in which two people dislike each other and both feel either positive or negative toward a third individual.

Phileos   Love of friendship.

Propinquity   Nearness in place.

Psychological Equity   The perception that a relationship is equitable, whether it is or not.

Random Pairs   Pairs in which each individual has an equal chance of being paired with any other individual.

Reinforcement-affect model   A model proposed to account for attraction that emphasizes stimulus (reinforcement) and cognitive (affect) variables.

Two-factor Theory   Any theory that emphasizes two concepts to account for behavior.

REFERENCES

Aronson, E. Who likes whom—and why. *Psychology Today,* August 1970, pp. 48–50, 74.

——— and D. Linder. Gain and loss of esteem as determinants of interpersonal attraction. *Journal of Experimental Social Psychology,* 1965, *1,* 156–71.

Berlyne, D. E. *Conflict, Arousal and Curiosity.* New York: McGraw-Hill Book Company, 1960.

Berscheid, E., T. Brothen, and W. Graziano. Gain-loss theory and the "Law of Infidelity":

Mr. Doting versus the admiring stranger. *Journal of Personality and Social Psychology,* 1976, *33,* 709–18.

———, K. Dion, E. Walster, and G. W. Walster. Physical attractiveness and dating choice: A test of the matching hypothesis. *Journal of Experimental Social Psychology,* 1971, *7,* 173–89.

——— and E. Walster. A little bit about love. In T. L. Huston (Ed.). *Foundations of Interpersonal Attraction.* New York: Academic Press, Inc., 1974.

——— and ———. Physical attractiveness. In L. Berkowitz (Ed.), *Advances in Experimental Social Psychology,* Vol. 7. New York: Academic Press, Inc., 1974, 157–215.

Berscheid, E., E. Walster, and G. Bohrnstedt. The body image report. *Psychology Today,* 1973, *7,* 119–31.

Bohannon, P. (Ed.). *Divorce and After.* Garden City, N.Y.: Doubleday & Company, Inc., 1971.

Brehm, J. W., M. Gaty, G. Geothals, J. McCrommon, and L. Ward. Psychological arousal and interpersonal attraction. Mimeo. Available from authors, 1970.

Brickman, P., P. Meyer, and S. Fredd. Effects of varying exposure to another person with familiar or unfamiliar thought processes. *Journal of Experimental Social Psychology,* 1975, *11,* 261–70.

Brockner, J., and W. C. Swap. Effects of repeated exposure and attitudinal similarity on self-disclosure and interpersonal attraction. *Journal of Personality and Social Psychology,* 1976, *33,* 531–40.

Byrne, D. Interpersonal attraction and attitude similarity. *Journal of Abnormal and Social Psychology,* 1961, *62,* 713–15.

———. Response to attitude similarity-dissimilarity as a function of affiliation need. *Journal of Personality,* 1962, *30,* 164–77.

———. *The Attraction Paradigm.* New York: Academic Press, Inc., 1971.

——— and G. L. Clore. A reinforcement model of evaluative responses. *Personality: An International Journal,* 1970, *1,* 103–128.

———, G. L. Clore, and P. Worchel. The effect of economic similarity-dissimilarity on interpersonal attraction. *Journal of Personality and Social Psychology,* 1966, *4,* 220–24.

———, C. R. Ervin, and J. Lamberth. Continuity between the experimental study of attraction and "real life" computer dating. *Journal of Personality and Social Psychology,* 1970, *16,* 157–65.

——— and W. Griffitt. Similarity and awareness of similarity of personality characteristics. *Journal of Experimental Research in Personality,* 1969, *3,* 179–86.

———, ———, and C. Golightly. Prestige as a factor in determining the effect of attitude similarity-dissimilarity on attraction. *Journal of Personality,* 1966, *34,* 434–44.

———, ———, and D. Stefaniak. Attraction and similarity of personality characteristics. *Journal of Personality and Social Psychology,* 1967, *5,* 82–90.

——— and J. Lamberth. Reinforcement theories and cognitive theories as complementary approaches to the study of attraction. In B. I. Murstein (Ed.), *Theories of Love and Attraction.* New York: Springer Publishing Co., Inc., 1971. Pp. 59–84.

———, ———, J. Palmer, and O. London. Sequential effects as a function of explicit and implicit interpolated attraction responses. *Journal of Personality and Social Psychology,* 1969, *13,* 70–78.

———, O. London, and K. Reeves. The effects of physical attractiveness, sex, and attitude similarity on interpersonal attraction. *Journal of Personality,* 1968, *36,* 259–71.

——— and D. Nelson. Attraction as a function of attitude similarity-dissimilarity: The effect of topic importance. *Psychonomic Science,* 1964, *1,* 93–94.

——— and ———. Attraction as a linear function of positive reinforcement. *Journal of Personality and Social Psychology,* 1965 (a), *1,* 659–63.

——— and ———. The effect of topic importance and attitude similarity-dissimilarity on attraction in a multistranger design. *Psychonomic Science,* 1965 (b), *3,* 449–50.

——— and R. Rhamey. Magnitude of positive and negative reinforcements as a determinant of attraction. *Journal of Personality and Social Psychology,* 1965, *2,* 884–89.

——— and T. J. Wong. Racial prejudice, interpersonal attraction, and assumed dissimilarity of attitudes. *Journal of Abnormal and Social Psychology,* 1962, *65,* 246–53.

Caplow, T., and R. Forman, R. Neighborhood interaction in a homogeneous community. *American Sociological Review,* 1950, *15,* 357–66.

Clore, G. L., and D. Byrne. A reinforcement-affect model of attraction. In T. L. Houston (Ed.), *Foundations of Interpersonal Attraction.* New York: Academic Press, Inc., 1974.

Dion, K., E. Berscheid, and E. Walster. What is beautiful is good. *Journal of Personality and Social Psychology,* 1972, *24,* 285–90.

Driscoll, R., K. E. Davis, and M. E. Lipitz. Parental interference and romantic love: The Romeo and Juliet effect. *Journal of Personality and Social Psychology,* 1972, *24,* 1–10.

Elder, G. H., Jr. Appearance and education in marriage mobility. *American Sociological Review,* 1969, *34,* 519–33.

Festinger, L., S. Schachter, and K. Back. *Social Pressures in Informal Groups: A Study of a Housing Community.* New York: Harper & Row, Publishers, 1950.

Galton, F. *Hereditary Genius: An Inquiry into Its Laws and Consequences,* 1870. (Republished New York, Horizon Press, 1952).

Glick, P. C., and A. J. Norton. Marrying, divorcing, and living together in the U.S. today. *Population Bulletin,* 1977, *32,* 1–38.

Gouaux, C. Induced affective states and interpersonal attraction. *Journal of Personality and Social Psychology,* 1971, *20,* 37–43.

Griffitt, W. Personality similarity and self-concept as determinants of interpersonal attraction. *Journal of Social Psychology,* 1969, *78,* 137–46.

——— and P. Guay. Object evaluation and conditioned affect. *Journal of Experimental Research in Personality,* 1969, *4,* 1–8.

——— and R. Veitch. Preacquaintance attitude similarity and attraction revisited: Ten days in a fallout shelter. *Sociometry,* 1974, *37,* 163–73.

Gross, A. E., and C. Crofton. What is good is beautiful. *Sociometry,* 1977, *40,* 85–90.

Harrison, A. A. Exposure and popularity. *Journal of Personality,* 1969, *37,* 359–77.

Heider, F. Attitudes and cognitive organization. *Journal of Psychology,* 1946, *21,* 107–112.

———. *The Psychology of Interpersonal Relations.* New York: John Wiley & Sons, Inc., 1958.

Hewitt, J. Liking and the proportion of favorable evaluations. *Journal of Personality and Social Psychology,* 1972, *22,* 231–35.

Hohmann, G. W. The effect of dysfunctions of the autonomic nervous system on experienced feelings and emotions. Paper presented at the Conference on Emotions and Feelings at New School for Social Research, New York, 1962.

Homans, G. C. *Social Behavior: Its Elementary Forms.* New York: Harcourt Brace Jovanovich, Inc., 1961.

Jacobs, L., E. Berscheid, and E. Walster. Self-esteem and attraction. *Journal of Personality and Social Psychology,* 1971, *17,* 84–91.

Jones, E. E. *Ingratiation,* New York: Appleton-Century Crofts, 1964.

Kenrick, D. T., and R. B. Cialdini. Romantic attraction: Misattribution versus reinforcement explanations. *Journal of Personality and Social Psychology,* 1977, *35,* 381–91.

Kirkpatrick, C., and S. Stone. Attitude measurement and the comparison of generations. *Journal of Applied Psychology,* 1935, *19,* 564–82.

Lamberth, J. Sequential variables as determinants of human performance with attitudinal reinforcers. *Psychonomic Science,* 1971, *22,* 350–52.

────── and D. Byrne. Similarity-attraction or demand characteristics? *Personality,* 1971, *2,* 77–91.

Landy, D., and H. Sigall. Beauty is talent: Task evaluation as a function of the performer's physical attractiveness. *Journal of Personality and Social Psychology,* 1974, *29,* 299–304.

Morse, S. J., H. T. Reis, and J. Gruzen. Hedonism and equity in heterosexual interaction. Paper presented at a symposium on "Exchange Theory and Interpersonal Relationships" at the American Psychological Association, Montreal, Canada, August 1973.

Mettee, D. R. Changes in liking as a function of the magnitude and affect of sequential evaluations. *Journal of Experimental Social Psychology,* 1971 (a), *7,* 157–72.

────── . The true discerner as a potent source of positive affect. *Journal of Experimental Social Psychology,* 1971 (b), *7,* 293–303.

────── and E. Aronson. Affective reactions to appraisal from others. In T. L. Houston (Ed.), *Foundations of Interpersonal Attraction.* New York: Academic Press, Inc., 1974.

Miller, A. G. Role of Physical attractiveness in impression formation. *Psychonomic Science,* 1970, *19,* 241–43.

Mills, J., and E. Aronson. Opinion change as a function of the communicator's attractiveness and desire to influence. *Journal of Personality and Social Psychology,* 1965, *1,* 173–77.

Moreland, R. L., and R. B. Zajonc. A strong test of exposure effects. *Journal of Experimental Social Psychology,* 1976, *31,* 370–76.

Morgan, C. L., and H. H. Remmers. Liberalism and conservatism of college students as affected by the depression. *School and Society,* 1935, *41,* 708–784.

Murstein, B. I. Physical attractiveness and marital choice. *Journal of Personality and Social Psychology,* 1972, *22,* 8–12.

Nahemow, L., and M. P. Lawton. Similarity and propinquity in friendship formation. *Journal of Personality and Social Psychology,* 1975, *32,* 205–213.

Newcomb, T. M. An approach to the study of communicative acts. *Psychological Review,* 1953, *60,* 393–404.

────── . Individual systems of orientation. In S. Koch (Ed.), *Psychology: A Study of a Science.* Vol. 3. New York: McGraw-Hill Book Company, 1959. Pp. 384–422.

────── and G. Svehla. Intra-family relationships in attitudes. *Sociometry,* 1937, *1,* 180–208.

────── . *The Acquaintance Process.* New York: Holt, Rinehart and Winston, 1961.

────── . Dyadic balance as a source of clues about interpersonal attraction. In B. I. Murstein (Ed.), *Theories of Attraction and Love.* New York: Springer Publishing Co., Inc., 1971.

Novak, D. W., and M. J. Lerner. Rejection as a consequence of perceived rejection. *Journal of Personality and Social Psychology,* 1968, *9,* 147–52.

Orne, M. T. On the social psychology of the psychological experiment: With particular reference to demand characteristics and their implications. *American Psychologist,* 1962, *17,* 776–83.

────── . Demand characteristics and the concept of quasi-controls. In R. Rosenthal and R. L. Rosnow (Eds.), *Artifacts in Behavioral Research.* New York: Academic Press, Inc., 1969. Pp. 143–79.

Palmer, J., and D. Byrne. Attraction toward dominant and submissive strangers: Similarity versus complementarity. *Journal of Experimental Research in Personality,* 1970, *4,* 108–115.

Pearson, K., and A. Lee. On the laws of inheritance in man. I. Inheritance of physical characters. *Biometrika,* 1903, *2,* 357–462.

Price, K. O., E. Harburg, and T. Newcomb. Psychological balance in situations of negative interpersonal attitudes. *Journal of Personality and Social Psychology,* 1966, *3,* 265–70.

Reik, T. *A Psychologist Looks at Love.* New York: Farrar & Rinehart (now Farrar, Straus & Giroux, Inc.), 1944.

Richardson, H. M. Studies of mental resemblance between husbands and wives and between friends. *Psychological Bulletin,* 1939, *36,* 104–120.

———. Community of values as a factor in friendships of college and adult women. *Journal of Social Psychology,* 1940, *11,* 303–312.

Rosenthal, R. *Experimenter Effects in Behavioral Research.* New York: Appleton-Century-Crofts, 1966.

———. Interpersonal expectations: Effects of the experimenter's hypothesis. In R. Rosenthal and R. L. Rosnow (Eds.), *Artifacts in Behavioral Research.* New York: Academic Press, Inc., 1969. Pp. 181–277.

Rubin, Z. Measurement of romantic love. *Journal of Personality and Social Psychology,* 1970, *16,* 265–73.

———. *Liking and Loving: An Invitation to Social Psychology.* New York: Holt, Rinehart and Winston, 1973.

Sachs, D. H., and D. Byrne. Differential conditioning of evaluative responses to neutral stimuli through association with attitude statements. *Journal of Experimental Research in Personality,* 1970, *4,* 181–85.

Saegert, S., W. Swap, and R. B. Zajonc. Exposure, context and interpersonal attraction. *Journal of Personality and Social Psychology,* 1973, *25,* 234–42.

Schachter, S. The interaction of cognitive and physiological determinants of emotional state. In L. Berkowitz (Ed.), *Advances in Experimental Social Psychology.* Vol. 1. New York: Academic Press, Inc., 1964.

——— and J. F. Singer. Cognitive, and social and physiological determinants of emotional state. *Psychological Review,* 1962, *69,* 379–89.

——— and L. Wheeler. Epinephrine, chloropromazin, and amusement. *Journal of Abnormal and Social Psychology,* 1962, *65,* 121–28.

Schiller, B. A quantitative analysis of marriage selection in a small group. *Journal of Social Psychology,* 1932, *3,* 297–319.

Schuster, E., and E. M. Elderton. The inheritance of physical characters. *Biometrika,* 1906, *5,* 460–69.

Sigall, H., and E. Aronson. Opinion change and the gain-loss model of interpersonal attraction. *Journal of Experimental Social Psychology,* 1967, *3,* 178–88.

——— and ———. Liking for an evaluator as a function of her physical attractiveness and nature of the evaluations. *Journal of Experimental Social Psychology,* 1969, *5,* 93–100.

Silverman, I. Physical attractiveness and courtship. *Sexual Behavior,* September, 1971, Pp. 22–25.

Taylor, D. A., I. Altman, and R. Sorrentino. Interpersonal exchange as a function of rewards and costs and situational factors: Expectancy confirmation-disconfirmation. *Journal of Experimental Social Psychology,* 1969, *5,* 324–39.

Tognoli, J., and R. Keisner. Gain and loss of esteem as determinants of interpersonal attraction: A replication and extension. *Journal of Personality and Social Psychology,* 1972, *23,* 201–204.

Valins, S. Cognitive effects of false heart-rate feedback. *Journal of Personality and Social Psychology,* 1966, *4,* 400–408.

Walster, E., V. Aronson, D. Abrahams, and L. Rothman. The importance of physical attractiveness in dating behavior. *Journal of Personality and Social Psychology,* 1966, *4,* 508–516.

———, and E. Berscheid. Adrenaline makes the heart grow fonder, *Psychology Today,* 1971, *5,* 47–62.

———, ———, and G. W. Walster. New directions in equity research. *Journal of Personality and Social Psychology,* 1973, *25,* 151–76.

————, G. Walster, and E. Berscheid. *Equity: Theory and Research.* Boston: Allyn & Bacon, Inc., 1978.

————, G. Walster, J. Piliavin, and L. Schmidt. "Playing hard-to-get": Understanding an elusive phenomenon. *Journal of Personality and Social Psychology,* 1973, *26,* 113–21.

————, G. W. Walster, and S. Traupmann. Equity and premarital sex. Unpublished manuscript, 1977. Quoted in E. Walster, G. W. Walster, and E. Berscheid. *Equity: Theory and Research.* Boston: Allyn & Bacon, Inc., 1978.

Williamson, R. C. *Marriage and Family Relations.* New York: John Wiley & Sons, Inc., 1966.

Wilson, W., and H. Nakajo. Preference for photographs as a function of frequency of presentation. *Psychonomic Science,* 1965, *3,* 577–78.

Winslow, C. N. A study of the extent of agreement between friends' opinions and their ability to estimate the opinions of others. *Journal of Social Psychology,* 1937, *8,* 433–42.

Zajonc, R. *Social Psychology: An Experimental Approach.* Belmont, Calif.: Wadsworth Publishing Co., Inc., 1966.

————. Attitudinal effects of mere exposure. *Journal of Personality and Social Psychology Monograph Supplement,* 1968, *9,* 1–27.

———— and D. W. Rajecki. Exposure and affect: A field experiment. *Psychonomic Science,* 1969, *17,* 216–17.

10

Altruism

By this time in your study of social psychology you may have come to the pessimistic realization that social psychologists are a lot like news people—they study what sells. Just as newspaper editors know that a nice multiple murder sells more

PLO cites Israel in bombing death

Bulletin Wire Services

Beirut, Lebanon — The Palestine Liberation Organization blamed Israel today for the bombing assassination of Abu Hassan, the guerilla leader reputed to have masterminded the terrorist attack at the 1972 Munich Olympics in which 11 Israeli athletes died.

A PLO spokesman charged that "Zionist agents" planted the remote control bomb that killed Ali Hassan Salameh, 38, security chief of the Al

Abu Hassan headed the list. As leader of the Black September guerilla group, he organized the massacre at the Munich Olympics, the Israelis have said.

Vowing vengeance, Al Fatah said in a statement yesterday: "The murderers will not escape."

Abu Hassan was considered very close to PLO leader Yasir Arafat and *Please Turn to Page 6*

Abu Hassan Salameh
...'most wanted list'

Salvitti is guilty in extortion case

By HARMON V. GORDON
Of The Bulletin Staff

A federal judge yesterday found Augustine A. Salvitti, former executive director of the Philadelphia Redevelopment Authority, guilty of extorting $21,000 from a New Jersey engineering firm that held a $1.4-million consultant contract with the authority.

The decision by U.S. District Judge Edward N. Cahn in Philadelphia came

six days after Salvitti reported to the federal prison at Allenwood, Lycoming County, Pa., to begin serving a three-year sentence for accepting a $27,500 kickback in a $1-million land deal.

The week-long trial in the engineering firm extortion ended Jan. 8. Cahn, who heard the case without a jury, had promised a decision in several weeks.

Salvitti was charged with extortion

Turmoil in Iran

Advisers urge the shah not to travel to the U.S.

Regency chief submits Resignation to Khomeini

Man drives van onto lake, drowns

A man drove a van onto an ice-covered lake in a Chester County park yesterday, stopped the vehicle, started running away and fell through the ice to his death.

The van later fell through the ice.

The victim was identified as Charles P. Welch, 25, of 123 Brookhill road, Newtown Square, Delaware County. Martha Montich, deputy Chester County coroner, said an autopsy would be performed today.

State police said they don't know why the man drove onto the lake or why he ran away from the van.

The incident occurred at 2.45 P.M. in Marsh Creek State Park in Upper Uwchlan Township. Police said Welch drove east on Lyndell road, then onto Marsh Creek Lake about 200 yards before stopping the van.

Park rangers, who witnessed the incident, went to the scene by boat but were unable to save Welch. He was pronounced dead at Coatesville Hospital.

Cyclist sues for $10,000

They're living in fear of a real disaster

These headlines were clipped from a recent issue of a newspaper and show the balance of negative to positive news contained there.

papers than the story of someone helping a blind person across the street, social scientists are aware of the pull of the negative and disastrous. There is a good deal of pressure on us to solve the problems that beset our countries and we find that by definition those problems are negative. People feel prejudiced against others and discriminate against them; those who can get power misuse it; those not in power slavishly obey orders; people aggress against one another. Even when we study attraction, I suspect people are more interested in "Who dislikes me?" rather than "Who likes me?"

There is no doubt that there is more effort spent by social scientists in studying the negative aspects of life than in studying the positive ones. Perhaps this is because in Canada and the United States we have been brought up with the idea that doing good, obeying the law, and living an upstanding life are values to be cherished. When people violate these norms by being antisocial it tweaks our curiosity and we strive to understand why.

There is, however, another class of behavior that mystifies us and these are just the opposite sorts of actions. Why does someone jump into a nearly frozen river to rescue an elderly person whose car has run off the road into the water? Why does someone stand up and face danger to help a woman who is being mugged by a gang? Why does a soldier throw himself on top of a live hand grenade in battle? Obviously, social norms of doing good, obeying the law, and living an upstanding life are not adequate to explain the behaviors just mentioned. Even though it is true that the religious backgrounds of those who settled Canada and the United States (primarily Judeo-Christian) emphasized moral behavior, self-sacrificing behavior is still unique enough to be newsworthy.

Social psychologists have preferred to refer to these types of self-sacrificing behavior as *altruism* or *prosocial behavior*. There is a good deal of research in developmental psychology into *moral development* (see Chapter 4 for a discussion). Basically, we are referring to the same thing when we speak of these three areas of research. Defining exactly what is meant by *altruism* or *prosocial behavior* is a little difficult but we will mean *the unselfish concern for the welfare of others* when we use either of the words.

To gain a little practice in determining what is an altruistic act and what is not, consider the following situations:

1. A young woman spurns a life of her own to care for an aging wealthy aunt and for twenty years she faithfully nurses her until her death. The deceased aunt leaves her sizable estate to her niece.
2. A young woman spurns a life of her own to care for an aging aunt. For twenty years she faithfully supports and nurses her aunt until her death. The deceased aunt leaves her sizable estate, which only her lawyer knew existed, to her niece.
3. A wealthy man gives a sizable amount of money to a private college in his city, but insists that the gift be anonymous.
4. A wealthy man leaves a sizable amount of money in his will to a private college in his city. Since the will does not stipulate that the benefactor remain anonymous, a building is named in his honor.
5. Albert Schweitzer spurned a chance for a brilliant career in either music or theology in Europe and went to serve humanity in an underdeveloped country in Africa. He became one of the most famous men of his day.
6. Martin Luthor King took extraordinary risks and made great personal sacrifices in the struggle for civil rights in the United States. He always counseled nonviolence and championed the cause of blacks everywhere. Yet at the time he was assassinated, he was one of the most powerful and revered men in the country.

Which of the actions listed above conform to the definition of altruism—unselfish concern for the welfare of others? The answer is that we really can't know without knowing why the individual did what he or she did. And that makes the study of altruism devilishly difficult.

There are several theories of human behavior that were not specifically developed to deal with prosocial behavior, but because of the uniqueness of such behavior are placed in contrast to each other most clearly when they deal with altruism. For that reason we will discuss the theories here prior to discussing the empirical research on the topic.

There is a class of theory that has grown up to deal with human behavior in general and has variously been called *social exchange* (Foa & Foa, 1974, 1975; Homans, 1961; Thibaut and Kelley, 1959) *equity theory* (Walster, Bersheid, and Walster, 1973; Walster and Walster, 1975) or the *justice motive* (Lerner, 1974, 1975, 1977). Since these three have certain elements in common, I will begin with social exchange theory and develop the other two from it.

To begin with, all three of these theories are hedonic. That is, they emphasize people's choosing to behave in a manner that they expect to be the most pleasurable or the least pleasurable to them. You may ask what these hedonic theories have to do with altruism, which is, after all, the unselfish concern for the welfare of others. There is evidence, as you will shortly see, which indicates that people engage in altruistic behavior because it is pleasurable to them. Why does someone donate large sums of money to an educational or religious institution? In some instances it is undoubtedly because of a promise to name a building after the donor, but there are a sufficient number of anonymous donations to make us wonder how universal such a motivation is.

At a level closer to most of us, why do we donate money to charities? There are innumerable fund-raising events aimed at stamping out diseases, helping those who are less fortunate than ourselves, and so forth. Every year millions of people contribute to such enterprises. Why they do so is the heart of altruism. I have taken the position that they do so because they want to and that fulfilling this desire to help others is pleasurable. This in no way debases their action, rather it argues that species *Homo sapiens* has come to the point where it is enjoyable to help others. Far from being a negative aspect of altruism, it seems to me that it is a very positive reason for helping. If it were pleasurable only to benefit oneself, then it seems to me that we humans would be functioning at a lower ethical level than when we find that one of life's pleasures is to help others. I think this approach is quite consistent with the higher stages of ethical development proposed by Kohlberg (see Chapter 4).

Social Exchange Theory

Social exchange theory is based on economics, except that in social exchange what individuals are exchanging is not goods and money but social resources. That statement must, however, be qualified to some degree, because goods and money do interact with social resources to determine behavior. For example, consider the case of a clerk who has worked in old Mr. Jones's shoe store for fifteen years. The neighborhood is going downhill and the clerk can go elsewhere and make more money. He refuses because he knows Mr. Jones cannot get anyone else to replace him, and in a couple of years, Mr. Jones can sell his store and retire on his savings and social security. Money and goods are all tied up together in this illustration, but the decision ultimately is a social exchange one.

One way of viewing the matter is to think of it in terms of Maslow's (1954) hierarchy of needs. Humans have basic physiological needs—food, water, air, and so

This helicopter is used by a bank to speed transactions around the city. It takes off from a building with a sign advertising a lottery—another sort of monetary transaction.

forth. Once these needs are met, at least at a minimal level, another set of needs must be met—shelter, clothing, and so forth. Once our physical needs are cared for, then social needs such as love, esteem, and achievement appear. It is, however, impossible to differentiate between the need to achieve and a more basic need such as food or shelter. In our society, the more we achieve, the more we are able to provide food and shelter. Thus, the movement from an economic theory of exchange to a social one is neither particularly startling nor is the line of demarcation between the two very clear-cut. Some of the things we want and need are economic in nature, some are social, and sometimes meeting the social needs helps achieve the meeting of the economic needs, and vice versa.

The basic idea behind social exchange theory is really quite simple. Each of us has social needs—love, friendship, social approval, esteem, and so forth. At the same time, we have certain social resources with which to obtain or satisfy these needs. We offer companionship, friendship, love, esteem, and so forth to others. According to Thibaut and Kelley, and Homans, individuals internally compute the rewards and costs in a social interaction and determine an outcome, which in turn helps them to decide whether to maintain the relationship.

INDIVIDUAL CHOICES

To clarify all this a bit, let us go back a step and consider a very simple case—one person and one decision. Let us assume that Erica is faced with a choice of deciding on a major in college. Erica's real interests lie in art. She wants to be a painter. If there were no other considerations Erica would major in art. Soon after deciding that she would major in art, Erica's father asks a very pointed question: "What kind of job can you get in art?" She realizes that she wants to paint, not get a job. However, she also would like to eat and so that is a consideration. Let us assume that we can scale Erica's feelings from − 10 (supreme agony) to + 10 (supreme ecstasy). Further, let us assume that Erica does not want to get married right after college to someone who could support her while she painted, and that Erica's parents cannot support her after college. Figure 10–1 gives the hypothetical scale values for several items that would go into making Erica's decision. Note that a change in the weight Erica puts on painting, or on security, or on marriage could easily tip the decision in another direction.

As you can see, things are relatively complicated even in a situation in which individual decisions are being made. But things get more complex as other people are added to the situation.

GROUP DECISIONS

Thibaut and Kelley (1959) argued that the best way to understand group decision making is to set up an *interaction matrix*, which merely indicates each participant's preferences for engaging in a range of behavior exchanges. The model proposed by Thibaut and Kelley is that participants exchange certain rewards, whether these be friendship, help with a task, or sex. At the same time, these rewards for the other person have certain *costs* associated with them—the task or friendship takes time and energy. In addition, by helping you or being your friend, the individual may be

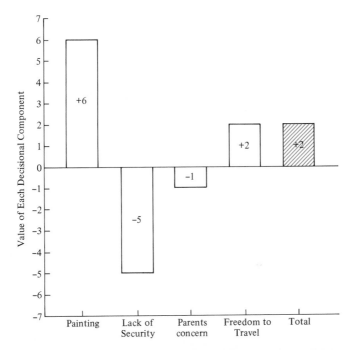

Figure 10–1 Hypothetical case of Erica deciding whether to major in art and become a painter. In this instance the positive aspects would outweigh the negative ones and her decision would be to become a painter.

One place where bargaining still occurs in present-day society is in the purchase of a car, particularly a large, luxury model.

missing out on other activities that are important and potentially rewarding. To this point, social exchange basically has followed an economic model. You want something and you pay something for it. That usually ends an economic transaction unless you've been cheated or some such thing. In our daily economic lives there isn't a built-in next step we go through—"did I get cheated?" When our economy was less rigidly controlled and there was more bartering and bargaining taking place, this next step was very natural. If a man had traded two mules for a horse he might wonder if he had been taken. But today, most of what we buy is priced and we either pay the price or don't buy the object.

In social exchange, however, there is no agreed upon "price" for each reward. Is ten minutes of a friend's time worth twenty minutes of an acquaintance's time in helping you get your car started? Questions like this really don't make sense, so Thibaut and Kelley tell us that the *outcome* of an interaction is the difference between total cost and reward. The outcome is very subjective, because it involves the individual's determination of costs and rewards and this is based on the individual's needs. To return to our illustration of the horse trader who traded two mules for a horse, he may have got a fine horse and still found that the outcome was not to his liking. For example, if he was trying to get a race horse, but instead traded for a very fine plow horse, he would be disappointed.

A number of interactions occur between two individuals and between each of our duo and other people. Whether a relationship between two individuals continues depends not on the absolute outcome of each of their interactions but on the *comparison level* each has. That is, there is a certain level of satisfaction that must be attained in a relationship for the relationship to continue. This accounts for the fact that a relationship may continue for some time and then break off.

THE MINIMAX STRATEGY

It has been assumed that individuals work within the framework of minimizing their costs and maximizing their rewards (Kelley, 1968; Sidowski, Wyckoff, and Tabory, 1956). This minimax strategy makes a lot of conceptual sense, so let us see how it works.

410

In an interaction between two people, there are some things that one enjoys but the other doesn't, and vice versa. Let us assume that two individuals are going to spend an evening together and there are three possibilities for their activity. They can go to a movie, watch television, or go to a concert. Each of the two, Harold and Ellen, has likes and dislikes. Again, assuming a scale from -10 to $+10$, their likes and dislikes are pictured in Figure 10-2. As you can see from the figure, if both employ the minimax strategy, Harold will go to the movies and Ellen will watch TV. If Ellen goes to the movies with Harold her costs will approach her rewards and she will be less satisfied than Harold will. Of course, the fact that both like to do things in each other's company has not yet entered into the equation.

All of this sounds very complicated. Does each one of us compute rewards and costs and keep a running log of outcomes and break off a relationship when the ledger sheet becomes too unbalanced? According to Thibaut and Kelley we don't carry a set of numbers around in our heads that detail each relationship, but something akin to this goes on when we decide which relationships to continue and which to terminate.

Resource Theory of Exchange

Uriel G. and Edna B. Foa, although not finding anything to quibble with concerning the basic ideas of social exchange theory, have argued that in social exchange the elements of exchange differ and that the difference must be taken into consideration. In economic transactions one party pays money for goods or services. The element of exchange is not in question. A number of years ago, when trading was still prevalent enough to have a major impact on our economy, the medium of exchange was not set. Therefore, it might be a horse for a mule, or a cow for a horse, six sheep for a donkey, and so forth. Still tangible, material objects were being offered for tangible, material objects. Even when we consider the fact that workers offer their labor for money, the employer intends to translate that work into money.

Figure 10–2 Outcomes of three activities for Harold and Ellen. Generally Ellen likes TV more than movies and both more than a concert. Harold generally likes movies more than TV. However, they both like doing things together, and conversing, more than doing things alone. From this matrix we can predict that Harold will probably go to the movies and Ellen will go along or stay at home and watch TV.

Now consider the case of social exchange. How far do you think you would get if you walked into a clothing store and told the owner "I am prepared to hold you in high esteem for one hour in exchange for that sport coat?" The two elements of exchange, esteem and a sport coat, are so different that it is impossible to seriously consider such an exchange.

The Foas' contribution to social exchange theory, and it is a major one, is that there are several classes of resources and that the rules for transactions between classes of resources differ. As they say,

> . . . we suggest that while all interpersonal encounters may indeed be perceived as transactions, the rules of exchange vary systematically for different types of transactions. Recognizing the existence of qualitative differences among transactions, we offer a system for sorting them into homogenous categories. Moreover, the notion that the rules of exchange vary *systematically* across types of transactions suggests that these types are organized into a distinct pattern, or structure, according to their relative similarity and dissimilarity. Thus similar transactions will have similar rules of exchange while dissimilar ones will follow a different set of rules. In this manner, economic and psychological exchanges, though not equated, are considered within the same framework. Hence allowances are made for the study of the interplay. [Foa and Foa, 1975, p. 2.]

The Foas have conceptualized social exchange media into six cognitive classes: love, services, goods, money, information, and status. Further, they assert that these resources can be categorized with respect to particularism and concreteness. *Particularism* refers to the quality of an individual's valuing and exchanging of a resource and to his or her relationship with another individual when doing so. For example, changing a clerk at a supermarket checkout line will not have much effect on your transaction, but changing your doctor or lawyer will. Love is the most particularistic

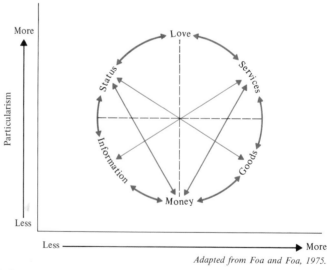

Adapted from Foa and Foa, 1975.

Figure 10-3 Six social resources classified by particularism and concreteness. The arrows in the diagram reflect some of the possible transactions.

resource and money the least. Concreteness can range from very concrete to very abstract. Goods and services are the most concrete, and status and information the most abstract, of the six resources. Figure 10-3 shows the resources plotted with respect to particularism and concreteness. As you can see from the figure, some resources are more likely than others to be exchanged for certain other resources (for example, status and love are more likely to be exchanged than are goods and love). A number of investigations have experimentally verified the Foas' conceptualization of resources in exchange theory (Foa, Megonigal, and Greipp, 1976).

Equity Theory

Equity theory may be properly seen as an extension of exchange theory in that it adds a dimension to social transactions, namely one of equity. Adams (1963, 1965) and Walster, Berscheid, and Walster (1973) point out that in society individuals have learned to meet a standard that is equitable and just to other members in the society. Thus, we somehow feel uncomfortable if we are receiving all of the favors being dispensed in a relationship and giving none in return. The relationship is not equitable and thus not very satisfying.

The reason for this equalizing of rewards, according to Walster et al., is that the group can maximize collective rewards by evolving a system for apportioning rewards and costs equitably among themselves. Note that equity theory is not saying that humans inherently want everyone treated well, but that the way for *most* people to be treated well is to have a system that equally distributes rewards and costs. Typically, groups will reward members who treat other members equitably and will increase the costs of (punish) individuals who treat other members inequitably.

A relationship is equitable when the positive outcomes (rewards) and negative outcomes (costs) for each individual are equal. Generally speaking, experimental evidence supports the idea that individuals do behave equitably. In some experiments, individuals have spontaneously shared an overabundance of rewards, and deprived partners have been quick to demand their fair share (Leventhal, Allen, and Kemelgor, 1969; Maxwell, Ratcliffe, and Schmitt, 1969). In addition, individuals who receive more than their fair share experience distress—usually guilt (Adams and Rosenbaum, 1962; Adams, 1963; Leventhal, et al., 1969); and those who receive less than their fair share are also distressed—usually angered (Jacques, 1961; Walster, Berscheid, and Walster, 1970; Leventhal et al., 1969; Thibaut, 1950).

Individuals in an inequitable relationship attempt to eliminate the distress that occurs because of the inequity by restoring equity. The more inequity that exists the more distress they feel (Brock and Buss, 1962; Lerner and Matthews, 1967) and the harder they seek to restore equity (Brock and Becker, 1966; Carlsmith and Gross, 1969). In an inequitable situation an individual can restore equity in one of two ways. First, he can alter his actions so the relationship becomes equitable. For example, an acquaintance of mine is a lawyer who has a good friend who is a plumber. They exchange legal services for plumbing work. If the plumber feels the relationship is inequitable because he is receiving more than he should, he can come around more often and check out the plumbing and make any necessary repairs until the relationship is equitable. The second form of restoring equity is to restore psychological equity by distorting the importance of the outcomes of the partner's contributions. For example, if the lawyer feels he is receiving more than he should be, he could say that good legal advice is more important than good plumbing and that without him his plumber friend would have been sued innumerable times. Whether this is actually the fact or not, the perception of equity has been restored.

Restoring an inequitable relationship to equity is a difficult task, because just the right amount of rewards and costs must be applied. To reward the person who has an excess of costs in a relationship too much will result in an inequitable relationship. In addition, for a person who is in an equitable relationship and has benefited from it, sometimes adequate compensation is not available. In such a case equity can be restored psychologically by derogating the costs to the other individual or by justifying them completely. To test the idea of adequate compensation, Berscheid and Walster (1967) allowed women who had done harm to another person to provide restitution. Some women were allowed to make only inadequate restitution to the harmed individual; some were allowed to make adequate restitution; still others were allowed only to overcompensate the harmed woman. Women who were allowed to make adequate restitution were much more likely to compensate the harmed women than were those who were allowed to make only inadequate restitution or else to overcompensate the other woman. This result, which was replicated by Berscheid, Walster, and Barclay (1969) has some interesting implications.

Probably the most important implication is that when an individual or group has been harmed, excessive reference to that harm where adequate restitution is not available may actually *reduce* the restitution that is granted. For example, certain minority groups in Canada and the United States have been discriminated against for many years (see Chapter 6). If the majority feels that adequate restitution is not available, then it is possible that continued reference to that discrimination will result in less, not more restitution.

The Justice Motive

A final approach to the problem of how people deal with each other has been proposed by Lerner and his associates (Braband and Lerner, 1975; Lerner, 1971a, 1974, 1975, 1977; Lerner and Lichtman, 1968; Lerner and Braband, 1973; Miller, 1977). The basic idea grew out of close scrutiny of two seemingly incompatible responses. At times humans can exhibit deep compassion and self-denying behavior, whereas at other times they act with indifference or callousness to equal suffering or even cause that suffering themselves. Lerner has attempted to solve this dilemma by suggesting that the way people act toward other people is dependent upon whether the suffering individual is seen as deserving of the fate received. Lerner argues that undeserved suffering elicits compassion and help, whereas deserved suffering results in indifference or even callousness. For example, people react with great sympathy, sadness, revulsion, and horror when a husband and father is brought down by an assassin's bullet (e.g., John F. Kennedy and Martin Luther King). On the other hand, many people are insistent that even husbands and fathers die when they are convicted of murder. In one instance the individual does not deserve his fate and in the other he does.

Lerner argues that the justice motive is learned during the process of socialization. The infant who originally demands immediate gratification for his or her needs learns to delay immediate gratification. As children mature, they also learn that justice is the best strategy for all. If everyone follows the principle of justice, then the largest number of individuals will obtain what they deserve—whether it is reward or punisment.

Comment

The question that probably is stirring in your mind is "How does equity theory differ from the justice motive?" The answer, it seems to me, is that the differences between the two are more apparent than real. It should be obvious that equity theory differs from exchange theory in that equity proposes that everyone should be treated fairly, whereas exchange argues that everyone tries to maximize her or his outcomes. However, the justice motive also appears to be based upon a motivation for fairness or equity. If equity and justice are equated, then the two theories are basically identical. If equity and justice are not equivalent concepts as they are identified by their proponents, then I fail to see the difference between the two.

Both equity theory and the idea of the justice motive developed in the 1960s as a response to exchange theory and they elaborate an important point—people tend to want to see an equitable distribution of resources among all people. Society, if it is to flourish, must provide for the good of all its members, not just a few.

Altruistic Behavior

Depending upon which element of human nature I wish to stress, I can start this section on altruistic behavior with a few examples. Let us consider these two:

An 18-year-old switchboard operator, alone in her office in the Bronx, is raped and beaten. Escaping momentarily, she runs naked and bleeding to the street, screaming for help. A crowd of 40 passersby gathers and watches as, in broad daylight, the rapist tries to drag her back upstairs. No one interferes. Finally, two policemen happen by and arrest her assailant. [Latané and Darley, 1970, p. 2.]

On a cold and dreary November day two unidentified men are driving on Philadelphia's West River Drive when they see the car ahead of them veer off the road and into the Schuylkill River. The two men immediately stop their car and jump into the river which is swift, cold and deep to drag an elderly lady out of her car to safety. They leave before the police get their names. [Reported on KYW, Philadelphia, Pa., November 3, 1977.]

Why do we observe such differences in behavior? Even though I have here but one example apiece of two different kinds of behavior, there are many other examples that could be given. Which kind of example describes human behavior most accurately? Are the behaviors shown in these two examples equally prevalent in society? It is to questions such as these that researchers in altruism have addressed themselves.

During the late 1960s, Bibb Latané and John M. Darley (Latané and Darley, 1970) carried out an ambitious research project which was aimed at understanding altruism. Its title, *The Unresponsive Bystander: Why Doesn't He Help?* provides a key to their analysis of the situation. But before we analyze their results and theoretical analysis, we need to look carefully at the research they carried out.

The simplest situations in which altruistic impulses can operate are not the ones that make newspaper headlines; rather they are the everyday occurrences and requests with which we all are familiar. Latané and Darley began their work with an examination of such situations.

HELPING IN NONEMERGENCY SITUATIONS

In a very simple field study, students in psychology classes at Columbia University went out on to the streets of New York and asked 1,520 passers-by for help or information. The students asked for the time, directions, change, the individual's name, or for a dime. Figure 10-4 shows the frequency of assistance received by the students. As you can easily see, a vast majority of people were willing to give the time and directions, somewhat fewer were willing (or able) to make change, but when it came to giving out the person's name or a dime, compliance with the request dropped dramatically. Yet if a reason for needing the dime was given (my wallet has been stolen) 72 percent helped, and if the individual prefaced the request for the stranger's name by giving his or her name, 59 percent complied with the request.

What happens when someone asks directions and is given the wrong information? Obviously, we have all been given misinformation when requesting directions and if

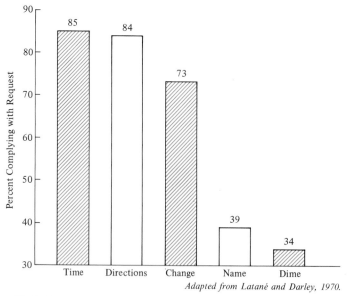

Adapted from Latané and Darley, 1970.

Figure 10-4 **Percentage of individuals complying with five different requests.**

Subway stations are ideal places for altruism research.

we follow it, we are usually greatly inconvenienced. Now, what do you do if you overhear someone giving directions which you know are wrong? Do you intervene and save the individual requesting information a good deal of inconvenience? To do so, of course, you must contradict the individual giving directions. Thus you have a knotty problem.

To determine people's reactions to misinformation, a prearranged situation was developed. Two students selected a New York subway rider and one of them (the confederate) sat near the individual. The student (the experimenter) looking bewildered, asked whether the train was going uptown or downtown. The confederate gave the wrong answer thus presenting the rider with a dilemma. Should the bewildered information seeker be allowed to ride the labyrinth subway system or should the misinformation be corrected? In addition, three different conditions were arranged. One third of the time, the bewildered rider asked the question of the confederate directly; one third of the time both the confederate and the subject were asked the question; and for another third of the time the question was addressed to the subject directly. In all cases the confederate immediately answered with the wrong information. If the question was addressed to the confederate, the subject corrected the misinformation 27 percent of the time, presumably leaving the bewildered rider to be lost in the subway 73 percent of the time. If the question was addressed to both individuals the misinformation was corrected half the time. If the question was addressed directly to the subject, 93 percent of the time he or she corrected the misinformation.

There is an emerging pattern of responses in these nonemergency situations. As the responsibility for the act or the justification for helping becomes clearer, then helping behavior increases. With the subway riders there is an obvious relationship between responsibility for the information and the percentage of times an individual corrects misinformation. As people give more justification for helping (by saying their wallet has been stolen or by giving their name) compliance with simple requests increases. Thus it appears that responsibility and justification for an act play a role in whether an individual will help.

Emergencies occur quite often; some are life-threatening and others are not. Altruism is generally thought of in terms of emergency situations. For example, the revulsion we feel when we hear about a young girl screaming while being stabbed to death, with no one responding makes headlines. So do daring and brave rescues, but somehow or other it seems that there are more horrifying occurrences than brave ones. Is this accurate or do we just remember the horrifying ones? Possibly another variable enters into the picture—maybe more of the negative stories are picked up by the news media.

Latané and Darley report a number of experiments in which individuals were faced with an emergency. Their responses are instructive.

The Smoke-Filled Room. The subjects in the smoke-filled room study were Columbia University students who were invited to take part in an interview about problems of urban life. The student was instructed to fill out some preliminary forms while waiting for the actual interview. Contact with students was made by telephone and they received all instructions on the phone. Thus, there was no personal contact with the experimenter. When the subject arrived in the experimental room, a large sign informed him he had come to the proper place, requested that he sit and wait for the interviewer, and instructed him to fill out the preliminary forms.

While the subject was filling out the forms, smoke was introduced into the room through a small vent in the wall. The smoke, which was chemical, was moderately textured and clearly visible. For the entire experimental period or until the subject took action, smoke continued to flow into the room. Enough smoke had filtered into the room after four minutes to obscure vision and produce a mildly acrid odor that interfered with breathing.

Of the 24 subjects who were alone in the room, half of them reported the smoke within two minutes and 75 percent of them had reported the smoke at the end of four minutes. By the end of six minutes, however, when the experiment was terminated, the other 25 percent of the subjects had not reported the smoke. Of course, smoke does not necessarily mean fire and the subjects who did not report the smoke also did not flee. They remained in the room doggedly filling out the preliminary forms as the density of the smoke increased. Presumably they did not view the smoke as an emergency.

There were two other conditions in this experiment. In the first, there were two passive confederates in the room filling out forms. These confederates had been instructed to notice the smoke when it appeared, shrug their shoulders, and return to work. Subjects in this condition reported the smoke only 10 percent of the time as compared to 75 percent reporting when the subjects were alone. Another condition was run in which there were three naïve subjects. As in the situation just reported, there were three people in the room when the smoke appeared, but all three of them were subjects and could be expected to become concerned at the sight of smoke. Of course, once one person in a group had reported the smoke, the other two would not be expected to report the smoke also because their information would be redundant. However, in only 38 percent of the groups did anyone report the smoke. This, of course, compares to the 75 percent reporting when subjects were alone.

The major conclusion that seemingly can be drawn from this study is that the

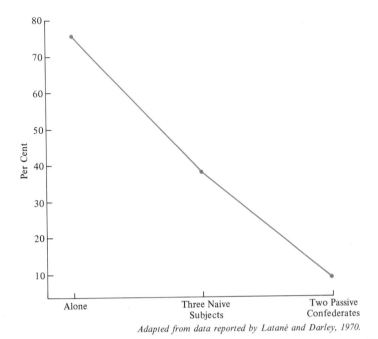

Adapted from data reported by Latané and Darley, 1970.

Figure 10–5 Percentage of subjects reporting smoke in a room when alone, with two other naïve subjects, or with two confederates who had been told to ignore the smoke.

presence of others *inhibits* activities that can be considered altruistic. Of course, since the subjects who did not report the smoke stayed in the building, the results are tentative. But clearly, the presence of others inhibited the reporting of the smoke. Figure 10–5 shows the results graphically. Note that the mere presence of others inhibited reporting and the presence of others specifically told to do nothing inhibited it even more. It seems reasonable to assume that a baseline figure for reporting the smoke is 75 percent, the mere presence of others dropped that figure to 38 percent, and the presence of others who purposely ignored the situation dropped the figure to 10 percent. This study indicates that if other people are present, individuals are less likely to respond in this particular situation.

Still, it is not possible to generalize from this study to emergency situations in general. The students who did not react to the smoke may not have perceived it as an emergency. There are other reasons for smoke than fire; steam from a heating unit or from cigarettes and cigars. Latané and Darley wanted to make clear that there was an emergency and thus they designed another experiment, one that involved a distressing emergency.

A Lady in Distress. The lady-in-distress study used the same general framework as the smoke-filled room study. While subjects were filling out a preliminary questionnaire, they were exposed to an emergency. In this experiment, the subjects were tested alone, with a friend, or with a stranger.

The experimental situation was designed to portray a great deal of realism. Male subjects were contacted and asked to participate in a survey being conducted by the Consumer Testing Bureau, a marketing research group that tested adult puzzles and games. When a subject arrived for the appointment he was met by a vivacious and attractive young woman who played the part of a market research representative. She showed him to the testing room which was separated from the office next door only by a collapsible cloth folding curtain wall. Through the open door to the next office the subject could see office furniture including a large, ramshackle bookcase with stacks of paper and equipment perched precariously on the top shelf. She then started the subject on filling out his questionnaires and told him she would return in 10 or 15 minutes.

While the subjects were working on their questionnaires the representative moved about in the office next door. After about four minutes she climbed up on a chair to get a book from the top shelf and then there was a loud crash, a woman's scream, the sound of a falling chair, and the following monologue:

"Oh, my God, my foot. . ." cried the representative. "I . . . I . . . can't move . . . it. Oh, my ankle. I . . . can't . . . can't . . . get . . . this thing off . . . me." She moaned and cried for about a minute longer, getting gradually more subdued and controlled. Finally, she muttered something about getting outside, knocked the chair around as she pulled herself up, and limped out, closing the door behind her. [Latané and Darley, 1970, p. 58.]

The whole sequence of events was taped to assure that each subject heard the same thing. Recall, the subject was separated from this action only by a thin curtain wall, with a door in it that could easily be opened.

Four conditions were run in this study. Subjects were run alone, or in pairs. There were three variations on the "pairs" theme. In one of them subjects were paired with a confederate who was instructed to look up when the crash came, stare quizzically at the curtain, shrug his shoulders and go back to work filling out his form. Another variation of the pairs was that both were naïve subjects and strangers to each other. The final condition was two naïve subjects who were friends.

Seventy percent of the subjects who were alone in the room offered some sort of assistance, either by coming into the office or calling out to offer help. When there was a passive confederate in the room with them, only 7 percent of the subjects offered assistance. Clearly, the presence of an unresponsive individual inhibited the altruistic behavior of the subjects in this experiment. When two strangers were together, help was offered by either one of them only 40 percent of the time. When two friends were present, help was offered 70 percent of the time. Whereas this seems to be as high as the "Alone" condition, it actually represents a drop because in these situations there were two persons, rather than one, who could have helped.

The results of this experiment seem clear. The presence of others inhibits helping behavior, and it is inhibited most by the presence of a passive individual, next most by a stranger, and least by a friend. However, friends did inhibit helping behavior.

In both the smoke study and the lady-in-distress study there was no villain. That is, an accident had occurred but no person could be seen as causing it. Since so many of the bystander apathy stories that we hear involve a villain, it seems appropriate to discuss a study in which money is stolen.

The Clumsy Thief. Subjects in the clumsy thief study were Columbia College freshmen who were brought to the same waiting room used in the two previous studies. Among the subjects was a short, clean-cut student wearing a conservative sport jacket and an open shirt. This was an accomplice who was to play the thief. Subjects were paid $2.00 to participate, and the receptionist apologized for the fact that interviews were running late and paid the subject immediately to save time. She took the money out of an envelope, which had several large bills and some small ones. To emphasize the amount of money in the envelope she asked if anyone had change for a twenty. She then put the envelope back on top of the desk where she was working and shortly afterward walked out to answer a call.

Shortly after the receptionist left the room the thief stood up, walked over to the desk, fumbled with a magazine that had been lying on top of it and then clumsily took the money out of the envelope and stuffed it in his jacket pocket. He then picked up the magazine and returned to his chair. The theft was staged in such a way that it was difficult to miss, although as we shall see, many subjects claimed not to have noticed.

There were two conditions. In one, the subject was alone and in the other, two subjects were in the room together. In the alone condition, 52 percent of the subjects claimed not to have seen the theft, whereas in the together condition, 25 percent of the pairs of subjects claimed not to have seen the theft. Of course we would expect the theft to be noticed more often when there are two people present than when there is only one. It seems strange that so many people did not notice such a clumsy theft, but the experimental situation was such that their word must be accepted and only those who admitted seeing the theft considered.

If the subject was alone and admitted seeing the theft, only 50 percent reported it. If there were two people together who noticed the theft, either one of them reported the theft only 25 percent of the time. Again, we would expect more, not less, of the pairs to report because there are two persons rather than one who could report.

SAFETY IN NUMBERS?

One of the interesting aspects of the studies reported by Latané and Darley is that subjects responded early or not at all. In each of the studies there was a relatively short period of time in which an individual could respond. Over 90 percent of all subjects who responded, responded in the first half of the relatively short period of time allowed to them. It seems that whatever the mental process people use to decide to intervene or not to intervene, the decision is made rather quickly.

Latané and Darley propose an intervention model that emphasizes several aspects of the individual and the situation. First, the individual must notice that something is wrong. If a person is concentrating on a personal matter or a problem of great importance, the emergency may not be noticed and if it is not, intervention will not take place. Second, the individual must interpret the noticed situation as an emergency or at least as one that needs intervention. Specifically, is the man lying in the gutter ill or is he a drunk napping? Is the smoke a sign of fire or of a faulty radiator? If the bystander interprets the situation as an emergency, then the decision must be made that he or she has a responsibility to respond. Next, the individual must decide on the form of assistance to be given and finally how to implement her or his decision. Figure 10–6 shows the steps schematically.

Latané and Darley anticipated that each step in intervention would be taken in order. However, the bystander is not committed to a course of action until help is offered. For example, upon seeing a car drive off into a river, the individual may think, "My God, that lady is going to drown if I don't jump in and save her. But the water is cold and the current is swift and I might drown myself. Maybe she's already

HELPING: CONCENTRATION OF RESPONSIBILITY

One of the issues raised by thoughtful analysis of altruism research is the generality of the diffusion of responsibility effect. We know that there are situations in which people do help—when there are many others available to help. For example, when an appeal is broadcast for blood at an area bloodbank, many people respond even though we all have blood and most of us are capable of donating it. Millions respond to appeals for charitable contributions, even though they know there are millions who are capable of helping. How can this be if, as has been suggested, the more people who view an emergency the less likely anyone is to help?

Wegner and Schaefer (1978) report an experiment that sheds some light on this apparent contradiction in altruistic behavior. Their notion is that when there are many more observers than victims, there is a diffusion of responsibility that inhibits people from helping. Note that many of the real-life examples we have referred to in this chapter that illustrate nonhelping occur in a situation where many people view one person in trouble. The Kitty Genovese case and the case of the Bronx switchboard operator mentioned earlier are but two examples. When, however, there are appeals for blood or money for a charitable foundation, there are, it is true, many potential donors. There are also many potential or actual victims. Possibly there is a concentration of responsibility when there are equal, or nearly equal, numbers of victims and helpers.

Wegner and Schaefer's study tested this notion by varying the number of bystanders and the number of helpers. Subjects participated in an experiment in an industrial setting. They were either the only one or in a group of three who had surpassed their quota of production and who would therefore be paid. They were exposed to either one or three other workers who had not met their quota and would not be paid. Following each of two work periods, subjects were allowed

the option of transferring some of their work credit to the worker(s) below quota. Thus the design was simple. Subjects were either alone or in a group of three and had something to give away. Half of each group were exposed to one worker who needed their help and half were exposed to a group of three workers who needed their help.

Subjects offered more help when they were alone than when they were in a group of three and they offered more help when there were three people who needed help than when just one needed it. The former effect replicates the diffusion of responsibility notion. That is, where there are more people to give assistance less is given than when there is just one. However, when there were three potential donors and three who needed help, there was more help given than when there were three potential helpers and one person who needed help.

The complexities of altruism are many. There does seem to be a diffusion of responsibility when the number of potential helpers is greater than the number of victims. However, as the number of potential donors and the number of victims begin to be more nearly equal, there seems to be a process of concentration of responsibility. Possibly when there are many helpers and one victim, the helpers feel their efforts aren't necessary. As the number of victims and potential helpers become more nearly equal, however, the potential helpers feel that their efforts will not only help, but are greatly needed.

Reference

Wegner, D. M., and D. Schaefer. The concentration of responsibility: An objective self-awareness analysis of group size effects in helping situations. *Journal of Personality and Social Psychology,* 1978, *36,* 147–55.

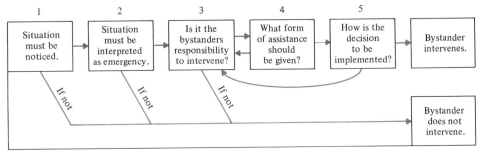

Adapted from Latané and Darley, 1970.

Figure 10–6 Schematic drawing of the steps in the decision to intervene. Arrows returning from steps 4 and 5 indicate cycling.

out of the car and on her way to the surface." This process is what Latané and Darley call *cycling.* That is, individuals seem to move through the decision process, but at some point they cycle back to an earlier step. In the example above, the person noticed the emergency, perceived it as an emergency, decided it was his responsibility to respond, but as soon as the form of assistance became clear he cycled back to indecision about his responsibility.

Interestingly enough, the crucial step seems to be the decision as to whether it is the bystander's responsibility to intervene. Latané and Darley suggest, and their research strongly supports the idea, that there is no safety in numbers. In most of the studies reported by these researchers, as in the ones detailed here, the more people there were present, the less assistance was offered. One explanation is that numbers diffuse each individual's sense of responsibility and there is less chance that help will be forthcoming from a crowd than from an individual. The old adage, "There's safety in numbers" may be true in some situations, but it seems that if you want help in an emergency you might be better off to have just one person observe it.

There are, however, other explanations for failing to help in an emergency situation. As it turns out, diffusion of responsibility does not seem to be the most reasonable explanation. Petty, Williams, Harkins, and Latané (1977) placed a poster offering free coupons for a McDonald's burger in an elevator and observed how many individuals took a coupon when they were alone or when someone else was present. They found that over 80 percent of the people helped themselves to a coupon when they were alone, whereas less than 40 percent took a coupon when someone else was present. These results, which cannot be explained by diffusion of responsibility, are strikingly similar to the helping behavior observed in emergency situations. If, as this suggests, diffusion of responsibility is not the explanation, what is? Petty et al. suggest that other social influence variables referred to by Latané and Darley (1970) may provide the answers.

Social Influence—The Key to Nonhelping?

It is easy and popular to attribute bystander inaction to apathy, indifference, or alienation from social norms; but it does not explain very much. If one person views an emergency and doesn't intervene, we probably never hear about it. If two people witness it and don't intervene, it's a negative situation. If 11, or 38, or hundreds view the emergency and don't intervene, it is a tragedy. Why is this? The sheer number of people who can be insensitive to the predicaments of others horrifies us.

Yet Latané and Darley point out that certain social influence processes work against an individual's helping if a group is present. In a crowd each person is aware that his or her behavior is being watched by others. The person may want to help, but even more the person does not want to "play the fool." For example, many people consider it bad manners to stare at an individual. Yet stare one must if he is going to realize that the person in an emergency is in trouble. This characteristic of social influence may delay the process of realizing that an emergency exists.

Once the individual has attended to the situation long enough to be sure that a cry of "Wolf" will not be inappropriate, he is now faced with a social influence process we discussed in Chapter 7, conformity. Assume that you are standing in a crowd of 50 people at a busy intersection waiting for the light to turn green. Directly in front of you a young man stabs another man. First, you must quit looking at the ground, or the buildings, or the traffic light and attend to the stabbing victim and his attacker, who is now fleeing. By the time you do attend and it registers in your brain as an emergency, you are most likely standing in a group of 49 other individuals who are doing nothing. The research on conformity clearly exemplified the extreme pressure that a unanimous group exerts on the individual. You are now in a situation where that unanimous pressure to conform is placed on your shoulders—as most people are. And do not act!

You however would not remain unresponsive. You would be one of the people who did respond and help. Latané and Darley conducted an experiment in which they described two emergency situations and asked subjects how they would respond. All subjects rated themselves as highly likely to respond and to do so whether others were present or not. Yet when the emergency situations were actually enacted, a substantial number of people did not respond. It is apparent that even though each of us is probably fairly sure that we would respond in an emergency, many of us would not. When the situation in the Asch conformity study or the Milgram obedience study (see Chapter 7) is explained to students, I seldom find anyone who says he or she would select the incorrect line or administer the heaviest electrical shock. What we think we will do and what we actually will do may be two quite different things.

Social Norms and Feelings—Altruistic Sources?

Leonard Berkowitz (1972) has pointed out that Blau (1964, 1968) dealt with the idea that reciprocity as it pertains to social exchange is a moral principle. A person who gains benefits from fellow humans is obligated to repay them and thus even altruistic acts are based upon potential profit. Berkowitz argues that there is a good deal of human behavior based on externally derived incentives; that is, on what the individual can gain by his or her behavior. "But there is probably a far greater incidence of selfless action in behalf of others—even in the absence of reciprocity or anticipated benefits—than the usual form of exchange theory would have us believe.

Some of this behavior, although not all, is influenced by the operation of social rules, internalized standards of conduct" (Berkowitz, 1972, p. 65).

Berkowitz points out the other side of the issue in research on altruism; many people *do* help. One of the points that has been underemphasized is that in many studies a substantial minority or even a majority of the individuals who had the opportunity helped in one way or another (Feldman, 1968; Latané & Darley, 1970; Pilivian, Rodin, and Pilivian, 1969). This is true even in a situation in which a considerable amount of pain is involved for the one who helps (Schwartz, 1970a).

The issue that Berkowitz addressed is an important one—do people respond just for external rewards? Or, to put it another way, are there social norms that cause us to act in altruistic ways? But first, external rewards must be dealt with.

EXTERNAL REWARDS FOR HELPING

Berkowitz points out that his early experiments in the area of atruism were based on the common-sense notion that many people in our society have acquired strong standards of conduct which dictate that they help others in need. These standards rely not on external rewards (material rewards or approval from others) but on internal norms (approval by self). Presumably, these people act altruistically for the good feelings they have about themselves when they do and to avoid the guilt they feel when they don't.

Other writers have suggested that altruistic behavior is normative in nature; but their work could be interpreted in at least two ways because the possibility that help was given in hope of return benefits was not ruled out (Berkowitz and Levy, 1956; Deutsch, 1949; Thomas, 1957).

In an attempt to rule out such an interpretation, Berkowitz reports three experiments (Berkowitz, 1957; Berkowitz and Daniels, 1963; Berkowitz, Klanderman, and Harris, 1964). In the first of these studies pairs of men were engaged in a joint endeavor. The greatest motivation toward an assigned task came when both the subject and his partner could gain a valuable prize for effective performance. When, however, only one partner could gain a prize, individuals were just as motivated when it was the partner who could receive the prize as when they, themselves, could receive the prize. In addition, they were more highly motivated when only one could receive the prize than when neither could receive a prize. Of course, it is still possible to assume that an individual works hard when only his or her partner can gain a prize in order to gain the partner's approval.

To explore this possibility, Berkowitz and Daniels (1963) informed subjects that their partners would not learn of any help they had given for several weeks or even months. The delay was meant to lessen the effect of any approval they might receive from their partners. If the partner didn't know they had helped, then the partner could not give them approval for that help. Consistent with the idea that there are norms to help, subjects worked hardest when their partner was most dependent on them, even though the partner would not find out about the help until much later. However, when given the opportunity to suggest changes in the experiment, subjects did express a desire to have some sort of incentive for themselves included. Thus subjects helped others, apparently because that was their social norm, but they would have appreciated a little something for themselves too.

There is, however, one other possible source of approval that the Berkowitz and Daniels study did not discount—that is, the experimenter's approval. Berkowitz, Klandermann, and Harris (1964) controlled for this possibility and were able to rule out the experimenter as a source of social approval that might affect subject performance. Thus, it seems that there is a social norm to help others.

HELPING AS A MORAL NORM

Latané and Darley are not the only ones to propose an analysis of helpingfulness that emphasizes noticing an emergency and assuming responsibility for action. Schwartz (1970b) demonstrated that male university student's acceptance of various moral norms was most strongly related to their peers' descriptions of how they actually behaved when they were sensitive to the feelings and thoughts of others and when they felt they had personal responsibility. Schwartz and Clausen (1970) assessed subjects' readiness to accept personal responsibility and found that many more subjects who were high in acceptance of personal responsibility than those who were low in it helped a peer who suffered an epileptic seizure.

Testing the Moral Norm. The notion that there is a moral norm to help rests on two kinds of evidence. The first is that many subjects exert a considerable effort for someone else even when there is little in it for them. Second, subjects, after participating in an experiment, typically verbalize a moral norm to help. When asked, they said they helped because one ought to help others. These responses, of course, may merely be an attempt to place their behavior in the best possible light. Berkowitz and his associates tested a number of possibilities concerning the existence of a social norm of helpfulness.

First, an attempt was made to manipulate the salience of the helpfulness norm. Women shoppers were interviewed about either their own and other people's helpfulness or whether they were smart consumers. It was assumed that people in the first group would be reminded of their social responsibility and thus be more helpful. Further, half of the women in each group were given frequent social approval (for positive remarks about helpfulness or for smart-consumer answers, depending upon the condition they were in). Within a minute of the end of the interview, a male college student approached each woman, telling her that his wallet disappeared and asking to borrow 40 cents for bus fare. Whether the woman had been interviewed about helpfulness or consumerism made no difference in how many helped the young man, but the women were more likely to give the student 40 cents if they themselves had been rewarded than if they had not been. Thus, this experiment did not support the idea of a social norm of helpfulness.

There were, however, two possible subtle factors at work to affect the results. First, it may be that women resent being stopped and interviewed in a shopping center. Most of them were probably in a hurry and this intrusion on their time is a negative influence. Evidence supporting this idea comes from a control condition of women who were not interviewed. They complied with the request for 40 cents about as often as the women who were interviewed and rewarded with social approval. The groups that varied were the ones that were interviewed but did not receive rewards in the form of social approval. These women gave the 40 cents significantly *less* than women in the three other groups. The second subtle influence that may have affected the results of this study was that any helpfulness response was rewarded, whether it was for helping or against helping.

Another study (reported in Berkowitz, 1972) indicated that rewarded ideas can affect later aid. Women shoppers in shopping centers were again the subjects. This time only the helpfulness interview was used and two conditions were established. In one condition, only helpful answers were rewarded by the interviewer; thus the interviewer tried to promote expressions of responsibility and charity. In another condition, only selfish and cynical answers were rewarded. The third group was a nonrewarded but interviewed control group. Immediately after the interview the women were approached by a student asking for 40 cents for bus fare. Sixty-six percent of the women who were rewarded for helpful ideas gave the student 40 cents, whereas only 28 percent of those women who were rewarded for cynical or selfish ideas gave the money. Fifty percent of the interviewed but not rewarded women gave the 40 cents. There were, however, some women who could not be induced to give very many helpful or nonhelpful ideas and they were excluded from the data reported above.

Another approach to heightening individuals' awareness of a social norm of helpfulness is to provide models. Recall that modeling has been shown to be extremely effective in teaching aggressive behavior (see Chapter 8). Berkowitz and Daniels (1964) found that subjects who believed others to be highly dependent upon them were most helpful when they (the subject) had been helped by a confederate (not the person they were to help). Macaulay (1970) shed more light on a model's role in influencing others. For one group, she had a model place money in a Volunteers of America Christmas box, and for the other group she had a model loudly insist that she would not donate to this charity. The greatest increase in donations came following the donating model, but the refusing model also caused an increase in donations when compared to a similar period of time when no model was present. In this instance, it seems that merely calling attention to the charity, even though refusing to donate, was enough to encourage a number of people who (presumably) believed in the charity to donate anyhow.

Other situational influences seemingly affect people's helpfulness. For example, Berkowitz and Connor (1966) and Isen (1970) report experiments in which people who had succeeded on a task were more likely to help someone else who needed that help. Seemingly, being successful put the person in a good mood and this warm glow generalized to helping other people.

Guilt. All unpleasant feelings do not reduce helpfulness. The guilt produced by violation of one's own moral standards has long been the subject of novelists, poets, and playwrights. Darlington and Macker (1966) found that persons who believed they had harmed someone else were relatively quick to agree to donate blood to a local hospital. In another study (Carlsmith and Gross, 1969), students who had just given electric shock to a peer agreed to do more work for a fictitious committee to save California's redwoods than those who delivered only loud noises to their peers. Interestingly enough, it seems that people who have accidentally injured a person are more willing to help someone other than the person they hurt (Freedman, Wallington, and Bless, 1967). That is, guilty subjects were more willing than nonguilty subjects to help another, but not the person they had hurt. In another experiment

Freedman et al. (1967) found that guilty subjects would help the person they had hurt only if they did not have to meet him or her. Presumably this is because the injured party may make a scene or cause some other unpleasantness.

Rawlings (1970) found that just knowing someone had been hurt earlier was enough to invoke helpfulness on the part of female students, even if they had not been responsible for the harm. Berkowitz suggests, however, that just seeing someone harmed is probably not sufficient to arouse protective feelings and behavior. Harking back to Lerner's just world and equity theory, the harm probably must be viewed as undeserved.

That is, sympathy or empathy must be aroused for any sort of guilt mechanism to be operative. Several psychologists have placed particular stress on the role of empathy in helpfulness and altruism. Aronfreed (1970) has even maintained that the term *altruism* should be reserved for those behaviors that are empathetic. Does that make sense? Empathy is the "intellectual identification with or vicarious experiencing of the feelings, thoughts or attitudes of another person." Aronfreed insisted that to be truly altruistic, behavior must not be impelled by hope of benefits from others.

There are a number of experiments which indicate that empathy is an important process in altruistic behavior. Hornstein (1970) reported an experiment in which subjects found an envelope on the street that contained a man's wallet with a check and $2.00 in it. Also in the envelope was a letter ostensibly from a man who had found the wallet and was returning it. The contents of the letter were varied so that the model (the person returning the wallet) was either similar to or dissimilar from the great majority of those who would find the envelope and the model's letter indicated he was either happy or unhappy about returning the wallet. Thus there were 4 conditions: Similar-Happy, Similar-Unhappy; Dissimilar-Happy and Dissimilar-Unhappy. The most wallets returned were in the Similar-Happy group (70 percent), whereas the least were in the Similar-Unhappy (10 percent). Thus subjects seemed to empathize with the similar model and were willing to return the wallet if he was happy about returning it and unwilling to return it if he were unhappy about returning it. Aderman and Berkowitz (1970) also present evidence for the importance of empathy in altruistic behavior. Students listened to a taped dialogue. Those who had been told to concentrate on a person in the dialogue who needed help and did not receive it or on a potential helper who had helped exerted the greatest effort when given the chance to help someone else.

What Sort of Person Is Helped?

Are you more likely to be helped if you are of one sex or another, are attractive, or possess some other characteristic that should be superfluous to altruism? The answer seems to be a resounding "Yes." For example, Daniels and Berkowitz (1963) found that subjects exerted considerably less effort for an unattractive peer than for an attractive one.

Pomazal and Clore (1973) report an interesting experiment in which a car was parked by the side of a highway with the trunk raised and a spare tire leaned against the car. Either a male or a female confederate was attempting to jack the car up and did not look at the passing cars or gesture for them to stop. When the victim was a male, only 2 percent of the cars stopped, whereas 25 percent of the cars stopped when

The man with his back to the camera crossed the street against the light and yelled and asked for help. No one helped, but someone did yell back.

the victim was a female. Almost all of those who stopped were males, and the typical male who stopped was over thirty-five, driving a pick-up or a camper or was alone. In a very similar study, West, Whitney, and Schnedler (1975) also found that females were helped much faster than males and almost always by males.

Another form of helping by the roadside is picking up a hitchhiker. Pomazal and Clore (1973) found that a female hitchhiker was offered a ride by 19 percent of the passing cars, whereas a male hitchhiker received offers from only 6 percent of the passing cars. Again, those offering rides were almost all males. Another study in California (Snyder, Grether, and Keller, 1974) found that females were offered more rides than males and again, almost exclusively by males. Finally, West and Brown (1975) found that males offered more rides to an attractive victim than to an unattractive one.

Of course, the fact that males are offering females help by the side of a highway or picking them up when they are hitchhiking may not be altruistic behavior. Snyder, Grether, and Keller (1974) raised the issue of sexual overtones when a lone male stops to pick up a lone female. Whether these acts were altruistic or not, it seems apparent that situational determinants such as attractiveness and sex influence helping behavior.

As Berkowitz (1972) points out, it is never possible to rule out entirely the possibility that individuals help each other for some external gain. In the studies reviewed in the preceding section this problem is quite apparent. Yet in more subtle ways it is possible for most of our seemingly altruistic behavior to have overtones of external reward. Let us consider this situation for just a moment.

The point of Berkowitz's argument concerning altruism is that there is a social norm to help. That is, in the process of being socialized, we are all taught to help others. Most human societies emphasize the importance of helping others. Indeed, the very fabric of most societies depends upon voluntary assistance to others. Even here, though, there is a reward that is potentially available to those who conform to society's norms—the smooth functioning of society. That is, we all live an easier and better life if society functions smoothly, and at times it takes a great deal of helping to keep society functioning smoothly. Therefore, in one sense, it may be argued that even a social norm of helping contains within it the seeds of external reward for the individual.

Attribution and Helping

Attribution theory (see Chapter 1) emphasizes an individual's perception of the situation, particularly with respect to causal factors, and the motivation of the person whose behavior is perceived. For example, if someone stops you on the street and asks for a dime, there are two basic questions that must be answered satisfactorally before you are likely to help. The first of these concerns your perceptions of why the individual needs the dime (causal factors) and what the individual intends to do with the dime. Earlier in this chapter we discussed a study by Latané and Darley in which Columbia University students stopped people on the street and asked for a dime. Only 34 percent of the people asked complied. If, however, the individual gave a reason for needing the dime ("my wallet was stolen") 72 percent of the people complied. They had some evidence about causal factors that resulted in the need for the dime. The second aspect of an attributional analysis of helping is what the receiver intends to do with the dime. If the request comes from a person who looks as if he will save it until he has enough to buy alcohol, you will probably be less likely to comply than you would if it appears that the individual needs the dime to call a friend.

Several studies have indicated that people are more willing to help another if the help is needed because of reasons beyond the individual's control (external locus of dependency) than if the help is needed because the individual decides he or she wants it (internal locus of dependency). For example, Schopler and Matthews (1965) conducted an experiment in which subjects were asked to help a subordinate. Half of the subjects were led to believe that the help was needed as part of the experimental procedure and half were led to believe that the subordinate decided to ask for help on his own volition. Subjects were more willing to help the subordinate who needed the help as part of the experimental procedure.

Ickes and Kidd (1976) point out that there is another factor that helps determine whether an individual will help or not. This factor is whether the potential helper's outcomes have been based on ability or chance. That is, when individuals have themselves succeeded on the basis of their own ability rather than chance they are more likely to help. Thus it appears that people who attribute their own success to their ability and are asked for help by someone who needs help through no fault of his or her own are most likely to help.

The research in this area has been concerned with helping in nonemergency situations and may or may not generalize to emergencies. There are, however, several possible common-sense explanations for the phenomena just described. First, it is fairly obvious that in American and Canadian society there is a premium placed upon individual achievement. The history of both countries is replete with tales of rugged individualists who overcame great odds and succeeded. These individuals, from whom most inhabitants of the two countries descend, were generally quick to help those who were in need because of factors beyond their control. They and we were not as quick to help those perceived as being capable but unwilling to help themselves.

The second phenomenon, helping when the helper's success is dependent on ability rather than chance, also makes sense. If an individual is in a position to help because of his or her ability then continued application of that ability will probably allow the person to continue to help. If, however, the individual is in a position to help because of chance, fortune may not be so kind in the future and the resources must be protected. Whether this is the type of analysis individuals engage in is not presently known, but such an analysis seems reasonable.

The heart of attribution theory is the way in which an individual perceives the situation. In a helping situation how does the potential helper view the person to be helped? How does the helper view his or her own situation? Once these questions are answered, then it is possible to predict more accurately the behavior of the potential helper.

Altruism—What Do We Know?

Up to this point, it may seem that altruism is a widely discussed but little understood phenomenon. That perception seems to me to be quite accurate. In a recent article, Pomazal and Jaccard (1976) have summarized the pattern of research in altruism rather nicely. These authors contend that the emphasis on a social norm of helping (such as that proposed by Berkowitz and his associates) is inadequate, and such an approach has been criticized by several others (Darley and Latané, 1970; Krebs, 1970; Schwartz, 1973). Subsequent to the research on social norms, a number of investigators turned their attention to situational factors that influence altruism, as exemplified in the attributional approach to altruism. It seems that the individual's perception of the need for help (Latané and Darley, 1968), the nature of the dependency relationship (Darley and Latané, 1968), the perceived costs of helping (Walster and Pilivian, 1972), and the mood of the individual (Isen and Levin, 1972) influence altruistic behavior. Furthermore, these variables, as well as demographic and individual differences variables (Gergen, Gergen, and Meter, 1972; Wispe and Freshley, 1971), seem to be related to helping behavior in complex ways.

It is clear that Berkowitz (1972), although proposing a normative approach to helping behavior, nevertheless argues that situational determinants are a strong factor in altruism. Thus, a recurring theme throughout most research on altruism is that it is heavily influenced by situational factors. Are we then to say that altruism is so

HAPPY AND HELPFUL: SAD AND . . . ?

Research has consistently indicated that positive mood states induce helpful behavior. That is, when people have been successful at a variety of tasks, when they have concentrated on happy thoughts, or when they have found some small object, they have been more helpful to others. Negative mood states have shown no such consistency. Manipulations intended to induce negative mood states have been shown to increase, decrease, or not affect helping behavior.

Weyant (1978) suggested that negative mood states are complex phenomena and that they interact with perceived reward value for helping. Specifically, he predicted that positive mood states lead to more helping than neutral mood states, but that negative mood states would lead to more helping than neutral states when costs for helping are low and benefits are high. When benefits for helping are low and costs are high, negative mood states should lead to less helping than neutral states. When both benefits and costs are low and when both benefits and costs are high for helping, negative mood states should lead to no more or less helping behavior than neutral mood states. Simply stated, Weyant proposed that when we are in a negative mood state, we will help more than when we are in a neutral mood state only if costs are low and benefits are high.

Weyant tested his hypothesis by inducing positive, neutral, and negative mood states in his subjects. This was done by giving subjects anagrams. In the positive mood state group, the anagrams were easy and subjects achieved a high degree of success. In the negative mood state group, the anagrams were quite difficult. Then both groups were given bogus statistics concerning the performance of average college students. The average number of anagrams solved in the positive mood group was considerably above the fictional mean for average college

students, whereas the mean for the negative mood group was considerably below that for average college students. Neutral mood group subjects were merely asked to rate the anagrams for pronounceability.

Costs and benefits were manipulated in the following way. Subjects were asked to help a charity by sitting at a table collecting donations (low cost) or going door-to-door soliciting donations (high costs). The charity was described either as the Little League (low benefit) or the American Cancer Society (high benefit). Thus, there were three mood states, two levels of cost, and two levels of benefits. The major measure of helping was the number of students in each condition who were willing to assist.

Subjects in the positive mood state groups offered to help more than subjects in the neutral mood state groups. The groups of interest are the negative mood groups. When the benefit was high and the cost low (sit at a desk for the American Cancer Society) 71 percent of the negative mood group and only 33 percent of the neutral mood group offered to help. When benefits were low and costs high (door-to-door for the Little League) 29 percent of the neutral group and only 5 percent of the negative group offered to help. When costs were high and benefits high or when costs and benefits were low, the negative and neutral groups did not differ in helping behavior. These results confirm Weyant's predictions that negative mood states interact with benefits and costs to influence helping. We should be aware that such states may be influencing people in nonlaboratory situations, explaining some of the variability in people's helping behavior.

Reference

Weyant, J. M. Effects of mood states, costs and benefits on helping. *Journal of Personality and Social Psychology*, 1978, *36*, 1169–76.

situationally bound that we can make no predictions about it? One of the interesting outgrowths in the study of situational factors affecting personality has been the realization that including situational factors adds to rather than detracts from our ability to predict. The situation is another variable and one that can help prediction greatly when it is properly understood.

Altruistic Development

It is a well-accepted tenet of psychology that a newborn infant is primarily, if not totally, motivated to satisfy his or her needs. This should not surprise us if we give the idea much thought; a newborn human infant is pitifully equipped to survive without assistance from other people. Left alone, the infant will die in a few hours.

Depending upon how altruism is defined, however, altruism may be present in children as early as the second year of life (Rheingold, Hay, and West, in press). At the very least, a form of sharing was discovered in children as early as two years of age by these investigators. Let us review what is known about the development of altruism.

Age

A number of investigations have reported that children's sharing increases between 6 and 12 years of age (e.g., Elliott, and Vasta, 1970; Emler and Rushton, 1974; Harris, 1971; Midlarsky and Bryan, 1967; Rushton, 1975; Rushton and Weiner, 1975). In addition to sharing, Green and Schneider (1974) reported that measures of helping also increased with age. At the same time, a number of investigators have found that competitiveness rather than cooperation increases with age, at least in Anglo-American cultures (Kagan and Madsen, 1971; Madsen, 1971; Madsen and Connor, 1973; Rushton and Weiner, 1975). Of course, it is possible that both cooperation and competitiveness increase between the ages of 6 and 12. General social activity increases during these ages and it is highly possible that the situation in which a child finds himself or herself is a major determinant of whether that child will cooperate or compete.

Several researchers have suggested that the increase in sharing behavior during middle childhood (6 to 12 years of age) might be linked to cognitive changes in the child which occur during the same period (Krebs, 1970; Rosenhan, 1972; Wright, 1971). Of particular interest are changes in the child's moral judgments. Flavell, Botkin, Fry, Wright, and Jarvis (1968) found evidence for a developmental shift from "egocentric" to "reciprocal" behavior during the 7–14 year age span. It may well be that moral judgment and generosity vary together. Rushton (1975) addressed the issue of whether moral judgment causes a change in generosity or merely covaries with generosity. He divided children into groups on the basis of a high or low level of moral judgment and found that children high in moral judgment were more generous than children low in moral judgment. This effect was evident on a retest done 8 weeks later, although it was somewhat weaker. Thus it seems that moral judgment affects generosity, rather than just covarying with it.

Observations of Models

There have been many demonstrations that exposing a child to an altruistic model enhances the child's subsequent altruistic behavior (e.g., Bryan and Walbek, 1970; Grusec, 1971, 1972; Staub, 1971). Just as observation of an aggressive model increases aggression (see Chapter 8), prosocial behavior is strongly influenced by observing an altruistic model. Krebs (1970) has argued, however, that if modeling studies that enhance altruistic behavior are to be interpreted as indicating that the child has internalized new learning, generality across situations and durability over time must be demonstrated. A number of studies have shown both generality to another situation and durability over time (Midlarsky and Bryan, 1972; Rosenhan, 1969; Rushton, 1975). Rushton (1975) showed that modeled behavior (either generous or selfish) produced strong durability over a two-month period. The children played a game and won 16 tokens with which they could buy a prize for themselves. They had also seen a generous model (one who gave half of his or her tokens to a charity), a selfish model (one who kept all of his or her tokens), or no model at all. Eight weeks later the children again played the game, again won 16 tokens, and were told they could contribute to a charity. On the retest, however, there was no model. (Figure 10–7 shows Rushton's results). It is apparent that even though the children

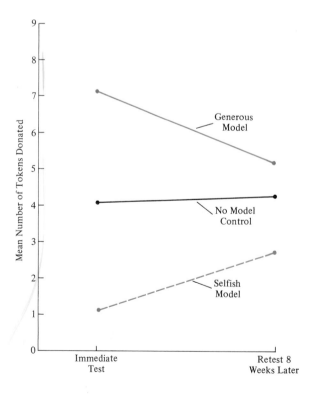

Figure 10–7 Mean number of tokens (out of 16) donated immediately and 8 weeks later by children after observing a generous model, a selfish model, or no model.

Data from Rushton, 1975.

who had observed a generous model did not donate as many tokens to charity as they had immediately after seeing the model, they still donated more tokens than did the control subjects and more than children who had seen a selfish model.

Conceptualizing Altruistic Development

Currently, there appear to be two viable ways of conceptualizing altruistic socialization. The cognitive-developmental-stage theory approach (Piaget, 1932; Kohlberg, 1969) and the cognitive-social-learning approach (Bandura, 1969; Mischel, 1973). Although these two viewpoints are often seen as being in conflict with one another, Rushton (1976) argues persuasively that the difference between the two may be more apparent than real. The cognitive-developmental account of altruistic development emphasizes the information a child gains and how he or she is able to process it. The social-learning approach emphasizes direct reinforcement and modeling. Rushton asserts: "So it appears that if the social learning theorists move further into cognitive processes and the cognitive developmentalists become more specific about their cognitive constructs, a useful integration might be possible. Certainly, neither approach can afford to ignore the empirical findings of the other" (Rushton, 1976, p. 911).

Rushton's argument is a sound one. Social learning theory has difficulty in explaining why direct reinforcement is not any more powerful in eliciting altruistic behavior than it is. On the other hand, cognitive-developmental-stage theory experiences difficulty when children's responses to moral judgment stories are compared to their behavior. For example, when a child has reached a given stage of cognitive moral development (see Chapter 4) that level of cognitive functioning should control his or her behavior. Unfortunately the generality of functioning at both the cognitive and the behavioral levels is quite low (Shantz, 1975). The problem faced by the cognitive-developmental-stage theorists is not unlike the problems faced by researchers in attitude and attitude change (see Chapter 5), who find that attitudes and behavior do not correlate very highly. Thus, the integration of the two theoretical approaches seems to be the most promising approach open to theorists and researchers.

The Trouble with Altruism

Why is there so much disarray in the field of atruism? People sometimes act out of the goodness of their hearts and do things for other people with no desire to collect something in return and sometimes they do not. The first behavior we label altruism and the second we call something else. It all seems such a simple matter that we should not have to devote a full chapter to it, let alone read the chapter and still not know where we stand.

If things were as simple as the preceding paragraph paints them, then altruism would indeed be a simple topic. But they are not, and it isn't. Let us explore the problem carefully.

Why do people respond to solicitations such as this one, to help others or to help themselves?

Intent

Undoubtedly the most difficult problem in determining an altruistic act is intent. When does someone offer to do something with no desire to collect anything in return? The answer to that depends upon what is meant by collecting something in return. For example, if you donate to a charity do you really expect nothing in return? Let us assume the charity will someday help discover cures for heart disease that may benefit you or someone you love. Possibly the person collecting is a neighbor and you want that person's social approval. The two rewards I've mentioned are external sources of reward; as you can see, it's hard to determine when someone is acting from an altruistic motive or from a selfish motive.

An even more difficult problem arises when we try to assess internal motivation. Possibly the individual gives to a charity or helps someone because it is pleasurable to do so. Is it altruism if someone helps another and gets a great deal of pleasure from doing so? This very issue has plagued altruism researchers and it should not. Berkowitz, among others, has carefully defined altruism as helping others without any thought for external reward. He has decided to leave the issue of internal reward alone and that appears to be a wise choice.

In Chapter 1 we dealt with a number of different theoretical approaches to human nature. Probably the one that recurs most often is hedonism, which asserts that humans do that which is pleasurable. For centuries, humanity has been taught by those who supposedly know about these things that hedonism is shallow, or evil, or both. Unfortunately, the hedonism that has been highlighted has been the advice to "Eat, drink, and be merry; for tomorrow we die." However, the philosophical theory of hedonism is that humans do what is pleasurable. What is pleasurable may be

CITY LIVING AND ALTRUISM

Popular belief joins with social science theory in asserting that city living has important, potentially negative, effects on individuals. One area of fascination for researchers has been the differences between urban and rural residents with regard to interpersonal trust and helping behavior. The fascination has occurred primarily because there seem to be few, if any, differences in interpersonal trust between the two groups, and yet city dwellers are seemingly less helpful.

House and Wolf (1978) reported results that are important for several reasons. First, they used archival data that are representative of the United States as a whole. Second, they used longitudinal data (1956 to 1972), and third, they were able to distinguish between an attitude of trust and trusting behavior. The data for this article were taken from the University of Michigan Survey Research Center during presidential elections from 1956 to 1972. Individuals were classified as living in (1) old, large cities; (2) new, large cities; (3) intermediate cities; (4) small towns; and (5) rural areas. Some of the questions asked during these surveys, which utilized a representative sample of the adult population of the United States, concerned the individuals' trust of other people. When these data were analyzed, it was apparent that individuals residing in different sized and type of cities did not differ in the trust they expressed toward others, nor did city residents differ from small-town and rural residents. Thus, these data support the idea that there is equal trust expressed regardless of place of residence.

When a survey is taken, interviewers go out, knock on doors, and ask people to answer questions. House and Wolf reasoned that the refusal rates in various different residential areas and across time would provide evidence on the issue of helpfulness. That is, do refusal rates vary by size of the city individuals reside in and across time?

The answer to the preceding question is a resounding "Yes." In 1956, 7.3 percent of the people who were asked to submit to an interview refused. By 1972, this number had almost doubled to 14.4 percent. With willingness to be interviewed as a measure of helpfulness, the people in the United States became far less helpful between 1956 and 1972. Furthermore, there were large differences in helpfulness based on the size of the city in which an individual lived. The largest rejection rate in 1956 was in small towns, with a 12.1 percent rate. This rate remained relatively constant through 1972. Large cities, old or new, showed large decreases in helpfulness. In 1956, approximately 8 percent of large city residents refused to be interviewed. By 1972, this number had grown to approximately 19 percent.

It appears that people say they trust others about as much in rural areas, small towns, and cities but are more helpful in rural areas and small cities than in large cities. House and Wolf tried to explain these differences and changes by utilizing other variables in their data (i.e., age, sex, population density, crime rate, and so forth). The major determinant of an unwillingness to help (by being interviewed) appears to be the rising crime rate. As they say,

> The caution, incivility, distrust and lack of concern for others that often characterizes urban behavior appears largely to result from a (probably correct) perception that interactions with others, especially strangers, can be dangerous. Further, the present data suggest that these behavioral differences between urbanites and nonurbanites are a relatively *recent* response to a *recent* epidemic of crime. [House and Wolf, 1978, p. 1040.]

Reference

House, J. S. and S. Wolf. Effects of urban residence on interpersonal trust and helping behavior. *Journal of Personality and Social Psychology,* 1978, *36,* 1029–43.

eating, drinking, or being merry, or it may be helping someone else with no thought of external reward. To assert that if humanity is unleashed, to act pleasurably, an orgy will result, is to assert a rather debased view of humanity. As a matter of fact, changes in our societies in Canada and the United States in the last century have freed most of us from working such long hours to meet basic needs that we do have time to follow pleasurable pursuits. If all hedonic impulses were of the eat, drink, and be merry sort, there would be many more true orgies than there are. As a matter of fact, many altruistic efforts are pleasurable and, to many people, more pleasurable than other types of activities. But should we refuse to classify an act as altruistic because the person who offers help derives pleasure from it? I think not.

Do Non-New Yorkers Help More?

Much of the research in altruism was motivated by events such as the murder of Kitty Genovese during which 38 people heard her screams and did not help. The title of Latané and Darley's (1970) book *The Unresponsive Bystander: Why Doesn't He Help?* illuminates their point of view concerning altruism. It emphasizes the fact that people don't help and tries to sort out the reasons why.

One outgrowth of this approach in research in altruism was an attempt to find places where people would help. The immediate hypothesis is that low levels of altruism exist in New York City, and moving the research to other cities or to smaller cities and finally to rural areas would show a dramatic increase in altruism. Some differences were noted, but in general, the results were about the same in most places.

In an attempt to locate people in a place where there was an optimal chance to find altruistic behavior, Darley and Batson (1973) ran a study at Princeton Theological Seminary in Princeton, New Jersey. Princeton is a small college town and if anyone is going to help, they reasoned, it should be men training to be Christian ministers. To make the situation even more salient, half of the subjects were told that they were to give a talk on the parable of the Good Samaritan, while the other half were told that they were to give a talk on the jobs in which seminary students would be most effective. Then another variable was introduced, one third of each group was told they were late and please hurry to another building where they were to talk, one third was told to go right on over to the other building, and the final third were told that it would be a few minutes before people were ready for them in the other building. Thus, there were six groups (two different talks and three degrees of time pressure.) Each subject on his way to deliver his talk, passed a victim sitting in a doorway, head down, eyes closed, and not moving. As the subject passed, the victim coughed twice and groaned. The dependent variable was whether the subject helped or not.

The results of the study are very interesting. It made no difference whether the seminarians were on their way to deliver a talk about jobs for seminarians or about the Good Samaritan. The only significant effect was that those who had time helped more than those who were in a hurry. The results are presented in Figure 10–8. The results in the figure show a graded helping score, which ranged from "failed to notice

Are people more helpful in small towns or large cities?

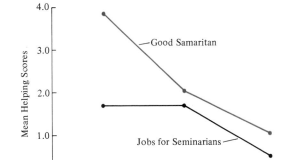

Figure 10–8 Mean graded helping scores for seminarians who were either early, needed now, or late and were to talk on either the Good Samaritan or Jobs for Seminarians.

From Darley and Batson, 1973.

the victim" to "after stopping, refused to leave the victim and insisted on taking him to the infirmary or for coffee." The range of scores was from 0 (for not noticing the victim) to 5. Of all subjects, 40 percent offered aid and 60 percent did not.*

Apparently, seminarians help no more than anyone else. However, I wonder if this emphasis on not helping is justified. The major decline in helping behavior among seminarians occurred when they were told to hurry because someone was waiting for them (only 10 percent helped). In the other two conditions, as in the majority of studies we have reviewed, approximately half (often times more) of the people helped. Berkowitz, in reviewing the literature on altruism has this to say:

> The exact proportion of help-givers in these studies does not really matter, of course; with the possible exception of the shop cashiers in the Feldman investigation, we do not know if the samples were even roughly representative of the people in a given community. What is important about the figures I have cited is that they are far from zero. Many persons do help their fellow man even when there are no obvious material benefits to be gained from this action. [Berkowitz, 1972, p. 67.]

Berkowitz's point is well taken. Many people do help and it is impossible to know exactly how many "many" is. However, it seems that many researchers and writers expect that everyone should behave altruistically. Obviously, everyone does not perform any other behavior, so why should we expect everyone to be altruistic? A more realistic picture may be that we would like for there to be more positive acts than there are negative ones; more who rescue others from death than there are those who kill others; more who contribute money and goods to those who need it than there are those who steal. Possibly there are many more positive acts than there are negative ones, but we just don't hear about them.

---

*Greenwald (1975) reanalyzed Darley and Batson's data and arrived at the conclusion that the message did make a difference (i.e., those who were to talk on the parable of the Good Samaritan helped more). The reanalysis is a complicated issue and beyond the scope of this book. You should be aware, however, that not everyone agrees with Darley and Batson's conclusions about the parable. The "hurry" conditions were not questioned by Greenwald, and Darley and Batson's conclusion about them appears acceptable.

The study of altruism itself raises an altruistic question. Why do psychologists study altruism? For altruistic ends (i.e., to help others), for selfish ends (i.e., to enhance their careers), or to gain knowledge? For whatever reason it is done, the research itself raises ethical questions.

The first issue faced by a researcher in prosocial behavior is that it is difficult to do the research in any but natural settings. For example, when a group of people are asked if they would help in an emergency, an overwhelming majority respond affirmatively. Yet we know that a much smaller percentage of people actually do help in a real emergency. Since most people do not tell the researcher how they would act in an emergency, either because they don't know or do not wish to say they wouldn't help, it becomes necessary to conduct the research in real-life settings.

Much altruism research makes use of the field experiment (see Chapter 2). The researcher finds an appropriate natural setting and stages a request for help, an accident, or some other incident in which help is needed. The people who happen to be in the area become the subjects for the experiment and their privacy is invaded with a staged incident.

The first issue, of course, is that people who happen to be in the vicinity of the incident become subjects. They are not given any choice in the matter, nor do any of them give their consent to be a subject. Furthermore, the subjects and anyone else passing by may be subjected to a staged robbery, accident, or assault. It is impossible to stop everyone who might see the incident and assure them that no damage was done.

These negative aspects of altruism research must be weighed against the potential advantage of the research. Is it worth bringing people into a psychological experiment unknowingly in order to learn more about prosocial behavior? Is it worth upsetting individuals with staged scenes of violence to learn more about altruism? These are, of course, the questions a researcher in the area of altruism should answer before proceeding with the work.

Equity and Altruism

An act is no less altruistic if someone gains pleasure from it. Is it any less altruistic if someone gains external reward from it? Most altruism researchers would assert that it is. We may say, however, that an act, done for external reward, may be just as helpful to the recipient as one done for no external reward. Thus, we are again back into the question of motivation—the motivation of the one doing the helpful act. And that is the difficulty with defining and researching altruism.

Walster, Walster, and Berscheid (1978) argue that the bystander takes the cost and the adequacy of helping into account before helping. They point out that Weiss, Boyer, Lombardo, and Stitch (1973) found that observers were quicker to make a response that was totally effective in helping than one that was ineffective. Other evidence comes from Lerner (1971b) who uses a public demonstration to illustrate how bystanders can be insensitive to even the most intense suffering of others.

Lerner first reminds his audience that many Americans and Canadians are suffering desperately and need help. He then hands each member of the audience a folder that contains a case history of a single family in Canada or the United States. Even though these families desperately need help, for one reason or another, the existing governmental agencies cannot help them. Each of the families lives under degrading conditions and needs the money for food and clothes, to eliminate intestinal worms, to heal sores, and so forth. Lerner then points out to his audience that they can do something. If each one of them holding a folder will donate $100 a month, the family in that folder can avoid the degradation, suffering, and even death. All that is required of the affluent members of Lerner's audiences of Americans and Canadians is that they cut back on their cigarettes, entertainment, liquor, movies, and dining out. Almost without exception the audiences refuse. Why?

Lerner, who has initiated the demonstration is quite sensitive in attempting to explain the motivations that go into a decision not to help. First and foremost, the potential cost is high. Not the few cigarettes or liquor or less entertainment. Rather when one sets out on such a course, where can we stop? Are we to continue giving $100 a month to more and more families until we live in the same situation that those described in the folders do? Obviously, many folders have been handed out, and these represent just a few cases in affluent countries. What about all the starving, sick people who live in degrading conditions in the Third World nations? The problem seems so mammoth that a single $100 a month is not sufficient.

On the other hand, it may well be that members of Lerner's audiences would enthusiastically support an equitable tax system that would cost them $100 a month but had a chance of alleviating the pain and suffering of all of the families in need (at least in Canada and the United States), not just one. It may be that many people in Lerner's audience redouble their efforts for an equitable system.

Depending upon how we wanted to view a refusal to help on the part of a member of Lerner's audience, we could argue that bystanders don't help or that they do help. This latter conclusion would be based on the assumption that audience members, or at least some of them, work toward developing a system that is more equitable for everyone.

Comment

Is that all that can be said about altruism? What we know rather definitively is that people sometimes act altruistically and sometimes don't. But you didn't need a whole chapter to know that. We also can say, with some degree of certainty, that when there is an emergency, people tend to be inhibited in helping by the presence of others. Some people argue that there is a social norm of helping but others say "No." Some argue that people behave altruistically to maintain equitable relationships. I have argued that when people are given a choice, they do that which is most pleasurable or least unpleasurable to them. Are any of these positions incompatible?

Well, it depends on the situation. It seems to me the equity position would have a hard time dealing with the extreme case of altruism in which one person gives up his or her life for someone else. Of course, the position I have espoused can say, "Well, under the circumstances, that is what the individual found least unpleasurable." To be honest, however, that isn't a very satisfying answer.

Which brings us to the whole point of these last few sentences. As of yet, there aren't that many satisfying answers about altruism. Research will undoubtedly tell us more in the future, but for now we are left with many unanswered questions. I should point out, however, that altruism is a rather recent addition to the area of social psychology. Most of the research has been done on it in the last 10–15 years. A behavior with as many ramifications as altruism will undoubtedly take much more research before it yields to the inquisitive researchers who wonder why and try to find out.

SUMMARY

1 Altruism or prosocial behavior is unselfish concern for the welfare of others. An act cannot be classified as altruistic without knowing the intent of the actor.
2 Social exchange is a theory, based on economics, which emphasizes that each of us has social needs and social resources, which we exchange with others. The resource theory of social exchange emphasizes the differences between the classes of social resources, and that the rules for transactions between classes of resources differ.
3 Equity theory is based on the assumption that relationships are governed by a societal need to treat equitably as many members of that society as possible. The greatest good for the greatest number demands that equity prevail. A relationship is equitable when rewards and costs for each individual are equal; when they are not it is inequitable.
4 Latané and Darley carried out an extensive research program in altruism that indicated that when responsibility is clear, many people help in nonemergency situations. In emergency situations, generally speaking, the more people who view the emergency, the less chance there is that at least one of them will help. This may be because of diffusion of responsibility, conformity, or the fear of making a socially undesirable mistake.
5 There is disagreement as to whether a social norm of helping exists. If such norms exist, they are not based on external rewards, but internal ones such as self-approval. Evidence seems to support the idea of some sort of altruistic norm in American and Canadian societies.
6 Attribution theory emphasizes that altruism must be viewed in the context of two basic questions. First, what are the causal factors that resulted in an individual's needing help, and, second, what motivates the individual to be helped? When the person who needs help is perceived to need it through no fault of his or her own and when it is assumed that the help will be used appropriately, help is most likely to be offered.

7 Altruism increases among children during middle childhood. Children can learn altruistic behavior by observing altruistic models. At least two theoretical approaches to prosocial behavior have been proposed, the cognitive-developmental-stage and the cognitive-social-learning theory.

8 The major problem in altruism research is intent. Sorting out whether an individual behaves altruistically in hope of gaining some external reward is difficult, but it is virtually impossible to determine when prosocial behavior leads to internal reward. Thus, many researchers have defined altruism as behavior not motivated by external reward.

9 Prosocial behavior is situationally controlled and research in altruism is fraught with ethical problems. It is almost essential to do much altruism research in the field with subjects who happen to be on the scene. The researcher must be careful to assure that no potential harm is likely and that the knowledge gained is substantial.

GLOSSARY

Altruism Unselfish concern for the welfare of others.

Cognitive-Developmental Model The model of altruistic socialization that emphasizes the information the child gains and how he or she processes it.

Cognitive-Social-Learning Model The model of altruistic socialization that emphasizes direct reinforcement and modeling.

Comparison Level In exchange theory, one standard for judging the goodness of outcomes.

Cycling The process of returning to an earlier stage in the decision-making process and repeating some or all of the stages in deciding whether or not to help.

Egocentric Regarding the self as the center of all things.

Empathy The intellectual identification with, or vicarious experiencing of, the feelings, thoughts, or attitudes of another person.

Equity Theory The theory that is based on the assumption that relationships are most satisfying when costs and rewards are equal for each person in the relationship.

Interaction Matrix A set of preferences for each individual from which behavior can be predicted.

Minimax Strategy In exchange theory the strategy of minimizing costs and maximizing rewards.

Outcome In exchange theory the result of an interaction that is the difference between total cost and reward.

Particularism In the resource theory of exchange the emphasis upon some resources (e.g., love) being tied to a particular individual.

Prosocial Behavior Behavior that is altruistic.

Reciprocal Given or felt by each individual toward the other.

Resource Theory of Exchange The theory of exchange that emphasizes the similarities and differences in the elements of exchange.

Social Exchange Theory A theory of behavior based on the assumption that individuals compute the rewards and costs in relationship to help determine whether to maintain that relationship.

The Justice Motive The assumption that the way people act toward others is dependent upon whether the individual in need of help is perceived as deserving of his or her fate.

REFERENCES

Adams, J. S. Toward an understanding of inequity. *Journal of Abnormal and Social Psychology,* 1963, *67,* 422–36.

———. Inequity in social exchange. In L. Berkowitz (Ed.), *Advances in Experimental Social Psychology.* Vol. 2. New York: Academic Press, 1965.

——— and W. E. Rosenbaum. The relationship of worker productivity to cognitive dissonance about wage inequity. *Journal of Applied Psychology,* 1962, *46,* 161–64.

Aderman, D., and L. Berkowitz. Observational set, empathy, and helping. *Journal of Personality and Social Psychology,* 1970, *14,* 141–48.

Aronfreed, J. The socialization of altruistic and sympathetic behavior: Some theoretical and experimental analyses. In J. R. Macauley and L. Berkowitz (Eds.), *Altruism and Helping Behavior.* New York: Academic Press, Inc., 1970. Pp. 103–126.

Bandura, A. *Principles of Behavior Modification.* New York: Holt, Rinehart and Winston, 1969.

Berkowitz, L. Effects of perceived dependency relationships upon conformity to group expectations. *Journal of Abnormal and Social Psychology,* 1957, *55,* 350–54.

———. Social norms, feelings, and other factors affecting helping and altruism. In L. Berkowitz (Ed.), *Advances in Experimental Social Psychology.* Vol. 6. New York: Academic Press, Inc., 1972. Pp. 63–108.

——— and W. H. Connor. Success, failure and social responsibility. *Journal of Personality and Social Psychology,* 1966, *4,* 664–69.

——— and L. R. Daniels. Responsibility and dependency. *Journal of Abnormal and Social Psychology,* 1963, *66,* 429–37.

——— and ———. Affecting the salience of the social responsibility norm: Effects of past help on the response to dependency relationships. *Journal of Abnormal and Social Psychology,* 1964, *68,* 275–81.

———, S. B. Klanderman, and R. Harris. Effects of experimenter awareness and sex of subject and experimenter on reactions to dependency relationships. *Sociometry,* 1964, *27,* 327–57.

——— and B. I. Levy. Pride in group performance and group-task motivation. *Journal of Abnormal and Social Psychology,* 1956, *53,* 300–306.

Berscheid, E., and E. Walster. When does a harm-doer compensate a victim? *Journal of Personality and Social Psychology,* 1967, *6,* 435–41.

———, ——— and A. Barclay. Effect of time on tendency to compensate a victim. *Psychological Reports,* 1969, *25,* 431–36.

Blau, P. M. *Exchange and Power in Social Life.* New York: John Wiley & Sons, 1964.

———. Social exchange. In D. L. Sills (Ed.). *International Encyclopedia of the Social Sciences.* Vol. 7. New York: Macmillan Publishing Co., Inc., 1968. Pp. 452–57.

Braband, J., and M. J. Lerner. A little time and effort—Who deserves what from whom? *Personality and Social Psychology Bulletin,* 1975, *1,* 177–81.

Brock, T. C., and A. H. Buss. Dissonance, aggression, and evaluation of pain. *Journal of Abnormal and Social Psychology,* 1962, *65,* 192–202.

———and———. Effects of justification for aggression in communication with the victim on past aggression dissonance. *Journal of Abnormal and Social Psychology,* 1964, *68,* 403–412.

———, and L. A. Becker. Debriefing and susceptability to subsequent manipulations. *Journal of experimental Social Psychology,* 1966, *2,* 314–323.

Bryan, J. H., and N. H. Walbek. Preaching and practicing self-sacrifice: Children's actions and reactions. *Child Development,* 1970, *41,* 329–53.

Carlsmith, J. M., and A. E. Gross. Some effects of guilt on compliance. *Journal of Personality and Social Psychology,* 1969, *11,* 232–39.

Darley, J. M., and C. D. Batson. From Jerusalem to Jerico. A study of situational and dispositional variables in helping behavior. *Journal of Personality and Social Psychology,* 1973, *27,* 100–108.

Darley, J., and B. Latané. Bystander intervention in emergencies: Diffusion of responsibility. *Journal of Personality and Social Psychology,* 1968, *8,* 377–83.

——— and———. Norms and normative behavior: Field studies of social interdependence. In J. Macaulay and L. Berkowitz (Eds.), *Altruism and Helping Behavior,* New York: Academic Press, Inc., 1970.

Darlington, R. B., and C. F. Macker. Displacement of guilt-produced altruistic behavior. *Journal of Personality and Social Psychology,* 1966, *4,* 442–43.

Deutsch, M. The effects of cooperation and competition upon group process. *Human Relations,* 1949, *2,* 129–52; 199–231.

Elliott, R., and R. Vasta. The modeling of sharing: Effects associated with vicarious reinforcement symbolization, age and generalization. *Journal of Experimental Child Psychology,* 1970, *10,* 8–15.

Emler, N. P., and J. P. Rushton. Cognitive-developmental factors in children's generosity. *British Journal of Social and Clinical Psychology,* 1974, *13,* 277–81.

Feldman, R. E. Response to compatriot and foreigner who seek assistance. *Journal of Personality and Social Psychology,* 1968, *10,* 203–14.

Flavell, J. H., P. T. Botkin, C. L. Fry, J. W. Wright, and P. E. Jarvis. *The development of role-taking and communication skills in children.* New York: John Wiley & Sons, Inc., 1968.

Foa, U. G., and E. B. Foa. *Societal Structures of the Mind.* Springfield, Ill., Charles C Thomas, Publisher, 1974.

——— and———. *Resource Theory of Social Exchange.* Morristown, N.J.: General Learning Press, 1975.

———, S. Megonigal, and J. R. Greipp. Some evidence against the possibility of utopian societies. *Journal of Personality and Social Psychology,* 1976, *34,* 1043–48.

Freedman, J., S. Wallingford, and E. Bless. Compliance without pressure: The effect of guilt. *Journal of Personality and Social Psychology,* 1967, *7,* 117–24.

Gergen, K., M. Gergen, and K. Meter. Individual orientations to pro-social behavior. *Journal of Social Issues,* 1972, *28,* 105–130.

Green, F. P., and F. W. Schneider. Age differences in the behavior of boys on three measures of altruism. *Child Development,* 1974, *45,* 248–51.

Greenwald, A. G. Does the Good Samaritan parable increase helping? A comment on Darley and Batson's no-effect conclusion. *Journal of Personality and Social Psychology,* 1975, *32,* 578–83.

Grusec, J. E. Power and the internalization of self-denial. *Child Development,* 1971, *42,* 93–105.

———. Demand characteristics of the modeling experiment: Altruism as a function of age and aggression. *Journal of Personality and Social Psychology,* 1972, *22,* 139–48.

Harris, M. Models, norms and sharing. *Psychological Reports,* 1971, *29,* 147–53.

Homans, G. C. *Social Behavior: Its Elementary Forms.* New York: Harcourt Brace Jovanovich, Inc., 1961.

Hornstein, H. A. The influence of social models on helping. In J. R. Macaulay and L. Berkowitz (Eds.), *Altruism and Helping Behavior.* New York: Academic Press, Inc., 1970. Pp. 29–41.

Ickes, W. J., and R. F. Kidd. An attributional analysis of helping behavior. In J. H. Harvey, W. J. Ickes, and R. F. Kidd (Eds.), *New Directions in Attribution Research.* Vol. 1. Hillsdale, N.J.: Earlbaum, 1976, 311–34.

Isen, A. M. Success, failure, attention and reactions to others: The warm glow of success. *Journal of Personality and Social Psychology,* 1970, *15,* 294–301.

Isen, A., and P. Levin. The effect of feeling good on helping: Cookies and kindness. *Journal of Personality and Social Psychology,* 1972, *21,* 384–88.

Jacques, E. *Equitable Payment.* New York: John Wiley & Sons, Inc., 1961.

Kagan, S., and M. C. Masden. Cooperation and competition of Mexican, Mexican-American, and Anglo-American children of two ages under four instructional sets. *Developmental Psychology,* 1971, *5,* 32–39.

Kelley, H. H. Interpersonal accomodation. *American Psychologist,* 1968, *23,* 399–410.

Kohlberg, L. Stage and sequence: The cognitive-developmental approach to socialization. In D. A. Goslin (Ed.), *Handbook of Socialization Theory and Research.* Chicago: Rand McNally & Company, 1969.

Krebs, D. Altruism—An examination of the concept and a review of the literature. *Psychological Bulletin,* 1970, *73,* 258–302.

Latané, B., and J. Darley. Group inhibition of bystander intervention. *Journal of Personality and Social Psychology,* 1968, *10,* 215–21.

———— and ————. *The Unresponsive Bystander: Why Doesn't He Help?* New York: Appleton-Century-Crofts, 1970.

Lerner, M. J. Justified self-interest and the responsibility for suffering: A replication and extension. *Journal of Human Relations,* 1971a, *19,* 550–59.

————. Deserving vs. justice: A contemporary dilemma. Research report no. 24. Department of Psychology, University of Waterloo, May 15, 1971b.

————. The justice motive: "Equity" and "parity" among children. *Journal of Personality and Social Psychology,* 1974, *29,* 539–50.

————. The justice motive in social behavior. *Journal of Social Issues,* 1975, *31,* 1–19.

————. The justice motive: Some hypotheses as to its forms and origins. *Journal of Personality,* 1977, *45,* 1–52.

———— and J. Braband. Children's preference for deceiving over self-interest: Rule following on the justice motive. Unpublished manuscript, University of Waterloo, 1973.

———— and R. R. Lichtman. Effects of perceived norms on attitudes and altruistic behavior toward a dependent other. *Journal of Personality and Social Psychology,* 1968, *9,* 226–32.

———— and G. Matthews. Reactions to the suffering of others under conditions of indirect responsibility. *Journal of Personality and Social Psychology,* 1967, *5,* 319–27.

Leventhal, G. S., J. Allen, and B. Kemelgor. Reducing inequity by reallocating rewards. *Psychonomic Science,* 1969, *4,* 295–96.

Macaulay, J. R. A skill for charity. In J. R. Macaulay and L. Berkowitz (Eds.), *Altruism and Helping Behavior.* New York: Academic Press, Inc., 1970. Pp. 43–59.

Madsen, M. C. Developmental and cross-cultural differences in the cooperation and competitive behavior of young children. *Journal of Cross-Cultural Psychology,* 1971, *4,* 365–71.

———— and C. Connor. Cooperative and competitive behavior of retarded and nonretarded children at two ages. *Child Development,* 1973, *44,* 175–78.

Maslow, A. H. *Motivation and Personality.* New York: Harper & Row, Publishers, 1954.

Maxwell, G., K. Ratcliff, and D. R. Schmitt. Minimizing differences in a maximizing differences game. *Journal of Personality and Social Psychology,* 1969, *12,* 158–63.

Midlarsky, E., and J. H. Bryan. Training charity in children. *Journal of Personality and Social Psychology,* 1967, *5,* 408–415.

———— and ————. Affect expressions and children's imitative altruism. *Journal of Experimental Research in Personality,* 1972, *6,* 195–203.

Miller, D. T. Personal deserving versus justice for others: An exploration of the justice motive. *Journal of Experimental Social Psychology,* 1977, *13,* 1–13.

Mischel, W. Toward a cognitive social learning reconceptualization of personality. *Psychological Review,* 1973, *80,* 252–83.

Petty, R. E., K. D. Williams, S. G. Harkins, and B. Latané. Social inhibition of helping yourself: Bystander response to a cheeseburger. *Personality and Social Psychology Bulletin,* 1977, *3,* 575–78.

Piaget, J. *The Moral Judgment of the Child.* London: Routledge & Kegan Paul, 1932.

Pilivian, I. M., J. Rodin, and J. A. Pilivian. Good Samaritanism: An underground phenomenon? *Journal of Personality and Social Psychology,* 1969, *13,* 289–99.

Pomazal, R. J., and G. L. Clore. Helping on the highway: The effects of dependency and sex. *Journal of Applied Social Psychology,* 1973, *3,* 150–64.

Pomazal, R., and J. J. Jaccard. An informational approach to altruistic behavior. *Journal of Personality and Social Psychology,* 1976, *33,* 317–26.

Rawlings, E. I. Reactive guilt and anticipatory guilt in altruistic behavior. In J. R. Macaulay and L. Berkowitz (Eds.), *Altruism and Helping Behavior.* New York: Academic Press, Inc., 1970. Pp. 163–77.

Rheingold, H. L., D. F. Hay, and M. J. West. Sharing in the second year of life. *Child Development,* in press.

Rosenhan, D. L. Some origins of concern for others. In P. Mussen, J. Langer, and M. Covington (Eds.), *Trends and Issues in Developmental Psychology,* New York: Holt, Rinehart and Winston, 1969.

————. Learning theory and prosocial behavior. *Journal of Social Issues,* 1972, *28,* 151–63.

Rushton, J. P. Generosity in children. Immediate and long term effects of modeling, preaching, and moral judgment. *Journal of Personality and Social Psychology,* 1975, *31,* 459–66.

————. Socialization and the altruistic behavior of children. *Psychological Bulletin,* 1976, *83,* 898–913.

———— and J. Weiner. Altruism and cognitive development in children. *British Journal of Social and Clinical Psychology,* 1975, *14,* 341–49.

Schopler, J., and M. Matthews. The influence of perceived causal locus of partners' dependence on the use of interpersonal power. *Journal of Personality and Social Psychology,* 1965, *2,* 609–612.

Schwartz, S. Normative explanations of helping behavior: A critique proposal and empirical test. *Journal of Experimental Social Psychology,* 1973, *9,* 349–64.

Schwartz, S. H. Elicitation of moral obligation and self-sacrificing behavior: An experimental study of volunteering to be a bone marrow donor. *Journal of Personality and Social Psychology,* 1970(a), *15,* 283–93.

————. Moral decision making and behavior. In J. R. Macaulay and L. Berkowitz (Eds.), *Altruism and Helping Behavior.* New York: Academic Press, Inc., 1970(b). Pp. 127–41.

———— and G. T. Clausen. Responsibility, norms and helping in an emergency. *Journal of Personality and Social Psychology,* 1970, *16,* 299–310.

Shantz, C. U. The development of social cognition. In E. M. Heatherington (Ed.), *Review of Child Development Research.* Vol. 5. Chicago: University of Chicago Press, 1975.

Sidowski, J., L. B. Wyckoff, and L. Tabory. The influence of reinforcement and punishment in a minimal social situation. *Journal of Abnormal and Social Psychology,* 1956, *52,* 115–19.

Snyder, M., J. Grether, and K. Keller. Staring and compliance: A field experiment on hitchhiking. *Journal of Applied Social Psychology,* 1974, *4,* 165–70.

Staub, E. A child in distress: The influence of nurturance and modeling on children's attempts to help. *Developmental Psychology,* 1971, *5,* 124–32.

Thibaut, J. W. An experimental study of the cohesiveness of underprivileged groups. *Human Relations,* 1950, *3,* 251–78.

——— and H. H. Kelley. *The Social Psychology of Groups.* New York: John Wiley & Sons, Inc., 1959.

Thomas, E. Effects of facilitative role interdependence on group functioning. *Human Relations,* 1957, *10,* 347–66.

Walster, E., E. Berscheid, and G. W. Walster. Reactions of an exploiter to the exploited: Compensation, justification, or self-punishment? In J. R. Macaulay and L. Berkowitz (Eds.), *Altruism and Helping Behavior.* New York: Academic Press, Inc., 1970.

———, ———, and ———. New directions in equity research. *Journal of Personality and Social Psychology,* 1973, *25,* 151–76.

——— and J. Pilivian. Equity and the innocent bystander. *Journal of Social Issues,* 1972, *28,* 165–89.

——— and G. W. Walster. Equity and social justice: An essay. *Journal of Social Issues,* 1975, *31,* 21–44.

———, G. W. Walster, and E. Berscheid. *Equity: Theory and Research.* Boston, Mass.: Allyn & Bacon, Inc., 1978.

Weiss, R. F., J. L. Boyer, J. P. Lombardo, and M. H. Stitch. Altruistic drive and altruistic reinforcement. *Journal of Personality and Social Psychology,* 1973, *25,* 390–400.

West, S. G., and T. J. Brown. Physical attractiveness, the severity of the emergency and helping; A field experiment and interpersonal simulation. *Journal of Experimental Social Psychology,* 1975, *11,* 531–38.

———, G. Whitney, and R. Schnedler. Helping a motorist in distress: The effects of sex, race and neighborhood. *Journal of Personality and Social Psychology,* 1975, *31,* 691–98.

Wispé, L., and H. Freshley. Race, sex, and sympathetic helping behavior: The broken bag caper. *Journal of Personality and Social Psychology,* 1971, *17,* 59–65.

Wright, D. *The Psychology of Moral Behavior.* Harmondsworth, Middlesex, England: Penguin Books, 1971.

11

Group Behavior

Group Behavior

The count is three and two, the bases are loaded and your team is behind by one run in the bottom of the ninth inning. Throughout this baseball game the umpires have made a number of calls the hometown fans don't agree with, and now, on a close pitch, the batter is called out, the game is over and you've lost. A barrage of debris rains down on the outfielders from the opposing team. You find yourself, in frustration, throwing anything you can get your hands on. Under normal circumstances you would not dream of trying to hurt someone; but now when you join in the chant of kill the umpire, you mean it. In Boston, Chicago, Los Angeles, Montreal, New York, Pittsburgh, Toronto, St. Louis, San Francisco, and many other cities in Canada and the United States group behavior gets nasty. People who would normally not engage in such activities go along with the group. Why?

There are many answers to that question; some we understand and some we don't. This chapter is an attempt to summarize some of the knowledge we have about groups. We will start with a sample of some of the things groups do and then we will analyze some of the important characteristics of groups.

What Do Groups Do—and Why?

Groups do many things. They influence people's behavior—for better or worse. They allow individuals to make decisions they ordinarily wouldn't make and, they sometimes come together because they are ordered to do so by a court to decide whether someone deserves to live or die.

This group of youngsters has come together with a specific goal—presenting a concert.

As indicated in Chapter 1, social facilitation was one of the earliest dominant forces in social psychological research for the first three decades of this century. Much of this work was done to solve a practical problem. This is not an unusual state of affairs in social psychology. Lewin wanted to influence housewives to prepare less popular foods for consumption during World War II; Milgram was interested in why many people in Nazi Germany had obeyed orders to kill others; and present-day social psychological researchers are interested in why people hurt, like, or help each other. The problem that generated much of the research on social facilitation was aimed at determining whether schoolwork and homework could be better performed by the student working alone or with others in the room working on the same task (Mayer, 1903; Burnham, 1905). Interest in this topic has continued to the present, although it has not recently dominated social psychological research as it once did.

From the time of Tripplett's (1898) early study with children, it has been apparent that some individuals are stimulated to work faster when others are present, some work slower, and some seem unaffected in their work by the presence of others. In general, children do better than adults in the presence of others (Feofanov, 1928); subjects with low intelligence are less stimulated to perform well by the presence of others (Abel, 1938); and subjects are less likely to become bored when working with someone else (Taylor, Thompson, and Spassoff, 1937). Moreover, if subjects think they will do well, they are likely to work harder when others are present (d'Amorim & Nutlin, 1972; Good, 1973) yet subjects who place high value on socially desirable behavior and are self-conscious generally perform more poorly when others are present (Taylor and Weinstein, 1974).

Competing Responses

If all of this seems confusing, research by Zajonc (1965) has gone a long way toward explaining the seeming contradictions. Zajonc reasoned that performance on a simple task, one an individual knew he or she could perform well, should be enhanced by the presence of others. On the other hand, a complex task should be more difficult to perform when others are present.

Zajonc's reasoning was straightforward and followed from a great deal of research in the general area of anxiety. When an individual is anxious, performance is enhanced on simple tasks, but inhibited on complex tasks (Spence, Farber, and McFann, 1956). A simple task is defined as one in which there are few competing responses, whereas a complex task is one in which there are many competing responses. For example, when you are learning to drive a stick-shift car, the first time you try to start the car after stopping at a red light in heavy traffic is very likely to result in disaster. As the light turns green you must raise your left foot to release the clutch while simultaneously depressing your right foot to give gas to the engine. These acts must be synchronized so that the car starts smoothly. For most of us, the first time we try this, if we're lucky the car bucks across the intersection and doesn't die in the middle. The reason for this is that we have several motions to perform and when they are new to us, there are many responses competing with the correct ones. For example, you may push down with your left foot, release the gas with your right foot, grind to a halt, throw up your hands and scream in frustration. But none of these actions gets your car out of that damned intersection.

And yet, after many days or weeks, or in some cases, months of practice, you can smoothly start your car from the busiest intersection without giving it a thought. What has happened? The incorrect competing responses have dropped out, and you are now making the correct responses.

Basically, Zajonc found that subjects who had few competing responses on a task did better when others were present, but that the presence of others caused a decrement in performance when there were many competing responses possible. To return to our illustration of driving a stick-shift car, when you are learning to drive the car, you will probably do better if you don't have an audience, but after you have learned to drive well, an audience should enhance your performance. Do you remember how easy it was to start your car, even soon after you had learned, when you stopped at a deserted intersection? The real disasters occur when there are cars all around and the driver in every one of them watches you make a fool of yourself.

EVALUATION APPREHENSION

Zajonc's explanation seems to answer a number of thorny questions about social facilitation, but it does not answer the question "Why"? Why do people become more anxious in the presence of others and, and in their presence, perform better on a simple task but worse on a complex one? One explanation for this phenomenon is what is referred to as evaluation apprehension, that is, concern over being judged by others. Cottrell, Wack, Sekerak, and Rittle (1968) found that subjects' dominant responses were facilitated only when others were present and watching them. Furthermore, social facilitation effects occurred only when subjects felt that their performance was being evaluated (Innes and Young, 1975; Martens and Landers, 1972). Thus, it seemed clear that for the presence of others to have an effect on people, it was necessary for the other people to be watching their performance and to be evaluating it. Things seemed to be tied up in a neat bundle. The nice, neat bundle, however, has a few frayed edges.

The most difficult data to account for are those showing that other animals are affected in much the same way we are by the presence of others. Zajonc, Heingartner, and Herman (1969) found that household cockroaches performed better in the presence of other cockroaches when a dominant response (for cockroaches) would facilitate their performance, and worse when a dominant response would impair their performance. Cockroaches were placed in a maze. At one end was a bright light from which cockroaches try to escape. If they were required to run straight ahead, a dominant response, they performed faster when four other cockroaches were present than when the other cockroaches were absent. If, however, they were required to make a right turn to escape the light they did worse when the four other cockroaches were present than when they were absent. Thus, the same results occurred with cockroaches as with humans. I would not like to have to argue the point that the cockroaches perform better when other cockroaches are present because they fear being judged by their peers.

SOCIAL FACILITATION AND DISTRACTION

Being distracted from a task hurts your performance, doesn't it? In the interesting world of social facilitation research the answer may be "No." Of course, that "No" is qualified by the distinction between simple and complex tasks. Recall that a simple task is one at which you are very proficient and a complex task is one at which you tend to make a number of errors.

Baron, Moore, and Sanders (1978) suggest that distraction might actually help your performance on a simple task but impair it on a complex task. Their analysis implies that the audience in social facilitation research increases drive (even though it is distracting) and thus enhances performance on a simple task and impairs it on a complex one. As we have discussed in the text, there is a good deal of evidence to support the effects of an audience on performance. The question of why is more difficult and even more intriguing if distraction leads to better performance on simple tasks.

Baron et al. utilized a paired-associates learning task to test the effects of social facilitation. Paired-associates learning is a task in which two words are paired and the subject's task is to learn the second word in the pair (response) when the first word (stimulus) is presented. Lists of words can be constructed that are either very simple or very complex. For example, if the stimulus and response words in the pairs making up the list are synonyms, the list would be very simple to learn. If, on the other hand, synonyms are in the list as stimulus and response words, but they are not paired with *each other,* the list would be very complex. To illustrate, consider two pairs; adept-skillful and barren-fruitless. If these two pairs were paired as just shown, they would be simple to learn. If, however, the pairs were adept-fruitless and skillful-barren, they would be more difficult. If the list were made up of 10 or 15 pairs, it would be very difficult indeed.

Baron et al. used simple and complex paired-associates lists and within each of these two groups half of the subjects were observed by one other person and half worked alone. A sensitive measure of paired-associates learning in social facilitation research is errors on the lists. With another person present subjects averaged .74 errors per pair on the simple list and 3.33 errors per pair on the complex list. Alone, subjects averaged 1.17 errors per pair on the simple list and 2.65 errors on the complex one. Thus, the presence of another person enhanced performance on the simple list and inhibited it on the complex one.

In addition to the paired-associates learning task, Baron et al. assessed each subject's distraction. Subjects were more distracted when another person was present than when they were alone and this was true for both the simple task group and the complex task group. It is not surprising to note that when subjects were faced with a complex task their performance was inhibited by being distracted. Obviously when you are distracted you do not perform as well as when you are not distracted. What is startling is that those individuals who learned the simple list were also distracted by the presence of another person, but they were superior in their performance to a group who learned the same list with no one else present.

Baron et al. attribute these results to an increase in arousal caused by the presence of another person. This arousal causes enhanced performance on simple tasks and impaired performance on complex ones. Thus distraction, on the right kind of task, can facilitate performance.

Reference

Baron, R. S., D. Moore, and G. S. Sanders. Distraction as a source of drive in social facilitation research. *Journal of Personality and Social Psychology,* 1978, *36,* 816–24.

Cottrell (1972) has proposed a mechanism to explain social facilitation in humans, cockroaches, and species in between. He has suggested that all animals, human and nonhuman, learn through experience that the presence of others raises different expectations than the absence of others. For example, most of us would not be willing to do things in the presence of others that we feel perfectly comfortable doing in the privacy of our own rooms. For instance, most of us feel perfectly comfortable in removing our clothes and stepping into a shower when we are alone, or possibly with one other person or a group under special circumstances (e.g., in a locker room). However, most of us would feel somewhat uncomfortable at removing all of our clothes in a group of people most of the time. This is because we have learned what is socially acceptable and socially unacceptable.

Other animals, including cockroaches, have also learned certain things about the presence of other individuals. For example, when there is a limited amount of food or water individuals in many species have learned that they will have to fight to get their share. Thus they have learned to anticipate certain consequences when others are present and they are often aroused because of this expectation. Therefore, they too perform tasks that require dominant responses better and do worse on tasks that do not require dominant responses when others are present. The presence of others has enormous consequences for our performance. It also has, however, other, rather frightening, consequences for behavior—to which we now turn.

Deindividuation

In a major contribution to the psychological effects of groups on behavior, Zimbardo (1970) called the attention of psychologists to the negative effects groups can have on behavior. Zimbardo points out that during the late 1960s self-destruction, the destruction of others, riots and mob violence, loss of value for life, and loss of behavior control increased dramatically. These increases represented a fundamental change in the quality of individual and mass hostility, inhumanity, and aggression from what it had been earlier in our lifetimes.

Most groups, even crowded and active ones, do not degenerate into negative behavior. Like this one, they enjoy themselves.

Zimbardo argued that what has enabled a large increase in these negative behaviors to occur is what he called deindividuation. This concept Zimbardo defined in the following way:

> Deindividuation is a complex, hypothesized process in which a series of antecedent social conditions lead to changes in perception of self and others, and thereby to a lowered threshold of normally restrained behavior. Under appropriate conditions what results is the "release" of behavior in violation of established norms of appropriateness.
>
> Such conditions permit overt expressions of antisocial behavior, characterized as selfish, greedy, power-seeking, hostile, lustful, and destructive. However, they also allow a range of "positive" intense feelings of happiness or sorrow, and open love for others. Thus emotions and impulses usually under cognitive control are more likely to be expressed when the input conditions minimize self-observation and evaluation as well as concern over evaluation by others. [Zimbardo, 1970, p. 251.]

To be fully understood, deindividuation must be seen in all three of its components—conditions that stimulate it, the feelings that characterize the process, and deindividuation behaviors. Figure 11-1 gives a schematic representation of the deindividuation process.

Even though this is a most important process in human behavior, Zimbardo points out that there were only two experiments and one conceptual article dealing with the phenomenon (Festinger, Pepitone, and Newcomb, 1952; Singer, Brush, and Lublin, 1965) prior to 1969. It should also be made clear that Zimbardo is referring to a process that involves much more than mob rule psychology. The process allows for both positive and negative behaviors, for behavior both in and out of a group; and Zimbardo has attempted to define the process in a scientifically testable way.

There are several elements of the model Zimbardo proposes that should be considered in greater detail.

ANONYMITY

The output of deindividuated behavior should become more likely as the individual feels more anonymous. If others can't identify you, then they can't single you out for criticism or punishment. This loss of identifiability can be accomplished in several ways: by being disguised, masked, lost in a crowd, dressed in a uniform, or "under cover of darkness." The appeal of the "invisible" pet or friend or of being invisible yourself is very prevalent in our society. Yet anonymity is also a thing to be feared. Each one of us prizes his or her uniqueness; many children are afraid of wearing a mask or seeing others in a mask. Being lost in a crowd can also be frightening. Anonymity is a two-edged sword.

RESPONSIBILITY

If others are present, the responsibility for an act is diffused, not attributable to any one person. In Chapter 10 we saw that altruistic behavior tends to be inhibited by the presence of others. The other side of this coin is that when antisocial behavior is committed in a group, the responsibility for that behavior is diffused. It has been reported that the Klansmen who murdered three civil rights workers in Mississippi in

Some Conditions Leading
to Process of
Deindividuation

Some Conditions of
Resulting Behaviors

457

Social Facilitation

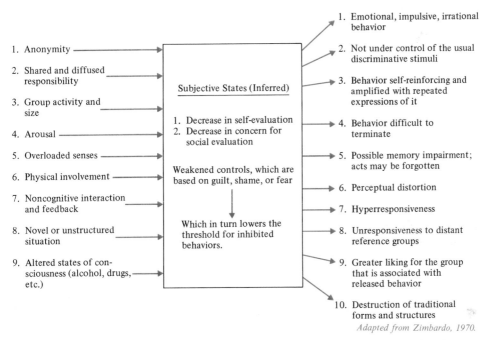

1. Anonymity

2. Shared and diffused
   responsibility

3. Group activity and
   size

4. Arousal

5. Overloaded senses

6. Physical involvement

7. Noncognitive interaction
   and feedback

8. Novel or unstructured
   situation

9. Altered states of con-
   sciousness (alcohol, drugs,
   etc.)

Subjective States (Inferred)

1. Decrease in self-evaluation
2. Decrease in concern for
   social evaluation

Weakened controls, which are
based on guilt, shame, or fear

Which in turn lowers the
threshold for inhibited
behaviors.

1. Emotional, impulsive, irrational
   behavior

2. Not under control of the usual
   discriminative stimuli

3. Behavior self-reinforcing and
   amplified with repeated
   expressions of it

4. Behavior difficult to
   terminate

5. Possible memory impairment;
   acts may be forgotten

6. Perceptual distortion

7. Hyperresponsiveness

8. Unresponsiveness to distant
   reference groups

9. Greater liking for the group
   that is associated with
   released behavior

10. Destruction of traditional
    forms and structures

Adapted from Zimbardo, 1970.

Figure 11–1 A schematic representation of the deindividuation process. Not all of the
conditions leading to the process nor all of the conditions of the resulting behaviors
need be present for deindividuation to be operative.

1964 passed the murder weapon from hand to hand so that the responsibility would
be shared equally (Huie, 1965). The Ku Klux Klan itself favors the wearing of white
sheets to insure anonymity and thus diffused responsibility.

GROUP PRESENCE

The presence of the group alone can help to assure anonymity and diffused
responsibility. But it has other functions it can serve in the process of deindividuation.
First, it can provide models for activity. One member of the group can be seen either
aggressing or acting altruistically, and others often will follow. The group can also
generate physical activity that is itself arousing. The milling and pushing and shoving
that occurs within a group can arouse people. On the other hand, huge masses of
people obediently standing in line or moving toward some other place have led to the
folk saying that people can be herded like sheep. The group can have either an
arousing or a calming effect upon the individuals in it.

TEMPORAL PERSPECTIVE

Statements such as "time seemed to stand still" or a person "lives for the moment"
impart some of the feelings that go with an increased perception of the present. "Time

seemed to fly" is another phrase that seeks to capture the idea that sometimes the present seems to gain more importance than either the past or the future. Behavior under these conditions is not trapped between past obligations and future liabilities.

AROUSAL

Extreme arousal seems to be a necessary condition for achieving a true state of "ecstasy." In many societies techniques have been developed that facilitate arousal prior to rites of war, self-sacrifice, and initiation. The war dance of many societies is probably the most common and best known of these techniques and consists of loud repetitive music, which is dominated by simple, powerful themes. Groups may dance for hours or even days, singing, shouting, and chanting enactments of symbolic confrontations with the enemy.

Cognitive, verbal, and intellectual activities serve to break the spell, and thus are incompatible with the spontaneous release that occurs in the subjective states of deindividuation. These activities must be overcome by intense *sensory stimulation* or the person must get so absorbed in the action that the only meaningful act is the action itself. Cognitive controls can also be undermined by placing individuals in a novel situation. Things that we would never do in the block where we live—in front of family, friends and neighbors—may be easily performed in a new situation. Rootless Americans who move frequently help break down cognitive controls on behavior. Finally, cognitive controls on behavior can be undermined by *altered states of consciousness* brought about by drugs. All these factors can combine to result in an increase in deindividuated behavior.

A sleepy village on Martha's Vineyard is crowded during the summer season, yet here the conditions for deindividuation do not occur and people do not engage in destructive behavior.

Deindividuated behavior must, for the theoretical construct to be plausible, show different patterns than contagion (see Chapter 8), extreme aggression, or the disinhibition of specific responses. As Zimbardo puts it,

> Virtually by definition, deindividuated behavior must have the property of being a high-intensity manifestation of behavior which observers would agree is emotional, impulsive, irrational, regressive, or atypical for the person in the given situation. But that is not enough. In addition, the behavior must not be under discriminative stimulus control. It must be unresponsive to features of the situation, the target, the victim, or the states of self which normally evoke a given level of response or a competing response. This is due to the combined effects of arousal, involvement in the act, and the direct pleasure derived from action-feedback, without regard for associated conditions which sanction or justify the action. [Zimbardo, 1970, p. 259.]

Zimbardo specifically identifies a screening effect utilized by an individual in a deindividuating circumstance. This screening blocks out feedback that is not affective and self-enhancing. That is, emotional stimuli are allowed into the system by the deindividuating individual's perceptions and then they are allowed to grow in intensity within the individual because nonaffective stimuli are blocked out. This affective reverberating feedback is pleasurable and thus self-reinforcing. Since it is self-reinforcing, each recurrence amplifies the earlier state of emotional arousal.

Evidence for such effects is cited by Zimbardo from three sources. First, Jacques Cousteau argues that the "dance of death" by sharks when they surround a passive victim is one of the most terrifying sights of all. After circling the victim for hours, when one shark attacks they all join together and tear the victim to shreds within moments. Black racer snakes when placed in a cage with live mice may wait a long or a short time before they kill the first mouse. But after striking the first one, they seem to kill at an ever faster rate until all (or most) of the mice are killed. Yoko Ono, John Lennon's wife, originated an audience participation act called "Cut Piece." She sat in front of the audience in a beautiful dress and invited the audience to cut it up with a pair of scissors. At first there was an awful silence and then they went wild. Once they had started they couldn't seem to stop. It was a terrible scene and she was left quite naked.

Deindividuated behavior is difficult to terminate once it starts because it has a self-reinforcing aspect and the screening of cognitive perceptions leaves it almost entirely under internal control. It may be that deindividuated behavior is easy to stop before it reaches a certain (as yet unspecifiable) level of intensity, but when the reverberating emotional arousal reaches a given level, it can't be turned off very easily.

A Pirandellian Prison

Probably the best-known experiment into deindividuation is one carried out by Zimbardo and his associates (Zimbardo et al., 1973). These investigators recruited 21 male subjects and assigned 10 of them to be prisoners and 11 to be guards. The prisoners were picked up by people in police cars, charged with a felony, warned of their constitutional rights, searched while spread-eagled against the squad car, handcuffed, and taken to the police station for booking. After fingerprinting each prisoner was left alone until he was blindfolded and taken to the "Stanford County Prison." The "prison" was specially constructed in the basement of the psychology building at Stanford University. At the prison, each prisoner was stripped, skin-searched, deloused, and issued a uniform, bedding, soap, and towel. The warden welcomed them to the prison by informing them of the rules and instructing them to obey them.

The 21 subjects, chosen from more than 75 volunteers, were mainly college students who answered an ad in a local newspaper that offered $15.00 a day for participation in a psychological study of prison life. A flip of a coin determined whether a subject would be a prisoner or a guard.

The mock prison was a deliberate attempt to simulate the psychological state of imprisonment in certain ways. Real prisoners typically report feeling powerless, dependent, frustrated, anonymous, and dehumanized. These characteristic states were reproduced where it was possible to do so, although obviously some of the events in real prisons such as racism, physical brutality, and enforced homosexuality were not features of the mock prison. Anonymity was promoted by attempting to minimize each prisoner's sense of identity and uniqueness. Prisoners wore smocks and nylon caps, each had his identity number and was required to address other prisoners by number, not name. In addition each prisoner's personal effects were removed and the prisoners were housed in clean but barren cells.

The guards were also made to feel anonymous. Their uniforms were identical and they wore silver reflector sunglasses so that eye contact could not be made with them. They had identical symbols of power—billy-clubs, handcuffs, and keys. Although the guards had no formal training in being guards, they moved easily into their roles. The guards' behavior was as important to the research project as that of the prisoners and because of this they were given wide latitude in managing the prisoners.

On the second morning of the experiment there was a prisoners' rebellion. The prisoners took off their caps, tore off their numbers, and barricaded themselves inside their cells by placing their beds against the doors. The guards were quite upset and called in two guards on standby duty, while the night shift stayed on to assist the day shift. They shot the prisoners with a stream of chilling carbon dioxide from a fire extinguisher, broke into each cell, stripped the prisoners naked, put the ring leaders in solitary confinement, and began to harass and intimidate all prisoners. To head off further insurrections the guards created a privileged cell for "good prisoners" and then put some of the trouble-makers into the privileged cell and some of the good prisoners into other cells. In this way they broke down the trust the prisoners had for each other and the prisoners never again acted in unity against the system.

This incident seemed to trigger arbitrariness in the guards' use of power. They made the prisoners obey petty orders, do meaningless tasks, and degrade each other. The prisoners slowly became resigned to their fate and even behaved in ways that seemed to justify the guards' abysmal behavior toward them. For example, fully half of the comments made by prisoners about other prisoners were nonsupportive and 85 percent of prisoners' evaluative statements about other prisoners were uncomplimentary or deprecating.

Within 36 hours one prisoner had to be released because of depression, disorganized thinking, and uncontrolled crying. On each of the next three days one prisoner was also released because of extreme anxiety symptoms. The only psychological dimension on which the prisoners who remained the full time and those released early differed was authoritarianism—the more authoritarian prisoners were better able to handle the prison situation.

The experiment had been planned to last two weeks but was terminated after six days. As Zimbardo puts it,

We were no longer dealing with an intellectual exercise in which a hypothesis was being evaluated in the dispassionate manner dictated by the canons of the scientific method. We were caught up in the passion of the present, the suffering, the need to control people, not variables, the escalation of power and all of the unexpected things that were erupting around and within us. We had to end this experiment. So our planned two-week simulation was aborted after only six (was it only six?) days and nights. [Zimbardo et al., 1973, p. 56.]

Comment

Zimbardo has identified and presented us with evidence for the effects of deindividuation. Whereas the process is not necessarily a group-related one, being in a group helps us to gain the anonymity, the arousal, and the support that are so vital a part of the process. The prison experiment presents another side of the deindividuation process and shows us another aspect of small groups.

Group Decision Making—Risky or Polarizing?

In 1961, James Stoner, a graduate student at MIT, undertook an ambitious project and discovered a reliable but nonobvious effect of group discussion. Stoner was interested in testing the long-standing notion that groups are more cautious and less daring than individuals. Stoner had six people at a time respond as individuals to a series of story problems called "choice-dilemma" items (developed by Kogan and Wallach, 1964). The subject was to advise the fictional character of each item as to how much risk could be taken in solving a given dilemma. For example, a sample of a dilemma is as follows (Myer and Lamm, 1976, p. 602):

George, a competent chess player, is participating in a national chess tournament. In an early match he draws the top-favored player in the tournament as his opponent. George has been given a relatively low ranking in view of his performance in previous tournaments. During the course of his play with the top-favored man, George notes the possibility of a deceptive though risky maneuver which might bring him a quick victory. At the same time, if the attempted maneuver should fail, George would be left in an exposed position and defeat would almost certainly follow.

Imagine you are advising George. Please check the *lowest* possibility that you would consider acceptable for the risky play in question to be attempted. George should attempt the play if the chances are at least

———— 1 in 10 that the play would succeed.

———— 2 in 10 that the play would succeed.

———— 3 in 10 that the play would succeed.

———— 4 in 10 that the play would succeed.

———— 5 in 10 that the play would succeed.

———— 6 in 10 that the play would succeed.

———— 7 in 10 that the play would succeed.

———— 8 in 10 that the play would succeed.

———— 9 in 10 that the play would succeed.

———— George should attempt the play only if it is certain (i.e., 10 in 10) that the play would succeed.

After each individual subject had marked his or her advice on all the items the six people assembled as a group and discussed each item until they reached agreement. On the whole the groups advised a more risky course of action than did the individual group members. That is, the group decision was about one scale unit or less more risky than the average of the individual decisions. Even though the amount of this difference was small, it did not support the contention that groups are more conservative in their judgments than individuals. Quite the contrary, these groups were more daring than individuals. The phenomenon was immediately dubbed the *risky shift* and set off a wave of investigations into group risk taking.

During the 1960s there were a mass of risky-shift studies carried out in at least a dozen different countries which were labeled by some a fruitless fad (Smith, 1972). Why was all the research done if it was to prove only a few years later to be seriously flawed?

Nonrisky Group Decisions

Even in the early research on the risky shift there were two choice-dilemma questions that consistently did not result in a shift to a more risky decision by a group. One of these resulted in no shift and the other resulted in a shift to a more conservative decision. This particular choice-dilemma item involved a personal choice—whether to marry after a marriage counselor had warned that the marriage would possibly be unhappy. In general, the average of the individual choices was riskier than the group choice.

On the whole, however, during the ten years of risky-shift research, it was generally agreed that groups make riskier decisions than individuals, and reasons for this phenomenon were sought. For example, Wallach, Kogan, and Bem (1964) attributed the risky shift to a diffusion of responsibility in the group. That is, when an individual makes a decision, she or he must live with the responsibility for that decision. But when a group makes a decision, the responsibility is spread around to several individuals. It was even suggested that such policy-making bodies as the United States National Security Council made riskier decisions than would one person deciding alone.

As research proceeded, however, and other choice-dilemma situations were investigated, it turned out that in other cases group decisions were more conservative than individual ones (Teger and Pruitt, 1967; McCauley et al., 1973; Knox and Safford, 1976). Thus, it seemed that the term *risky shift* was a misnomer and represented an overgeneralization.

Group Polarization

If groups sometimes make riskier decisions than individuals and sometimes make more conservative decisions than individuals, how can we make sense out of the results? Possibly it is the situation itself. In certain types of situations (for example, personal decisions) groups are more conservative than individuals. This sort of approach, however, leaves more questions unanswered than it answers.

Certain researchers into group-induced shifts have argued that groups do not reliably change to riskier or more conservative decisions; rather they become more polarized (Lamm, Trommsdorff, and Rost-Schaude, 1973; Myers, 1975; Myers and Kaplan, 1976; Myers and Lamm, 1976). That is, the group shifts to a more extreme position in the direction the individuals in the group already favor. If their view is correct, the reason the whole research area became known as risky shift is that in most of the choice dilemmas that Stoner (and others following him) used, the individuals in group initially favored a course of action that was somewhat on the risky side. When the group met the interaction increased each individual's assurance that that particular course of action was correct. Therefore, the group decision was more risky on most of the items. But if the group had originally favored a slightly conservative course of action on Stoner's choice of dilemma items, the shift would have been in the expected (conservative) direction and much of the research that has gone on would not have been carried out. Thus, one of the accidents that occur in scientific work seems to have added to our understanding of group decision-making processes.

Under what circumstances do group decisions become polarized? Actually, there are quite a number of areas in which it seems that groups polarize their initial opinions; but attitudes, ethical decisions, person perception, and negotiation behavior are the four areas we will discuss.

ATTITUDES

In 1941, Robinson conducted lengthy discussion groups with students on attitudes toward two subjects: pacifism and capital punishment. The students were initially quite pacifistic and following the discussion the group had shifted to an even more pacifistic stance although the change was not statistically significant. On attitudes toward capital punishment, to which the students were initially opposed, there was a significant shift toward more opposition to it. Moscovici and Zavalloni (1969) found that French students who had initially positive attitudes toward DeGaulle and negative attitudes towards Americans became more polarized after discussion. In addition, attitudes towards social issues and life-situation dilemmas have shown similar effects (Gouge and Fraser, 1972; Myers and Bishop, 1970).

ETHICAL DECISIONS

Each one of us often faces many ethical decisions, ranging from simple decisions concerning contributing to charity all the way to decisions that seriously, adversely, and immediately affect another individual or group. A number of studies that have investigated diverse ethical decisions, such as whether one should be more concerned with one's own welfare or that of humanity in general, whether an underaged teenager should order a drink, and how much time or money to invest in a worthy cause, have all indicated a group polarization effect (Myers and Lamm, 1976). That is, after group discussion the decision made was more extreme in the direction favored by the individuals prior to the discussion.

PERSON PERCEPTION

Myers (1975) had subjects evaluate faculty members as "good" or "bad" and then had them distribute a hypothetical pay increase among the individuals. Then the individual subjects were allowed to discuss the issue in groups and following this discussion, their decisions were more polarized. Doise (1970) described a stimulus person as relatively introverted or extroverted by having subjects read a descriptive paragraph about the individual. After group discussion, there was greater polarity in the group impressions of extroversion-introversion. Thus it seems that our perceptions of other people's qualities can be made more extreme by group discussion.

NEGOTIATING

Negotiating has long been an art and a skill that is highly valued. With the increase in labor negotiations, negotiations between nations, and conflicts between large groups, teams now negotiate more serious matters than individuals do. Is it possible that these teams (which are groups that engage in discussions among themselves) also show group polarization effects? There are minimal data, but they are intriguing. Rabbie and Visser (1972) instructed union bargaining teams to set expectation levels both as individuals and then as a group. When the issues were important and the bargaining position strong, individuals aspired to higher payoffs than when the issues were less important and the bargaining position weak. This is not particularly surprising since we would expect negotiators to try to attain more when the issues were important and the union had a strong case. What is important, however, is that after group discussion, the positions became more extreme.

Lamm and Sauer (1974) observed a similar polarization effect. Individuals were asked to distribute eighteen profit units between themselves and another player. On the average, the individuals proposed that they should receive 64 percent and the other player 36 percent. After discussing the issue with other individuals with whom they were not competing, they increased their demands to almost 70 percent, leaving slightly over 30 percent for the other player.

There seems to be evidence that a group polarization effect does occur in negotiations. Since, almost by definition, negotiating teams favor their side of the issue, this polarizing effect may make settlements more difficult. For example, consider a situation in which a union is negotiating with management for a new contract. Usually, the members of the union team favor a relatively high wage increase, if for no other reason than that they stand to receive the increase personally. Now the group comes together and a polarization effect occurs resulting in a higher initial demand than the group as individuals would have made. The reverse effect is happening with the management team. It is their job to keep wages down and their initial offer may be well below what the individuals would have offered if they had not discussed the issue.

There is a growing trend in labor negotiations to use a single, impartial arbitrator when the two sides have deadlocked. This individual listens to the final proposal of each side and then chooses one of them. The two proposals cannot be altered and one or the other must be selected. The single arbitrator is, of course, not subject to group polarization effects. The increasing popularity of the trend may be a counterbalance to the polarization effects groups have when it is essential that two groups reach an agreement. This is, of course, speculation—but interesting speculation.

Group Polarization—Why Does It Occur?

There are several ways in which we can view the effects of group polarization, but probably the most appealing theoretical explanation is what Myers and Lamm have called *informational influences theory*. This view asserts that cognitive learning occurs during exposure of the minority to the majority viewpoint during discussion. During the course of a group discussion there will typically be pro and con arguments, and these will be roughly in the proportion of those who espouse each side of the issue. Thus there usually will be a predominance of arguments on the majority side. For each individual in the group, some of the arguments will be roughly in the proportion of the pro and con advocates in the group. Therefore, these arguments will move the group in the direction of the majority.

To illustrate, let us assume that there is a discussion group of ten people who are expected to come to a group decision about abortion. The initial views of the ten individuals are seven in favor of it and three opposed. Now let us assume that the group discusses the issue for an hour. Some of the points made will not be new and persuasive but they will probably be roughly in the seven to three proportion. The new and persuasive arguments will also be roughly in the same proportion. After an hour's discussion the group will have heard approximately seven new and persuasive arguments for abortion and three against it. Thus any change in the group will probably be to make the proabortion majority more extreme or to move the antiabortion minority to a less extreme position. Either of these will result in the group polarization effect. It has been established that the content of the discussion carried on in a group is highly correlated with the prediscussion positions taken by group members and this in turn predicts the shift that will occur after the discussion (Bishop and Myers, 1974; Ebbesen and Bowers, 1974; Morgan and Aram, 1975; Vinokur and Burnstein, 1974).

Yet why should it be argued that new and persuasive information causes the change rather than just the fact that the minority members realize they are in the minority? Several experiments (Burnstein and Vinokur, 1973; Eagly, 1974) have indicated that when information alone is presented, with subjects having no knowledge of the speakers' real attitudes, the group polarization effect occurs. This indicates that it is indeed the information that is causing the shift in group opinion.

The idea that groups make more risky decisions than individuals has been replaced by the realization that group decision making tends to polarize (i.e., to move to a more extreme position in the direction initially favored by the majority). There are, however, two theoretical explanations.

One of these explanations, informational influence, is based on the assumption that when a group discusses an issue there are a given number of persuasive arguments on each side of the issue. For example, if the issue were abortion, there would be a number of pro- and a number of antiabortion arguments. During the course of the discussion, participants voice their opinions concerning the issue. If there is a majority of proabortion individuals in the group, on the average they will voice their opinions in proportion to their numbers. Thus, there will be more proabortion arguments than antiabortion ones and the group will move to a more extreme position in the proabortion direction.

The second explanation, normative influence, has been conceptualized in terms of social comparison processes. These theories assume that relatively extreme attitudes are socially desirable and a person who presents himself or herself in such a fashion will gain social approval. In some situations, it is socially desirable to be extreme in a risky direction, whereas other situations call for prudence. The individual voices an opinion he or she feels is appropriately extreme (in a risky or prudent direction) and listens to the other individuals in the group. There usually are others more extreme and it is socially desirable to move toward them. Thus a group polarizes after discussion.

Vinkour and Burnstein (1978) point out that both of these interpretations of the polarization phenomenon explain it quite well. What would each predict, however, if the groups were very nearly evenly split on the issue? Then the effect would differ depending upon which theory you subscribed to. The persuasive arguments approach would argue for a small amount of shift in the direction that had more readily available arguments. That is, some issues in certain populations seem to have more arguments on one side or the other. For example, in a population of women who were members of the National Organization of Women (NOW) one would expect more proabortion arguments than in a group of highly devout Roman Catholic women. Thus, depending on the group and the topic, the persuasive arguments theory would predict that the group as a whole would polarize in the direction of the side that had more persuasive arguments even in a split group. There would, however, be a marked depolarization of attitudes between the two disagreeing subgroups. That is, the subgroups would move closer to each other after discussion.

Normative influence would predict that in the situation where the group is evenly split, as there is no majority to influence the entire group, there will be a breakup into two competing subgroups. Consistent with social comparison theory, there will be two groups with which an individual can compare himself or herself. Thus, the two subgroups should become more extreme in their views, leading to no lessening of the differences between the subgroups.

Vinkour and Burnstein tested these notions by creating split groups and found that there was some total-group polarization in the direction of the previously known preponderance of arguments in the population being studied. There was, however, an even greater depolarization between the subgroups. That is, the subgroups came closer together after the discussion than they had been before. These results favor a persuasive arguments interpretation.

Reference

Vinkour, A., and E. Burnstein. Depolarization of attitudes in groups. *Journal of Personality and Social Psychology*, 1978, *36*, 872–85.

There is a substantial body of evidence which argues for the notion that cognitive learning must occur for the group polarization effect to surface. There is also evidence to suggest that the passive receipt of arguments outside of interactive discussion generally does not produce as much group-opinion shift as does the situation in which group members are allowed actively to enter the discussion (Bishop and Meyers, 1974; Burnstein and Vinokur, 1973; St. Jean, 1970; St. Jean and Percival, 1974). Listening to a group discussion also tends to elicit less shift than actual participation in that discussion (Bell and Jamieson, 1970; Lamm, 1967). Moscovici, Doise, and Dulong (1972) and Moscovici and Lecuyer (1972) have shown that instructions and seating patterns that interfere with the natural group interaction also reduce the group polarization effect.

It seems apparent that more group shift will occur when individuals are exposed to cognitive learning that favors one side or another in an argument. Furthermore, the shift in group opinion will be enhanced if group members are allowed to participate in the discussion.

Comment

In spite of the early misnaming of an important research area, shifts in group decisions after discussion do occur. That these shifts are not in the direction of greater risk is relatively unimportant. That they do occur is vitally important to social psychologists and most other people in the world. We have already discussed the potential effects on union negotiations, negotiations between countries, and so forth. There is another situation—one in which you may find yourself involved some day. The particular groups I refer to are juries and most of us will some day find ourselves involved either through participation as a juror, as a lawyer practicing before juries, or much less likely, as a plaintiff or defendant having important matters decided by this group.

Groups Making Decisions—Juries

During the 70s interest in the jury as a decision-making group grew enormously among social scientists. For example, I tracked down 83 articles, books, or papers dealing with the jury decision-making process. Seven of them were published prior to 1960, 10 in the 60s, and 66 in the first $7\frac{1}{2}$ years of the 70s. What brought about this burgeoning interest in juries? Answers to questions such as these are never simple, but I suspect one of the reasons is that the legal community was ready to listen to what social scientists had to say about juries.

For example, there has long been an interest concerning jury size among court officials. Traditionally, juries have had twelve members, but if six, eight or ten could do the job just as well, then that would represent a large savings in time, trouble, and money to a lot of people. There is a growing movement to reduce the size of juries, and some of the research done by social scientists has been cited by the Supreme Court of the United States (e.g., Williams *vs.* Florida, 1970) as one of the reasons for seeking reduction in jury size.

Most of the empirical research on juries has been done in the United States, but it is, nevertheless, applicable to Canadian juries. Both systems originated in English common law. The changes made in the system in Canada and the United States are strikingly similar, with two exceptions. Civil juries are used much less frequently in Canada than in the United States, although when used in Canada they tend to have six members; and lawyers do not have as much freedom in questioning prospective jurors in Canada as they do in the United States. Particularly in criminal cases, with which this section primarily deals, juries in the two countries are strikingly similar.

There are still other reasons for studying juries. They are naturally and frequently occurring groups that have a specific job and are instructed to come to a decision, in most cases a unanimous decision. The researcher knows what stimulus material all members of the group have been exposed to, and theoretically at least, they are only supposed to base their decision on that material. Since juries seem to be such excellent candidates for group study, why haven't they been studied extensively? There are several problems with studying juries.

First and foremost, jury deliberations are secret, and the only way a researcher can determine what went on during jury deliberations is to ask the jurors after the decision has been reached. However, courts in some jurisdictions prohibit jurors from discussing their deliberations. It is difficult to find all twelve jurors after they are dismissed and getting them all to discuss their deliberations is often impossible, even if the court does not threaten them with a penalty for doing so. Finally, even if jurors are willing and able to discuss their deliberations, their perceptions of what actually went on in the jury room may be distorted.

Even with all of the difficulties involved in studying jury decisions, it has become possible to do so. Let us look at the techniques that have been used to overcome some of the difficulties.

Studying Juries

A classic study was published in the 1960s that has guided much of jury research since the time (Kalven and Zeisel, 1966). Much of the book was concerned with agreement between juries' decisions and the presiding judge's opinions. However, in one of the later chapters of that book, Kalven and Zeisel reported interviews with members of more than 250 juries and came to the conclusion that in more than nine out of ten cases the jury verdict conforms to the initial majority. In fact, Kalven and Zeisel were so convinced of the evidence they presented that they made this comment:

The deliberation process might well be likened to what the developer does for an exposed film; it brings out the picture, but the outcome is pre-determined. On this view the deliberation process offers fascinating data on human behavior and should reward systematic study. The topic, however, is not so much how juries decide cases but how small groups produce consensus. From what we have been able to perceive thus far, the process is an interesting combination of rational persuasion, sheer social pressure, and the psychological mechanism by which individual perceptions undergo change when exposed to group discussion. [Kalven and Zeisel, 1966, p. 489.]

As we have mentioned, Kalven and Zeisel were not primarily interested in jury decisions or more specifically in the way juries reached their decisions. Even though they clearly stated that their ideas concerning the deliberative process were a radical hunch (Kalven and Zeisel, 1966, p. 489), neither they nor anyone else seems to have taken this cautionary note seriously. What has happened is that most jury studies have not had juries deliberate—if the outcome is a foregone conclusion, why do it? In most studies, the case has been presented and then individuals have been asked to indicate their opinion of guilt or innocence. From those individual indications an inference has been made that an equivalent percentage of juries would convict or acquit. For example, Jones and Aronson (1973) had 234 individuals serve as jurors and presented a written synopsis of a rape or attempted rape to them. After subjects had read the case each one was asked to recommend the number of years imprisonment the defendant should receive ranging from "less than one" to "more than forty." Furthermore, one third of the subjects were told the victim was married, another third were told she was a virgin, and the final third were told she was a divorcee.

The intent of the study was to determine whether the defendant would be more harshly punished if he actually committed a rape as contrasted to attempting to rape his victim and whether the status of the victim would affect the severity of the sentences meted out. Figure 11–2 shows the results. As can be seen from the figure, actual rape is punished more severely than attempted rape, and the rape of a married woman is dealt with more severely than if the woman is a virgin or divorced. With regard to attempted rape, it appears that the only significant difference occurs when the woman is a divorcee. Then the defendant's sentence is lighter. Presumably, subjects who thought the defendant was innocent could only check the "less than one year" sentence. All information in this study was presented to the "jury" by means of a written synopsis.

As you can readily see, the case presented by Jones and Aronson (and many others) depends heavily for its validity upon Kalven and Zeisel's radical hunch that deliberations don't alter the decisions of jury members. This whole idea is quite inconsistent with everything we have discussed in this chapter, except the group polarization effect. In essence, the notion of group polarization and jury deliberations bringing out the already exposed negative of majority opinion are quite compatible.

FLAWS IN THE RADICAL HUNCH

The whole notion of group polarization does not stand or fall on the basis of jury deliberations. However, it is quite possible that juries don't follow the group polarization model in spite of the seeming compatibility between Kalven and Zeisel's hunch and the model. Let us closely examine the data upon which Kalven and Zeisel based their hunch.

During the larger project upon which their book is based, Kalven and Zeisel examined the first ballot of 225 juries and found that "in instances where there is an

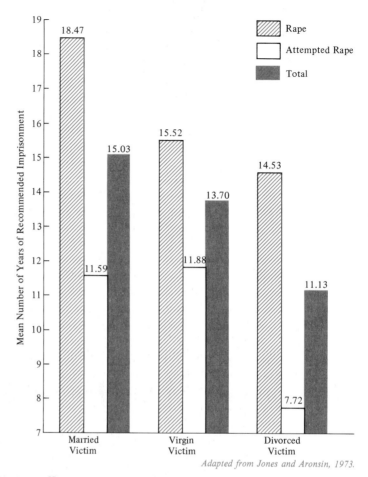

Adapted from Jones and Aronsin, 1973.

Figure 11-2 Mean number of years of imprisonment recommended for a man accused of rape or attempted rape of three different categories of victims.

initial majority either for conviction or for acquittal, the jury in roughly nine out of ten cases decides in the direction of the initial majority" (Kalven and Zeisel, 1966, p. 488).

Two glaring weaknesses are apparent in these data. First, the researchers had to interview jurors after they had finished deliberating. These sorts of retrospective data need to be treated with extreme caution for several reasons. First, jurors may actually forget what happened during the course of deliberations, particularly if those deliberations extended over a relatively long period of time. Second, jurors' perspectives of what they thought early in the deliberations may be highly colored by what occurred later in the deliberations. For example, a juror who actually felt the defendant was guilty early in the deliberations but later changed his or her opinion might forget the early opinion and assert that the opinion had remained unswervingly innocent since the beginning of the deliberations. Finally, some jurors may not wish to admit that they had been convinced to change their opinions during deliberations.

A second and far more damaging potential weakness in Kalven and Zeisel's data concerns the timing of the first ballot by each of the 225 juries. Remember, it was on the basis of the majority on this ballot that they could predict the juries' verdict in over 90 percent of the cases. However, juries decide when they will cast their first ballot, and they can do it as soon as they enter the jury room, after it is apparent that there is a consensus, or anywhere in between. Thus, none, some, or even all of the deliberations could have been concluded when the first ballot was taken. The later it was taken in the deliberations, the higher the correlation with the final verdicts—but unfortunately Kalven and Zeisel neglect to tell us how much deliberation had occurred when the first ballot was taken. Evidently they did not even collect data on when each jury first balloted.

Thus it seems premature on the basis of Kalven and Zeisel's data to assert that the deliberative phase of the juries' work is unimportant. It may be unimportant although, as I said earlier, if this is the case it contradicts virtually all of the research reported in this chapter. As you will recall, throughout this chapter we have seen that individuals in groups interacting with each other have enormous effect on group behavior. It would be ironic if, in this area where even our laws assume that jurors will influence each other, individuals actually have little or no effect on each other.

In fact, recent evidence which we have collected indicates that deliberations are vitally important. Over the last several years I have been interested in jury decisions and have concentrated on the value of the deliberative phase of juries. You may think it unusual that social scientists took Kalven and Zeisel's radical hunch at face value and proceeded to conduct research based on it, but when you consider the complications of conducting research on jury deliberations you may reconsider your judgment.

Assessing the Effect of Jury Deliberations

Even though there are hundreds of juries deliberating every day, these juries are open to social scientists only after they have finished their deliberations. In fairness to those being tried, the courts have been adamant in recent years in their refusal to allow scientific study of a deliberating jury. In many respects this may be a blessing in disguise, because it has forced researchers to devise new and more appropriate means of studying juries. One of these new research methodologies has been to videotape trials so that they may be repeated exactly. No two trials are exactly alike—even a retrial of the same case differs from the original trial. In staging mock trials we have found it virtually impossible to present the same trial twice even when we write a script for it! Our experience is that the lawyer who loses the case the first time will alter the case the second time to improve her or his chance of winning.

However, during the mid 1970s we experimented with videotaping trials and presenting this *exact replay* of a trial to a number of different juries. We found that juries that viewed the trial live did not differ in the verdicts they reached from those that viewed the videotapes. At about this time we became aware of the extensive researchers of Gerald Miller and his associates (Miller, 1974, 1975, 1977; Miller et al., 1975a, 1975b), who had already obtained strong evidence for the comparability of jury decisions when the trial was viewed live and on tape. This further convinced us that videotapes were a viable way to present an unchanging stimulus (the trial) to a number of different juries.

However, the same problem for which Kalven and Zeisel were earlier open to criticism still remained. To assess accurately the effects of deliberation on the jury, we needed to know what the members of the jury thought immediately after the trial and prior to the start of their deliberations. In Pennsylvania, where we were conducting our research, there is a law which allows the judge to instruct the jury to ballot immediately after the trial is finished but before they have started deliberating. We have utilized this law but have not announced the results of the ballot to the jury. Thus we know exactly what each member of the jury thinks about the guilt or innocence of the victim prior to deliberations.

Contrary to Kalven and Zeisel's radical hunch, we found that deliberations do have a decided effect on our juries (Lamberth, Kreiger, and Walbridge, 1975; Lamberth and Kirby, 1974; Lamberth and Krieger, 1976). One way of looking at the situation is to compare the figures Kalven and Zeisel give with our own. This is done in Table 11–1. As that table shows, Kalven and Zeisel's prediction scheme does not hold up very well when a predeliberation ballot is used.

Basically the story is the same for student jurors and actual jury pool members from the Court of Common Pleas of Philadelphia (see Table 11–1). Kalven and

Table 11–1 Predicted and obtained verdicts for twenty-one juries

Jury[a]	Predeliberation Ballot			Verdict	
	Guilty	Neutral	Not Guilty	Predicted[b]	Obtained
1	7	1	4	Guilty	*Hung
2	3	0	9	Not Guilty	Not Guilty
3	2	2	8	Not Guilty	Not Guilty
4	4	3	5	Not Predictable	Hung
5	5	1	6	Not Guilty	Not Guilty
6	3	1	8	Not Guilty	Not Guilty
7	8	0	4	Guilty	*Hung
8	6	1	5	Guilty or Hung	*Not Guilty
9	2	1	9	Not Guilty	Not Guilty
10	5	0	7	Not Guilty	Not Guilty
11	5	0	7	Not Guilty	*Hung
12	2	2	8	Not Guilty	*Hung
13	6	2	4	Guilty	Guilty
14	3	3	6	Not Guilty	*Hung
15	2	0	10	Not Guilty	Not Guilty
16	3	2	7	Not Guilty	Not Guilty
17	4	1	7	Not Guilty	*Hung
18	3	1	8	Not Guilty	Not Guilty
19	0	2	10	Not Guilty	Not Guilty
20	1	1	10	Not Guilty	*Hung
21	3	0	9	Not Guilty	Not Guilty

[a] Students were used as jurors for the first eleven juries whereas jury pool members from the Court of Common Pleas of Philadelphia made up the jurors for the other ten juries.
[b] Predictions are based on Kalven and Zeisel's prediction scheme.
* Indicates an incorrect prediction.

Trial before a jury of one's peers is a right guaranteed to anyone accused of a crime who resides in a country whose legal system is based on English Common Law. As we have seen in Chapter 6, and in this chapter, that theoretical guarantee is not always honored in practice. Women, blacks, and non-property owners are but three groups who have, at one time or another, been denied this right. These groups are identifiable and classifiable, and since it is obvious that they are being excluded from juries as a group, steps can be taken to remedy the situation. There are other, more subtle, ways that individuals can be denied a jury of their peers.

A peer is someone who is your equal in rank. A second definition is more explicit, "a person who is equal to another in abilities, qualifications, etc." (*Random House College Dictionary,* 1975). What does it mean to have peers on a jury? Should the jurors be the same age, race, sex, and so forth as the defendant? Courts have not interpreted a jury of peers in that way, but as research into jury decision making progresses, certain variables are clarified.

Authoritarianism characterizes a personality type typified by nine traits (see Chapter 6). Basically, authoritarians are closed-minded and conservative. They also tend to be older than equalitarians. As most individuals brought to trial are between the ages of 18 and 25, having older persons who are authoritarians may not result in a jury of peers. Is it possible, however, to categorize authoritarians as a group on the basis of their behavior as jurors?

Bray and Noble (1978) reported an experiment in which authoritarians tended to vote guilty more often than did equalitarians. Lamberth, Krieger, and Shay (1979) found that authoritarians were crucial in the decision-making process. In accordance with Bray and Noble, Lamberth et al. found that authoritarians, more than equalitarians, were likely to change their attitude toward the defendant's guilt during the course of deliberations. That is, authoritarians were more likely than others to change their view of the defendant's guilt when the majority of the other jurors disagreed with them. Surprisingly enough, when asked after the deliberations to name the jurors who had most influenced them, authoritarians who changed their view were most often influenced by other jurors who were equalitarian. In addition, several studies have found that authoritarians are more punitive when the jury they serve on is called on to assess punishment.

How are we to make sense out of all of this? Carefully read the description of authoritarians in Chapter 6. Note that the authoritarian is extremely concerned with being identified with the in-group. When a jury begins to solidify in its deliberations, the in-group is the majority. The majority pressures the minority to conform. (Recall from Chapter 7 that authoritarianism was a personality characteristic associated with obedience in Elms and Milgram's work.) Thus, the authoritarian is more likely than others to support the in-group and change his or her attitude to conform with theirs. It should be noted that the authoritarian does not typically just change his or her vote to conform, but when asked later is convinced of the accuracy of the new position.

I should emphasize that neither I, nor anyone else that I know of, is advocating exclusion of authoritarians from juries. There are, however, certain aspects of authoritarians' behavior that lead one to entertain the idea that some authoritarians may not be deciding the case solely on the basis of the evidence presented. Even though this is the ideal of the jury system, there is evidence to suggest that few, if any, jurors decide cases solely on the basis of the evidence presented.

References

Bray, R. M., and A. M. Noble. Authoritarianism and decisions of mock juries: Evidence of jury bias and group polarization. *Journal of Personality and Social Psychology,* 1978, *36,* 1424–30.

Lamberth, J., E. Krieger, and S. Shay. Juror decision making: A case of attitude change mediated by authoritarianism. Unpublished manuscript, Temple Univ., 1979.

Zeisel's predictions are wrong approximately 38 percent of the time! Far from being able to accurately predict the final verdict from the first ballot in roughly nine out of ten cases, our data indicate that in only six out of ten cases can the initial ballot predict the final verdict with great accuracy.

There are several possibile reasons for this discrepancy. It is possible that the juries we have selected are unique and that further study with other juries will alter the proportion of incorrect predictions. Yet the fact that two distinctly different populations of jurors was sampled (students and jury pool members) weakens such an argument. At the moment, it seems that either the retrospective nature of Kalven and Zeisel's data or the difference in when the first ballot was taken is a much more likely candidate for explaining the difference between these two positions.

Many other researchers have decried the lack of realism in jury research done by social scientists. For example, Davis, Bray, and Holt (1977) have pointed out several deficiencies in research into jury decisions including unrealistic modes of presenting the trial, the population from which jurors are drawn, and the fact that most researchers do not allow a deliberative phase. The results of the research into jury size (six versus twelve) has been mixed, with Bermant and Coppock (1973) and the Institute of Judicial Administration (1972) finding no differences in the decisions of six- and twelve-person juries, whereas Mills (1973) found substantial differences. Zeisel and Diamond (1974) incisively critiqued all three studies on the basis of nonrandom sampling of cases. It seems that in two of the studies, counsel had a choice between 6- and 12-person juries and chose twelve-person juries for their larger, more complex cases.

Comment

Our explorations into group decision making, jury style, must seem primitive or at least chaotic. They are! This is the state of affairs, because we are seeing the emergence of a new research area and until researchers come to some decisions among themselves about how to go about conducting the research, it always seems chaotic. It's like watching a family on their first camping vacation unload and begin to set up camp. At first chaos reigns. With some agreement about how to do things, who will do what, and so forth, the family can, after some practice, pitch camp in a short time.

Except for the fact that the amount of time it takes to iron out the wrinkles is measured in years rather than days, starting research in a new area is quite comparable. At the moment, people are arguing about who should do what and whether most of the work that has already gone on was needed or is even very useful. The problems in jury research are compounded by the fact that there are two disciplines (law and social science) involved and that each has its own way of going about doing things.

There is, however, an air of excitement about research in a new area. Ten or twenty years from now people will probably look back and comment on the primitive methods and techniques being used today, but right now it's fun and exciting. And, after all, that's rather important itself.

Group Characteristics

The 8:02 A.M. is a very crowded commuter train between Paoli and Philadelphia. Every morning, beginning a few minutes before departure time, approximately three hundred individuals, mostly men, gather to wait for the train. Careful observation shows that (1) most of the passengers wait in a specific spot next to the track (depending upon which car they wish to board); (2) each individual rides in the same car in approximately the same seat every day; (3) there is little conversation among the riders; and (4) each passenger leaves his car from the same exit each day. It takes this train 27 minutes to reach Philadelphia, and so this group of people spend about $2\frac{1}{2}$ hours a week together.

Various patterns of behavior emerge to the careful observer. Most people on the train read the *Philadelphia Inquirer,* whereas a lesser, but still substantial, number read the *New York Times* and the *Wall Street Journal.* A few work, a few sleep, but only those people who seem to know each other in a different context (e.g., at work, from some social gathering, and so forth) converse. When the train reaches its destination, even though the aisles may be crowded with people moving toward an exit, if a person stands in front of his seat, he is almost immediately allowed into the line moving toward the exit. This aspect of the behavior of passengers is quite noticeable and differs from the behavior of most people in a line. Think about lines at the supermarket check-out stands, to get tickets (even tickets for the 8:02) or virtually any other type of line—people normally do not allow, let alone invite, others to cut into the line in front of them. Quite the contrary, people become quite angry when someone cuts in line.

The description I've given of the riders of the 8:02 is intended to get you ready for a very important question—"Do the riders of the 8:02 constitute a group?" According to the dictionary they do, because the definition of group given there is "any assemblage of persons or things; cluster; aggregation," and certainly the riders of the 8:02 are an assemblage of persons.

The 8:02 preparing to leave Paoli station.

Social psychologists, however, have been somewhat more specific about the elements that constitute a group. Let's look at psychological definitions of groups and see if the riders of the 8:02 form a group.

Psychological Definitions of Groups

There is no definitive boundary between a cluster of people and a group from a psychological point of view, nor is there a clear-cut distinction between small groups and large groups. There is a good deal of agreement that for a collection of individuals to be considered a group, there must be interaction among the individuals, but this interaction can take several froms. Four features of group life typically emerge as a collection of individuals becomes a group (Znaniecki, 1939; Sherif, 1954). These are (1) the members of the group share motives and goals that point the direction in which the group will move; (2) norms set by the members of the group set boundaries within which relationships may be established and activities carried on; (3) roles become established with continuing interaction; and (4) a network of likes and dislikes develops among group members.

Small groups may vary in size and probably the most common definition of a small group is the one given by Bales (1950, p. 33):

A small group is defined as any number of persons engaged in interaction with each other in a single face-to-face meeting or a series of meetings, in which each member receives some impression or perception of each other member distinct enough so that he can, either at the time or in later questioning, give some reaction to each of the others as an individual person, even though it be only to recall that the other person was present.

Homans (1950, p.1) has this to say about groups:

We mean by a group a number of persons who communicate with one another over a span of time, and who are few enough so that each person is able to communicate with all the others, not at secondhand, through other people, but face-to-face.

Even though these definitions were written in the same year and sound quite different, they are amazingly similar. They agree that the group must be small enough to permit face-to-face interaction and communication, and they both imply some goal, either ongoing or one that can be reached in one meeting. This type of group has been referred to as a *primary* group (Cooley, 1909).

Typically, groups have been analyzed from three different perspectives: process, structure, and change. When the focus is on group *process,* our interest is in the act-by-act sequence of events as it unfolds over time. This longitudinal approach to the study of groups has emphasized categories of behavior within the group. The *structure* of a group is constantly changing and thus to focus on it means that a cross-sectional approach is used. That is, at some chosen time the group leadership, interactions, norms, and so forth are analyzed. It is understood that the same group

may reflect different patterns of leadership, interaction, and norms at a different time. The analysis of *social change* focuses on these changes in the structure of the group.

For purposes of explaining group behavior and studying it, we could start with any of the three perspectives. However, it seems easier to understand how a group functions at a given time prior to studying how the group changes and how an act-by-act sequence unfolds over time. So we will view groups first from the structure perspective, then from the perspective of change, and finally we will discuss group process.

Group Structure

Groups come together for diverse purposes and in diverse ways. Some are formed by orders from a superior and some occur seemingly spontaneously because there is a common goal that a group desires. Some groups that come together under orders are work groups, military units, juries, and so forth. Groups that band together because of individual needs are volunteer groups such as service clubs, churches, charitable organizations, street gangs, and the like. Even though these groups may form in quite different ways, one of the elements that almost invariably emerges in a group is a leader. A leader may be appointed by a higher authority as in a military unit, or be elected as in a jury, or emerge by consensus or by displaying leadership characteristics, as in a street gang.

A second element of group structure is the roles members of the group play in the functioning of the group. As groups grow in size and complexity, individuals tend to specialize in some aspect of the functioning of the group. Actually, leadership may be no more than a specific role in the group, albeit an important one. But as specialized aspects of behavior occur in a group, the expectations for behavior in these specialties are represented by the roles that members of the group take on. As roles develop, it is possible that an informal structure may lead to conflicting role expectations. Furthermore, the structure of the group is greatly influenced by who likes or dislikes whom. The liking and disliking occurs primarily because the more popular people in a group tend to occupy roles that they wish to occupy.

Leadership

Although most groups have a single leader, leadership is sometimes divided among more than one individual. When this occurs the division is often made by having a *task* leader and a *socioemotional* leader. A task leader is primarily concerned with performance of the task at hand, whereas the socioemotional leader (who is usually the best-liked person) is often concerned with affectional relationships and member satisfaction (Hare, 1976).

LEADERSHIP TRAITS

Leadership research, dating from the 1920s, indicates that leaders typically have higher ratings on "good" traits that all members of the group are supposed to have. For example, good leaders are expected to be more enthusiastic, intelligent, dominant, self-confident, and equalitarian than group members—but group members are expected to exhibit these characteristics also (Goodenough, 1930; Gibb, 1947; Borgatta, 1954; Cattell and Stice, 1954; Kipnis and Lane, 1962; Harrison, Rawls, and Rawls, 1971; Mitchell, 1971; Vertreace and Simmons, 1971; Smith and Cook, 1973; Sorrentino, 1973; Zigon and Cannon, 1974). The specific traits that may be valued in

This group obviously has a leader, but who is he? You would have to know whether this was a social group or a work group before you could answer the question.

a leader can and do vary with the characteristics of the group. For example, a group of conservatives would not value liberalism in their leader. It is necessary to understand the traits that are important to the group in determining which traits the group's leader will exhibit.

Even though a group leader tends to have more of all positive attributes than any other members of the group, these traits cannot be so extreme that the potential leader is considered a deviate. For example, a B student is often the leader on college campuses rather than the "straight-A grind," who also may be referred to as the "curve-wrecker" (Davie and Hare, 1956). The person who does most of the talking wins most of the decisions and becomes the leader of the group (e.g., Levin, 1973; Regula and Julian, 1973; Stang, 1973) unless the individual talks so much that other members of the group are antagonized.

A self-oriented leader is a rather hostile person who needs to be the center of group activity. Group-oriented leaders, on the other hand, are able to reduce group tensions, work toward a goal, and even take a follower's role when that is appropriate (Anderson, 1939; Hare, 1957). Leaders who emerge in leaderless groups tend to be more self-oriented than leaders who are appointed to head the group. This probably occurs because it takes more dominating behavior to become a leader than it does to maintain a leadership role once it is established. In laboratory groups, leaders who are elected tend to gain more acceptance than do leaders who take over (Raven and French, 1958; Blake and Mouton, 1961; Read, 1974). This, of course, is understandable in that group members have had a role in the selection of the elected leaders.

LEADERSHIP FUNCTIONS

The major function of a group leader has been referred to as that of "completer" by Schutz (1961). By this Schutz means that the leader must have the necessary skills, emotional involvement, social ability, and concern for the goals of the group to keep it functioning. Have you ever belonged to a group in which the leader was unable or unwilling to be a completer? In such instances the group either ceases to function or another leader emerges.

An extensive questionnaire was formulated by Hemphill (1949) to study leadership qualities. Respondents were asked to give a description of the different groups to which they belonged and also to report observations of the leader's behavior. Five functions were identified that were characteristic of leaders of all groups. First, the leader was to advance the purpose of the group, and second, to administrate. Next, the leader was expected to inspire greater activity or to set the standards for the group. Fourth, the leader was supposed to make individual members feel secure in the group, and finally to act without regard to his or her's own self-interest. A number of studies since have identified some or all of the leadership functions enumerated by Hemphill.

In the military, the individual's rank determines both the leadership expectations an individual has of himself and those others have of him. For example, in the air corps ratings by superior officers of airplane commanders were negatively correlated with the officer's "consideration" score, which was based on his friendship and mutual trust with crew members. That is, commanders who received high ratings from their superior officers received lower consideration ratings from their men. Many military organizations stress an organization that maintains a certain social distance between leaders and followers. The rationale for this is that commanders may be called upon to make decisions that very likely will result in injury or death to their men. Thus, the organizational structure is hindered when emotional bonds develop that would alter command decisions necessary to the proper functioning of the group (Fiedler, 1957).

POWER

Leaders have more power and influence than group members. Generally speaking, the person who has power in a group is imitated, more often approached by others, and is liked by his or her associates. Research has shown that the power and influence of an individual will increase if that person is put in a position of leadership in a group (Maier & Solem, 1952). Conversely, an individual will attempt to exert more influence when put in a position of leadership (Gerard, 1957; Kipnis, 1972). And the more an individual attempts to influence other people, the more successful he or she will be at influencing them.

There is, then, a certain circularity to power and leadership, just as there is a certain circularity to wealth and making money. There is more than a small amount of truth in the old saying, "The rich get richer and the poor get poorer." By the same token, people expect a leader to be powerful. The leader expects the leader to be powerful and tries to influence others. The more other people and the leader expect the leader to be powerful and the more the leader attempts to influence others and is successful, the more powerful the leader becomes.

Leadership on the 8:02

We began our discussion of groups with a description of the 8:02 from Paoli to Philadelphia. We will return to it as we proceed through our analysis of groups. Whereas we have discussed the role of leadership in groups, the definitions of small groups we reviewed earlier do not demand that a group have a leader to be classified as a group. Obviously, the 8:02 does not have a leader or even several individuals who take on different leadership roles. It may be argued that the reason for this is the members of the 8:02 club have no goal—but they do. Their goal is to arrive in Philadelphia fairly early each morning so that they can go to work, class, or some other activity. The fact that they have no leader or leaders does not necessarily exclude these three hundred people from the group category.

Roles

As groups tend to grow in size and complexity, the individuals who are members of the group tend to specialize. The specialization may be in elements of the task of the group or in socioemotional aspects of group interaction. As roles in the group emerge, these specialities add an element of structure to the group. Obviously, this is less important in a group that is formally organized (such as a plane crew or infantry platoon) and takes on much more importance in informal groups that develop.

But what is a role? Basically there are two ways a role can be viewed. Some authors (Newcomb, 1950; Sarbin, 1954) use the term *role* to mean the behavior that

From which of these would you expect a leader to come, the mansion or the ghetto?

an individual directs toward fulfilling expectations. However, many more researchers (Bates, 1956; Levinson, 1959; Southall, 1959; Hare, 1976) use *role* to refer to the set of expectations shared by group members concerning the behavior exhibited by a person who occupies a given position in the group. We will use *role* in this latter sense. Thus, certain people find themselves in the role of leader or member, or in a most interesting role that we shall discuss in a moment, that of the joker. Since the role of the leader has already been discussed, we will turn now to the other two roles.

THE MEMBER

Membership in a group carries with it certain rights and obligations. One particularly telling piece of evidence of this is that group members become very upset when there is a silent member. Silent members will cause dissatisfaction among other group members, although this dissatisfaction will be reduced if it is made clear at the outset that certain members will not participate at all (Smith, 1957). But if the silence appears to be indifference and neglect, the group will be very concerned (Rosenthal and Cofer, 1948). The reason for this is rather obvious—if very many members do not function, the group is ineffective.

A good deal of attention has been given to the newcomer in a group. The newcomer will have an easier time of it if any or all of the following occur: (1) group members are expecting change (Ziller, Behringer, and Jansen, 1961); (2) the new member is not too different from other group members (Ziller, Behringer, and Goodchilds, 1960); and (3) group members have already had a pleasant time together (Heiss, 1963). All of this should not be too surprising to you if you recall your own experience in groups. A new member poses a certain threat to the group while also offering certain benefits. Few groups retain a highly stable membership for very long. People's interests change, they move to other parts of the city or to other cities, and so forth, they die. Thus any group must eventually have new members to keep going, but new members bring unknown consequences.

THE JOKER

Another role that has been identified in some groups is that of the clown or joker. Actually, this role has a long history in groups and a very special task. True, the joker is supposed to be witty, but the task is more difficult than just being witty. The joker ideally presents ideas and insights from a slightly different point of view under the cover of humor. According to Hare (1976) the joker must be able to grasp the tragic nature of life before he or she can grasp its comic side. Having achieved this, and using humor as a tool, the joker is ideally equipped to provide special insights and help to the group.

Cloyd (1964) found that the following characteristics were identified as composing the joker's role: humorous, liberal, challenges others opinions, gets off the subject, egotistical and cynical. Evidently there are certain functions which can be handled under the guise of humor that would be unacceptable if handled in other ways. Generally speaking, members of groups that have a joker like the group better than those who do not have one (Goodchilds and Smith, 1964). Thus the role of joker is a very important one for successful functioning of the group, because certain activities such as disagreeing, presenting new and different ideas, and so forth are more palatable to the other members when they are served with a touch of humor.

483

Group Structure

Roles on the 8:02

Probably the clearest distinction between a group as it has traditionally been viewed by psychologists and a collection of individuals is that the collection of individuals has no structure. For example, except for the employees of the railroad, everyone on the train plays the same role. There are no leaders, jokers, or other sorts of specialized group members. Each member of the group is just that, a member. After they have paid their money for a ticket they really do not perform any functions for the group. Thus, the riders of the 8:02 are not really a group but rather a collection of individuals.

However, if you reread the definitions of small groups given early in this chapter, you will note that those do not clearly specify a group structure that would exclude the riders of the 8:02 from the category of a group. Thus, we need to add to those definitions the concept of structure and consequently certain roles that individuals play in the group. Riders on the train have activities that they engage in, such as working, reading the paper or talking, but these are for their own ends and do not benefit the other riders. So the riders of the 8:02 really are engaging in elementary collective behavior, not group behavior. That is, the activities carried on on the 8:02 could just as well be done anywhere else and the only person(s) it would affect would be the individual(s) involved.

Interpersonal Choice

Individuals within a group indicate their interpersonal choices toward other members of the group in a variety of ways. One of the simplest is by frequency of association. Another expression of interpersonal choice is through elections and still another is through expressing views toward other people.

The expression of interpersonal choice in most instances has a large measure of interpersonal attraction involved. This is especially true of social groups, but less true of certain aspects of other types of groups. For example, if the goal of the group is to do battle successfully with an enemy, the most liked person would not necessarily be selected as the leader. It is highly possible that the most disliked person would be selected, or someone who fell in between, because battle skills would be the primary basis for choice.

Even in this extreme an instance, however, liking or disliking for a person might well play a part—because people have difficulty electing someone whom they dislike. Thus, military organizations do not allow leaders to be elected. In government, politicians are often elected because they are liked more or the opponent is disliked more, not because of their abilities to lead. In one major city in the United States a mayor was reelected after accusing one of his enemies of lying, agreeing to a lie detector test that cleared his enemy and indicated he, the mayor, was lying. Many people agreed that the mayor's other achievements had not been so outstanding nor so meaningful to the city as to warrant his reelection. Rather, he was liked by a majority of the voters. Small wonder that the military does not entrust the serious business of national defense to elected leaders.

THE SOCIOGRAM

The major tool used to study interpersonal choice in groups has been sociometric ratings. *Sociometric* generally means the interpersonal choices that group members have revealed to an observer or experimenter. Sociometry was introduced by Moreno (1953). Sociometric ratings are often expressed in a sociogram. Assume a group of six children in nursery school whose names are Lisa, Jeanie, Laura, Timmy, Doug, and Steven. Each child is told that the group is going to go on a field trip and asked which of the other children he or she would like to have go on the trip. The results would look something like Table 11–2. A sociogram, which is merely a pictorial representation of each child's choices, can then be drawn. Figure 11–3 is a sociogram of the choices made by our six nursery school children.

Basically, the sociogram is a very useful instrument in determining group attraction or likes and dislikes for other characteristics of a group. By changing the wording of the question asked, the sociogram can reflect group leadership choices, work choices, and so on. Therefore the sociogram can be seen as an expansion of individual measuring devices to encompass the whole group. For example, the Interpersonal Judgment Scale (see Chapter 9) used in much research on interpersonal attraction would be extremely cumbersome to use with a group—each individual would have to fill out a scale for every other group member. The sociogram simplifies the task of determining group choices.

Comment

Group structure, you will remember, is only the first perspective in our understanding of groups, although an essential one. We have taken a short look at a cross section of groups—how they function at any one time by emphasizing group leadership, roles, and interpersonal choice. The picture we get from each study is necessarily distorted because groups are constantly changing. New individuals enter the group, existing members assume new roles, tasks and goals change, and time changes the members.

Table 11–2 Hypothetical choices of six children to include on a field trip

Child	Choices
Lisa	Jeanie, Timmy, Doug
Jeanie	Lisa, Laura, Timmy, Doug, Steven
Laura	Lisa, Jeanie, Timmy, Doug
Timmy	Lisa, Doug, Steven
Doug	Lisa, Jeanie, Timmy
Steven	Lisa, Timmy, Doug

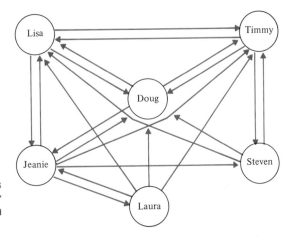

Figure 11–3 Sociogram of choices made by nursery school children for children to accompany them on a field trip.

Group Change

How do groups alter their goals, their membership, their roles, and so forth? Actually, prior to understanding how groups alter these functions, we need to understand what methods groups use to establish them. Typically, the functions we are referring to are called norms, and their development is a process of social control or social influence. In Chapter 7 we discussed social influence with emphasis upon compliance, conformity, and obedience. Our discussion of group change will re-emphasize much of the material covered in Chapter 7.

Group Norms

Group members tend to form group norms and then conform to them. Norms are rules of behavior that have been accepted as legitimate by members of a group. They

This is a group of children who might develop a sociogram such as the one discussed in the text.

specify the kinds of behavior that are expected of group members and they are derived for the most part from the goals that the group has set for itself. When a set of goals is given, norms define the kind of behavior that is consistent with or necessary for the realization of those goals (Bates and Cloyd, 1956). When the norms refer to the expectations for a single individual they define that individual's role.

The Development of Norms

Each person who joins in the formation of a group has a certain set of expectations about the goals of the group and how it is going to reach those goals. These expectations join with the expectations of other group members as the group begins to form. Much of the task of a group early in its development has to do with rules about what is and what is not appropriate behavior. A group must come to some decision about norms and goals, about *means* and *ends,* before it can proceed to complete its task. After groups do this—and they do if they are successful—then individuals who do not agree with the norms have four choices. They can conform, change the norms, remain as deviates, or leave the group.

Conforming

The research on conforming to group norms that is typically cited in monographs about small groups (for example, see Hare, 1976) is that of Sherif on the autokinetic phenomenon, Asch's and Crutchfield's studies of conformity, and Milgram's study of obedience, among others. However, the major research on conformity has already been discussed in Chapter 7, including the work of Sherif, Asch, Crutchfield, and Milgram. We need not repeat or even recapitulate that information, but you need to reread it to understand the enormous pressures that can be brought to bear on an individual by a group and the effects such pressure has on conformity.

You recall that Asch and Crutchfield utilized unanimous groups opposing an individual and that the power of the group is great. It is this power that is brought to bear to enforce norms. However, also recall that Milgram in his studies of obedience found that groups had a liberating effect—that is when other members of a group chose not to obey, it assisted the individual in resisting orders to obey. Thus, the group seemingly can function in two ways—to force conformity or to liberate an individual from the need to obey—but these two functions serve the same purpose, to do what the group wants.

Changing Group Norms

As group norms were formed through group interaction, they can be changed in the same way (Lippett, Watson, and Westley, 1958). The most effective way to change group opinion is through group discussion rather than through lectures or directives. During World War II, Kurt Lewin and his colleagues found that group discussion was the most effective way to get housewives to change to low-priority food (e.g., Lewin, 1943, 1947, 1951). Since that time a number of researchers have reported changes in a variety of behaviors, the most recent examples being changes in personality patterns (e.g., Foulds, 1972; Leith and Uhlemann, 1972; Nobler, 1972). These more recent studies have resulted from the joining together of social and clinical psychology to work in group therapy.

When different types of discussion groups are compared, the most effective in changing opinions are those in which the opportunities for discussion are maximized. Usually the amount of discussion is controlled by a democratic leader who urges all members to take part (Preston and Heintz, 1949; Maier and Solem, 1952; Hare, 1953). If the discussion leader is the "natural" leader of the group, there will be more opinion change than if the leader is placed in the group only for this purpose (Torrance and Mason, 1956).

Apparently, the important element that occurs during discussion of a change in norms is the opportunity to break down the old value system before adopting a new one (Alpert and Smith, 1949). This is not just an intellectual process but an emotional one as well. Therefore time needs to be allowed for group members to adjust to the new set of norms, and discussion seems to serve that purpose. Interestingly enough, the greatest resistance to change in group norms occurs just prior to yielding to the new norms (Redl, 1948). It is almost as if one last effort is made to retain the old norms and then the new norms are accepted.

An intensified version of the process of breaking down old values and replacing them with new ones was developed for use with prisoners of war during the Korean War (Lifton, 1956, 1961; Schein, 1956, 1960; Schein, Schneier, and Barker, 1961). The Chinese were extremely effective in breaking down American prisoners, and during the Viet Nam War the North Vietnamese continued that success. In November of 1977, President Carter signed a bill that took these successes into account and changed the requirements of a prisoner of war. Realizing that the techniques of opinion change had been greatly improved over the years, the new code of conduct no longer requires that a prisoner give only his name, rank, and serial number.

When groups have established norms, it is possible, although somewhat cumbersome to get them to change these norms. There are still times, however, when the group refuses to change its norms, or an individual changes his or her norms faster than the group does. One of the most striking large-scale clashes between individual and group norms occurred in the United States during the Viet Nam War. In the early 1960s when the United States sent in advisers to the South Vietnamese Army, few United States citizens knew or cared about it. As these advisers grew in number and the aid became an all-out war effort, there were initially but a few who objected. By the time the war ended, there were an enormous number of United States citizens who opposed the war. To be sure, by the end of the war, it was not a deviate position to oppose the war, but in the mid- to late 1960s it was. The entire history of that conflict has not yet been written, but many know first-hand the intensity of feeling that can be generated when group norms change.

Remaining a Deviate in the Group

We have discussed the pressures brought to bear on an individual by a group to conform—particularly when that group is unanimous (see Chapter 7). Typically, rather than having unanimous groups in real life, there may be a large group aligned against the deviates. Outside of laboratory work, rarely is a deviate faced with unanimous opposition. Nevertheless, the role of a deviate in a group is a difficult one.

Deviates typically perceive their opinions as being closer to those of the group than they actually are (Travers, 1941; Gorden, 1952), and may not be aware of the extent of their deviancy (Newcomb, 1943; Festinger, Schacter, and Back, 1950). This means that the deviate is not under as much pressure to conform as the group would like, because he or she is unaware of the extent of the deviateness. The group, on the other hand, must reexamine its concept of reality (Festinger 1954) if it is to tolerate a deviant member. To avoid doing this, the group will pressure the deviate to conform. The group's success in obtaining conformity from the deviate is a function of how specific the group's limits are, the penalties for deviation, and how important group membership is to the deviate. Punishment for deviance is greatest when the group is of primary importance to the individuals involved. For example, if the group is a group of workers and the deviance of the member is "rate-busting," the punishment can be severe indeed.

When the group first discovers that an individual is a deviate, interaction wih the individual increases. However, it falls off if the deviate begins to conform or if the group comes to the conclusion that the individual is a lost cause (Festinger and Thibaut, 1951; Berkowitz and Howard, 1959; Allen, 1965). The rejection of a deviate seems to be almost a universal phenomenon (Schachter et al., 1954; Israel, 1956). In some cases, however, the persistent deviate can win over other members of the group. There is experimental evidence for the part played by Henry Fonda in the movie, *Twelve Angry Men* in which one juror successfully opposed the majority and influenced the other eleven jurors to side with him in their verdict. If the deviate eventually conforms, more support is given to him or her (Levine, Saxe, and Harris, 1973).

Small groups will reject deviant members if the group can survive more effectively without them. Sometimes, however, a deviant member has skills that are needed for the survival or success of the group. When this occurs, group members may change their norms to conform to the deviance of the member. For example, if a small group is playing basketball, the owner of the only ball may be allowed to violate group norms or to make new ones. The alternative for other group members is to destroy the group by having no ball with which to play. Basically, in addition to the skills or things that the deviant member possesses, the deviant member's status and the strength of the group's expectations for conformity will influence reactions to the deviant (Zeisel, 1963; Wahrman, 1970; Frank and Wolman, 1973).

Comment

Group change is relatively difficult. A deviate member must possess powers of persuasion or other enticements that are powerful enough to sway the rest of the group. In many cases, changing group norms proves to be an impossible task and members leave the group. There is not a great deal of research into deviate members leaving a group. One reason for this is that much laboratory research deals with only a very small number of group meetings. Defections from groups in real life occur for many reasons other than the deviance of the member. For example, the aims of the group may not be what the member had first perceived, the individual's interests may change, or any number of other events may cause a group member to "drop out." Thus defections from groups is not well understood.

Group Process

Group process refers to the interaction among members of a group that occurs as the group continues to meet and work toward its goals. Research on group interaction first necessitates some sort of classification system. Bales (1950) developed the most popular classification scheme and we will briefly describe it. The problem in doing research on group interaction is that there must be some agreement as to how a conversation or statement, an action, or any other behavior is classified. Bales's twelve categories are shown in Table 11-3. Categories 1-3 and 10-12 are *social*-emotional, with the first three being positive and the other three being negative. There are six *task* behavior categories, with 4-6 being problem solving attempts and 7-9 being questions. Different groups utilize different proportions of behavior described by each category, so there is no way of saying that a group should display so much of a behavior described by one particular category to be a well-functioning group. The classification scheme is merely meant to describe group behavior in a coherent way.

Table 11-3 Bale's twelve categories for categorizing group behavior

Category Name	Examples
1. Shows Solidarity	Jokes, raises others' status, gives help, rewards.
2. Shows Tension Release	Laughs, shows satisfaction.
3. Shows Agreement	Passively accepts, understands, concurs, complies.
4. Gives Suggestion	Directs, implying autonomy for others.
5. Gives Opinion	Evaluates, analyzes, expresses feeling, wishes.
6. Gives Information	Provides orientation, repeats, clarifies, confirms.
7. Asks for Information	Seeks orientation, repetition, confirmation.
8. Asks for Opinion	Seeks evaluation, analysis, expression of feeling.
9. Asks for Suggestion	Seeks direction, possible ways of action.
10. Shows Disagreement	Passively rejects, behaves formally, withholds help.
11. Shows Tension	Asks for help, withdraws "out of field."
12. Shows Antagonism	Deflates others' status, defends or asserts self.

In long-standing groups, the social class or personality of the members, the style of leadership, or other factors may produce characteristic differences between groups in their patterns of talk and social-emotional activity. Morris (1966) reports that 60 percent of the distribution of group activity is determined by the type of task the group faces. That is, a production group and a discussion group may well differ in group activity, but the majority of the difference is accounted for by the difference in their tasks.

Group Size

Another variable that influences group process is group size. Among college students, as group size increases, duration, frequency, and intimacy of contact decrease (Fischer, 1953). Typically, the larger the group, the less satisfying the group experiences (Gerard and Hoyt, 1974; Lundgren and Bogart, 1974). Why should this be so? There are several reasons to expect social-emotional group experiences to be less satisfying as group size increases.

First, as more people become group members it is more difficult to maintain face-to-face contact with each one of them. For example, as the group increases in size each member has less time available to communicate. Second, the total amount of discussion decreases as a group becomes quite large. Evidently there is some sort of inhibition against speaking to a fairly large group.

Not only does the total amount of participation, and the amount of participation per member, decrease as group size increases, but the distribution of participation also varies (Bales et al., 1951; Reynolds, 1971). In groups of three to eight, all members generally address some remarks to the group as a whole but typically only the top participator addresses more to the group as a whole than to specific other members. As group size increases, group members participate less frequently, whereas the most vocal participator (often the leader) addresses the group more. Thus, instead of each member participating in fairly equal amounts, as a group gets larger, the leader more and more dominates the participation.

Another and possibly more relevant way to view group size is to consider the number of relationships possible as group size increases. Individual relations, that is relationships that are one-to-one, increase much more rapidly than does group membership. For example, in a three-member group, there are three possible individual relationships, whereas in a six-member group this number increases to fifteen. But, as you are well aware, individual relationships are not the only type of relationships possible in a group. There are relationships between individuals and subgroups, subgroups and other subgroups, and so on. These relationships give a clearer picture of the increasing complexity of possible relationships as group size increases. Figure 11–4 shows the increase in the number of relationships possible as group size is increased. As you can see, adding one person to a five-person group adds 211 possible relationships, and adding one more person to that group increases the number of possible relationships by 665.

It would appear that groups wouldn't get much larger than five or six people if we merely considered the number of possible relationships. However, many groups cannot carry out their tasks with five or six people. For example, juries typically must

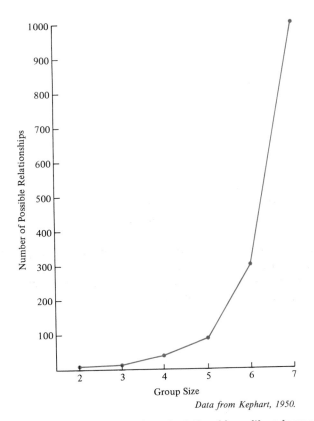

Figure 11–4 Increase in potential number of relationships with an increase in group size.

have twelve persons, undergraduate classes in many universities must have a minimum of ten students, and certain types of work crews must have more than five or six people to get the job done. In groups that become very large, a leader emerges. The emergence of a leader allows for the reduction in psychological complication of group size to a series of pair relationships with the leader coordinating them (Hare, 1976).

Comment

Groups are an interesting and commonplace phenomenon. All of you probably belong to at least several groups: the class you are in, the family to which you belong, a social group of one sort or another. In the past you have probably belonged to innumerable groups. Some groups, such as the family, tend to last for an extended period of time, whereas the lifespan of other groups can be counted in hours. Groups differ from a collection of individuals. By now, it should be evident that the riders on the 8:02 are a collection of individuals, not a group. The makeup of groups—their structure, process and norms—clearly informs us that the riders of the 8:02 are not a group. They could, however, become a group. For example, if the fares on the train were raised dramatically, a few simple changes might result in a most effective group.

SUMMARY

1 Social facilitation is the process by which performance is influenced by the presence of others. Zajonc has proposed a theory of social facilitation that emphasizes competing responses. It seems that many species perform tasks with dominant responses better, and tasks that do not utilize dominant responses worse, when others are present.

2 Deindividuation is the process by which social conditions lead to changes in perception of self and of others and thereby to a lowered threshold of normally restrained behavior. Conditions that lead to deindividuated behavior are anonymity, lessened responsibility, group presence, altered temporal perspective, and arousal. Deindividuated behavior, once started, is difficult to terminate because it has a self-reinforcing aspect.

3 Group decisions are sometimes more risky and sometimes more conservative than individual decisions. Evidence seems to indicate that group decisions are more polarized than individual ones; that it, groups shift to a more extreme position in the direction the individuals in the group already favor. Group decisions about attitudes, ethical decisions, person perception, and negotiating seem to show this polarization.

4 One theory of group polarization is the *informational influences theory,* which asserts that cognitive learning occurs during exposure of the minority to the majority viewpoint during discussion. There will generally be more majority than minority arguments and thus the group will polarize in the direction initially favored by the majority.

5 The jury is an ideal vehicle for studying group decision making because it is a naturally occurring phenomenon, charged with reaching a decision, and it is possible to determine where each individual stood prior to the beginning of deliberations. Research into the jury decision-making process, although in its infancy, has indicated that deliberations are vitally important.

6 Group structure often includes a leader, the roles members play, and the interpersonal choices shown by group members for each other. Good leaders have an excess of the characteristics valued in group members and they have more power and influence than other group members. The sociogram is a tool used to study and to depict graphically interpersonal choice in groups.

7 Group norms are rules of behavior that have been accepted as legitimate by members of a group and are formed by the expectations of individual members joining together. Changing group norms is difficult and this is done by breaking down old values and replacing them with new ones. When a member's expectations become more extreme than the group's, the member can try to change those norms, remain a deviate in the group, or leave the group.

8 Group process is the interaction among members of a group that occurs as the

group continues to meet and work toward its goals. Bales has developed a classification scheme to categorize group interaction. One of the most important variables influencing group process is the size of the group.

GLOSSARY

Choice Dilemma Items used in risky-shift research that asked the subject to indicate his or her choice when faced with a specific dilemma.

Deindividuation The depersonalizing effects of being in a group, in which perceptions of self and others change to allow behavior that is normally restrained.

Evaluation Apprehension Concern over being judged by others.

Group A number of persons who communicate, face-to-face, over a period of time in pursuing a common goal or goals.

Group Norms Rules of behavior that have been accepted as legitimate by members of a group.

Group Polarization The hypothesis that groups shift to a more extreme position in the direction the individuals in the group already favor.

Group Process The interaction among members of a group that occurs as the group continues to meet and work toward its goals.

Informational Influence Theory The theory developed to account for group polarization, which asserts that cognitive learning occurs during exposure of the minority to the majority viewpoint during discussion.

Joker A role in many groups in which the occupant presents ideas and insights from a different point of view under the cover of humor.

Retrospective Data Data collected after an event has occurred, which depend on the subject's memory of the event.

Risky Shift The area of research that proposed that group decisions were more risky than individual ones. Subsequent research has shown that groups do not always make decisions that are riskier.

Role The set of expectations shared by group members concerning the behavior exhibited by a person who occupies a given position in the group.

Social Facilitation The effects on performance of the presence of others.

Socioemotional Leader A leader who is primarily concerned with the affectional relationships and satisfaction of group members.

Sociogram A pictoral representation of a group's interpersonal choices.

Task Leader A leader who is primarily concerned with the performance of the group's task.

REFERENCES

Abel, T. *M.* The influence of social facilitation on motor performance at different levels of intelligence. *American Journal of Psychology,* 1938, *51,* 379–89.

Allen, V. L. Conformity and the role of the deviant. *Journal of Personality,* 1965, *33,* 584–97.

Alpert, B., and P. A. Smith. How participation works. *Journal of Social Issues,* 1949, *5,* 3–13.

Anderson, H. H. Dominance and social integration in the behavior of kindergarten children and teachers. *Genetic Psychology Monographs.* 1939, *21*, 287–385.

Bales, R. F. *Interaction Process Analysis: A Method for the Study of Small Groups.* Cambridge, Mass.: Addison-Wesley, Publishing Co., Inc., 1950.

———— et al., Channels of communication in small groups. *American Sociological Review,* 1951, *16*, 461–68.

Bates, A. P., and J. S. Cloyd. Toward the development of operations for defining group norms and members' roles. *Sociometry,* 1956, *19*, 26–39.

Bates, F. L. Position, role, and status: A reformulation of concepts *Social Forces,* 1956, *34*, 313–21.

Bell, P. R., and B. D. Jamieson. Publicity of initial decisions and the risky shift phenomenon. *Journal of Experimental Social Psychology,* 1970, *6*, 329–45.

Berkowitz, L., and R. C. Howard. Reactions to opinion deviates as affected by affiliation need (n) and group member interdependence. *Sociometry,* 1959, *22*, 87–91.

Bermant, G., and R. Coppock. Outcomes of six- and twelve-member jury trials: An analysis of 128 civil cases in the State of Washington. *Washington Law Review,* 1973, *48*, 593–96.

Bishop, G. D., and D. Myers. Informational influence in group discussion. *Organizational Behavior and Human Performance,* 1974, *12*, 92–104.

Blake, R. R., and J. S. Mouton. Comprehension of in and out-group positions under intergroup competition. *Journal of Conflict Resolution,* 1961, *5*, 304–310.

Borgatta, E. F. Analysis of social interaction and socioeconomic perception. *Sociometry,* 1954, *17*, 7–31.

Burnham, W. H. The hygiene of home study. *Pedagogical Seminary,* 1905, *12*, 213–30.

Burnstein, E., and A. Vinokur. Testing two classes of theories about group-induced shifts in individual choice. *Journal of Experimental Social Psychology,* 1973, *9*, 123–37.

Cattell, R. F., and G. F. Stice. Four formulae for selecting leaders on the basis of personality. *Human Relations,* 1954, *7*, 493–507.

Cloyd, J. S. Functional differentiation and the structure of informal groups. *Sociological Quarterly,* 1964, *5*, 243–50.

Cooley, C. H. *Social Organization.* New York: Charles Scribner's Sons, 1909.

Cottrell, N. B. Social facilitation. In C. G. McClintook (Ed.), *Experimental Social Psychology.* New York: Holt, Rinehart and Winston, 1972.

————, D. L. Wack, G. J. Sekerak, and R. H. Rittle. Social facilitation of dominant responses by the presence of an audience and the mere presence of others. *Journal of Personality and Social Psychology,* 1968, *9*, 245–50.

d'Amorim, M. A., and J. R. Nuttin. (The perception of one's own successes and failures in function of the outcomes of a partner: The influence of task involvement and level of aspiration in male and female subjects.) *Psychologica Belgica,* 1972, *12*, 9–31.

Davie, J. S., and A. P. Hare. Button-down college culture. A study of undergraduate life at a men's college. *Human Organization,* 1956, *14*, 13–20.

Davis, J. H., R. M. Bray, and R. W. Holt. The empirical study of social decision processes in juries. In J. Tapp & F. Levine (Eds.), *Law, Justice and the Individual in Society: Psychological and Legal Issues.* New York: Holt, Rinehart and Winston, 1977.

Doise, W. L'importance d'une dimension principale dans les jugements collectifo, *l'Année Psychologique,* 1970, *70*, 151–59.

Eagly, A. H. Comprehensibility of persuasive arguments as a determinant of opinion change. *Journal of Personality and Social Psychology,* 1974, *29*, 758–73.

Ebbensen, E. B., and R. J. Bowers. Proportion of risky to conservative arguments in a group discussion and choice shift. *Journal of Personality and Social Psychology,* 1974, *29*, 316–27.

Feofanov, M. P. (The question of investigating the structural characteristics of the group.) *Zhurnal Psikhologii, Pedologii i Psikhotekhniki,* 1928, *1*, 107–120.

Festinger, L. Theory of social comparison processes. *Human Relations,* 1954, *7,* 117–40.

———, A. Pepitone, and T. Newcomb. Some consequences of deindividuation in a group. *Journal of Abnormal and Social Psychology,* 1952, *47,* 382–89.

———, S. Schachter, and K. Back. *Social pressures in informal groups: A study of human factors in housing.* New York: Harper and Row, Publishers, 1950.

——— and J. Thibaut. Interpersonal communication in small groups. *Journal of Abnormal and Social Psychology,* 1951, *46,* 92–99.

Fiedler, F. A. A note on leadership theory: The effect of social barriers between leaders and followers. *Sociometry,* 1957, *20,* 87–94.

Fischer, P. H. An analysis of the primary group. *Sociometry,* 1953, *16,* 272–76.

Foulds, M. B. The growth center model. Proactive programs of a university counseling service. *Comparative Group Studies,* 1972, *3,* 77–88.

Frank, H. H., and C. Wolman. Gender deviancy in male peer groups. Proceedings of the 81st Annual Convention of the American Psychological Association, 1973, *8,* 1063–64.

Gerard, H. B. Some effects of status, role clarity, and group goal clarity upon the individual's relations to group process. *Journal of Personality,* 1957, *25,* 475–88.

——— and M. F. Hoyt. Distinctiveness of social categorization and attitude toward ingroup members. *Journal of Personality and Social Psychology,* 1974, *29,* 836–42.

Gibb, C. A. The principles and traits of leadership. *Journal of Abnormal and Social Psychology,* 1947, *42,* 267–84.

Gladstone, R. Authoritarianism, social status, transgression and punitiveness. Proceedings of the 77th annual convention of the American Psychological Association, 1969, *4,* 287–88.

Good, K. J. Social facilitation: Effects on performance anticipation evaluation, and response competition on free associations. *Journal of Personality and Social Psychology,* 1973, *28,* 270–75.

Goodchilds, J. D., and E. E. Smith. The wit and his group. *Human Relations,* 1964, *17,* 23–31.

Goodenough, F. L. Interrelationships in the behavior of young children. *Child Development,* 1930, *1,* 29–48.

Gorden, R. L. Interaction between attitude and the definition of the situation in the expression of opinion. *American Sociological Review,* 1952, *17,* 50–58.

Gouge, C., and C. Fraser. A further demonstration of group polarization. *European Journal of Social Psychology,* 1972, *2,* 95–97.

Hare, A. P. Small group discussions with participatory and supervisory leadership. *Journal of Abnormal and Social Psychology,* 1953, *48,* 273–75.

———. Situational differences in leader behavior. *Journal of Abnormal and Social Psychology,* 1957, *55,* 132–35.

———. *Handbook of small group research* (2nd Ed.). New York: The Free Press, 1976.

Harrison, C. W., J. R. Rawls, and D. J. Rawls. Differences between leaders and nonleaders in six-to-eleven-year old children. *Journal of Social Psychology,* 1971, *84,* 269–72.

Heiss, J. S. The dyad views the newcomer: A study of perception. *Human Relations,* 1963, *16,* 241–48.

Hemphill, J. K. Situational factors in leadership. *Ohio State University Educational Research Monographs,* 1949, *32.*

Homans, G. C. *The Human Group.* New York: Harcourt Brace Jovanovich, Inc., 1950.

———. *Social Behavior: Its Elementary Forms.* New York: Harcourt Brace Jovanovich, Inc., 1961.

Huie, W. B. *Three Lives for Mississippi.* New York: WCC Books, 1965.

Innes, J. M., and R. F. Young. The effect of presence of an audience, evaluation apprehension and objective self-awareness on learning. *Journal of Experimental Social Psychology,* 1975, *11,* 35–42.

Institute of Judicial Administration. A comparison of six-and-twelve-member juries in New Jersey superior and county Courts, 1972.

Israel, J. *Self-evaluation and Rejection in Groups: Three Experimental Studies and a Conceptual Outline.* Stockholm: Almqvist and Wiksell, 1956.

Jones, C., and E. Aronson. Attribution of fault to a rape victim as a function of respectability of the victim. *Journal of Personality and Social Psychology,* 1973, *26,* 415–19.

Kalven, J., Jr., and H. Zeisel, *The American Jury.* Boston; Little, Brown and Company, 1966.

Kephart, W. M. A quantitative analysis of intragroup relationships. *American Journal of Sociology,* 1950, *60,* 544–49.

Kipnis, D. Does power corrupt? *Journal of Personality and Social Psychology,* 1972, *24,* 33–41.

Kipnis, D., and W. P. Lane. Self-confidence and leadership. *Journal of Applied Psychology,* 1962, *46,* 291–95.

Knox, R. E., and R. K. Safford. Group caution at the race track. *Journal of Experimental Social Psychology,* 1976, *12,* 317–24.

Kogan, N., and M. A. Wallach. *Risk Taking: A Study in Cognition and Personality.* New York: Holt, Rinehart and Winston, 1964.

Lamberth, J., and D. A. Kirby. The lawyer's dilemma: Authoritarianism and jury selection. Paper presented at the meeting of the Midwestern Psychological Association, Chicago, May 1974.

———— and E. Krieger. Deliberations: A crucial aspect of jury research. Paper presented at the meeting of the Psychonomic Society St. Louis, November 1976.

————, E. C. Krieger, and R. H. Walbridge. Jury verdicts of authoritarians and equalitarians in simulated criminal trials. Paper presented at the meeting of the Psychonomic Society, Denver, November 1975.

Lamm, H. Will an observer advise higher risk taking after hearing a discussion of the decision problem? *Journal of Personality and Social Psychology,* 1967, *6,* 467–71.

Lamm, H., and C. Sauer. Discussion-induced shift toward higher demands in negotiation. *European Journal of Social Psychology,* 1974, *4,* 85–88.

————, G. Trommsdorff, and E. Rost-Schaude. Group-induced extremization: Review of evidence and a minority-change explanation. *Psychological Reports,* 1973, *33,* 471–84.

Leith, W. R., and M. R. Uhlemann. The shaping group approach to stuttering. A pilot study. *Comparative Group Studies,* 1972, *3,* 175–99.

Levin, J. Bifactor analysis of a multitrait-multimethod matrix of leadership criteria in small groups. *Journal of Social Psychology,* 1973, *89,* 295–99.

Levine, J. M., L. Saxe, and H. Harris. Amount of initial disagreement as a determinant of reaction to a shifting attitudinal deviate. Proceedings of the 81st Annual Convention of the American Psychological Association, 1973, *8,* 157–58.

Levinson, D. J., Role personality and social structure in the organizational setting. *Journal of Abnormal and Social Psychology,* 1959, *58,* 170–80.

Lewin, K. Forces behind food habits and methods of change. *Bulletin of the National Research Council,* 1943, *108,* 35–65.

————. Frontiers in group dynamics: Concept, method and reality in social science, social equalibria, and social change. *Human Relations,* 1947, *1,* 5–41.

————. *Field Theory in Social Science.* New York: Harper & Row, Publishers, 1951.

Lifton, R. J. "Thought reform" of western civilians in Chinese Communist prisons. *Psychiatry,* 1956, *19,* 173–95.

————. *Thought Reform and the Psychology of Totalism: A Study of 'Brainwashing' in China.* New York: W. W. Norton & Company, Inc., 1961.

Lindzey, G., and E. F. Borgatta. Sociometric measurement. In G. Lindzey (Ed.), *Handbook of*

Social Psychology. Cambridge, Mass.: Addison-Wesley Publishing Co., Inc., 1954, 405–448.

Lippitt, R., J. Watson, and B. Westley. *The Dynamics of Planned Change: A Comparative Study of Principles and Techniques.* New York: Harcourt Brace Jovanovich, Inc., 1958.

———— and R. K. White. An experimental study of leadership and group life. In G. E. Swanson, T. M. Newcomb, and E. L. Hartley (Eds.), *Readings in Social Psychology,* New York: Holt, Rinehart and Winston 1952, 340–55.

Lundgren, D. C., and D. H. Bogart. Group size, member dissatisfaction, and group radicalism. *Human Relations,* 1974, *27,* 339–55.

Maier, N. R. F., and A. R. Solem. The contribution of a discussion leader to the quality of group thinking: The effective use of minority opinions. *Human Relations,* 1952, *5,* 277–88.

Martens, R., and D. M. Landers. Evaluation potential as a determinant of coaction effects. *Journal of Experimental Social Psychology,* 1972, *8,* 347–59.

Mayer, A. (On the schoolchild's work alone and in groups.) *Archiv fur die Gesamte Psychologie,* 1903, *1,* 276–416.

McCauley, C., C. L. Stitt, K. Woods, and D. Lipton. Group shift to caution at the race track. *Journal of experimental Social Psychology,* 1973, *8,* 80–86.

Miller, G. R. Televised trials: How do juries react? *Judicature,* 1974, *58,* 242–46.

————. Jurors' responses to videotaped trial materials: Some recent findings. *Personality and Social Psychology Bulletin,* 1975, *1,* 561–69.

————. The effects of videotaped trial materials on juror response. In G. Bermant, C. E. Nemeth, and N. Vidmar (Eds.), *Psychology and the Law: Research Frontiers.* Lexington, Mass.: D. C. Heath & Company, 1977, Pp. 185–208.

Miller, G. R., D. C. Bender, F. G. Boster, B. T. Florence, N. E. Fontes, J. E. Hocking, and H. E. Nicholson. The effects of video-tape testimony in jury trials. *Brigham Young University Law Review,* 1975 (a), *1,* 331–73.

————, F. G. Boster, N. E. Fontes, D. J. Lefebvre, and M. S. Poole. Jurors' responses to videotaped trial materials—Some further evidence. *Michigan State Bar Journal,* 1975 (b), *54,* 278–82.

Mills, L. R. Six-member and twelve-member juries: An empirical study of trial results. *University of Michigan Journal of Law Reform,* 1973, *6,* 671–711.

Mitchell, T. R. Cognitive complexity and group performance. *Journal of Social Psychology,* 1971, *86,* 35–43.

Moreno, J. L. *Who Shall Survive?* (Revised Edition). Beacon, N.Y.: Beacon House, 1953.

Morgan, C. P., and J. D. Aram. The preponderance of arguments in the risky shift phenomenon. *Journal of Experimental Social Psychology,* 1975, *11,* 25–34.

Morris, C. G. Task effects on group interaction. *Journal of Personality and Social Psychology,* 1966, *4,* 545–54.

Moscovici, S., W. Doise, and R. Dulong. Studies in group decision II: Differences of positions, differences of opinion and group polarization. *European Journal of Social Psychology,* 1972, *2,* 385–400.

———— and R. Lecuyer. Studies in group decision: I: Social space, patterns of communication and group consensus. *European Journal of Social Psychology,* 1972, *2,* 221–44.

———— and M. Zavalloni. The group as a polarizer of attitudes. *Journal of Personality and Social Psychology,* 1969, *12,* 125–35.

Myers, D. G. Discussion-induced attitude polarization. *Human Relations,* 1975, *28,* 699–714.

———— and G. D. Bishop. Discussion effects on racial attitudes, *Science,* 1970, *169,* 778–89.

———— and M. F. Kaplan. Group-induced polarization in simulated juries. *Personality and Social Psychology Bulletin,* 1976, *2,* 63–66.

———— and H. Lamm. The group polarization phenomenon. *Psychological Bulletin,* 1976, *83,* 602–627.

Newcomb, T. M. *Personality and Social Change.* New York: Holt, Rinehart and Winston, 1943.

————. Role behavior in the study of individual personality and of groups. *Journal of Personality,* 1950, *18,* 273–89.

Nobler, H. Group therapy with male homosexuals. *Comparative Group Studies,* 1972, *3,* 161–78.

Preston, M. G., and R. K. Heintz. Effects of participatory versus supervisory leadership on group judgment. *Journal of Abnormal and Social Psychology,* 1949, *44,* 345–55.

Rabbie, J. M., and L. Visser. Bargaining strength and group polarization in intergroup polarization. *European Journal of Social Psychology,* 1972, *2,* 401–416.

Raven, B. H., and J. R. P. French, Jr. Group support, legitimate power and social influence, *Journal of Personality,* 1958, *26,* 400–409.

Read, P. B. Source of authority and the legitimation of leadership in small groups. *Sociometry,* 1974, *37,* 189–204.

Redl, F. Resistance in therapy groups. *Human Relations,* 1948, *1,* 307–313.

Regula, C. R., and J. W. Julian. The impact of quality and frequency of task contributions on perceived ability. *Journal of Social Psychology,* 1973, *89,* 115–22.

Reynolds, P. D. Comment on "The distribution of participation in group discussions" as related to group size. *American Sociological Review,* 1971, *36,* 704–706.

Robinson, K. F. An experimental study of the effects of group discussion upon social attitudes of college students. *Speech Monographs,* 1941, *8,* 34–57.

Rosenthal, D., and C. N. Cofer. The effect on group performance of an indifferent and neglectful attitude shown by one group member. *Journal of Experimental Psychology,* 1948, *38,* 568–77.

St. Jean, R. A reformulation of the value hypothesis in group risk taking. Proceedings of the 78th Annual Convention of the American Psychological Association, 1970, *5,* 339–40.

———— and E. Percival. The role of argumentation and comparison processes in choice shifts: Another assessment. *Canadian Journal of Behavioral Science,* 1974, *6,* 297–308.

Sarbin, T. R. Role theory. In G. Lindzey (Ed.), *Handbook of Social Psychology.* Cambridge, Mass.: Addison-Wesley Publishing Co., Inc., 1954. Pp. 223–58.

Schachter, S., et al. Cross-cultural experiments on threat and rejection. *Human Relations,* 1954, *7,* 403–439.

Schein, E. H. The Chinese indoctrination program for prisoners of war: A study of attempted brainwashing: *Psychiatry,* 1956, *19,* 149–72.

————. Interpersonal communication, group solidarity, and social influence. *Sociometry,* 1960, *23,* 148–61.

————, I. Schneier, and C. H. Barker. *Coercive Persuasion.* New York: Norton, 1961.

Schutz, W. C. The ego, FIRO theory and the leader as completer. In L. Petriello and B. M. Bass (Eds.), *Leadership and Interpersonal Behavior.* New York: Holt, Rinehart and Winston, 1961. Pp. 48–65.

Sherif, M. Integrating field work and laboratory in small group research. *American Sociological Review,* 1954, *19,* 759–71.

Singer, J. E., C. A. Brush, and S. C. Lublin. Some aspects of deindividuation identification and conformity. *Journal of Experimental Social Psychology,* 1965, *1,* 356–78.

Smith, E. E. The effects of clear and unclear role expectations on group productivity and defensiveness. *Journal of Abnormal and Social Psychology,* 1957, *55,* 213–17.

Smith, M. B. Is experimental social psychology advancing? *Journal of Experimental Social Psychology,* 1972, *8,* 86–96.

Smith, R. J., and P. E. Cook. Leadership in dyadic groups as a function of dominance and incentives. *Sociometry,* 1973, *36,* 561–68.

Sorrentino, R. M. An extension of theory of achievement motivation to the study of emergent leadership. *Journal of Personality and Social Psychology,* 1973, *26,* 356–68.

Southall, A. An operational theory of role. *Human Relations,* 1959, *12,* 17–34.

Spence, K. W., I. E. Farber, and H. H. McFann. The relation of anxiety (drive) level to performance in competitional and noncompetitional paired-associates learning. *Journal of Experimental Psychology,* 1956, *52,* 296–305.

Stang, D. J. Effect of interaction rate on ratings of leadership and liking. *Journal of Personality and Social Psychology,* 1973, *27,* 405–408.

Stoner, J. A. F. A comparison of individual and group decisions involving risk. Unpublished master's thesis, Massachusets Institute of Technology, 1961.

Taylor, J. H., C. E. Thompson, and D. Spassoff. The effect of conditions of work and various suggested attitudes on production and reported feelings of tiredness and boredom. *Journal of Applied Psychology,* 1937, *21,* 431–50.

Teger, A. I., and D. G. Pruitt. Components of group risk taking. *Journal of Experimental Social Psychology,* 1967, *3,* 189–205.

Torrance, E. P., and R. Mason. The indigenous leader in changing attitudes and behavior. *International Journal of Sociometry,* 1956, *1,* 23–28.

Travers, R. M. W. A study in judging the opinions of groups. *Archives of Psychology,* 1941, *47,* No. 266.

Triplett, N. The dynamogenic factors in pacemaking and competition. *American Journal of Psychology,* 1898, *9,* 507–533.

Vertreace, W. C., and C. H. Simmons. Attempted leadership in the leaderless group discussion as a function of motivation and ego involvement. *Journal of Personality and Social Psychology,* 1971, *19,* 285–89.

Vinokur, A., and E. Burnstein. The effects of partially shared persuasive arguments on group induced shifts: A problem solving approach. *Journal of Personality and Social Psychology,* 1974, *29,* 305–315.

Wahrman, R. High status, deviance and sanctions. *Sociometry,* 1970, *33,* 485–504.

Wallach, M. A., N. Kogan, and D. J. Bem. Diffusion of responsibility and level of risk taking in groups. *Journal of Abnormal and Social Psychology,* 1964, *68,* 263–74.

White, R. K., and R. Lippitt. *Autocracy and democracy.* New York: Harper & Row, Publishers, 1960.

Williams *vs.* Florida (1970). United States Supreme Court Reports (Lawyers' Edition), *26,* 446–86.

Zajonc, R. B. Social facilitation: *Science,* 1965, *149,* 269–74.

———, A. Heingartner, and E. M. Herman. Social enhancement and impairment of performance in the cockroach. *Journal of Personality and Social Psychology,* 1969, *13,* 83–92.

Zeisel, H. What determines the amount of argument per juror? *American Sociological Review,* 1963, *28,* 279.

——— and S. S. Diamond. Convincing empirical evidence on the six-member jury. *University of Chicago Law Review,* 1974, *41,* 281–95.

Zigon, F. J., and J. R. Cannon. Processes and outcomes of group discussion as related to leader behaviors. *Journal of Educational Research,* 1974, *67,* 199–201.

Ziller, R. C., R. D. Behringer, and D. Goodchilds. The minority newcomer in open and closed groups. *Journal of Psychology,* 1960, *50,* 75–84.

———, ———, and M. J. Jansen. The newcomer in open and closed groups. *Journal of Applied Psychology,* 1961, *45,* 55–58.

Zimbardo, P. G. The human choice: Individuation, reason, and order versus deindividuation impulse and chaos. In W. J. Arnold and D. Levine (Eds.), *Nebraska Symposium on Motivation,* 1969. Lincoln: University of Nebraska Press, 1970.

————, W. C. Banks, C. Haney, and D. Jaffe. A Pirandellian prison: The mind is a formidable jailer. *New York Times Magazine,* April 8, 1973, pp. 38–60.

Znaniecki, F. Social groups as products of participating individuals. *American Journal of Sociology,* 1939, *44,* 789–812.

12

Environmental Psychology

Social psychology emphasizes the person interacting with his or her environment. For many years our discipline has emphasized the psychological environment. This is evident in Allport's definition (1968, p. 3) of the field "as an attempt to understand how the thought, feeling, or behavior of individuals are influenced by the actual, imagined, or implied presence of others." Undoubtedly it is true that the bulk of social psychology deals with interactions among people. Yet we are finding that the presence of others has an enormous impact on our lives even after they are gone.

Have you ever had the experience of going to a remote area to get away from it all? Time spent in the pristine wilderness or on a deserted, desolate beach is a valued, if seldom attained experience. However, few of us get so far away from civilization that the evidences of our fellow humans cannot be seen. Litter, destruction, and other such objectionable reminders that others have been around seemingly follow us wherever we go. Even those bold adventures who sail the seas on rafts or boats made of esoteric materials find the seas filled with pollution. We are being forced to be more aware of our environment and its impact upon us.

The psychological environment is inextricably linked with the physical environment. As more people live on the planet, we find conditions becoming overcrowded, resources being depleted, and the environment polluted. Psychologists have turned their attention to a number of these issues. We cannot cover all of them here but will examine the effects of population density and of heat and humidity on behavior, and attempts to conserve resources and lessen pollution by changing behavior. Since 1970 was the decade of environmentalism, many of these issues are still new, while one, the concern over population density, has had a somewhat longer history.

Population Density

It is difficult to know precisely, but it is estimated that there were only about 5 million people living on the earth 10,000 years ago. It took all but about 200 of those years for the world's population to reach one billion (Demeny, 1974). By 1976 the world population reached 4 billion and it continues to grow at slightly over 2 percent a year. Figure 12–1 shows graphically what it means for the world's population to

This beach is deserted, but it contains the evidence of human occupation.

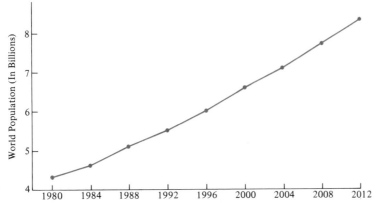

Figure 12-1 **Hypothetical increase in world population calculated at 2 percent increase a year. At that rate the world's population doubles about every 35 years.**

increase at 2 percent a year. The alarming fact is that, at that rate, the world's population doubles every 35 years. Thus, in 1976 the population was 4 billion, in 2012 it will be 8 billion, 16 billion in 2049, 32 billion in 2084, and so on. It is obvious that if the population continues to increase at 2 percent a year, calamity will strike before too many more doublings have occurred. Whatever the solution to the problem of population growth, it is apparent that we will continue to live in ever-more-crowded conditions for many more years.

What are the effects of population density? Certainly most of us would rather have some space to move around in, yet in both Canada and the United States we cluster in geographically small, crowded urban areas. For most individuals, however, this sort of crowding is voluntary. There are still great expanses of space that we may enjoy. At the present time, space is not a scarce commodity.

As a matter of fact, resources do not make themselves felt in any negative way until they are scarce. Buttel (1976) argues that social scientists in North America have not taken scarcity of resources seriously until recently because the continent was rich in those resources. Most of us did not consider gasoline an important commodity until recent years when we became aware of an impending energy shortage. This was forcefully driven home by the Arab oil embargo of the United States in the winter of 1973–74 and the shortages that became painfully evident in 1979. In certain sections of the country long lines to obtain gasoline were the rule and the concept of scarcity became important to us. Certainly, a portion of the problem associated with the energy shortage can be attributed to reckless consumption. Yet the sheer number of people using the available resources also can be seen as part of the cause.

Pollution and litter are also partly due to ignorance, greed, and an uncaring attitude toward the air, water, and earth upon which we depend. Industries and cities pour filthy wastes into waterways that once were clean. It would cost a great deal of money to clean up those wastes, and the industries and cities involved argue that such money is unavailable. The soil erodes and becomes polluted because of poor land management techniques, insecticides and other poisons that are used to control pests

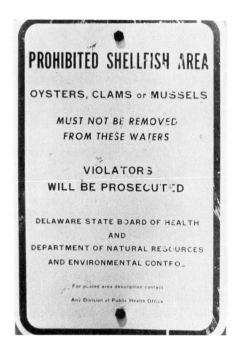

Shellfish cannot be removed from the area because the waters are polluted. Even so vast a resource as the ocean is not immune to pollution.

and increase crop yield, and because people find it easier to throw their wastes out of a car window than to use litter bags. Part of the problem, again, is caused by ignorance or greed, but another part can be traced to the large number of people alive and using the land today. That is not to argue that the existence of as many people as there are in the world today necessarily pollutes, but it certainly makes the fragile balance among living creatures harder to maintain.

Thr problem of dealing with large numbers of people in small geographical areas is not new. Japan and the Netherlands have long had densely populated areas. In Canada and the United States the problem is still far from acute, although the growing density of some urban areas in both countries may be leading to problems. Freedman (1975) has pointed out what should be obvious: density becomes an important problem when it occurs in conjunction with drastically curtailed resources. Under these conditions depressed areas become slums, which in turn become ghettos.

The effects of population density may be properly seen as the basic environmental problem we face. If the population of the world continues to increase at the present rate, Asimov (1975) has estimated that the entire mass of the universe we know today will consist of human bodies by about the year 8675. Something will happen before that impossible event occurs, but we do not yet know what it will be. There may be an enormously destructive war, or population growth may be curtailed. Barring some event or events that reduce the inexorable increase in population, long before the time Asimov describes, famine and starvation will check the increasing population. We are not in a position to know what will happen, but we are in a position to discuss some of the questions that have been raised with regard to psychological issues concerning space.

One of the most pervasive concerns with increasing population has been the effects of crowding (or overcrowding) on people. One of the early warning signals about the effects of overcrowding on humans came from research on rats and was sounded by Calhoun (1961, 1962a, 1962b). The general approach was to place several male and female rats in a colony and allow them to reproduce. Adequate food and water were always available and the colony grew. But as the conditions become more crowded, normal rat behavior began to be replaced by bizarre behavior: pansexualism, cannibalism, warfare, general hostility, and disorientation. Infant mortality increased to more than 90 percent of those born. The colony had become so crowded that extreme disruption of behavior took place. There was adequate food and water for all the rats so the conditions Calhoun referred to as a behavioral sink occurred because of overcrowding.

If overcrowding disrupts behavior in rats to such a great extent, what does it do to humans? We have few, if any, scientific observations on behavior in extremely crowded conditions that are not contaminated by other variables. Prisons, prisoner of war camps, nuclear submarines, and so forth, are places in which humans are crowded together. In prisons and prisoner of war camps, however, there are so many other factors working that it is virtually impossible to sort out the causative agents. Nuclear submarines, on the other hand, are manned by men who have volunteered for the duty. Thus it is impossible to make generalized predictions from their behavior.

There has been, however, a growing interest among psychologists in overcrowding and its effects on people. Actually, it is probably incorrect to refer to this research as strictly research on overcrowding, because the effects of sparse population are also of interest. As early as the 1930s, Hediger (1934, 1950) introduced the concept of a series of zones that animals seemed to maintain around themselves. Hall (1959) was stimulated by this work to inquire into humans' use of space in their social interactions. The work of Hall, which defined four separate zones of interpersonal activity, may be seen as the impetus for much of the research that has been carried out since that time. The four zones were the intimate (from physical contact to 18 inches), personal distance (1½ to 4 ft.), social distance (4 to 12 ft.), and public distance (12 to 25 ft.).

Personal Space

Interaction distance is the straight-line distance between two parties to a social interaction. The term *personal space* has long been used to identify the area within an invisible boundary, surrounding each individual, through which others should not pass. It moves with us, and depending on the situation in which we find ourselves, it can expand or contract. The term *personal space* has been used in a variety of different ways with different meanings. But in this book the term is used in the way just defined.

Why do we keep a "bubble" of space around us and why does it expand and contract? Some of the explanation is undoubtedly found in Hall's four interaction zones, which are distinguished by distance. An intimate activity is generally carried out in very close proximity to the other person, whereas personal, social, and public activities are carried out at greater distances. Many intimate activities violate personal space. However, there are two basic reasons for such a bubble. It keeps us from being too close or too far away. If we are too close, it is possible that we will become overstimulated and that our normal channels of perception will not function properly. For example, if we are too close to someone or something, vision becomes blurred. On the other hand, it is difficult to communicate if we are too far away from someone. Vision, hearing, and our other senses work more effectively at moderate distances. Thus standing or sitting at a moderate distance from another person facilitates communication.

Some of the most influential research into the effects of violating personal space was undertaken by Robert Sommer (Felipe and Sommer, 1966; Sommer, 1969). In a 1500-bed mental institution, Sommer violated the personal space of a number of patients by approaching and seating himself about 6 inches from them. If the subject moved, Sommer also moved to maintain a very close interaction distance. Control subjects were unobtrusively observed from a distance and their personal space was not violated. The primary response to spatial invasion was flight. After only 2 minutes one third of the experimental subjects had moved whereas no control subjects moved in the first 2 minutes. Half of the experimental, but only 8 percent of the control subjects, had moved after 9 minutes. After 20 minutes 35 percent of the control subjects and 65 percent of the experimental subjects had moved. Thus, it appears that even among extremely withdrawn patients enough emotion was generated by the simple intrusion of their personal space to cause them to leave. Konečí, Libuser, Morton, and Ebbenson (1975) and Patterson, Mullens, and Romano (1971), in a nonhospital setting, show essentially the same results as those obtained by Sommer.

From the investigation of Hall and Sommer, research on personal space has burgeoned and interest in it has grown among psychologists as well as the general populace. The idea that each one of us carries a bubble of space around with us that we consider our own is intriguing. Equally intriguing is the idea that we will flee if our interpersonal space is violated. This particular aspect of personal space, flight when the space is violated, is one that distinguishes it from territoriality. In addition, personal space is relatively portable, whereas territoriality is not, personal space has the person's body at the center, whereas territory does not, and the boundaries of territory are usually marked whereas the boundaries of personal space are invisible.

Theories of Personal Space

There are several theories to account for personal space; that is, why people keep an area of space around themselves. Argyle and Dean (1965) proposed an equilibrium theory, which emphasizes reaching equilibrium between approach and avoidance forces. There are four prominent features of any interaction between two people: the amount of eye contact, interaction distance, the intimacy of topics discussed, and the amount of smiling. Each dimension is seen as subject to both approach and avoidance forces. For example, a woman may want to look at the other person to gain information but may fear revealing something about herself by maintaining eye contact. These competing forces establish an equilibrium somewhere between constant eye contact and complete avoidance of contact. Changes in any one of the four dimensions result in changes in another dimension to achieve the desired level of intimacy. According to Hayduk (1978) the theory has received rather extensive testing with mixed results. It remains a popular theory in spite of this, probably because it is neat and simple (Patterson, 1973). Dosey and Meisels (1969, p. 93) say,

Personal space may be conceived in the sense of a body-buffer zone . . . that can be used . . . for protective purposes. This applies to threats to one's self-esteem as well as to the threat of bodily harm.

The greater the perceived threat, the greater distance the person will place between himself and another person. The threat may be physical or emotional. There have been a number of investigations that have supported the theory, but according to Hayduk (1978) the support has been neither extensive or universal enough to view protection theory as adequate.

Nesbitt and Steven (1974, p. 106), recalling Hall's (1966) comments that individuals experience each other more intensely at close distances, say,

Accordingly, in a high intensity environment, it might be expected that individuals would stand farther apart in an attempt to moderate the total amount of stimulation they are subjected to. In a deprived stimulus environment, individuals might stand closer together. The basis of the above argument is that extremes of environmental stimulation, and particularly high levels of stimulation are aversive and stressful.

There is limited evidence for this stimulation theory and it is mixed. Desor (1972) and Nesbitt and Steven (1974) generally support the theory, but results by Seta, Paulus, and Schkade (1976) qualify the relationship between stimulation and personal space.

What Variables Affect Personal Space?

A great deal of research effort has gone into the task of determining variables that influence personal space. According to Hayduk (1978), the basic factors influencing personal space are sex, age, culture, and acquaintance and liking. Each one has been tested and there is some evidence concerning their effects.

SEX

It has been widely reported that male-female space is less than female-female space, which is less than male-male space. Hayduk (1978) reviewed 35 separate studies that investigated sex and interpersonal space and the overall report is mixed. The vast majority of the studies found support or conditional support for the effect of sex on interpersonal space. However, there were so many studies in the conditional support category, as well as 8 studies that did not support the expected relationship, that caution is still advised in asserting the pattern of the influence of sex on interpersonal space.

Age

The basic assumption is that personal space is a learned phenomenon and develops by the age of 12. That is, by age 12 children are utilizing and responding to personal space in much the same way adults do. The evidence for this proposition is strong and consistent. Of the 7 studies Hayduk (1978) reports, all support the idea.

Culture

There is clear-cut evidence that culture has an effect on personal space. For example, several investigators (Hall, 1966; Little, 1968; Sommer, 1969; Watson and Graves, 1966) found that Latin Americans, French, Greeks, and Arabs use smaller interaction distances than is comfortable for people from the United States, England, Sweden, and Switzerland. Difficulties can arise in communicating with someone who has a space bubble that is different in size from yours. Have you ever found yourself in a situation where someone is conversing with you and continues to move closer to you even though you may retreat? In all probability your bubble is larger than his and when he is comfortable you move back, which causes him to move forward, and so on until you find yourself trapped against a wall.

The evidence for the effect of subculture on personal space in the United States is not nearly so clear. This probably is because race, socioeconomic status, and ethnicity are confounded. In addition, children who are of a specific racial or ethnic background may learn about personal space from the dominant culture as well as their own subculture. Evidence for such an idea is found in Jones and Aiello (1973) who hypothesized that black children would stand closer together than white children. This held true for first-grade children, but had diminished by third grade, and seemed to reverse by fifth grade. Patterson (1974) has suggested that socioeconomic status may be more of an influence on personal space than subculture. This probably occurs because people from a given socioeconomic class have more similar living conditions (which in turn affect personal space). Consistent with this idea Scherer (1974) found that both lower-class whites and blacks interact at closer distances than do middle-class whites and blacks.

Liking

Personal space is smaller when the people involved like each other. Several studies have supported this conclusion fully while two have provided tentative support. Why should people decrease their personal space requirements when interacting with a liked person? It seems obvious that people who like each other should interact at closer distances. Intimate relationships are more likely to occur and thus less distance will be utilized. Liking and sex do appear to interact to affect personal space (Byrne, Baskett, and Hodges, 1971).

As indicated at the beginning of this section, invasion of personal space results in flight or withdrawal. But what other effects does it have? There is fairly good evidence

INTERPERSONAL TOUCH

Personal space is the area within an invisible boundary surrounding each individual through which others should not pass. We become very uncomfortable when others violate our personal space. There are, however, times when we want our personal space violated. For example, a couple who are very much in love do not observe the boundaries of each other's interpersonal space. In addition, touch has long been considered to be one of the most powerful forms of nonverbal communication; we must violate another's personal space if we are to touch another person.

Whitcher and Fisher (1979) report an intriguing study on the effects of touch in a hospital setting. The subjects for the experiment were 48 patients who entered a major university hospital for elective surgery. The touch was administered by nursing personnel in the course of their regular duties. Patients not included in the study were not deprived of tactile stimulation. Rather, specific touching was added to the hospital routine for experimental patients. There were two groups (touch vs. no touch) of male (19) and female (29) patients involved in the study.

Normal hospital routine called for a nurse to close off a curtain around the patient's bed and introduce herself and explain that she was going to inform the patient about his or her surgery. The first touch in the touch group came as the nurse was introducing herself; she touched the patient's hand for a few seconds. Toward the end of the teaching session the nurse gave the patient a booklet further explaining the details of surgery. As she did so, she touched the patient's arm and maintained the contact for approximately one minute if the patient was in the touch group. Of course, if the patient was in the no-touch group, she did not administer either of these touches.

Several measures were taken to evaluate the effectiveness of touching the patient. An affective measure assessed the patient's feelings concerning hospitalization and surgery. In addition,

a measure of satisfaction with preoperative instructions and attraction toward the nurse were taken. Behavioral measures included the amount of the booklet read by patients and a measure of reciprocation of touch. The nurse reached out but did not touch the patient and the patient's reaction was measured. Finally, postoperative physiological measures (pulse, blood pressure, and temperature) were taken.

Patients who were touched showed an interesting pattern of responding. In general, touching of female patients appeared to be beneficial in that they were less worried about complications in surgery, thought the nurse was more interested in them, read more of the booklet, and had lower blood pressure than control females. Males in the touch condition, however, reacted more negatively than did control subjects.

Earlier research has indicated that low preoperative anxiety results in more favorable postoperative physiological responses. The study by Whitcher and Fisher indicates that it is possible to reduce anxiety in females by carefully manipulated touch. It is possible that male and female patients view touch by the nurse differently; that is, they may view it in a dependent context and thus, to male patients, as a negative stimulus.

The results of the Whitcher and Fisher study are suggestive; it may be that so simple a process as the touching of a patient tends to alleviate fears and enhance postoperative recovery. That the same results did not occur with male patients means that further work on and a better understanding of the therapeutic aspects of touch are necessary.

Reference

Whitcher, S. J., and J. D. Fisher. Multidimensional reaction to therapeutic touch in a hospital setting. *Journal of Personality and Social Psychology*, 1979, *37*, 87–96.

that invasion of personal space results in stress or anxiety (Middlemist, Knowles, and Matter, 1976; Worchel and Teddlie, 1976), but that task performance and aggressiveness may not be affected by inappropriate amounts of personal space (Evans and Howard, 1972; Freedman, Levy, Buchanan, and Price, 1972). It should be pointed out, however, that many experiments that investigate aggression or task performance and personal space do not allow severe invasions of personal space because of the space it takes to perform the task in the experiment. That is, many such experiments require a minimum amount of space to assess task performance or to measure aggressiveness, and there may not be a severe enough violation of personal space to show results.

Comment

The bubble of space we carry around with us is quite an interesting phenomenon. It is, however, just as complex as it is interesting. Therefore, there will have to be considerably more research before we can be as sure as we would like to be about what influences personal space, and how it affects other behaviors. Research has indicated that just as it is uncomfortable to have our personal space invaded, it is also uncomfortable to invade other's personal space (Barefoot, Hoople, and McClay, 1972; Efran and Cheyne, 1974). Of course, violating someone else's personal space means that we also violate our own.

Is Crowding Detrimental?

When is a room crowded? The answer to that question depends on a number of factors, including the activity being carried out, the particular people in the room, and so forth. For example, a cocktail party would appear quite uncrowded if each individual had 10 square feet of space available, whereas that would be just about right for a classroom and very crowded for an activity that required a great deal of physical movement. Rooms full of friends seem less crowded than rooms full of enemies. Stokols (1972) has argued that to be crowded an individual must recognize a disparity between the space available for an activity and the space required for that activity. Thus high density may bring about a feeling of being crowded, but it does not necessarily do so.

Ashcraft and Scheflen (1976, p.84) have this to say about crowding:

Crowding is an unpleasant subjective experience, but at the same time we know very little about its consequences for man.

History records the story of the Black Hole of Calcutta. In 1756 Fort Williams, the British settlement in Calcutta, was captured by Siraj-ud-daula. One hundred forty-six prisoners were forced into the fort's guardroom, an area equaling 18×14.10 feet (or one British square rod), where they were held overnight. In the morning only twenty-three remained alive. Usual explanations for the one hundred twenty-three deaths point to the intense heat and suffocation. But what were the effects of crowding?

Freedman (1975, p.1), on the other hand, takes a different view:

. . . How can this be if crowding is so bad? The answer, according to research accumulated over the past few years, is that high population density has been much maligned, at least as it affects humans. Intuitions, speculations, political and philosophical theory appear to be wrong in this respect. Under some circumstances crowding may have disastrous effects on rats, mice, rabbits, and other animals, but crowding does not have a generally negative effect on humans. People who live under crowded conditions do not suffer from being crowded. Other things being equal, they are no worse off than other people.

Schmitt (1957, 1966) correlated five measures of population density with nine measures of social pathology. The measures of population density were population per acre, number of dwelling units with 1.51 or more persons per room, average household size, the number of married couples without their own household, and the number of multiple-dwelling units with more than four units. In his first study all of these measures correlated with both adult crime rate and juvenile delinquency rates in 29 Honolulu census tracts. Schmitt (1966) used all nine indicators of social pathology in his second study which were (1) death rate; (2) infant mortality rate; (3) suicide rate; (4) incidence of tuberculosis; (5) incidence of venereal disease; (6) admissions to mental hospitals; (7) illegitimate birth rate; (8) juvenile delinquency rate; and (9) adult crime rate. Four of the five indicators of population density correlated significantly and positively with all nine measures of social pathology. Only household size failed to correlate with the measures of social pathology. Schmitt further found that population per acre was the strongest indicator of social pathology and this held true even when the sample was stratified by educational level and income. This indicates that even when socioeconomic factors are held constant, population per acre is related to measures of social pathology.

Freedman, Klevansky, and Ehrlich (1971) questioned the adequacy of Schmitt's classification system for socioeconomic status. Winsborough (1965) found essentially no relationship between population density and infant mortality rate, death rate, incidence of tuberculosis, public assistance rate, and public assistance rate to persons under 18 years of age. Do Chicago and Honolulu differ enough to show such differences or are Freedman et al. (1971) correct? Possibly neither of these answers is accurate. There could be enough differences in the studies themselves to yield differential results.

How Crowded Is Crowded?

Even though there may be large concentrations of people, do individuals feel crowded? The most densely populated country in the world is Holland, which has half an acre for every person living there. Japan, South Korea, Holland, and England are all more than one hundred times as densely populated as Canada and more than 10 times as densely populated as the United States. Does this mean the United States is about 10 times as densely populated as Canada? Technically, yes. There are, however,

One place where crowding is not a
problem is in space.

vast areas of Canada in which few people choose to live because of extreme weather
conditions. There are equally sparsely populated areas of the United States. So it
should be obvious that just determining how much space there is per person in a
country does not tell us much.

Let's look at it another way. In prison cells in the United States there are supposed
to be 38.5 square feet per person, which we may take as a minimum amount of space
that is considered healthful. In Washington, D.C., jail cells actually have 19 square
feet per person. World War II troop ships and a typical nightclub have about 10
square feet per person, a theater has about 7 square feet per person and a nine-
teenth-century London slum is estimated to have had about 9 square feet. The Nazi
concentration camp at Belsen had 3 square feet per person whereas the Black Hole of
Calcutta and the New York subway at rush hour each had about 2 square feet per
person. Figure 12–2 shows these facts graphically.

It is obvious that there is not a direct relationship between amount of space
available and negative outcomes. For example, 84 percent of the people in the Black
Hole of Calcutta died, whereas not even its severest critics claim that anywhere near
that many people die in the New York subway system at rush hour. It should be
noted, however, that riders on the New York subway are in those conditions for only
a few minutes each day, and that ventilation and heat are better controlled. It is
obvious that those people in the Black Hole of Calcutta were prisoners, unsure of
their fate, and that New York rush hour subway riders are much more sure of the
outcome of their crowded conditions. The point I am making is that crowding is a
complex variable, not one that can be easily understood. It is obvious that many
variables that affect the feeling of being crowded enter into the equation.

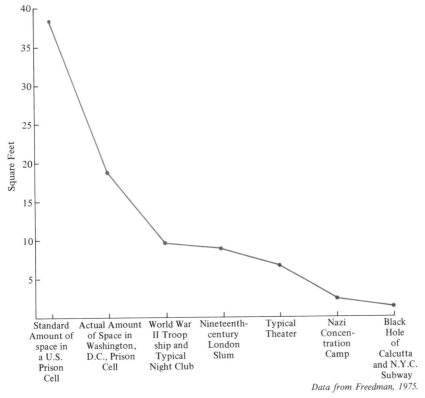

Data from Freedman, 1975.

Figure 12-2 Typical amounts of space per person in various situations.

Research on Crowding

According to Linder (1976), controlled observational studies of the effects of density on human behavior are very rare and the results are tentative. Hutt and Vaizey (1966) observed children playing in both large and small groups. The children were observed in the same playroom with the same play material at hand. In large groups children were observed to be less socially oriented and more aggressive than children playing in the small groups. The authors interpreted this as a function of increased density in the large groups. However, as Linder points out, it may have been a function of the increased numbers of children in the large groups, rather than the increased density.

As noted earlier, crowding is a complex variable and great care must be taken in experimenting on its effects to assure that extraneous variables do not enter in. Here is an excellent example. If the same room is used as an experimental area, then two variables are being altered when density is varied. That is, there is less space for each person under high-density conditions, but there are also more people. Any effects that occur may be the result of higher density, more people, or a combination of both. To control for such an extraneous variable (more people) different-sized rooms must be

RESPONDING TO CROWDING: LEARNED HELPLESSNESS?

The research on crowding and its effects on motivation of those who are crowded has properly moved into more realistic settings. Even though many psychologists can point to experimental evidence to support their intuitive disagreement with Freedman's density-intensity hypothesis, the motivational effects of crowding in situations people confront daily are of most importance.

Baum and his associates (Baum, Aiello, and Calesnick, 1978; Baum and Koman, 1976; Baum and Valins, 1977) have investigated the way people respond to social and spatial effects on perceptions of crowding. In one particularly interesting study, Baum et al. (1978) investigated the effects of perceived crowding in college dormitories on motivation.

Subjects from two different residential settings of equal density participated in a modified Prisoner's Dilemma game (see Chapter 7). Even though the density of the two settings was identical, they were arranged differently. One setting (long-corridor dormitory) grouped residents around a shared lounge, bathroom, and hall spaces in relatively large numbers (32–40 individuals). The short-corridor dormitory grouped smaller numbers (6–20 individuals) around the shared living spaces.

Baum et al. (1978) were particularly interested in the concept of learned helplessness (see Chapter 1) on behavior. They hypothesized that long-corridor students are subjected to unpredictable and uncontrollable stress because of the volume of people they must interact with in daily dormitory life. Compared to short-corridor students, long-corridor students generally encounter from two to five times more people when leaving their rooms, going to the bathroom, relaxing, and so forth. "Helplessness" training may begin when students in long-corridor dormitories realize that their efforts to regulate social contacts are not very effective. It is assumed that students will attempt to reestablish control for a time and then exhibit behavior that is characteristic of learned helplessness.

Baum et al. tested long- and short-corridor students on the modified Prisoner's Dilemma game after 1, 3, and 7 weeks of residence in the dormitories. The modification to the Prisoner's Dilemma game was specifically designed to test for learned helplessness. On any trial a subject could make a competitive or cooperative response as in the basic game. In this version there was another option, which was labeled withdrawal. If the player chose the withdrawal option, he or she was assured of losing very little and possibly nothing. There was, however, no possibility of winning anything. The Prisoner's Dilemma game with this withdrawal option has been specifically found to reflect a motivational deficit analogous to learned helplessness. Under conditions that result in learned helplessness (training on unsolvable problems) subjects tend to withdraw more and compete less than do subjects previously exposed to solvable problems.

Since it was expected that the "helplessness" training (i.e., exposure to the long-corridor dormitories) would take some time, no differences between long- and short-corridor subjects were expected in withdrawals after 1 and 3 weeks, but an increase in withdrawals in the long-corridor subjects was expected by week 7.

From week 1, short-corridor residents were less competitive and more cooperative than long-corridor residents. Across time both long- and short-corridor residents decreased their competitiveness. Short-corridor residents became more cooperative as their competitiveness decreased, whereas long-corridor residents did not. The startling results occurred in week 7. Responses for long-corridor residents during week 3 had been 66 percent competitive, 17 percent cooperative and 17 percent withdrawal. This compared to 48 percent competitive, 39 percent cooperative and 13 percent withdrawal responses for short-corridor residents. The comparable results for week 7 were 54 percent competitive, 10 percent cooperative and 36 percent withdrawal responses for long-corridor residents and 37 percent competitive, 52 percent cooperative and 11 percent withdrawal responses for short-corridor residents. Thus, long-corridor residents decreased competitiveness by withdrawing, whereas short-corridor residents reduced competitiveness by cooperating between weeks 3 and 7.

Other measures taken during this study indicate that long-corridor students reported more crowding, frequent unwanted interactions, less satisfaction, and more problems than did short-corridor students. These data, coupled with the results of the Prisoner's Dilemma game strongly suggest that even perceived crowding is associated with motivational deficits. Specifically, this prolonged exposure appears to result in behavior closely associated with learned helplessness.

References

Baum, A., J. R. Aiello, and L. E. Calesnick. Crowding and personal control: Social density and the development of learned helplessness. *Journal of Personality and Social Psychology*, 1978, *36*, 1000–1011.

Baum, A., and S. Koman. Differential response to anticipated crowding: Psychological effects of social and spatial density. *Journal of Personality and Social Psychology*, 1976, *34*, 526–536.

Baum, A., and S. Valins. Architecture and social behavior: *Psychological studies of social density.* Hillsdale, N.J.: Erlbaum, 1977.

used with the same number of people. For example, 10 people in a room containing 100 square feet of space are much less crowded than 10 people in a room containing 50 square feet. As long as the shapes of the rooms are held constant, the effects when a group is in the smaller room may be attributed to crowding.

CROWDING AND DENSITY

As work has progressed in this area of research it has become necessary to distinguish between crowding and density. I have alluded to the fact that sometimes you feel crowded in a small group in a large room and don't feel crowded in a large group in a small room. *Density* is an objective physical state that involves potential inconvenience because of restricted movement or lack of privacy. *Crowding* is a psychological state of stress that occurs when the individual becomes sensitive to the restrictions imposed by high density (Stokols, 1972). The state of most interest to psychologists is crowding, although the two concepts are inseparable.

Experimental research in crowding has concentrated on the effects of crowding on human behavior and the results have indicated that crowding is not always negative. For example Cozby (1973) found that high density is perceived positively at a party and negatively while studying. There are three areas of social behavior in which crowding has been investigated: feelings, attraction, and performance.

FEELING AND CROWDING

What effect do crowded conditions have on each of these states? Griffitt and Veitch (1971) reported that subjects in high-density conditions expressed more negative affect than did subjects in low-density conditions. Sundstrom reported subjects were less comfortable in a high-density situation. Haller (1972) held the size of groups constant, but varied the amount of space available for each individual by varying the size of the room with movable partitions. He then measured affect on a pleasurable-unpleasurable dimension. He found that, generally speaking, the more space there was, up to about 13 square feet per person, the more pleasurable the affect was. At 16 square feet per person, however, the experience became less

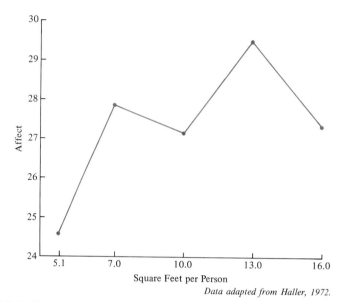

Data adapted from Haller, 1972.

Figure 12-3 Affect as a function of density. The higher the affect score, the more pleasurable the feelings.

pleasurable. Figure 12–3 shows Haller's results. It seems that low density leads to more pleasurable feelings, at least up to a point. Haller speculated that the exact amount of space where affect would be maximized would vary depending upon the activity involved. His situation most closely approximated a classroom; he measured several classrooms and found that there were about 10 square feet per person in those rooms. Thus, it may be that optimal feelings are obtained in roughly the same amount of space individuals have become used to for a given activity. Smith and Lawrence (1978) report that even subjects who are alone react negatively to restrictive spatial conditions (crowding).

Paulus, Cox, McCain, and Chandler (1975) had inmates at a Federal correctional institution fill out a scale that measured affective responses to their physical surroundings. High density was defined as inmates living in dormitories that accommodated 26 to 44, while low-density inmates lived in single cells. It was found that high-density subjects were more negative to their immediate surroundings than were low-density inmates.

It is possible that the negative affective response to high density is limited to males. Two investigators have found that males report more negative affect under high-density conditions whereas females are more negative toward low-density situations (Freedman, Levy, Buchanan, and Price, 1972; Ross, Layton, Erickson, and Schopler, 1973). Schettino and Borden (1976) reported that males and females reacted quite differently to high-density conditions in college classrooms. Under high-density conditions, males reported greater aggressiveness, whereas females reported more nervousness and crowdedness as density increased. Ross et al. (1973) suggest that research on personal space may provide a clue as to why there is a differential reaction to crowding by males and females. That is, there is a different socialization process operative for men and women. Women are trained to be more dependent and to express love and affection for each other more openly. Males are trained to be independent and not express affection for other males openly. Under high-density conditions females may be more used to the invasion of personal space that occurs than are males and better able to cope with it.

One criticism that has been leveled at crowding research has been that subjects are in high-density conditions for only short periods of time. For example, most of the studies referred to in this section have subjects in high-density conditions for from 5 minutes to several hours. It may be that any effects that manifest themselves in a short time will become more powerful over more extended periods. Two studies are particularly important. Smith and Haythorn's (1972) subjects were subjected to crowded or uncrowded conditions for 21 days. Generally speaking, more crowded conditions resulted in more stress and anxiety. A surprising result of this study, however, was that more crowded conditions led to less hostility toward others in the group than did less crowded conditions. There may be some sort of interpersonal interaction between increased stress, anxiety, and high density that reduces the hostility toward others who are in the same situation. The old adage, "Misery loves company" may better be stated "Misery loves company and is less hostile toward it." Zuckerman, Schmitz, and Yesha (1977) report a study of students living in dormitories on a college campus. Students who had more space indicated that they were less crowded, were in a better mood, and had a better relationship with their roommates than did students with less space. The differences in space were not great (198 square feet for low density and 173 square feet for high density) and the design of the two dormitories may have added to the greater feelings of crowding in one dormitory than in the other. However, the evidence presented by Smith and Haythorn (1972) and by Zuckerman et al. (1977) indicates that the effects of long-term crowding may well be noxious.

CROWDING AND LIKING

Griffitt and Veitch (1971) placed subjects in either a hot and crowded room or a cool and uncrowded room and obtained their evaluations of a stranger about whom they had limited information. With the information about the stranger held constant, both heat and density influenced how much the subjects liked the stranger. However, high-density conditions (4.06 square feet per person) resulted in the most negative evaluations of the stranger. Sundstrom (1975) reported that subjects were less willing to affiliate and discuss intimate topics in high-density than in low-density conditions. Valins and Baum (1973) and Baum and Valins (1973) studied the experience of crowding in two types of dormitories with the same amount of space but with different levels of social stimulation. They found that students in the dormitory with excessive levels of social stimulation felt more crowded and tried to reduce involvement with others. That is, they avoided others on their floors, experienced greater discomfort in the presence of others, and sat farther away from strangers in a laboratory setting. These studies combined with the evidence reported by Zuckerman et al. (1977) indicate that density does affect attraction.

CROWDING AND PERFORMANCE

One of the most important and controversial areas of concern with the effects of density is performance. The assumption that overcrowding adversely affected performance was almost universally accepted until Freedman and his associates published a series of articles and books that questioned that assumption (Freedman, 1975; Freedman, Klevansky, and Ehrlich, 1971; Freedman, Levy, Buchanan, and Price, 1972). These investigators, although starting with the assumption that crowding was aversive and detrimental to performance, were surprised to find little evidence to support their assumption. Freedman (1975, p. 7) says,

Indeed the research on which this book is based has produced two major findings. First, high density (crowding) does not have generally negative effects on humans. Overall, with other factors equated, living, working, or spending time for any reason under conditions of high density does not harm people. It does not produce any kind of physical, mental, or social pathology. People who experience high density are just as healthy, happy, and productive as those who experience lower density.

More to the point for our present purposes, Freedman (1975, p. 89) says,

It has been shown that population density bears little or no relationship to any kind of pathology among humans. While conditions of high density, either in a neighborhood or within one's own dwelling, obviously have substantial effects on how one lives, they do not appear to have generally negative consequences. Under more controlled circumstances, research demonstrates that people can function quite well when very crowded and isolated for considerable periods of time. Indeed, at least within the limits used in these studies, increasing the density has, if anything, positive effects—reducing hostility and stress. Density has also been shown to have no effect on performance on a wide variety of tasks, thus making it seem highly unlikely that it produces stress in the usual sense of the word.

There is evidence from other sources to support Freedman's claim concerning performance and density. For example, Kutner (1973), Sherrod (1974), and Stokols, Rall, Pinner, and Schopler (1973) found no effects of being crowded on the quality of task performance. Valins and Baum (1973), Sherrod (1974), and Epstein and Karlin (1975) found aftereffects of crowding on task performance.

Recently, however, there has been a growing series of studies that question Freedman's assumptions. Paulus, Annis, Seta, Schkade, and Matthews (1976) found that density results in a decrement in performance on a complex task. Saegert (1974) and Aiello, Epstein, and Karlin (1975) have reported increased palmar sweating and increased electrodermal activity for subjects in high-density conditions. In addition, Langer and Saegert (1977) found a decrement in performance under high-density conditions in a field study.

MAKING SENSE OF THE CROWDING AND PERFORMANCE DATA

What are we to make of these contradictory data? Probably the best approach is to be wary of a simple answer to a complex problem. To illustrate, consider what happens to performance in an arousing situation. According to at least one theory, there are two possible outcomes depending upon the complexity of the task being performed. Hull–Spence drive theory (Hull, 1951; Spence, 1960; Spence and Spence,

1966) postulates that arousal or anxiety enhances performance on simple tasks but causes a decrement in performance on complex tasks. The explanation for this seemingly contradictory prediction is that simple tasks do not have competing responses that are incorrect whereas complex ones do. For example, a football player whose only assignment is to block the man who lines up in front of him has a simple task and therefore any arousal should assist him in his task. However, someone learning to drive a stick-shift car has an enormously complex task. The driver must put the car in gear and simultaneously release the clutch with the left foot and apply pressure to the gas with the right foot just to get the car started. No matter how many times this process is repeated on lonely roads, the first time a new driver tries it at a busy intersection is almost a guarantee of disaster. At best the car bucks across the intersection; more often it ends up stalled in the middle of the cross-street with honking, irate motorists blocked all around.

Hull–Spence theory explains the foregoing in rather simple terms. A response that is simple or highly practiced will be enhanced by arousal or anxiety. A response that is complex or unpracticed will suffer if the person is aroused. Simple or well-practiced tasks have only the correct response available whereas complex tasks have many responses that can be made in addition to the correct one. These competing but incorrect responses are more likely to be emitted when the individual is aroused or anxious. Thus arousal energizes the individual to do a simple task quickly, but interferes with a complex one.

Haller (1974) tested the notion that crowding is an arousing stimulus by giving subjects either an easy task or a complex one to perform under crowded or un-crowded conditions. The task he used was two sets of paired associates. Learning paired associates is a classical performance task in which the first (stimulus) word of the pair is presented to the subject who must respond with the second (response) word. The lists were constructed in such a way that the stimulus and correct response words were either very easy (noncompetitional list) or very difficult (competitional list). That is, in the noncompetitional list the stimulus and correct response words were virtually synonyms. In the competitional list, synonyms were used, but they were not used as pairs. Table 12–1 gives the lists. If overcrowding is aversive, it would be expected that subjects in overcrowded conditions should do better on the non-competitional list and worse on the competitional list than subjects who are un-crowded.

Subjects learned either the competitional or noncompetitional list in crowded (4.91 square feet per person) or uncrowded (12.61 square feet per person) conditions. One measure of learning the lists is the number of trials it takes to learn each list (trials to criteria). The crowded subjects learned the noncompetitional list more quickly and the competitional list more slowly than did uncrowded subjects. The results are presented in Figure 12–4. The crucial interaction shown in the figure did not quite reach the level of significance psychologists automatically accept. Generally a probability that indicates the obtained results could have occurred by chance only 5 times out of a hundred ($p = .05$) is the convention used. Haller's results indicated his results could have occurred by chance 6 times in a hundred ($p = .06$). However, several other measures of performance support Haller's interpretation. Thus, according to Haller, overcrowding does lead to detrimental effects.

Table 12-1 Pairs of words used in competitional and noncompetitional lists by Haller (1974)

Competitional List		Noncompetitional List	
Stimulus	*Response*	*Stimulus*	*Response*
tranquil	placid	tranquil	placid
gypsy	opaque	pious	devout
undersized	wholesome	stubborn	headstrong
quiet	double	wicked	evil
arid	grouchy	insane	crazy
little	minute	little	minute
petite	yonder	frigid	arctic
desert	leading	adept	skillful
barren	fruitless	barren	fruitless
migrant	agile	distant	remote
serene	headstrong	mammoth	oversize
roving	nomad	roving	nomad

Checking the Scorecard

Here it may be wise to try to bring things into perspective in what must seems to be a sea of confusion. There are several factors that appear to influence the possible effects of overcrowding. The first and most obvious of these is "How crowded is

Figure 12-4 Trials to criteria for competitional and noncompetitional lists under crowded and uncrowded conditions. The interaction supports the idea that crowding is arousing.

Data adapted from Haller, 1974.

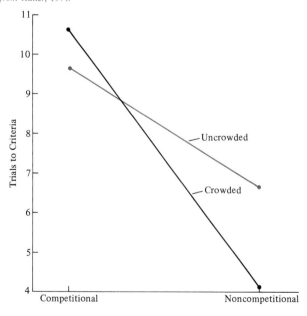

crowded." A look at the literature shows that one researcher's crowded conditions are another researcher's uncrowded ones. Table 12–2 gives the square feet per person allotted in selected laboratory experiments for crowded and uncrowded conditions. As a cursory check of Table 12–2 shows, experimenters have not been very consistent in labeling crowded and uncrowded conditions across studies. Freedman and his associates have had huge variations in the amount of space designated crowded and uncrowded, to some extent because these experimenters have allowed group size to vary.

Group size is itself a variable that interacts with density in most crowding studies. However, as several researchers have pointed out (Freedman, 1975; Linder, 1976; Schettino and Borden, 1976), group size and group density are two different things. As Schettino and Borden (1976, p. 67) say,

In a recent review of the crowding literature, Lawrence (1974) noted that "the field is confused—by definitions, by conflicting data, and as psychology often is, by popular conjecture" (p. 717). In part these inconsistencies stem from a failure to distinguish between two important variables of the group setting, (1) Group Size: the number of people in the situation, and (2) Group Density: the compactness of the group. Many of the studies reported in the literature have manipulated only one of these factors or confounded them.

A third source of difficulty in the crowding literature is the fact that different situations demand different amounts of space. Five square feet of space per person at a cocktail party may not be perceived as crowded, whereas it most certainly would be

Table 12–2 Amount of space provided for crowded and uncrowded conditions in 12 selected experiments

	Square Feet per Person			
Study	Crowded		Uncrowded	
1. Freedman, Klevansky & Ehrlich, 1971	3.9–7	(5–9)	17.8–32*	(5–9)
2. Freedman, et al., 1972	6.3	(4)	18.1	(4)
3. Freedman, Henska, Levy, Buchanan, & Price, 1972	10–16.7*	(6–10)	30–50*	(6–10)
4. Freedman, Henska & Levy (Reported in Freedman, 1975)	7–11.7*	(6–10)	15–25*	(6–10)
5. Freedman, Henska & Levy (Reported in Freedman, 1975)	8.8–11.7*	(6–8)	18.8–25*	(6–8)
6. Freedman & Staff (Reported in Freedman, 1975)	8.7–10.8*	(4–5)	20.4–25.5*	(4–5)
7. Griffith & Veitch, 1971	3.9–5.25*	(12–16)	12.6–21*	(3–5)
8. Ross, et al., 1973	6.2	(8)	16.7	(8)
9. Paulus, et al., 1976	11.8	(8)	50	(4)
10. Baum & Koman	6.6	(10)	13.4	(10)
11. Sundstrom, 1975	4.5	(6)	38	(6)
12. Haller, 1975	4.9	(11)	12.6	(11)

*Groups of different sizes were run in a room that did not vary in size. Thus, different amounts of space per subject were available depending upon the group size being run. Numbers in parentheses are the number(s) of people in the groups.

crowded in a classroom. Thus any attempt to make sense out of the crowding literature must build on the different amounts of space necessary to perform the task at hand.

Theories of Overcrowding

There are several theories of overcrowding, but we will deal with only two. One takes the point of view that overcrowding is a drive-arousing stimulus whereas the other does not.

FREEDMAN'S DENSITY-INTENSITY THEORY

Freedman (1975) has proposed what he terms a density-intensity theory. Here is his explanation of the theory (Freedman, 1975, pp. 89–90).

I propose that crowding by itself has neither good effects nor bad effects on people but rather *serves to intensify the individual's typical reactions to the situation.* If he ordinarily would find the circumstances pleasant, would enjoy having people around him, would think of the other people as friends, would in a word have a positive reaction to other people, he will have a more positive reaction under conditions of high density. On the other hand, if ordinarily he would dislike the other people, find it unpleasant having them around, feel aggressive toward them and in general have a negative reaction to the presence of other people, he will have a more negative reaction under conditions of high density. And if for some reason he would ordinarily be indifferent to the presence of other people, increasing the density will have little effect one way or the other. Thus, people do not respond to density in a uniform way, they do not find it either always pleasant or always unpleasant. Rather, their response to density depends almost entirely on their response to the situation itself. Density acts primarily to make this response, whatever it is, stronger.

Freedman's approach is unique and yet not entirely convincing. If his analogy is followed to its logical conclusion, happy workers would be placed in higher-density work environments and unhappy ones in less-crowded conditions. By the same token, depressed people should stay away from crowds and elated ones should invite crowding. Further, such an analysis does not allow for precision in predicting behavior. That is, the individual's state of mind must be known prior to being able to predict the effects of crowding on that person. Since this can be one of three states, negative, positive, or neutral, virtually any effect of crowding is possible. Most convincing of all, however, are the studies referred to earlier in this chapter, which have increasingly found negative effects of crowding (e.g., Griffitt and Veitch, 1971; Haller, 1974; Langer and Saegert, 1977; Paulus et al., 1976; Saegert, 1974; Sundstrom, 1975).

HALLER'S SOCIAL LEARNING THEORY

Haller points out that both Stokols (1972) and Carey (1972) have distinguished between density and crowding. Density refers to the number of people present in a given space; crowding is a stimulus that is determined by a person's perception of density. Thus, density is a physical stimulus and crowding is a psychological stimulus. The best way to view overcrowding, according to this approach, is to consider physical space in reference to psychological space. Haller prefers to term the physical variable density *available space;* he uses the term *acceptable space* to refer to the psychological dimension of crowding.

Available space is a physical variable and quite easily conceptualized and defined. It is a function of the physical space available and the number of persons present, and can be expressed in number of square feet per person.

Acceptable space is a much more complex variable and is a learned expectation concerning spatial norms. At least five variables can affect acceptable space. The first of these is *functional space,* which refers to the amount of space functionally available to an individual. It does not necessarily have a one-to-one relationship with physical space, because it can be affected by such variables as furniture arrangement (Mehrabian, 1968), partitions in the area (Desor, 1972), eye contact (Argyle and Dean, 1965) and even the proportions of the room (Daves and Swaffer, 1971; Desor, 1972). Available space is not affected by these variables. As an example, consider an airport waiting room. If 20 people are sitting in a room that is 20 feet wide and 40 feet long they have the same amount of available space regardless of how the chairs are arranged. However, if their chairs are arranged in 2 rows, back to back, each person has more functional space than if the rows are four feet apart facing each other.

The psychological presence of others also affects acceptable space. (The number of others present is considered in the measurement of available space.) At least 3 variables determine whether the presence of others will have a positive or negative effect on acceptable space; the individual's attraction toward the others, their sex, and their evaluation potential. Spatial research has consistently shown that people maintain closer distances when they like someone than when they dislike the other person (Byrne, Baskett, and Hodges, 1971; Duke and Nowicki, 1972; Holahan and Levinger, 1971; Little, Ulehla, and Henderson, 1965). With regard to the sex variable, acceptable space is greatest for subjects in male-male situations, smaller for female-female situations, and smallest for heterosexual situations (Duke and Nowicki, 1972; Hartnett, Bailey, and Gibson, 1970; Leibman, 1970). Additionally, if the others present are perceived as potential evaluators, their presence will serve to affect performance (Martens and Landers, 1972) and increase acceptable space.

Three other variables that affect acceptable space are activity, time, and personality characteristics. The amount of space needed for a casual conversation, working, and playing tennis vary quite dramatically. Therefore, the activity engaged in is one of the most clear-cut determinants of acceptable space. Time is a difficult variable to deal with in overcrowding. Haller and Lamberth (1973) suggested that extremely crowded conditions in a laboratory may at first be novel to a subject but after some time become aversive. On the other hand, people who live in extremely crowded conditions may adapt to them. Remember in Figure 12–2 that people lived in Nazi concentration camps for a long time with very little space. Personality characteristics are known to affect personal space. High authoritarians and high-test anxious persons maintain larger personal space when compared to low authoritarians and low-test anxious persons (Frankel and Barrett, 1971; Karabenick and Meisels, 1972).

Given these definitions of available space, acceptable space, and the variables that affect them, Haller proposes that crowding is a function of the ratio of available space to acceptable space. That is,

$$\text{Crowding} = \frac{\text{Available Space}}{\text{Acceptable Space}}$$

If the available space is less than the acceptable space, then the ratio is less than 1 and, by definition, is crowded. As can readily be seen, ratios very near to one may not be perceived as overcrowded, but as the ratios become smaller than one overcrowding results.

As an example, let us use Haller's data from Figure 12–3. Remember that a subsequent check of the average amount of space in a classroom resulted in a figure of approximately 10 square feet per person, so we will use that as our estimate of acceptable space. When the available space was 10 square feet (a crowding ratio of 1.00) and when it was 7 feet (a crowding ratio of 0.7) the affective ratings were between 27 and 28. However, when the available space dropped to 5.1 square feet (a crowding ratio of 0.5), the affective ratings dropped to 24.50. Thus dropping the ratio to 0.7 had no effect on affective ratings, but a ratio of 0.5 did.

Although Haller restricted his discussion to overcrowding, the model can be seen as a generalized one, which accounts for spatial effects. When the ratio is more than one, undercrowding occurs. It is possible that too much space has behavioral consequences as well.

Haller's model of overcrowding is at once flexible and testable. That is, it can account for a variety of different situations and it specifies conditions under which the model can be tested. As Haller (1974, p. 50) says,

. . . According to the overcrowding concepts described above, the model implies that crowding can be achieved in more than one way. If all variables determining acceptable space are held constant, then decreasing the available space increases the amount of overcrowding. Likewise, if available space is held constant, then increasing the acceptable space also increases the amount of overcrowding. In either case, the behavioral result is predicted to be the same if the ratio is the same because the proportion is considered to be the effective stimulus. That is, the model implies that the perceived amount of crowding is the same for a given proportion, regardless of which variable or combination of variables is altered to obtain that proportion.

Comment

Overcrowding is a complex variable, one that will not easily be understood. Undoubtedly there are those who will find Freedman's theory persuasive although I do not. As is probably quite clear by now, it seems to me that the flexibility, clear specification, and testability of Haller's theory make it a far more likely candidate to explain this very complex phenomenon.

Conservation

Conservation of the natural resources of the world can take many forms. Whether it be saving seals, redwoods, or whales, there is a great deal of publicity given to efforts made by conservationists. There are, however, many more natural resources

WHEN IS A CROWD A CROWD?

The subjective feeling of being crowded is not identical to population density. As we discussed in this chapter, sometimes you feel crowded when there is a relatively large amount of space per person, and other times you don't feel crowded when there is a relatively small amount of space per person. What are the factors that influence that perception? Or, to phrase the question another way, in Haller's analysis of crowding what are the factors that contribute to the concept of acceptable space? We don't know all of the factors and we are just beginning to study them. Rodin, Solomon, and Metcalf (1978) report a series of two experiments designed to investigate the relationship between crowding and perceptions of personal control.

Control of the environment appears to be a central feature to much of human behavior. Does it, however, affect our perceptions of how crowded a situation is? Rodin et al. designed an experiment in an elevator. Where did you stand the last time you entered an elevator? Many people move to a position directly in front of the control panel of buttons, presumably because this gives them a feeling of controlling the elevator. Subjects in this experiment were 45 males and 27 females who entered an elevator in the Yale University library. Four confederates were used and they filled the back wall of the elevator, and in one condition the position in front of the control panel and the front center of the elevator. This forced the subject to the right front of the elevator on the side that did not contain a control panel. Another group was run in which the subject was forced into the position in front of the control panel. People in the control position found the elevator to be less crowded than did those individuals in the identical position across the elevator who did not have a control panel in front of them. Thus, the control variable affected perceptions of density.

A second experiment studied the effects of control of a group on perceptions of density. Six person groups were formed, given several tasks to do, and one person was given the role of coordinator and one the role of terminator. The coordinator was responsible for initiating and facilitating group processes. The terminator was responsible for determining when a task was finished, for deciding and announcing the group's decision if one was called for, and for moving the group on to the next task. Thus there were four subjects in each group who had little or no control over the group and two who did exercise control. One of the controllers exercised an initiating role and one exercised a terminating role. Half of the groups were run in a high-density room (approximately 20 square feet) and half in a low-density room (approximately 47 square feet).

As in the previous experiment, those in positions of control rated the room as less crowded than did subjects who exercised no control. These differences were more pronounced in the small room than in the large one. In general, terminators rated the room more positively than coordinators in the small room and more negatively than coordinators in the large room. This seems reasonable because in low-density rooms there is less stress and the groups function more efficiently and the coordinator's role is more important. Under the stress of high density, the terminator must exercise more control and thus views the situation more positively.

Both these experiments lend support to the idea that one of the factors influencing perceptions of density is control of the situation.

Reference

Rodin, J., S. Solomon, and J. Metcalf. Role of control in mediating perceptions of density. *Journal of Personality and Social Psychology*, 1978, *36*, 988–99.

that need to be conserved. The air we breathe is polluted, as is the water we drink. The ozone layer that protects us from radiation from the sun may be endangered. All of these natural resources, although endangered, are remote from our psychological lives. That is, we are aware of the dangers, but most of us can influence them only indirectly or minutely. There is little we as individuals can do directly about the slaughter of baby seals, the destruction of the ozone layer, or the extinction of any species of animal. We can support conservation efforts with our contributions and our time, we can support legislation that protects natural resources, and so forth. Nevertheless, the efforts seem rather remote.

There are other conservation issues that we can address more directly. For example, the world's reserves of oil and natural gas are limited and the government of the United States energy policy has emphasized conservation. Conservation of this type extends to all energy sources and can be a very personal thing for each of us. Sitting in long gasoline lines, paying utility bills that have doubled or tripled in the last few years, and hearing constant reminders about conserving energy by driving more slowly, insulating our homes and so forth, makes this sort of conservation one we can easily identify with. But can we do very much about the problem?

Several psychologists at Princeton University have begun a research program aimed at conservation of electricity. As electricity is generated in several ways, with the burning of oil being a major source, significant changes in electrical usage could have major consequences for conservation.

Predicting Energy Consumption from Attitudes

In Chapter 5, the relationship between attitudes and behavior was discussed. In that chapter it was pointed out that one of the most persuasive arguments against continued attitude research was that attitudes and behavior do not correlate very well. Seligman, Kriss, Darley, Fazio, Becker, and Pryor (in press) have presented

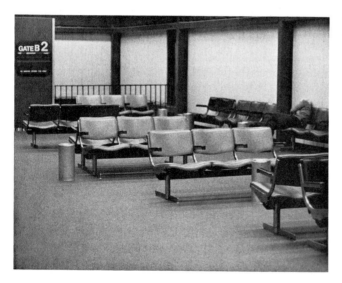

The chairs in this airport departure lounge are arranged to utilize space without giving the impression of crowding.

The top, left photo shows the site of the Ecology House built in an effort to conserve resources. It is built entirely underground, which reduces utility use substantially. The top, right photo shows the solar panels that further reduce fossil fuel use. As you can see, only the solar panels and the lamppost mar the wild landscape. The bottom photo shows all the rooms in the house open on an atrium and there is no feeling of being underground.

evidence that has a bearing on the relationship between attitudes and behavior on energy conservation.

Seligman et al. (in press) point out that attitudinal surveys carried out previously (e.g., Newman and Day, 1975) have been concerned with the percentage of respondents who have claimed to reduce their energy consumption. These surveys have not been specifically related to how self-reported conservation relates to their attitudes about conservation. Even though these surveys are conducted at regular intervals for up to several years (Milstein, 1976), the important connection between attitudes and behavior is not explicitly made. Seligman et al. (in press, p. 4) had quite a different goal in mind for their efforts, as they explicitly state:

527

The purpose of the present research was to begin the first step toward establishing the relationship between attitudes toward energy use and actual residential energy consumption. It is important to do this because once we have derived reliable attitudinal predictors of real energy consumption, subsequent research can begin to design energy campaigns that are explicitly directed at changing these attitudes. It is only after we know what attitudes are relevant to energy consumption that we can sensibly investigate experimentally the practicality of energy campaigns to change attitudes and energy consumption levels.

As this quotation makes clear, Seligman and his associates are very interested in the problem of energy conservation. They utilize survey techniques, and will use attitude-change techniques that have been developed through many years of basic social-psychological research. As in almost all successful and well-designed applied research efforts, the knowledge gained through years of basic research will be utilized.

Surveying Attitudes About Energy

In a research project on attitudes about energy, two different surveys were utilized, with 126 couples living in two- or three-bedroom townhouses responding. The first survey was given to 56 couples and then was refined and expanded before being given to 69 more couples. The resulting picture of these homeowners' attitudes toward energy revealed that six attitudes or clusters of attitudes were held by a sufficiently large number of the respondents to be considered representative. The first and most important was a personal comfort factor. For example, one item that taps this dimension was "I find I can't relax or work well unless the house is air-conditioned in the summer." A second dimension that was important was the respondent's belief that science could solve the energy crisis.

The third important factor was the individual's opportunity to play an important role in conserving energy. A fourth important factor is the effort it takes to save energy, and the resultant financial savings associated with energy conservation. The final two dimensions are a health factor and one that is concerned with the legitimacy of the energy crisis.

Predicting Actual Energy Consumption

The next step in the research reported by Seligman and his associates was to determine actual energy consumption for each household and its relationship to the attitudes surveyed. It was possible to determine that approximately 60 percent of the energy used by these respondents was associated with the six factors just mentioned. The most important factor was the individual's comfort, with health being next most important. Together these two factors accounted for approximately 53 percent of the variance in energy consumption by these families. The four other attitudinal factors isolated in the survey did not prove to be reliable predictors of energy consumption. The research has certain implications for energy conservation.

The implications of the results for energy conservation campaigns are clear. If the strongest determinant of residential summer energy consumption is the individual's need to live in a comfortable temperature, then that issue is what should be addressed. Individuals should be better informed about how to cool their houses without air-conditioning, e.g., regulating the use of window shades and drapes, opening windows in the evening as soon as outside temperature begins to drop, using window and attic fans, etc. Without doubt, once the comfort issue is recognized for its importance in energy conservation, imaginative and effective campaigns will be developed. [Seligman et al., in press, p. 18.]

Comment

It is possible to ascertain the relationship between attitudes and behavior, at least with regard to energy conservation. It remains to be seen whether effective campaigns designed to decrease energy consumption by changing attitudes can be developed. Certainly the information developed by Seligman and his associates lays a potentially valuable groundwork for such a campaign.

One interesting result of the Seligman et al. article is that comfort is shown to be so much more important than the financial savings that might result from energy conservation. Such a finding argues against the success of a campaign to reduce consumption based on the threat of increasing the price of energy. Of course, if the price is increased substantially, so that maintaining a comfortable temperature in the home interferes with other creature comforts, the picture may well change. That is, if the cost of energy is increased so much that the homeowner has to choose between being cool at home and all outside entertainment, a cool home may not seem so valuable. But unless a national policy for energy conservation is going to increase the cost of energy substantially, the importance of comfort may well overcome price.

Reducing Residential Energy Consumption

As part of the same program of research Seligman and Darley (1977) and Becker (in press) have reported on attempts to reduce energy consumption by two relatively simple means: feedback and goal setting. Consider for a moment electrical usage. How much electricity does it take to burn a light bulb for an hour? How much electricity is taken in turning on a light? Is it better to leave a light burning if you will not be using it for 5 minutes or to turn it off and turn it back on when you need it? How much electricity does it require to operate an electric range? A refrigerator? A clothes washer? A toaster? Most of us cannot answer such questions with any degree of accuracy. Neither can we estimate how to save energy. Most homeowners know that they burn a certain amount of electricity a month because their electric bill says they do. This is expressed in kilowatt-hours—a term that means virtually nothing to most individuals.

Feedback has been repeatedly shown to be effective in improving performance (Ammons, 1956; Bilodeau and Bilodeau, 1961). It can provide information about the type, extent, and direction of errors so they can be corrected. For example, consider the case of an individual shooting at a target. If the only feedback given is that the target was missed without also indicating that the shot went over or under, to the left or right, the archer can only guess at what sort of correction is needed to hit the target on the next shot. If, in addition, this information is delivered only once a month, it will not be very effective in improving the archer's marksmanship. Yet the feedback that is given to residential energy users is no more complete than that.

In addition to feedback, there is another variable which may affect performance—goals. There may be an implicit goal among all of us to conserve energy, but making that goal more explicit may also be helpful.

In the first of these two studies (Seligman and Darley, 1977), homeowners were given daily feedback about how much electricity they were using. Each day the electric meter was read and a percentage of expected electrical usage based on weather conditions and previous electrical usage by the homeowner was computed. This information was then recorded on a display mounted just outside the kitchen window. Thus homeowners could quickly check and determine whether they were using more or less electricity than expected. This relatively simple feedback scheme resulted in a 10.5 percent reduction in the homeowner's electrical usage.

Becker (in press) repeated the feedback aspect in his study but also added explicit goals. That is, he asked one group to reduce their energy consumption by 2 percent and another group to reduce their energy consumption by 20 percent. In addition he also asked two other groups to reduce their energy consumption by 2 percent and 20 percent but they were given no feedback as to how they were doing. Using both feedback and a difficult goal (20 percent reduction) resulted in a 13.0 percent reduction in the amount of electricity used. The other groups—an easy goal with feedback and easy and difficult goals with no feedback—did not result in any significant reduction in electrical usage. The results of the two studies combined suggest that homeowners in the Seligman and Darley study developed an implicit moderately difficult goal for themselves.

Comment

Reductions in energy consumption of the magnitude obtained by Seligman and Darley (1977) and Becker (in press) are of great significance. It has been estimated that 20 percent of the total energy used in the United States is used in private residences (Ross and Williams, 1976). If so simple a technique as giving feedback and setting goals can reduce that consumption by 13 percent between 2 and 3 percent of the total energy used in the United States could be saved. As feedback of this sort can be easily automated and presented, the total potential savings available are enormous.

If this approach is combined with attempts to change attitudes about energy conservation as advocated by Seligman and his associates, even more savings are possible. It is not inconceivable that this work could result in total energy savings of 5 percent or even more in the United States. Undoubtedly, as work into these psychological aspects of energy conservation continues, more savings will be realized. For example, there is a psychological variable—perhaps more than one—at work in the popularity of large cars with large engines. Although it is true that these cars are faster and more impressive than their smaller, less powerful, counterparts, they also consume much more gasoline. Alterations in the psychological factors that enter into the decision to buy a large car are another way in which psychologists can aid in conserving valuable natural resources.

Environmental Pollution

Environmental pollution is a problem that afflicts both Canada and the United States, but is not viewed by most individuals as a problem that they themselves cause. It is easy to say that industry pollutes rivers and oceans. It is equally easy to contend that the air we breathe is polluted by others. There have been efforts to call attention to each individual's involvement in pollution. For example, the motto of a well-known antipollution group is "People Start Pollution, People Can Stop It." Psychologists have attempted to modify behaviors for pollution control by utilizing several techniques. One of the most prevalent techniques is operant conditioning. Littering behavior has been the prime target of these efforts, although patronage of mass transit, reduction of energy consumption, and recycling have also been studied (Tuso and Geller, 1976). For purposes of clarity and brevity we shall discuss the antilittering and recycling studies.

Litterbugs

We may seldom see litterbugs at work, but the results of their actions are everywhere. By the side of highways, on beaches, in parks, on the streets and just about everywhere people congregate, litter accumulates. Why do people litter and, more importantly, can something be done about it? Psychologists have been interested primarily in altering littering behavior. For example Finnie (1973) decreased littering by increasing the number of trash receptacles along a highway and a city sidewalk and by decorating the trash barrels in a city. Dodge (1972) increased the frequency of appropriate disposition of litter in a small city with an antilitter campaign that used posters, handouts, bumper stickers, and so forth. Burgess, Clark, and Hendee (1971) increased the number of children that gathered litter in litterbags at a movie theater by announcing specific instructions for using the litterbags. These studies are important because they demonstrate that prompting people to dispose of litter properly is effective in decreasing littering.

Geller and his associates (Geller, 1973, 1975, Geller, Witmer, and Orebaugh, 1976; Geller, Witmer, and Tuso, 1977) have been extremely active in research aimed at reducing littering. The research has compared the effectiveness of various antilitter messages. For example Geller (1973, 1975) distributed handbills to individuals entering a movie theater or a grocery store. The handbills had either no antilitter message, a general antilitter message, (i.e., "Please dispose of properly") or a specific antilitter message that designated the location of trash receptacles. In general, the specific instructions were most effective in reducing litter, but general instructions were also helpful.

Geller, Witmer, and Tuso (1977) investigated several variables that might influence littering in a grocery store. In a carefully controlled field experiment males' and females' littering behavior was compared when there were instructions on the handbills to dispose of them in a specified location for recycling purposes. Careful tabulation of the disposition of all handbills was kept and it was found that specific instructions to recycle rather than litter decreased littering. The results are presented in Figure 12–5. (Males and females did not differ in their littering.) Thus it seems apparent that a simple prompt in the form of an antilittering message is effective in reducing littering.

If It's Clean, Will It Stay Clean?

There is something about a clean environment which, it seems, encourages cleanliness. One of the most striking features of San Francisco, at least to those of us who live in the East, is its cleanliness. The streets are clean, the cars are clean, and the air seems cleaner. How do San Franciscans do it? I am not sure how the whole city stays clean, but there is some evidence that people work to keep clean areas clean. For example, Finnie (1973) recorded the frequency that hot dog wrappers were disposed of improperly in Philadelphia. Four areas of the city were selected, two clean and two dirty. One clean area and one dirty area had trash cans available, whereas the other two areas did not. In the clean area with a trash can, 15 percent of the hot dog eaters littered; 34 percent littered in the clean area without a trash can; 33 percent littered in a dirty area with a trash can, and 51 percent littered in a dirty area without a trash can. Finnie concluded that environment (clean vs dirty) and trash can availability are of equal importance in litter control.

Geller, Witmer, and Tuso (1977) investigated the effects of clean and dirty environments on littering more systematically. These investigators conducted a study in two grocery stores. Handbills advertising specials of the week were handed out to

Not all littered areas are this bad. This scene is within a very few blocks of a main artery in a major city.

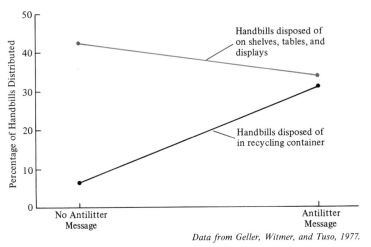

Figure 12-5 Percentage of handbills disposed of properly under conditions of no prompting or of antilittering prompting.

shoppers as they entered the supermarket and the disposal of the handbills was recorded. These did not contain instructions for disposal, and those given to males were marked differently than those given to females. In addition, on half the experimental days a "dirty" condition was implemented. A total of 140 handbills were placed around the store to suggest that earlier shoppers had disposed of their handbills on the floor, shelves, and display tables. Thus it was possible to compare the amount of littering that occurred when the store was clean and when it was dirty. When the store was littered, 5 percent of the individuals disposed of their handbills on the floor, whereas only 1 percent disposed of them on the floor when the store was clean. Males and females did not differ in the amount of floor littering that they did.

It does appear that if a place is clean, it will be kept clean. In many ways this should not be surprising. One of the more influential components of behavior is what has been termed modeling (see Chapter 8). If people see others performing a behavior, they are much more likely to engage in that behavior also. As we have seen in Chapter 11, Zimbardo attributes many antisocial activities to large groups of people who see others engaging in certain antisocial behaviors. Thus it should come as no surprise to us that modeling affects littering behavior.

Strictly speaking, however, modeling does not account for all of the littering observed by Geller, Witmer, and Tuso. Recall that the stores were prelittered. That is, the handbills were distributed throughout the store to look as though people had dropped them. In only a few instances, in which one customer saw another customer actually dispose of a handbill improperly, did anyone see a model litter. The effects of the littering were sufficient to increase dramatically the number of handbills dropped on the floor. This result is important in any attempt to reduce litter. It argues that cities which are kept clean will have an easier job of maintaining that cleanliness. If, as both the Finnie (1973) and the Geller et al. (1977) studies indicate, dirty places are littered more and clean ones are kept clean by the populace, then keeping a city clean means that it will be easier to maintain that cleanliness.

Another way to reduce trash pollution is to recycle containers, paper, and so forth. Not only does this approach decrease the amount of trash, but it also conserves natural resources by reusing materials. Paper, aluminum, and many other commodities can be reused. In an effort to reduce litter, some states in the United States have passed laws that prohibit the sale of beverages in nonreturnable containers. This is an important component in the effort to reduce litter and conserve natural resources, but there are many commodities that are not amenable to such a solution.

The recycling of paper is of great potential benefit to conservation efforts. Many articles that use paper can use recycled paper. The more recycled paper that is used, the fewer trees will have to be cut to provide the raw material for new paper. The ramifications of a recycling policy are enormous. The question is, however, how to get people to recycle products.

Even though many recycling programs have been developed, solid wastes have been reduced by less than 1 percent by even the most efficient ones (Hall and Ackoff, 1972). Thus, it seems that some other incentive may be necessary to increase the efficiency of recycling programs. Geller, Chaffee, and Ingram (1975) found that giving raffle tickets for each paper delivery to a recycling center or engaging two dormitories in a contest to see which one could contribute the most paper resulted in increased paper collected at the recycling center.

In the programs aimed at reducing litter, Geller and his associates concentrated on environmental variables, e.g., instructions for disposal of wastes, trash cans, and clean or dirty environments. Witmer and Geller (1976) point out that recycling will probably be more influenced by reinforcement contingencies for bringing recyclable

A recycling center.

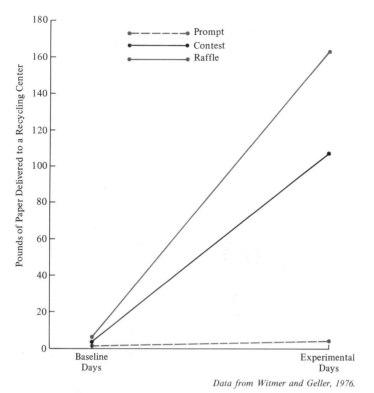

Data from Witmer and Geller, 1976.

Figure 12-6 Comparison of increase in amount of paper per day delivered to a recycling center under an environmental contingency (prompt) and under two reinforcement contingencies.

products to a recycling center. They set out to test one environmental contingency and two reinforcement contingencies.

Six dormitories served as the experimental setting. Two dormitories, one male and one female, were prompted to recycle paper. Two other dorms, one male and one female, were given one raffle ticket for each pound of paper brought to the recycling center. Prizes for the raffles ranged in value from $3.00 to $20.00. The final two dorms, both male, engaged in a contest with the winning dorm each week receiving a $15.00 prize. Baseline measurements were taken before and after the various experimental contingencies.

The results are shown in Figure 12–6. It is obvious that the prompt condition had almost no effect on the amount of paper delivered to the recycling center. However, both the contest and the raffle conditions increased the amount of paper delivered. Even though it appears that the raffle condition was more effective in increasing the amount of paper delivered to the recycling center, an experimental artifact may have caused these results. One of two dormitories paired for the contest was an R.O.T.C. dorm and the other was not. The R.O.T.C. dorm delivered less than 10 pounds a day over the three-week period and the civilian dorm decreased its amount each week although still delivering enough paper to win the contest. The civilian dorm had a purpose for the $15.00. They used it to buy beer and throw a party each week. Parties were not allowed in the R.O.T.C. dorm. Thus it may be that if the R.O.T.C. dorm had had a purpose for the money and a real contest had ensued, the contest dorms would have delivered as much or more paper than the raffle dorms.

The importance of this artifact needs to be investigated. Even though merchants donated the prizes given away in the raffle, 10 prizes were given away each week. The prizes ranged in price from $3.00 to $20.00. Thus it is obvious that the contest condition was considerably less expensive than the raffle condition. If a real contest were developed—that is, two groups competing for the prize—then it might be more economical to encourage paper recycling with contests.

It is clear that the problems associated with recycling, unlike reducing litter, are not affected to any great extent by prompts. Apparently some sort of reward condition is needed, although the reward need not be extremely valuable. There are, of course, other goals that may be used to promote recycling. Organizations may choose to hold paper collection drives (or any other type of recyclable drive) as a money-raising activity. The price of these materials fluctuates, but often it is helpful to the organization's treasury as well as the environment to encourage recycling.

Comment

The world we live in is an interesting and unique one. Apparently it is far more fragile than had been previously thought, and we are quite sensitive to both our physical and our psychological environment. As more research is carried out in such areas as personal space, crowding, and the effects of overpopulation, it is becoming increasingly apparent that we and our environment are inextricably interwoven. The human race lives on a planet whose resources are being taxed by the sheer numbers of us. What we will do when those resources are depleted, as some say they surely will be soon, is an open question. In the interim, several solutions to the problems of the environment have been suggested.

Probably the most important step is to stabilize the population of the world. No matter what other steps are taken, a population that continues to expand at a rapid rate will make all other efforts futile. With a stable population, however, some of the efforts discussed in this chapter, along with many others, may be effective in protecting the fragile environment.

The proper disposal of waste and the reuse of materials to protect the natural resources of the earth are two ways in which the environment can be protected. We have not discussed air, water, and noise pollution in this chapter simply because it is not possible to cover all areas of environmental concern. Certainly air and water pollution are health hazards, are hazards to all living things on the earth, and must be curbed if life in the form we now know it is to continue. The importance and the complexity of environmental problems cannot be overemphasized. Environmental problems must and can be solved and this chapter has been an attempt to give you some insight into the work psychologists are doing to solve them.

1 The world's population is growing at the rate of about 2 percent a year, which means that it doubles every 35 years. Resources do not normally make themselves felt in any negative way until they are scarce. An ever increasing population must eventually face resource shortages.

2 Personal space is the area around each individual through which others should not pass. Research has indicated that individuals will flee if their personal space is invaded. Theories to account for personal space include the equilibrium theory, perceived threat, and stimulation theory.

3 It seems likely that male-female space is less than female-female space, which is less than male-male space. Culture affects personal space; also people tend to stand closer to people they like than to people they dislike.

4 There is some disagreement concerning the effects of crowding, but the evidence seems to support the contention that it is harmful. Crowding is a complex variable and too many or too few people in a given area can cause unpleasant feelings, reduce liking, and may impair performance.

5 Much of the disagreement concerning the effects of crowding on behavior may stem from the fact that experimenters are not consistent in the number of square feet per person that is labeled crowded, group size is allowed to vary and different activities require different amounts of space.

6 Freedman has proposed a density-intensity theory of overcrowding that emphasizes the intensifying effects on any emotion of being crowded. Haller has proposed a social learning theory that defines crowding as the ratio of available space to acceptable space.

7 Conservation is an important area of environmental psychology. Research has indicated that the attitudes of homeowners toward energy can be categorized and that comfort is the most important consideration. This finding argues against the effectiveness of an energy conservation plan based on the avoidance of increased cost.

8 Reductions in energy consumption are possible when feedback is given and goals are set. Most individuals do not know how much electricity is used in their home until the monthly bill arrives. Setting a goal for energy prediction and giving frequent feedback result in substantial savings.

9 Littering can be reduced by prompting people to dispose of litter properly and by keeping areas clean.

10 Recycling is an efficient way to protect natural resources and to reduce litter, yet it is not extensively utilized. Research indicates that reinforcement is effective in increasing the amount of paper brought to recycling centers.

GLOSSARY

Acceptable Space   A learned expectation concerning spatial norms.

Available Space   A physical variable that is a function of the number of persons present and the amount of space available.

Competing Response A response that is incorrect.

Competitional List A paired associates' learning task with many competing responses.

Complex Task A task that has many competing responses.

Crowding A psychological state of stress that occurs when the individual becomes sensitive to the restrictions imposed by high density.

Density An objective physical state that involves potential inconvenience because of restricted movement or lack of privacy.

Density-intensity Theory A theory of overcrowding which states that whatever emotion is being felt, overcrowding intensifies it.

Functional Space The amount of space functionally available to an individual.

Interaction Distance The straight-line distance between two parties to a social interaction.

Intimate Zone From physical contact to 18 inches apart.

Noncompetitional List A paired associates' learning task with few competing responses.

Paired Associates A performance task in which the first word of a pair is presented to the subject, who must respond with the second word in the pair.

Personal Distance From 18 inches to 4 feet.

Personal Space An area surrounding each individual through which others should not pass.

Public Distance From 12 to 25 feet.

Recycling Reusing resources by collecting and, if necessary, reprocessing them.

Simple Task A task that does not have many competing responses.

Social Distance From 4 to 12 feet.

REFERENCES

Aiello, J. R., Y. M. Epstein, and R. A. Karlin. The effects of crowding on electrodermal activity. *Sociological Symposium,* Fall 1975, 32–40.

Allport, G. W. The historical background of modern social psychology. In G. Lindzey and E. Aronson (Eds.), *Handbook of Social Psychology.* Vol. I (2nd Edition). Reading, Mass.: Addison-Wesley Publishing Co., Inc., 1968, Pp. 1–70.

Ammons, R. B. Effects of knowledge of performance: A survey and tentative theoretical formulation. *Journal of General Psychology,* 1956, *54,* 279–99.

Argyle, M., and J. Dean. Eye-contact, distance, and affiliation. *Sociometry,* 1965, *28,* 289–304.

Ashcraft, N., and A. E. Scheflen. *People Space: The Making and Breaking of Human Boundaries.* Garden City, N.Y.: Anchor Books, 1976.

Asimov, I. Colonizing the heavens. *Saturday Review,* 1975, *2,* 12–13, 15–17.

Barefoot, J. C., H. Hoople, and D. McClay. Avoidance of an act which would violate personal space. *Psychonomic Science,* 1972, *28,* 205–206.

Baum, A., and S. Valins. Residential environments; group size and crowding. *Proceedings of the American Psychological Association,* 81st Annual Convention, 1973, 211–12.

Becker, L. J. Reducing residential energy consumption through feedback and goal setting. *Journal of Applied Psychology,* in press.

Bilodeau, E. A., and I. McD. Bilodeau. Motor-skills learning. *Annual Review of Psychology,* 1961, *12,* 243–80.

Burgess, R. L., R. N. Clark, and J. C. Hendee. An experimental analysis of anti-litter procedures. *Journal of Applied Behavior Analysis,* 1971, *4,* 71–75.

Buttel, F. H. Social science and the environment: Competing theories. *Social Science Quarterly,* 1976, *57,* 1976.

Byrne, D., G. D. Baskett, and L. Hodges. Behavioral indicators of interpersonal attraction. *Journal of Applied Social Psychology,* 1971, *1,* 137–49.

———, ———, and ———. Behavioral indicators of interpersonal attraction. *Journal of Applied Social Psychology,* 1972, *7,* 43–48.

Calhoun, J. B. Phenomena associated with population density. *Proceedings of the National Academy of Science,* 1961, *47,* 428–29.

———. Population, density and social pathology. *Scientific American,* 1962(a), *206:* 139–48(a).

———. A "behavioral sink." In E. L. Bliss (Ed.), *Roots of Behavior.* New York: Harper & Row, Publishers, 1962 (b).

Carey, G. W. Density, crowding, stress, and the ghetto. *American Behavioral Scientist,* 1972, *15,* 495–509.

Cozby, P. C. Effects of density, activity, and personality on environmental preferences. *Journal of Experimental Research in Personality,* 1973, *1,* 45–60.

Daves, W. F., and P. W. Swaffer. Effect of room size on critical interpersonal distance. *Perceptual and Motor Skills,* 1971, *33,* 926.

Demeny, P. The populations of under developed countries. *Scientific American,* 1974, *231,* 148–59.

Desor, J. A. Toward a psychological theory of crowding. *Journal of Personality and Social Psychology,* 1972, *21,* 79–83.

Dodge, M. C. Modification of littering behavior: An explanatory study. Unpublished Master's Thesis, Utah State University, 1972.

Dosey, M. A., and M. Meisels. Personal space and self-protection. *Journal of Personality and Social Psychology,* 1969, *11,* 93–97.

Duke, M. P., and S. Nowicki. A new measure and social learning for interpersonal distance. *Journal of Experimental Research in Personality,* 1972, *6,* 119–32.

Efran, M. G., and J. A. Cheyne. Affective concomitants of the invasion of shared space: Behavioral, physiological, and verbal indicators. *Journal of Personality and Social Psychology,* 1974, *29,* 219–26.

Epstein, Y. M., and R. A. Karlin. Effects of acute experimental crowding. *Journal of Applied Social Psychology,* 1975, *5,* 34–53.

Evans, G. W., and R. B. Howard. A methodological investigation of personal space. In W. J. Mitchell (Ed.), *Environmental Design: Research and Practice* (*Proceedings of the EDRA III/AR VIII Conference*). Los Angeles: University of California Press, 1972.

Felipe, N. J., and R. Sommer. Invasions of personal space. *Social Problems,* 1966, *14,* 206–214.

Finnie, W. C. Field experiments in litter control. *Environment and Behavior,* 1973, *5,* 125–28.

Frankel, A. A., and J. Barrett. Variations of personal space as a function of authoritarianism, self-esteem, and racial characteristics of a stimulus situation. *Journal of Consulting and Clinical Psychology,* 1971, *37,* 95–98.

Freedman, J., A. S. Levy, R. W. Buchanan, and J. Price. Crowding and human aggression. *Journal of Experimental Social Psychology,* 1972, *8,* 528–48.

Freedman, J. L. *Crowding and Behavior.* New York: The Viking Press, Inc., 1975.

———, S. Klevansky, and P. Ehrlich. The effect of crowding on human task performance. *Journal of Applied Social Psychology,* 1971, *1,* 7–25.

Geller, E. S. Prompting anti-litter behaviors. *Proceedings of the 81st Annual Convention of the American Psychological Association,* 1973, *8,* 901–902.

————. Increasing desired waste disposals with instructions. *Man-Environment Systems,* 1975, *5,* 125–28.

————, J. L. Chaffee, and R. E. Ingram. Promoting paper-recycling on a university campus. *Journal of Environmental Systems,* 1975, *5,* 39–57.

————, J. F. Witmer, and A. L. Orebaugh. Instructions as a determinant of paper-disposal behaviors. *Environment and Behavior,* 1976, *8,* 417–39.

————, ————, and M. A. Tuso. Environmental interventions for litter control. *Journal of Applied Psychology,* 1977, *62,* 344–51.

Griffitt, W., and R. Veitch. Hot and crowded: Influence of population, density and temperature on interpersonal affective behavior. *Journal of Personality and Social Psychology,* 1971, *17,* 92–98.

Hall, E. T. *The Silent Language.* Doubleday & Company, Inc., 1959.

————. *The Hidden Dimension.* Garden City, N.Y. Doubleday & Company, Inc., 1966.

Hall, J. R., and R. L. Ackoff. A systems approach to the problems of solid waste and litter. *Journal of Environmental Systems,* 1972, *2,* 351–64.

Haller, J. Room density as a function of affect and attraction. Unpublished Master's Thesis, University of Oklahoma, 1972.

————. The energization properties of overcrowding. Unpublished doctoral dissertation, University of Oklahoma, 1974.

————, and J. Lamberth. Room density as a determinant of affect and attraction. Paper presented at the annual meeting of the Southwestern Psychological Association, Dallas, 1973.

Hartnett, J. J., K. G. Bailey, and F. W. Gibson. Personal space as influence by sex and type of movement. *Journal of Psychology,* 1970, *76,* 139–44.

Hayduk, L. A. Personal space: An evaluative and orienting overview. *Psychological Bulletin,* 1978, *85,* 117–34.

Hediger, H. Zur biologie und psychologie der flecht bei tieren. *Biologisches Zentralblatt,* 1934, *54,* 21–40.

————. *Wild Animals in Captivity.* London: Thornton Butterworth Ltd., 1950.

Holohan, C., and G. Levinger. Psychological versus spatial determinants of social schema distance: A methodological note. *Journal of Abnormal Psychology,* 1971, *78,* 232–36.

Hull, C. L. *Essentials of Behavior.* New Haven, Conn.: Yale University Press, 1951.

Hutt, C., and M. J. Vaizey. Differential effects of group density on social behavior. *Nature,* 1966, *209,* 1371–72.

Jones, S. E., and J. R. Aiello. Proxemic behavior of black and white first-, third-, and fifth-grade children. *Journal of Personality and Social Psychology,* 1973, *25,* 21–27.

Karabenick, S. A., and M. Meisels. Effects of performance evaluation on interpersonal distance. *Journal of Personality,* 1972, *40,* 275–87.

Konečni, V. J., L. Libuser, H. Morton, and E. B. Ebbensen. Effects of a violation of personal space on escape and helping response. *Journal of Experimental Social Psychology,* 1975, *11,* 288–99.

Kutner, D. J., Jr. Overcrowding: Human responses to density and visual exposure. *Human Relations,* 1973, *26,* 31–50.

Langer, E. J., and S. Saegert. Crowding and cognitive control. *Journal of Personality and Social Psychology,* 1977, *35,* 175–82.

Lawrence, J. Science and sentiment: Overview of research on crowding and human behavior. *Psychological Bulletin,* 1974, *81,* 712–20.

Leibman, M. The effects of sex and race norms on personal space. *Environment and Behavior,* 1970, *2,* 208–246.

Linder, D. E. Personal space. In J. W. Thibaut, J. T. Spence, and R. C. Carson (Eds.), *Contemporary Topics in Social Psychology.* Morristown, N.J.: General Learning Press, 1976.

Little, K. B., F. J. Vlehla, and C. Henderson. Value congruence and interaction distance. *Journal of Social Psychology,* 1965, *75,* 249–253.

Little, K. B. Cultural variations in social schemata. *Journal of Personality and Social Psychology,* 1968, *10,* 1–7.

Martens, R., and D. M. Landers. Evaluation potential as a determinant of coaction effects. *Journal of Experimental Social Psychology,* 1972, *8,* 347–59.

Mehrabian, A. Relationship of attitude to seated posture, orientation and distance. *Journal of Personality and Social Psychology,* 1968, *10,* 26–30.

Middlemist, R. D., E. S. Knowles, and C. F. Matter. Personal space invasion in the lavatory: Suggestive evidence for arousal. *Journal of Personality and Social Psychology,* 1976, *33,* 541–46.

Milstein, J. S. Attitudes, knowledge, and behavior of American consumers regarding energy conservation with some implications for governmental action. Federal Energy Office, Office of Energy Conservation and Environment, Washington, D.C., 1976.

Nesbitt, P. D., and G. Steven. Personal space and stimulus intensity at a Southern California amusement park. *Sociometry,* 1971, *34,* 114–21.

Newman, D. K., and D. Day. *The Stevens energy consumer.* Cambridge, Mass.: Ballinger, 1975.

Patterson, M. L. Compensation in nonverbal immediacy behaviors: A review. *Sociometry,* 1973, *36,* 237–52.

———. Factors affecting interpersonal spatial proximity. Paper presented at the annual meeting of the American Psychological Association, New Orleans, September 1974.

———, S. Mullens, and J. Romano. Compensatory reactions to spatial intrusion. *Sociometry,* 1971, *34,* 114–21.

Paulus, P., A. B. Annis, J. J. Seta, J. K. Schkade, and R. W. Matthews. Density does affect task performance. *Journal of Personality and Social Psychology,* 1976, *34,* 248–53.

Paulus, P. B., V. Cox, G. McCain, and J. Chandler. Some effects of crowding in prison environment. *Journal of Applied Social Psychology,* 1975, *5,* 86–91.

Ross, M., B. Layton, B. Erickson, and J. Schopler. Affect, facial regard, and reactions to crowding. *Journal of Personality and Social Psychology,* 1973, *28,* 69–76.

Ross, M. H., and R. H. Williams. Energy efficiency: Our most underated energy resource. *The Bulletin of the Atomic Scientists,* November 1976, 30–38.

Saegert, S. The effects of spatial and social density on arousal, mood and social orientation. Unpublished doctoral dissertation, University of Michigan, 1974.

Scherer, S. E. Proxemic behavior of primary school children as a function of their socioeconomic class and subculture. *Journal of Personality and Social Psychology,* 1974, *29,* 800–805.

Schettino, A. P., and R. J. Borden. Sex differences in response to naturalistic crowding: Affective reactions to group size and group density. *Personality and Social Psychology Bulletin,* 1976, *2,* 67–70.

Schmitt, R. C. Density, delinquency, and crime in Honolulu. *Sociology and Social Research,* 1957, *41,* 274–76.

———. Density, health, and social disorganization. *Journal of American Institute of Planners.* 1966, *32,* 38–40.

Seligman, C., and J. M. Darley. Feedback as a means of decreasing residential energy consumption. *Journal of Applied Psychology,* 1977, *62,* 363–68.

————, M. Kriss, J. M. Darley, R. H. Fazio, L. J. Becker, and J. B. Pryor. Predicting residential energy consumption from homeowner's attitudes. *Journal of Applied Social Psychology,* in press.

Seta, J. J., P. B. Paulus, and J. K. Schkade. Effects of group size and proximity under cooperative and competitive conditions. *Journal of Personality and Social Psychology,* 1976, *34,* 47–53.

Sherrod, D. R. Crowding, perceived control, and behavioral afteraffects. *Journal of Applied Social Psychology,* 1974, *4,* 171–86.

Smith, F. J., and J. E. S. Lawrence. Alone and crowded: The effects of spatial restrictions on measures of affect and simulation response. *Personality and Social Psychology Bulletin,* 1978, *4,* 139–42.

Smith, S., and W. M. Haythorn. Effects of compatibility, crowding, group size, and leadership seniority on stress, anxiety, hostility, and annoyance in isolated groups. *Journal of Personality and Social Psychology,* 1972, *22,* 67–79.

Sommer, R. *Personal space: The basis of behavioral design.* Englewood Cliffs, N.J.: Prentice-Hall, 1969.

Spence, J. T., and K. W. Spence. The motivational components of manifest anxiety, drive and stimuli. In C. D. Spielberger (Ed.), *Anxiety and Behavior.* New York: Academic Press, Inc., 1966.

Spence, K. W. *Behavior Theory and Learning.* Englewood Cliffs, N.J.: Prentice-Hall, Inc., 1960.

Stokols, D. On the distinction between density and crowding: Some implications for future research. *Psychological Review,* 1972, *79,* 275–77.

————, M. Rall, B. Pinner, and J. Schopler. Physical, social and personal determinants of the perception of crowding. *Environment and Behavior,* 1973, *6,* 87–115.

Sundstrom, E. An experimental study of crowding: Effects of room size, intrusion, and goal blocking on nonverbal behavior, self-disclosure, and self-reported stress. *Journal of Personality and Social Psychology,* 1975, *32,* 645–54.

Tuso, M. A., and E. S. Geller. Behavior analysis applied to environmental/ecological problems: A review. *Journal of Applied Behavior Analysis,* 1976, *9,* 526 (Ms. No. 02828).

Valins, S., and A. Baum. Residential group size, social interaction and crowding. *Environment and Behavior,* 1973, *5,* 421–40.

Watson, O. M., and T. D. Graves. Quantitative research in proxemic behavior. *American Anthropologist,* 1966, *68,* 971–85.

Winsborough, H. H. The social consequences of high population density. *Law and Contemporary Problems,* 1965, *30,* 120–26.

Witmer, J. F., and E. S. Geller. Facilitating paper recycling: Effects of prompts, raffles and contests. *Journal of Applied Behavior Analysis,* 1976, *9,* 315–22.

Worchel, S., and C. Teddlie. The experience of crowding: A two-factor theory. *Journal of Personality and Social Psychology,* 1976, *34,* 34–40.

Zuckerman, M., M. Schmitz, and A. Yesha. Effects of crowding in a student environment. *Journal of Applied Social Psychology,* 1977, *7,* 67–72.

Applied Social Psychology

13

The distinction between basic and applied research is a thin one. The scientist who is working to solve a puzzle and follows the leads that will, in his or her estimation, provide the most knowledge or are of most interest to the individual is doing basic research. The same scientist who has a problem in mind and sets out to solve that

543

problem is doing applied research. For example, the scientist who is interested in aggression and spends thirty years studying the topic and following the leads he or she finds most interesting is doing basic research. Another scientist who is interested in the increasing incidence in aggressive crimes and spends thirty years trying to find a way to reduce such crimes is doing applied research. It may be that both scientists will perform similar or even identical experiments in the course of their research. Basic and applied research cannot be distinguished by the actual research that is done, rather the distinction between the two is a function of the end the researcher has in mind.

It may seem to you that social psychology, by its very nature, is all applied research. That is, because there are so many social problems in the world, the social psychologist must be attempting to solve problems. In point of fact, much of the research we have discussed in this book was aimed at solving problems and much was not. There is more rapid "fall-out" from basic research discoveries in social psychology than in many other sciences. For example, a physicist may discover the laser and then uses will be found for it many years later. If a social psychologist found a way to eliminate prejudice and discrimination, its implementation would be much more rapid because its uses are so obvious. Thus, in one sense, all of social psychology is applied—or will be as soon as breakthroughs come. Look back over the major topics covered in this book and note how relevant each one is to everyday life. A breakthrough in socializing children, changing attitudes, alleviating prejudice or undue pressures for conformity, reducing aggression, or increasing attraction would be implemented very rapidly.

Ironically, however, there is a climate in Canada and the United States that allows such attacks on research as the one by Senator William Proxmire. Proxmire's attack was specifically aimed at the research of Ellen Berscheid and Elaine Walster as outrageous wastes of the taxpayers' money. What Proxmire objected to for two reasons, was the scientific study of love. First, Proxmire argued that no matter how much money was spent, the scientists wouldn't get an answer anyone would believe. That Proxmire was not entirely convinced of the validity of his argument is attested to by his next statement, which was "I'm against it because I don't want the answer." Obviously, if the answer cannot be found, Senator Proxmire need not worry about getting an answer he doesn't want. These two statements by Proxmire, however, point out a very important element in research in the social sciences.

Human Nature and Lawfulness

The "You can't answer it and even if you could I don't want to know" syndrome is a very important part of the life of a social scientist. Proxmire was taken to task for his blast at Berscheid's grant by James Reston of the *New York Times*. Reston (1975, p. 13) said that the funding of such research "could be the best investment of Federal money since Mr. Jefferson made the Louisiana Purchase." Reston's arguments were based on the assumption that a better understanding of marriage, divorce, and population growth would be invaluable to our society. Proxmire (1975, p. 14)

If the $133,000 spent for the study was genuinely being spent for the purposes Mr. Reston asserts, there might be some merit in the Federal Government's funding it. But the summary of the project written by the National Science Foundation which led me to make my criticism doesn't mention marriage, divorce, or population growth. Instead, it talks of "dependency variables," and "dyadic relationships."

Unfortunately, Senator Proxmire didn't seem to know that a dyad is "a couple or pair" and Dr. Berscheid *possibly* could have avoided the situation if she had said she was interested in why intimate relationships begin and why they do or do not continue. If you review the work of Berscheid and the Walsters in Chapter 9, you will note that Mr. Reston seems to be the more perceptive individual of the two.

Most social psychologists assume that human behavior follows certain laws, that these laws can be discovered, and we do want to know what they are. Possibly Senator Proxmire does not want to know why two people fall in love, but many of us do. If we know why people fall in love and then either stay there or fall out of love, we'll have an opportunity to cut the soaring divorce rate. The accompanying reduction in emotional trauma to the couple, and even more importantly to the children involved, would be worth a lot.

There are two issues that I have raised in this discussion and possibly it would help if we sorted them out. First, there is the issue of whether human behavior is based on natural laws and, if so, whether these laws can be discovered and utilized. This is basically an emotional issue. Social scientists say that it is, and they want to know the laws, while some other individuals are uncomfortable with the idea that our behavior follows a "lawful" pattern. I could point to innumerable instances of social scientists predicting human behavior to prove it is lawful. However, the only people I would convince, I fear, are those who already agree. Those who disagree could and do point to innumerable instances of behavior that cannot be predicted to support their contention.

Second, there is the issue of basic and applied research. Proxmire is arguing against knowledge, which is the fundamental tenet of basic research, when he says he doesn't want to know why two people fall in love. However, he does seem to be saying that he wants to know more about divorce. The irony is that the knowledge gained in research in love could be applied to help solve the problem of divorce. Thus, Proxmire does not want the basic knowledge but does want solutions to problems. It is not unusual for people to be uninterested in knowledge but interested in solutions. Unfortunately for them, the knowledge precedes the solutions.

Applied Research

Applied research is a problem-solving endeavor and there are an enormous number of societal problems that need to be solved. Many of them have been mentioned in other chapters. Now, however, we will spend this chapter reviewing specific problem oriented-research areas.

The general areas I have chosen to highlight are human sexual behavior, criminal justice, and smoking. The three are not tightly bound together except that they are applied and there is exciting research going on in each area. The very diversity of these three topics will, I hope, give you a flavor of applied social psychology.

Human Sexual Behavior

The major scientific approach to sex research prior to 1960 was the Kinsey reports on male and female sexuality (Kinsey, Pomeroy, and Martin, 1948; Kinsey, Pomeroy, Martin, and Gebhard, 1953). These reports (which were discussed in Chapter 2) were surveys of men and women's sexual practices. They contained a disadvantage that all self-report measures contain—they relied on the memory and truthfulness of the respondents. In spite of these drawbacks, Kinsey and his associates did a most impressive job, against difficult pressures, of cataloging the sexual practices of the 1940s. If Senator Proxmire does not want to know about love in the 1970s you can imagine how much the politicians of Kinsey's day wanted to know about sex—at least publicly.

Scientists always work within the society in which they live. If the topic of their investigation is controversial or taboo, it makes their work much more difficult. The history of research into sexual practices in Canada and the United States is and has been controversial. Therefore individuals who wished to study the subject have had to exercise caution. For example, in their early work Masters and Johnson (1966) sought no publicity, and when it came there were expressions of outrage and anger from many individuals. These investigators brought individuals and couples into the laboratory and observed as they engaged in various sexual acts while their physiological responses were monitored. The outcries against such experimentation were loud; yet their work was vitally important. As Byrne and Byrne (1977, p. 58) say,

It was easy enough to express shock at this work or to be amused by the idea of white-coated researchers peering eagerly at their busy subjects. One scene in the play *Oh! Calcutta!* makes fun of such a situation: the male and female subjects engage in intercourse attached to electrodes as the doctor and nurse sing a love song. Despite such satire and a good many angry condemnations, the findings of Masters and Johnson have had a tremendous influence both on sexual therapy and on the average person's understanding of sex.

Changes in Sexual Themes

If you read the Kinsey report, it is hard in the light of present-day literature, candor, and media presentations to find anything shocking about it. Yet when the work of Kinsey and his associates was published, it interested, embarrassed, and shocked many people. It also became a best-seller even though by today's standards it is rather dull reading.

Prior to the Kinsey report, the publication of James Joyce's *Ulysses* (1914) and D. H. Lawrence's *Lady Chatterley's Lover* (1928) laid the groundwork for sexual candor in literature. Until 1708 there were no laws against explicit sexual material in literature (Byrne and Byrne, 1977) when such attempts began in England. Shortly thereafter strict antipornography statutes were enacted throughout the world, which have been softened in the last several years. Court battles and censorship were unsuccessfully employed against *Ulysses* and *Lady Chatterley's Lover.* Since the court decision in 1933 to admit *Ulysses* to the United States, sexual candor has increased in respectable literature. Byrne (1977) briefly summarizes the changes in the literature of the period between 1933 and the late 1970s. He concludes that there appears to be little possibility of an increase in sexual candor in literature because all restraints have been abandoned.

Pictorial representations of sexual activity have also increased. Nudity in magazines was limited to bare-breasted women in *National Geographic* and nudist magazines prior to the early 1950s when *Playboy* was first published. From what are now considered very modest pictures, a number of magazines have proceeded to showing nude shots of both males and females. However, the explicitness of literature has not yet been reached, in that these publications do not show intercourse or any other overt sexual activity involving more than one person.

Movies have undergone changes in the direction of explicitness that are more analogous to literature than they are to magazine depiction of sex. In 1934 a production code of ethics was adopted by moviemakers in Hollywood. The code was extremely restrictive by present-day standards. Movies produced in accordance with this code portrayed married couples sleeping in twin beds, short kisses with only lip contact allowed, and one foot of one person firmly planted on the floor when two individuals talked to each other on the same bed. In the late 1940s and 1950s movie producers were beginning to rebel at such restrictions. The box office success of *The Outlaws,* in which Jane Russell showed more cleavage than the code allowed, and of *The Moon is Blue,* which violated the code with respect to language (for example, the word *virgin* was spoken) helped to weaken the restrictions. During the 1960s the code continued to crumble and it was replaced in 1968 with a rating system that serves primarily to restrict film content on the basis of the age of the viewer. Whether it was intended or not, the rating system allows anything to be shown in an *X*-rated movie. Sexual explicitness in movies since the new rating system has matched that of literature.

Sexual Research

At the same time that literature, photographs, and movies have been undergoing changes, research methods in the sexual practices of the human species have also undergone changes. At the turn of the century Sigmund Freud (1962, 1963) began to explore and theorize about the role sex played in his patients' lives. Not only the general public, but much of the scientific community was scandalized by such speculations. During this time the work of Kraft-Ebing (1894) and Ellis (1899) was clinical in nature and dealt with abnormality to assure that it was disassociated from the lives of most people. There were surveys of sexual behavior prior to that of Kinsey and his associates (Davis, 1929; Hamilton, 1929; Terman, Buttenwieser, Ferguson, Johnson, and Wilson 1938), but they did not attract the attention of the general public.

The experimental study of human sexual behavior developed much later and very tentatively. For example, Clark (1952) showed male subjects "cheesecake" photos and their responses consisted of Thematic Apperception Test stories. By the late 1960s and 1970s experimental research into sexual activities had expanded, utilizing more female subjects, more explicit stimuli, and response measures that either measure or ask subjects about physiological changes in their genitals as well as asking about their sexual behavior outside the laboratory (Byrne, 1976).

Sexual Attitudes and Sexual Behavior

With all of the sexual changes in literature, magazines, movies, and even stuffy research laboratories, it seems reasonable to assume that attitudes toward sex and sexual behavior are also changing. In 1972, Morton Hunt surveyed 2000 individuals concerning their sexual attitudes and behaviors. The sample surveyed was, as closely as possible, representative (see Chapter 2) of the total population with regard to sex, age, race, marital status, education, occupation, and geographic area. The results of the survey are both interesting and informative. Let us consider a few examples to see how sexual behavior and attitudes toward sex have changed or not changed in the past several decades.

Premarital Intercourse

Attitudes toward premarital intercourse have changed markedly in the last several years. The Roper polling agency surveyed the United States in 1937 and in 1959 concerning this question. In both surveys 22 percent said it was all right for both men and women, 8 percent said it was all right for men only, and over 50 percent said it was all right for neither. Hunt's poll asked the question somewhat more systematically, varying the degree of emotional attachment between the couple. Depending on the degree of emotional attachment, from 60 to 84 percent of the males approved premarital intercourse for males and from 44 to 81 percent felt it was acceptable for females. The females surveyed were less permissive, but from 37 to 73 percent approved premarital intercourse for males and 20 to 68 percent felt it was all right for females.

With regard to behavior, in Kinsey's study over one quarter of unmarried males had not experienced intercourse by age 25. In Hunt's sample, only 3 percent of unmarried males had not experienced intercourse by age 25. In Kinsey's sample, between 42 and 47 percent of the women who were married before or by the age of 25 had had premarital intercourse. The comparable figure for Hunt's sample was 81 percent.

Interestingly enough in both the 1940s and the 1970s more people engage in premarital intercourse than approve of it. There is the possibility that differences in the way the questions were asked account for such differences. However, a maximum

For many years it has been assumed, with some support from Kinsey, that females are not as aroused by erotic material as are males. This assumption has been questioned in recent years and more research has occurred into the question of erotica and arousal. Apparently, men and women are equally aroused by erotica, but specific themes are more arousing to one sex than the other. For example, a picture of a nude male is more arousing to females than to males.

Griffitt and Kaiser (1978) reported a study in which affect, sex guilt, and gender were identified. Affect is generally used by psychologists to denote arousal or emotional feelings. Sex guilt refers to the amount of guilt a subject associates with sexual thoughts and activity and is often measured using Mosher's sex-guilt scale. Then, of course, Griffitt and Kaiser assessed any potential differences between males and females on these measures.

One of the problems that faces sex researchers is the social desirability of responses to erotica. Canada and the United States have long been countries in which sex is a taboo topic and a "double-standard" existed. That is, males were expected to be sexually active (or this behavior was tolerated) prior to marriage, whereas females were not. This state of affairs in the society leads to certain problems for the researcher interested in the effects of erotic material. One example should suffice; until very recently, it could be assumed that males had more experience with erotic materials than did females and that females would be less likely to seek out such erotic material. This resulted, of course, from the societal view that females should be protected from erotica.

Griffitt and Kaiser overcame some of these problems by introducing a discrimination learning task into their experiment. Subjects are shown a card with a circle and square on it, one black, one white, one on the left, the other on the right and one large, one small. In a series of cards, each has a circle and a square, but position, color, and size vary. The subject's task is to determine which dimension has been arbitrarily chosen by the experimenter and within that dimension, which is actually correct. For example, size may be the proper dimension and large the correct response. Research has shown that subjects can learn this task fairly easily for a variety of reinforcements.

Eight groups were formed; males and females, high and low sex-guilt, and experimental or control. In the experimental group each time the subject made a correct choice, he or she was shown an erotic scene, whereas an incorrect choice led to a picture of a geometric design. Control subjects received a geometric design regardless of the choice they made. High sex-guilt subjects made fewer correct responses (which led to erotic scenes) than did low sex-guilt subjects. Further, males tended to make more choices that led to erotic scenes than did females.

At the conclusion of the learning task subjects were asked to report their affective state during the learning phase of the experiment. This "Feelings Scale" tapped such dimensions as excited, sad, pleasant, and so forth. Low sex-guilt subjects and males, in general, reported more positive affect than did high sex-guilt subjects and females. Further, Griffitt and Kaiser determined that affect was probably the primary determinant of erotica-producing choices. Thus, even though sex-guilt and gender influence how you feel about erotic material, your feelings appear to be the variable that determines whether you will choose to view erotic material.

Reference

Griffitt, W., and D. L. Kaiser. Affect, sex guilt, gender, and the rewarding-punishing effects of erotic stimuli. *Journal of Personality and Social Psychology,* 1978, *36,* 850–58.

of 84 percent of males approved premarital intercourse for males and 97 percent had engaged in it, whereas the analogous figures for females were 68 and 81 percent.

HOMOSEXUALITY

If more people engage in premarital intercourse than approve of it, the same cannot be said for homosexual activity. Hunt posed the simplistic proposition to his respondents "Homosexuality is wrong." This view represents the unequivocal moral norm that has been associated with this matter in Western cultures since early Christian times. Over half of all the women and nearly half of all the men in Hunt's sample disagreed. This is one of the few areas in which women take a less traditional view than do men. With regard to homosexual activity, however, Hunt found it no more prevalent than did Kinsey.

SWINGING

If you were to believe the stories in newspapers and magazines, the conclusion that many sophisticated married couples swing (swap mates for sexual purposes) would be almost unavoidable. The whole idea was virtually unmentionable until recently, so there are no data on individuals' attitudes on the subject or on their behavior in Kinsey's time. Hunt, however, reports that 38 percent of the men and 25 percent of the women surveyed felt that mate swapping was not wrong. That many may not feel that it is wrong, but they must feel that it is inappropriate for them and their marriage because only 2 percent of the married males in Hunt's sample and less than 2 percent of the married females had ever engaged in the practice. Here again, the behavior of individuals is not nearly so permissive as their attitudes would lead us to believe. Furthermore, Hunt reports that the vast majority of married people—including the youngest age groups—are not at all inclined to grant their mates permission for extramarital sexual activity.

COMMENT

How are we to view these data? With alarm? With satisfaction? That, of course, is a very personal question. There are those who argue that increasingly permissive sexual attitudes will lead to decadence reminiscent of ancient societies which purportedly strangled in evil. Hunt takes a different point of view.

To the majority of Americans, sexual liberation thus means the right to enjoy all parts of the body, the right to employ caresses previously forbidden by civil or religious edict and social tradition, and the right to be sensuous and exuberant rather than perfunctory and solemn—but all within the framework of meaningful relationships. Sex, for the great majority of Americans—including the liberated—continues to express loving feelings or to engender them, or both. It has not been successfully disjoined from love and remade into a simple appetite, except by a tiny minority of swingers.

This ought not surprise us, after all, for there is a wealth of evidence in the literature of psychology to show that the physical care and love given the child by the mother and the father promote digestion and other autonomic functions, create a sense of health and well-being, and thus build into the nervous system a deep, abiding linkage between sensuous well-being and the state of loving. And being laid down in our nervous structure so early in life, this synthesis of sex and affection is not likely to be dissolved by the liberation of American sexuality from its heritage of guilt and shame. [Hunt, 1974, p. 38.]

Learning About Sex

Throughout this book the issue of how children learn—morality, attitudes, aggression, and so forth—has been raised. The question of how children learn about sex is equally as important, if not more so. Morality, attitudes, aggression, and other behaviors children learn are not considered innate by most psychologists. There are few, if any, people who would disagree with the contention that sexual impulses are inborn and that their fulfillment is important for the continuation of the species. The logical outcome of an innate sexual drive is that virtually every human will feel sexual drives at one time or another in life. Therefore one approach to teaching children about sex is "don't." If it is natural, why do they need to be taught? What is wrong with such an approach?

We could argue that eating and elimination are natural drives, so let nature take its course. Certainly, in teaching a child about nutrition or table manners we do not alter the basic physiological drive. However, it would be a strange society if we went around grabbing at any and every bit of food when we were hungry, eating it with hands, tongues, and mouths off any surface. A child who reacted in this way would be considered abnormal. If elimination were done whenever and wherever the individual felt the urge, we would live in a filthy, unsanitary mess. Parents take great pains to teach their children how and what to eat, and toilet training is one of the greatest concerns of parents of toddlers. Yet some urge that sex should not be taught.

Messenger (1971) studied a community off the Irish coast that is extremely repressive in its approach to sex. In Inis Beag sex is never discussed in the home when children are about, menstruation causes extreme trauma in many young girls' lives, menopause induces "madness," and males even drown because of so-called modesty about sexual matters. The islanders take the attitude that sexual activity is natural and after marriage nature will take its course. Intercourse between husbands and wives is always initiated by the husband and takes place without either partner removing their underclothes. Women consider intercourse a marital duty and to refuse a mortal sin, yet orgasm for females is virtually unknown.

The first menstrual flow for a young girl is traumatic because neither she nor her mother understands it. The physiological origins of the menopause are equally unknown and island women have been known to retire from life in their mid-40s to ward off this condition. The society is so sexually inhibited that all but infants do not bathe; rather they wash their feet, lower legs, hands, lower arms, necks, and faces on Saturday night. This assures the protection of the society from nudity. Men do not learn to swim because to do so would mean baring portions of their bodies. Since the men spend much of their time at sea in canoes, the inability to swim undoubtedly causes many deaths by drowning.

To be sure, Inis Beag is an extreme example of sexual repression and myth. Yet in Canada and the United States innumerable young people have grown up depending upon sources outside of the home—peers, school, literature—to learn about sex because of a reluctance on the part of their parents to discuss the issue with them. One of the reasons for this undoubtedly is religious. The dominant religion in Canada and the United States—Christianity—has taken a highly inhibited approach toward sex, at least in many of its churches, denominations, and sects. Sex education, discussions of sex, and sexual practices are much more inhibited than are other basic physiological drives.

PORNOGRAPHY AND OBSCENITY—A CASE STUDY

Erotic literature, photographs, and movies have long been the subject of extensive controversy in Canada, the United States, and many other countries. In 1967 President Lyndon Johnson of the United States appointed a Commission on Obscenity and Pornography to study the issue and to determine if pornography and obscenity were harmful. Evidently, the powers in charge by 1970 when the Commission reported (President Nixon and Congress) felt that the task of the Commission was to find *that* obscenity and pornography were harmful. The Commission found surprisingly little evidence to suggest that pornography and obscenity were harmful, and there were hints in the data that erotic materials may, under certain circumstances, be helpful.

The results of the study were so unexpected in certain circles that a great controversy arose. President Nixon denounced the Commission's report and city, state, and Federal legislatures introduced tough, new antipornography laws. Just what did the Commission say and why? The Commission supported research projects and based on the results of these surveys and experimental studies concluded that obscenity and pornography increased normal sexual activity but did not lead to new or unique

Adult book stores offer many sorts of titillation.

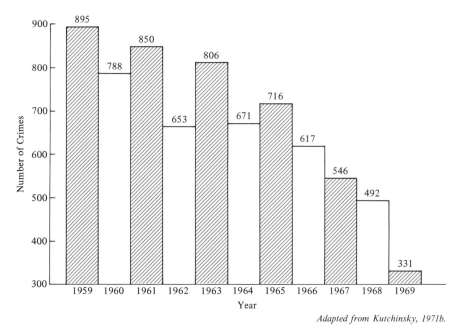

Adapted from Kutchinsky, 1971b.

Figure 13-1 Heterosexual crimes reported to Copenhagen police from 1959 to 1969.

forms of sex. That is, persons who viewed erotic material were more likely to increase for short periods of time whatever sexual activity they normally engaged in (masturbation, intercourse, and so on) (Byrne and Byrne, 1977). One of the most startling and controversial aspects of the Commission's report had to do with studies conducted in Denmark, which indicated a decrease in sex crimes as pornography became more available through the 1960s and finally completely legal in 1969 (Ben-Veniste, 1971; Kutchinsky, 1971a, 1971b).

Denmark—A Special Case? The most publicized results of studies in Denmark are illustrated by Figure 13–1, which shows the incidence of heterosexual crimes registered by the police in Copenhagen between 1959 and 1969. As can be seen, there is a dramatic drop in sex crimes reported to the police during the period. Kutchinsky interprets these data very carefully, pointing out that there are several possible explanations for these statistics. However, he does suggest that there is a possible relationship between the legalization of pornography and sex crimes.

The rationale for such a relationship is that pornography is utilized by those who would otherwise seek release in illegal ways (peeping, exhibitionism, rape, and so forth). This position makes explicit a long-time assumption that the reduction in arousal by any method may generalize to other behaviors. That is, if the potential sex offender can reduce his general level of arousal by utilizing pornography, there will be less necessity to reduce that arousal through criminal means. As Ward and Woods (1972) say,

It seems to us that the implications of the Danish studies in general and, in particular, of the finding concerning offences against female children are of tremendous importance.

Certainly, as we have said, these conclusions are tentative and subject to the qualifications we expressed before. But if in fact it appears possible to reduce substantially the incidence of sexual offences against children by legalizing pornography, then serious thought indeed must be given to this possibility by any government.

There have been others who have urged caution in making public policy on the basis of these data (Eysenck, 1972; Gummer, 1971; Holbrook, 1972). The pornography issue is an emotionally loaded one and sometimes researchers on both sides of the issue let their feelings influence their conclusions. It has not been my practice to cite studies in this book and then attempt to refute their conclusions. However, there is enough literature around that seems to be guided more by feelings than data to justify one illustration of such a problem.

Court (1977) has assessed the statistics in Denmark and studied the patterns of liberalization of laws concerning pornography in four other countries and Copenhagen. He then tabulated the rates per 100,000 population of rape and attempted rape in these geographic areas. As a control country, a country that has retained strict pornography laws, he compared Singapore to the other five. His results are shown in Figure 13–2. Court argues that these statistics support the notion that increased

Figure 13-2 Rate per 100,000 population of rapes and attempted rapes reported to the police.

Adapted from Court, 1977.

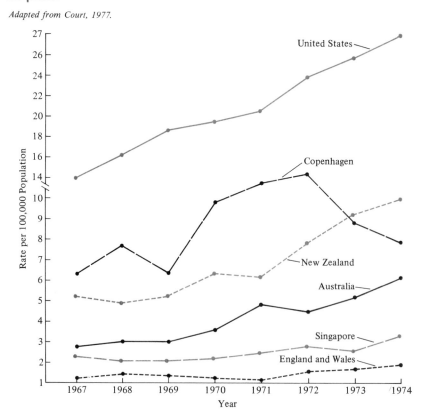

permissiveness with regard to pornography may decrease sexual crimes in general, but there is an increase in rape and attempted rape. To quote Court,

> Pornagraphy is now more readily available in Western countries than it was a decade ago. Over the same period as this transition has occurred, there has been an increased reporting of rape and attempted rape in those countries. This paper seeks to establish whether the relationship between these two observations is more than fortuitious.
>
> Three components of the data presented suggest that the trends in reported rape figures bear an important relationship in the circulation of pornographic materials:
>
> **(a)** after periods of relatively stable level of reporting (i.e., a linear trend) an upward trend in rate per 100,000 of population occurs in those countries;
> **(b)** the upward trend appears to coincide with, or closely follow, the availability of pornography in the community;
> **(c)** this upward trend was not found in a country, Singapore, where control has been exercised even though the base-rate of reports was comparable. [Court, 1977, pp. 152–53.]

Frankly, a close study of Court's data do not support his conclusions. There appear to be rather sharp increases in the rate of reported rape and attempted rape in two countries that coincide with liberalization of pornography laws (Australia in 1970 and New Zealand about 1971). For example, Australia had a 73 percent increase in rape and attempted rape between 1970 and 1974, whereas New Zealand had a 60 percent increase between 1971 and 1974. However, Singapore, the control country, had a 50 percent increase between 1970 and 1974.

The decade of the 70s has been a time of increased publicity about rape and a great emphasis upon more thorough reporting of the crime. Women's groups have organized to pressure for more humane treatment of rape victims. Therefore it is not surprising that more women are reporting rape and attempted rape to the police. To try to tie such an increase to more permissive attitudes toward pornography is unwarranted. It is, as I said earlier, an example of how strong feelings about a subject can influence the way in which a researcher views his data.

Sexual Freedom and Political Repression

On the other hand, several sources have utilized the data reported in Figure 13–1 to argue rather uncritically for the legalization of pornography (Byrne and Byrne, 1977; Faust, 1973; Howard, 1975; Simmons, 1972). Byrne (1976) argues that as people become more familiar with unique stimuli, these stimuli become more acceptable. He presents a model by which formerly unacceptable sexual activity can become commonplace. Furthermore, Byrne and Byrne (1977) argue that sexual repression and political repression go together. As they say,

> In various places in this book, there have been contrasts between prosex and antisex orientations—in examining divergent cultures, in assessing the attitudes and beliefs of individuals, and in determining the very different emotional responses that can be elicited by erotic stimulation. Now we come to perhaps the most important consideration of all—the implications of these differing sexual orientations for the broader aspects of our society. Let it be said initially that the evidence is primarily of an indirect nature and open to multiple

interpretations. Nevertheless, our conclusion is that sexual freedom is associated with political freedom whereas sexual restrictiveness is associated with political tyranny. [Byrne and Byrne, 1977, p. 351.]

The idea the Byrnes espouse, although not new, is quite interesting. Since their argument pertains to the present and not past societies, it does not seem fruitful to argue that there have been sexually free and politically repressed countries in history. The Byrnes are arguing that the freedom to engage in sexual practices, and more specifically to have free access to any sexual material, goes hand in hand with other political freedoms. One gauge of an individual's freedom in a society is how freely available explicit sexual material is. It does seem important to examine some of the ramifications of sexual freedom with respect to the availability of erotic material.

Modeling and Erotica

Several chapters of this book have dealt with the enormous impact that observational learning has on individuals. One effect of the free publication and sale of erotic material that has not been adequately considered is learning via modeling. Let us consider an erotic movie that shows explicit sexual scenes between consenting adults who enjoy the activity and in general show sex as an emotionally positive experience. Anyone who sees such a movie will probably learn about the positive aspects of sex.

However, much pornography involves aggressive activity. Sadism, rape, or the use of children for adult sexual pleasure all allow viewers to learn about aggressive sexual activity. In the same way that I argued against aggression on television, in the movies, and in literature, I would argue that aggressive sexual activity should be controlled, at the very least until we understand more about it. If, as seems apparent with other forms of explicit aggression, its free dissemination should be curtailed. I should hasten to add that this seems in no way contrary to what the Byrnes (1977) argue. They define abormal sexuality as "a sex-related behavior that causes psychological distress or unwanted physical pain for an individual, any force to compel another to engage in sexual activity or any unwitting engagement in sexual activity (such as peeping)" and are opposed to it.

Viewing pornography for sale in a shop window can be distressing to many people. Should the distress this causes them be allowed to interfere with the freedom of others to purchase nonaggressive erotica? The answer to such a question is a difficult one. However a practical solution could be achieved by having specific stores, with public display prohibited, set aside for the sale of unaggressive erotica. This may seem an infringement of freedom but in certain states alcohol is sold in state liquor stores under carefully controlled conditions. People grouse about the price of alcohol in state stores but not about the concept of lack of freedom associated with its control.

In any society the tensions between freedom and the good of the society as a whole create problems. Certainly with regard to sexual behavior we can agree with those who argue for more enlightenment. However, the freedom of those who oppose explicit sexual material being freely available must also be considered. When even its adherents do not have hard data, the dissemination of erotic material should be approached cautiously. Possibly complete freedom with regard to erotica is the best approach, but because of the aggressive content of much erotica, I doubt it. A more open, less repressive attitude toward sexual behavior in Canada and the United States should be beneficial to the society. The questions that must be answered before such steps can be taken are important ones.

Why Sex Research?

There is no truth to the popularly expressed idea that sex researchers are dirty old men who get their kicks from peeping at keyholes. I can say this because a number of sex researchers are women, and more importantly, careful research into such problems as sexual dysfunction, male-female differences in sexual arousal and activity, changing attitudes toward sex and pornography, are all important behavioral issues that need to be understood and dealt with in an informed way, not in ignorance. There is, however, an even more important issue that has permeated sex, probably since it was first discussed. Byrne (1977) has said it best:

> ... there is a special problem related to sexual activity which carries a critical set of concerns that cry out for solution. As you may know, copulation can result in babies if the participants are of the opposite sex and if they do not utilize appropriate contraceptive techniques. In light of that revelation, it is astonishing but true that sexually active teenagers tend to use contraceptive procedures that are unreliable and they do so only sporadically or not at all (Eastman, 1972). Three-fourths of all first pregnancies occur prior to marriage, and less than 20 percent of the couples involved use any method of contraception (Zelnick and Kantner, 1974). According to a 1976 report by the Alan Guttmacher Institute, one million American teenagers become pregnant each year, resulting in almost half a million out-of-wedlock births and 300,000 abortions. The remaining legitimate births tend to occur in hasty, unplanned marriages characterized by disrupted education (Baizerman, Sheehan, Ellison, and Schlessinger, 1971) divorce within four years (Semmens, 1970), child abuse by unhappy young mothers (Kempe and Helfer, 1968), and a rate of suicide among teenage mothers ten times that of the general population (Cvetkonich, Grote, Bjorseth, and Sarkissian, 1975). [Byrne, 1977, pp. 7–8.]

That paragraph alone is an eloquent answer to the question this section asks.

Crime

Technically crime is "an action or an instance of negligence that is deemed injurious to the public welfare or morals or to the interests of the state and that is legally prohibited" (*The Random House College Dictionary,* Rev. Ed.). This broad definition of crime includes jaywalking, speeding, smoking pot, selling pornography, burglary, armed robbery, rape, and murder. It also includes the so called "white-collar crimes," such as embezzlement, obstruction of justice, and bribery. Just as the behaviors subsumed under the name *crime* are quite diverse, diverse persons commit them. Even more startling is the punishment convicted criminals receive. Typically, convicted white-collar criminals receive very short jail sentences, whereas a poor burglar may receive a sentence several times as long for stealing a fraction of the money.

This statue in front of the police building in Philadelphia emphasizes the helping aspect of police. Many citizens, however, view the police as a defense against crime.

These are but a few of the problems and anomalies associated with crime. Crime is a serious problem. For example, in the United States violent crimes increased over 100 percent between 1960 and 1969. Although the increase slowed somewhat in the early 70s, violent crime still rose 13 percent between 1970 and 1972 (U.S. Bureau of Census, 1973). There are those who argue that the increase in crime reflects the "baby boom" that followed World War II (Bazelon, 1977). That is, most crime is committed by young people between 18 and 25 or 30, and since these persons were born between 1946 and 1950, they would be in their crime-prone years between 1964 and 1980. Thus, if we can just hold out until these young people mature, or are put away for good or some such thing, violent crimes should decrease. Bazelon (1977) argues that this is a misguided view and one that is dangerous.

Undoubtedly the causes of crime are many. Many years ago it would be argued that criminals had some serious personality defect and should be punished for their crimes. Today more voices are being raised to disagree with such an approach (Bazelon, 1977; Cohn, 1969; Culbertson, 1977; Danzinger and Wheeler, 1975; Eckhardt, 1977). What are the critics saying and why?

The Failure of the Correctional System

Prior to answering the question of what the critics of a retributional system are saying, we must see why they are saying it. This is one of those unfortunate situations that has festered for years and is only taken seriously when it erupts into the public view. Stated bluntly, our system of punishing offenders has not worked. This is

558

CAN JUVENILE DELINQUENTS BE REHABILITATED?

According to Gendreau and Ross (1979) the vast majority of commentators on the juvenile delinquent scene have taken the position that "nothing works." That is, juvenile delinquents cannot be rehabilitated. This view, according to these researchers is strangely illogical. Juvenile delinquents, according to almost everyone, learn their inappropriate behavior; why can't they learn behavior that is more appropriate? Gendreau and Ross surveyed the literature of juvenile rehabilitation and report the results that follow.

Family intervention is based on two simple ideas; the sooner the problem behavior is treated the better, and the treatment should involve the family and the school. This approach explicitly states that the characteristics the individual possesses combine with the situation the individual lives in to produce problem behavior. In one excellent example of family intervention, it was assumed that the modification of family interaction was the key to changing behavior. The therapists modeled appropriate roles for the family, teaching them how to negotiate, communicate, develop alternatives to maladaptive behavior, differentiate rules from requests, and so forth. The recidivism rates for these delinquents, when compared to client-centered therapy groups, psycho-dynamic treatment, and no treatment controls, were 21 percent to 47 percent lower after 6 to 18 months. These are quite impressive figures and are just one example of the success of the family intervention approach.

Contingency management is the name given to attempts to alter behavior by rewarding appropriate behavior. One large-scale program has been carried out that uses a token economy levels system. A token economy is a system in which an individual is given tokens for appropriate behavior. The levels system is simply a series of levels the delinquents work through, each with more freedom than the preceding one, until they are at the "homeward bound" level. Thus earning tokens in the lowest level allows the individual to function adequately there and then move up to a higher level. If you think about it for a moment, this approach is much like a job. Appropriate behaviors at all levels are rewarded with money (tokens) and overall success at a lower level leads to promotions (movement to a higher level). When compared to delinquents committed to the Kansas Boys' School and to delinquents on probation, contingency management delinquents had a 35 percent lower recidivism rate after a year.

Gendreau and Ross present much more evidence for successful juvenile delinquent rehabilitation programs than I have cited here. They point out that correctional researchers are utilizing multiple methods rather than a single one. Impressively, they point out that since 1973 they were unable to find a study that reported significant results that relied on a single method. They make the point that individuals differ and that different treatments will be effective in altering inappropriate behavior.

The point made by Gendreau and Ross is that there are possibilities for the rehabilitation of juvenile offenders. These must take the characteristics of the individual and the situation seriously and strive to change both. Interestingly enough, in this final chapter of the book, we are still dealing with the interaction of individual and situation, which is how we defined social psychology in Chapter 1.

Reference

Gendreau, P., and B. Ross. Effective correctional treatment: Biblio-therapy for cynics. *Crime and Delinquency,* 1979 (in press).

---

evidenced by the recidivism rate (rate of return to prison). The correctional system has received publicity only when it does not protect those who are outside of it from those who are classed as criminals. Seemingly, no one cared what happened to those who were imprisoned, unless and until they were released and again committed crimes. The brutality, dehumanization, terror, lack of privacy, and other indignities that occurred within prison walls were unimportant. When criminals committed crimes again, they became important.

According to Culbertson (1977), our correctional system does not work—that is does not rehabilitate offenders—because of external and internal problems. These problems, when elucidated are shocking and thought-provoking.

Durkheim (1938) argued that crime is a fundamental condition of social life and that it helps to maintain an essential factor in the social order, the collective conscience. Griswold, writing in *An Eye for an Eye* (Griswold, Misenheimer, Powers, and Tromanhauser, 1970) argues as follows:

> With the absolute certainty of offending many people, I have to say that the American people want, desire, lust for and need crime and criminality. They need, albeit on a subconscious level, an easily identifiable group whom they can look down upon, feel superior to, castigate, segregate and inflict emotional, psychological and physical punishment upon. The public needs its criminally deviant individuals so that through an act of catharsis they can expunge their own guilt feelings, and every once in a while call up from the darker side of their souls all the repressed hate and fury that dwells within.

Reasons and Kapland (1975) argue that crime provides a supply of criminals sufficient to maintain the criminal justice system, provides employment in prisons for 70,000 persons many of whom would find it difficult to find jobs elsewhere, provides slave labor for prison industries, reduces unemployment rates, and provides subjects for drug research. Gans (1971) notes that punishing criminals serves the function of upholding the legitimacy of conventional norms and proving that moral deviance does not pay. Schur (1969) points out that crime is an important economic force in society. Many people make a living from crime; some by committing it but probably more by combating, punishing, incarcerating, studying, and writing about it. The firearms industry is an example of an economic gain realized through crime. Some of the desired goods and services provided by criminals are prostitution, gambling, and drugs. Schur's position is that at least some crimes have become respectable and others fill a societal need. If he is correct, then the correctional system is bound to fail because it is being asked to rehabilitate the criminal to a standard above that of a large segment of American society.

As if these external forces were not enough to assure the failure of any correctional system, Culbertson points out several internal problems as well. According to Schrag (1974), the greatest deficiency in the field of corrections is the lack of a theoretical framework. That is, administrators are practice-oriented and have no real interest in theory development. They are further hampered by not knowing whether society wants correctional institutions to be warehouses of people for a given period of time, punishment-oriented, or rehabilitative in orientation. With so little direction failure is almost a certainty.

The correctional process also suffers from a lack of negative feedback. As Miller (1955) points out, negative feedback is necessary if a system is to continue to exist and function. The correctional system is characterized by closed systems, and the criticism that negative feedback provides is important. Yet the absence of criticism allows the governing boards to discount evidence that is contrary to their decisions, ignore the ethical and moral consequences of decisions, and to create an illusion of unanimity on

A prison is cold and forbidding. It does not, however, seem to be a deterrent to crime.

decisions that is partly the result of conformity pressures. Finally, the correctional institutions have been guided by the medical model: that crime is a disease. As Martinson (1974, p. 49) says: "Our present treatment programs are based on a theory of crime as a 'disease'—that is to say, as something foreign and abnormal in the individual which can presumably be cured."

With a lack of direction compounded by the roles filled for society by correctional institutions and their inmates, it is small wonder that they have had little deterent effect on crime. In fact, it may be argued that their main function is as an educational institution with the major offering being "crime techniques." The only point upon which most social scientists seem to agree is that correctional institutions and crime are an important part of the economic fabric of the United States.

The Causes of Crime

Why do people become criminals? Because they are evil? Because they are sick? Because they become overly emotional? Because they are poor? These, and many other explanations of criminal activities have been suggested. There is, however, a

561

growing emphasis on crime as an outgrowth of poverty. Two particularly cogent arguments come from a United States Federal Judge and a Congressman.

Bazelon, the judge, argues that our correctional institutions have not worked and will not work. He points out that more than 3 percent of the United States' nonwhite male population between the ages of 18 and 34 were in prison in 1970. This is six times the figure for white males of the same age. He contrasts these figures to those for unemployment of black teenagers, aged 16 to 19, which amounted to 34 percent in 1970, and 45 percent in poverty areas of large cities. He sees a connection between the boredom, lack of income, squalid living conditions in which those unemployed youth live, and crime. If there is no other employment for these young people, crime provides it.

Eckhardt, the Congressman, points out that the United States' criminal laws derive from another era when most people were self-employed. As the society has changed from an agricultural to a postindustrial one, the vast majority of people live in urban areas and are employed by others. Unemployment is now an important factor in the life of many Americans. As Eckhardt says,

Oscar Wilde may not have been too far off the mark when he asserted that "starvation, not sin, is the parent of modern crime." A 1974 study done by the Library of Congress, for instance, found a strong correlation between prison admissions and the annual unemployment rate in the United States. That report found that "the unemployment rate can statistically describe over eighty percent of the year-to-year variation in prison admissions at the federal level, and seventy-nine percent at the state level." [Eckhardt, 1977, p. 35.]

However, poverty has been around a long time. Why should it have more impact on crime now than it did in other times in history? Part of the answer undoubtedly lies in the changing economic system in the United States. There is another way to conceptualize poverty and that involves the individual's perception of his or her relative economic standing.

THE GAP MODEL

Danziger and Wheeler (1975) present a model of the economic influence on crime that emphasizes the gap between the individual's income and the average income of the society. People in Canada and the United States may have an income well in excess of most people in Third World countries and still consider themselves poor. This occurs because they compare themselves to the average income in their own country. For example, Piore (1973) found that Boston firms were unable to attract employees from the local labor market for low-wage, low-skilled factory jobs but found that these same jobs induced immigration from Puerto Rico. People in the bottom portion of the economic order are likely to view their incomes as inadequate.

When individuals view themselves in relationship to a reference group and realize that they fall below the average of that group they can react in two ways. First, they can respond by working longer hours and trying to bring themselves up to the average of the reference group. Secondly, they can become frustrated and withdraw from legal activities and turn to illegal ones. If the situation is such that it is very difficult for them to attain the average of the reference, it is more likely that illegal

One theory of the economic influences on crime emphasizes the gap between these two types of environments.

activities will be the course of action chosen. For blacks, discrimination in the United States is so prevalent that unemployment rates drop only slightly and wages increase only slowly with increased education, the vehicle that has lifted other minority groups out of poverty (Harrison, 1972).

Even though poverty has not changed over the years, instant communications have changed individuals' reference groups. That is, as the media in general, and television in particular, have become more pervasive, poor people are shown how other people in the society live—and they are shown in full color on a regular basis. As poor people realize just how far they are below the average (or at least what

563

television depicts as the average level of living), then illegal activities become more attractive as the only way to bring themselves up to the average.

Urban Structure and Criminal Mobility

One of the interesting and depressing by-products of such an analysis is that crimes will occur close to where poor people live. Capone and Nichols (1974; 1975; 1976) have investigated the distance criminals travel to commit different crimes in Dade County, Florida. Robbery trip distances were calculated for each of 825 offenders by locating the residence of each criminal and then computing the distance to the scene of the robbery. They found that unarmed trips are shorter than armed ones, but that most crimes occur close to the residence of the criminal. The data base these investigators used as 825 robbery trips (642 robberies) that occurred in metropolitan Miami in 1971. Figure 13–3 shows the results graphically. These data document one of the reasons poverty areas are also high crime areas.

Comment

The literature on crime, its causes, and prevention, is becoming more attuned to economic factors as contrasted to moral or medical factors. The idea that criminals are sinful or sick is giving way to the idea that criminals are poor. As a matter of fact, most probably are poor; certainly the ones who end up in prison are. In 1973 in

Crime is frequent in ghetto areas, and some cities use mounted patrolmen to combat it.

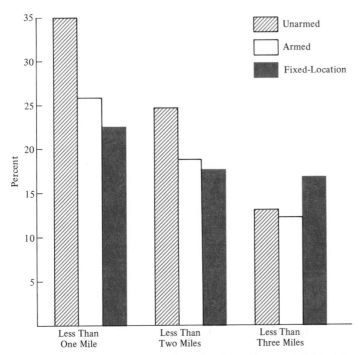

Figure 13-3 Percentage of unarmed, armed, and fixed-location crimes committed in Dade County, Florida, in 1971 as a function of distance traveled to commit the crime. Fixed-location robberies refer to crimes committed in stores, hotels, gas stations, etc., as contrasted to crimes committed against moving targets.

Washington, D.C., nearly 70 percent of those arrested for robbery and 50 percent of all courtroom defendants were unemployed. In addition those who are unable to raise enough money to make bail go to prison more often and get much longer prison sentences than those who do make bail (Eckhardt, 1977).

If the individuals who argue that crime is an economic problem rather than a moral one are correct, then the solution to crime must also lie in the economic realm. This, of course, is what many are arguing, particularly black leaders who rank ghetto unemployment as the number one problem facing blacks in the United States.

Crime Prevention and Victimization: An Attributional Analysis

Kidder and Cohn (in press) have reported on a large-scale research project into the causes and cures of crime. Instead of relying solely on the experts for their data, they used participant observations and interviews conducted in a variety of settings. The research project was interdisciplinary and depended heavily on survey research techniques (see Chapter 2). Three cities, one on the West Coast, one in the Midwest, and one on the East Coast, were the areas in which the research was conducted. The researchers attended community crime prevention programs, city block meetings, and civic association meetings, and talked with civic leaders, merchants, police officers, housewives, children, and "people-on-the-street."

Social problems have root causes and superficial ones (Nearing, 1965) or "prior" and "immediate" ones (Brickman, Ryan, and Wortman, 1975). Kidder and Cohn have tried to illuminate the same ideas by referring to "distal" (situated away from) and "proximal" (situated toward the point of origin) causes of crime. Distal forces, which presumably act on offenders several steps removed from their criminal behavior, are neighborhood deterioration and unemployment. Proximal forces, which are more closely tied to the criminal behavior of offenders, are alcohol and drugs. There are also distal and proximal causes for victims. The safety of the neighborhood in which an individual lives or works is a distal cause, whereas the precautions taken by an individual for protection are proximal causes.

One of the intriguing aspects of the work by Kidder and Cohn is that they consider both criminal and victim; therefore their analysis includes both the causes of crime and the causes of victimization. Although it is true that, if all criminal activity were halted, there would be no victims, since there is crime there are causes of victimization. Moreover, these authors stress the attributional aspect of their research. Crime is one area in which the attributions of the victims are extremely important for control; and therefore the attributional approach of viewing crime as a cluster of symptoms is most appropriate. The research on attributions for success and failure (cf. Weiner, Frieze, Rukla, Reed, Rest, and Rosenbaum, 1971) has identified two important dimensions in people's personal theories: internal versus external and stable versus unstable causes. The same dimensions have been useful in understanding causal attributions about insomnia, schizophrenic delusions, feelings of sexual adequacy, and many other problems (Ross, Rodin, and Zimbardo, 1969; Storms and Nisbett, 1970; Valins and Nisbett, 1972).

CURING THE CAUSES OF CRIME

According to Kidder and Cohn, people are easily able to tell researchers what they believe to be the causes of crime. For example, Kidder and Cohn report the causes of crime most frequently mentioned in their survey, and two other surveys. The two most frequently mentioned proximal causes of crime were drugs (and alcohol) and insufficient law enforcement. There were three basic distal causes; economic (including unemployment and poverty), boredom on the part of young people, and lack of parental guidance. Thus when people speak out about the causes of crime, they focus on the criminal and more specifically the environment that breeds youthful offenders. For example, unemployment is one of the reasons young people are bored and the use of alcohol and other drugs may be the only way an individual can escape the effects of poverty for a few hours.

If people responded logically to this state of affairs, they would demand that the conditions that breed crime be cleaned up. To combat crime people would demand that unemployment be reduced, that conditions which allow people to live in poverty be attacked, or that alcohol and other drugs be made less readily available. To one extent or another, some of these solutions are being demanded, but not always in the name of crime prevention. For example, during the middle and late 1970s community groups were bringing pressure to bear on banks to stop "redlining" neighborhoods.

Redlining refers to banks' outlining on a map certain neighborhoods that are deteriorating and are poor loan-risk areas. When banks do this and refuse to make loans for the purchase or improvement of homes in the neighborhood, the area deteriorates even more rapidly.

However, people are not always logical and the measures that are most often taken to control crime concern the victim not the criminal (Dubow, McCabe, and Kaplan, 1976). For example, people do not venture out at night, they purchase locks, burglar alarms, guns, dogs, and the like, they report crimes or suspicious-looking people to the police, they form citizen patrols, organize blocks, or seek improved street lighting. Each of these responses focuses not on the criminal, but on protecting the victim. Ironically, people-on-the-street agree with Bazelon and Eckhardt about the causes of crime, but they do not organize to demand eradication of the conditions that permit crime to occur. Many years ago it was discovered that mosquitoes carry certain deadly diseases. Eradication of mosquito breeding grounds was implemented to control the diseases. Eradication of the root causes of crime would probably also be effective. Yet people choose to swat each individual mosquito rather than fight crime at its source. Why is this?

Kidder and Cohn argue that one of the major reasons for this is that society has altered its emphasis. In the 60s programs were implemented to seek out and eliminate the root causes of crime. In the 1970s, however, the emphasis has shifted to the prevention of victimization. For example, in 1969 the Law Enforcement Assistance Administration of the United States Justice Department spent $63 million on crime victimization prevention. Seven years later that figure had risen to $810 million.

Why has there been a shift in emphasis from prevention of crime to prevention of victimization? Kidder and Cohn contend that both individuals and crime-prevention programs are guided by efficiency. If individuals and programs do not report positive results they conclude they are helpless (Seligman, 1975; Wortman and Brehm, 1975). They go on to say,

> While failure to produce the desired effects can make individuals feel frustrated or helpless, it actually threatens the survival of programs whose funds were granted on the basis of a promise of success. Cochran, Gordon, and Campbell (in press) argue that when program administrators' jobs are threatened by program evaluations, those administrators are quite likely to produce statistics that make their programs look successful. The collective wisdom among community organizers who have worked in the area of crime and victimization prevention is that "crime is not a good organizing issue . . . because it's a difficult issue on which to show obvious results". . . What many "crime prevention" programs have done, however is define their goal not as crime reduction or even victimization reduction but very simply as the numbers of blocks, organized, numbers of horns or whistles distributed, numbers of engraving tools used, or numbers of Operation ID stickers passed out. These statistics are easy to collect, easy to report to funding agencies, and provide impressive numbers. [Kidder and Cohn, in press, pp. 22.]

Comment

Crime is a many-faceted, real, and terrifying problem. If the arguments made by a number of people in different professions are accurate, the root causes of crime are

One of the areas of interest to applied social psychologists is the effects of stress on health. Stress, of course, comes from a variety of modern sources: the fast pace of living, change in our environment, crowding, fear of crime, and so forth. This interest in stress has increased as social psychologists have become more involved in field research, more concerned with physical health, and more aware of the increasing sources of stress in our environment.

Kobasa (1969) suggests recent research has shown that recent life histories of hospitalized persons show more stressful events than do the life histories of matched controls. Research of this sort has led to a popular preoccupation with the relationship between stress and health. That is, the popular press prints scales of stressful life events and if you score at a relatively high level, you are told the chances are 60 percent or 80 percent that you will become ill. Kobasa warns of two things: the studies upon which such predictions are made are correlational in nature, and there are many people who are highly stressed who do not become sick. With respect to correlational studies, recall that correlation does not imply causality; that is, one variable (stress) does not necessarily cause the effects of the second variable (sickness) just because they are correlated.

Kobasa studied individuals who had been stressed but stayed healthy as well as persons who had been stressed and became ill. She hypothesized that individual characteristics as well as the life situations the individuals face would affect the relationship between stress and health for individuals. More specifically, she predicted that of those people under stress, those who have a greater sense of control over their lives will remain healthier than those who are alienated and those who view it as a threat.

A sample of 100 high-stress/low-illness and 100 high-stress/high-illness individuals was selected from a pool of middle- and upper-level executives of a large public utility. The subjects were then administered a battery of personality tests to test the hypothesis just stated. It should be pointed out that the executives first filled out two scales to determine stress and degree of illness in the past three years. The two groups, high-stress/low-illness and high-stress/high-illness were then selected and the personality battery was administered after the stress-illness relationship had been determined. This sort of design allows only for analysis of differences in personality characteristics after the stress and illness. To the extent that stress and illness changed the personality characteristics measured, they (the personality characteristics) are not predictive of stress and illness.

The high-stress executives who did become ill more often did not differ from the high-stress executives who did not become ill in terms of age, job level, and number of years in the job, but they did differ on some personality characteristics. High-stress/low-illness executives are more hardy (more achievement oriented, with a greater sense of role consistency, greater endurance, and a greater commitment to self), show a more vigorous attitude toward the environment, have a greater sense of meaningfulness, and are higher in internal locus of control, than high-stress/high-illness executives.

It does seem that stress is related to illness but the relationship is not one-to-one. The high-stress/low-illness group had a stress rating that would put them in the category of 80 percent chance of illness (just as the high-stress/high-illness group did) but they did not suffer nearly as much illness as the high-stress/high-illness group. Stress is important, but it interacts with other elements in the individual in producing illness.

Reference

Kobasa, S. C. Stressful life events, personality, and health: An inquiry into hardiness. *Journal of Personality and Social Psychology*, 1979, 37, 1–11.

not being adequately faced. A judge, a United States Representative, sociologists, psychologists, and the man-on-the-street seem to agree about the root causes of crime. These causes, however, are not being attacked with much vigor. Rather than eradicating the breeding grounds of crime—poverty, unemployment, and so forth—ineffectual measures are taken that show quick results. It seems to me, however, that as long as conditions exist that allow criminals to develop—indeed make it almost necessary for some people to turn to crime—all the dogs, guns, burglar alarms, neighborhood groups, and prisons will not eradicate the problem. As long as criminal activity is the only way to keep from living in poverty, there will be plenty of criminals available to take the place of those who are imprisoned. Long-lasting solutions must attack the problem at its roots.

Smoking

One of the most frequent questions directed to me in a social psychology class is "What is normal behavior?" To be sure, I suspect that the student asking the question is "testing the water" to determine whether his or her behavior is normal. When we consider society in Canada and the United States, and particularly what society condones and condemns, it is small wonder that people are confused. For example, drugs that presumably relax individuals, such as marijuana and cocaine, are illegal, but alcohol is legal. Is there any evidence that the legal drug is less harmful or less debilitating than the illegal ones? Quite the contrary—alcohol has been indicted in gastrointestinal disorders and fatal liver dysfunction, as well as coordination inhibition sufficient to cause thousands of fatal accidents a year. Put another way, alcohol kills many thousands of people every year in Canada and the United States.

Cigarette smoking and societal reaction to it are even more confusing. Over the last 30 years it has become more apparent that smoking is harmful to health. Cigarette smoking has been implicated in cancer, heart disease, and emphysema, to

This sign in a pediatrician's office points out that smoking is harmful to children and they learn to smoke by observing adults.

FOR THE HEALTH OF · OUR CHILDREN, PLEASE · DON'T SMOKE.

Cigarettes are dispensed side by side with ice cream, candy, and cold drinks.

name but three fatal conditions with which it is associated. Yet cigarettes are freely available in both Canada and the United States. Furthermore, the United States Department of Health, Education and Welfare announced (January 1978) a massive multimillion dollar compaign to reduce smoking while the United States Department of Agriculture continues to provide millions of dollars in subsidy payments to farmers who grow tobacco. No wonder people are confused.

Stanley Schachter and his associates have published a series of articles that deal with smoking, not from the point of view of society's reaction to smoking, but from the individual smoker's viewpoint. The studies incorporate physiological data and social psychological data, as well as field and laboratory research, in attempting to unravel several mysteries surrounding smoking. The results of the studies don't really provide a solution to the problem of smoking, but they move in the direction of better understanding the phenomenon.

The Contradictions of Smoking

If a smoker is asked why he or she smokes, the answer will probably be that it's relaxing. Ikard, Green, and Horn (1968) found that 80 percent of smokers described their smoking as pleasurable and relaxing. However, the Surgeon General's Report (United States Department of Health, Education, and Welfare, 1964) stated that smoking causes an increase in heart rate of from 15 to 25 beats per minute and an increase in blood pressure. These physiological measures contradict the general impression smokers have that smoking a cigarette is relaxing, because they indicate arousal. Nesbitt (1973) reported that smoking increases pulse rate in smokers and nonsmokers, that smokers were better able than nonsmokers to endure a stressful situation (such as being shocked) when smoking but less able to do so when not smoking. Thus it appears that the smokers' reports that smoking is relaxing *and* a concurrent increase in physiological responses are both accurate. Herman (1974) reported that light smokers and heavy smokers respond differently to cigarette deprivation and salience cues. Schachter and his associates began with these relatively sparse bits and pieces and worked to understand the smokers' behavior.

NICOTINE REGULATION

Cigarette smoking is a difficult habit to change. It has usually been assumed that the addictive agent is nicotine, although the research evidence on this matter has been inconclusive. The basic premise behind this research has been that if nicotine is the active addictive agent, then smokers will regulate the amount of nicotine consumed. There have been at least 10 studies on human subjects with results that find little or no indication of nicotine regulation (Finnegan, Larson and Haag, 1945; Goldfarb, Jarnik and Glick, 1970) in contrast to which Ashton and Watson (1970) reported that subjects puffed considerably more with low-nicotine than with high-nicotine cigarettes. In between these two extremes are a number of studies that found some evidence that smokers regulated their nicotine content, but crudely and imprecisely.

Schachter (1977) suggested that one of the reasons for the conflicting evidence on this matter is that smokers are erroneously lumped into one category whereas light and heavy smokers may differ in their addiction to nicotine. To test this idea Schachter selected 11 smokers. Seven of them were heavy smokers and 4 were light smokers. Heavy smokers were defined as smoking 20 or more cigarettes a day, whereas light smokers smoked 15 or fewer cigarettes a day. Each subject was given cigarettes to smoke for two four-day periods—from Saturday morning to Tuesday night. During one of these periods each smoker received low-nicotine (.3 mg nicotine per cigarette) cigarettes to smoke and during the other four-day period each smoker received high-nicotine (1.3 mg nicotine per cigarette) cigarettes to smoke. Every heavy smoker smoked more low-nicotine cigarettes than high-nicotine cigarettes, indicating that these individuals were regulating their nicotine intake. Of the four light smokers, two increased their consumption of low-nicotine cigarettes as compared to high-nicotine ones and two actually smoked fewer low-nicotine than high-nicotine cigarettes.

At least for the subjects in Schachter's experiment, heavy smokers appear to regulate nicotine intake. Why, then, has there been inconsistent evidence concerning nicotine regulation? Schachter points out that of the 10 studies concerning nicotine regulation, the four that gave the most consistent evidence were conducted in England (Ashton and Watson, 1970; Frith, 1971; Johnston, 1942; Russell, Wilson, Patel, Cole, Feyeraband, 1973). Cigarettes are much more expensive in England and salaries are generally lower there than in the United States. In relation to take-home pay, cigarettes may cost the individual more than three times as much in Britain as in the U.S. Schachter speculates that the nonaddicted light smoker in England may have given up the habit and not been included in studies of nicotine regulation conducted in that country. Thus, results for studies in the two countries may differ.

REGULATING MECHANISM

Schachter, Kozlowski and Silverstein (1977) note that nicotine is readily absorbed by the body, that some of it is chemically altered by the liver, kidneys, and lungs and the rest excreted in the urine. Furthermore, the acidity or alkalinity of the urine influences how much nicotine is excreted. If the urine is acid, about 35 percent of the nicotine will be excreted, if it is normal about 7 percent of the nicotine will be excreted, whereas only about 1 percent of nicotine will be excreted in alkaline urine (Beckett, Rowland, and Triggs, 1965; Beckett and Triggs, 1967). Thus, it may be assumed that if nicotine level is the agent that regulates smoking, increasing the amount of nicotine excreted in the urine should cause individuals to increase their smoking.

Schachter, Kozlowski, and Silverstein (1977) administered bicarbonate of soda, ascorbic acid or acidulin, or cornstarch to alkalize, acidify, or leave unaltered the ph of heavy smokers' urine. Smokers whose urine was alkalized or who received cornstarch as a placebo did not alter their smoking behavior. Subjects whose urine was acidified significantly increased their smoking. Figure 13–4 shows the percentage of change in cigarette smoking per day by subjects on each drug. As two different drugs were used to acidify the urine of subjects, and both resulted in an increase in smoking, it is possible to state with some confidence that more nicotine excreted by acidic urine results in more smoking for heavy smokers.

Schachter, Kozlowski, and Silverstein were concerned with the large differences in smoking by different heavy smokers. That is, some smokers who are placed in the heavy-smoker category may smoke as little as one pack a day, whereas other heavy smokers smoke three or more packs a day. The researchers suggest that smokers with

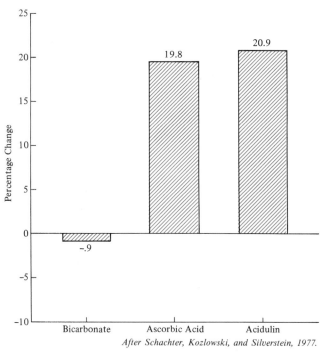

After Schachter, Kozlowski, and Silverstein, 1977.

Figure 13-4 Percentage increase or decrease in smoking from amount smoked by the placebo takers when taking bicarbonate of soda, ascorbic acid, or acidulin.

more acidic urine will eliminate nicotine more quickly and smoke more cigarettes to keep a high nicotine level. To test this assumption the ph of smokers' urine when they were not on drugs was correlated with the number of cigarettes smoked during that period. As expected the correlation was −.63. That is, as the ph of the smokers' urine lowered (became more acid) the number of cigarettes consumed rose. This finding, although suggestive, should be regarded with some caution. A correlation merely shows that a relationship exists, it does not indicate whether a more acid urine causes more smoking or more smoking causes an increase in acidity of the urine. Until more research is done it is impossible to say whether alkalizing the urine of heavy smokers would have the effect of lowering cigarette consumption.

SMOKING AND URINARY PH AT PARTIES

Although most smokers can relate with some accuracy the amount they smoke, they also realize that certain situational variations alter their smoking. Silverstein, Kozlowski, and Schachter (1977) investigated the amount of smoking and urinary ph on days smokers went to a party. A common-sense definition of a party was used. That is, any gathering that involved casual or free movement among the participants, if the purpose of the event was to have a "good time" by seeing old friends or meeting new people was classified as a party. The number of cigarettes smoked on days when an individual went to a party and when he or she did not, as well as the urinary ph of the smokers at bedtime comprised the data of this study. On social days, smokers smoked 12 percent more cigarettes and their urinary ph was significantly more acid than on nonsocial days.

There are several possible explanations for these data. First, party days are typically longer than nonparty days and the increase in smoking may be due to the fact that the smoker is awake longer. However, when cigarettes per hour are computed for party and nonparty days, subjects averaged 1.85 cigarettes per hour on social days and 1.73 cigarettes per hour on nonsocial days. Thus, it seems that just the increase in hours the subject is awake on party days does not account for all of the increase in smoking. Similarly, urinary ph appears to follow a cycle in which it is highly acidic upon waking, becomes alkaline during the first few hours after waking, and for at least some subjects, decreases to more acidic levels at bedtime.

To investigate the possible causes of more acidic urine on party days, Silverstein, Kozlowski, and Schachter (1977) convinced 15 people to urinate before and after a party and 9 of the 15 people to urinate about the same time of day on days they did not attend a party. For both smokers and nonsmokers urine ph was lower (more acidic) following a party than before one. On days when subjects did not attend a party their urine ph did not change over the hours the party had been held. Thus, it can be said that going to a party has an acidifying effect on urine ph. What is it about going to a party that increases urine acidity? Schachter and his colleagues reasoned that it might well be stress and began to investigate the effects of stress on cigarette smoking and urinary ph.

STRESS

Up to this point in the study of cigarette smoking by Schachter and his colleagues, field studies had been used. Now, however, it became necessary to move into the

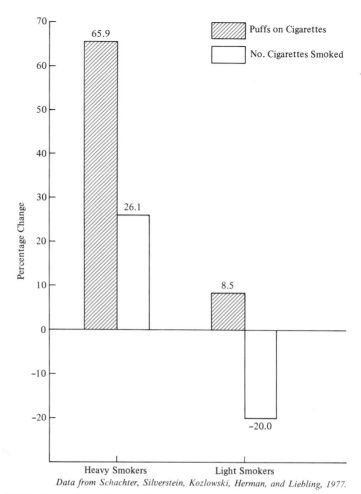

Data from Schachter, Silverstein, Kozlowski, Herman, and Liebling, 1977.

Figure 13-5 Percentage change (increase or decrease) in number of cigarettes smoked and number of puffs taken for heavy and light smokers compared to a low-stress group.

laboratory because there were too many variables that could increase urine acidity and cigarette smoking. The laboratory allowed the precision and control necessary to isolate one variable that seemed most important and to determine its effects upon smoking.

Schachter, Silverstein, Kozlowski, Herman, and Liebling (1977) stressed heavy and light smokers to determine the effects of stress on smoking. Two levels of stress were used. High stress was defined as the delivery of a series of electrical shocks to the subjects until they became so painful the subject asked the experimenter to stop. Low stress was defined as the delivery of electrical shock to the subject until the subject was able to feel the shock; the intensity was not increased further although more shocks were delivered to equate for the number of shocks given to the high-stress group.

Subjects in the high-stress group smoked more cigarettes during the experimental session and took significantly more puffs on their cigarettes than did subjects in the low-stress condition. Of particular interest in the present study is the difference between heavy and light smokers. McArthur, Waldron, and Dickinson (1958) reported that 70 percent of heavy smokers but only 30 percent of light smokers said they smoked more under pressure. The results from the Schachter et al. (1977) study are presented in Figure 13–5. The results show that heavy smokers smoke more cigarettes and take more puffs under high-stress conditions than do heavy smokers in the low-stress condition. Obviously such a relationship does not exist for light smokers.

In a carefully controlled situation, Schachter et al. (1977) have demonstrated that stress increases cigarette smoking in heavy smokers, but there are still several possible causal explanations. Schachter and his associates interpret this increase in smoking as an attempt by heavy smokers to keep a constant level of nicotine. This notion implies that stress increases urinary acidity, which in turn increases the amount of nicotine excreted by the body. To keep nicotine levels high, heavy smokers smoke more. Recall that light smokers (Schachter, 1977) do not seem to regulate nicotine level and would not be expected to smoke more while being stressed if this explanation is accurate.

To test the idea that an increase in stress leads to an increase in urine acidity, Schachter et al. (1977) moved back to a field setting. This time they convinced 10 people to urinate just before presenting a colloquium, defending their Ph.D. thesis, or taking comprehensive examinations and again at the same time of day when they were not under stress. Nine of the 10 subjects had more acidic urine on stress days than on control days and this was so for both smokers and nonsmokers.

Two important facts about stress and smoking have emerged to this point in the research reported by Schachter and his associates. First, stress increases smoking and stress increases urine acidity. However, there are many reasons for changes in urinary ph. For example, light and heavy exercise, as well as simply standing, acidify urine, the kinds of food eaten and the time since eating alter ph (Wesson, 1969). Therefore there are several possible explanations for the data and Schachter, Silverstein, and Perlick (1977) explored some of them.

The Relationship Between Stress and Smoking

The task now faced by Schachter and his associates was to pit the psychological state of stress against urine acidity. To do this stress and urine ph must be manipulated independently and it seemed essential to return to the laboratory to achieve the control necessary to sort out these two variables.

Subjects were 48 smokers who were given either bicarbonate of soda (to alkalize their urine) or a placebo. Additionally half of each group were placed in a high-stress condition and half were placed in a low-stress condition. The stress conditions were the same as those used by Schachter, Silverstein, Kozlowski, Herman, and Liebling (1977). In that study low-stress subjects received shock that they could just feel whereas high-stress subjects were shocked until it was sufficiently painful to them to ask the experimenter to stop.

In the placebo condition, high-stress acidifies urine but low-stress subjects show no such effect. In the bicarbonate conditions, urine ph increases (becomes more alkaline) and stress has no effect on it. The data on cigarettes smoked and number of puffs parallels that of urinary ph. In the placebo condition high-stress subjects tend to smoke more cigarettes and take more puffs than do low-stress subjects. However, with bicarbonate of soda, subjects do not smoke more cigarettes nor take more puffs under high stress than low stress. The data are presented graphically in Figure 13–6.

Prior to asserting that bicarbonate of soda decreases smoking we must be careful to reiterate the mechanism Schachter and his colleagues are proposing. They argue that smokers (particularly heavy smokers) smoke to maintain an optimal level of nicotine in the body. Smoking can be increased by acidifying urine, which causes the elimination of nicotine. Conversely it can be decreased by alkalizing the urine, which in turn retains more nicotine. However, if nicotine is at a very low level, variations in urine acidity should have no effect on smoking.

Nicotine Deprivation. Issac and Rand (1972) have demonstrated that nicotine is at or near zero after a night's sleep. They have also demonstrated that it takes several hours to bring the nicotine in the bloodstream up to a constant level. Therefore, nicotine in the body is lower in the morning than at any other time during the day. It follows then that if Schachter and his associates were to run the experiment we have

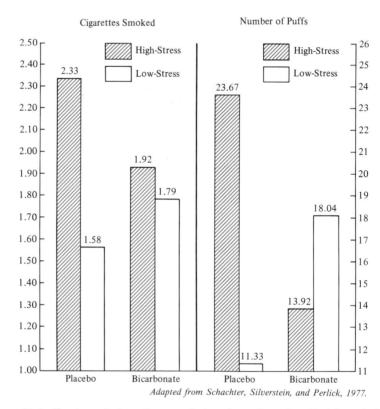

Adapted from Schachter, Silverstein, and Perlick, 1977.

Figure 13-6 Number of cigarettes smoked and number of puffs taken during a 35-minute period under high- and low-stress conditions after taking bicarbonate of soda or a placebo.

NO SMOKING

Certain situational factors may inhibit smokers; however, a "no smoking" sign is often not one of them.

just discussed in the morning, there should be no effect of either stress or ph of urine on smoking. They did replicate the experiment in the morning and found that bicarbonate does alkalize urine but that stress has no effect on urine ph. Most important, they found that neither bicarbonate nor stress had any effect on the number of cigarettes smoked or the number of puffs taken. Furthermore, morning subjects smoke more cigarettes and puff more than do afternoon subjects. These results support the argument that nicotine level regulation is a major physiological mechanism in smoking.

Comment

Schachter and his associates have very deliberately and cautiously tried to fit some of the pieces of the smoking puzzle together. Earlier in this section I commented on society's confusion about smoking. It is probably true that individual smokers are equally confused. On the one hand, they want to smoke, but they don't want to contract the fatal afflictions associated with smoking. Why then do many thousands of them continue to smoke? Schachter and his associates attribute it to nicotine addiction. That is, smokers (particularly heavy ones) are sensitive to nicotine and smoke to increase plasma levels of nicotine if they are low. Therefore, smokers smoke more in the morning, when their urine is acid and large amounts of nicotine are being excreted. This acidic condition can be caused by drugs that are themselves acid (for example, vitamin C) or by stress. This increase in acidity can be counteracted by taking bicarbonate of soda. Whereas it is probably good advice for a smoker to take Alka-Seltzer before rather than after a party, you should recall that this only helps maintain a high nicotine level, which has been achieved earlier in the day. Bicarbonate of soda has no effect on smoking until a constant level is reached. After that level has been reached, bicarbonate should help the smoker reduce his or her cigarette consumption.

Interestingly enough, Schachter and his associates point out even more ironies in the area of smoking. For example, New York City taxes cigarettes on the basis of their tar and nicotine content. If the heavy smoker switches to a low-nicotine brand to avoid paying the tax for higher-nicotine cigarettes, he or she will smoke more cigarettes to attain a constant level of plasma nicotine. The smoker then gets the same amount of tar and nicotine but a good deal more of such combustion by-products as are implicated in increased risk of arteriosclerosis, heart disease, and fetal damage (Larson, Haag, and Silvette, 1961; Surgeon General's Report, 1972). Furthermore, it will be more difficult for the heavy smoker to get a sufficient dose of nicotine and thus he or she is in mild withdrawal all of the time. Schachter's (1977) facetious comment that keeping heavy smokers in withdrawal explain the rise in muggings, rape, and general mayhem since the statute was introduced is, of course, overstating the case. However, the situation does point out the difficulty of legislating behavior and the unintended by-products of doing so.

SUMMARY

1 Basic research is research aimed at providing the most knowledge whereas applied research has a problem-solving orientation. Social scientists generally assert that human behavior is lawful and seek to discover those laws through research.

2 The major scientific approach to human sexual behavior prior to 1960 was the Kinsey reports. Masters and Johnson's work in the 1960s at first brought outrage and then served as the basis of better understanding of human sexual functioning and for therapy in the 1970s.

3 There have been enormous changes in the handling of sexual themes in literature, magazine photographs, and movies in the last several decades. In literature virtually all restraints have been abandoned, but magazine photographs have not become as explicit as literature. Movies, on the other hand, have reached almost the level of explicitness of literature. Sexual attitudes and behavior of people in the United States have undergone changes in the past several decades.

4 Pornography and obscenity were found in a report by the Commission on Obscenity and pornography not to be harmful for adults and possibly to have some positive aspects.

5 Crime has been blamed on evil, illness, excessive emotions, and poverty, but presently many people argue that poverty is the most pervasive cause of crime. The U.S. correctional system does not work and violent crimes continue to increase. People most frequently attribute crime to drugs, insufficient law enforcement, economic factors, and lack of parental control, but they tend to fight crime with measures that do not combat the root causes.

Smoking cigarettes is neither relaxing nor safe. Heavy smokers appear to regulate their nicotine intake whereas light smokers do not. The regulating mechanism appears to be associated with urinary pH.

Under stress, heavy smokers smoke more cigarettes and take more puffs than they do when they are not under stress. For light smokers, stress does not appear to increase smoking. In addition, stress increases urinary acidity.

Apparently heavy (but not light) smokers smoke to maintain an optimal level of nicotine in the body. Smoking can be increased by acidifying urine or decreased by alkalizing it. If nicotine is at a low level, however, variations in urine acidity have no effect on smoking.

GLOSSARY

Abnormal Sexuality A sex-related behavior that causes psychological distress or unwanted physical pain for an individual, any force to compel another to engage in sexual activity, or any unwitting engagement in sexual activity (such as peeping).

Applied Research Research that is aimed at problem solving.

Basic Research Research that is aimed at increasing knowledge.

Crime An action or an instance of negligence that is deemed injurious to the public welfare and that is legally prohibited.

Distal Situated away from.

Dyadic Relationships Relationships between two individuals.

Homosexuality Sexual activity with another person of the same sex.

Menopause The period when a female stops menstruating. This usually occurs at about age 45 or 50 and she is then no longer able to reproduce.

Menstruation The periodic discharge of blood and mucous tissue from the uterus that occurs approximately every 28 days from puberty to menopause.

Nicotine A colorless liquid that is highly toxic and contained in tobacco.

Obscenity Sexual actions, words, or pictures that are disgusting to the perceiver.

pH The concentration of hydrogen ions in a solution. High pH indicates alkalinity, low pH acidity.

Pornography Obscene literature, art, or photography without accompanying artistic merit.

Premarital Intercourse Sexual intercourse prior to marriage.

Prostitution Engaging in sexual intercourse for money.

Proximal Situated toward the point of origin.

Recidivism Repeated relapse into an activity such as crime.

Swinging The behavior of married couples who swap partners for sexual purposes.

Ashton, H., and D. W. Watson. Puffing frequency and nicotine intake in cigarette smokers. *British Medical Journal,* 1970, *3,* 679–81.

Baizerman, M., C. Sheehan, D. B. Ellison, and E. R. Schlessinger. *Pregnant Adolescents: A review of literature with abstracts 1960–1970.* Washington, D.C. Consortium on Early Childbearing and Childbearing Research Utilization and Sharing Project, 1971.

Bazelon, D. L. Criminals are the final result of "Our failing social justice system." *The Center Magazine,* July/August, 1977.

Beckett, A. H., M. Rowland, and E. G. Triggs. Significance of smoking in investigations of urinary excretion rates of amines in man. *Nature,* 1965, *207,* 200–201.

———— and E. G. Triggs. Enzyme induction in man caused by smoking. *Nature,* 1967, *216,* 587.

Ben-Veniste, R. Pornography and sex-crime: The Danish experience. *Technical Reports of the Commission on Obscenity and Pornography,* Vol. 6 Washington, D.C., U.S. Government Printing Office, 1971.

Brickman, P., K. Ryan, and C. B. Wortman. Causal chains: Attribution of responsibility as a function of immediate prior causes. *Journal of Personality and Social Psychology,* 1975, *32,* 1060–67.

Byrne, D. Sexual imagery. In H. Money and H. Musaph (Eds.), *Handbook of Sexology.* Amsterdam: Excerpta Medica, 1976.

————. Sexual changes in society and science. In D. Byrne and L. A. Byrne (Eds.), *Exploring Human Sexuality.* New York: Harper & Row, Publishers, 1977, Pp. 12–23.

————. Social psychology and the study of sexual behavior. *Personality and Social Psychology Bulletin,* 1977, *3,* 3–30.

———— and L. A. Byrne (Eds.). *Exploring Human Sexuality.* New York: Harper & Row, Publishers, 1977.

Capone, D., and W. W. Nichols. The journey to crime: A preliminary analysis of robbery trips in Dade County. Paper presented at the meetings of the Association of American Geographers, Southeastern Division, November 1974.

———— and ————. Crime and distance: An analysis of offender behavior in space. Proceedings, Association of American Geographers, 1975, *7,* 45–49.

———— and ————. Urban structure and criminal mobility. *American Behavioral Scientist,* 1976, *20,* 199–213.

Clark, R. A. The projective measurement of experimentally induced levels of sexual motivation. *Journal of Experimental Psychology,* 1952, *44,* 391–99.

Cochran, N. A., A. Gordon, and D. T. Campbell. *Numbers in bureaucracies: Reflections on the positivist stampede.* Arlington Heights, Ill.: A. H. M. Publishing Company. In press.

Cohn, A. W. Metacorrection: State of the art. In A. W. Cohn (Ed.), *Problems, Thoughts and Processes in Criminal Justice Administration.* Hackensack, New Jersey, National Council on Crime and Delinquency, 1969.

Court, J. H. Pornography and sex-crimes. A re-evaluation in light of recent trends around the world. *International Journal of Criminology and Penology,* 1977, *5,* 129–57.

Culbertson, R. G. Corrections: The state of the art. *Journal of Criminal Justice,* 1977, *5,* 39–46.

Cvetkovich, G., B. Grote, A. Bjorseth, and J. Sarkissian. On the psychology of adolescents' use of contraceptives, *Journal of Sex Research,* 1975, *11,* 256–70.

Danziger, S., and D. Wheeler. The economics of crime: Punishment or income redistribution. *Review of Social Economy,* 1975, *33,* 113–31.

Davis, K. B. *Factors in the Sex Life of 2,200 Women.* New York: Harper & Row, Publishers, 1929.

Dubow, F. L., E. J. McCabe, and J. Kaplan. A review of the literature on reactions to crime. Technical Report. Northwestern University, 1976.

Durkheim, E. *The Rules of Sociological Method.* New York: Macmillan Publishing Co., Inc. 1938.

Eastman, W. F. First intercourse. *Sexual Behavior,* 1972, *2,* 22–27.

Eckhardt, B. Two hundred years of social and economic change have shaped our crime problem. *The Center Magazine,* July/August, 1977:

Ellis, H. *Studies in the Psychology of Sex* (1899). New York: Random House, Inc., 1936.

Eysenck, H. J. *Psychology Is About People.* London, The Penguin Press, 1972.

Faust, B. Why don't humanists do their homework? *Australian Humanist,* 1973, *28,* 4–7.

Finnegan, J. K., P. S. Larson, and H. B. Haag. The role of nicotine in the cigarette habit. *Science,* 1945, *102,* 94–96.

Freud, S. *Three Contributions to the Theory of Sex* (1905). New York: E. P. Dutton & Co., Inc. 1962.

———. *The Sexual Enlightenment of Children.* New York: Collier Books, 1963.

Frith, C. D. The effect of varying the nicotine content of cigarettes on human smoking behavior. *Psychopharmacologia,* 1971, *19,* 188–92.

Gans, H. J. The uses of poverty: The poor pay all, *Social Policy,* 1971, *1,* 20–24.

Goldfarb, T. L., M. E. Jarvik, and S. D. Glick. Cigarette nicotine content as a determinant of human smoking behavior. *Psychopharmacologia,* 1970, *17,* 89–93.

Griswold, H., M. Misenheimer, A. Powers, and E. Tromanhauser. *An Eye for an Eye.* New York: Holt, Rinehart and Winston, 1970.

Gummer, J. S. *The Permissive Society.* London: Cassell Publishers, 1971.

Hamilton, G. V. *A Study in Marriage.* New York: Boni, 1929.

Harrison, B. *Education, Training and the Urban Ghetto.* Baltimore: The Johns Hopkins University Press, 1972.

Herman, C. P. External and internal cues as determinants of the smoking behavior of light and heavy smokers. *Journal of Personality and Social Psychology,* 1974, *30,* 664–72.

Holbrook, D. *Sex and Dehumanization.* London: Sir Isaac Pitman & Sons Ltd., 1972.

Howard, L. R. C. Obscenity and the forensic psychologist, *New Behavior,* July 3, 1975.

Hunt, M. *Sexual Behavior in the 1970s.* Chicago: Playboy Press, 1974.

Ikard, F. F., D. E. Green, and D. Horn. The development of a scale to differentiate between types of smoking as related to the management of affect. Paper presented at the annual meeting of the Eastern Psychological Association, Washington, D.C., April 1968.

Issac, P. F., and M. J. Rand. Cigarette smoking and plasma levels of nicotine. *Nature,* 1972, *236,* 308.

Johnston, L. M. Tobacco smoking and nicotine. *Lancet,* 1942, *2,* 742.

Kempe, R. R., and C. H. Helfer. *The Battered Child.* Chicago: University of Chicago Press, 1968.

Kidder, L. H., and E. S. Cohn. Public views of crime and crime prevention. In I. H. Frieze, D. Bar-Tal, and J. Carroll (Eds.), *New Approaches to Social Problems: Applications of Social Psychology and Attribution Theory for Understanding How People View the Causes of Events.* San Francisco: Josey-Bass, in press.

Kinsey, A. C., W. B. Pomeroy, and C. E. Martin. *Sexual Behavior in the Human Male.* Philadelphia: W. B. Saunders Company, 1948.

———, ——— C. E. Martin, and P. H. Gebhard. *Sexual Behavior in the Human Female.* Philadelphia: W. B. Saunders Company, 1953.

Kraft-Ebing, R. von. *Psychopathia Sexualis* (1886). Philadelphia: F. A. Davis, 1894.

Kutchinsky, B. Pornography in Denmark: Pieces in a jigsaw puzzle collected around New Year, 1970. *Technical Reports of the Commission on Obscenity and Pornography,* Vol. 4,

Washington, D.C., U.S. Government Printing Office, 1971 (a).

————. Towards an explanation of the decrease in registered sex crimes in Copenhagen. *Technical Reports of the Commission on Obscenity and Pornography,* Vol. 7, Washington, D.C., U.S. Government Printing Office, 1971 (b).

Larson, P. S., H. B. Haag, and H. Silvette. *Tobacco.* Baltimore: The Williams & Wilkins Company, 1961.

Martinson, R. What works? Questions and answers about prison reform. *Public Interest,* 1974, Spring, 22–54.

Masters, W. H., and V. E. Johnson. *Human Sexual Response.* Boston: Little, Brown and Company, 1966.

McArthur, C., E. Waldron, and J. Dickinson. The psychology of smoking. *Journal of Abnormal and Social Psychology,* 1958, *56,* 267–75.

Messenger, J. C. Sexual repression: Its manifestations. In D. S. Marshall and R. C. Suggs (Eds.), *Human Sexual Behavior.* Englewood Cliffs, N.J., Prentice-Hall, Inc., 1971, Pp. 14–20.

Miller, J. G. Toward a general theory for the behavioral sciences. *American Psychologist,* 1955, *10,* 513–31.

Nearing, S. *The Conscience of a Radical.* Harborside, Me.: Social Science Institute, 1965.

Nesbitt, P. D. Smoking, physiological arousal, and emotional response. *Journal of Personality and Social Psychology,* 1973, *25,* 137–44.

Piore, M. The role of immigration in industrial growth: A case study of the origins and character of Puerto Rican migration to Boston. Department of Economics Working Paper No. 112, Massachusetts Institute of Technology, May 1973.

Proxmire, W. The love students. *New York Times,* March 23, 1975, p. 14.

Reasons, C. E., and R. L. Kaplan. Tear down the walls? Some functions of prisons. *Crime and Delinquency,* 1975, *21,* 360–72.

Reston, J. Proxmire on love. *New York Times,* March 14, 1975, p. 13.

Ross, L. D., J. Rodin, and P. G. Zimbardo. Toward an attribution therapy: The Reduction of fear through induced cognitive-emotional inattribution. *Journal of Personality and Social Psychology,* 1969, *12,* 279–88.

Russell, M. A. H., C. Wilson, V. A. Patel, P. V. Cole, and C. Feyerabend. Comparison of effect on tobacco consumption and carbon monoxide absorption of changing to high and low nicotine cigarettes. *British Medical Journal,* 1973, *4,* 512–16.

Schachter, S. Nicotine regulation in heavy and light smokers. *Journal of Experimental Psychology: General,* 1977, *106,* 5–12.

————, L. T. Kozlowski, and B. Silverstein. Effects of urinary ph on cigarette smoking. *Journal of Experimental Psychology:* General, 1977, *106,* 13–19.

————, B. Silverstein, L. T. Kozlowski, C. P. Herman, and B. Liebling. Effects of stress on cigarette smoking and urinary ph. *Journal of Experimental Psychology: General,* 1977, *106,* 24–30.

————, ————, and D. Perlick. Psychological and pharmacological explanations of smoking under stress. *Journal of Experimental Psychology: General,* 1977, *106,* 31–40.

Schrag, C. Theoretical foundations for a social science of corrections. In D. Glaser (Ed.), *Handbook of Criminology.* Chicago: Rand-McNally & Company, 1974. Pp. 705–43.

Schur, E. M. *Our Criminal Society.* Englewood Cliffs, N.J., Prentice-Hall, Inc., 1969.

Seligman, M. E. P. *Helplessness.* San Francisco: W. H. Freeman and Company, Publishers, 1975.

Semmens, J. P. Marital sexual problems of teenagers. In J. P. Semmens and K. E. Krants (Eds.), *The Adolescent Experience,* London: Macmillan & Company Ltd., 1970.

Silverstein, B., L. T. Kozlowski, and S. Schachter. Social life, cigarette smoking, and urinary pH. *Journal of Experimental Psychology: General,* 1977, *100*, 20–23.

Simmons, G. L. *Pornography Without Prejudice.* London: Abelard Schuman, 1972.

Storms, M. D., and R. E. Nisbett. Insomnia and the attribution process. *Journal of Personality and Social Psychology,* 1970, *16*, 319–28.

Surgeon General's Report. *The Health Consequences of Smoking.* Washington, D.C.: U.S. Department of Health, Education, and Welfare, 1972.

Terman, L. M., P. Buttenwieser, L. W. Ferguson, W. B. Johnson, and D. P. Wilson. *Psychological Factors in Marital Happiness.* New York: McGraw-Hill Book Company, 1938.

United States Bureau of the Census. *Statistical Abstract of the United States,* 1973 (94th Edition), Washington, D.C., 1973.

United States Department of Health, Education, and Welfare. Smoking and Health. (Tech. Rep. of the Advisory Committee to the Surgeon General of the Public Health Service). Public Health Service Publication No. 1103. Washington, D.C.: U.S. Government Printing Office, 1964.

Valins, S., and R. E. Nisbett. Attribution processes in the development and treatment of emotional disorders. In E. E. Jones, D. E. Kanouse, H. H. Kelley, R. E. Nisbett, S. Valins, and B. Weiner (Eds.), *Attribution: Perceiving the Causes of Behavior.* Morristown, N.J.: General Learning Press, 1972, 137–49.

Ward, P., and G. Woods. *Law and Order in Australia,* Sydney: Angus and Robertson, 1972.

Weiner, B., I. Frieze, A. Rukla, L. Reed, S. Rest, and R. M. Rosenbaum. *Perceiving the Causes of Success and Failure.* Morristown, N.J.: General Learning Press, 1971.

Wesson, L. G. *Physiology of the Human Kidney.* New York: Grune & Stratton, Inc., 1969.

Wortman, C. B., and J. W. Brehm. Response to uncontrollable outcomes: An integration of reactance theory and the learned helplessness model. In L. Berkowitz (Ed.), *Advances in Experimental Social Psychology,* 1975, *8*, 277–336.

Zelnick, M., and J. F. Kantner. The resolution of teenage first pregnancies. *Family Planning Perspectives,* 1974, *6*, 74.

Authors Index

585

Subject Index

traditional vs. nontraditional, 393
World population, 502–503, 504
Written surveys, 53–56
Wynne-Edwards model of animal social
  behavior, 98–99

Yielding, 272–73
  defined, 272

Zero correlation, 60, 61
Zero-sum games, 302

Articles Published in the *Journal of Abnormal and Social Psychology* and the *Journal of Personality and Social Psychology* on Selected Topics between 1944 and 1978

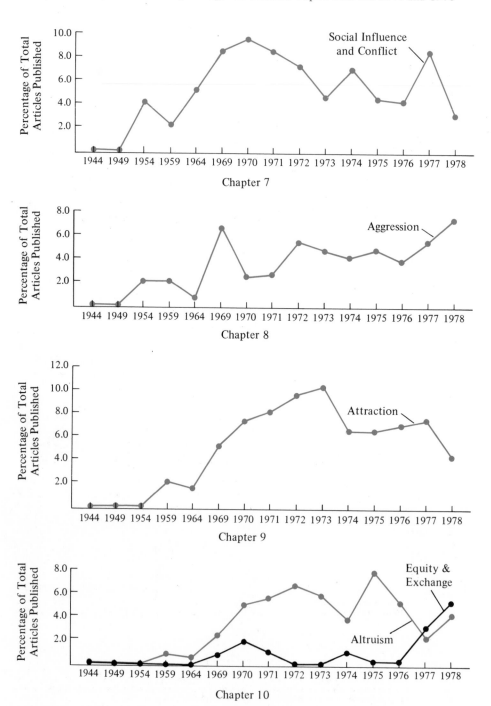